5TH EDITION

WORLD HERITAGE SITES

A FIREFLY BOOK

Published jointly by the United Nations Educational, Scientific and Cultural Organization (UNESCO), 7, place de Fontenoy, 75352 Paris 07 sp, France, and Firefly Books Ltd. 2014

Text © UNESCO 2014
Maps © Collins Bartholomew Ltd 2014
Photographs © as per credits on page 895-896

First printing

Publisher Cataloging-in-Publication Data (U.S.)

A CIP record for this title is available from the Library of Congress

Library and Archives Canada Cataloguing in Publication

A CIP record for this title is available from Library and Archives Canada

Published in the United States by
Firefly Books (U.S.) Inc.
P.O. Box 1338, Ellicott Station
Buffalo, New York 14205

Published in Canada by
Firefly Books Ltd.
50 Staples Avenue, Unit 1
Richmond Hill, Ontario L4B 0A7

Printed and bound in China

The ideas and opinions expressed in this publication are those of the authors and are not necessarily those of UNESCO and do not commit the Organization.

The designations employed and the presentation of material throughout this publication do not imply the expression of any opinion whatsoever on the part of UNESCO concerning the legal status of any country, territory, city or area or of its authorities or concerning the delimitation of its frontiers or boundaries.

All mapping in this book is generated from Collins Bartholomew digital databases.

For more information on World Heritage, please contact:
UNESCO World Heritage Centre
7 place de Fontenoy
75352 Paris 07 SP, France
Tel: (33) 01 45 68 15 71
Fax: (33) 01 45 68 55 70
e-mail: wh-info@unesco.org
http://whc.unesco.org

5TH EDITION

WORLD HERITAGE SITES

A COMPLETE GUIDE
TO 981 UNESCO
WORLD HERITAGE SITES

FIREFLY BOOKS

How to use this book

The page on which the information on a World Heritage site can be found is accessed in a number of ways – by consulting the continent maps on which all the sites are located, or by reference to either the alphabetical or country index. All entries are presented in a similar manner and are arranged chronologically by the year in which they were first inscribed on the World Heritage List.

The diagram below indicates the individual components of each entry and explains the colour coding used to distinguish whether a site is classified as natural, cultural or mixed.

Site title
gives the official UNESCO World Heritage title for each entry.

Red band
represents entries classified as cultural sites.

Locator map
shows the location of the site in a wider region.

Blue band
represents entries classified as mixed sites.

Timeline
on every page highlights the year in which the sites were first inscribed.

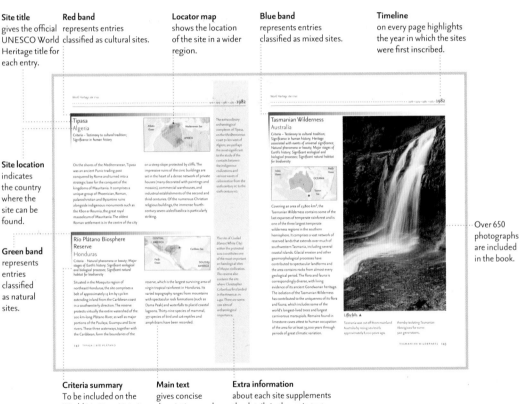

Site location
indicates the country where the site can be found.

Green band
represents entries classified as natural sites.

Over 650 photographs are included in the book.

Criteria summary
To be included on the World Heritage List, sites must be of outstanding universal value and meet at least one out of ten selection criteria. Full criteria explanation can be found on pages **870–1**.

Main text
gives concise descriptions and information about each site.

Extra information
about each site supplements the details in the main text.

Contents

6 Foreword

8 World Heritage sites – mapped by continent

25 World Heritage sites – descriptions, locations and photographs

870 UNESCO's World Heritage Mission Statement, inscription criteria and information about UNESCO Worldwide

874 Country index

882 Index

895 Acknowledgements

Foreword
by Irina Bokova
Director-General of UNESCO

©UNESCO

The World's Heritage provides us with a unique map of the world – a map where the traditional boundaries between States are blurred, that highlights the links binding humanity, and which reveals the intimate relationship between culture and nature, between human genius and natural beauty. The 1972 World Heritage Convention is the foremost international treaty for the protection of major natural and cultural heritage around the world. For four decades, the Convention has helped to safeguard extraordinary places for the enlightenment and enjoyment of future generations.

Today, 981 sites are inscribed on the World Heritage List. Located in 160 countries, they include 759 cultural, 193 natural, and 29 mixed sites – all of which have been recognized for their 'outstanding universal value'. Each site is anchored in a unique cultural and natural context, while being woven into the wider history of humanity and the world,

as motifs in the tapestry of a common, irreplaceable heritage.

India's Taj Mahal, the Serengeti in Tanzania, and Machu Picchu in Peru have iconic status. Other World Heritage sites are less well-known – the Old Town of Lijiang, China, whose architecture draws on several cultures over many centuries; the volcanic island of Surtsey in Iceland that was formed in the 1960s; the outstanding ancient rock art of Tsodilo in Botswana; and the 60 active glaciers of the Olympic National Park in the United States of America. The diversity of World Heritage sites is simply astounding. All are there to be discovered anew – starting within these pages, through these maps and striking photographs.

These pages tell also the story of the evolution of the World Heritage Convention itself, with the emergence of new categories of sites. Cultural landscapes record the relationship between nature and culture over time. The Rice Terraces of the Philippines and the Tokaj Wine Region Historic Cultural Landscape in Hungary bear witness to techniques of cultivating land that preserve biodiversity while supporting livelihoods. Other cultural landscapes reveal powerful spiritual bonds between people and their environment, such as the monasteries and the sacred cedar trees of Lebanon's Ouadi Qadisha (the Holy Valley) and the Forest of the Cedars of God (Horsh Arz el-Rab), and the Royal Hill of Ambohimanga in Madagascar. All such sites highlight the creative interaction between communities and the world in which they live.

Recent years have seen the rise of transboundary sites (they number 29 today), located in two or more countries, and jointly nominated and managed. The Wadden Sea in Germany and the Netherlands and the Talamanca Range-La Amistad Reserves / La Amistad National Park in Costa Rica and Panama illustrate this new spirit of collaboration and cooperation.

The inscription of a site is the beginning of a journey. UNESCO works to monitor, provide technical assistance and share knowledge, but ultimate responsibility for conservation lies with States. World Heritage sites can be tremendous vectors for dialogue, development and knowledge. When accommodation, transportation, guiding and business are developed in a sustainable manner, heritage tourism can be extremely beneficial to the site and the communities living in and around it – both socially and economically.

Today's young people are tomorrow's custodians. The World Heritage Centre has launched innovative initiatives to make them aware of the need to preserve heritage and encourage them to take action. Through the Patrimonito cartoons for children and the World Heritage Volunteers programme, it is important that young people are being engaged with early.

Protecting heritage lies at the heart of UNESCO's mandate. It is important for fostering a dialogue among cultures, it is a foundation for reconciliation amongst peoples and it contributes to the sustainable development of societies. In a world of change, world heritage is a reminder of all that unites humanity. I trust this updated edition of The World's Heritage will provide readers with a better understanding of our planet's cultural and bio-diversity, which UNESCO works every day to safeguard for the benefit of all.

Irina Bokova

World Heritage Sites
Europe

Belarus
Architectural, Residential and Cultural Complex of the Radziwill Family at Nesvizh p748▾; Belovezhskaya Pushcha / Białowieża Forest p61; Mir Castle Complex p635; Struve Geodetic Arc p747▲.

Cyprus
Choirokoitia p554▾; Painted Churches in the Troodos Region p210▾; Paphos p101.

Denmark
Jelling Mounds, Runic Stones and Church p426▾; Ilulissat Icefjord p708 (see map on p15); Kronborg Castle p608; Roskilde Cathedral p452.

Estonia
Historic Centre (Old Town) of Tallinn p509; Struve Geodetic Arc p747▲.

Finland
Bronze Age Burial Site of Sammallahdenmäki p599▲; Fortress of Suomenlinna p378; Old Rauma p368▾; High Coast / Kvarken Archipelago p630▲; Petäjävesi Old Church p436▾; Struve Geodetic Arc p747▲; Verla Groundwood and Board Mill p486▾.

Germany
Aachen Cathedral p33; Abbey and Altenmünster of Lorsch p379▲; Bauhaus and its Sites in Weimar and Dessau p484▲; Bergpark Wilhelmshöhe p866; Berlin Modernism Housing Estates p784▾; Castles of Augustusburg and Falkenlust at Brühl p193▲; Classical Weimar p549; Collegiate Church, Castle and Old Town of Quedlinburg p441▲;

Cologne Cathedral p474; Fagus Factory in Alfeld p826▲; Frontiers of the Roman Empire: Upper German-Raetian Limes p273; Garden Kingdom of Dessau-Wörlitz p610▲; Hanseatic City of Lübeck p281; Historic Centres of Stralsund and Wismar p690▲; Luther Memorials in Eisleben and Wittenberg p503▲; Margravial Opera House Bayreuth p856▲; Maulbronn Monastery Complex p407▾; Messel Pit Fossil Site p456▾; Mines of Rammelsberg and Historic Town of Goslar and Upper Harz Water Management System p387; Monastic Island of Reichenau p640▾; Museumsinsel (Museum Island), Berlin p578; Muskauer Park / Park Muzakowski p719▾; Old town of Regensburg with Stadtamhof p753; Palaces and Parks of Potsdam and Berlin p346; Pilgrimage Church of Wies p176▾; Prehistoric Pile Dwellings around the Alps p839▲; Primeval Beech Forests of the Carpathians and the Ancient Beech Forests of Germany p772; Roman Monuments, Cathedral of St Peter and Church of Our Lady in Trier p251; Speyer Cathedral p128▾; St Mary's Cathedral and St Michael's Church at Hildesheim p225▾; The Wadden Sea p804; Town Hall and Roland on the Marketplace of Bremen p727; Town of Bamberg p406; Upper Middle Rhine Valley p684; Völklingen Ironworks p441▾; Wartburg Castle p589; Würzburg Residence with the Court Gardens and Residence Square p132; Zollverein Coal Mine Industrial Complex in Essen p667▾.

continued on page 12

Azores
(Portugal)

Key to maps

● Cultural site

● Natural site

● Mixed site

234 Page number reference

▲▾ top/bottom of page

The maps in this section are laid out by geographical continent. Please see the maps on page 872 for UNESCO's regional areas.

Madeira
(Portugal)

Canary Islands
(Spain)

Only countries States Parties to the World Heritage Convention are labelled on these maps. United Nations countries boundaries shown as of August 2013. Twenty-nine properties are nominated and managed by more than one State Party.

NORWAY

SWEDEN

FINLAND

RUSSIAN FEDERATION

ESTONIA

LATVIA

DENMARK

LITHUANIA

RUS. FED.

BELARUS

GERMANY

POLAND

UKRAINE

TURKEY

CYPRUS

232▼
747▲
497
747▲
504▼
716▲
392▼
742
104
630▲ 630▲
81
742
847▲
667▲
368▲ 599▲
436▼
747▲
486▼
356▲
432▼
408▲
371
404▲ 435▲
378
509
747▲ 344
744
643▼
646
725▲
459
383
426▼
608
640▲
544
747▲
420
396
553
452
350
396
728 427
804
281
690▲
772
615
715▼
635
727
547
421
748▼
503▲
772
866
441▲
578
784▲
526
61
747▲
826▲
484▲
346
610▲
89
382▲ 868▼
347
225▲
387
719▼
675▲
752▲
868▼
589
675▲
30
702
564
747▲
132
549
36
868▼
456▼
856▲
40
594
868▼ 772
827
379▲
406
753
868▼
407▼
839▲
839▲
865▲
839▲ 176▼
640▼
747▲
828
442
226
237▼
225▲
292
550
230
329
856▼
333
210▼
101 554▼

e large-scale map on pages 10–11

Scale 1 : 20 000 000

9

FRANCE

BELGIUM

LUXEMBOURG

SWITZERLAND

AUSTRIA

SLOVENIA

CZECH REPU

CROA

ANDORRA

MONACO

Corsica
(France)

Sardinia
(Italy)

SAN
MARINO

HOLY
SEE

ITALY

Sicily
(Italy)

MALTA

Only countries States Parties to the World Heritage Convention are
labelled on these maps. United Nations countries boundaries shown
as of August 2013.
Twenty-nine properties are nominated and managed by more than
one State Party.

10

World Heritage Sites
Europe

Albania
Butrint p389; Historic Centres of Berat and Gjirokastra p732▼.

Andorra
Madriu-Perafita-Claror Valley p732▲.

Austria
City of Graz – Historic Centre and Schloss Eggenberg p585; Fertö / Neusiedlersee Cultural Landscape p664▼; Hallstatt-Dachstein / Salzkammergut Cultural Landscape p531; Historic Centre of the City of Salzburg p498; Historic Centre of Vienna p678; Palace and Gardens of Schönbrunn p502; Prehistoric Pile Dwellings around the Alps p839▲; Semmering Railway p551▲; Wachau Cultural Landscape p641.

Belgium
Belfries of Belgium and France p575; Flemish Béguinages p562▼; Historic Centre of Brugge p650; La Grand-Place, Brussels p555; Major Mining Sites of Wallonia p855▼; Major Town Houses of the Architect Victor Horta (Brussels) p648▼; Neolithic Flint Mines at Spiennes (Mons) p652; Notre-Dame Cathedral in Tournai p655▲; Plantin-Moretus House-Workshops-Museum Complex p745▼; Stoclet House p805▲; The Four Lifts on the Canal du Centre and their Environs, La Louvière and Le Roeulx (Hainault) p554▲.

Bosnia and Herzegovina
Mehmed Paša Sokolović Bridge in Višegrad p779; Old Bridge Area of the Old City of Mostar p734.

Bulgaria
Ancient City of Nessebar p165; Boyana Church p60▼; Madara Rider p69▲; Pirin National Park p179; Rila Monastery p178; Rock-Hewn Churches of Ivanovo p69▼; Srebarna Nature Reserve p168▲; Thracian Tomb of Kazanlak p49▼; Thracian Tomb of Sveshtari p234▲.

Croatia
Cathedral of St James in Šibenik p627; Episcopal Complex of the Euphrasian Basilica in the Historic Centre of Poreč p516▼; Historic City of Trogir p533; Historical Complex of Split with the Palace of Diocletian p82; Old City of Dubrovnik p86; Plitvice Lakes National Park p57; Stari Grad Plain p790▼.

Czech Republic
Gardens and Castle at Kroměříž p565▼; Historic Centre of Český Krumlov p386; Historic Centre of Prague p384; Historic Centre of Telč p392▲; Holašovice Historical Village Reservation p551▼; Holy Trinity Column in Olomouc p637; Jewish Quarter and St Procopius' Basilica in Třebíč p704▼; Kutná Hora: Historical Town Centre with the Church of St Barbara and the Cathedral of Our Lady at Sedlec p469; Lednice-Valtice Cultural Landscape p493; Litomyšl Castle p588▲; Pilgrimage Church of St John of Nepomuk at Zelená Hora p443; Tugendhat Villa in Brno p681▼.

continued on page 13

Scale 1 : 10 000 000   11

Europe (continued from page 8)

Iceland
Surtsey p789▾; Þingvellir National Park p709.

Ireland
Brú na Bóinne – Archaeological Ensemble of the Bend of the Boyne p401▲; Skellig Michael Monastery p492.

Latvia
Historic Centre of Riga p544; Struve Geodetic Arc p747▲.

Lithuania
Curonian Spit p615; Kernavė Archaeological Site (Cultural Reserve of Kernavė) p715▾; Struve Geodetic Arc p747▲; Vilnius Historic Centre p421.

Netherlands
Defence Line of Amsterdam p488; Droogmakerij de Beemster (Beemster Polder) p580; Historic Area of Willemstad, Inner City and Harbour, Curaçao p528▾ (see map p16); Ir. D.F. Woudagemaal (D.F. Wouda Steam Pumping Station) p566; Mill Network at Kinderdijk-Elshout p523; Rietveld Schröderhuis (Rietveld Schröder House) p636▲; Schokland and Surroundings p449▲; Seventeenth-century canal ring area of Amsterdam inside the Singelgracht p818; The Wadden Sea p804.

Norway
Bryggen p43; Rock Art of Alta p232▾; Røros Mining Town and the Circumference p104; Struve Geodetic Arc p747▲; Urnes Stave Church p81; Vegaøyan – the Vega Archipelago p716▲; West Norwegian Fjords – Geirangerfjord and Nærøyfjord p742.

Poland
Auschwitz Birkenau German Nazi Concentration and Extermination Camp (1940-1945) p40; Castle of the Teutonic Order in Malbork p547; Centennial Hall in Wrocław p752▲; Belovezhskaya Pushcha / Białowieża Forest p61; Churches of Peace in Jawor and Swidnica p675▲; Historic Centre of Kraków p30; Historic Centre of Warsaw p89; Kalwaria Zebrzydowska: the Mannerist Architectural and Park Landscape Complex and Pilgrimage Park p594; Medieval Town of Toruń p526; Muskauer Park / Park Muzakowski p719▾; Old City of Zamość p382▾; Wieliczka and Bochnia Royal Salt Mines p36; Wooden Churches of Southern Małopolska p702; Wooden Tserkvas of the Carpathian Region in Poland and Ukraine p868▾.

Portugal
Alto Douro Wine Region p662; Central Zone of the Town of Angra do Heroismo in the Azores p162▾; Convent of Christ in Tomar p175; Cultural Landscape of Sintra p447; Garrison Border Town of Elvas and its Fortifications p851; Historic Centre of Évora p258; Historic Centre of Guimarães p682▲; Historic Centre of Oporto p482; Landscape of the Pico Island Vineyard Culture p731; Laurisilva of Madeira p602; Monastery of Alcobaça p337; Monastery of Batalha p177; Monastery of the Hieronymites and

Tower of Belém in Lisbon p163; Prehistoric Rock-Art Sites in the Côa Valley and Siega Verde p563▾; University of Coimbra – Alta and Sofia p863▲.

Russian Federation (see also p24)
Architectural Ensemble of the Trinity Sergius Lavra in Sergiev Posad p420; Church of the Ascension, Kolomenskoye p427; Cultural and Historic Ensemble of the Solovetsky Islands p392▾; Curonian Spit p615; Ensemble of the Ferrapontov Monastery p643▾; Ensemble of the Novodevichy Convent p728; Historic and Architectural Complex of the Kazan Kremlin p646; Historic Centre of Saint Petersburg and Related Groups of Monuments p344; Historic Monuments of Novgorod and Surroundings p383; Historical Centre of the City of Yaroslavl p744; Kizhi Pogost p356▲; Kremlin and Red Square, Moscow p350; Struve Geodetic Arc p747▲; Virgin Komi Forests p449▾; White Monuments of Vladimir and Suzdal p396.

Spain
Alhambra, Generalife and Albayzín, Granada p202; Aranjuez Cultural Landscape p658▾; Archaeological Ensemble of Mérida p410; Archaeological Ensemble of Tárraco p621▾; Archaeological Site of Atapuerca p647▲; Burgos Cathedral p200; Catalan Romanesque Churches of the Vall de Boí p644▾; Cathedral, Alcázar and Archivo de Indias in Seville p266; Cave of Altamira and Paleolithic Cave Art of Northern Spain p220▲; Cultural Landscape of the Serra de Tramuntana p839▾; Doñana National Park p430▲; Garajonay National Park p250▲; Heritage of Mercury: Almadén p858▲; Historic Centre of Cordoba p198; Historic City of Toledo p242; Historic Walled Town of Cuenca p505; Ibiza, Biodiversity and Culture p572; La Lonja de la Seda of Valencia p485▲; Las Médulas p535▲; Monastery and Site of the Escurial, Madrid p193▾; Monuments of Oviedo and the Kingdom of the Asturias p217; Mudéjar Architecture of Aragon p256; Old City of Salamanca p328; Old Town of Ávila with its Extra-Muros Churches p233; Old Town of Cáceres p253; Old Town of Segovia and its Aqueduct p209; Palau de la Música Catalana and Hospital de Sant Pau, Barcelona p528▲; Palmeral of Elche p639; Poblet Monastery p366; Prehistoric Rock-Art Sites in the Côa Valley and Siega Verde p563▾; Pyrénées - Mont Perdu p508▾; Renaissance Monumental Ensembles of Úbeda and Baeza p697▾; Rock Art of the Mediterranean Basin on the Iberian Peninsula p562▲; Roman Walls of Lugo p649▲; Route of Santiago de Compostela p397; Royal Monastery of Santa María de Guadalupe p416▲; San Cristóbal de La Laguna p587▾; San Millán Yuso and Suso Monasteries p535▾; Santiago de Compostela (Old Town) p211; Teide National Park p766; University and Historic Precinct of Alcalá de Henares p568; Tower of Hercules p806; Vizcaya Bridge p758; Works of Antoni Gaudí p182.

Sweden
Agricultural Landscape of Southern Öland p640▲;

Birka and Hovgården p404▲; Church Village of Gammelstad, Luleå p504▲;); Decorated Farmhouses of Hälsingland p847▲; Engelsberg Ironworks p408▲; Hanseatic Town of Visby p459; High Coast / Kvarken Archipelago p630▲; Laponian Area p497; Mining Area of the Great Copper Mountain in Falun p667▲; Naval Port of Karlskrona p553; Rock Carvings in Tanum p432▾; Royal Domain of Drottningholm p371; Skogskyrkogården p435▲; Struve Geodetic Arc p747▲; Varberg Radio Station p725▲.

Turkey
Archaeological Site of Troy p550; City of Safranbolu p442; Göreme National Park and the Rock Sites of Cappadocia p230; Great Mosque and Hospital of Divriği p225▲; Hattusha: the Hittite Capital p237▾; Hierapolis-Pamukkale p329; Historic Areas of Istanbul p226; Nemrut Dağ p292; Neolithic Site of Çatalhöyük p856▾; Selimiye Mosque and its Social Complex p828; Xanthos-Letoon p333▾.

Ukraine
Ancient City of Tauric Chersonese and its Chora p865▲; Kiev: Saint-Sophia Cathedral and Related Monastic Buildings, Kiev-Pechersk Lavra p347; L'viv – the Ensemble of the Historic Centre p564; Primeval Beech Forests of the Carpathians and the Ancient Beech Forests of Germany p772; Residence of Bukovinian and Dalmatia Metropolitans p827; Struve Geodetic Arc p747▲; Wooden Tserkvas of the Carpathian Region in Poland and Ukraine p868▾.

United Kingdom
Blaenavon Industrial Landscape p620▾; Blenheim Palace p270; Canterbury Cathedral, St Augustine's Abbey and St Martin's Church p327; Castles and Town Walls of King Edward in Gwynedd p257▾; City of Bath p290; Cornwall and West Devon Mining Landscape p757; Derwent Valley Mills p675▾; Dorset and East Devon Coast p671; Durham Castle and Cathedral p246; Frontiers of the Roman Empire: Antonine Wall and Hadrian's Wall p254; Giant's Causeway and Causeway Coast p244; Gough and Inaccessible Islands p468▾ (see map on p18); Heart of Neolithic Orkney p570; Henderson Island p321▾ (see map p21); Historic Town of St George and Related Fortifications, Bermuda p621▲ (see map on p15); Ironbridge Gorge p239; Liverpool – Maritime Mercantile City p707▾; Maritime Greenwich p507; New Lanark p659; Old and New Towns of Edinburgh p470; Palace of Westminster and Westminster Abbey including Saint Margaret's Church p272; Pontcysyllte Aqueduct and Canal p801; Royal Botanic Gardens, Kew p692; Saltaire p665; St Kilda p241; Stonehenge, Avebury and Associated Sites p254; Studley Royal Park including the Ruins of Fountains Abbey p248; Tower of London p312.

Europe (continued from page 11)

France

Abbey Church of Saint-Savin sur Gartempe p168▼; Amiens Cathedral p117; Arles, Roman and Romanesque Monuments p131; Belfries of Belgium and France p575; Bordeaux, Port of the Moon p775; Bourges Cathedral p381; Canal du Midi p480; Cathedral of Notre-Dame, Former Abbey of Saint-Rémi and Palace of Tau, Reims p372; Chartres Cathedral p65; Cistercian Abbey of Fontenay p121▲; Episcopal City of Albi p813; Fortifications of Vauban p794; From the Great Saltworks of Salins-les-Bains to the Royal Saltworks of Arc-et-Senans, the production of open-pan salt p153▲; Gulf of Porto: Calanche of Piana, Gulf of Girolata, Scandola Reserve p174; Historic Centre of Avignon: Papal Palace, Episcopal Ensemble and Avignon Bridge p444; Historic Fortified City of Carcassonne p514; Historic Site of Lyons p561; Jurisdiction of Saint-Emilion p600; Lagoons of New Caledonia: Reef Diversity and Associated Ecosystems p788▼ (see map on page 21); Le Havre, the city rebuilt by Auguste Perret p738▲; Mont-Saint-Michel and its Bay p58; Nord–Pas de Calais Mining Basin p850▲; Palace and Park of Fontainebleau p113; Palace and Park of Versailles p62; Paris, Banks of the Seine p360; Pitons, cirques and remparts of Reunion Island p812 (see map on page 18); Place Stanislas, Place de la Carrière and Place d'Alliance in Nancy p169; Pont du Gard (Roman Aqueduct) p229; Prehistoric Pile Dwellings around the Alps p839▲; Prehistoric Sites and Decorated Caves of the Vézère Valley p44▼; Provins, Town of Medieval Fairs p669; Pyrénées - Mont Perdu p508▼; Roman Theatre and its Surroundings and the 'Triumphal Arch' of Orange p120; Routes of Santiago de Compostela in France p557▼; Strasbourg – Grande île p334; The Causses and the Cévennes, Mediterranean agro-pastoral Cultural Landscape p826▼; The Loire Valley between Sully-sur-Loire and Chalonnes p622; Vézelay, Church and Hill p66.

Greece

Acropolis, Athens p282; Archaeological Site of Aigai (modern name Vergina) p504▲; Archaeological Site of Delphi p262; Archaeological Site of Mystras p341; Archaeological Site of Olympia p336; Archaeological Sites of Mycenae and Tiryns p574; Delos p353; Historic Centre (Chorá) with the Monastery of Saint John, the Theologian, and the Cave of the Apocalypse on the Island of Pátmos p603; Medieval City of Rhodes p324; Meteora p332; Monasteries of Daphni, Hosios Loukas and Nea Moni of Chios p342▼; Mount Athos p309; Old Town of Corfu p771; Paleochristian and Byzantine Monuments of Thessalonika p313▼; Pythagoreion and Heraion of Samos p388▼; Sanctuary of Asklepios at Epidaurus p315; Temple of Apollo Epicurius at Bassae p240▼.

Holy See

Historic Centre of Rome, the Properties of the Holy See in that City Enjoying Extraterritorial Rights and San Paolo Fuori le Mura p92; Vatican City p180.

Hungary

Budapest, including the Banks of the Danube, the Buda Castle Quarter and Andrássy Avenue p274; Caves of Aggtelek Karst and Slovak Karst p456▲; Early Christian Necropolis of Pécs (Sopianae) p619▼; Fertö / Neusiedlersee Cultural Landscape p664▼; Hortobágy National Park - the Puszta p583▼; Millenary Benedictine Abbey of Pannonhalma and its Natural Environment p479; Old Village of Hollókő and its Surroundings p293; Tokaj Wine Region Historic Cultural Landscape p686.

Italy

Archaeological Area and the Patriarchal Basilica of Aquileia p565▲; Archaeological Area of Agrigento p542; Archaeological Areas of Pompei, Herculaneum and Torre Annunziata p524; Assisi, the Basilica of San Francesco and Other Franciscan Sites p632; Botanical Garden (Orto Botanico), Padua p532▲; Castel del Monte p506▲; Cathedral, Torre Civica and Piazza Grande, Modena p520, Church and Dominican Convent of Santa Maria delle Grazie with 'The Last Supper' by Leonardo da Vinci p95; Cilento and Vallo di Diano National Park with the Archeological sites of Paestum and Velia, and the Certosa di Padula p558▲; City of Verona p618; City of Vicenza and the Palladian Villas of the Veneto p428; Costiera Amalfitana p538; Crespi d'Adda p465; Early Christian Monuments of Ravenna p487; Eighteenth-Century Royal Palace at Caserta with the Park, the Aqueduct of Vanvitelli, and the San Leucio Complex p527; Etruscan Necropolises of Cerveteri and Tarquinia p729▼; Ferrara, City of the Renaissance, and its Po Delta p453; Genoa: Le Strade Nuove and the system of the Palazzi dei Rolli p759▲; Historic Centre of Florence p134; Historic Centre of Naples p448; Historic Centre of Rome, the Properties of the Holy See in that City Enjoying Extraterritorial Rights and San Paolo Fuori le Mura p92; Historic Centre of San Gimignano p358; Historic Centre of Siena p460; Historic Centre of the City of Pienza p495; Historic Centre of Urbino p567; Isole Eolie (Aeolian Islands) p625; Late Baroque Towns of the Val di Noto (South-Eastern Sicily) p690▼; Longobards in Italy. Places of the power (568-774 AD) p824; Mantua and Sabbioneta p797; Medici Villas and Gardens in Tuscany p860▲; Monte San Giorgio p704▲; Mount Etna p869▲; Piazza del Duomo, Pisa p265; Portovenere, Cinque Terre, and the Islands (Palmaria, Tino and Tinetto) p513; Prehistoric Pile Dwellings around the Alps p839▲; Residences of the Royal House of Savoy p541; Rhaetian Railway in the Albula / Bernina Landscapes p784▲; Rock Drawings in Valcamonica p76▲; Sacri Monti of Piedmont and Lombardy p695▲; Su Nuraxi di Barumini p546▼; Syracuse and the Rocky Necropolis of Pantalica p750▼; The Dolomites p807; The Sassi and the park of the Rupestrian Churches of Matera p399;

The Trulli of Alberobello p501; Val d'Orcia p724; Venice and its Lagoon p268; Villa Adriana (Tivoli) p595; Villa d'Este, Tivoli p673; Villa Romana del Casale p546▲.

Luxembourg

City of Luxembourg: its Old Quarters and Fortifications p424.

Malta

City of Valletta p93; Hal Saflieni Hypogeum p98▲; Megalithic Temples of Malta p96.

Montenegro

Durmitor National Park p107; Natural and Culturo-Historical Region of Kotor p84.

Republic of Moldova

Struve Geodetic Arc p747▲.

Romania

Churches of Moldavia p412▲; Dacian Fortresses of the Orastie Mountains p597; Danube Delta p362; Historic Centre of Sighişoara p592; Monastery of Horezu p408▼; Villages with Fortified Churches in Transylvania p404▼; Wooden Churches of Maramureş p581.

San Marino

San Marino Historic Centre and Mount Titano p782.

Serbia

Gamzigrad-Romuliana, Palace of Galerius p776; Medieval Monuments in Kosovo p717▼; Stari Ras and Sopoćani p76▼; Studenica Monastery p250▼.

Slovakia

Bardejov Town Conservation Reserve p645; Caves of Aggtelek Karst and Slovak Karst p456▲; Historic Town of Banská Štiavnica and the Technical Monuments in its Vicinity p414; Levoča, Spišský Hrad and the Associated Cultural Monuments p417; Primeval Beech Forests of the Carpathians and the Ancient Beech Forests of Germany p772; Vlkolínec p418; Wooden Churches of the Slovak part of the Carpathian Mountain Area p795▲.

Slovenia

Heritage of Mercury: Idrija p858▲; Prehistoric Pile Dwellings around the Alps p839▲; Škocjan Caves p261▲.

Switzerland

Abbey of St Gall p176▲; Benedictine Convent of St John at Müstair p159▼; La Chaux-de-Fonds / Le Locle, Watchmaking Town Planning p800▲; Lavaux, Vineyard Terraces p777; Monte San Giorgio p704▲; Old City of Berne p157; Prehistoric Pile Dwellings around the Alps p839▲; Rhaetian Railway in the Albula/Bernina Landscapes p784▲; Swiss Alps Jungfrau-Aletsch p660; Swiss Tectonic Arena Sardona p787;Three Castles, Defensive Wall and Ramparts of the Market-Town of Bellinzone p610▼.

The former Yugoslav Republic of Macedonia

Natural and Cultural Heritage of the Ohrid Region p77.

World Heritage Sites
North America and the Caribbean

Barbados
Historic Bridgetown and its Garrison p829▲.

Belize
Belize Barrier Reef Reserve System p483.

Canada
Canadian Rocky Mountain Parks p194; Dinosaur Provincial Park p48; Gros Morne National Park p302; Head-Smashed-In Buffalo Jump p118▲; Historic District of Old Québec p206; Joggins Fossil Cliffs p796▲; Kluane / Wrangell-St Elias / Glacier Bay / Tatshenshini-Alsek p52; Landscape of Grand Pré p849▲; L'Anse aux Meadows National Historic Site p37▼; Miguasha National Park p599▼; Nahanni National Park p38▲; Old Town Lunenburg p463; Red Bay Basque Whaling Station p865▼; Rideau Canal p773; SGang Gwaay p133▲; Waterton Glacier International Peace Park p450; Wood Buffalo National Park p170.

Costa Rica
Area de Conservación Guanacaste p596▼; Cocos Island National Park p516▲; Talamanca Range-La Amistad Reserves / La Amistad National Park p162▲.

Cuba
Alejandro de Humboldt National Park p672▲; Archaeological Landscape of the First Coffee Plantations in the South-East of Cuba p649▼; Desembarco del Granma National Park p583▲; Historic Centre of Camagüey p785▼; Old Havana and its Fortification System p146; San Pedro de la Roca Castle, Santiago de Cuba p548▲; Trinidad and the Valley de los Ingenios p323; Urban Historic Centre of Cienfuegos p749; Viñales Valley p593▼.

Dominica
Morne Trois Pitons National Park p515.

Dominican Republic
Colonial City of Santo Domingo p343.

El Salvador
Joya de Cerén Archaeological Site p416▼.

Guatemala
Antigua Guatemala p73; Archaeological Park and Ruins of Quirigua p130▼; Tikal National Park p88▼.

Haiti
National History Park – Citadel, Sans Souci, Ramiers p139▲.

Honduras
Maya Site of Copán p90; Río Plátano Biosphere Reserve p142▼.

Mexico
Agave Landscape and Ancient Industrial Facilities of Tequila p754; Ancient Maya City of Calakmul, Campeche p687▲; Archaeological Monuments Zone of Xochicalco p605; Archeological Zone of Paquimé, Casas Grandes p563▲; Camino Real de Tierra Adentro p816▼; Central University City Campus of the Universidad Nacional Autónoma de México (UNAM) p770▲; Earliest 16th-Century Monasteries on the Slopes of Popocatepetl p432▲; El Pinacate and Gran Desierto de Altar Biosphere Reserve p864▼; El Tajin, Pre-Hispanic City p394; Franciscan Missions in the Sierra Gorda de Querétaro p703▲; Historic Centre of Mexico City and Xochimilco p284▲; Historic Centre of Morelia p369; Historic Centre of Oaxaca and Archaeological Site of Monte Albán p286; Historic Centre of Puebla p284▼; Historic Centre of Zacatecas p419▲; Historic Fortified Town of Campeche p577; Historic Monuments Zone of Querétaro p496; Historic Monuments Zone of Tlacotalpan p548▼; Historic Town of Guanajuato and Adjacent Mines p318; Hospicio Cabañas, Guadalajara p534; Islands and Protected Areas of the Gulf of California p733; Luis Barragán House and Studio p722▲; Monarch Butterfly Biosphere Reserve p791; Pre-Hispanic City and National Park of Palenque p299; Pre-Hispanic City of Chichen-Itza p330; Pre-Hispanic City of Teotihuacan p288; Pre-Hispanic Town of Uxmal p489; Prehistoric Caves of Yagul and Mitla in the Central Valley of Oaxaca p817▲; Protective town of San Miguel and the Sanctuary of Jesús Nazareno de Atotonilco p781▼; Rock Paintings of the Sierra de San Francisco p419▼; Sian Ka'an p267; Whale Sanctuary of El Vizcaino p401▼.

Nicaragua
León Cathedral p829▼; Ruins of León Viejo p619▲.

Panama
Archaeological Site of Panamá Viejo and Historic District of Panamá p529; Coiba National Park and its Special Zone of Marine Protection p745▲; Darien National Park p130▲; Fortifications on the Caribbean Side of Panama: Portobelo-San Lorenzo p99; Talamanca Range-La Amistad Reserves / La Amistad National Park p162▲.

Saint Kitts and Nevis
Brimstone Hill Fortress National Park p596.

Saint Lucia
Pitons Management Area p711.

United States of America
Cahokia Mounds State Historic Site p151▲; Carlsbad Caverns National Park p446; Chaco Culture p285; Everglades National Park p53; Grand Canyon National Park p54; Great Smoky Mountains National Park p164; Hawaii Volcanoes National Park p264; Independence Hall p64; La Fortaleza and San Juan National Historic Site in Puerto Rico p166; Kluane / Wrangell-St Elias / Glacier Bay / Tatshenshini-Alsek p52; Mammoth Cave National Park p126▲; Mesa Verde National Park p28; Monticello and the University of Virginia in Charlottesville p304; Olympic National Park p128▲; Papahānaumokuākea p814▼; Redwood National Park p103; Statue of Liberty p187; Taos Pueblo p380▲; Waterton Glacier International Peace Park p450; Yellowstone National Park p34; Yosemite National Park p184▲.

Only countries States Parties to the World Heritage Convention are labelled on these maps. United Nations countries boundaries shown as of August 2013. Twenty-nine properties are nominated and managed by more than one State Party.

708

Greenland
(Denmark)

170

C A N A D A

865▼ 37▼

302

94
◄94   48
118▲
450

599▼

206   796
        849▲
        463

34

773

UNITED STATES
OF AMERICA   187
                    64

151▲   304

126▲   621▲
       164   Bermuda (UK)

54   28
   285 380▲
   446

563▲

733

MEXICO   53

733   146   749   Puerto Rico (USA)   ANTIGUA AND
                            593▼ 323 785▼   672▲   139◄   166   BARBUDA
       781▼   649▲   343   SAINT KITTS AND NEVIS
       419▲   CUBA   548▲ HAITI   596   596
       816▼   583▲   DOMINICAN   515   DOMINICA
   754 318 703▲ 770▲, 722▲   JAMAICA   REPUBLIC   SAINT LUCIA   711
   534   288 394   SAINT VINCENT AND   829▲ BARBADOS
   369 791 432▲   330   THE GRENADINES
   284▲ 284▼ 548▼   489 267   GRENADA   TRINIDAD
       605 286   577   687▲ BELIZE   AND
            817▲   299 88▲ 483 HONDURAS   TOBAGO
                                       130▼ 142▼
                          73
                          90
GUATEMALA   416▲   619▲ NICARAGUA
EL SALVADOR   829▲
                          596▲
Cocos Island   162▲   99
(COSTA RICA)   162▲ 529 130▲
       516▲   COSTA RICA 745▲
              PANAMA

Scale 1 : 37 500 000   15

496

528▼ Curaçao (Netherlands)

184▼
473▼
426▲

VENEZUELA

841▼
756▼
COLOMBIA
473▼
458
32▼
171▲
ECUADOR
576▼

398▼ 644▲

431 GUYANA
687▼
658▲
SURINAME

624

537

668▲

356▼
238
214
210▲
800▼ 326
PERU 296
172
158
434
617
634 BOLIVIA
556▼
348▲
367▲
289
736
705
CHILE
Galápagos Islands
(Ecuador)
26

Rapa Nui (Chile)
454

374▲
150

809▲
208
579▼
681▲
674 280
681▲
588▼
579▼
223 108
606
844
606
235
188
407▲
159▲ 159▲

PARAGUAY

BRAZIL

636▼
656

628
628
647▼

URUGUAY
472

696▲
762▲

ARGENTINA

620▲
590

607▲

111

Only countries States Parties to the World Heritage
Convention are labelled on these maps. United Nations
countries boundaries shown as of August 2013.
Twenty-nine properties are nominated and managed by
more than one State Party.

Scale 1 : 37 000 000

World Heritage Sites
South America

Argentina
Cueva de las Manos, Río Pinturas p607▲; Iguazu National Park p188; Ischigualasto / Talampaya Natural Parks p628; Jesuit Block and Estancias of Córdoba p647▼; Jesuit Missions of the Guaranis: San Ignacio Miní, Santa Ana, Nuestra Señora de Loreto and Santa María Mayor (Argentina), Ruins of Saõ Miguel das Missões (Brazil) p159▲; Parque Nacional Los Glaciares p111; Península Valdés p590; Quebrada de Humahuaca p705.

Bolivia
City of Potosí p289; Fuerte de Samaipata p556▼; Historic City of Sucre p367▲; Jesuit Missions of the Chiquitos p348▲; Noel Kempff Mercado National Park p636▼; Tiwanaku: Spiritual and Political Centre of the Tiwanaku Culture p634.

Brazil
Atlantic Forest South-East Reserves p606; Brasilia p280; Brazilian Atlantic Islands: Fernando de Noronha and Atol das Rocas Reserves p668▲; Central Amazon Conservation Complex p624; Cerrado Protected Areas: Chapada dos Veadeiros and Emas National Parks p681▲; Discovery Coast Atlantic Forest Reserves p579▼; Historic Centre of Salvador de Bahia p208; Historic Centre of São Luís p537; Historic Centre of the Town of Diamantina p588▼; Historic Centre of the Town of Goiás p674; Historic Centre of the Town of Olinda p150; Historic Town of Ouro Preto p108; Iguaçu National Park p235; Jesuit Missions of the Guaranis: San Ignacio Miní, Santa Ana, Nuestra Señora de Loreto and Santa María Mayor (Argentina), Ruins of Saõ Miguel das Missões (Brazil) p159▲; Pantanal Conservation Area p656; Rio de Janeiro: Carioca Landscapes between the Mountain and the Sea p844; Sanctuary of Bom Jesus do Congonhas p223; São Francisco Square in the Town of São Cristóvão p809▲; Serra da Capivara National Park p374▲.

Chile
Churches of Chiloé p620▲; Historic Quarter of the Seaport City of Valparaíso p696▲; Humberstone and Santa Laura Saltpeter Works p736; Rapa Nui National Park p454; Sewell Mining Town p762▲.

Colombia
Coffee Cultural Landscape of Colombia p841▼; Historic Centre of Santa Cruz de Mompox p473▲; Los Katíos National Park p426▲; Malpelo Fauna and Flora Sanctuary p756▼; National Archeological Park of Tierradentro p473▼; Port, Fortresses and Group of Monuments, Cartagena p184▼; San Agustín Archeological Park p458.

Ecuador
City of Quito p32▼; Galápagos Islands p26; Historic Centre of Santa Ana de los Ríos de Cuenca p576▼; Sangay National Park p171▲.

Paraguay
Jesuit Missions of La Santísima Trinidad de Paraná and Jesús de Tavarangue p407▲.

Peru
Chan Chan Archaeological Zone p238; Chavín (Archaeological site) p210▲; City of Cuzco p158; Historic Centre of Lima p326; Historic Sanctuary of Machu Picchu p172; Historical Centre of the City of Arequipa p617; Huascarán National Park p214; Lines and Geoglyphs of Nasca and Pampas de Jumana p434; Manú National Park p296; Río Abiseo National Park p356▼; Sacred City of Caral-Supe p800.

Suriname
Central Suriname Nature Reserve p658▲; Historic Inner City of Paramaribo p687▼.

Uruguay
Historic Quarter of the City of Colonia del Sacramento p472.

Venezuela
Canaima National Park p431; Ciudad Universitaria de Caracas p644▲; Coro and its Port p398▼.

MOROCCO
857
717▲
543
522▲
119
494
218
666 305
478▲
340▼

379▼
142▼
1094
148▼
53▼
335
148▼
97▼ 46
220▼
317 72
80
145▼ TUNISIA
261▼
149 144

ALGERIA
145▲
234▼

LIBYA

136▼

EGYPT
49▲ 78
738▼ 70
688▲
74
56
56

MAURITANIA
MALI

SENEGAL
121▼
29 626▲
832▼ 755▲
698▼ 755▲
116▼
845▲
GAMBIA
GUINEA
GUINEA-BISSAU

310
321▲ 725▼
340▲
Burkina
FASO
805▼

367▼

862▲

854

NIGER
CHAD

SUDAN
695▼
836

ERITREA
98▼
37▲
60▲ 32▲
102▼ DJIBOUTI
752▼

106▲
ETHIOPIA
833
517
106▲ 517

485▼
726▲
232▲ 741▼

587▲

313▲

CENTRAL
AFRICAN REPUBLIC

94▼

UGANDA
478▼ 430▼ 663▲
838
508▲
KENYA
682▼
782▼
832▲

SIERRA
LEONE
126▲
139▼
LIBERIA

153▼
44▲ 94▲ 44▲
855▲ 44▼

GHANA
TOGO

BENIN
NIGERIA

CAMEROON
308▼ 848
848
848
781▲ CONGO

DEM. REP.
OF THE
CONGO

517

422
45 RWANDA
97▼ 42▼ 278
BURUNDI 112▲
755▼

612

CÔTE
D'IVOIRE

SAO TOME AND
PRINCIPE

GABON

186▼
186▲

TANZANIA

137▼ 116▲

SEYCHELLES
17

133▼
COMOROS

CAPE VERDE
799▲

ANGOLA

ZAMBIA
186▲ 756▼
190
MALAWI
365

778▼
77
778▲
778▼
352
663▲
778▼
778▼

338
668▼ ZIMBABWE MOZAMBIQUE
257▲ 240▼
696▼ 693▼

MADAGASCAR

770▼

NAMIBIA BOTSWANA
869▼
593▲
593▲
593▼ 747▼ 575▼
611
SWAZILAND

MAURITIUS
760
812 792

764▼
569▼
720
SOUTH
AFRICA
LESOTHO

Reunion Island
(France)

Only countries States Parties to the World Heritage
Convention are labelled on these maps. United Nations
countries boundaries shown as of August 2013.
Twenty-nine properties are nominated and managed by
more than one State Party.

Gough Island (UK)
468▼

18

Scale 1 : 50 000 000

World Heritage Sites
Africa

Algeria
Al Qal'a of Beni Hammad p109▲; Djémila p148▲; Kasbah of Algiers p379▼; M'Zab Valley p145▼; Tassili n'Ajjer p145▲; Timgad p148▼; Tipasa p142▲.

Benin
Royal Palaces of Abomey p232▲.

Botswana
Tsodilo p668▼.

Burkina Faso
The Ruins of Loropéni p805▼.

Cameroon
Dja Faunal Reserve p308▼; Sangha Trinational p848.

Cape Verde
Cidade Velha, Historic Centre of Ribeira Grande p799▲.

Central African Republic
Manovo-Gounda St Floris National Park p313▲; Sangha Trinational p848.

Chad
Lakes of Ounianga p854.

Congo
Sangha Trinational p848.

Congo, Democratic Republic of the
Garamba National Park p94▼; Kahuzi-Biega National Park p97▲; Okapi Wildlife Reserve p478▼; Salonga National Park p186▲; Virunga National Park p45.

Côte d'Ivoire
Comoé National Park p153▼; Historic Town of Grand-Bassam p855▲; Mount Nimba Strict Nature Reserve p126▼; Taï National Park p139▼.

Egypt
Abu Mena p49▲; Ancient Thebes with its Necropolis p74; Historic Cairo p78; Memphis and its Necropolis – the Pyramid Fields from Giza to Dahshur p70; Nubian Monuments from Abu Simbel to Philae p56; Saint Catherine Area p688▲; Wadi Al-Hitan (Whale Valley) p738▼.

Ethiopia
Aksum p98▼; Fasil Ghebbi, Gondar Region p60▲; Harar Jugol, the Fortified Historic Town p752▼; Konso Cultural Landscape p833; Lower Valley of the Awash p102▼; Lower Valley of the Omo p106▼; Rock-Hewn Churches, Lalibela p32▲; Simien National Park p37▲; Tiya p106▲.

Gabon
Ecosystem and Relict Cultural Landscape of Lopé-Okanda p781▲.

Gambia
Kunta Kinteh Island and Related Sites p698▼; Stone Circles of Senegambia p755▲.

Ghana
Asante Traditional Buildings p94▲; Forts and Castles, Volta, Greater Accra, Central and Western Regions p44▲.

Guinea
Mount Nimba Strict Nature Reserve p126▼.

Kenya
Fort Jesus, Mombasa p832▲; Lake Turkana National Parks p517; Lamu Old Town p682▼; Mount Kenya National Park/Natural Forest p508▲; Kenya Lake System in the Great Rift Valley p838; Sacred Mijikenda Kaya Forests p782▼.

Lesotho
Maloti-Drakensberg Park p611.

Libya
Archaeological Site of Cyrene p136▼; Archaeological Site of Leptis Magna p144; Archaeological Site of Sabratha p149; Old Town of Ghadamès p261▼; Rock-Art Sites of Tadrart Acacus p234▼.

Madagascar
Rainforests of the Atsinanana p778▼; The Royal Hill of Ambohimanga p663▼; Tsingy de Bemaraha Strict Nature Reserve p352.

Malawi
Chongoni Rock-Art Area p756▲; Lake Malawi National Park p190.

Mali
Cliff of Bandiagara (Land of the Dogons) p340▲; Old Towns of Djenné p310; Timbuktu p321▲; Tomb of Askia p725▼.

Mauritania
Ancient Ksour of Ouadane, Chinguetti, Tichitt and Oualata p478▲; Banc d'Arguin National Park p340▼.

Mauritius
Aapravasi Ghat p760▼; Le Morne Cultural Landscape p792▲.

Morocco
Archaeological Site of Volubilis p543; Historic City of Meknes p494; Ksar of Aït-Ben-Haddou p305; Medina of Essaouira (formerly Mogador) p666; Medina of Fez p119; Medina of Marrakesh p218; Medina of Tétouan (formerly known as Titawin) p522▲; Portuguese City of Mazagan (El Jadida) p717▲; Rabat, Modern Capital and Historic City: a Shared Heritage p857.

Mozambique
Island of Mozambique p365.

Namibia
Namib Sand Sea p869▼; Twyfelfontein or /Ui-//aes p770▼.

Niger
Aïr and Ténéré Natural Reserves p367▼; Historic

Centre of Agadez p862▲; W National Park of Niger p485▼.

Nigeria
Osun-Osogbo Sacred Grove p741▼; Sukur Cultural Landscape p587▲.

Senegal
Bassari Country: Bassari, Fula and Bedik Cultural Landscapes p845▲; Djoudj National Bird Sanctuary p121▼; Island of Gorée p29; Island of Saint-Louis p626▲; Niokolo-Koba National Park p116▼; Saloum Delta p832▼; Stone Circles of Senegambia p755▲.

Seychelles
Aldabra Atoll p133▼; Vallée de Mai Nature Reserve p171▼.

South Africa
Cape Floral Region Protected Areas p720; Fossil Hominid Sites of South Africa p593▲; iSimangaliso Wetland Park p575▼; Maloti-Drakensberg Park p611; Mapungubwe Cultural Landscape p693▲; Richtersveld Cultural and Botanical Landscape p764▼; Robben Island p569▼; Vredefort Dome p747▼.

Sudan
Archaeological Sites of the Island of Meroe p836; Gebel Barkal and the Sites of the Napatan Region p695▼.

Tanzania
Kilimanjaro National Park p278; Kondoa Rock-Art Sites p755▼; Ngorongoro Conservation Area p42▲; Ruins of Kilwa Kisiwani and Ruins of Songo Mnara p116▲; Selous Game Reserve p137; Serengeti National Park p112; Stone Town of Zanzibar p612.

Togo
Koutammakou, the Land of the Batammariba p726▲.

Tunisia
Amphitheatre of El Jem p80; Dougga / Thugga p530; Ichkeul National Park p97▼; Kairouan p335; Medina of Sousse p317; Medina of Tunis p72; Punic Town of Kerkuane and its Necropolis p220▼; Site of Carthage p46.

Uganda
Bwindi Impenetrable National Park p422; Rwenzori Mountains National Park p430▼; Tombs of Buganda Kings at Kasubi p663▲.

Zambia
Mosi-oa-Tunya / Victoria Falls p338.

Zimbabwe
Great Zimbabwe National Monument p240▲; Khami Ruins National Monument p257▲; Mana Pools National Park, Sapi and Chewore Safari Areas p186▼; Mosi-oa-Tunya / Victoria Falls p338; Matobo Hills p696▼.

PALAU
● 858▼

786▲

**PAPUA
NEW GUINEA**

127

311

699

122

429▼

AUSTRALIA

830

39

368▲

306

260

125

609
763
808

808

429▼

718

808

143
808

Only countries State Parties to the World Heritage
Convention are labelled on these maps. United Nations
countries boundaries shown as of August 2013.
Twenty-nine properties are nominated and managed by
more than one State Party.

World Heritage Sites
Oceania

Australia
Australian Convict Sites p808; Australian Fossil Mammal Sites (Riversleigh / Naracoorte) p429▼; Fraser Island p393; Gondwana Rainforests of Australia p260; Great Barrier Reef p122; Greater Blue Mountains Area p609; Heard and McDonald Islands p522▼ (not on map); Kakadu National Park p127; Lord Howe Island Group p136▲; Macquarie Island p506▼ (not on map); Ningaloo Coast p830; Purnululu National Park p699; Royal Exhibition Building and Carlton Gardens p718; Shark Bay, Western Australia p368▲; Sydney Opera House p763; Tasmanian Wilderness p143; Uluru-Kata Tjuta National Park p306; Wet Tropics of Queensland p311; Willandra Lakes Region p125.

Fiji
Levuka Historical Port Town p863▼.

Kiribati
Phoenix Islands Protected Area p821.

Marshall Islands
Bikini Atoll, Nuclear Test Site p809▼.

New Zealand
New Zealand Sub-Antarctic Islands p556▲; Te Wahipounamu – South West New Zealand p354; Tongariro National Park p349.

Palau
Rock Islands Southern Lagoon p858▼.

Papua New Guinea
Kuk Early Agricultural Site p786▲.

Solomon Islands
East Rennell p558▼.

Vanuatu
Chief Roi Mata's Domain p795▼.

SOLOMON ISLANDS

558▼

VANUATU 795▼

788▼

New Caledonia (France)

FIJI 863▼

808

136▲

FEDERATED STATES OF MICRONESIA

809▼ MARSHALL ISLANDS

KIRIBATI

821

PAPUA NEW GUINEA

SOLOMON ISLANDS

SAMOA

FIJI

NIUE

TONGA

COOK ISLANDS

Scale 1 : 100 000 000

Henderson Island (UK)

321▼

NEW ZEALAND

349

354

354

354

354

556▲

Scale 1 : 27 000 000

601▲
GEORGIA
481▲
ARMENIA
435▲ 437
655▼ 500
630▲ 698▲
AZERBAIJAN 607▲
792▼ 767▼
215▲ 810▼
815 746▲
697▲ 691
767▲ 762▼ 835
IRAQ 868▲ 850▼
835 ISLAMIC REP.
88▲ 846
KUWAIT 803▲ 38▼
798 714 835
68 835 835 710
820 746▼
BAHRAIN 849▼ 864▲
SAUDI QATAR
ARABIA UNITED ARAB
EMIRATES
835
322 760▲
303 760▲ 760▲
760▲
OMAN
245 614
152
398▲ YEMEN

KAZAKHSTAN

786▼

693▼
842
557▼
M O N

750▼
348▼
UZBEKISTAN 707▲ 729▲
867▲ 867▼
405 670 867▲ 867▲
778▲ 817▼ 803▼ 867▲
573 629
861▼
TAJIKISTAN
683 703▼
AFGHANISTAN
110▼
109▼
532▼
124
PAKISTAN 576▼
333▲
102▲ 425
765▲ 403 196▼
216 413 NEPAL 85
118▼ 814▲ 161 512▼ 576▼
860▼ 247 154 50 215▼
BHUTAN 224
222
249 688▼
730 342▼ BANGLADESH
694▼ 228
156 271▲ 512▼
723 160 MYANMAR
271▼
847▼
308▲
237▲ 252
847▼
204
576▼ 847▼ 276
INDIA
MALDIVES 847▼ 138 151▼
363 140
314 823
320 316 SRI LANKA

298▲

C H

712

Socotra (Yemen)
785▲

Jammu and Kashmir: Dotted line represents approximately the
Line of Control in Jammu and Kashmir agreed upon by India and
Pakistan. The final status of Jammu and Kashmir has not been
agreed upon by the parties.

Only countries States Parties to the World Heritage Convention
are labelled on these maps. United Nations countries boundaries
shown as of August 2013.

Twenty-nine properties are nominated and managed by more
than one State Party.

SEE INSET

INSET:

837▼ 236
761
761
100
569▲
192 191 SYRIAN
205 ARAB
LEBANON 197 39 REPUBLIC
680 739
793 739
843▼ 105
694▲
ISRAEL 114
853 221
oPt* 739 Jerusalem 713
676
740 JORDAN
212
834

*occupied
Palestinian
territory

Scale 1 : 12 000 000

World Heritage Sites
Asia, Middle East and Arabian Peninsula

Afghanistan
Cultural Landscape and Archaeological Remains of the Bamiyan Valley p703▼; Minaret and Archaeological Remains of Jam p683.

Armenia
Cathedral and Churches of Echmiatsin and the Archaeological Site of Zvartnots p655▼; Monasteries of Haghpat and Sanahin p500; Monastery of Geghard and the Upper Azat Valley p630▼.

Azerbaijan
Gobustan Rock Art Cultural Landscape p767▼; Walled City of Baku with the Shirvanshah's Palace and Maiden Tower p607▼.

Bahrain
Pearling, Testimony of an Island Economy p849▼; Qal'at al-Bahrain – Ancient Harbour and Capital of Dilmun p746▼.

Bangladesh
Historic Mosque City of Bagerhat p228; Ruins of the Buddhist Vihara at Paharpur p222; The Sundarbans p512▼.

Cambodia
Angkor p390; Temple of Preah Vihear p789▲.

China
Ancient Building Complex in the Wudang Mountains p429▲; Ancient City of Ping Yao p540; Ancient Villages in Southern Anhui – Xidi and Hongcun p653; Capital Cities and Tombs of the Ancient Koguryo Kingdom p722▼; Chengjiang Fossil Site p845▼; China Danxia p811; Classical Gardens of Suzhou p518; Cultural Landscape of Honghe Hani Rice Terraces p861▲; Dazu Rock Carvings p584; Fujian Tulou p788▲; Historic Centre of Macao p737; Historic Ensemble of the Potala Palace, Lhasa p425; Huanglong Scenic and Historic Interest Area p395; Imperial Palaces of the Ming and Qing Dynasties in Beijing and Shenyang p277; Imperial Tombs of the Ming and Qing Dynasties p616; Jiuzhaigou Valley Scenic and Historic Interest Area p380▼; Historic Monuments of Dengfeng, in the 'Centre of Heaven and Earth' p810▲; Kaiping Diaolou and Villages p774; Longmen Grottoes p654; Lushan National Park p484▼; Mausoleum of the First Qin Emperor p300; Mogao Caves p298▲; Mount Emei Scenic Area, including Leshan Giant Buddha Scenic Area p481▲; Mount Huangshan p357; Mount Qingcheng and the Dujiangyan Irrigation System p648▲; Mount Sanqingshan National Park p796▼; Mount Taishan p297; Mount Wutai p802; Mount Wuyi p598; Mountain Resort and its Outlying Temples, Chengde p436▲; Old Town of Lijiang p510; Peking Man Site at Zhoukoudian p298▼; Sichuan Giant Panda Sanctuaries – Wolong, Mt Siguniang and Jiajin Mountains p751; Site of Xanadu p852▲; South China Karst p768; Summer Palace and Imperial Garden in Beijing p552; Temple and Cemetery of Confucius and the Kong Family Mansion in Qufu p433; Temple of Heaven: an Imperial Sacrificial Altar in Beijing p559; The Great Wall p294; Three Parallel Rivers of Yunnan Protected Areas p700; West Lake Cultural Landscape of Hangzhou p831; Wulingyuan Scenic and Historic Interest Area p382▲; Xinjiang Tianshan p867▲; Yin Xu p759▼; Yungang Grottoes p672▼.

continued on page 24

Scale 1 : 38 000 000

Asia, Middle East and Arabian Peninsula (continued)

Georgia
Bagrati Cathedral and Gelati Monastery p435▼; Historical Monuments of Mtskheta p437; Upper Svaneti p481▼.

India
Agra Fort p161; Ajanta Caves p156; Buddhist Monuments at Sanchi p342▲; Champaner-Pavagadh Archaeological Park p730; Chhatrapati Shivaji Terminus (formerly Victoria Terminus) p723; Churches and Convents of Goa p237▲; Elephanta Caves p271▼; Ellora Caves p160; Fatehpur Sikri p247; Great Living Chola Temples p276; Group of Monuments at Hampi p252; Group of Monuments at Mahabalipuram p204; Group of Monuments at Pattadakal p308▲; Hill Forts of Rajasthan p860▲; Humayun's Tomb, Delhi p403; Jantar Mantar p814▲; Kaziranga National Park p224; Keoladeo National Park p216; Khajuraho Group of Monuments p249; Mahabodhi Temple Complex at Bodh Gaya p688▼; Manas Wildlife Sanctuary p215▼; Mountain Railways of India p576▲; Nanda Devi and Valley of Flowers National Parks p333▲; Qutb Minar and its Monuments, Delhi p413; Red Fort Complex p765; Rock Shelters of Bhimbetka p694▼; Sun Temple, Konârak p183; Sundarbans National Park p271▲; Taj Mahal p154; Western Ghats p847▼.

Indonesia
Borobudur Temple Compounds p376; Cultural Landscape of Bali Province: the Subak System as a Manifestation of the 'Tri Hita Karana' Philosophy p859; Komodo National Park p370; Lorentz National Park p604▲; Prambanan Temple Compounds p373; Sangiran Early Man Site p503▼; Tropical Rainforest Heritage of Sumatra p712; Ujung Kulon National Park p374▼.

Iran, Islamic Republic of
Armenian Monastic Ensembles of Iran p792; Bam and its Cultural Landscape p710; Bisotun p762▼; Golestan Palace p868▲; Gonbad-e Qābus p850▼; Masjed-e Jāmé of Isfahan p846; Meidan Emam, Esfahan p38▼; Pasargadae p714; Persepolis p68; Sheikh Safi al-Din Khānegāh and Shrine Ensemble in Ardabil p810▼; Shushtar Historical Hydraulic System p803▲; Soltaniyeh p746▲; Tabriz Historic Bazaar Complex p815; Takht-e Soleyman p691; Tchogha Zanbil p88▲; The Persian Garden p835▼.

Iraq
Ashur (Qal'at Sherqat) p697▲; Hatra p215▲; Samarra Archaeological City p767▲.

Israel
Bahá'í Holy Places in Haifa and the Western Galilee p793; Biblical Tels – Megiddo, Hazor, Beer Sheba p739; Incense Route – Desert Cities in the Negev p740; Masada p676; Old City of Acre p680; Sites of Human Evolution at Mount Carmel: The Nahal Me'arot/Wadi el-Mughara Caves p843▼; The White City of Tel-Aviv – The Modern Movement p694▲.

Japan
Buddhist Monuments in the Horyu-ji Area p415▲; Fujisan, Sacred Place and Source of Artistic Inspiration p867▼; Gusuku Sites and Related Properties of the Kingdom of Ryukyu p643▲; Himeji-jo p409; Hiraizumi – Temples, Gardens and Archaeological Sites Representing the Buddhist Pure Land p840; Hiroshima Peace Memorial (Genbaku Dome) p477; Historic Monuments of Ancient Kyoto (Kyoto, Uji and Otsu Cities) p438; Historic Monuments of Ancient Nara p560; Historic Villages of Shirakawa-go and Gokayama p462▲; Itsukushima Shinto Shrine p486▲; Iwami Ginzan Silver Mine and its Cultural Landscape p764▲; Ogasawara Islands p841▲; Sacred Sites and Pilgrimage Routes in the Kii Mountain Range p726▼; Shirakami-Sanchi p415▼; Shiretoko p748▲; Shrines and Temples of Nikko p604▼; Yakushima p400.

Jerusalem (Site proposed by Jordan)
Old City of Jerusalem and its Walls p114.

Jordan
Petra p212; Quseir Amra p221; Um er-Rasas (Kastrom Mefa'a) p713; Wadi Rum Protected Area p834▼.

Kazakhstan
Mausoleum of Khoja Ahmed Yasawi p707▲; Petroglyphs within the Archaeological Landscape of Tamgaly p729▲; Saryarka – Steppe and Lakes of Northern Kazakhstan p786▼.

Korea, Democratic People's Republic of
Complex of Koguryo Tombs p715▲; Historic Monuments and Sites in Kaesŏng p862▼.

Korea, Republic of
Changdeokgung Palace Complex p521; Gochang, Hwasun and Ganghwa Dolmen Sites p626▼; Gyeongju Historic Areas p642; Haeinsa Temple Janggyeong Panjeon, the Depositories for the Tripitaka Koreana Woodblocks p462▼; Historic Villages of Korea: Hahoe and Yangdong p822; Hwaseong Fortress p536; Jeju Volcanic Island and Lava Tubes p780; Jongmyo Shrine p468▲; Royal Tombs of the Joseon Dynasty p799▼; Seokguram Grotto and Bulguksa Temple p457.

Kyrgyzstan
Sulaiman-Too Sacred Mountain p803▼.

Lao People's Democratic Republic (Laos)
Town of Luang Prabang p464; Vat Phou and Associated Ancient Settlements within the Champasak Cultural Landscape p679.

Lebanon
Anjar p205; Baalbek p191; Byblos p192; Ouadi Qadisha (the Holy Valley) and the Forest of the Cedars of God (Horsh Arz el-Rab) p569▲; Tyre p197.

Malaysia
Archaelogical Heritage of the Lenggong Valley p852▼; Gunung Mulu National Park p638; Kinabalu Park p631; Melaka and George Town, Historic Cities of the Straits of Malacca p790▲.

Mongolia
Orkhon Valley Cultural Landscape p719▲; Petroglyphic Complexes of the Mongolian Altai p842; Uvs Nuur Basin p693▼.

Nepal
Chitwan National Park p196; Kathmandu Valley p50; Lumbini, the Birthplace of the Lord Buddha p512▲; Sagarmatha National Park p85.

Oman
Aflaj Irrigation Systems of Oman p760▲; Archaeological sites of Bat, Al-Khutm and Al-Ayn p322; Bahla Fort p303; Land of Frankincense p614.

Pakistan
Archaeological Ruins at Moenjodaro p102▲; Buddhist Ruins of Takht-i-Bahi and Neighbouring City Remains at Sahr-i-Bahlol p110; Fort and Shalamar Gardens in Lahore p124; Historic Monuments at Makli, Thatta p118▼; Rohtas Fort p532▼; Taxila p109▼.

Palestine (oPt) Member of UNESCO since 23 Nov 2011
Birthplace of Jesus: Church of the Nativity and the Pilgrimage Route, Bethlehem p853.

Philippines
Baroque Churches of the Philippines p402; Historic Town of Vigan p582; Puerto-Princesa Subterranean River National Park p601▼; Rice Terraces of the Philippine Cordilleras p466; Tubbataha Reefs Natural Park p412▼.

Qatar
Al Zubarah Archaeological Site p864▲.

Russian Federation (see also p12)
Central Sikhote-Alin p664▲; Citadel, Ancient City and Fortress Buildings of Derbent p698▲; Golden Mountains of Altai p557▲; Lake Baikal p476; Lena Pillars Nature Park p843▲; Natural System of Wrangel Island Reserve p716▼; Putorana Plateau p819; Uvs Nuur Basin p693▼; Volcanoes of Kamchatka p490; Western Caucasus p601▲.

Saudi Arabia
Al-Hijr Archaeological Site (Madâin Sâlih) p798; At Turaif District in ad-Dir'iyah p820.

Sri Lanka
Ancient City of Polonnaruwa p140; Ancient City of Sigiriya p151▼; Golden Temple of Dambulla p363; Central Highlands of Sri Lanka p823; Old Town of Galle and its Fortifications p320; Sacred City of Anuradhapura p138; Sacred City of Kandy p314; Sinharaja Forest Reserve p316.

Syrian Arab Republic (Syria)
Ancient City of Aleppo p236; Ancient City of Bosra p105; Ancient City of Damascus p39; Ancient Villages of Northern Syria p837▼; Crac des Chevaliers and Qal'at Salah El-Din p761; Site of Palmyra p100.

Tajikistan
Proto-urban Site of Sarazm p817▼; Tajik National Park (Mountains of the Pamirs) p861▼.

Thailand
Ban Chiang Archaeological Site p388▲; Dong Phayayen-Khao Yai Forest Complex p741▲; Historic City of Ayutthaya p359; Historic Town of Sukhothai and Associated Historic Towns p375; Thungyai-Huai Kha Khaeng Wildlife Sanctuaries p364.

Turkmenistan
Kunya-Urgench p750▲; Parthian Fortresses of Nisa p778▲; State Historical and Cultural Park 'Ancient Merv' p573.

United Arab Emirates
Cultural Sites of Al Ain (Hafit, Hili, Bidaa Bint Saud and Oases Areas) p835▲.

Uzbekistan
Historic Centre of Bukhara p405; Historic Centre of Shakhrisyabz p629; Itchan Kala p348▼; Samarkand – Crossroad of Cultures p670.

Vietnam
Citadel of the Ho Dynasty p837▲; Complex of Hué Monuments p411; Ha Long Bay p440; Hoi An Ancient Town p586; Central Sector of the Imperial Citadel of Thang Long - Hanoi, p816▲; My Son Sanctuary p579▲; Phong Nha-Ke Bang National Park p706.

Yemen
Historic Town of Zabid p398▲; Old City of Sana'a p245; Old Walled City of Shibam p152; Socotra Archipelago p785▲.

The World Heritage sites,
ordered by the year they were
first inscribed on the List.

World Heritage site since

· ·1978

Galápagos Islands
Ecuador

Criteria – Natural phenomena or beauty; Major stages of Earth's history; Significant ecological and biological processes; Significant natural habitat for biodiversity

Situated in the Pacific Ocean approximately 1,000 km from the South American mainland, the Galápagos Archipelago of nineteen major islands and their marine reserve have been called a unique 'living museum and showcase of evolution'. Located at the confluence of three ocean currents, the Galápagos are a 'tossed salad' of marine species.

Volcanic processes formed the islands, most of which are volcanic summits, some rising over 3,000 m from the Pacific floor. They vary greatly in altitude, area and orientation and these differences, combined with their physical separation, contributed towards the species diversity and endemism on particular islands. Ongoing seismic and volcanic activity reflects the processes that formed the islands and it was these processes, together with the islands' extreme isolation, that led to the development of unusual animal life – such as the marine iguana, the giant tortoise and the flightless cormorant – that inspired Charles Darwin's theory of evolution following his visit in 1835.

The western part of the archipelago experiences intense volcanic and seismic activity. The larger islands typically comprise at least one gently sloping shield volcano, culminating in collapsed craters or calderas.

Long stretches of shoreline are only slightly eroded, but in many places faulting and marine erosion have produced steep cliffs and lava, coral or shell sand beaches.

There is coastal vegetation along beaches, salt-water lagoons and low, broken, boulder-strewn shores, and mangrove swamps dominate protected coves and lagoons. The arid zone that lies immediately inland dominates the Galápagos landscape. The humid zone emerges above the arid zone through a transition belt in which elements of the two are combined. It is very damp and is maintained in the dry season by thick, garua fogs. A fern-grass-sedge zone covers the summit areas of the larger islands where moisture is retained in temporary pools.

The endemic fauna includes invertebrate, reptile, marine and bird species. There are a few indigenous mammals. All the reptiles, except for two marine turtles, are endemic.

Marine environments are highly varied and are associated with water temperature regimes reflecting differences in nutrient and light levels. These range from warm temperate conditions brought on by vigorous upwelling (Cromwell Current) and a moderately cool, warm temperate-subtropical influence (Peru Flow).

An endemic Galápagos giant tortoise. Adults in the wild can grow up to 1.2 m in length and live for 150 years. There are now only eleven subspecies remaining from the original twelve.

A Sally Lightfoot (Graspus Graspus) crab which is endemic to the Galápagos Islands and lives on the rocky shore, feeding on algae and dead fish, birds and seals.

The Heritage site is situated on the Galápagos Submarine Platform and consists of about 120 islands in total. The larger islands in the group are Isabela, Santa Cruz, Fernandina, Santiago and San Cristobal.

World Heritage site since

· **1978**

Mesa Verde National Park
USA

Criteria – Testimony to cultural tradition

NORTH
AMERICA

Pacific
Ocean

Atlantic
Ocean

Standing on the Mesa Verde plateau in southwest Colorado at a height of more than 2,600 m is this concentration of ancestral Pueblo Indian dwellings. Their originality derives in part from the unique local topography of mesas, or tablelands, intersected by deep canyons, that dictated their construction. The dwellings were also designed to cope with the challenging local climate: a semi-arid environment with irregular rainfall and extremes of temperature between day and night.

The dwellings were built by the Anasazi Indians, ancestors of the Pueblos, between the sixth and twelfth centuries, and the earliest habitations are found largely on the plateau. Later, villages grew in and around the cave-studded sides of the cuestas where erosion had left protective overhanging cliffs. Some of these imposing stone-built cliff dwellings comprise more than 100 rooms. In all, some 4,400 sites have been recorded.

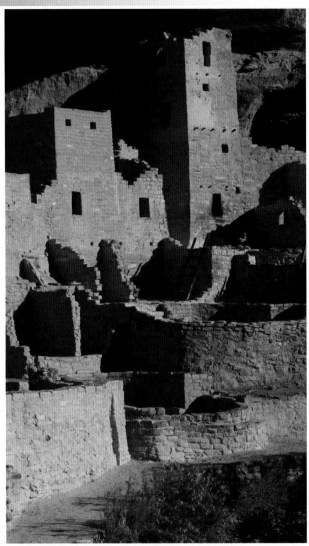

▲
The Mesa Verde site has been protected by the Federal Antiquities Act since 1906.

The cliff-side villages had specific functions: agricultural, handicraft and religious.

The Anasazi developed irrigation techniques to cultivate the cereal crops that were central to their diet. At their civilisation's high point, they produced high-quality ceramics, weaving and wickerwork made from yucca fibre.

World Heritage site since

· 1978

Island of Gorée
Senegal

Criteria – Heritage associated with events of
universal significance

The island of Gorée, which lies off the coast of Senegal opposite Dakar, is a memorial to the African diaspora. From the fifteenth to the nineteenth century, it was the largest slave-trading centre on the African coast. Ruled in succession by the Portuguese, Dutch, English and French, its architecture is characterized by the contrast between the grim slave-quarters and the elegant houses of the slave traders. An estimated 20 million Africans passed through the island between the mid-1500s and the mid-1800s. A small slave-house contained 150–200 slaves, who would often have to endure months in appalling conditions before being shipped to the Americas. Today it continues to serve as a reminder of human exploitation and as a sanctuary for reconciliation.

Slave houses contained cells, 2.6 m square, in which fifteen to twenty men would be chained to the wall by their neck and arms. Attached to the chain was a large iron ball which the men would have to carry when they were allowed, once a day, to relieve themselves.

▼

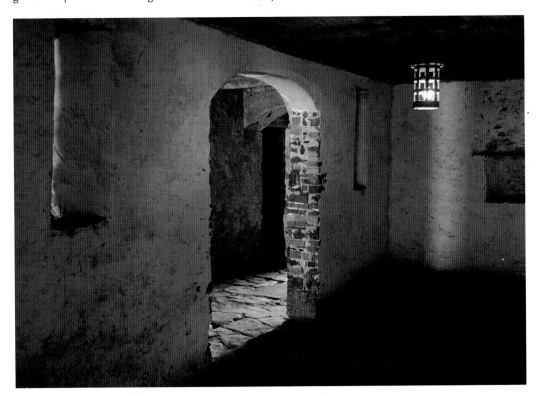

Historic Centre of Kraków
Poland
Criteria – Significance in human history

North Sea
Baltic Sea
EUROPE

The historic centre of Kraków, the former capital of Poland, is an outstanding example of medieval architecture. The thirteenth century merchants' town has Europe's largest market square and numerous historical houses, palaces and churches with magnificent interiors. Remnants of the fourteenth-century fortifications, the medieval site of Kazimierz with its ancient synagogues, Jagellonian University and the Gothic Wawel Cathedral all testify to the town's fascinating history.

The layout of Kraków is based on four core areas: Stare Miasto, or old town, around the market square; the Wawel, site of the imperial palace; the urban district of Kazimierz; and the Stradom quarter.

Stare Miasto is characterized by a rigid grid of perfectly orthogonal streets, a layout ordered by Bolesław the Chaste in 1257 when he decided to unify the various peoples scattered around the hill of the Wawel. All that remains now of the medieval enclosure walls is the gate and the wall that was built in 1499 near the main city gate.

The old town is separated from the old district of Kazimierz, which was an island until 1880. Kazimierz formed the Jewish quarter of Kraków until the Second World War.

The city's university quarter is the oldest in Poland and among the oldest in Europe. Students at Jagellonian University have included Copernicus and Karol Wojtyła (Pope John Paul II).

The limestone hill of the Wawel that lies above Kraków's historic centre is the site of a complex housing some of the city's most important buildings, including the Royal Palace. Today the palace accommodates a museum displaying tapestries, the Royal Treasury, standards and antique furniture. Wawel Cathedral, where the kings of Poland were buried, also stands here.

At the entrance to the Wawel lies the start of the ancient Royal Way of monuments and remarkable historical buildings, leading to the heart of the old city: the market square (Rynek Główny). Extending 200 m along each side, this is one of the largest medieval public squares in Europe. One side is dominated by the Gothic church of the Assumption of the Virgin Mary while in the centre is the Sukiennice, the ancient cloth market.

Wawel Cathedral (the Basilica of Saints Stanisław and Waclaw) was for centuries the scene of the main events of the Polish royal families – coronations, weddings, funerals and burials.

In the part of the Wawel Castle accessible on the river Wisła there is a small park at the base of the hill with the cave of the legendary Krak, prince and head of a Slav tribe.

In the Second World War the 64,000-strong Jewish community of Kazimierz was deported, eventually to the nearby concentration camps at Auschwitz; only 6,000 returned at the end of the war.

Rock-Hewn Churches, Lalibela
Ethiopia

Criteria – Human creative genius; Interchange of values; Testimony to cultural tradition

The eleven medieval monolithic churches of this thirteenth-century 'New Jerusalem' are situated in a mountainous region in the heart of Ethiopia near a traditional village with circular-shaped dwellings. The churches are carved from solid rock and are recessed below ground level. Lalibela is a high place of Ethiopian Christianity, tended by Coptic priests and still today a place of pilgrimage and devotion.

The rock churches are connected by maze-like tunnels, with a small river running between them called the Jordan. Churches on one side of the Jordan represent the earthly Jerusalem; those on the other side represent the heavenly Jerusalem.

◄ The Bete Giorgis Church.

City of Quito
Ecuador

Criteria – Interchange of values; Significance in human history

Quito, the capital of Ecuador, was founded in the sixteenth century on the ruins of an Inca city and stands at an altitude of 2,850 m. Despite the 1917 earthquake, the city has the best-preserved, least altered historic centre in Latin America. The monasteries of San Francisco and Santo Domingo, and the Church and Jesuit College of La Compañía, with their rich interiors, are pure examples of the 'Baroque school of Quito', which is a fusion of Spanish, Italian, Moorish, Flemish and indigenous art.

Quito is built on uneven land traversed by two deep ravines (quebradas). One of the ravines is arched over partly to preserve the alignment of the streets, the drainage of which escapes through a cleft in the ridge northward to the plain of Tumbaco.

◄ Santo Domingo Monastery and Church.

Aachen Cathedral
Germany

Criteria – Human creative genius; Interchange of values; Significance in human history; Heritage associated with events of universal significance

With its columns of Greek and Italian marble, bronze doors, octagonal basilica and cupola, the Palatine Chapel of Aachen was from its inception regarded as an exceptional architectural achievement. It was the largest domed structure to be built north of the Alps since antiquity. Construction began around 790–800 under the Emperor Charlemagne, who was buried there. Throughout the Middle Ages it remained one of the prototypes of religious architecture and German emperors continued to be crowned there until 1531. Its present form has evolved over the course of more than a millennium. Two parts of the original complex have survived: the Coronation Hall, which is currently located in the Town Hall, built in the fourteenth century, and the Palatine Chapel, around which the cathedral would later be built.

When he began work on the Palatine Chapel, Charlemagne's dream was to create a 'new Rome'. Two hundred years later, when he was canonized, pilgrims began flocking to the town to see his tomb and the relics he had gathered. The town's ties with Charlemagne are reflected in numerous architectural memorials.

Yellowstone National Park
USA

Criteria – Natural phenomena or beauty; Major stages of Earth's history; Significant ecological and biological processes; Significant natural habitat for biodiversity

Yellowstone National Park covers 9,000 km² of a vast natural forest of the southern Rocky Mountains in the North American west. The park holds half of the world's known geothermal features, with over 10,000 examples, and is equally renowned for its wildlife which includes grizzly bears, wolves, bison and wapitis.

Established as America's first national park in 1872, Yellowstone boasts an impressive array of geothermal phenomena, with geysers, lava formations, fumaroles, hot springs and waterfalls, lakes and canyons. There are more than 580 geysers – the world's largest concentration, and two-thirds of all those on the planet. The source of these phenomena lies under the ground in the area's geological origins: Yellowstone is part of the most seismically active region of the Rocky Mountains, a volcanic 'hot spot'.

Crustal uplifts 65 million years ago formed the southern Rocky Mountains and volcanic outflows were common until around 40 million years ago. A more recent period of volcanism began in the region about 2 million years ago, when thousands of cubic kilometres of magma filled immense chambers under the plateau and then erupted to the surface. Three cycles of eruption produced huge explosive outbursts of ash. The latest cycle formed a caldera 45 km wide and 75 km long when the active magma chambers erupted and collapsed. The crystallizing magma is the source of heat for hydrothermal features such as geysers, hot springs, mud pots and fumaroles.

Most of the area was glaciated during the Pleistocene (from 1.8 million to 10,000 years ago, when the last ice age ended) and many glacial features remain. The park lies at the headwaters of three major rivers – Yellowstone, Madison and Snake. Yellowstone Lake at 2,357 m is North America's largest lake at high elevation, while Lower Yellowstone Falls is the highest of more than forty named waterfalls in the park.

Great elevational differences produce a range of plant communities, from semi-arid steppe to alpine tundra. The park has seven species of coniferous tree, especially lodgepole pine, and 1,100 species of vascular plant, including an endemic grass. Thermal areas have unique assemblages of thermal algae and bacteria.

Yellowstone has six native species of ungulate, including elk. There has been intensive study and management of grizzly bear for thirty years, and regulations also protect native fish.

Castle Geyser is located in the Upper Geyser Basin in Yellowstone National Park. The geyser is thought to be approximately 5,000 years old, and will erupt hot water for 20 minutes up to a height of 27 m, once every 12 hours.

The Yellowstone Plateau, now a forested area of 6,500 km² with an average elevation of 2,000 m, was formed out of the accumulation of rhyolite magma. The plateau is flanked on the north, east and south by mountains rising to 4,000 m.

Ninety-six per cent of the Yellowstone National Park lies in Wyoming, three per cent in Montana and one per cent in Idaho.

Archaeological investigations show that human groups visited the park area for 10,000 years but none made it a permanent home.

World Heritage site since

· ·1978

Wieliczka and Bochnia Royal Salt Mines
Poland
Criteria – Significance in human history

The Wieliczka Salt Mine, located in southern Poland near the city of Kraków, has been worked as a source of rock salt since the late thirteenth century. Spread over nine levels, it has 300 km of galleries, connecting more than 2,000 excavation chambers.

Over the centuries, miners have established a tradition of carving sculptures out of the native rock salt. As a result, the mine contains entire underground churches, altars, bas-reliefs, and dozens of life-size or larger statues. It also houses an underground museum and has a number of special-purpose chambers such as a sanatorium for people suffering from respiratory ailments. The subterranean lake, open to tourists since the fifteenth century, completes this curious complex.

Bochnia Royal Salt Mines and the Wieliczka Saltworks Castle used for the management of the property were added as extensions to the site in 2013.

The largest of the underground chapels, the Chapel of the Blessed Kinga, is located 101 m below the surface; it is over 50 m long, 15 m wide and 12 m high, with a volume of 10,000 m³.

▼

Simien National Park
Ethiopia

Criteria – Natural phenomena or beauty;
Significant natural habitat for biodiversity

With its abundance of creviced basalt rock, Simien serves as an ideal water catchment area, replenished by two wet seasons and the Mayshasha River. Consequently the park is rich in a wide range of wildlife and vegetation.

Massive erosion over many years on the Ethiopian plateau has created one of the most spectacular landscapes in the world, with jagged mountain peaks, deep valleys and sharp precipices dropping some 1,500 m. The park is home to some extremely rare animals such as the Gelada baboon, the Simien fox and the Walia ibex, a goat found nowhere else in the world.

◄

Gelada baboon

L'Anse aux Meadows National Historic Site
Canada

Criteria – Heritage associated with events of universal significance

The area has been home to many different cultures. The earliest signs of human activity go back roughly 5,000 years to the Dorset and Groswater paleoeskimo. It was from here that exploration around the Gulf of St Lawrence and into Vinland by the Vikings led to the first encounters between Europeans and North American Aboriginal peoples.

Located at the tip of the Great Northern Peninsula on the Island of Newfoundland, L'Anse aux Meadows is the oldest known European settlement and the only authenticated Viking site on the American continent. Here, archaeologists have unearthed evidence of European exploration in North America dating back around 1000 years, well before Columbus or Cabot.

In 1960, Helge and Anne Stein Ingstad, with the help of local fisherman George Decker, uncovered the remnants of eight wood-framed, peat-turf buildings similar to those found in Greenland and Iceland.

A forge, four workshops, and numerous artefacts have been found – a cloak pin, needle and spindle whorl indicate Norse origin and the presence of women in camp, while the metal slag found indicates the first forging of iron in the New World. Wood debris and nail fragments point to ship repair as one of the main activities by Vikings at L'Anse aux Meadows, which is likely the 'gateway to Vinland' mentioned in the sagas.

World Heritage site since

· ·1978

Nahanni National Park
Canada

Criteria – Natural phenomena or beauty; Major
stages of Earth's history

Located in the southwest corner of the
Northwest Territories, along the course
of the South Nahanni and Flat rivers, the
park lies in a diverse mountainous area
comprising mountain ranges, rolling
hills, rugged plateaus, deep canyons and
spectacular waterfalls, as well as a globally
significant limestone cave system. The
park has many unique geological features
including tufa mounds known as the
Rabbitkettle Hotsprings, which rise in a
succession of terraces to a height of 27 m.
There are also wind-eroded sandstone
landforms known as the Sand Blowouts, and
large areas that have remained unglaciated
for more than 100,000 years. The park is
home to animals of the boreal forest, such
as bald eagles, grizzly bears and caribou.

Parks Canada is
working with the
Dene and Metis
people to expand
Nahanni National
Park Reserve. The
expanded park
will protect more
wildlife habitat
and outstanding
geological features.

World Heritage site since

· ·1978 ·1979

Meidan Emam, Esfahan
Islamic Republic of Iran

Criteria – Human creative genius; Traditional
human settlement; Heritage associated with
events of universal significance

The Royal Square (Meidan Emam) of
Esfahan is a monument of Persian socio-
cultural life during the Safawid period. Built
by Shah Abbas the Great at the beginning
of the seventeenth century, it is bordered
on each side by four monumental buildings
linked by a series of two-storey arcades: to
the north the Portico of Qeyssariyeh (1602–
19), to the south the Royal Mosque (1612–30),
to the east the Mosque of Sheyx Loffollah
(1602–18), and to the west the pavilion of
Ali Qapu, a small fifteenth-century Timurid
palace, enlarged and decorated by the shah
and his successors. All of these architectural
elements of the Meidan-e Shah, including
the arcades, are adorned with a profusion of
painted ceramic tiles.

The Royal Square
was the heart of
the Safawid capital.
Its vast sandy
esplanade was used
for promenades,
assembling troops,
playing polo,
celebrations and
public executions. On
all sides, the arcades
house shops. Above
the portal of the large
bazaar of Qeyssariyeh
is a tribune that
accommodates
musicians giving
public concerts.

World Heritage site since

· 1978 · **1979**

Ancient City of Damascus
Syrian Arab Republic

Criteria – Human creative genius; Interchange of values; Testimony to cultural tradition; Significance in human history; Heritage associated with events of universal significance

Damascus preserves a few traces of its long history prior to the Arabic conquest, including some from the Roman period.

Over the centuries guilds of craftsmen and merchants established themselves around the city's **Great Mosque**, (pictured below) while the important Christian minority consolidated itself in the northeast quarters, around the churches and sites associated with the conversion of St Paul.

Founded in the third millennium BC, Damascus is considered to be the oldest city and oldest capital of the world. It is the cradle of historical civilizations, constituting an ancient beacon of science and art over time, and a reference for systems of architecture and town planning over several thousand years.

Damascus had many rulers, including King David of Israel and Alexander the Great, before it became part of the Arab world as the capital of Umayyad caliph in 636.

In the Middle Ages it was the centre of a flourishing craft industry, specializing in swords and lace.

The city has some 125 monuments from the different periods of its history, one of the most spectacular being the eighth century Great Mosque of the Umayyads, built on the site of an Assyrian sanctuary.

Auschwitz Birkenau, German Nazi Concentration and Extermination Camp (1940–1945)
Poland

Criteria – Heritage associated with events of universal significance

Auschwitz-Birkenau was the principal and most notorious of the six concentration and extermination camps established by Nazi Germany to implement its Final Solution policy which had as its aim the mass murder of the Jewish people in Europe. It was built in Poland under Nazi German occupation initially as a concentration camp for prisoners of war. Between the years 1942–4 it became the main mass extermination camp where Jews were tortured and killed for their so-called racial origins. In addition to the mass murder of well over a million Jewish men, women and children, and tens of thousands of Polish victims, Auschwitz also served as a camp for the racial murder of thousands of Roma and Sinti and prisoners of several European nationalities. The Nazi policy of spoliation, degradation and extermination of the Jews was rooted in a racist and anti-Semitic ideology propagated by the Third Reich.

Auschwitz-Birkenau was the largest of the concentration camp complexes created by the Nazi German regime and was the one which combined extermination with forced labour. At the centre of a huge landscape of human exploitation and suffering, the remains of the two camps of Auschwitz I and Auschwitz II-Birkenau, as well as its Protective Zone were placed on the World Heritage List as evidence of this inhumane,

cruel and methodical effort to deny human dignity to groups considered inferior, leading to their systematic murder. The camps are a vivid testimony to the murderous nature of the anti-Semitic and racist Nazi policy that brought about the annihilation of more than 1.2 million people in the crematoria, 90 per cent of whom were Jews.

The fortified walls, barbed wire, railway sidings, platforms, barracks, gallows, gas chambers and crematoria at Auschwitz-Birkenau show clearly how the Holocaust, as well as the Nazi German policy of mass murder and forced labour took place. The collections at the site preserve the evidence of those who were premeditatedly murdered, as well as presenting the systematic mechanism by which this was done. The personal items in the collections are testimony to the lives of the victims before they were brought to the extermination camps, as well as to the cynical use of their possessions and remains. The site and its landscape has high levels of authenticity and integrity since the original evidence has been carefully conserved without any unnecessary restoration.

Auschwitz-Birkenau, monument to the deliberate genocide of the Jews by the Nazi regime (Germany 1933–45) and to the deaths of countless others, bears irrefutable evidence to one of the greatest crimes ever perpetrated against humanity. It is also a monument to the strength of the human spirit which in appalling conditions of adversity resisted the efforts of the German Nazi regime to suppress freedom and free thought and to wipe out whole races. The site is a key place of memory for the whole of humankind for the holocaust, racist policies and barbarism; it is a place of our collective memory of this dark chapter in the history of humanity, of transmission to younger generations and a sign of warning of the many threats and tragic consequences of extreme ideologies and denial of human dignity.

World Heritage site since

· 1978 · **1979**

Ngorongoro Conservation Area
Tanzania

Criteria – Significance in human history; Natural phenomena or beauty; Major stages of Earth's history; Significant ecological and biological processes; Significant natural habitat for biodiversity

The huge and perfect crater of Ngorongoro is one of the largest inactive, unbroken and unflooded calderas in the world. Its diverse landforms and altitudes and its variable climate have resulted in the development of several distinct habitats: scrub heath and the remains of dense montane forests on its steep slopes, with grassy plains, lakes, swamps and woodland on the crater floor. Around 25,000 large animals live in the crater, including the highest density of mammalian predators in Africa.

Ngorongoro Conservation Area also includes Empakaai Crater, filled by a deep lake, and the active volcano of Oldonyo Lenga. At nearby Olduvai Gorge, excavations uncovered the existence of one of our more distant ancestors, Homo habilis. Laitoli Site, also in the area, is one of the main localities of early hominid footprints, dating back 3.6 million years. Leopard and the endangered African elephant, mountain reedbuck, flamingo, wildebeest and buffalo are among the species that live on the crater rim.

▲
Ngorongoro crater is, on average, 16–19 km wide, its floor is 264 km^2 and its rim soars to 400–610 m.

One of the Park's wildebeest with flamingos in the background.
▼

World Heritage site since

· 1978 · **1979**

Bryggen
Norway
Criteria – Testimony to cultural tradition

Bryggen is the old wharf of the city of Bergen. With its traditional wooden buildings and street patterns, Bryggen is a relic of an ancient wooden urban structure once common in Northern Europe and is a reminder of the town's importance as part of the trading empire of the powerful North German and Baltic Hanseatic League from the fourteenth to the mid-sixteenth century.

Over the centuries several devastating fires, the most recent in 1955, have ravaged

Bryggen today. ▼

the traditional wooden houses. However, rebuilding has traditionally followed old patterns and methods, so leaving its main structure preserved, and the town retains its medieval appearance. Some sixty-two buildings remain of this former townscape.

Today, Bergen is the only overseas trading post of the Hanseatic League whose original structures still remain within the city limits and cityscape.

The Hanseatic League took control of Bergen in 1350 and the German colonists who arrived thereafter directly influenced the appearance of Bryggen, with buildings constructed along the narrow streets running parallel to the dock.

The urban unit revolves around a courtyard (gård) common to several three-level wooden houses whose gabled façades and lateral walls and roofs are covered with shingles.

World Heritage site since

· 1978 · **1979**

Forts and Castles, Volta, Greater Accra, Central and Western Regions
Ghana

Criteria – Heritage associated with events of universal significance

The remains of fortified trading-posts, established between 1482 and 1786, can still be seen along the coast of Ghana between Keta and Beyin. They were links in the trade routes established by the Portuguese in many areas of the world during their era of great maritime exploration. Accra was first settled at the end of the sixteenth century when the Ga people migrated there. These early inhabitants engaged in farming and lagoon fishing, with sea fishing taken up during the middle of the eighteenth century. During the slave trade Accra took on greater importance owing to the nearby forts, many of which were owned and controlled by the Dutch, a prominence that lasted until the abolition of the slave trade in 1807.

The forts and castles at Accra were of great strategic value and were occupied at different times by European traders and adventurers from Portugal, Spain, Denmark, Sweden, Holland, Germany and Britain.

Prehistoric Sites and Decorated Caves of the Vézère Valley
France

Criteria – Human creative genius; Testimony to cultural tradition

The Vézère Valley contains 147 prehistoric sites dating from the Palaeolithic and twenty-five decorated caves. It is particularly interesting from an ethnological and anthropological, as well as an aesthetic point of view because of its cave paintings, especially those of the Lascaux Cave, whose discovery in 1940 was of great importance for the history of prehistoric art. The hunting scenes show some 100 animal figures, which are remarkable for their detail, rich colours and lifelike quality.

The depictions of animals involved in the hunt helped to assure or reassure the hunters of great success. The Lascaux Cave is closed to the public, but a replica has been created at Montignac, 200 m from the original cave, where two of the galleries have been reproduced: the Great Hall of the Bulls and the Painted Gallery.

◄
Lascaux Cave.

World Heritage site since

· 1978 · **1979**

Virunga National Park
Dem. Rep. of the Congo

Criteria – *Natural phenomena or beauty; Major stages of Earth's history; Significant natural habitat for biodiversity*

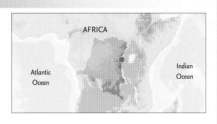

AFRICA

Atlantic
Ocean

Indian
Ocean

The areas of lowest and highest rainfall in the Democratic Republic of the Congo are in Virunga National Park.

The park is home to mountain gorillas, and before the recent war, there were some 20,000 hippopotamuses living in its rivers. Its wetlands are a wintering ground for some bird species from Siberia.

Virunga National Park lies at the border of several biogeographic zones and comprises an outstanding diversity of habitats. The range of altitudes in the park, which covers an area of 7,900 km², adds to a habitat variety ranging from swamps and savannas to the Rwenzori snowfields at a height of over 5,000 m; and from lava plains to the afromontane forests on the slopes of volcanoes. There are hot springs in the Rwindi plains, and some of the Virunga Massif volcanoes, such as Nyiragongo (3,470 m), are still active.

At the time of inscription on the World Heritage List, the rivers of Virunga had probably the largest hippopotamus concentration in Africa.

The savanna of the Rwindi area is home to elephant, buffalo, antelope, warthog, lion and various monkeys. The Semiliki Valley and the Virunga mountains are the habitat of gorilla, chimpanzee and okapi. The park also includes important wetlands, which are recognized under the Ramsar Convention on Wetlands and are important transit and wintering areas for some bird species.

◀
Mountain gorilla 'Bonane' holds her newborn in Virunga National Park.

World Heritage site since

· 1978 · **1979**

Site of Carthage
Tunisia

Criteria – Interchange of values; Testimony to
cultural tradition; Heritage associated with
events of universal significance

EUROPE

Mediterranean Sea

AFRICA

Carthage is one of the most famous historic
sites of the Roman Empire with a period of
domination that spanned several centuries,
making it one of the largest and longest-
lasting of the ancient empires.

At a time when the sea was the most
efficient means of travel and
communication, Carthage's two first-class
harbours gave it a distinct advantage over
other city states. The Carthaginians
developed superb shipbuilding and sailing
skills that were the basis of a centuries-long
naval and mercantile domination. They also
supported what was at its height a great
trading empire that spanned the
Mediterranean. The Carthaginians traded
in silver, lead, ivory and gold, beds and
bedding, simple pottery, jewellery,
glassware, African wild animals, fruit and
nuts. The huge wealth Carthage acquired
saw it become the home to a brilliant
civilization and one of the largest cities in
the pre-industrial world.

The city was founded in the ninth
century BC by Phoenician traders from
Tyre, in modern Lebanon, and by the sixth
century BC had conquered and controlled
much of the southern Mediterranean: the
North African coast from modern Morocco
to the borders of modern Egypt, Sardinia,
Malta, the Balearic Islands, and western
Sicily. This expansion inevitably brought
Carthage into conflict with the other
dominant regional powers – the empires
first of Greece and then of Rome, and the
three battled for control over territories.
Competition over Sicily sparked the war
against Greece lasting for more than 200
years; this ended in victory for the
Carthaginians. The wars against Rome,
known as the Punic Wars, were divided into
three periods between 264 BC and 146 BC,
when the Romans finally triumphed. They
razed Carthage, imposing strict controls
over further settlement; in the process
much of the evidence and artefacts of the
ancient city was destroyed.

In the first century AD the Roman Emperor
Augustus founded the city anew, as Colonia
Julia Carthago. This second, Roman
Carthage grew on the ruins of the first and
prospered quickly, becoming second only to
Rome in splendour and wealth.

The city's ultimate decline was confirmed
in AD 439 with the occupation by the Vandals
and finally in AD 637 when it was captured by
Arabs and destroyed. Carthage never
regained its importance, largely because of
the concentration of power in nearby Tunis.

Both images show
sections of the
Antonine Baths at
Carthage, with the
top one showing
fragments of the
ruined 'caldarium'
(the hottest room)
and the steam room.

The refounded first
century city of Julia
Carthago illustrated
the splendour and
wealth of Rome, and
exerted considerable
influence on the
development of
structural architecture
and of characteristic
Punic and Roman
town planning. It is
also an important
testimony to Punic
history and
constitutes an
interesting example
of the Punic city.

The Punic port is the
best place to visit, as
Carthage was a port
that was stronger on
the seas than the
Roman Empire for
many years.

Dinosaur Provincial Park
Canada

Criteria – Natural phenomena or beauty; Major
stages of Earth's history

Dinosaur Provincial Park contains some of
the most important fossil discoveries ever
made from the 'Age of Reptiles' – in
particular, about thirty-nine species of
dinosaur, dating back some 75 million years.
The park stands at the heart of Alberta's
badlands, a beautiful, barren and deeply
eroded area of sparse vegetation.

During the late Cretaceous period
75 million years ago, the landscape of the
area was very different, with lush forests and
rivers flowing into a warm inland sea. Its low
swamps were home to a variety of animals,
including dinosaurs. The conditions were
also perfect for the preservation of their
bones as fossils.

The badlands now provide habitat for a
number of ecologically specialized plant
species. The mild winter microclimate
coupled with an abundant food supply,
supports native ungulates and over
165 species of bird have been recorded.

▲

Erosion has left exposed Cretaceous
shales and sandstones and created
extensive badlands, the largest in
Canada.

Geological strata of the Dinosaur
Park Formation yielded many of the
dinosaur remains for which the park
is renowned. Between 1979 and
1991, a total of 23,347 fossil
specimens were collected, including
300 dinosaur skeletons.

World Heritage site since

· 1978 · **1979**

Abu Mena
Egypt
Criteria – Significance in human history

The church, baptistry, basilicas, public buildings, streets, monasteries, houses and workshops in this early Christian holy city were built over the tomb of the martyr Menas of Alexandria, who died in AD 296. The Thermal Basilica, built in the fifth century to accommodate the increasing number of Christian pilgrims, was used to store the curative waters for the surrounding heated baths and pools.

By AD 600, the oasis at Abu Mena had become a pilgrimage destination, centred on the great basilica complex. Archaeological excavations have revealed an entire town with houses and cemeteries, which exhibit an important fusion of East and West religious influences.

◄

The ancient public baths of Abu Mena.

Thracian Tomb of Kazanlak
Bulgaria
Criteria – Human creative genius; Testimony to cultural tradition; Significance in human history

Discovered in 1944, this Hellenistic tomb is located in Bulgaria's romantic Valley of Roses. Part of a large necropolis with more than 500 burial mounds, it lies near Seuthopolis, the capital city of the Thracian king Seutes III. The art and archaeological discoveries of the site reflect a rich culture that was at its peak in the fifth to third centuries BC. The pattern of the particularly fine Kazanlak Tomb murals shows that they were not painted spontaneously: the paintings are a carefully premeditated artistic composition executed in accordance with a precise project. The architecture and the pattern of the composition were prepared together as an integrated work of art. It is clear that both were the work of one person – an artist-architect.

The murals of the Kazanlak Tomb are particularly important because they are the only entirely preserved work of Hellenistic art that has been found in exactly the state in which it was originally designed and executed.

World Heritage site since

· 1978 · **1979**

Kathmandu Valley
Nepal

Criteria – Testimony to cultural tradition;
Significance in human history; Heritage
associated with events of universal significance

ASIA

Arabian
Sea

Bay of
Bengal

Kathmandu Valley
has seven
monumental zones
with three historical
palaces within their
urban settings (the
cities of Kathmandu,
Patan and Bhaktapur),
two Hindu centres
(Pashupati and
Changu Narayan) and
two Buddhist centres
(Swayambunath and
Boudhanath).

Kathmandu, the
Nepalese capital, is
the country's political
and commercial hub
and is an exotic and
fascinating showcase
of culture, art and
tradition. The valley in
which the cities of
Kathmandu, Patan
and Bhaktapur stand
is roughly an oval
bowl encircled by
green, terraced hills
dotted with compact
clusters of red tiled-
roofed houses.

The world-famous Kathmandu Valley has a
concentration of monuments unique and
unparalleled in the world. It is the principal
centre of settlement in the hill area of
Nepal and is a prime cultural focus of the
Himalaya. The Kathmandu Valley
monumental zones represent a highly
developed architectural expression of the
religious, political and cultural life of the
area.

The seven groups of monuments and
buildings include: the Durbar Square of
Hanuman Dhoka (or Hanuman Gate) in
Kathmandu, the Durbar Square of Patan
and the Durbar Square of Bhaktapur; the
Buddhist stupas of Swayambhu and of
Bauddhanath; and the Hindu temples of
Pashupati and Changu Narayan.

Pashupati is Nepal's most renowned
Hindu cremation site. Changu Narayan
Temple is an impressive double-roofed
temple which is said to be the most ancient
temple of the Hindu god Vishnu in the
Kathmandu Valley.

The city of Kathmandu is a melting pot for
the nation's population and its unique
architectural heritage, palaces, temples and
courtyards have inspired many writers,
artists, and poets, both foreign and
Nepalese. It boasts a unique symbiosis of
Hinduism, Buddhism and Tantrism in its

culture, which is still as alive today as it was
hundreds of years ago. The religious
influence can be openly seen in the city.
Most of the principal monuments are in
Durbar Square, the city's social, religious
and urban focal point, built between the
twelfth and the eighteenth centuries by the
ancient Malla kings of Nepal. Some of the
most interesting are the Taleju Temple, Kal
Bhairab, Nautalle Durbar, Coronation
Nasal Chowk, and the Gaddi Baithak, the
statue of King Pratap Malla, the Big Bell,
Big Drum and the Jaganath Temple.

Patan (or Lalitpur), just across the holy
Bagmati River about 14 km east of
Kathmandu city, is of great historic and
cultural interest, and the city of Bhaktapur
(or Bhadgaon) stands at an altitude of
1,401 m.

Pashupati Temple is one of the most
important Hindu temples as well as Nepal's
most sacred Hindu shrine and one of the
subcontinent's greatest sites for the god
Shiva in a sprawling collection of temples,
ashrams, images and inscriptions raised
over the centuries along the banks of the
sacred Bagmati River.

Durbar Square of ▶
Patan.

Kluane / Wrangell-St Elias / Glacier Bay / Tatshenshini-Alsek
Canada and USA

Criteria – *Natural phenomena or beauty; Major stages of Earth's history; Significant ecological and biological processes; Significant natural habitat for biodiversity*

Pacific Ocean

NORTH AMERICA

Atlantic Ocean

Geologically the mountains are part of the Pacific mountain system and include the 130 km-long Bagley ice field, the second-highest peak in the USA (Mount St Elias) and the largest piedmont glacier on the North American continent (Malaspina Glacier).

A unique area of mountain peaks, foothills, glacial systems, lakes, streams, valleys and coastal landscapes make up these spectacular parks stretching from British Columbia and Yukon Territory in Canada across the border to Alaska in the United States.

The Wrangell-St Elias region has the largest array of glaciers and ice fields outside the polar region. These glacial features and the high mountains of the Wrangell-St Elias, Chugach and Kluane ranges have resulted in the region being called the Mountain Kingdom of North America.

The variety of climatic zones and elevations have produced three major biomes or ecological areas: coastal coniferous; northern coniferous; and alpine tundra. The great variety of birds and wildlife, including grizzly bears, caribou and Dall's sheep, reflects this habitat diversity. There are freshwater fish and all five species of Alaskan Pacific salmon spawn in park or preserve waters.

Braided river.
▼

Everglades National Park
USA

Criteria – Major stages of Earth's history;
Significant ecological and biological processes;
Significant natural habitat for biodiversity

NORTH
AMERICA

Pacific
Ocean

Atlantic
Ocean

The vegetation and flora of south Florida have long fascinated scientists and naturalists and were a primary reason for the establishment of the park.

Everglades National Park, pictured below, on the southern tip of the Florida Peninsula has been called 'a river of grass flowing imperceptibly from the hinterland into the sea'. Its exceptional variety of water habitats has made it a sanctuary for large numbers of birds and reptiles, including threatened species such as the manatee.

The park lies at the interface between temperate and subtropical America, between fresh and brackish water and between shallow bays and deeper coastal waters. Consequently it hosts a complex of habitats supporting a high diversity of flora and fauna including many endemic to this area.

The Everglades protect 800 species of land and water vertebrates, over 400 bird species and sixty known species of reptile, amphibian and insect. Over 275 species of fish mostly inhabit the marine and estuarine waters and there are great numbers of economically valuable crustaceans.

Hammocks or tree islands are dominated by tropical and temperate hardwood species. The most important trees are mangroves, taxa, slash pine and cypress. Prairies can be dominated by sawgrass, muhley grass, or cordgrass in coastal areas.

World Heritage site since

• 1978 • **1979**

Grand Canyon National Park
USA

Criteria – Natural phenomena or beauty; Major
stages of Earth's history; Significant ecological and
biological processes; Significant natural habitat for
biodiversity

NORTH
AMERICA

Pacific
Ocean

Atlantic
Ocean

The Grand Canyon, carved nearly 1,500 m
deep into the rock by the Colorado River, is
the most spectacular gorge in the world. Its
horizontal strata retrace the geological
history of the past two billion years as it cuts
across the Grand Canyon National Park. It
also contains prehistoric traces of human
adaptation to a particularly harsh
environment.

The Grand Canyon dominates the national
park, which was created in 1919 by an act of
Congress and was one of the first national
parks in the United States. The steep,
twisting gorge, 1.5 km deep and 445.8 km
long, was formed during some 6 million
years of geological activity and erosion by
the Colorado River on the raised Earth's
crust (2.5 km above sea level). The gorge,
which ranges from 200 m–30 km wide,
divides the park into the North Rim and
South Rim: the buttes, spires, mesas and
temples in the canyon are in fact mountains,
looked down upon from the rims.

Erosion is ongoing and seasonal and
permanent rivers produce impressive
waterfalls and rapids of washed-down
boulders along the length of the canyon and
its tributaries. The horizontal geological
strata that erosion has exposed span some
2,000 million years of geological history,
providing evidence of the four major
geological eras: early and late Precambrian,
Palaeozoic, Mesozoic and Cenozoic.

The canyon is also a vast biological
museum in which there are five different life
and vegetation zones. Over 1,000 plant
species have so far been identified including
several officially listed as threatened. The
park is also home to 76 mammal, 299 bird
and 41 reptile and amphibian species, and
some 16 fish species inhabit the Colorado
River and its tributaries.

Archaeological remains show the
adaptation of human societies to the area's
severe climate and landscape, with evidence
of settlement. The park contains more than
2,600 documented prehistoric ruins,
including evidence of Archaic cultures (the
earliest known inhabitants), Cohonina
Indians along the South Rim, and Anasazi
Indians on both the South Rim, North Rim,
and within the Inner Canyon. Hualapai and
Havasupai Indians moved into the canyons
at this time, remaining undisturbed until the
arrival of the Anglo-Americans in 1860.

▶ Low sunlight helps to
reveal the canyon's
horizontal strata.

The Grand Canyon
area was first
protected in 1893 as a
forest reserve in which
mining, lumbering
and hunting
continued to be
allowed. It was
upgraded to a game
reserve in 1906, giving
protection to the
wildlife, and
redesignated a
National Monument
in 1908.

Altitudinal range
provides a variety of
climates and habitats,
ranging from desert
to mountain
conditions.

Fossil remains found
in the park include
early plants, marine
and terrestrial
specimens, early
reptiles and some
mammals.

Nubian Monuments from Abu Simbel to Philae
Egypt

Criteria – Human creative genius; Testimony to cultural tradition; Heritage associated with events of universal significance

This part of southern Egypt, extending from Aswan to the Sudanese border, is an area of outstanding archaeological importance containing magnificent ancient monuments, including the temples of the Pharaoh Ramses II at Abu Simbel and the Sanctuary of Isis at Philae.

Built by Ramses at Abu Simbel in Nubia to reaffirm the Egyptian Empire's ownership of what was then its southern neighbour, the Great Temple has four colossal statues of the pharaoh carved into the rock and fastened to the cliff wall. Nearby is the Little Temple, dedicated to the Goddess Hathor in memory of the pharaoh's wife Queen Nefertari.

In the 1960s the sites faced inundation by the river Nile as a consequence of the construction of the Aswan High Dam. UNESCO launched a successful international campaign to save the temples, which led to their removal to higher ground.

Interior of the Great Temple of Ramses II at Abu Simbel. ▲

▲

In addition the site includes the temples of Amada, Derr, Ouadi Es Sebouah, Dakka, Maharraqah, Talmis and Beit el Ouali and the Kiosk of ak-Kartassi.

West colonnade of the Sanctuary of Isis at Philae.

Plitvice Lakes National Park
Croatia

Criteria – Natural phenomena or beauty; Major stages of Earth's history; Significant ecological and biological processes

Plitvice Lakes National Park contains a series of outstandingly beautiful lakes, caves and waterfalls. There are approximately twenty interlinked lakes between Mala Kapela Mountain and Pljesevica Mountain.

The park's features were formed over thousands of years by the waters flowing over the limestone and chalk and depositing barriers of travertine rock, in the process creating natural dams; these in turn created the lakes, caves and waterfalls. These

geological processes continue today.

Varying altitudes and soils support a variety of plants. The dense forests of the park are rich in wildlife and are home to brown bears, wolves and many rare bird species. Archaeological remains show evidence of human settlement by an Illyrian tribe dating from 1000 BC.

To preserve the natural characteristics of the lakes, the park was extended in 2000, taking in more of the area's drainage system.

The lake system is divided into the upper and lower lakes. The upper lakes lie in a dolomite valley surrounded by thick forests and interlinked by numerous waterfalls. The lower lakes, smaller and shallower, lie on the limestone bedrock and are surrounded only by sparse underbrush.

▼

Mont-Saint-Michel and its Bay
France

Criteria – Human creative genius; Testimony to cultural tradition; Heritage associated with events of universal significance

Atlantic Ocean

EUROPE

This small rock outcrop, 900 m in circumference at its base and 80 m at its peak, stands about 2 km off the coast on sandy ground that is exposed at low tide.

Its exceptional situation between land and sea has determined the establishment and development of Mont-Saint-Michel, and the practical and aesthetic solutions to the challenges of its natural environment.

The abbey dominates and is controlled by a tiny village clinging to the foot of the mount.

Mont-Saint-Michel is one of the most important sites of medieval Christian civilization. The Gothic-style Benedictine abbey dedicated to the archangel Saint Michel and the village that grew up in the shadow of its great walls are together known as the 'Wonder of the West'. It is unequalled, as much because of the coexistence of the abbey and its fortified village within the confined limits of a small island, as for the originality of the placement of the buildings which give Mont-Saint-Michel its unforgettable silhouette. Built between the eleventh and sixteenth centuries, the abbey is a technical and artistic tour de force, having adapted to the problems posed by its unique position and site: perched on a rocky islet in the midst of vast sandbanks exposed to powerful tides between Normandy and Brittany. Mont-Saint-Michel forms an architectural complex of great originality, built by successive restructurings and additions throughout the Middle Ages.

In 966 Benedictine monks from St Wandrille founded the monastery of Saint-Michel-au-Péril-de-la-Mer on a granite tidal island in the bay of Mont-Saint-Michel. A sanctuary dedicated to Saint Michel had already existed on this location for a long time. The oldest part of the present abbey, the small pre-Romanesque church of Notre-Dame-sous-Terre, undoubtedly dates back to the tenth century. There are Romanesque influences in the nave of abbey church and in a group of convent buildings, including the chaplain's residence and the covered gallery of the monks, dating from the twelfth century.

However it was the architectural advances of the later medieval Gothic period that allowed the island's restricted area to be used to best advantage, in the high walls, soaring masses and airy pinnacles which so harmoniously crown the sharp silhouette of the rock. The new group of Romanesque convent buildings that were built from 1204, merit the name Merveille (Marvel) for the elegance of their conception. They comprise the chaplain's residence of the twelfth century; the celebrated rooms known as Salles des Hôtes and des Chevaliers, with rib vaults that spring from the central colonnades; and, on the uppermost floor beside the refectory, the cloister, which is open on one side to the sea.

Fasil Ghebbi, Gondar Region
Ethiopia

Criteria – Interchange of values; Testimony to cultural tradition

The fortress-city of Fasil Ghebbi is an outstanding testimony of the modern Ethiopian civilisation on the northern plateau of Tana. In the sixteenth and seventeenth centuries, this was the residence of the Ethiopian emperor Fasilides and his successors. Surrounded by a 900-m-long wall, the city contains palaces, churches, monasteries and unique public and private buildings marked by Hindu and Arab influences, subsequently transformed by the Baroque style brought to Gondar by the Jesuit missionaries. Beyond the confines of the city is a fine bathing palace, a two-

storeyed battlemented structure situated beside a rectangular pool of water which was supplied by a canal from the nearby river. It was reached by a stone bridge, part of which could be raised for defence.

The main castle, which stands today in a grassy compound surrounded by later fortresses, was built in the late 1630s and early 1640s. With its huge towers and looming battlemented walls, it resembles a piece of medieval Europe transposed to Ethiopia.
◄

Boyana Church
Bulgaria

Criteria – Interchange of values; Testimony to cultural tradition

Located on the outskirts of Sofia, Boyana Church consists of three buildings. The eastern church was built in the tenth century, then enlarged at the beginning of the thirteenth century by Sebastocrator Kaloyan, who ordered a second two-storey building to be erected next to it. The frescoes in this second church, painted in 1259, make it one of the most important

collections of medieval paintings. The ensemble is completed by a third church, built at the beginning of the nineteenth century. This site is one of the most complete and perfectly preserved monuments of east European medieval art.

Boyana's frescoes are an early example of the icon-painting style which strongly influenced the Tirnovo artistic school. The icon-style murals that became widespread in the Serbian, Russian and Mount Athos (Greece) monasteries during the fourteenth to sixteenth centuries are closely related to this innovation.

Belovezhskaya Pushcha / Białowieża Forest
Belarus and Poland

Criteria – Natural phenomena or beauty

The Białowieża Primeval Forest dates back to 8000 BC and is the only remaining example of the original forests which once covered much of Europe. Located on the watershed of the Baltic and Black seas, this immense forest range consisting of evergreens and broadleaved trees is the home of some remarkable animal life, including rare mammals such as the wolf, the lynx and the otter, as well as some 300 European Bison, a species which was reintroduced into the park in 1929. The birdlife includes corncrake, white-tailed eagle, white stork, peregrine falcon and eagle owl. Białowieża National Park comprises about one-tenth of the entire forest. It is the oldest national park in Poland and one of the oldest in Europe.

Almost 90 per cent of the Białowieża National Park is covered with 'old growth' virgin stands of mixed broadleaved and conifer forests.

Over 900 vascular plant species have been recorded, including 26 tree and 138 shrub species. Almost two-thirds are indigenous.

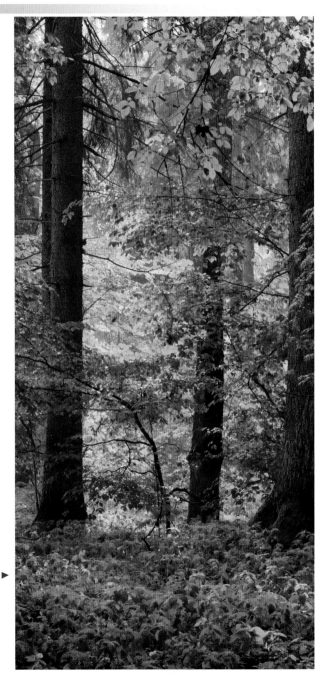

World Heritage site since

· 1978 · **1979**

Palace and Park of Versailles
France

Criteria – Human creative genius; Interchange of values; Heritage associated with events of universal significance

The Palace of Versailles. ▶

The Palace of Versailles, built and embellished by several generations of the foremost French architects, sculptors, decorators and landscape architects, was one of the largest royal palaces in the world and provided the model of the ideal royal residence for over a century. The prestigious ensemble of the palace, the Trianons and the Park of Versailles is the result of a century and a half of works commissioned by the kings of France and entrusted to their greatest artists. Versailles was the principal residence of the French kings from Louis XIV to Louis XVI (from 1682–1789) and became both the source and symbol of absolute royal power during the Ancien Régime.

Versailles was originally a small village some 20 km southwest of Paris, set in a wooded region chosen by Louis XIII as his personal hunting preserve. The modest brick and stone château that the king ordered built here in 1623 was two storeys tall and surrounded by a moat. Enlargements followed but the strongest imprint was left by Louis XIII's son, Louis XIV. Under the direction of Louis Le Vau, the king's architect, a programme of expansion and new building began in the 1660s. The decoration of the palace interior was supervised by the painter Charles Le Brun who, with teams of painters, decorators and craftsmen, created a remarkable complex of frescoes, marbles, stuccoes, gilded bronzes, fabrics, furniture and accessories in the palace halls.

After 1678 Versailles was considerably enlarged and radically modified by Jules Hardouin Mansart. He successfully introduced a sober and colossal architecture, homogeneous and majestic, that is inseparable even today from the memory of the 'Sun King', Louis XIV. It was during this phase of building that the palace developed the appearance that is recognizable now.

The gardens, which complete the palace, developed along with the general construction. They were designed by André Le Nôtre, who was responsible for the creation of the typology of the French garden, an open system of axial paths extending as far as the eye can see, punctuated geometrically by parterres of flowers and low hedges, little streams, large ponds and fountains.

The Orangerie and the Grand Trianon are the work of Jules Hardouin Mansart, who was assisted by Robert de Cotte in the construction of the Royal Chapel, a masterpiece of French Baroque.

The creations at Versailles during the eighteenth century are among the most perfect and most celebrated realizations of the Louis XV and Louis XVI styles: the Petit Trianon by Jacques-Ange Gabriel (1751), the decoration of the apartments of Louis XV by Verbeck and Rousseau, and the apartments and the Hameau of Marie-Antoinette by Mique.

Independence Hall
USA

Criteria – Heritage associated with events of
universal significance

Independence Hall in Philadelphia may be
considered the birthplace of the United
States of America: it was here that the
Declaration of Independence was signed in
1776, the Articles of Confederation uniting
the thirteen colonies were ratified in 1781,
and the Constitution setting out the nation's
basic laws was adopted in 1787, after George
Washington had presided over the debate,
which ran from May to September. The
universal principles of freedom and
democracy set forth in these documents are
of fundamental importance to American
history and have also had a profound impact
on law-makers around the world. The
building has undergone many restorations,
notably by Greek revival architect John
Haviland in 1830, and by a committee from
the National Park Service in 1950, returning
it to its 1776 appearance.

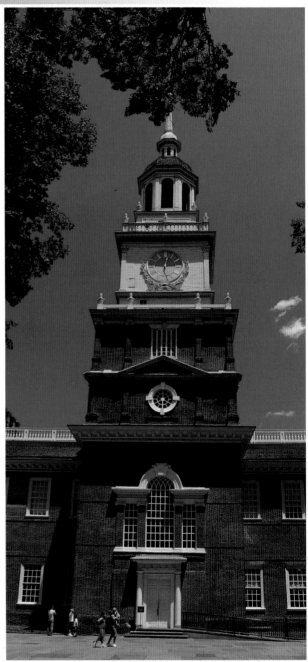

The building, finished in
1753, is a modest brick
structure with a steeple
that was intended to
hold a 943 kg bell. The
bell has however
cracked twice and
stands silently on the
ground in a special
shelter. A reproduction
now hangs in the
steeple. ▶

World Heritage site since

· 1978 · **1979**

Chartres Cathedral
France

Criteria – Human creative genius; Interchange of values; Significance in human history

Chartres Cathedral has retained in near totality its original stained-glass windows. The 55 lower windows are made up of large compartmentalized glass medallions in which are inscribed scenes of narrative cycles, while large figures, intended to be viewed from a distance, fill the 91 upper windows: in total there are 1,359 subjects ranged over 146 windows.

▼

Partly built, starting in 1145, and then reconstructed over a 26-year period after the fire of 1194, Chartres Cathedral marks the high point of French Gothic art. It is a place of pilgrimage, attracting throngs from all over the Christianized West. The cathedral, with its vast nave in pure ogival style, its porches adorned with fine sculptures from the mid-twelfth century, and the magnificent twelfth and thirteenth-century stained-glass windows, all in remarkable condition, combine to make it a masterpiece. Chartres Cathedral has exerted a considerable influence on the development of Gothic art both within and outside France. The fundamental design of the building was imitated at Cologne (Germany), Westminster (United Kingdom) and León (Spain).

Vézelay, Church and Hill
France

Criteria – Human creative genius; Heritage
associated with events of universal significance

The twelfth-century monastic church of the
Madeleine of Vézelay is a masterpiece of
Burgundian Romanesque art and
architecture. Believed to be the resting
place of the relics of St Mary Magdalene,
it has also been an important place of
pilgrimage since medieval times. The hill
of Vézelay was a site of devotion where
medieval Christian spirituality produced an
outflowing of expression, from prayer and
the epic poem to the Crusades for which it
was an important backdrop.

Established in the ninth century as a
Benedictine abbey on the hill at Vézelay, the
church came to prominence in the mid-
eleventh century when the belief spread that
it held the relics of St Mary Magdalene, the
penitent. Consequently Vézelay became a
popular pilgrimage destination, all the more
frequented because of its situation on one
of the routes leading to the great
pilgrimage site of Santiago de Compostela
in northwest Spain. The afflux of pilgrims
profited the town, which during the twelfth
century had 8,000–10,000 inhabitants, a
considerable population for the period.

Vézelay became a centre of great
importance in the Christian west. On Easter
Sunday in 1146 it hosted the assembly called
to celebrate the departure of the Second
Crusade and St Bernard preached to King

Louis VII, Queen Eleanor and a host of
nobles, prelates and people gathered on the
hill. In 1190 the kings of France and
England, Philippe II and Richard I, the
Lionheart, united their armies at Vézelay and
left together for the Third Crusade. In 1217
Francis of Assisi chose the hill of Vézelay to
found the first Franciscan establishment on
French soil; and Louis IX of France, King
Saint-Louis, who was especially devoted to
the Madeleine of Vézelay, visited on four
separate occasions.

With its sculpted capitals and portal, the
superb church remains the most striking
witness to this illustrious history. In
particular, it was the sculpted portal
between the nave and the narthex, its
enclosed porch, that brought universal
renown to Vézelay. The central tympanum
above the doorway bears the Mission of the
Apostles, an allegorical reference to the
importance of the Crusades. The breadth
and the complexity of the subject were
well-matched by the inventiveness and
passion of its sculptor who has produced
one of the major monuments of Western
Romanesque art.

The origins of Vézelay
are linked with the
memory of a knight
around whom a
legend had grown up.
Around AD 860 Girart
de Roussillon, the
hero of the epic poem
which bears his name,
founded a monastery
on the banks of the
Cure together with his
wife, Berthe. Ravaged
some years later by
the Normans, the
establishment, a
Benedictine abbey,
was rebuilt on the
summit of a
neighbouring hill, the
site of its present
location.

World Heritage site since

· 1978 · **1979**

Persepolis
Islamic Republic of Iran

Criteria – Human creative genius; Testimony to cultural tradition; Heritage associated with events of universal significance

According to Plutarch, the Greeks carried away the Persepolis treasures on 20,000 mules and 5,000 camels.

The magnificent ruins of Persepolis lie at the foot of Kuh-i-Rahmat (Mountain of Mercy), about 650 km south of the present capital city of Teheran. Founded by Darius I in 518 BC, Persepolis was the capital of the Achaemenid Empire. It was built on an immense half-artificial, half-natural terrace, where an impressive palace complex was constructed, inspired by Mesopotamian models. It seems that Darius planned this impressive complex not only as the seat of government but also, and primarily, as a show place and a spectacular centre for the receptions and festivals of the Achaemenid kings and their empire. What remains today, dominating the city, is the immense stone terrace (530 m by 330 m), backed against the mountains. The importance and quality of the monumental ruins make it a unique archaeological site.

Persepolis was the example par excellence of the dynastic city, the symbol of the Achaemenid dynasty, which is why it was burned by the Greeks of Alexander the Great in 330 BC.
▼

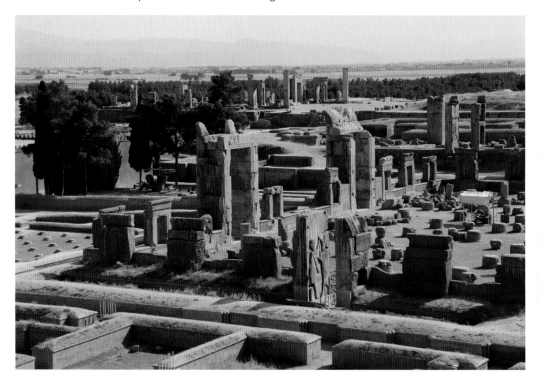

World Heritage site since

· 1978 · **1979**

Madara Rider
Bulgaria

Criteria – Human creative genius; Testimony to
cultural tradition

The Madara Rider is a majestic horseman
carved 23 m above ground level in an almost
vertical 100 m high cliff. The horseman is
thrusting a spear into a lion lying at his
horse's feet, while a dog runs after the
horseman. Madara was the principal sacred
place of the First Bulgarian Empire before
Bulgaria's conversion to Christianity in the
ninth century. The Madara Horseman was
carved at the very beginning of the eighth
century, about three decades after the
foundation of the Bulgarian State in AD 681.
The sculpture thus marks a triumph: the
Byzantine Empire had recognised the new
state. The relief is not an abstract artistic
scene but a powerful symbolic
representation of a specific historical and
cultural transition.

In creating these
remarkable figures,
first the sculptor
outlined the images
with a 1.5 cm wide and
2 cm deep groove in
the rock. Then he
hewed out the
surrounding surface
so that the figures
project from it. Finally
he covered the figures
in red plaster to
outline them even
more clearly against
the rock.

Rock-Hewn Churches of
Ivanovo
Bulgaria

Criteria – Interchange of values; Testimony to
cultural tradition

This remarkable complex of rock-hewn
churches, chapels, monasteries and cells lies
in the valley of the Roussenski Lom River,
near the village of Ivanovo. The first hermits
dug out small cells and churches here
during the twelfth century. Then, in the
thirteenth century, Bulgaria once again
embraced Orthodox Christianity. The first
Patriarch was the monk Gioacchino, who
shared with Tsar Ivan Ansen II the plan to
expand the Bulgarian church. Before taking
over the Patriarchal throne he had lived as a
hermit in one of the Ivanovo caves, and the
monk achieved such a high level of sanctity
that the Tsar commissioned him to
construct a larger monastery at the site,
which greatly enhanced the Tsar's image
as a merciful monarch.

After 1396, the
monastery of Ivanovo
fell into ruins and was
abandoned. The solid
limestone out of
which it was carved
enabled it to resist the
weather, saving its
remarkable labyrinth
of cells, rooms,
churches and frescoes
to this day. The
fourteenth-century
murals testify to the
exceptional skill of the
artists belonging to
the Tarnovo School of
painting.

World Heritage site since

· 1978 · 1979

Memphis and its Necropolis – the Pyramid Fields from Giza to Dahshur
Egypt

Criteria – Human creative genius; Testimony to cultural tradition; Heritage associated with events of universal significance

The Great Sphinx of ▶ Giza and the Pyramid of Khafre (Chephren).

The necropolis of Saqqara dates back to the period of the formation of the pharaonic civilization.

At Giza the solar barge, one of the oldest boats preserved today, was discovered intact in the complex around the pyramid of Cheops.

The pyramid is a symbol of the Sun, the great god Ra, whose cult became pre-eminent from the Fourth Dynasty; the Pyramid Texts, found in the funerary chambers of the tombs dating from the end of the Old Kingdom, speak of the transformation of the dead king into the Sun.

The capital of the Old Kingdom of Egypt in the third millennium BC, Memphis was one of the Seven Wonders of the Ancient World. The area of pyramid fields that served as the its necropolis contains a number of exceptional monuments that bear witness to the status of Ancient Egypt as one of the most brilliant civilizations of this planet.

The first sovereign of the unified Egyptian kingdom, Menes (or Narmer), was said to have ordered the construction of a new capital in the Nile Delta area around 3100 BC. It was from Menes that the name of Mennufer (City of Menes) came. The temple of Ptah built there was the most important sanctuary dedicated to this primary god of Creative Force, and its ruins are all that survive today of the grandeur of Memphis, as it was known to the ancient Greeks.

Nearby Saqqara was the necropolis of the city and the largest in the land, and it is the site of the first great stone pyramid. The pyramid was built as a mausoleum for the pharaoh Djoser, founder of the Third Dynasty, who ruled from around 2668 BC. Designed by his architect and vizier, Imhotep, it is the oldest step pyramid in the world. It stands in a funerary complex enclosed by a 10-m-high wall.

To the south lies the necropolis of Dahshur. The founder of the Fourth Dynasty, Snefru, who reigned from around 2613 BC, built here. During his twenty-nine year reign he transformed the structure of Egyptian royal tombs: he chose the now familiar pyramid shape with a square base. He built both the Red Pyramid, named after its reddish-coloured limestone, and the Rhomboid (or Bent) Pyramid, with its double-angled slope on each of the four faces; this was apparently an intermediate form. Another innovation of Snefru was the construction of an annex within the pyramid.

To the north, the great pyramids of Giza were built by Snefru's son Khufu or Cheops, and his successors Khafre (Chephren) and Menkaure (Mycerinus). The 'Horizon of Cheops' was the name given to the Pharaoh's tomb, the oldest and largest. The other two pyramids were known in antiquity as 'Great is Chepren' and 'Divine is Mycerinus' respectively. Each tomb forms part of the classic funerary complex first built by Snefru.

Medina of Tunis
Tunisia

Criteria – Interchange of values; Testimony to
cultural tradition; Traditional human settlement

The Medina of Tunis has exerted an
outstanding influence on the development
of architecture, sculpture and urban
planning. This group of buildings is rare, as
most historic Islamic centres have suffered
serious destruction and reconstruction over
the centuries, whereas Tunis still preserves
its homogeneity. The Medina of Tunis
extends over 2.7 km² and includes most of
the 700 historic monuments of the city,
including palaces, mosques, mausoleums
and fountains. It is divided between the
central core, which still bears traces from the
period of its foundation (the eighth century),
and two quarters dating back to the
thirteenth century. Today the medina is still
inhabited, but by only a small percentage of
the city's total population.

The medina is where the
main mosque of Tunis,
Zitouna, is located. Its
name means 'olive tree',
and comes from the
mosque's founder who
taught the Koran under
an olive tree. It was first ▶
erected in the ninth
century by the Aghlabid
rulers, but its most
famous part, the
minaret is a nineteenth-
century addition.

World Heritage site since

· 1978 · **1979**

Antigua Guatemala
Guatemala

Criteria – Interchange of values; Testimony to
cultural tradition; Significance in human history

CENTRAL
AMERICA

Caribbean Sea

Pacific
Ocean

Much of Antigua's
architecture today
dates from the
seventeenth and
eighteenth centuries
and provides us with
a colonial jewel in the
Americas.

Antigua Guatemala is an outstanding
example of preserved colonial architecture.
Built 1,500 m above sea level in an
earthquake-prone region, Antigua, the capital
of the Captaincy-General of Guatemala, was
founded in the early sixteenth century as
Santiago de Guatemala. It was the seat of
Spanish colonial government for the
Kingdom of Guatemala, which included
much of present-day Central America. It was
also the cultural, economic, religious and
educational centre for the entire region
until the capital was moved to present-day
Guatemala City after the damaging
earthquakes of 1773. In the space of under
three centuries the city, which was built on
a grid pattern inspired by the Italian
Renaissance, acquired a number of superb
monuments, many of which are preserved
today as ruins.

The Church of our
Lady of Mercy in
Antigua Guatemala.
▼

World Heritage site since

· 1978 · **1979**

Ancient Thebes with its Necropolis
Egypt

Criteria – Human creative genius; Testimony to cultural tradition; Heritage associated with events of universal significance

Thebes was the capital of Egypt at the height of its greatest power and magnificence, the Middle and New Kingdoms that lasted over a thousand years from around 2134–1070 BC. It contains the finest relics of ancient Egyptian history, art and religion. With the temples and palaces at Karnak and Luxor and, across the river, the necropolises of the Valley of the Kings and the Valley of the Queens, Thebes is a striking testimony to Egyptian civilization at its height.

Hundreds of rulers glorified the city with architecture, obelisks and sculpture. Thebes of the Living, on the right bank of the Nile, is identifiable in the fabulous site of Luxor and Karnak, and temples built here were dedicated to the divine triad of Montu, Amon and Mut. The celebration of death took shape in the necropolis of Thebes of the Dead on the Nile's left bank.

From the Middle Kingdom to the first century AD the city was sacred to the god Amon, the supreme Sun God, and temples of incomparable splendour and size were dedicated to him. The temple of Luxor, built by Amenophis III and Ramses II, was connected to the enormous sanctuary of Karnak by a long processional avenue lined by sphinxes leading to its entrance. The monumental Karnak complex is composed

of three temples: one consecrated to Mut, mother goddess of Egypt and wife of Amon; one to the warrior god Montu; and one to Amon.

On the opposite bank of the river Thebes of the Dead grew for almost fifteen centuries. Great funerary temples were built at the foot of the hills, entirely separate from their corresponding tombs which were dug into the mountains to keep them safe from violation and tomb robbers. To the north were erected the Temple of Deir el-Bahari, built by Queen Hatshepsut, dedicated to Amon-Re (one of the identities of Amon), and the temple consecrated to Hathor, the goddess of sweetness and joy who was venerated in the form of a cow.

The colossi of Memnon, massive twin statues of Amenhotep III facing eastwards over the river Nile, and the magnificent frescoes within the tombs are much admired by visitors to the site.

The Great Hypostyle Hall of Columns in the Temple of Amun at the Karnak Temple Complex. There are 134 columns, resembling papyrus stalks, in 16 rows. Each column is covered in hieroglyphics or battle scenes.

The tombs of the pharaohs and of their dignitaries, priests and princesses are hidden in the bowels of the mountains of Thebes of the Dead and form the great cemeteries of al-Asasif, al-Khokha, Qurnet Mura, Deir al-Medina, the Valley of the Kings and the Valley of the Queens.

Among the underground tombs of the Valley of Kings, the British explorers Howard Carter and Lord Carnarvon found in 1922 a small tomb that soon became the most renowned in Egypt, that of the young pharaoh Tutankhamun.

Rock Drawings in Valcamonica
Italy

Criteria – Testimony to cultural tradition; Heritage associated with events of universal significance

Valcamonica, situated in the Lombardy plain, has one of the world's greatest collections of prehistoric petroglyphs – more than 140,000 symbols and figures carved in the rock over a period of 8,000 years, depicting themes connected with agriculture, navigation, war and magic. Several periods of carving can be identified: Upper Palaeolithic (c. 8000 BC), with scenes depicting hunting and early civilisation;

Neolithic (4000–3000 BC), in which the first depictions of a religious nature appear; and Eneolithic (3000–2000 BC), with highly detailed hunting and rural scenes and scenes depicting female initiation rituals. After 1000 BC the isolation of the area ended and battle scenes are carved into the rocks as well as drawings showing huts, wagons, harvests and weapons.

The rock engravings of Valcamonica constitute an extraordinary figurative documentation of prehistoric customs and mentality. The study of these configurations in stone has made a considerable contribution to the fields of prehistory, sociology and ethnology.

Stari Ras and Sopoćani
Serbia

Criteria – Human creative genius; Testimony to cultural tradition

On the outskirts of Stari Ras, the first capital of Serbia, there is an impressive group of medieval monuments consisting of fortresses, churches and monasteries. Situated on a hill at the border between the small kingdom of Raska and the Byzantine Empire, this city drew its strength from its strategic location and its mixture of Eastern and Western influences. Its many monuments make up a single architectural complex that testifies to the city's

architectural and cultural prime, which lasted until the early fourteenth century. The Church of St Peter, built in the ninth century on the foundations of an Illyrian cemetery and an early Christian basilica, is an example of early Christian architecture, and was the religious centre of Serbia for several centuries.

The monastery of Sopoćani, was built in 1260 by King Uros I as a family resting place. Surmounted by a cupola, it has exceptional frescoes which provide invaluable historical evidence about this ancient royal lineage.

Natural and Cultural Heritage of the Ohrid region

The Former Yugoslav Republic of Macedonia

Criteria – Human creative genius; Testimony to cultural tradition; Significance in human history; Natural phenomena or beauty

Ohrid is one of the most ancient human settlements in Europe. More than 250 archaeological sites with material remains dating from between the Neolithic period and the late Middle Ages have been excavated.

Writing, education and Slavic culture – all spread out from Ohrid in the seventh to nineteenth centuries. It is a cultural centre of great importance for the history not only of this part of the Balkan Peninsula, but for world history and literature in general. The city and its historic-cultural region are located in a natural setting of exceptional beauty, while its architecture represents the best preserved and most complete ensemble of ancient urban architecture of the Slavic lands. It also has the oldest Slav monastery, St Pantelejmon, and more than 800 Byzantine-style icons dating from the eleventh to the fourteenth century. After those of the Tretiakov Gallery in Moscow, this is considered to be the most important collection of icons in the world.

St Pantelejmon monastery, fully restored in 2002.
▼

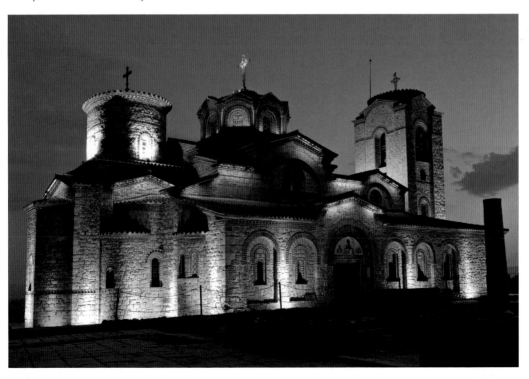

Historic Cairo
Egypt

Criteria – Human creative genius; Traditional human settlement; Heritage associated with events of universal significance

Mediterranean Sea   ASIA

AFRICA

Arabian Sea

The Mosque and ▶ Madrasa of Sultan Hassan.

Few other cities in the world are as rich in old buildings: the historic centre on the east bank of the river Nile includes 600 classified monuments that date from the seventh century through Cairo's golden age in the fourteenth century, right up to the twentieth century. Collectively they reflect the strategic, political, intellectual and commercial importance of the city.

The ancient capitals of al-Fustat, al Qatai and al-Qahira are included in Historic Cairo.

Lying at the heart of modern, urban Cairo lies one of the world's oldest Islamic cities. Cairo, which was founded in the tenth century, was the new capital and centre of the Islamic world, and its wealth of architectural treasures – mosques, madrasas, palaces and caravanserais, hammams and fountains – reflect its importance at that time.

In the seventh century AD, after the death of the Prophet Muhammad, the founder of Islam, Arab armies marched with speed to conquer neighbouring lands. In 640 Caliph Omar with his army reached the Nile and founded his own capital of al-Fustat; this was the first capital in Egypt under Arab rule.

Over the following centuries of factional battles for supremacy the capital was moved, first in 870 to al Qatai to the north east, where the Great Mosque of Ibn-Tulun was built. With its large courtyard surrounded by porticoes and punctuated by elegantly decorated arches, this mosque was the only building of the period to survive and remains one of the finest monuments in historic Cairo.

In AD 969, during the Fatimid era, Cairo (al-Qahira) was established as the capital. This was the start of a great period of city splendour. The present-day quarter of al-Azhar has contemporary monuments,

including the three large gates and the huge, square towers of the city's walls and five mosques. Among these, the Mosque of al-Hakim, compact and severe, is the last example of a military mosque. The Mosque of al-Azhar was built between 970 and 972 under the Caliph Muizz to serve as a sanctuary and as a meeting place; it also housed a university which became the most important centre for Islamic studies.

In the following centuries Egypt had successive changes of dynasties and rulers, including Saladin, the successful leader of the Islamic forces in the Third Crusade of 1189–1192, who constructed the Citadel which remained the heart of Egyptian government until the nineteenth century. Cairo thrived under the dynasty of the Mamelukes, rulers from 1250–1517. In addition to religious structures the sultans of that time built splendid mausoleums in the City of the Dead, the huge cemetery to the east of the city proper, and one of a number of cemeteries within this World Heritage site.

In 1517, the Ottomans defeated the Mamelukes and during their rule from the sixteenth to the nineteenth centuries many impressive buildings, such as the magnificent mosque of Muhammad Ali, were erected.

World Heritage site since

· 1978 · **1979**

Amphitheatre of El Jem
Tunisia

Criteria – Significance in human history; Heritage associated with events of universal significance

EUROPE

Mediterranean Sea

AFRICA

The impressive ruins of the largest colosseum in North Africa are found in the small village of El Jem, known in classical times as Thysdrus, located 60 km south of Sousse. It is one of the most accomplished examples of Roman amphitheatre construction, approaching the status of the Colosseum in Rome. Built during the first half of the third century, it may have accommodated up to 60,000 spectators.

Elliptical in form, it is constructed from large stone blocks and probably comprised four floors. The theatre was never completed, because of political rivalries and lack of funds within the Empire. Later it served as a stronghold: it was the last Berber bastion against Arab invaders. Following the Roman period, the amphitheatre was used at various times as a citadel and was twice attacked by cannon fire.

The amphitheatre is well preserved and little altered, one of the last surviving monuments of this type from the Roman world. Underneath it run two passageways, in which animals, prisoners and gladiators were kept until the moment when they were brought up into the bright daylight to perform what was in most cases the last show of their lives.

▼

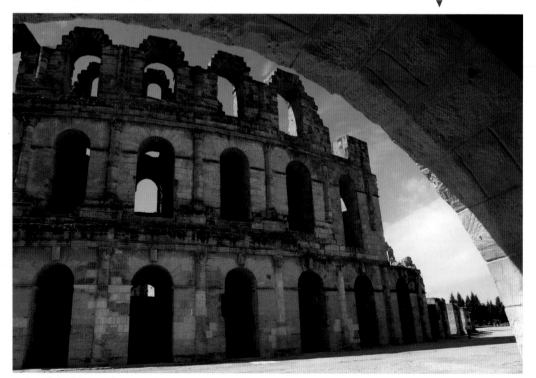

World Heritage site since

· 1978 · **1979**

Urnes Stave Church
Norway

Criteria – Human creative genius; Interchange of
values; Testimony to cultural tradition

The wooden stave church of Urnes, built in
the twelfth and thirteenth centuries, is an
outstanding example of traditional
Scandinavian wooden architecture. It brings
together traces of Celtic art, Viking traditions
and Romanesque architectural design. The
stave churches constitute one of the most
elaborate types of wood construction in
northern Europe. They are constructed just
from wood – even the roof is covered with
wooden shingles. At Urnes, the structure
uses wood for the columns, capitals and
semicircular arches to replicate the style of
stone Romanesque architecture. On the
outside, there are outstanding panels of
eleventh-century carved strapwork taken
from an earlier stave church built here. Inside
is an amazing series of twelfth-century
figurative capitals and a wealth of medieval
liturgical objects. The embellishments of the
seventeenth century and the restoration of
1906–1910 preserved its authenticity.

Christianity was
introduced into
Norway by St Olav in
the eleventh century.
The stave church at
Urnes stands in a
glacial valley on the
north bank of
Sognefjord, and is the
finest example of a
medieval stave church
from around thirty
that remain in
Norway.

▼

World Heritage site since

· 1978 · **1979**

Historical Complex of Split with the Palace of Diocletian
Croatia

Criteria – Interchange of values; Testimony to cultural tradition; Significance in human history

EUROPE

Adriatic
Sea

Tyrrhenian
Sea

A view of the historic ▶
complex of Split with
St Dominus' Bell
Tower in the
foreground.

The ancient city of Split is renowned for the massive palace built at the turn of the fourth century AD by the Roman Emperor Diocletian. Unique in scale and completeness, it is integrated into an array of important medieval buildings including the cathedral, twelfth- and thirteenth-century Gothic palaces, and other palaces in Renaissance and Baroque style.

In the early Middle Ages the town was built within the palace until commercial prosperity inspired its growth and spread outside in the thirteenth and the fourteenth centuries. A new centre developed along the western walls of the palace, which was fortified in the fourteenth century. Later, in the seventeenth century, a new defence system with projecting bastions was erected.

Much of the Roman and medieval town exists today. On the eastern side of the palace lies the Porta Argentea (Silver Gate) with the church of St Dominic on the opposite side. The Silver Gate gives access to the Plain of King Tomislav and thence to the peristil (peristyle), the central open-air courtyard area of the palace.

In the eastern part of the peristyle is the Mausoleum of Diocletian (today's Cathedral of St Dominus dedicated to St Mary); its original octagonal form is complete and a dome, once covered by mosaics, forms the roof. The monumental wooden gateposts and the stone pulpit from the thirteenth century represent the oldest monuments in the cathedral.

A small temple opposite the mausoleum, probably dedicated to Jupiter, became the baptistry in the early Middle Ages. Only the closed part of the temple (the cella), with its richly decorated portal, has been preserved.

Diocletian Street runs north from the peristyle to the Porta Aurea (Golden Gate); Agubio Palace, with a Gothic portal and inner yard is to the left. To the right, in Papaliceva Street, is the Papalic Palace (fifteenth century), the most important example of Gothic architecture in Split.

Kresimir Street leads from the peristyle to the Porta Ferrea (Iron Gate) in the west; Cindro Palace (seventeenth century), the city's most beautiful Baroque palace, lies on the right. Beyond the Iron Gate is the square Narodni Trg (Piaca), centre of the medieval commune and the liveliest square of modern Split. Of the original Gothic houses at the northern end of the square, only the Town Hall which opened in 1443 survives.

Diocletian's Palace is internationally important not only for its level of preservation but also for the buildings of succeeding historical periods within and around it that together form the fabric of old Split.

Diocletian spent his later years after his retiral in the palace that he built between AD 293 and 305 near his Dalmatian birthplace. The most valuable example of Roman architecture on the eastern Adriatic, its form and the arrangement of the buildings within, represent a transitional style of imperial villa, Hellenistic town and Roman camp.

World Heritage site since

· 1978 · **1979**

Natural and Culturo-Historical Region of Kotor
Montenegro

Criteria – Human creative genius; Interchange of values; Testimony to cultural tradition; Significance in human history

This natural harbour on the Adriatic coast in Montenegro was an autonomous city of the Byzantine Empire until the late twelfth century, when it became a free city of medieval Serbia. From 1420 it was under Venetian control and was then occupied by the French from 1807–1914.

The region of Kotor has played an exceptionally important role in the diffusion of Mediterranean culture in the Balkans along the southern Adriatic coast. Its art, goldsmithing and architecture schools have had a long-lasting influence on the region. Founded by the Romans, Kotor developed in the Middle Ages into an important commercial and artistic centre and many empires battled for control of the city. Its most impressive building is St Tryphon

Cathedral, built in 1166, damaged during the 1667 earthquake and then restored. Most of Kotor's palaces and houses, many Romanesque churches and all of neighbouring Dobrota's palaces and Perast's main buildings have suffered from earthquakes. Kotor was evacuated by all its inhabitants after the most recent, on 15 April 1979. An intensive restoration programme has now been completed and the city is flourishing again.

St Tryphon Cathedral and part of the old town of Kotor, viewed from above.
▼

Sagarmatha National Park
Nepal

Criteria – Natural phenomena or beauty

ASIA

Arabian Sea

Bay of Bengal

This is an exceptional area with dramatic mountains, glaciers and deep valleys, dominated by Mount Everest (Sagarmatha), the highest peak in the world (8,848 m), and is the homeland of the Sherpa, with their unique culture. The park is fan-shaped and enclosed on all sides by high, geologically young mountain ranges. The deeply incised valleys cut through sedimentary rocks and underlying granites to drain southwards into the Dudh Kosi and its tributaries, which form part of the Ganges River system. Most of the park (69 per cent) comprises barren land above 5,000 m, 28 per cent is grazing land and about 3 per cent is forested. The low number of mammals is almost certainly the result of human activities. Several rare species, such as the snow leopard and the lesser panda, are found in the park.

There are approximately 2,500 Sherpa people living within the park. They belong to the Nyingmapa sect of Tibetan Buddhism, which was founded by the revered Guru Rimpoche who was, according to legend, born of a lotus in the middle of a lake. There are several monasteries in the park, the most important being Tengpoche.

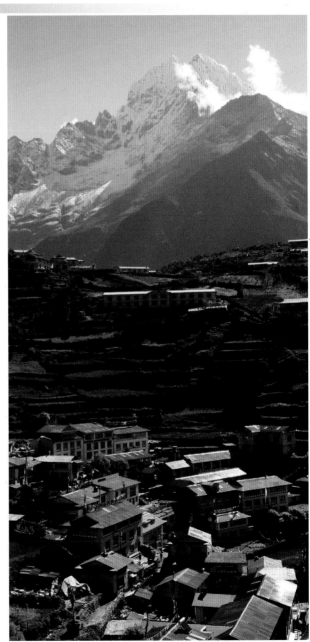

▲
Namche Bazar village.

World Heritage site since

· 1978 · **1979**

Old City of Dubrovnik
Croatia

Criteria – Human creative genius; Testimony to
cultural tradition; Significance in human history

The distinctive ▶
rooftops of Dubrovnik,
many of which were
reconstructed after the
1990s' armed conflict.

The 'Pearl of the Adriatic', Dubrovnik was an
important Mediterranean power from the
thirteenth century. The city's self-
confidence, wealth and culture are reflected
in its beautiful Gothic, Renaissance and
Baroque churches, monasteries, palaces and
fountains, many of which are survivors of a
massive earthquake in 1667. UNESCO is
currently coordinating a major restoration
programme to restore Dubrovnik's
architecture, damaged in armed conflict in
the 1990s after the break-up of the
communist state of Yugoslavia, of which it
had been part.

From the city's founding in the seventh
century, it was under the control of the
Byzantine Empire. Sovereignty passed to
Venice in 1205 after the crusaders sacked
Constantinople, until 1358 when Venice
ceded control and Dubrovnik became part
of the Hungarian-Croatian kingdom. It
operated effectively as a republican free
state, reaching its peak in the fifteenth and
sixteenth centuries. But an economic crisis
in Mediterranean shipping and, particularly,
a catastrophic earthquake in April 1667
destroyed the well-being of the republic.
It proved a turning point for the previously
powerful city.

Dubrovnik is a remarkably well-preserved
example of a late-medieval walled city, with a
regular street layout. Among the
outstanding medieval, Renaissance and
Baroque monuments within the magnificent
fortifications and the monumental gates to
the city are the eleventh century Town Hall
(now the Rector's Palace); the Franciscan
Monastery (completed in the fourteenth
century, but now largely Baroque in
appearance) with its imposing church; the
Dominican Monastery; the cathedral (rebuilt
after the earthquake); the customs house
(Sponza); and a number of other Baroque
churches, such as that of St Blaise, the patron
saint of the city.

The original World Heritage site consisted
solely of the defences and the intra-mural
city. It was later extended to include the Pile
medieval industrial suburb, a planned
development of the fifteenth century, and
the Lovrijenac Fortress, set on a cliff, which
was probably begun as early as the eleventh
century but owes its present appearance to
building work in the fifteenth and sixteenth
centuries. Also included were the Lazarets,
built in the early seventeenth century to
house potential plague-carriers from abroad;
the late fifteenth-century Kase moles, built to
protect the port against southeasterly gales;
and the Revelin Fortress, dating from 1449,
which was built to command the town moat
on its northern side.

Dubrovnik was
founded on an island
in the seventh century
by refugees from the
Latin city of
Epidaurum, who
named their
settlement Laus (from
the Latin lausa, 'rock').
Dubrovnik's old name
of Ragusa (or Rausa),
originated from the
name Laus. Across the
river, at the foot of Srđ
Mountain, the Slavs
later developed their
own settlement
named Dubrovnik
(from the Croatian
word dubrava, 'oak
woods'). The two
settlements were
united in the twelfth
century when the
channel separating
them was filled in.

World Heritage site since

· 1978 · **1979**

Tchogha Zanbil
Islamic Republic of Iran
Criteria – Testimony to cultural tradition;
Significance in human history

The ruins of the holy city of the Kingdom of
Elam, surrounded by three huge concentric
walls, are found at Tchogha Zanbil. Founded
c. 1250 BC, the city remained unfinished after it
was invaded by Ashurbanipal, as shown by the
thousands of unused bricks left at the site.

◄
The site contains the
best preserved and the
largest of all
the ziggurats of
Mesopotamia. Today
the ziggurat is over
25 m high, but with its
last two stages (since
destroyed) it would
originally have risen to
a height of 60 m.

Tikal National Park
Guatemala
Criteria – Human creative genius; Testimony to
cultural tradition; Significance in human history;
Significant ecological and biological processes;
Significant natural habitat for biodiversity

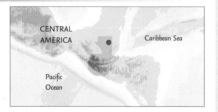

Tikal National Park protects some 221 km²
of rainforest and possesses a great wealth of
animal life. In the heart of this jungle lies
one of the major sites of Mayan civilization,
inhabited from the sixth century BC to the
tenth century AD. The ceremonial centre
contains superb temples and palaces, and
public squares accessed by means of ramps.
Remains of dwellings are scattered
throughout the surrounding countryside.

At its height from AD 700–800, the city
supported a population of 90,000 Mayan
Indians. There are over 3,000 separate
buildings, including religious monuments
decorated with hieroglyphic inscriptions,
and tombs. The ruined city reflects the
cultural evolution of Mayan society from
hunter-gathering to farming, with an
elaborate religious, artistic and scientific
culture.

The reserve contains
the largest area of
tropical rainforest in
Guatemala and
Central America, with
a wide range of
unspoilt natural
habitats. Tikal is a
well-known site for
viewing jungle
animals, especially the
howler monkey and
the spider monkey,
large numbers of
which often
congregate around
the Mayan site.

World Heritage site since

· 1978 · 1979 · **1980**

Historic Centre of Warsaw
Poland

Criteria – Interchange of values; Heritage
associated with events of universal significance

The historic centre of the Polish capital
Warsaw was almost completely rebuilt after
fighting during the Second World War
destroyed 85 per cent of the Old Town. The
city is an outstanding example of a near-
total reconstruction of a span of history
covering the thirteenth to the twentieth
centuries.

Poland was occupied by German Nazi
troops in 1939 and its capital was the scene
of two large-scale insurrections: the 1943
Warsaw Ghetto Uprising of the Jewish

population; and the general Warsaw
Uprising of August 1944. After the 1944
Uprising, occupying forces systematically
destroyed the city in reprisal. From these
total ruins, between 1945 and 1966, Warsaw's
historic centre was reconstructed.

Almost every building in Warsaw Old Town
is of a unique architectural style, from
Gothic to Baroque. All have been restored:
among the more famous are the market
square, city walls and Barbican as well as the
Royal Castle and numerous churches.

The reconstruction
of the city was
meticulously planned
in a five-year
programme that
began after the war.
Among the references
utilized to reconstruct
the Old Town, it is
believed that paintings
of Warsaw streetscapes
by the Italian artist
Canaletto were used.

The precise
reconstruction of
the historic centre
showcases the
restoration techniques
of the later twentieth
century.

◄

Kanonia Square is
next to Warsaw's main
square. It is triangular
in shape and contains
Warsaw's narrowest
house (the yellow
house in the corner).
This was an attempt
by the seventeenth/
eighteenth century
owners to pay less
property tax (which
depended on the width
of the property's street-
facing wall and the
number of windows
that wall had).

Maya Site of Cópan
Honduras

Criteria – Significance in human history;
Heritage associated with events of universal
significance

CENTRAL
AMERICA

Caribbean Sea

Pacific
Ocean

SOUTH
AMERICA

Mayan civilization
developed from
around 2000 BC and
at the height of its
power in Central
America (around AD
250–900), Cópan was
the largest and most
influential city in the
southeastern area.

The ruins of Cópan are among the most
important sites of the indigenous American
Mayan civilization, with temples, plazas and
terraces that are among the most
characteristic of any complex of Mayan
architecture and building.

There is evidence that Cópan was
inhabited from 2000 BC onwards, but its full
flourishing, along with other Mayan cities,
came in the period AD 250–900, with
important advances in mathematics,
astronomy and hieroglyphic writing, as well
as major cultural developments.

Cópan's ruined citadel and imposing
public squares reveal the three main stages
of city development, during which the
temples, plazas, altar complexes and ball
courts that can be seen today, evolved. For
unknown reasons the site was abandoned
shortly after AD 900.

Discovered in 1570 by the Spanish
conquistador Diego García de Palacio, the
ruins of Cópan were not excavated until the
nineteenth century.

Cópan is under threat
from river erosion,
agricultural activity
and earthquakes,
while its natural
surroundings are
being threatened by
the infringement of
the neighbouring
town of Cópan Ruins.

◄ ►

A Mayan temple, left,
and a carved stone
pillar, right, in the
ruins of Cópan.

World Heritage site since

· 1978 · 1979 · **1980**

Historic Centre of Rome, the Properties of the Holy See in that City Enjoying Extraterritorial Rights and San Paolo Fuori le Mura
Holy See and Italy

Criteria – Human creative genius; Interchange of values; Testimony to cultural tradition; Significance in human history; Heritage associated with events of universal significance

EUROPE

Adriatic Sea

Tyrrhenian Sea

Founded, according to legend, by Romulus and Remus in 753 BC, Rome was first the centre of the Roman Republic, then of the Roman Empire, and from the fourth century the capital of the Christian world.

In 1990 the World Heritage site in Rome was extended out to the seventeenth-century city walls built by Pope Urban VIII.

The World Heritage site in the historic centre of Rome comprises outstanding buildings and monuments from ancient and medieval Roman history. These include the forums, the Mausoleum of Augustus, the Mausoleum of Hadrian, the Pantheon (pictured below), Trajan's Column and the Column of Marcus Aurelius, and the religious and public buildings of papal Rome.

The 1929 Lateran Treaty between Italy and the Holy See that established Vatican City State also confirmed that some properties termed 'extraterritorial' and situated on Italian soil would remain the property of the Holy See. Those extraterritorial properties comprise a series of unique artistic achievements: Santa Maria Maggiore, St John Lateran and St Paul Outside the Walls. All were architecturally and artistically influential in the Christian world for centuries. Also included are several remarkable palaces: the Cancelleria, the Palazzo Maffei, the Palazzo di San Callisto and the Palazzo di Propaganda Fide.

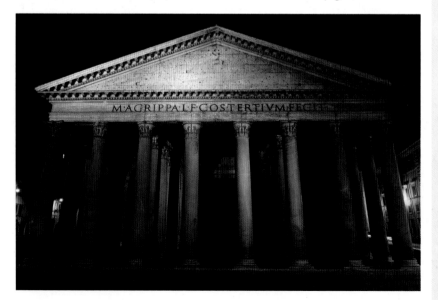

M·AGRIPPA·L·F·COS·TERTIVM·FEC

◄

The Pantheon is one of the best preserved ancient Roman buildings. The original Pantheon was built in c. 27 BC by Agrippa but was destroyed in AD 80 by fire. The current building dates from c. AD 125 during Emperor Hadrian's reign.

World Heritage site since

· 1978 · 1979 · **1980**

City of Valletta
Malta

Criteria – *Human creative genius; Heritage associated with events of universal significance*

EUROPE

AFRICA

Mediterranean Sea

The three islands of Malta were long fought over for their perceived strategic importance in the Mediterranean and were held successively by Phoenicians, Greeks, Carthaginians, Romans, Byzantines, Arabs, and the Order of the Knights of St John, who ruled for over two centuries.

Valletta is inextricably linked to the military, charitable and religious Order of St John of Jerusalem, the Knights Hospitaller. The Knights were based in Malta from 1530 to 1798 and left a strong mark, bequeathing the capital with a grid of broad, straight streets lined with hundreds of well-planned monuments. The result is that at a total size of just 0.5 km², Valletta is one of the most concentrated historic areas in the world.

The city's design is late Renaissance with a grid-based street layout, fortified and bastioned walls modelled around its peninsular site, and the planned building of great monuments in well-chosen locations. Churches and palaces, museums and theatres, gardens and piazzas retain their original features almost completely. Remarkably, the city has undergone no important modifications since 1798, when the Knights left.

Valletta, Malta. ▼

World Heritage site since

· 1978 · 1979 · **1980**

Asante Traditional Buildings
Ghana

Criteria – Traditional human settlement

AFRICA

Atlantic
Ocean

The majority of the Asante villages were destroyed during the nineteenth century in the wars undertaken by these people against British domination between 1806 and 1901. The royal mausoleum (Barem) was burned by Baden-Powell in 1895.

To the northeast of Kumasi, these buildings are the last material remains of the great Asante civilization, which reached its high point in the eighteenth century. Since the dwellings are made of earth, wood and straw, they are vulnerable to the onslaught of time and weather. There exist today only a few of the traditional homes and temples, of which the majority are less than 100 years old. These are constructed with a framework of poles and wooden imposts linked by bamboo slats which support the thatched roof. The floor is of puddled clay. The main façade is built of earth over a core of wood and has a balustrade, imposts and sometimes windows. The decoration consists of geometric, floral, animal or anthropomorphic motifs.

Garamba National Park
Dem. Rep. of the Congo

Criteria – Natural phenomena or beauty;
Significant natural habitat for biodiversity

AFRICA

Atlantic
Ocean

Indian
Ocean

Lying on the watershed between the river Nile and the river Congo the park is a vast undulating plateau broken up by inselbergs (generally of granitic formation) and sizeable marshland depressions.

The park's immense savannas, grasslands and woodlands, interspersed with gallery forests along the river banks and the swampy depressions, are home to flagship species such as the Northern white rhinoceros and the Congo giraffe, which are found nowhere else. High concentrations of elephants are also found here.

◄

Hippos in the 'maternité' pool in Garamba National Park.

World Heritage site since

· 1978 · 1979 · **1980**

Church and Dominican Convent of Santa Maria delle Grazie with 'The Last Supper' by Leonardo da Vinci

Italy

Criteria – Human creative genius; Interchange
of values

EUROPE

Mediterranean Sea

Ionian
Sea

The fifteenth-century Renaissance Church
and Convent of Santa Maria delle Grazie in
Milan, pictured below, is a striking
monument in itself, made all the more
remarkable by bearing on the fabric of a wall
one of the supreme art masterpieces: 'The
Last Supper' by Leonardo da Vinci.

Da Vinci was commissioned in 1495 to paint
a mural on the north wall of the refectory and
finished work in 1497. The painting depicts

the moment in the Gospel of John 13:21
immediately after Jesus says, 'One of you will
betray me'. In composition, perspective and
execution the painting broke with tradition
and heralded a new era in the history of art.

It was not technically a fresco in that
Leonardo worked on dry plaster, sealing the
wall and painting in tempera. Within years
the painting began to deteriorate and
repeated conservation has been carried out.

Within the building,
the genius of
Leonardo da Vinci is
seen especially in the
use of light and
strong perspective.
The three windows
and the landscape
beyond create a
luminosity that, set
against the backlight,
illuminates the
characters from the
side as well. The result
is a combination of
particularly classical
Florentine and
chiaroscuro
perspectives.

World Heritage site since

· 1978 · 1979 · **1980**

Megalithic Temples of Malta
Malta
Criteria – Significance in human history

EUROPE

AFRICA   Mediterranean Sea

Professor Lord Renfrew, a leading prehistorian, described the megalithic temples of Malta and Gozo as 'the oldest free-standing monuments in the world'. They are also remarkable for their diversity of form and decoration.

The elaborate rituals to which the temples are testimony are a remarkable manifestation of the human spirit, especially on a remote island at such an early date.

The seven megalithic temples that make up this World Heritage site on Malta and Gozo are outstanding examples of structures that represent a major development in culture, art and technology. All date from the third millennium BC and each is the result of an individual development, differing from the others in plan, execution and construction techniques.

The two temples of Ggantija on the island of Gozo are notable for their gigantic Bronze Age structures. On Malta, the temples of Hagar Qim, Mnajdra and Tarxien are unique architectural masterpieces, given the limited resources available to their builders. The Ta'Hagrat and Skorba complexes show how the tradition of temple-building was handed down in Malta. Each one is remarkable for diversity of form and decoration.

Section of the Temple of Hagar Qim. ▼

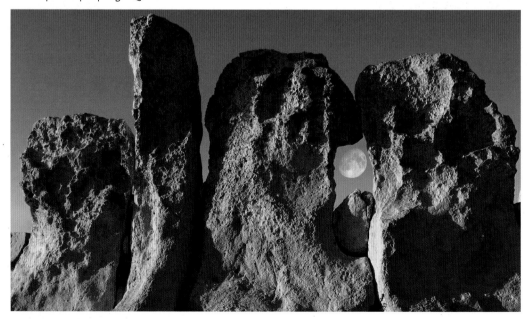

Kahuzi-Biega National Park
Dem. Rep. of the Congo
Criteria – Significant natural habitat for biodiversity

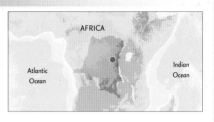

A vast area of primary tropical forest dominated by two spectacular mountains, Kahuzi (3,308 m) and Biega (2,790 m), the park has a diverse and abundant fauna. It consists of a smaller sector on the eastern side, covering part of the Mitumba Mountains, and a larger western sector in the central Congo basin. The two zones are connected by a narrow corridor. The western zone is forested by equatorial rainforest, with transition forest between 1,200 m and 1,500 m. In the eastern zone, six different primary vegetation types have been distinguished. The park was established to protect 200–300 eastern lowland (Grauer's) gorilla occurring mainly in the forests at 2,100–2,400 m, but also in the lower rainforest.

The park's mosaic of biotypes makes it an excellent gorilla habitat, but it is also home to other primates including eastern chimpanzee, and numerous Cercopithecinae and Colobinae. Other mammals include elephant, forest hog and many antelope and duiker.

Ichkeul National Park
Tunisia
Criteria – Significant natural habitat for biodiversity

The Ichkeul lake and wetland are a major stopover point for hundreds of thousands of migrating birds, such as ducks, geese, storks and pink flamingos, who come to feed and nest there. Ichkeul is the last remaining lake in a chain that once extended across North Africa. Due to increased salinity in the lake and marshes, conservation efforts in recent years, including a high-quality scientific monitoring programme, have resulted in improved water quality, leading toward the restoration of vegetation critical to the functioning of the ecosystem, the gradual return of wintering and breeding birds, and the recovery of fish populations.

Ichkeul National Park consists of an isolated and wooded massif, Djebel Ichkeul, and a brackish permanent lake, Lake Ichkeul, the area of which varies with the seasons. Ichkeul is recognized as being extremely diverse largely due to the wide variety of habitats.

◄

World Heritage site since

· 1978 · 1979 · **1980**

Hal Saflieni Hypogeum
Malta

Criteria – Testimony to cultural tradition

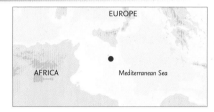

EUROPE

AFRICA   Mediterranean Sea

The Hypogeum is an enormous
subterranean structure excavated c. 2500 BC.
The megalithic walls are constructed of
cyclopean masonry – large irregular blocks
of chalky coralline stone without mortar.
The workmanship is all the more impressive
when it is considered that the chambers
were meticulously carved using only flint
and stone tools. The principal rooms
distinguish themselves by their domed
vaulting and by the elaborate structure of
false bays inspired by the doorways and
windows of contemporary terrestrial
constructions. Curvilinear and spiral
paintings in red ochre are still visible in some
areas. The carved façade is magnificent and
the quality of its architecture is in a
remarkable state of preservation. Perhaps
originally a sanctuary, the Hypogeum
became a necropolis in prehistoric times.

Hal Saflieni
Hypogeum is a
cultural property of
exceptional
prehistoric value. The
only known example
of a subterranean
structure of the
Bronze Age, it was
only discovered
accidentally in 1902 by
a stonemason laying
housing foundations.

Aksum
Ethiopia

Criteria – Human creative genius; Significance in
human history

ASIA

AFRICA

Atlantic
Ocean

Indian Ocean

The ruins of the ancient city of Aksum are
found close to Ethiopia's northern border.
They mark the location of the heart of
ancient Ethiopia, when the Kingdom of
Aksum was the most powerful state
between the Eastern Roman Empire and
Persia. The massive ruins, dating from
between the first and the thirteenth
centuries AD, include giant monolithic
stelae, royal tombs and the ruins of ancient
castles. Long after its political decline in the
tenth century, Ethiopian emperors
continued to be crowned in Aksum.

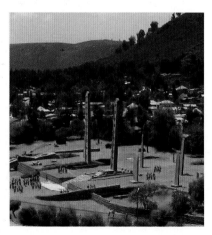

◄

Transported to Rome
by the troops of
Mussolini in 1937, the
stela 2 was returned by
the Italian
Government in April
2005. Weighing 150
tons and 24 m high, it
is around 1,700 years
old and a symbol of
the Ethiopian people's
identity.

World Heritage site since

· 1978 · 1979 · **1980**

Fortifications on the Caribbean Side of Panama: Portobelo – San Lorenzo

Panama

Criteria – Human creative genius; Significance in human history

The forts came under regular attack and were rebuilt three times: after their capture by the privateer Henry Morgan in 1668 and by British Admiral Vernon in 1739, and again in 1761. However, trade routes had changed and the fort suffered no new attacks.

The group of seventeenth- and eighteenth-century fortifications of the Caribbean coast of Panama are magnificent examples of contemporary Spanish colonial military architecture, located in a natural setting of great beauty. The forts of Portobelo and San Lorenzo formed part of the defence system of the Spanish Crown to guard the access to the Isthmus of Panama that was crucial to Europe's trade with its colonies.

Portobelo's forts, castles, barracks and batteries created a defensive line around its bay and protected the harbour, while the works at San Lorenzo guarded the mouth of the Chagres River.

The forts are now in a poor state of preservation. The Pan American Institute of Geography and History is among the international organizations acknowledging the importance of the Portobelo and San Lorenzo sites as an essential link in the understanding of American history.

Fort Geronimo, Portobelo.
▼

World Heritage site since

· 1978 · 1979 · **1980**

Site of Palmyra
Syrian Arab Republic

Criteria – Human creative genius; Interchange of values; Significance in human history

Caspian Sea

Mediterranean Sea

ASIA

The grand colonnade, 1,100 m in length, which links the temple of Bel with the so-called Camp of Diocletian, is the monumental axis of the city, with its open central street flanked by covered lateral passages.

An oasis in the Syrian desert, northeast of Damascus, Palmyra contains the monumental ruins of a great city that was one of the most important cultural centres of the ancient world. From the first to the second century, the art and architecture of Palmyra, standing at the crossroads of several civilizations, married Graeco-Roman techniques with local traditions and Persian influences. The city offers the consummate example of an ancient urbanized complex, for the most part protected, with its large public monuments such as the Agora, the Theatre and the temples. Alongside these, the inhabited quarters are preserved, and there are immense cemeteries outside the fortified enceinte. Palmyra exerted a decisive influence on the evolution of neoclassical architecture and modern urbanization.

Part of the ruined city of Palmyra.
▼

World Heritage site since

· 1978 · 1979 · **1980**

Paphos
Cyprus

Criteria – Testimony to cultural tradition;
Heritage associated with events of universal
significance

The Tombs of the
Kings, in Kato Paphos,
is a necropolis carved
out of solid rock with
some tombs decorated
with Doric pillars.
Spread over a vast area,
these impressive
underground tombs
date back to the fourth
century BC. High
officials rather than
kings were buried here.

Paphos has been inhabited since the
Neolithic period. It was a centre of the cult
of Aphrodite and of pre-Hellenic fertility
deities. According to legend, Aphrodite's
birthplace was on this island, and her temple
was erected here by the Mycenaeans in the
twelfth century BC. The remains of villas,
palaces, theatres, fortresses and tombs
mean that the site is of exceptional
architectural and historic value. The mosaics
of Nea Paphos are among the most
beautiful in the world. Excavations have also
unearthed the spectacular third- to fifth-
century mosaics of the Houses of Dionysus,
Orpheus and Aion, and the Villa of Theseus,
buried for sixteen centuries and yet
remarkably intact. The mosaic floors of
these noblemen's villas are considered
among the finest in the Eastern
Mediterranean.

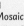
Mosaic floor from the
Villa of Theseus,
depicting Theseus' fight
with the minotaur in
the labyrinth. The villa
dates from the second
half of the second
century AD and
contained 100 rooms.

World Heritage site since

· 1978 · 1979 · 1980

Archaeological Ruins at Moenjodaro
Pakistan

Criteria – Interchange of values; Testimony to cultural tradition

The ruins of the huge city of Moenjodaro – built entirely of unbaked brick in the third millennium BC – lie in the Indus valley. The acropolis, set on high embankments, the ramparts, and the lower town, which is laid out according to strict rules, provide evidence of an early system of town planning.

◄
Moenjodaro is the most ancient and best-preserved urban ruin on the Indian subcontinent. It has exercised a considerable influence on the subsequent development of urbanization on the Indian peninsula.

Lower Valley of the Awash
Ethiopia

Criteria – Interchange of values; Testimony to cultural tradition; Significance in human history

The Awash valley contains one of the most important groupings of palaeontological sites on the African continent. The remains found at the site, the oldest of which date back at least four million years, provide evidence of human evolution which has modified our conception of the history of humankind. The most spectacular discovery came in 1974, when fifty-two fragments of a skeleton enabled the famous Lucy to be reconstructed.

◄
In life, Lucy would have stood about 1 m tall and weighed 27–30 kg. By dating the deposits in which her fossilised remains were found, she is estimated to have lived 3.18 million years ago.

Redwood National Park
USA

Criteria – Natural phenomena or beauty;
Significant ecological and biological processes

Redwood National Park comprises a region
of coastal mountains bordering the Pacific
Ocean north of San Francisco. It is covered
with a magnificent forest of coastal redwood
trees, the tallest and most impressive trees in
the world. The park was established
specifically to protect these trees, because it
is only here and in Oregon that they now
survive. Descendants of the giant evergreens
that grew during the age of the dinosaurs,
redwoods thrived in moist temperate regions
of the world. They take 400 years to mature
and some of the survivors are more than
2,000 years old. The park's marine and land
life are equally remarkable, in particular the
sea lions, the bald eagle and the endangered
California brown pelican.

Archaeological surveys, test excavations, research and consultations conducted over the past twenty years have resulted in the recording of fifty prehistoric archaeological sites, nineteen historic sites and at least twenty-one places of significance to local Indian communities. The archaeological sites span 4,500 years and represent changing settlement and subsistence systems.

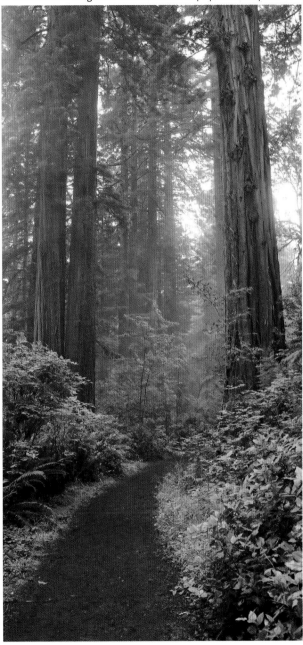

▼ Redwood trees can grow to around 100 m in only a few hundred years.

World Heritage site since

• 1978 • 1979 • 1980

Røros Mining Town and the Circumference

Norway

Criteria – Testimony to cultural tradition; Significance in human history; Traditional human settlement

Røros is in a remarkably complete state of preservation. An engraving of the town as seen from the slag heaps in the 1860s is virtually the same as a 1970s photograph taken from the same viewpoint.

The history of the town of Røros is linked to the copper mines. Established in the seventeenth century, they were exploited for 333 years until 1977. Completely rebuilt after its destruction by Swedish troops in 1679, Røros contains about 2,000 wooden one- and two-storey houses and a smelting house. Many of these buildings have preserved their blackened wooden façades, giving the town a medieval appearance. The site was inscribed on the World Heritage List in 1980 and extended in 2010.

The extension is a serial site and comprises the Town and its industrial-rural cultural landscapes; Femundshytta, a smelter with its associated area; and the Winter Transport Route. Surrounded by a buffer zone, coincident with the area of privileges (the Circumference) granted to the mining enterprise by the Danish-Norwegian Crown (1646), the property illustrates the establishment and flourishing of a lasting culture based on copper mining in a remote region with a harsh climate.

A modern day view of Røros.
▼

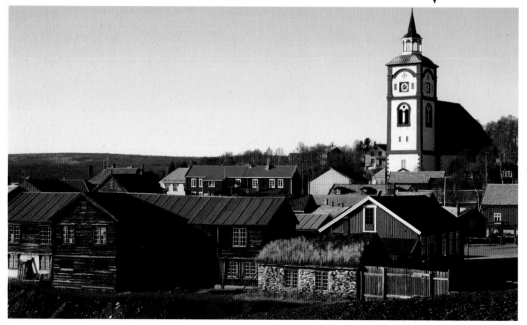

World Heritage site since

· 1978 · 1979 · **1980**

Ancient City of Bosra
Syrian Arab Republic

Criteria – Human creative genius; Testimony to cultural tradition; Heritage associated with events of universal significance

Bosra is associated with important events in the history of ideas and beliefs: according to tradition its bishop took part in the Council of Antioch, while the Prophet Muhammad came there twice and, at the time of his first visit, is said to have learned the precepts of Christianity from a Nestorian monk named Bahira.

Bosra, once the capital of the Roman province of Arabia, was an important stopover on the ancient caravan route to Mecca. A magnificent second-century Roman theatre, early Christian ruins and several mosques and madrasas are found within its great walls. The Roman theatre, pictured below, probably built under Trajan, is enclosed by the walls and towers of a citadel fortified between 481 and 1231. From outside it could be an Arab fortress, with great square towers built from enormous blocks of stone, but right at its heart lies this ancient theatre, with room for 15,000 spectators. The cathedral of Bosra, completed in 513 by Archbishop Julianus, has influenced Christian and, to a lesser extent, Islamic architectural forms. The Mosque of Omar, restored in 1950, is one of the rare buildings of the first century of the Hegira preserved in Syria.

The Roman theatre of Bosra.
▼

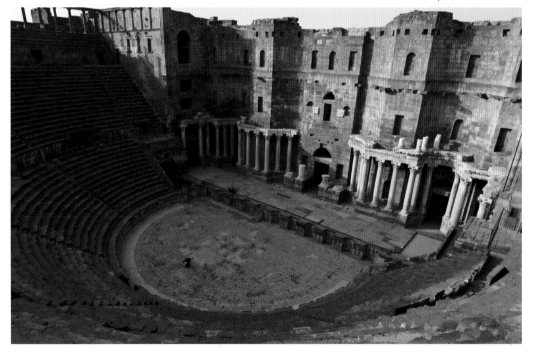

World Heritage site since

• 1978 • 1979 • **1980**

Tiya
Ethiopia

Criteria – Human creative genius; Significance in
human history

Tiya is among the most important of
approximately 160 archaeological sites
discovered so far in the Soddo region, south
of Addis Ababa. The site contains thirty-six
monuments, including thirty-two carved
stelae covered with symbols, most of which
are difficult to decipher. They are the
remains of an ancient Ethiopian culture
whose age has not yet been precisely
determined.

◄
Tiya contains several
representational
configurations
including low relief
carvings of sword
designs and one of a
human figure. The
stelae could also have
had a funerary
significance, as there
are tombs scattered
around the carvings.

Lower Valley of the Omo
Ethiopia

Criteria – Testimony to cultural tradition;
Significance in human history

Evidence of the
oldest-known
humanoid
technological activity
has been found in this
region, as well as
stone objects
attesting to an
encampment of
prehistoric human
beings that is among
the oldest known
today.

A prehistoric site near Lake Turkana, the
lower valley of the Omo is renowned the
world over. The discovery of Australopithecine
fossils there has been of fundamental
importance in the study of human
evolution. The area is unlike any other place
on Earth in that so many different types of
people have inhabited such a small area of
land over many millennia. It is believed that
it was the crossroads of a wide assortment
of cultures where early humans of many

different ethnicities passed as they migrated
to and from lands in every direction.

◄
Drinking mixture
being prepared for
coming of age 'Bull
Jumping' ceremony.

World Heritage site since

· 1978 · 1979 · **1980**

Durmitor National Park
Montenegro

Criteria – Natural phenomena or beauty; Major stages of Earth's history; Significant natural habitat for biodiversity

EUROPE

Adriatic
Sea

Black
Sea

This breathtaking national park was formed by glaciers and is traversed by rivers and underground streams. Along the Tara River canyon, which has the deepest gorges in Europe (1,300 m), the dense pine forests are interspersed with clear lakes. The park comprises the Mount Durmitor plateau and the valley formed by the canyon of the Tara River, one of the last wild rivers in Europe. There are numerous examples of weathering processes, rock shapes and land features characteristic of karstic, fluvial and glacial

erosion. Because of its location and range in altitude, the park is influenced by both Mediterranean and alpine microclimates, resulting in an exceptional range of flora and fauna. The park contains one of the last virgin black pine forests in Europe. The Tara and its tributaries, as well as the lakes, contain a large number of salmon.

The park supports a rich karstic flora with many rare and endemic plants. There are thirty-seven species endemic to the area and six specific to Durmitor. Forest fauna includes the brown bear, wolf, wild boar, wild cat, chamois, various species of eagle, capercaillie, black grouse and rock partridge.

Black Lake, below the slopes of Mount Durmitor, is the largest and deepest lake in the park.
▼

World Heritage site since

· 1978 · 1979 · **1980**

Historic Town of Ouro Preto
Brazil

Criteria – Human creative genius; Testimony to cultural tradition

Pacific Ocean

SOUTH AMERICA

Atlantic Ocean

Located 513 km north of Rio de Janeiro, Ouro Preto (Black Gold), pictured below, played a leading role in Brazil's Golden Age in the eighteenth century. It was created by thousands of soldiers of fortune eager to exploit local gold deposits; they were followed by many artists who produced works of outstanding quality, such as the Church of São Francisco de Assis by Antônio Francisco Lisboa (Aleijadinho), a masterpiece of Brazilian architecture.

A 'Mining Baroque' style developed which successfully fused Brazilian influences with European Baroque and Rococo. At its centre is Tiradentes Square containing imposing public and private buildings, such as the old Parliament House (1784) and the Palace of the Governors. In the closing years of the eighteenth century it became a centre of the movement for the emancipation of Brazil from colonial rule known as Inconfidência Mineira.

Ouro Preto was shaped by the grouping together of small settlements (arriais) in a hilly landscape, forming an irregular urban layout that follows the contours of the landscape. With the exhaustion of the gold mines in the nineteenth century, the city's influence declined but many churches, bridges and fountains remain as a testimony to its past prosperity.

World Heritage site since

· 1978 · 1979 · **1980**

Al Qal'a of Beni Hammad
Algeria

Criteria – Testimony to cultural tradition

The Al Qal'a encompasses a large number of monumental remains, including the Great Mosque. This is one of the largest in Algeria: its minaret is 25 m high and its prayer room has thirteen aisles with eight bays.

The ensemble of preserved ruins known as the Al Qal'a of Beni Hammad is situated on the southern flank of the Jebel Maâdid 1,000 m above sea level in a setting of striking beauty. It bears exceptional witness to a cultural tradition: it is one of the most interesting and most precisely dated monumental complexes of the Islamic civilisation and provides an authentic picture of a fortified Muslim city. The first capital of the Hammadid emirs, it was established in 1007 by Hammad, son of Bologhine, the founder of Algiers. The city was abandoned in 1090 when it was menaced by a Hilalian invasion, and finally destroyed in 1152 by the Almohads. It enjoyed particular splendour during the eleventh century.

Taxila
Pakistan

Criteria – Testimony to cultural tradition; Heritage associated with events of universal significance

Situated strategically on a branch of the Silk Road that linked China to the West, Taxila flourished economically and culturally. Buddhist monuments in the valley became destinations for pilgrims from as far afield as Central Asia and China.

From the ancient Neolithic tumulus of Saraikala to the ramparts of Sirkap second century BC and the city of Sirsukh first century AD, Taxila illustrates the different stages in the development of a city on the Indus that was alternately influenced by Persia, Greece and Central Asia and which, from the fifth century BC to the second century AD, was an important Buddhist centre of learning.

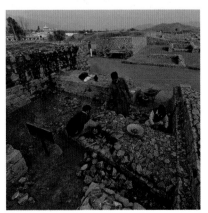

◄

Archaeologists excavating a site in Taxila.

Buddhist Ruins at Takht-i-Bahi and Neighbouring City Remains at Sahr-i-Bahlol
Pakistan

Criteria – Significance in human history

The Buddhist monastic complex of Takht-i-Bahi (Throne of Origins) was founded in the early first century. Owing to its location on the crest of a high hill, it escaped successive invasions and is still exceptionally well preserved. Nearby are the ruins of Sahr-i-Bahlol, a small fortified city dating from the same period. The complex consists of four main groups: the Court of Stupas,

embellished with a series of tall niches enshrining Buddhist statues; the early monastic complex with residential cells around an open court; the temple complex with a main stupa in the middle of a courtyard; and the tantric monastic complex with an open courtyard in front of a series of dark cells with low openings for mystical meditation, in keeping with tantric practice.

The complex is the most impressive and complete Buddhist monastery in Pakistan. In 1871, many sculptures were found at Takht-i-Bahi. Some depicted stories from the life of the Buddha while others, more devotional in nature, included the Buddha and Bodhisattava.

Hill-top ruins of Takht-i-Bahi.
▼

Parque Nacional Los Glaciares

Argentina

Criteria – Natural phenomena or beauty; Major stages of Earth's history

The Parque Nacional Los Glaciares is an area of exceptional natural beauty, with rugged, towering mountains and numerous glacial lakes.

This vast alpine area includes the Patagonian ice field: at over 14,000 km² it is the largest ice mantle outside Antarctica and occupies about half of the park. It has a total of forty-seven glaciers while a further 200 smaller glaciers are independent of the main ice field.

Los Glaciares is the best place in South

America to see glaciers in action. Glacial activity is concentrated around two main lakes, Argentino and Viedma. Lake Argentino, 160 km long, is particularly spectacular, with three glaciers dumping their massive blue icebergs into the lake with thunderous splashes.

The most impressive wildlife in the park are the birds: the waterfowl include swans, ducks, geese and flamingos, while overhead glides the huge Andean condor.

In Los Glaciares, the effects of retreating and advancing glaciers can be clearly seen. The Perito Mereno glacier, pictured below, often advances so far that its snout cuts off the normal escape stream of Lake Rico, forming a natural dam which inundates vast areas. When the glacier retreats in the heat of summer a wall of water roars down the valley.

▼

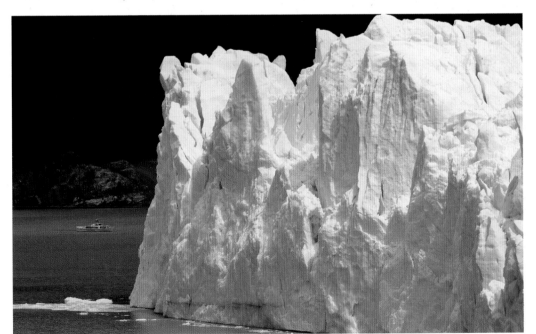

World Heritage site since

· 1978 · 1979 · 1980 · **1981**

Serengeti National Park
Tanzania

Criteria – Natural phenomena or beauty;
Significant natural habitat for biodiversity

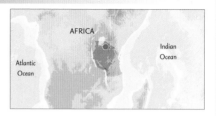

AFRICA

Atlantic
Ocean

Indian
Ocean

The vast plains of the Serengeti comprise 15,000 km² of savanna and open woodland. They contain the largest herds of grazing animals in the world and the carnivores that prey on them, providing a wildlife spectacle that is second to none.

The annual migration is dominated by wildebeest, gazelles and zebras, each harvesting the grass most suited to it. The herds are followed by prides of lion numbering up to 3,000 individuals, hyenas and jackals.

The great herds are continuously moving through the entire ecosystem but the sight is most impressive in May and June, when millions of animals travel en masse from the central plains to the permanent water holes on the western side of the park.

Serengeti is contiguous with Ngorongoro Conservation Unit, an area of 5,280 km² that was declared a World Heritage site in 1979.

Characteristic larger mammals of the Serengeti include leopard, cheetah, African elephant, black rhino, hippopotamus and giraffe, pictured below. Smaller mammals include numerous species of bat, bushbaby, monkey and baboon, aardvark, hare, porcupine, fox, mongoose, otter, wildcat, bushpig and rodent. Reptiles include Nile crocodile, Nile monitor lizard, python, cobra and puff adder. Over 500 bird species include raptors, vultures and over 20,000 water birds.

World Heritage site since

· 1978 · 1979 · 1980 · **1981**

Palace and Park of Fontainebleau

France

Criteria – Interchange of values; Heritage
associated with events of universal significance

Standing at the heart of a vast forest in the Île-de-France, Fontainebleau was transformed from a medieval royal hunting lodge into a dazzling Italianate palace that became one of the most important and prestigious sites of the French court. Surrounded by an immense and beautiful park, Fontainebleau combines Renaissance and French artistic influences. Its architecture and decor were influential on the artistic evolution not only of France but of Europe as a whole.

Fontainebleau was first enlarged and embellished by François I who commissioned artists from Renaissance Italy to begin work in 1528. The fashion of painting, stucco work, sculpture and statuary at Fontainebleau gave its name to a style that became influential throughout Europe in the sixteenth and seventeenth centuries. Successive modifications continued until in the nineteenth century the palace complex reached its present layout with five courtyards, arranged irregularly and surrounded by wings of buildings and gardens.

Royal domicile, 'house of the centuries' – Fontainebleau retains the imprint of every reign and style. Henri IV, Louis XIII, Louis XV and Louis XVI carried on the embellishment of this beautiful palace, which Napoleon I preferred above all others.

▼

Old City of Jerusalem and its Walls
Jerusalem (Site proposed by Jordan)

Criteria – Interchange of values; Testimony to cultural tradition; Heritage associated with events of universal significance

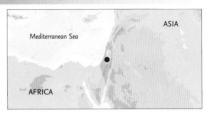

The golden-domed ▶ building is the Dome of the Rock and is one of the earliest surviving Islamic monuments.

As a holy city for Judaism, Christianity and Islam, Jerusalem has always been of enormous symbolic importance. Among its hundreds of historic monuments are key sites for each religious community: the Temple Mount (known as the Haram ash-Sharif for the Muslims) and the Western Wall for Jews; the Church of the Holy Sepulchre and the Via Dolorosa for Christians and for Muslims, the Dome of the Rock and Al-Aqsa Mosque on the Haram ash-Sharif. Jerusalem's symbolic importance for three of the world's religions has prompted power struggles that have lasted for centuries.

It is considered that the First Temple was built on Mount Moriah, or Temple Mount, by King Solomon and was completed in 957 BC. It was destroyed in 586 BC by Nebuchadnezzar II of Babylon. In 515 BC the Second Temple was completed and during the Roman rule, Herod the Great (73–4 BC) enlarged it, the famous Western Wall being part of the supporting structure for the levelled platform on which the temple stood. The Romans destroyed the Second Temple in AD 70 and established a citadel in the area, the Aelia Capitolina.

Jerusalem's period of Christian rule, from the fourth century, was one of its most peaceful and prosperous epochs. Among the Christian shrines was the Church of the Holy Sepulchre, completed in 335, marking the site of the crucifixion, tomb and resurrection of Jesus and the most sacred place in the Christian world.

The Arabs captured Jerusalem in 638 and the new rulers commissioned the Dome of the Rock. Intended as a shrine rather than a mosque, it was completed around 691 and is one of the most ancient Islamic buildings in existence. Close by, the Al-Aqsa Mosque was built between the late seventh and early eighth centuries.

This era of peaceful coexistence ended in 969 when control of the city passed to the Egyptian Arab Fatimids who systematically destroyed all synagogues and churches. Their prohibition on Christian pilgrimage became a contributing cause of the Crusades that culminated in the Christians' capture of Jerusalem in 1099. During the Christian Kingdom, the Dome of the Rock was converted to a Christian shrine (Templum Domini), the Church of the Holy Sepulchre was rebuilt, and hospices and monasteries were founded.

The Tower of David, ▶ the Citadel, Jerusalem.

World Heritage site since

· 1978 · 1979 · 1980 · **1981**

Ruins of Kilwa Kisiwani and Ruins of Songo Mnara
Tanzania
Criteria – Testimony to cultural tradition

The remains of two great East African ports admired by early European explorers are situated on two small islands near the coast. From the thirteenth to the sixteenth century, the merchants of Kilwa dealt in gold, silver, pearls, perfumes, Arabian crockery, Persian earthenware and Chinese porcelain; much of the trade in the Indian Ocean thus passed through their hands.

These sites are of prime importance to the understanding of the Swahili culture and the Islamization of the east coast of Africa. They include the remarkable Great Mosque, constructed in the twelfth century of coral tiles imbedded in a core of puddled clay.

◄

Ruins of Kilwa's fort or gezira (prison).

Niokolo-Koba National Park
Senegal
Criteria – Significant natural habitat for biodiversity

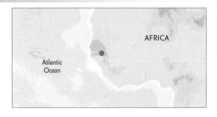

Niokolo-Koba National Park covers almost 10,000 km² of the Guinea savanna of Senegal, with significant areas of bush land and gallery forest along both banks of the upper Gambia River. This varied landscape is home to an incredible range of wildlife, with over seventy species of mammal, 329 bird, thirty-six reptile, twenty amphibian and vast numbers of invertebrates. Derby's eland, an endangered species, is the world's largest

antelope. Other important species include chimpanzee, leopard, dwarf crocodile and hippopotamus. The park is the last refuge in Senegal for giraffe and elephant, of which there is a large population. Niokolo-Koba is large enough to demonstrate the key aspects of the functioning Guinea savanna ecosystem, and to ensure the survival of its many endangered species.

Niokolo-Koba National Park covers 9,130 km² of the Guinea savanna of Senegal, with significant areas of bush land and gallery forest along both banks of the upper Gambia River. The area is rich in wildlife, including lions that are reputed to be Africa's largest.

World Heritage site since

· 1978 · 1979 · 1980 · **1981**

Amiens Cathedral
France

Criteria – Human creative genius, Interchange of values

Amiens Cathedral, in the heart of Picardy, is one of the largest classic thirteenth-century Gothic churches. It is notable for the coherence of its plan, the beauty of its three-tier interior elevation, and the particularly fine display of sculptures on the principal façade and in the south transept.

Building of Notre Dame d'Amiens began in 1220, two years after its Romanesque predecessor was destroyed by fire. Its builders used the technical knowledge and experience of other church builders to construct their cathedral quickly, resulting in a uniform style that is very rare: the nave, the largest part of the church, was completed in 1245.

The great height of the cathedral and its design allow in an exceptional amount of light. Despite its vast amount of stained glass, the building survived the First World War virtually unscathed.

The western façade, which is flanked by two square towers without spires, has three portals decorated with the elaborate statuary for which the cathedral is famous (**the central one is pictured above**).

From 1292–1375 the cathedral was enhanced by a series of chapels built between the buttresses of the side aisles. This style of the seven radiating chapels became a model for other cathedrals.

World Heritage site since

· 1978 · 1979 · 1980 · **1981**

Head-Smashed-In Buffalo Jump
Canada

Criteria – Heritage associated with events of universal significance

Among the many buffalo hunting techniques of the Plains Peoples, the Buffalo Jump was perhaps the most effective. When a bison herd was in proper position, young men well-instructed in animal behaviour, the "buffalo runners," enticed the animals towards the kill. They did so by dressing in the skins of calves and imitating the sound of a calf separated from its mother. Behind and upwind of the herd, fellow runners in wolf or coyote pelts moved the herd onward with their calls. Moving closer to the cliff edge, the herd was funnelled into converging lines of stone cairns where other band members shouted and waved large robes to frighten the buffalo into a headlong stampede. Confronted with the plunge over the cliff, the lead buffalo were forced over the precipice by the pressure of the herd racing behind.

In a typical hunt, dozens of animals were killed in the fall from the cliff or by the weapons of the hunters waiting below. For days after, the spoils of the kill were processed in the butchering camp, ensuring survival of the hunting group for another season.

Historic Monuments at Makli, Thatta
Pakistan

Criteria – Testimony to cultural tradition

The capital of three successive dynasties and later ruled by the Mughal emperors of Delhi, Thatta was constantly embellished from the fourteenth to the eighteenth century. Covering a distance of about 12 km, the site preserves an imposing monumental complex with the remains of the city itself in the valley and those of the necropolis at the edge of the Makli plateau. The remains of the city and its necropolis provide a unique view of civilization in Sind.

Within the broad family of Islamic monuments, those of Thatta represent a particular type, notable for the fusion of diverse influences into a local style. The effect of the Grand Mosque of Shah Jahan with its complex of blue and white buildings capped by ninety-three domes is unique.
◀

The tomb of Prince Sultan Ibrahim bin Norza Mohammad Isa Tarkhan has stood here since the eleventh century.

World Heritage site since

· 1978 · 1979 · 1980 · **1981**

Medina of Fez
Morocco

Criteria – Interchange of values; Traditional
human settlement

Fez is a jewel of Spanish-Arabic civilization,
an outstanding and well-preserved example
of an ancient city. The Medina of Fez is
densely packed with monuments – *madrasas*
(schools), *fondouks* (shops), palaces,
residences, mosques and fountains.

Founded in the ninth century and home to
the oldest university in the world, Fez el Bali
(the name of the old city) has two distinct
centres on the right and left banks of the
river Fez, settled by Arab refugees from
Córdoba in Spain and from Kairouan (in
modern-day Tunisia). In the fourteenth
century a Jewish quarter, the Mellah, was
joined to the newly founded city. The urban
fabric and principal monuments in the
Medina date from this period.

Previously the capital of Morocco, Fez lost
that status to Rabat in 1912.

A medina typically
forms a distinct quarter
in many North African
cities. It is generally the
oldest part of a city,
with walls and
labyrinthine streets.

The Medina of Fez is
thought to be the
largest car-less urban
area in the world.

▲
The minaret and city walls in Fez Medina.

World Heritage site since

· 1978 • 1979 • 1980 • **1981**

Roman Theatre and its Surroundings and the 'Triumphal Arch' of Orange
France

Criteria – Testimony to cultural tradition; Heritage associated with events of universal significance

The most striking feature of the theatre is the stage wall 'scenae frons'. This would originally have been covered with marble slabs and decorated with bas-reliefs, carved friezes, statues in niches and columns. Their purpose was not purely decorative because the projections and cavities in the wall would have helped to eliminate the problem of echoes.

The Triumphal Arch.
▼

Situated in the Rhone valley, the ancient theatre of Orange, with its 103 m-long façade, is one of the best preserved of all the great Roman theatres. The theatre was closed by imperial command in 391: by this time Christianity had become the *de facto* state religion and the Church opposed all pagan spectacles. The theatre was abandoned and later sacked and pillaged by barbarians. It was only in the nineteenth century that it slowly recovered its original splendour, thanks to the restoration work begun in 1825. The Triumphal Arch, pictured below, located to the north of the town, is one of the most beautiful and interesting surviving examples of a provincial triumphal arch from the reign of Augustus. It is decorated with low reliefs commemorating the establishment of the Pax Romana.

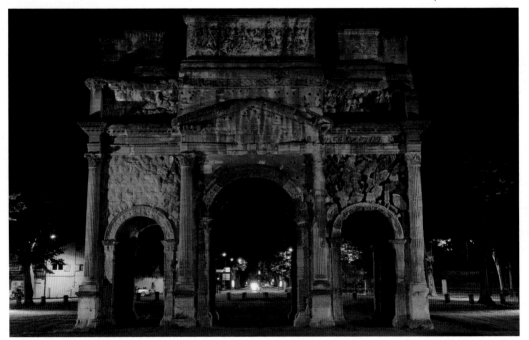

Cistercian Abbey of Fontenay
France
Criteria – Significance in human history

The Fontenay gardens were completely redesigned in the 1970s by the garden architect Peter Holmes, who created a magnificent landscape of greenery and plants to bring out the abbey buildings. The beauty of the gardens adds an extra charm to the old Romanesque stone buildings of Fontenay.

Fontenay Abbey is located in northern Burgundy, 80 km north of Dijon in a small marshy valley a few kilometres from Montbard. It was founded by St Bernard in 1119 and built from 1130 onwards, making it one of the oldest Cistercian monasteries in Europe. With its church, cloister, refectory, sleeping quarters, bakery, and ironworks, it is an excellent illustration of the ideal of self-sufficiency practised by the earliest communities of Cistercian monks.

The forge, dated to the end of the twelfth century, recalls the part which the Cistercians played in technological progress during the Middle Ages: this is one of the oldest industrial buildings in France. Despite the transformations undergone in the thirteenth, fifteenth, and sixteenth centuries, the Abbey of Fontenay, restored after 1906, has the appearance today of a generally authentic and well-preserved whole.

Djoudj National Bird Sanctuary
Senegal
Criteria – Natural phenomena or beauty; Significant natural habitat for biodiversity

The park is one of the first sources of fresh water for more than three million migrant birds after crossing 2000 km of the Sahara. The waters also hold populations of crocodile and African manatee.

Situated in the Senegal River delta, the Djoudj Sanctuary is a wetland of 160 km², comprising a large lake surrounded by streams, ponds and backwaters. It forms a living but fragile sanctuary for some 1.5 million birds, such as the white pelican, the purple heron, the African spoonbill, the great egret and the cormorant.

◄

Great Egret.

Great Barrier Reef
Australia

Criteria – Natural phenomena or beauty; Major stages of Earth's history; Significant ecological and biological processes; Significant natural habitat for biodiversity

The Great Barrier Reef viewed from above.

The Great Barrier Reef is a site of remarkable variety and beauty on the northeast coast of Australia. It is the world's most extensive stretch of coral reefs. The great diversity of its fauna reflects the maturity of an ecosystem that has evolved over millions of years on the northeast continental shelf of Australia.

The site contains a huge range of species including over 1,500 species of fish, about 360 species of hard coral and 5,000 species of mollusc, plus a great diversity of sponges, sea anemones, marine worms and crustaceans. About 215 species of birds are found in its islands and cays. Extending to Papua New Guinea, the reef system comprises some 2,900 individual reefs covering more than 20,000 km², including 760 fringing reefs. The reefs range in size from under 0.01 km² to over 100 km² and vary in shape to provide the most spectacular marine scenery on Earth. There are approximately 600 continental islands including many with towering forests and freshwater streams, and some 300 coral cays and unvegetated sand cays. A rich variety of landscapes and seascapes, including rugged mountains with dense and diverse vegetation, provide spectacular scenery.

The form and structure of the individual reefs show great variety. There are two main classes: platform or patch reefs, resulting from radial growth; and wall reefs, resulting from elongated growth, often in areas of strong currents. There are also the many fringing reefs where growth is established on subtidal rock of the mainland coast or continental islands.

The site includes major feeding grounds for the endangered dugong and nesting grounds of world significance for four species of marine turtle including the endangered loggerhead turtle. Given the severe pressures on these species elsewhere, the Great Barrier Reef may be a last stronghold. It is also an important breeding area for humpback and other whale species.

A wide range of fleshy algae occurs, often small and inconspicuous but highly productive and heavily grazed by turtles, fish, molluscs and sea urchins. In addition, calcareous algae are an important component of reef building processes. Fifteen species of seagrass grow throughout the area, forming over 3,000 km² of seagrass meadows and providing an important food source for grazing animals, such as dugongs and turtles.

The Great Barrier Reef is important in the historic and contemporary culture of the Aboriginal and Torres Strait Islander groups of the coastal areas of northeast Australia. The contemporary use of and association with the Marine Park plays an important role in the maintenance of their cultures and there is a strong spiritual connection with the ocean and its inhabitants. New species continue to be discovered throughout the Great Barrier Reef. A new species of dolphin, the Australian snub-nose dolphin, was discovered in 2005 within inshore areas, but only in low numbers. A recent survey of the inter-reef areas has found at least four new species of fish and one of the sponges that commonly occurs is likely to be a new genus.

A clown fish. ▶

World Heritage site since

· 1978 · 1979 · 1980 · **1981**

Fort and Shalamar Gardens in Lahore
Pakistan

Criteria – Human creative genius; Interchange of values; Testimony to cultural tradition

The complex of fairytale-like buildings surrounding the Court of Shah Jahan, and especially the Shah Burj or Shish Mahal, make it one of the most beautiful palaces in the world. Built in 1631–2, it sparkles with mosaics of glass, gilt, semi-precious stones and marble screening.

The Fort and Shalamar Gardens in Lahore are a unique artistic realization which, while bearing exceptional testimony to the Mughal civilization, have exercised a considerable influence long after their creation in the Punjab and throughout the Indian subcontinent. The first historic references to Lahore Fort, situated northwest of the city, date from before the eleventh century. Destroyed and rebuilt several times by the Mughals from the thirteenth to the fifteenth centuries, it was definitively rebuilt and reorganized starting with the reign of Emperor Akbar (1542–1605). Based on the twenty-one monuments preserved within its boundaries, it comprises the most beautiful repertory of the forms of Mughal architecture, whose evolution may be followed over more than two centuries. The elegance of the splendid gardens, built on three terraces with lodges, waterfalls and large ornamental ponds, is unequalled.

Shalamar Gardens.
▼

World Heritage site since

· 1978 · 1979 · 1980 · **1981**

Willandra Lakes Region
Australia

Criteria – Testimony to cultural tradition; Major
stages of Earth's history

The Willandra Lakes Region is a remarkable
example of a site where the economic and
cultural life of Homo sapiens can be partly
reconstructed, showing a fascinating
interaction between Aboriginal people and
the changing natural environment. The
fossil remains of a series of lakes and sand
formations that date from the Pleistocene
(2.5 million to 5,000 years ago) can be found
in this region, together with archaeological
evidence of human occupation dating from

45–60,000 years ago. It is a unique landmark
in the study of human evolution on the
Australian continent. Several well-preserved
fossils of giant marsupials and other
animals, some of which are now extinct,
have also been found here. The site includes
the entire lake and river system from Lake
Mulurulu, the latest to hold water, to the
Prungle Lakes, dry for more than 15,000
years.

When the Willandra
Billabong Creek
ceased to flow, the
lakes dried in series
from the Prungle
Lakes in the south to
Lake Mulurulu in the
north over several
thousand years. As
each lake evaporated,
it became an
independent system
undergoing a basic
transformation from
fresh water to saline
water to dry lake bed.

Lake Mungo Lunette. Erosion of this dune has
exposed extensive evidence of Aboriginal occupation
over the millennia. ▼

World Heritage site since

· 1978 · 1979 · 1980 · **1981**

Mammoth Cave National Park
USA

Criteria – Natural phenomena or beauty; Major stages of Earth's history; Significant natural habitat for biodiversity

Mammoth Cave National Park, located in the state of Kentucky, has the world's largest network of natural limestone caves and underground passageways, carved by twenty-five million years of cave-forming action by the Green River and its tributaries. The park and its underground network of more than 560 km of surveyed passageways is the most extensive and diverse cave ecosystem in the world, with over 200 species indigenous to the network of caves, and forty-two species adapted to life in total darkness. Surface features are also important and Big Woods, a temperate deciduous oak-hickory dominated forest, is reputed to be one of the largest and best remaining examples of the ancient forests of eastern North America that once covered most of Kentucky.

Almost every type of cave formation is known within the site and the geological processes involved in cave formation are continuing. Mammoth boasts superlative examples of chambers, shafts, stalagmites, stalactites, as well as gypsum 'flowers' and 'needles'.

Mount Nimba Strict Nature Reserve
Côte d'Ivoire and Guinea

Criteria – Significant ecological and biological processes; Significant natural habitat for biodiversity

Located on the borders of Guinea, Liberia and Côte d'Ivoire, Mount Nimba rises above the surrounding savanna. Its slopes are covered by dense forest at the foot of grassy mountain pastures. They harbour an especially rich flora and fauna, with endemic species such as the viviparous toad, and chimpanzees that use stones as tools.

The park includes significant portions of Mount Nimba, a geographically unique area with more than 200 endemic species. These species include multiple types of duikers, big cats and civets.

◄

The critically endangered Mount Nimba toad.

World Heritage site since

· 1978 · 1979 · 1980 · **1981**

Kakadu National Park
Australia

Criteria – *Human creative genius; Heritage associated with events of universal significance; Natural phenomena or beauty; Significant ecological and biological processes; Significant natural habitat for biodiversity*

This spectacular living cultural landscape has been cared for continuously by Aboriginal people – called Bininj/Mungguy - for more than 50,000 years. Their deep spiritual connection to the land dates back to the creation time and Kakadu is inscribed on the World Heritage List for both its cultural and natural values.

Kakadu's rock art, pictured right, and archaeological sites record the way of life of the region's inhabitants, from the hunter-gatherers of prehistoric times to the Aboriginal people still living there today.

Bininj/Mungguy believe that during the creation time, ancestral beings known as the first people, or Nayahunggi, journeyed across the landscape. The ancestors created the landforms, plants, animals and Aboriginal people we see today, and they left language, ceremonies, kinship, and rules to live by.

The park covers a huge 20,000 km² and moving through the park, the landscape changes dramatically, from the soaring sandstone escarpment to floodplains, monsoon forests, savanna woodlands and tidal flats. These environments provide habitat for a wide range of rare plant and animal species, some of which are found nowhere else in the world.

Kakadu's landscapes undergo dramatic seasonal changes. Wet season rains create a vast shallow wetland sea for hundreds of square kilometres, where ducks, geese and wading birds abound. As the floodplains start to dry, huge numbers of these waterbirds congregate around the permanent rivers and billabongs.

Because of its diversity, from marine and coastal habitats (which are home to turtles and dugongs) through to the stone country, Kakadu offers a fantastic cultural and wildlife experience.

One-third of Australia's bird species and almost one-fifth of its mammal species are found in Kakadu. Millions of waterbirds make seasonal use of the floodplains. Kakadu's great diversity of invertebrates includes 55 species of termite, at least 350 species of ant and more than 160 species of grasshopper.

Olympic National Park
USA

Criteria – Natural phenomena or beauty;
Significant ecological and biological processes

Renowned for the diversity of its ecosystems, Olympic National Park contains glacier-clad peaks interspersed with alpine meadows surrounded by an extensive forest, the best example of temperate rainforest in the Pacific Northwest. The park is divided into two segments: a mountainous core and a separate coastal strip. The mountains contain about sixty active glaciers; the area is unique because it is the lowest latitude in the world at which glaciers begin, at an elevation lower than 2,000 m. The coastal strip stretches along 80 km of wilderness beach, characterized by rocky headlands and a wealth of intertidal life, and the arches, caves and buttresses are evidence of the continuous battering of the waves. The coniferous forest of Olympic is of prime commercial interest and practically all the original forest outside the park has been harvested.

▶ *Olympic National Park has an extensive temperate rainforest dominated by conifers.*

The main danger to the integrity of the site is, oddly, one of its attractions: the mountain goats, introduced in the 1920s. They have increased erosion, reduced and altered plant cover, such that more resistant or less palatable species have become dominant. As a result three of the endemic plants may now be endangered.

Speyer Cathedral
Germany

Criteria – Interchange of values

Speyer Cathedral exerted a considerable influence on the development of Romanesque architecture in the eleventh and twelfth centuries, and also on the evolution of the principles of building restoration in Europe and in the world from the eighteenth century to the present. A basilica with four towers and two domes, it was founded by Conrad II in 1030 and remodelled at the end of the eleventh century. It is one of the most important Romanesque monuments from the time of the Holy Roman Empire. The cathedral was the burial place of the German emperors for almost 300 years. A huge stone font, with a capacity of 1,560 litres, stands on the square in front of the main portal of the cathedral. This font once symbolized the borderline between the diocese and the city.

In 1689 the cathedral was seriously damaged by fire, and it was reconstructed in the Romanesque style. The Bavarian King Ludwig I commissioned the painting of the interior. A new western block was added in 1854–8, a Romanesque pastiche. Starting in 1957, nineteenth-century paintings and the layers of painted plaster were removed to restore its eleventh-century form.

World Heritage site since

• 1978 • 1979 • 1980 • **1981**

Darien National Park
Panama

Criteria – *Natural phenomena or beauty; Significant ecological and biological processes; Significant natural habitat for biodiversity*

Forming a land-bridge between the Central and South American continents, Darien National Park contains an exceptional variety of habitats – sandy beaches, rocky coasts, mangroves, swamps, and lowland and upland tropical forests – containing remarkable wildlife. The area has been under protection since 1972, with the establishment of Alto Darién Protection Forest, and was declared a national park in 1980. It extends along about 80 per cent of the Colombian border and includes part of the Pacific coast. Access is by river and heavy truck. The area is both anthropologically and historically rich, with two major indigenous groups – Chocó and Kuna Indians – and a number of smaller groups still living by traditional practices. Today, conservation of Indian culture is included as a management objective.

The park's remarkably varied fauna is largely unstudied and includes bush dog, giant anteater, jaguar, ocelot, capybara and howler monkey. Harpy eagles are also found in the park, as are cayman and American crocodile.

Archaeological Park and Ruins of Quirigua
Guatemala

Criteria – *Human creative genius; Interchange of values; Significance in human history*

Quirigua's monumental complexes are remarkable for their elaborate system of pyramids, terraces, and staircases. The ruins contain some outstanding eighth-century monuments and an impressive series of carved stelae. These are the principal written chronicles of this lost civilisation, as well as the key to their highly advanced calendar system. Like most Mayan monuments, they were erected to commemorate the passage of time, and significant historic events. Inhabited since the second century AD, by the reign of Cauac Sky (723–84), Quirigua had become the capital of an autonomous and prosperous state. The extraction of jade and obsidian in the upper valley of the Rio Motagua, which was tightly controlled, gave rise to a profitable goods trade with the coastal ports of the Caribbean.

Quirigua's huge stone monolithic sculptures were artfully carved without the benefit of metal tools; stone chisels, driven by other stones or wooden mallets, were the only tools available. They include the largest known quarried stone in the Maya world, which stands 10.6 m tall and weighs over 59 tons.

World Heritage site since

· 1978 · 1979 · 1980 · **1981**

Arles, Roman and Romanesque Monuments
France

Criteria – Interchange of values; Significance in human history

Arles is an especially significant example of the appropriation of a classical Roman city by a medieval European civilization. It has some impressive Roman monuments, of which the earliest – the arena, the theatre and the cryptoporticus (subterranean galleries) – date back to the first century BC. The Roman theatre could hold 10,000 people in thirty-three rows of seats, and the arena 20,000 spectators. Gladiator fights and animal hunts took place here until the end of the fifth century. During the fourth century Arles experienced a second golden age, as attested by the Baths of Constantine and the necropolis of Les Alyscamps. In the eleventh and twelfth centuries, Arles once again became one of the most attractive cities in the Mediterranean. Within the city walls, the church of St-Trophime, pictured below, with its cloister, is one of Provence's major Romanesque monuments.

In Roman times Arles was surrounded by graveyards, including one known as Les Alyscamps. This cemetery became important when the Christian martyr St Genest and the first bishops of Arles were buried there. In 1040 the site became the St-Honorat priory, one of the required stops on the pilgrimage route to Santiago de Compostela in Spain.

Church of St-Trophime. ▼

Würzburg Residence with the Court Gardens and Residence Square
Germany

Criteria – Human creative genius; Significance in human history

This magnificent Baroque palace – one of the largest and most beautiful in Germany and surrounded by wonderful gardens – was created under the patronage of the Prince-Bishops of Schönborn and was home to one of the most brilliant courts of Europe during the eighteenth century. The main part of the Residence was built between 1720 and 1744 and decorated internally between 1740 and 1770. The most renowned architects of the time – the Viennese Lukas von de Hildebrandt and the Parisians Robert de Cotte and Germain Boffrand – drew up plans that were supervised by the official architect of the Prince Bishop, Balthasar Neumann. Sculptors and stucco-workers came from Italy, Flanders and Munich. The Venetian painter Giovanni Battista Tiepolo decorated the staircase and the walls of the Imperial Hall with frescoes.

Tiepolo painted the staircase vault with a fresco that depicts Apollo and the Four Continents. In the portion of the fresco representing Europa, he included portraits of those responsible for the design of the Residence: Neumann (portrayed as an artillery colonel), Tiepolo with his son Giandomenico and the Prince-Bishop supported by Fame and crowned by Virtue.

SGang Gwaay
Canada

Criteria – Testimony to cultural tradition

Pacific
Ocean

NORTH
AMERICA

Atlantic
Ocean

SGang Gwaay Llnagaay (Ninstints) is a village site of the Haida people and part of the Gwaii Haanas National Park Reserve and Haida Heritage Site in the Queen Charlotte Islands (Haida Gwaii) of British Columbia. The Haida people lived on SGang Gwaay (Anthony Island) for thousands of years, but the population was decimated by disease by the 1880s. Most of the village has been taken by nature and returned to the forest. What is left is unique in the world: remains of a nineteenth-century Haida village where the remnants of twenty-three houses and thirty-two memorial or mortuary poles depict a rich and flamboyant society. The protected area epitomises the rugged beauty and ecological character of the Pacific coast, and commemorates the living culture of the Haida people and their relationship to the land and sea, offering a tangible key to their oral traditions.

Gwaii Haanas is on the spring migration route of the grey whales which spend their summers in feeding grounds in the Bering Sea. Killer whales (orcas), humpback and minke whales are also seen in the waters surrounding Gwaii Haanas, along with Pacific white-sided dolphins, steller sea lions and harbour seals.

Aldabra Atoll
Seychelles

Criteria – Natural phenomena or beauty; Significant ecological and biological processes; Significant natural habitat for biodiversity

AFRICA

Indian Ocean

The atoll is comprised of four large coral islands which enclose a shallow lagoon; the group of islands is itself surrounded by a coral reef. Due to difficulties of access and the atoll's isolation, Aldabra has been protected from human influence and thus retains some 152,000 giant tortoises, the world's largest population of this reptile.

Aldabra is the least-disturbed large island in the Indian Ocean and the only place in the world where a reptile is the dominant herbivore. The only endemic mammal is a flying fox.

◄

Giant Tortoise.

World Heritage site since

· 1978 · 1979 · 1980 · 1981 · **1982**

Historic Centre of Florence
Italy

Criteria – Human creative genius; Interchange of values; Testimony to cultural tradition; Significance in human history; Heritage associated with events of universal significance

The Duomo ▶
dominates the
Florence skyline.

The Medicis, Florence's great patrons and benefactors, ruled the Grand Duchy of Tuscany until the family died out in 1737. Florence became part of the Kingdom of Italy in 1859 and was the country's political capital for a short time, between 1865 and 1870.

The historic centre of Florence may be viewed from the surrounding hills, especially Piazzale Michelangelo (just under the Romanesque Basilica of San Miniato), or Fiesole; both offer some of the most spectacular views in the Arno valley.

Florence is the symbol and cradle of the Renaissance and its beautiful historic centre may best be described as a treasure chest of works of art and architecture. Its 600 years of extraordinary artistic activity can be seen in a wealth of buildings and artefacts, especially the cathedral Santa Maria del Fiore (the Duomo), the church of Santa Croce, the Uffizi Gallery and the Medicis' Pitti Palace, now a gallery with paintings by great masters such as Giotto, Brunelleschi, Botticelli and Michelangelo.

Founded in 59 BC as a Roman colony known as Florentia, the free commune of Florence gradually gained supremacy over rival towns in Tuscany until, in the fifteenth century, the city reached the apex of its splendour. Defined by the fourteenth-century walls, and built up thanks to the enormous business and economic power Florence achieved, the two succeeding centuries were its golden age. Under the powerful Medici family, its rulers in the fifteenth and sixteenth centuries, Florence exerted a major influence on the development of architecture and the monumental arts, first in Italy and then throughout Europe.

The spiritual focus of the city is the Cathedral Piazza of Santa Maria del Fiore;

Giotto's campanile is on one side and the Baptistry of St John in front, with the Gates of Paradise by Lorenzo Ghiberti.

To the north lies the Palazzo Medici-Riccardi by Michelozzo and St Lawrence's Basilica by Brunelleschi, their sacristies designed by Donatello and Michelangelo. Further on are the Museum of St Mark's, with Fra Angelico's masterpieces, the Galleria dell'Accademia with Michelangelo's David (1501–4) and the Santissima Annunziata Piazza with the Lodge of the Holy Innocents by Brunelleschi.

On the south side of the cathedral is the political and cultural centre of Florence, with the Palazzo Vecchio, and the Galleria degli Uffizi nearby. Close to these are the Museo del Bargello and the Basilica of the Holy Cross. Across the Ponte Vecchio, over the river Arno, is the Oltrarno quarter, with the Pitti Palace and Boboli Gardens. Also in the Oltrarno, is the Holy Ghost Basilica by Filippo Brunelleschi and the Carmelite Church, with its frescoes by Masolino, Masaccio and Filippino Lippi. To the west of the cathedral stand the imposing Strozzi Palace and the Basilica of Santa Maria Novella, its façade designed by Leon Battista Alberti.

World Heritage site since

· 1978 · 1979 · 1980 · 1981 · **1982**

Lord Howe Island Group
Australia

Criteria – Natural phenomena or beauty;
Significant natural habitat for biodiversity

A remarkable example of isolated oceanic
islands, born of volcanic activity more than
2,000 m under the sea, the Lord Howe
Island Group boasts an exceptional diversity
of spectacular and scenic landscapes within
a small area. The sheer slopes of its volcanic
mountains and the dramatic rock formation
Ball's Pyramid rise out of an underwater
world that is one of the most beautiful in

the world. The isolation of this special place
at the junction of tropical and temperate
latitudes has led to tremendous biodiversity.
This group of islands is one of the major
breeding sites for seabirds in the southwest
Pacific and is home to numerous endemic
species of flora and fauna.

The Lord Howe Island
Group supports
the southernmost
true coral reef in
the world, which
differs considerably
from more northerly
warm water reefs. It
is unique in being a
transition between the
algal and coral reef,
due to fluctuations
of hot and cold water
around the island.

Archaeological Site of
Cyrene
Libya

Criteria – Interchange of values; Testimony
to cultural tradition; Heritage associated with
events of universal significance

A colony of the Greeks of Thera, Cyrene was
one of the principal cities in the Hellenic
world. It was Romanized and remained a
great capital until the earthquake of AD 365.
The site contains the three monumental
complexes of the sanctuary of Apollo, the
Acropolis and the Agora, and preserves a
necropolis complex which is numbered
among the most extensive and varied of the
ancient world. A thousand years of history is
written into its ruins.

Once given by Mark
Anthony to Cleopatra,
Cyrene is not only
one of the cities of the
Mediterranean world
around which myths,
legends and stories
have been woven
over more than 1,000
years, but it is also
one of the most
impressive complexes
of ruins in the entire
world.

◄

Temple of Zeus,
Cyrene.

World Heritage site since

· 1978 · 1979 · 1980 · 1981 · **1982**

Selous Game Reserve
Tanzania

Criteria – Significant ecological and biological processes; Significant natural habitat for biodiversity

AFRICA

Atlantic
Ocean

Indian
Ocean

Some 400 species of animal are known, and in 1986 approximately 750,000 large animals of 57 species were recorded.

The Selous Game Reserve is a 50,000 km² ecosystem and one of the largest wildlife reserves in the world. It is noted particularly for the range of its wildlife – large numbers of elephant, black rhinoceros, cheetah, giraffe, impala, hippopotamus and crocodile live in this immense sanctuary – and for its remoteness, being relatively undisturbed by humans.

The reserve, which includes Mikumi National Park and Kilombero Game Controlled Area, has a variety of vegetation zones, ranging from dense thickets to open wooded grasslands. The deciduous miombo woodland is dominant, providing the world's best example of this vegetation type. Soils are relatively poor and infertile and winters bring drought, but despite these facts, the reserve has a higher density and species diversity than any other miombo woodland area, thanks to its size, the diversity of its habitats, the availability of food and water, and the lack of human settlement.

In 1994, in the reserve and surrounding buffer area, there were 52,000 of the endangered African elephant, 50 per cent of the country's total, which is now growing again after years of decline due to ivory poaching.

Impalas in the reserve.
▼

Sacred City of Anuradhapura
Sri Lanka

Criteria – Interchange of values; Testimony to cultural tradition; Heritage associated with events of universal significance

Anuradhapura, a political and religious capital that flourished for 1,300 years, is one of the principal shrines of Buddhism. Abandoned and hidden away in dense jungle for many years, the splendid site, with its palaces, monasteries and monuments, is now accessible again.

Founded in the fourth century BC, Anuradhapura quickly became both the capital of Ceylon, as the country was then called, and the sacred city of Buddhism on the island. It has remarkable monuments, particularly the huge dagabas (relic chambers), set on circular foundations and surrounded by a ring of monolithic columns, much like Sinhalese stupas.

The city was attacked by waves of invaders from southern India and was finally abandoned in 993. It stands as a permanent manifesto of the culture of Sri Lanka, impervious to outside influences.

The religious significance of Anuradhapura was confirmed when a cutting from the 'tree of enlightenment', under which the Buddha meditated and gained enlightenment, was brought to the city in the third century BC. The cutting flourished and today, the bodhi tree spreads out over the centre of the site from a sanctuary near the Brazen Palace.

Jetavanaramaya dagaba
▼

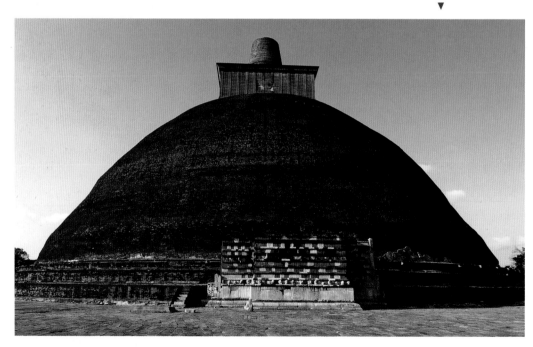

World Heritage site since

· 1978 · 1979 · 1980 · 1981 · **1982**

National History Park – Citadel, Sans Souci, Ramiers
Haiti

Criteria – Significance in human history; Heritage associated with events of universal significance

Situated within the National History Park created by presidential decree in 1978, these buildings enjoy splendid natural setting of mountainous peaks covered with luxuriant vegetation.

These Haitian monuments date from the beginning of the nineteenth century, when Haiti proclaimed its independence. The Palace of Sans Souci, the buildings at Ramiers and, especially, the Citadelle Henry serve as universal symbols of liberty, as they were the first to be built by black slaves who had gained their freedom. The Citadelle, constructed at an altitude of 970 m and covering a surface area of about 10,000 m², is one of the best examples of the art of military engineering of the early nineteenth century. It was designed specifically to allow an integrated use of artillery capabilities; an elaborate system of cisterns supplied water; and colossal defensive walls rendered this citadel impregnable. It can shelter a garrison of up to 5,000 men.

Taï National Park
Côte d'Ivoire

Criteria – Natural phenomena or beauty; Significant natural habitat for biodiversity

The park contains some 1,300 species of higher plants, of which 54 per cent occur only in the Guinea zone. Vegetation is predominantly dense evergreen forest of a Guinean type characterized by tall trees (40–60 m) with massive trunks. Plants thought to be extinct, such as Amorphophallus staudtii, have been discovered in the area.

The park is one of the last remaining portions of the vast primary forest that once stretched across present-day Ghana, Côte d'Ivoire, Liberia and Sierra Leone, and is the largest island of forest remaining in West Africa. Its rich natural flora, and threatened mammal species such as the pygmy hippopotamus and eleven species of monkeys, are of great scientific interest. The park lies in southwest Côte d'Ivoire about 200 km south of Man and 100 km from the coast, between the Cavally River (which marks the western border with Liberia) and the Sassandra River on the east. There is a gradation from north to south, with the southern third of the park being the moistest and richest area, especially of leguminous trees.

Ancient City of Polonnaruwa
Sri Lanka

Criteria – Human creative genius; Testimony to cultural tradition; Heritage associated with events of universal significance

A carving of Buddha ▶ in Polonnaruwa.

Polonnaruwa bears witness to several civilizations, notably that of the conquering Cholas, disciples of Brahmanism, and of the Sinhalese sovereigns of the twelfth and thirteenth centuries.

The city is a Buddhist shrine. The tooth of Buddha, a remarkable relic placed in the Atadage, or Temple of the Tooth Relic, by King Vijayabahu I, was considered the talisman of the Sinhalese monarchy. Its removal by King Bhuvanaikabahu II to Kurunegala at the end of the thirteenth century only confirmed the decline of Polonnaruwa.

Polonnaruwa was the second capital of Ceylon (now Sri Lanka) after the destruction of Anuradhapura in 993. This immense new capital created by the megalomaniac sovereign, Parakramabahu I, in the twelfth century, is one of history's most astonishing urban creations, both because of its unusual dimensions and because of the very special relationship of its buildings with their natural setting. In addition to the monumental ruins of Parakramabahu's fabulous garden city, Polonnaruwa contains the Brahmanic monuments built in the eleventh century by the Chola invaders from southern India.

After the destruction of Anuradhapura by Rajaraja, Polonnaruwa, a temporary royal residence during the eighth century, became the capital. The conquering Cholas constructed monuments to their religion (Brahmanism), and especially temples to Shiva where fine bronze statues, today in the Museum of Colombo, were found. The reconquest of Ceylon by Vijayabahu I did not put an end to the city's role as capital: it became covered, after 1070, with Buddhist sanctuaries, of which the Atadage, the Temple of the Tooth Relic which held the tooth of the Buddha, is the most renowned.

The apogee of Polonnaruwa occurred in the twelfth century AD when two sovereigns endowed it with monuments. Parakramabahu I (1153–1186) created within the boundary walls a garden city, where palaces and sanctuaries prolonged the enchantment of the countryside. This required the construction of a series of sophisticated irrigation systems; these systems are still used today. In addition, other notable monuments were built during his reign: the Lankatilaka, an enormous brick structure which has preserved a colossal image of Buddha; the Gal Vihara, with its gigantic rock sculptures which is among the masterpieces of Sinhalese art; and the Tivanka Pilimage, where wall paintings of the thirteenth century illustrate the *jataka* (narratives of the previous lives of Buddha).

The successor to Parakramabahu, Nissamkamalla I, ruler until 1196, built monuments that were less refined than those of his predecessor but nonetheless splendid: the Rankot Vihara, an enormous stupa or relic chamber 175 m in diameter and 55 m high, is one of the most impressive; its plan and its dimensions are reminiscent of the dagabas at Anuradhapura.

After this golden age the city fell into a long decline until government finally moved to Kurunegala at the end of the thirteenth century.

World Heritage site since

· 1978 · 1979 · 1980 · 1981 · **1982**

Tipasa
Algeria

*Criteria – Testimony to cultural tradition;
Significance in human history*

The extraordinary archaeological complexes of Tipasa, on the Mediterranean coast 70 km west of Algiers, are perhaps the most significant to the study of the contacts between the indigenous civilizations and various waves of colonization from the sixth century BC to the sixth century AD.

On the shores of the Mediterranean, Tipasa was an ancient Punic trading post conquered by Rome and turned into a strategic base for the conquest of the kingdoms of Mauritania. It comprises a unique group of Phoenician, Roman, palaeochristian and Byzantine ruins alongside indigenous monuments such as the Kbor er Roumia, the great royal mausoleum of Mauritania. The oldest Roman settlement is in the centre of the city on a steep slope protected by cliffs. The impressive ruins of the civic buildings are set in the heart of a dense network of private houses (many decorated with paintings and mosaics), commercial warehouses, and industrial establishments of the second and third centuries. Of the numerous Christian religious buildings, the immense fourth-century seven-aisled basilica is particularly striking.

Río Plátano Biosphere Reserve
Honduras

Criteria – Natural phenomena or beauty; Major stages of Earth's history; Significant ecological and biological processes; Significant natural habitat for biodiversity

The site of Ciudad Blanca (White City) within the protected area constitutes one of the most important archaeological sites of Mayan civilization. The reserve also contains the site where Christopher Columbus first landed in the Americas in 1492. There are some 200 sites of archaeological importance.

Situated in the Mosquita region of northeast Honduras, the site comprises a belt of approximately 15 km by 150 km extending inland from the Caribbean coast in a southwesterly direction. The reserve protects virtually the entire watershed of the 100 km-long Plátano River, as well as major portions of the Paulaya, Guampu and Sicre rivers. These three waterways, together with the Caribbean, form the boundaries of the reserve, which is the largest surviving area of virgin tropical rainforest in Honduras. Its varied topography ranges from mountains with spectacular rock formations (such as Dama Peak) and waterfalls to placid coastal lagoons. Thirty-nine species of mammal, 377 species of bird and 126 reptiles and amphibians have been recorded.

World Heritage site since

· 1978 · 1979 · 1980 · 1981 · **1982**

Tasmanian Wilderness
Australia

Criteria – Testimony to cultural tradition;
Significance in human history; Heritage
associated with events of universal significance;
Natural phenomena or beauty; Major stages of
Earth's history; Significant ecological and
biological processes; Significant natural habitat
for biodiversity

Covering an area of 13,800 km², the
Tasmanian Wilderness contains some of the
last expanses of temperate rainforest and is
one of the three largest temperate
wilderness regions in the southern
hemisphere. It comprises a vast network of
reserved lands that extends over much of
southwestern Tasmania, including several
coastal islands. Glacial erosion and other
geomorphological processes have
contributed to spectacular landforms and
the area contains rocks from almost every
geological period. The flora and fauna is
correspondingly diverse, with living
evidence of its ancient Gondwanan heritage.
The isolation of the Tasmanian Wilderness
has contributed to the uniqueness of its flora
and fauna, which includes some of the
world's longest-lived trees and largest
carnivorous marsupials. Remains found in
limestone caves attest to human occupation
of the area for at least 35,000 years through
periods of great climatic variation.

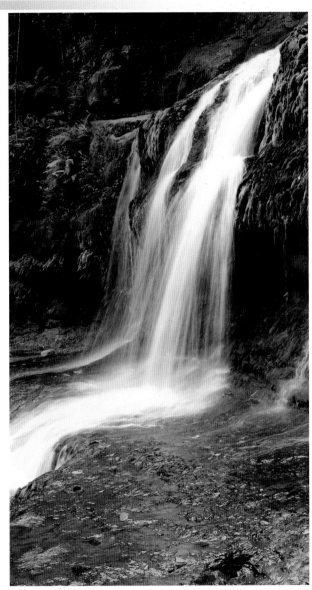

Liffey falls. ▲

Tasmania was cut off from mainland
Australia by rising sea levels
approximately 8,000 years ago,
thereby isolating Tasmanian
Aborigines for some
500 generations.

World Heritage site since

·· 1978 • 1979 • 1980 • 1981 • **1982**

Archaeological Site of Leptis Magna
Libya

Criteria – Human creative genius; Interchange of values; Testimony to cultural tradition

Leptis Magna was one of the most beautiful cities of the Roman Empire, with its imposing public monuments, harbour, marketplace, storehouses, shops and residential districts. It was enlarged and embellished by Septimius Severus, who was born there and later became emperor. It is still one of the best examples of Severan urban planning. Thereafter, Leptis fell prey to the same vicissitudes of fortune as the majority of the coastal cities of Africa. Pillaged from the fourth century and reconquered by the Byzantines who transformed it into a stronghold, it definitively succumbed to the second wave of Arab invasion, that of the Hilians in the eleventh century. Buried under drifting sands, the city has been disengaged, piece by piece, over the course of a long archaeological exploration.

The city, which was constructed during the reign of Augustus and Tiberius but which was entirely remodelled along very ambitious lines under the Severan emperors, incorporates major monumental elements of that period. The forum, basilica and Severan arch rank among the foremost examples of a new Roman art, strongly influenced by African and Eastern traditions.

Leptis Magna Theatre with the ruins of the market, the forum and the harbour in the background.
▼

World Heritage site since

· 1978 · 1979 · 1980 · 1981 · **1982**

Tassili n'Ajjer
Algeria

Criteria – Human creative genius; Testimony to cultural tradition; Natural phenomena or beauty; Major stages of Earth's history

Tassili, a mountainous region in the centre of the Sahara, is a strange lunar landscape of deep gorges, dry river beds and 'stone forests'. During the prehistoric period Tassili had a very different climate, with abundant game, regular rainfall and fertile land. In 1933 one of the most important groupings of prehistoric cave art in the world was discovered here. More than 15,000 drawings and engravings record the climatic changes, the animal migrations and the evolution of

human life on the edge of the Sahara from 6000 BC to the first centuries AD. This art covers several periods, each of which corresponds to a particular fauna, yet each can equally be characterized by stylistic differences, without reference to an ecosystem.

At the end of the Upper Pleistocene period there were huge lakes in this region, fed by rivers whose dry beds can still be seen. The plants and animals found on the plateaus bear witness to former wetter periods. Relict species surviving in wet microclimates include fish and shrimp and, until the 1940s, the dwarf Saharan crocodile, many thousands of kilometres from the nearest population in Egypt.

M'Zab Valley
Algeria

Criteria – Interchange of values; Testimony to cultural tradition; Traditional human settlement

The five ksour (fortified cities) in the M'Zab Valley preserve a traditional human habitat of the tenth century. Simple, functional and perfectly adapted to the environment, the architecture of M'Zab was designed for community living, while respecting the structure of the family. The pattern of the life in the M'Zab Valley included a seasonal migration. Each summer the population moved to palm groves, where the 'summer

cities' were marked by a looser organization, the highly defensive nature of the houses, the presence of watchtowers, and a mosque without a minaret, comparable with those in the cemeteries. The settlement of the M'Zab Valley has exerted considerable influence on architects and city planners of the twentieth century, from Le Corbusier to Pouillon.

Each of the five M'Zab miniature citadels is encircled by walls and dominated by a mosque, whose minaret functioned as a watchtower. The mosque, with its arsenal and grain stores, was conceived as a fortress, the last bastion of resistance in the event of a siege.

World Heritage site since

· 1978 · 1979 · 1980 · 1981 · **1982**

Old Havana and its Fortification System
Cuba

Criteria – Significance in human history;
Traditional human settlement

The Castillo de la Real Fuerza is the oldest extant colonial fortress in the Americas: its west tower is crowned by a bronze weathervane dating back to 1632.

The Plaza de Armas has been the seat of authority and power in Cuba for 400 years. The imposing Palacio de los Capitanes Generales on the west side of the square is one of Cuba's most majestic buildings and is now the City Museum. Calle Obispo, which runs off the Plaza de Armas, was a haunt of Ernest Hemingway.

Havana was the last city the Spanish conquistadors founded in Cuba and is the finest surviving Spanish complex in the Americas. The city's situation made it a perfect gathering point for the annual treasure fleets bound for Spain from Mexico and Peru and it became the front door to the vast Spanish colonial empire. The modern-day city is a large metropolis but its old centre retains an interesting mix of Baroque and neoclassical monuments, and a homogeneous ensemble of private houses with arcades, balconies, wrought-iron gates and internal courtyards.

Havana was established at its present location in 1519 and by 1550 it had become the most important city on the island, a position it has held ever since. It became one of the Caribbean's main centres for shipbuilding and has been Cuba's capital since 1607.

Spain fortified the city in the 1760s when Europe's Seven Years' War spilled over into the Americas; those fortifications can still be seen today. Havana was allowed to trade freely, growing in wealth through the eighteenth and nineteenth centuries, remaining physically untouched by the wars of independence in Central and South America in the first half of the nineteenth century. After political agitation throughout the nineteenth century, Cuba finally gained its independence from Spain in 1902. Havana suffered little damage during periods of unrest, including the Cuban Revolution of the 1950s, and the old city stands today much as it was 100 years ago or more.

The Cuban government has been involved in efforts to restore the character of a colonial city to the historic centre. Many of Old Havana's finest buildings have been converted into museums, and there are churches, palaces, castles, revolutionary monuments and markets to visit. The fortress of La Fuerza has been restored, as have the palaces of the Segundo Cabo and of Los Capitanes Generales. Restoration is slowly extending to residential areas.

The pattern of early urban planning still exists with the city's four large squares: Plaza de La Cathedral, Plaza de San Francisco, Plaza Vieja and Plaza de Armas. There is also a notable complex of seventeenth–nineteenth-century buildings. The Plaza de la Catedral, with the towers of the Catedral de San Cristóbal de La Habana dominating the square, is one of the city's most outstanding sights.

World Heritage site since

· 1978 · 1979 · 1980 · 1981 · **1982**

Djémila
Algeria

Criteria – Testimony to cultural tradition;
Significance in human history

Situated 900 m above sea level, Djémila, or Cuicul, is one of the world's most beautiful Roman ruins. The classic formula of Roman urban planning was adapted to the physical constraints of the site: at both ends of the *cardo maximus*, the backbone of the city, are two gates. In the centre is the forum, an enclosed square surrounded by buildings essential to the functioning of civil life. Aristocratic dwellings set with rich mosaics

multiplied during the course of the second century in this central quarter. However, this cramped defensive situation, hemmed in by walls, hindered the development of the city. In the mid-second century AD the city therefore expanded to the south, where a new quarter, rich in both public buildings and private dwellings, was established.

Christianity was implanted in the southern quarter at an early date. The remains of a group of episcopal buildings have been located there: two basilicas, a baptistry, a chapel and several houses, the residence of the bishop and the priest.

Timgad
Algeria

Criteria – Interchange of values; Testimony to cultural tradition; Significance in human history

Timgad, which lies on the northern slopes of the Aurès mountains in a site of great natural beauty, is a consummate example of a Roman military colony created *ex nihilo* by the Emperor Trajan in AD 100. With its square enclosure measuring 355 m on each side and its precise orthogonal design based on the *cardo* and *decumanus* (the two perpendicular routes running through the city), it is an excellent example of Roman town planning at its height. Large public

buildings in the south of the city include the forum and its annexes (*basilica* and *curia*), temples, a theatre with a seating capacity of 3,500, a market and baths. In the northeast sector, there are other baths and a public library.

Timgad's development was meticulously planned. The streets were paved with large rectangular slabs of limestone, and particular attention was paid to the disposition of public conveniences. The houses, including many immense private residences, sparkled under a décor of sumptuous mosaics.

World Heritage site since

· 1978 · 1979 · 1980 · 1981 · **1982**

Archaeological Site of Sabratha
Libya
Criteria – Testimony to cultural tradition

Mediterranean Sea

ASIA

AFRICA

A Phoenician trading post that served as an outlet for the products of the African hinterland, Sabratha was part of the short-lived Numidian kingdom of Massinissa before being Romanized and rebuilt in the second and third centuries AD. The spectacular ruins highlight its wealth in Roman times, which saw the construction of grandiose monuments, of which the most renowned is the theatre (pictured below), probably built during the reign of

the Emperor Commodus (AD 161–192), with a capacity of 5,000 seats. The best conserved part is the frons scena, at the back of the stage, which has been reconstructed with original fragments and is divided into three levels with overlapping marble columns. Near the theatre stands the amphitheatre, and other monuments include the temples of Liber Pater, Serapis, Hercules and Isis, the Basilica of Justinian and the Capitolium.

The decline of Sabratha began in the fourth century: commerce with Africa was less active, it was wracked by religious quarrels, and much of the city was destroyed by earthquakes, particularly that of AD 365. The Vandals invaded Sabratha in 455 and the city was definitively abandoned after the Arab invasions of the seventh and eleventh centuries.

Roman Theatre at Sabratha.
▼

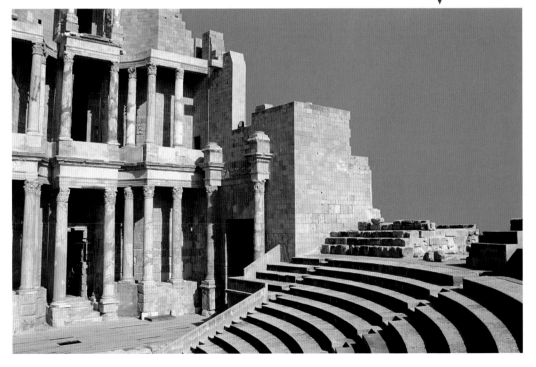

World Heritage site since

· 1978 • 1979 • 1980 • 1981 • **1982**

Historic Centre of the Town of Olinda
Brazil

Criteria – Interchange of values; Significance in human history

Founded in 1537 by the Portuguese, the town's history is linked to the sugar cane industry. Rebuilt after being looted by the Dutch, its basic urban fabric dates from the eighteenth century. The harmonious balance between the buildings, gardens, twenty Baroque churches, convents and numerous small passos (chapels) all contribute to Olinda's particular charm. From the sixteenth century, few of the churches and convents built by religious missions survive.

Among the more important of the eighteenth-century buildings are the Episcopal Church, the Jesuit College and Church (now the Church of Graça), the Franciscan, Carmelite, Benedictine and other monasteries, convents and churches. The studied refinements of the décor of these Baroque architectural structures contrasts with the charming simplicity of the houses, which are painted in vivid colours or faced with ceramic tiles.

Over recent decades, Olinda – a city much appreciated by artists – has been the object of numerous preservation measures. Outstanding buildings such as the Church of Graça, with the former Jesuit College, the **Convent do Carmo (pictured below)**, and the Episcopal Palace have all been restored.

Cahokia Mounds State Historic Site
USA

Criteria – Testimony to cultural tradition;
Significance in human history

Cahokia Mounds, some 13 km northeast of St Louis, Missouri, is the largest pre-Columbian settlement north of Mexico. It was occupied primarily during the Mississippian period 800–1400, when it covered nearly 16 km² and included some 120 mounds (earthworks). It is a striking example of a complex chiefdom society, with many satellite mound centres and numerous outlying hamlets and villages.

This agricultural society may have had a population of 10–20,000 at its peak between 1050 and 1150. Primary features at the site include Monks Mound, the largest prehistoric earthwork in the Americas, covering over 50,000 m² and standing 30 m high.

Cahokia has numerous large oval-shaped pits arranged in arcs of circles. Archaeologists believe that posts set in these pits lined up with the rising sun at certain times of the year, serving as a calendar, called Woodhenge.

Ancient City of Sigiriya
Sri Lanka

Criteria – Interchange of values; Testimony to cultural tradition; Significance in human history

The ruins of the capital built by the parricidal King Kassapa I (477–495) lie on the steep slopes and at the summit of a granite peak standing some 370 m high, the 'Lion's Rock', which dominates the jungle from all sides. A series of galleries and staircases emerging from the mouth of a gigantic lion constructed of bricks and plaster provide access to the site.

The 'Sigiri graffiti' are poems inscribed on the rock, and are among the most ancient texts in the Sinhalese language. They show the considerable influence exerted by the city on the literature and thought of ancient Ceylon.

◄

Sigiriya or Lion's Rock.

Old Walled City of Shibam
Yemen

Criteria – Testimony to cultural tradition;
Significance in human history; Traditional
human settlement

Surrounded by a fortified wall, the sixteenth-century city of Shibam is one of the oldest and best examples of urban planning based on the principle of vertical construction, giving the city the nickname of 'the Manhattan of the desert'. The city is built on a hillock, which has allowed it to escape the devastating floods of Wadi Hadramaut. Its plan is almost rectangular; and it is enclosed by earthen walls within which blocks of

dwellings, also built from earth, have been laid out on a grid. The tallest house is eight storeys and the average is five, and the buildings for the most part date from the sixteenth century. However, some older houses and large buildings still remain from the first centuries of Islam, such as the Friday Mosque, built in 904, and the castle, built in 1220.

In Shibam there are some mosques, two ancient sultan's palaces and more than 500 buildings all made uniform by the material of which they are constructed: unfired clay blocks which continue to be made locally.

▼

From the Great Saltworks of Salins-les-Bains to the Royal Saltworks of Arc-et-Senans, the production of open-pan salt
France

Criteria – Human creative genius; Interchange of values; Significance in human history

The Great Saltworks of Salins-les-Bains, where brine has been extracted since the Middle Ages features three buildings above ground: salt stores, the Amont well building and a former dwelling.

It is linked to the Royal Saltworks of Arc-et-Senans, a factory designed with the same sense of architectural quality as that of a palace. It is a temple to labour, perfectly illustrating the cultural changes that came about with the birth of industrial society. Located near Besançon, the Royal Saltworks was designed by Claude-Nicolas Ledoux. Its construction, begun in 1775 and completed in 1779 during the reign of Louis XVI, was the first major achievement of industrial architecture, reflecting the ideal of progress of the Enlightenment. This vast semicircular complex was designed to permit a rational and hierarchical organization of work and was to have been followed by the building of an ideal city, the city of Choux, a project that was never realized.

The Royal Saltworks' exceptional architecture included a system of double canals composed of wooden cylinders which drew saline water from Salons, 21 km away. At Arc-et-Senans the water was evaporated in immense vats heated night and day by a wood fire.

World Heritage site since

··· 1978 • 1979 • 1980 • 1981 • 1982 • **1983**

Comoé National Park
Côte d'Ivoire

Criteria – Significant ecological and biological processes; Significant natural habitat for biodiversity

One of the largest protected areas in West Africa, this park is characterized by its great plant diversity. It is one of the few remaining natural areas in the region that is large enough to ensure the ecological integrity of the species contained within the site. The park comprises the land between the Comoé and Volta rivers, with a mean altitude of 250–300 m and a series of ridges rising to 600 m. The Comoé and its tributaries form the principal drainage; the river runs through the park for 230 km. Due to the presence of the Comoé, the park contains plants which are normally found only much farther south, such as shrub savannas and patches of thick rainforest.

The park provides an outstanding example of an area of transitional habitat from forest to savanna. Its remarkable variety of habitats is home to a high number of mammal species, including eleven species of monkey.

Taj Mahal
India

Criteria – Human creative genius

Situated on the right ▶
bank of the Yamuna
River, the Taj Mahal
stands in a vast
Mughal garden of
some 0.17 km^2
bounded by four
minarets. The unique
Mughal style
combines elements
and styles of Persian,
Central Asian and
Islamic architecture.
Its octagonal structure
is capped by a bulbous
dome. The architectural
precision is balanced
by the delicate white
marble decoration of
floral arabesques,
decorative bands and
calligraphic
inscriptions.

The Taj Mahal is the jewel of Muslim art in
India and one of the universally admired
masterpieces of the world's heritage. An
immense mausoleum of white marble, it
was built in Agra between 1631 and 1648 by
order of the Mughal emperor Shah Jahan
in memory of his third and favourite wife.

The Taj Mahal partially owes its renown
to the moving circumstances of its
construction. To perpetuate the memory
of Mumtaz Mahal, who died in 1631, Shah
Jahan had this funerary mosque built.

The monument, begun in 1632, was
finished in 1648. Unverified legends
attribute its construction to an international
team of several thousands of masons,
marble workers, mosaicists and decorators
working under the orders of the architect of
the emperor, Ustad Ahmad Lahori using
building materials from all over India and
central Asia.

The Darwaza, or gateway, was completed
in 1648. It is a three-storey red sandstone
structure with a lofty central arch and two-
storeyed wings on either side. Its walls are
inscribed with verses from the Koran in
Arabic in black calligraphy. The small domed
pavilions on top are Hindu in style and
signify royalty. The gate was originally lined
with silver, now replaced with copper, and

decorated with 1,000 nails whose heads
were contemporary silver coins.

The Bageecha, or gardens, are planned
along classical Mughal char-bagh style. Two
cypress-tree-lined canals quarter the garden
into equal squares. The garden is laid out in
such a way as to maintain perfect symmetry.

The Taj Mahal stands in the north end of
the garden on two bases, one of sandstone
and above it a square platform in a
chequerboard design topped by a huge
white marble terrace. On the corners are
four minarets.

Two identical red sandstone buildings
stand on either side; the western one is the
masjid (mosque), which sanctifies the area
and provides a place of worship. The rauza,
the mausoleum itself, is square with
bevelled corners. Each corner has a small
dome while in the centre the main double
dome is topped by a brass finial. The main
chamber inside is octagonal with a high
domed ceiling. This chamber contains false
tombs of Mumtaz and Shah Jahan, both
inlaid with precious stones.

World Heritage site since

• 1978 • 1979 • 1980 • 1981 • 1982 • **1983**

Ajanta Caves
India

Criteria – Human creative genius; Interchange of values; Testimony to cultural tradition; Heritage associated with events of universal significance

Five of the Ajanta caves were temples, and twenty-four were monasteries thought to have been occupied by 200 monks and artisans.

The caves were forgotten until their rediscovery by a British tiger-hunting party in 1819.

With its two groups of monuments corresponding to two important periods in Indian history, the caves bear exceptional testimony to the evolution of Indian art.

The Ajanta Caves are cave monuments cut out of hillside rock, first dating from the second and first centuries BC. The paintings and sculptures of Ajanta, considered to be masterpieces of Buddhist religious art, have had a considerable artistic influence.

The caves, situated 100 km northeast of Ellora, are cut into the volcanic lava of the Deccan in the forest ravines of the Sahyadri Hills and are set in beautiful wooded surroundings. They contain carvings that depict the life of Buddha, and their carvings and sculptures are considered to mark the beginning of classical Indian art.

The twenty-nine caves were first excavated around 200 BC and work went on for several hundred years until they were abandoned in 650 AD in favour of another site of cave monuments, at Ellora.

World Heritage site since

• 1978 • 1979 • 1980 • 1981 • 1982 • **1983**

Old City of Berne
Switzerland
Criteria – Testimony to cultural tradition

EUROPE

Atlantic
Ocean

Adriatic
Sea

Mediterranean
Sea

One of Berne's most recognizable symbols is the Zytglogge, the ornately decorated thirteenth-century clocktower with its moving gilded figure striking the hour.

Since 1848, large public monuments have been built which emphasize Berne's capital-city status: the Bundeshaus, Museum of Fine Arts, Historical Museum, University, Municipal Theatre, etc.

Founded in the twelfth century on a hill site looped by the Aare River, Berne (pictured below) developed over the centuries in line with an exceptionally coherent planning concept that continues to the present day.

The buildings in the Old City, dating from a variety of periods, include fifteenth-century arcades and sixteenth-century picturesque fountains, as well as towers and walls. The cathedral was constructed during the seventeenth century, when many patrician houses were built from sandy limestone; towards the end of the eighteenth century, almost 80 per cent of the constructed zones were renewed.

Like many European capitals, Berne today offers a contrast (particularly acute on the Bubenbergplatz) of old monuments and contemporary buildings; but it preserves in localized areas, traditional old streets with arcades, the majority of which are pedestrianized.

World Heritage site since

• 1978 • 1979 • 1980 • 1981 • 1982 • **1983**

City of Cuzco
Peru

Criteria – Testimony to cultural tradition;
Significance in human history

Inca mythology attributes the foundation of the city to the Inca Manco Cápac: according to tradition the golden sceptre that the sun had given him was thrust into the fertile soil of Cuzco to designate the emplacement of the capital.

Set in a fertile valley high in the Peruvian Andes, Cuzco (pictured below) was the historic capital of the Incas, the largest civilization in the Americas before the arrival of Europeans.

The city developed under its ruler Pachacutec (1438–71) into a complex urban centre with distinct religious and administrative functions; its surrounding area had separate zones for agricultural, artisanal and industrial production. Its sixteenth-century Spanish conquerors preserved its structure while building over its political and religious monuments.

Cuzco is today an amalgam of Inca capital and colonial city. Of the first, it preserves impressive vestiges, especially its plan: walls of meticulously cut granite or andesite, rectilinear streets within the walls, and the ruins of the Sun Temple. Of the colonial city, there remain the whitewashed squat houses, the palace and churches with their marvellous fusion of Spanish Baroque and Inca influences.

World Heritage site since

• 1978 • 1979 • 1980 • 1981 • 1982 • **1983**

Jesuit Missions of the Guaranis: San Ignacio Miní, Santa Ana, Nuestra Señora de Loreto and Santa María Mayor (Argentina), Ruins of Saõ Miguel das Missões (Brazil)
Argentina and Brazil
Criteria – *Significance in human history*

The ruins of San Ignacio Miní, founded in 1611, are the most eminent example of a *reducción* preserved on Argentinian territory. They are accessible and in a relatively good state of preservation, incorporating churches, a residence of the Fathers, and schools.

The remains of these five Jesuit missions, built in the land of the Guaranis during the seventeenth and eighteenth centuries, are illustrative of a significant period in the history of Argentina and Brazil. The ruins of Saõ Miguel das Missões in Brazil and those of San Ignacio Miní, Santa Ana, Nuestra Señora de Loreto and Santa María la Mayor in Argentina lie in the heart of a tropical forest. All these Guarani *reducciones* (settlements) are laid out on the same model: the church, the residence of the Fathers, and the regularly spaced houses of the Indians are arranged around a large square. However, each of the *reducciones* is characterized by a specific layout and a different state of conservation.

Benedictine Convent of St John at Müstair
Switzerland
Criteria – *Testimony to cultural tradition*

The convent bears exceptional testimony to a Carolingian civilization and art which has disappeared. It is one of the most coherent examples of conventual architecture and painting of the Carolingian period and the early Middle Ages.

The Convent of Müstair, which stands in a valley in the Grisons, is a good example of Christian monastic renovation during the Carolingian period. In the convent church, the removal of the Gothic ceiling (1908–9) and of the whitewash (1947–51) brought to light important vestiges of frescoes dating from the Romanesque period (c. 1150–70) and the Carolingian period (c. 800). This is now recognised as the most important cycle of painting from this period. These figurative paintings (scenes from the Old and New Testaments) are of a fine aesthetic quality and are particularly important in understanding the evolution of certain Christian iconographic themes, such as the Last Judgement. Other precious artworks include stucco statues and reliefs from the eleventh century.

World Heritage site since

· 1978 · 1979 · 1980 · 1981 · 1982 · **1983**

Ellora Caves
India

Criteria – Human creative genius; Testimony to cultural tradition; Heritage associated with events of universal significance

The Ellora Caves not only bear witness to the three great religions of ancient India (Buddhism, Brahminism and Jainism), they also illustrate the spirit of tolerance which permitted these three religions to establish their sanctuaries and their communities in a single place. The thirty-four monasteries and temples of Ellora, extending over more than 2 km, were dug side by side in the wall of a high basalt cliff, not far from Aurangabad, in Maharashtra. The caves, with their uninterrupted sequence of remarkable reliefs, sculptures and architecture dating from AD 600–1000, bring the civilization of ancient India to life. The caves of the Brahmin group are no doubt the best known of Ellora with the 'Cavern of the Ten Avatars' and especially the Kailasha Temple, an enormous complex most likely undertaken during the reign of Krishna I.

Progressing from south to north along the cliff, one discovers successively the twelve caves of the Buddhist group (between c. AD 600 and 800), comprising monasteries and a single large temple, then the caves of the Brahmin group (c. 600–900), and finally the Jain group (c. 800–1000).

Rock carved images of Buddha in meditation in cave number twelve.
▼

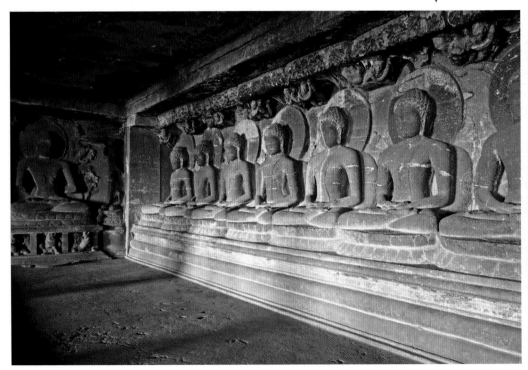

World Heritage site since

• 1978 • 1979 • 1980 • 1981 • 1982 • **1983**

Agra Fort
India

Criteria – Testimony to cultural tradition

The wall has two gates, the Delhi Gate and the Amar Singh Gate. The original and grandest entrance was through the Delhi Gate, which leads to the inner portal called the Hathi Pol or Elephant Gate. The entrance to the fort is now only through the Amar Singh Gate.

Near the gardens of the Taj Mahal stands the sixteenth-century Mughal monument known as the Red Fort of Agra. With its walls of red sandstone rising above a moat and interrupted by graceful curves and lofty bastions, the fortress encompasses within its enclosure walls of 2.5 km the imperial city of the Mogul rulers. It comprises many fairy-tale palaces, such as the Jahangir Palace and the Khas Mahal; audience halls, such as the Diwan-i-Khas; and two very beautiful mosques. Like the Delhi Fort, that of Agra is one of the most obvious symbols of the Mogul grandeur which asserted itself under Akbar, Jahangir and Shah Jahan. Several of the buildings are made from pure marble with beautiful carvings; all of these monuments mark the high point of an Indo-Muslim art strongly marked by influences from Persia.

World Heritage site since

· 1978 · 1979 · 1980 · 1981 · 1982 · **1983**

Talamanca Range-La Amistad Reserves / La Amistad National Park
Costa Rica and Panama

Criteria – Natural phenomena or beauty; Major stages of Earth's history; Significant ecological and biological processes; Significant natural habitat for biodiversity

The Cordillera de Talamanca is the highest and wildest non-volcanic mountain range in Central America. The mountains contain the largest tracts of virgin forest in Costa Rica.

Tropical rainforests have covered this area since the last glaciations, about 25,000 years ago. The park includes lowland tropical rainforest and cloudforest, and four communities not found elsewhere in Central America: subalpine paramo forests, pure oak stands, glacial lakes and high-altitude bogs. Species diversity is perhaps unequalled in any other reserve of equivalent size in the world. Signs of tapir, a species as yet unrecorded in Costa Rica, are abundant on the Panama side of the border. All Central American wild cats are found including puma, ocelot, jaguarundi, tiger cat and jaguar, as well as the Central American squirrel monkey. A green and black high-altitude viper, that has rarely been seen or collected, is present. Four different Indian tribes inhabit this property, which benefits from close cooperation between Costa Rica and Panama.

Central Zone of the Town of Angra do Heroismo in the Azores
Portugal

Criteria – Significance in human history; Heritage associated with events of universal significance

Angra has preserved the better part of its monumental heritage and a homogenous urban ensemble. Its original vernacular architecture is perfectly adapted to unique climatic conditions.

Angra do Heroismo played a highly significant role in maritime exploration from the fifteenth to the nineteenth centuries. Situated on the island of Terceira in the Azores archipelago, the site was protected from the prevailing winds by a series of hills and had two natural basins: that of the Beacon and that of the Anchorage (Angra) from which the village took its name. The port was an obligatory port of call for fleets from Africa and the Indies, and is an eminent example of the maritime framework that allowed exchanges between the world's great civilizations. The 400-year-old San Sebastião and San João Baptista fortifications are unique examples of military architecture. Damaged by an earthquake in 1980, Angra is now being restored.

World Heritage site since

· 1978 · 1979 · 1980 · 1981 · 1982 · **1983**

Monastery of the Hieronymites and Tower of Belém in Lisbon
Portugal

Criteria – Testimony to cultural tradition; Heritage associated with events of universal significance

The interior of the church of Belém incorporates three naves of equal height. The ribs of the vaulting spring from their piers, all of which are covered with sculptures where the luxurious Gothic flora is muted with decorative elements of the Renaissance.

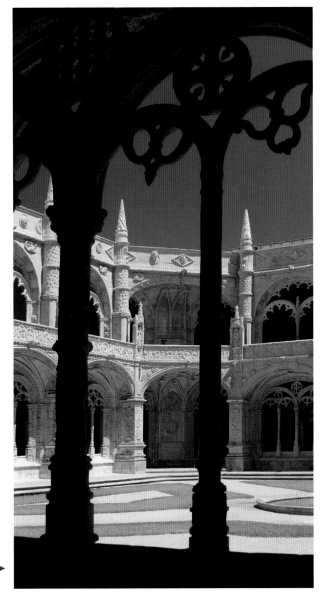

Standing at the entrance to Lisbon harbour, the Monastery of the Hieronymites, construction of which began in 1502, exemplifies Portuguese art at its best. The very rich ornamentation carved on the columns and walls – animals, vegetables, and twining ropes – earns this monument its fame.

The nearby Tower of Belém, built around 1514 to commemorate Vasco da Gama's expedition, is a reminder of the great maritime discoveries that laid the foundations of the modern world. The cross of the Knights of Christ is repeated on the parapets of this fortress, while the watchtowers that flank it are capped with ribbed cupolas inspired by Islamic architecture.

Created by the dynasty of Avis at its height, the complex of Belém is one of the most representative monuments to Portuguese power during the time of the Great Discoveries.

The two-storey cloisters of the Monastery of the ▶ Hieronymites.

World Heritage site since

· 1978 · 1979 · 1980 · 1981 · 1982 · **1983**

Great Smoky Mountains National Park
USA

Criteria – Natural phenomena or beauty; Major stages of Earth's history; Significant ecological and biological processes; Significant natural habitat for biodiversity

Great Smoky Mountains National Park is the most important natural area in the eastern United States and is of world importance as an example of temperate deciduous hardwood forest. Stretching over more than 2,000 km², this exceptionally beautiful park is home to more than 3,500 plant species, including almost as many species of tree, 130, as in all of Europe.

The name 'Smoky' comes from the natural fog that often forms in the morning or after rainfall.

Many endangered animal species are also found there, including probably the greatest variety of salamanders in the world. The dominant topographic feature of the park is the range of the Great Smoky Mountains with sixteen peaks over 1,829 m. Since the park is relatively untouched, it gives an idea of temperate flora before the influence of humankind.

The park contains evidence of four pre-Columbian Indian cultures: Mississippian, Woodland, Archaic and palaeo-Indian. The early Woodland culture period is of special archaeological importance because it shows the first evidence of organized horticulture in North America, with primitive agriculture on river floodplains.

▼

Ancient City of Nessebar
Bulgaria

Criteria – Testimony to cultural tradition;
Significance in human history

Situated on a rocky peninsula on the Black
Sea, Nessebar has been occupied for over
3,000 years. Originally a Thracian
settlement, at the beginning of the sixth
century BC, it became a Greek colony. The
city's remains from the Hellenistic period
include the acropolis, a temple of Apollo,
an agora and a wall from the Thracian
fortifications. Until its capture by the Turks
in 1453, Nessebar was one of the most
important Byzantine towns on the west
coast of the Black Sea. From this period
come monuments of exceptional quality:
for example, the Stara Mitropolia, a large
basilica without transept rebuilt in the ninth
century, the Church of the Virgin and the
Nova Mitropolia, founded in the eleventh
century and continually embellished until
the eighteenth century. Nessebar was
enriched in the nineteenth century by
numerous houses in the 'Plovdiv style', with
stone foundations and broad wooden eaves.

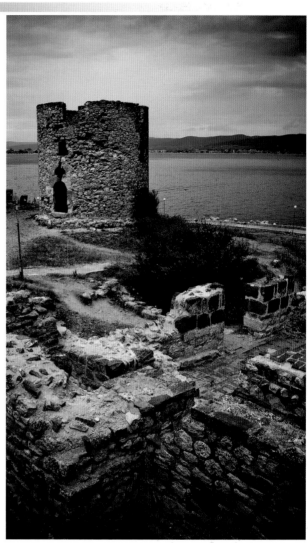

▲
The ruins of an ancient bastion and walls in Nessebar.

Nessebar, one of the oldest towns in
Europe, still exudes the spirit of
numerous ages and peoples –
Thracians, Hellenes, Romans, Slavs,
Byzantines and Bulgarians. Its
cobbled streets, well-kept medieval
churches, and timbered houses from
the nineteenth century illustrate its
chequered past. Nessebar's churches
can be best described as a cross
between Slav and Greek Orthodox
architecture.

World Heritage site since

• 1978 • 1979 • 1980 • 1981 • 1982 • **1983**

La Fortaleza and San Juan National Historic Site in Puerto Rico

USA

Criteria – Heritage associated with events of universal significance

Founded in 1521, San Juan was the second city established by the Spanish in the Americas. It stands at a strategically important point in the Caribbean, and between the fifteenth and nineteenth centuries a series of defensive structures was built to protect the city and the Bay of San Juan. The city defences represent a fine display of European military architecture adapted to harbour sites on the American continent.

For the explorers and the colonists of the New World who came from the east, Puerto Rico was an obligatory stopping-place in the Caribbean. From this evolved its primordial strategic role at the beginning of the Spanish colonization. The island was for centuries a stake disputed by the Spanish, French, English and Dutch. The fortifications of the Bay of San Juan, the magnificent port to which Puerto Rico owes its name, bear witness to its long military history.

La Fortaleza, completed in 1540, was the first of the defensive fortifications to be built to protect Spain's interests against Carib Indians, pirates and enemy warships. It is a vast system with ramparts, fortlets and fortresses, attesting formerly to its effectiveness and today to its historic significance. The main components of this

defensive system are La Fortaleza, El Morro (see photograph on the right) and San Cristóbal.

La Fortaleza is an exemplary monument of Hispano-American colonial architecture. It served as an arsenal, prison, and residence for the Governor-General of the island. El Morro, also built to protect San Juan Bay, stands on a rocky peak of land on the western extremity of the island. This triangular fort developed into a masterpiece of military engineering with stout walls, carefully planned steps and ramps for moving men and artillery. By the end of the eighteenth century, more than 400 cannon defended the fort, making it almost impregnable. San Cristóbal, with its dependencies, is another accomplished example of the military architecture of the second half of the eighteenth century.

San Juan National Historic Site includes forts, bastions, powder houses, walls and El Cañuelo Fort, also called San Juan de la Cruz – defensive fortifications that once surrounded the old colonial portion of San Juan, Puerto Rico. El Cañuelo Fort is located on the Isla de Cabras at the western end of the entrance to San Juan Bay.

▶ The walls of Fort San Felipe del Moro (El Morro) in San Juan.

By the nineteenth century, the old city had become a charming residential and commercial district. The city itself, with its institutional buildings, museums, houses, churches, plazas and commercial buildings, is part of the San Juan Historic Zone which is administered by municipal, state and federal agencies.

The entire historic site of San Juan with its different monumental components maintains, at present, a balance between constructed and non-constructed zones.

World Heritage site since

· 1978 · 1979 · 1980 · 1981 · 1982 · **1983**

Srebarna Nature Reserve
Bulgaria
Criteria – Significant natural habitat for
biodiversity

EUROPE

Black Sea

Until 1949, the lake
was connected to the
river Danube. Its
disconnection
prevented annual
flooding and the level
of the lake fell one
metre per year.
However, the lake was
reconnected with the
Danube by canal in
1978 to prevent water
levels from becoming
too low and to restore
the lake's fish
population.

The Srebarna Nature Reserve is a freshwater
lake adjacent to the Danube and extending
over 6 km². The reserve was set up primarily
to protect the rich diversity of wildfowl,
which represent half of all Bulgarian bird
species. It is the breeding ground of almost
a hundred species of bird, many of which
are rare or endangered. Some eighty other
bird species migrate and seek refuge there
every winter. Sixty-seven plant species can
be found in Srebarna Nature Reserve,
including water lily and a number of rare
marsh plants. Reeds occupy two-thirds of
the reserve and form a thick barrier around
the lake. They form reed-mace islands which
birds use for nesting.

Abbey Church of Saint-Savin sur Gartempe
France
Criteria – Human creative genius; Testimony to
cultural tradition

EUROPE

Atlantic
Ocean

Saint-Savin sur
Gartempe is the
second-oldest church
still standing in
France. It boasts the
largest Romanesque
frescoes in Europe.

Known as the 'Romanesque Sistine Chapel',
the Abbey Church of Saint-Savin contains
many beautiful eleventh- and twelfth-
century murals which are still in a
remarkable state of preservation. During
the reign of Charlemagne the bodies of two
martyrs, Savin and Cyprian, who had been
persecuted in the fifth century, were
discovered under miraculous circumstances
by Baidilius, Abbot of Marmoutier, who
ordered a church built to shelter the holy
remains. By coincidence, Charlemagne
decided to have a castle erected next to the
sanctuary. Because the abbey was sheltered
by the castle it escaped pillage from the
Viking raids and survives to this day. The
beautifully proportioned building dates to
the end of the eleventh century, but includes
some older parts, such as the crypts of the
saints.

Place Stanislas, Place de la Carrière and Place d'Alliance in Nancy
France

Criteria – *Human creative genius; Significance in human history*

These three squares in Nancy represent the oldest and most typical example of a modern capital where an enlightened monarch proved to be sensitive to the needs of the public. Built between 1752 and 1756 by a brilliant team led by the architect Heré, this was a carefully conceived project that succeeded in creating a capital that not only enhanced the sovereign's prestige but was also functional. The foundation stone of the first building in the square was officially laid in March 1752 and the royal square solemnly inaugurated in November 1755. In addition to some prestigious architecture conceived to exalt a sovereign with triumphal arches, statues, and fountains, the project provided the public with three squares that gave access to the town hall, the courts of law, and the Palais des Fermes as well as to other public buildings.

▲
Fountain of Amphitrite in Place Stanislas.

The project was carried out under the patronage of Stanislas Leszczynski, unhappy pretender to the Polish throne and father-in-law of Louis XV, King of France. Stanislas received, as a recompense for his abdication, the Dukedom of Lorraine for life. He 'reigned' (peacefully) from Nancy from 1737 to 1766.

World Heritage site since

· 1978 · 1979 · 1980 · 1981 · 1982 · **1983**

Wood Buffalo National Park
Canada

Criteria – Natural phenomena or beauty;
Significant ecological and biological processes;
Significant natural habitat for biodiversity

The forty-seven mammal species in the park include **North American Bison (pictured below)**, black bear, woodland caribou, Arctic fox, moose, grey wolf, lynx, snowshoe hare, muskrat, beaver and mink, while 227 bird species have been recorded, including great grey owl and snowy owl, willow ptarmigan, redpoll, crossbill and boreal chickadee.

Situated in a vast wilderness area, Wood Buffalo was created specifically to protect North American bison, one of the largest free-roaming, self-regulating herds in existence. The park is also the natural nesting place of the whooping crane and contains the world's largest inland delta, located at the mouth of the Peace and Athabasca rivers. The park has four main landscape features: a glacially eroded plateau; glaciated plains; a major freshwater delta; and alluvial river lowlands (including a unique salt mudflat in dry weather). Vegetation is typical of the boreal forest zone with white spruce, black spruce, jack pine and tamarack predominant. The upper surface of the plateau is about 1,500 m above the rest of the park and supports a spruce-willow-birch upland tundra community. Some areas of prairie occur. The park contains the largest undisturbed grass and sedge meadows in North America.

World Heritage site since

· 1978 · 1979 · 1980 · 1981 · 1982 · **1983**

Sangay National Park
Ecuador

Criteria – Natural phenomena or beauty; Major stages of Earth's history; Significant ecological and biological processes; Significant natural habitat for biodiversity

The site is situated in the Cordillera Oriental region of the Andes in central Ecuador. With its outstanding natural beauty and two active volcanoes, Tungurahua (5,016 m) and Sangay (5,230 m), the park illustrates the entire spectrum of ecosystems, ranging from tropical rainforests to glaciers, with striking contrasts between the snowcapped peaks and the forests of the plains. A third volcano, El Altar (5,139 m), is considered extinct. Major rivers drain eastwards into the Amazon Basin and are characterized by dramatic variations in level. Numerous waterfalls occur, especially in the hanging valleys of the glaciated zone and along the eastern edge of the Cordillera. The area's isolation has encouraged the survival of indigenous species such as the mountain tapir and the Andean condor.

The park's varied vegetation zones offer homes to many rare and vulnerable fauna species. At the highest altitudes mountain tapir, puma, guinea pig and Andean fox occur. Elsewhere spectacled bear, jaguar, ocelot, margay, pudu and giant otter are found.

Vallée de Mai Nature Reserve
Seychelles

Criteria – Natural phenomena or beauty; Major stages of Earth's history; Significant ecological and biological processes; Significant natural habitat for biodiversity

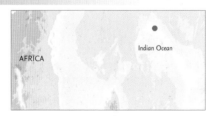

Vallée de Mai is a valley in the heart of Praslin National Park, an area which was untouched until the 1930s and still retains primeval palm forest in a near-natural state. This palm forest includes the endemic species coco de mer, the bearer of the largest nut in the world. The other five species of endemic palm are also found here, the only place in the Seychelles where they all occur together. Notable bird species include the endemic black parrot, which is totally dependent on the Vallée de Mai and the surrounding palm forest. In a densely populated island, the survival of the Vallée de Mai in itself is a remarkable achievement; too small to be self-sustaining, its present status is due to some replanting of coco de mer.

A rich body of legend has developed around the coco de mer, often with religious significance. In the nineteenth century the British General Gordon produced detailed 'proof' that the Vallée de Mai was the Garden of Eden and that coco de mer was the tree of knowledge.

World Heritage site since

• 1978 • 1979 • 1980 • 1981 • 1982 • **1983**

Historic Sanctuary of Machu Picchu
Peru

Criteria – Human creative genius; Testimony to cultural tradition; Natural phenomena or beauty; Significant ecological and biological processes

Machu Picchu stands 2,430 m above sea level in an extraordinarily beautiful setting in the middle of a tropical mountain forest. The city was probably the greatest urban achievement of the Inca Empire at its height: its giant walls, terraces and ramps seem as if they have been cut naturally in the continuous rock escarpments. The natural setting, on the eastern slopes of the Andes, encompasses the upper Amazon basin with its rich diversity of flora and fauna.

Set on the vertiginous site of a granite mountain sculpted by erosion and dominating a meander in the Rio Urubamba, Machu Picchu is a world-renowned archaeological site. Its construction, set out according to a very rigorous plan, comprises one of the most spectacular creations of the Incas, the largest civilization in the Americas before the arrival of Europeans. It appears to date from the period of the two great Inca rulers, Pachacutec Inca Yupanqui (1438–71) and Tupac Inca Yupanqui (1472–93). The function of this city, which is over 100 km from the Inca capital, Cuzco, is still unknown. Without making a judgement as to their purpose, several individual quarters may be noted in the ruins: a 'farmers' quarter near the colossal terraces whose slopes were cultivated and transformed into hanging gardens; an 'industrial' quarter; a 'royal' quarter and a 'religious' quarter.

The Historic Sanctuary of Machu Picchu covers 325 km² in some of the scenically most attractive mountainous territory of the Peruvian Andes. It was the last stronghold of the Incas, is of superb architectural and archaeological importance, and remains one of the most important cultural sites in Latin America. The site's stonework is a first-class example of the use of a natural raw material to create outstanding architecture totally appropriate to the surroundings.

The surrounding valleys have been cultivated continuously for well over 1,000 years, providing one of the world's greatest long-term examples of a productive man–land relationship. The people living around Machu Picchu continue a way of life closely resembling that of their Inca ancestors, being based on potatoes, maize and llamas. Machu Picchu also provides a secure habitat for several endangered species, notably the spectacled bear.

Machu Picchu bears, ▶ with Cuzco and the other archaeological sites of the valley of the Urubamba (Ollantautaybo, Runcuracay, Sayacmarca, Phuyupamarca, Huiñay Huayna, Intipucu and others), a unique testimony to the Inca civilization. Machu Picchu in particular is an outstanding example of man's interaction with his natural environment.

World Heritage site since

· 1978 • 1979 • 1980 • 1981 • 1982 • 1983

Gulf of Porto: Calanche of Piana, Gulf of Girolata, Scandola Reserve
France

Criteria – Natural phenomena or beauty; Major stages of Earth's history; Significant natural habitat for biodiversity

This reserve, on the central western coast of Corsica, includes a coastline of astonishing beauty studded with offshore islets and sea pillars rising out of translucent waters. On the shore there are hidden coves and long beaches of fine sand, sea grottoes and high cliffs of blood-red porphyry. Seagulls, cormorants and sea eagles can be found there. The clear waters, with their islets and inaccessible coves, host a rich marine life. The reserve is divided into two sectors: the

Elpa Nera inlet (between Pointe Bianca and Pointe Validori) and the Scandola peninsula. The vegetation is an outstanding example of typical Mediterranean maquis (shrubland). This is replaced by arborescent plants at an altitude of 200 m and oaks replace this in certain areas. This area conserves traditional agriculture and grazing activities, and contains complete systems of architecturally interesting fortifications.

Scandola Nature Reserve contains a rich sedentary and migrant fauna including the peregrine falcon, osprey and Eleonora falcon, with Cory's shearwater and Audouin's gull occurring in the littoral zone. The marine environment contains considerable numbers of spiny lobster and a wide range of littoral and sublittoral invertebrates and fish.

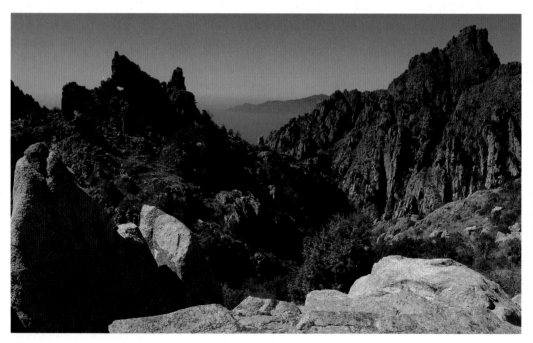

Convent of Christ in Tomar
Portugal

Criteria – Human creative genius; Heritage
associated with events of universal significance

The Convent of Christ, originally conceived
as a symbolic monument to the
Reconquista, the retaking of Portuguese
territory from Islamic rule, became the most
spectacular example of highly decorated
Manueline architecture. During the second
half of the twelfth century, the Knights
Templar came to Tomar to assist in the
Reconquista. Their original church, built at
the end of the twelfth century by the first
great Master of the Templars, Gualdim Pais,
was based on a polygonal ground plan of
sixteen bays with a central octagonal choir
and an ambulatory, typical of Templar
architecture. It was under Manuel I that the
choir was lavishly decorated and Diego de
Arruda created the enormous nave built
above the chapter room. The prodigious
exterior decoration combines with
stupefying ease Gothic and Moorish
influences.

When, in the fourteenth century, the Order of the
Knights Templar was abolished and replaced by the
Knights of the Order of Christ, Tomar lost none
of its importance. Successive embellishments
rendered it one of the most prestigious monuments
in Portugal.

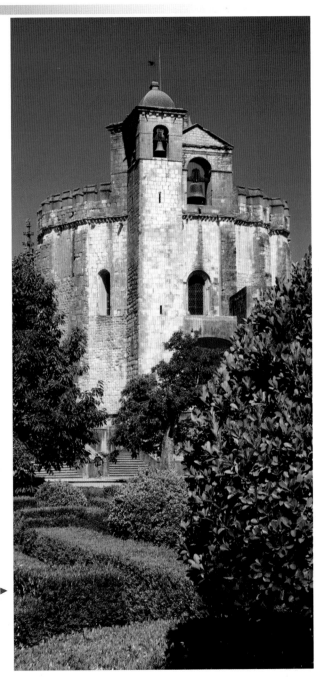

World Heritage site since

· 1978 · 1979 · 1980 · 1981 · 1982 · **1983**

Abbey of St Gall
Switzerland

Criteria – Interchange of values; Significance in
human history

The Abbey of St Gall is a perfect example
of a great Carolingian monastery and was,
from the eighth century to its secularization
in 1805, one of the most important in
Europe. Its library is one of the richest and
oldest in the world with more than 160,000
books and many precious manuscripts. It
has 400 volumes more than 1,000 years
old and the earliest-known architectural
plan drawn on parchment. An abbey has
existed on this site since 719 and successive
restructurings of its buildings attest to its
ongoing religious and cultural function.
From 1755–68, the conventual area was
rebuilt in Baroque style. The cathedral and
the library are the main features of this
remarkable architectural complex, reflecting
twelve centuries of continuous activity.

In 747, the abbot
Othmar established
a community of
Benedictine monks
in the place made
famous by St Gall.
By the ninth century,
the Abbey of St Gall
was one of the most
renowned centres of
Western culture and
science.

Pilgrimage Church of Wies
Germany

Criteria – Human creative genius; Testimony to
cultural tradition

The sanctuary of Wies, a pilgrimage church
in the beautiful setting of an Alpine valley, is
a masterpiece of Rococo art. The hamlet of
Wies, near Steingaden in Bavaria, was the
setting of a miracle in 1738: a simple wooden
image of Christ, mounted on a column,
appeared to some of the faithful to be in
tears. A wooden chapel was initially built
to house the miraculous statue. However,
pilgrims from Germany and abroad became
so numerous that the Abbot of Steingaden
decided to construct a splendid sanctuary.
Accordingly, work began in 1745 under
the direction of the celebrated architect,
Dominikus Zimmermann. The choir was
consecrated in 1749 and the remainder of
the church finished by 1754.

The prodigious stucco
decoration is the
work of Dominikus
Zimmermann,
assisted by his brother
Johann Baptist. The
lively colours of the
paintings bring out
the sculpted detail,
while the frescoes
and stuccowork
interpenetrate to
produce a décor
of unprecedented
richness. The ceilings,
painted as trompe-
l'œil, appear to open
on to an iridescent
sky, across which
angels fly.

World Heritage site since

· 1978 · 1979 · 1980 · 1981 · 1982 · **1983**

Monastery of Batalha
Portugal

Criteria – Human creative genius; Interchange of values

The Monastery of the Dominicans of Batalha was built to commemorate the victory of the Portuguese over the Castilians at the battle of Aljubarrota in 1385. It was to be the Portuguese monarchy's main building project for the next two centuries, out of which a highly original, national Gothic style evolved. The majority of the complex dates from the reign of João I, when the church (finished in 1416), the royal cloister, the chapterhouse, and the funeral chapel of the founder were constructed. The last great period of Batalha coincided with the reign of Manuel I, who built the monumental vestibule and the principal portal, and restored the royal cloister, creating a masterpiece of Manueline art. The arcades were embellished with finely carved tracery displaying the emblems of Manuel I, the Cross of the Order of Christ and the armillary sphere.

The church's interior maintains a sober Gothic majesty that has remained undisturbed by later additions. The nave and aisles are separated by thick pillars crowned by capitals with plant motifs. The chancel windows, decorated with beautiful sixteenth-century stained glass, project a diffused light that gives a feeling of great spirituality.

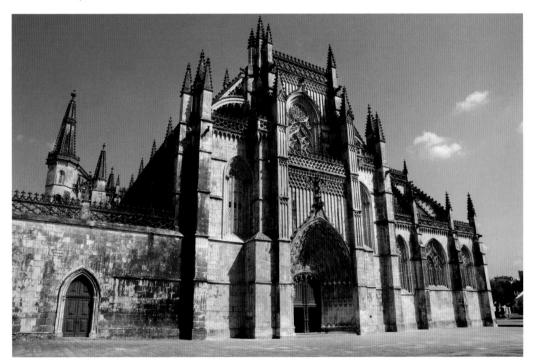

World Heritage site since

· 1978 · 1979 · 1980 · 1981 · 1982 · **1983**

Rila Monastery
Bulgaria

Criteria – Heritage associated with events of
universal significance

EUROPE

Black Sea

Rila Monastery was founded in the tenth
century by St John of Rila, a hermit whose
ascetic dwelling and tomb became a holy
site. It was transformed into a monastic
complex that played an important role in the
spiritual and social life of medieval Bulgaria.
Destroyed by fire at the beginning of the
nineteenth century, the monastery was
rebuilt between 1834 and 1862. Only the
Hrelyu Tower, built in 1355 by Stefan Hrelyu,

a local prince, survives from an earlier
period. The remaining nineteenth-century
structures occupy a vast irregular square,
with two entrances, both decorated with
frescoes. In the centre is the Cathedral of
Our Lady of the Assumption, built in 1833.
The buildings that surround it contain four
chapels, a refectory and some 300 cells for
the monks, a library and rooms for the
guests of the monastery.

During the Ottoman
Turkish domination of
Bulgaria, the monastery
became a bulwark of
national identity. It was
a destination for
pilgrimages from all
over the Balkan region,
especially after 1469,
when the relics of
St John of Rila were
brought here. Its
reconstruction in the
nineteenth century
symbolized an
awakening of a Slavic
cultural identity.

Rila Monastery fresco.
▼

World Heritage site since

· 1978 · 1979 · 1980 · 1981 · 1982 · **1983**

Pirin National Park
Bulgaria

Criteria – Natural phenomena or beauty; Major stages of Earth's history; Significant ecological and biological processes

EUROPE

Black Sea

The presence of limestone rocks, the southerly position of the range and close proximity to the Aegean, coupled with its relative isolation, have made Pirin National Park an important refuge for many species. In 2010, the site was extended to include an area of 400 km² in the Pirin Mountains.

Extending over an area of 274 km² in southwest Bulgaria, Pirin National Park has a limestone landscape, with lakes, waterfalls, caves and pine forests. The rugged mountains, with some seventy glacial lakes scattered throughout them, are home to hundreds of endemic and rare species, many of which are representative of the Balkan Pleistocene flora. There are many rivers and waterfalls. Generally, the timberline has developed as a result of

human interference over a long period and descends as low as 2,000 m, but in some places reaches 2,200–2,300 m. In the subalpine zone there are thickets of dwarf mountain pine and Juniperus sibirica. Above 2,400–2,600 m is a layer of alpine meadows, stony slopes, screes and rocks. There is a wide variety of animal species including many endemic species and glacial relicts among the invertebrate fauna.

Vatican City
Holy See

Criteria – Human creative genius; Interchange of values; Significance in human history; Heritage associated with events of universal significance

St Peter's was founded as a longitudinal basilica with five aisles, with a transept, apse, and large atrium with quadriporticus.

The basilica was reconstructed in the sixteenth century under the guidance of the most brilliant architects of the Renaissance. The remains of Constantine's original basilica still exist, with fragments of the circus of Caligula and Nero, and an entire first century AD Roman necropolis where Christian sepulchres are placed side-by-side with pagan tombs.

The Vatican City, one of the most sacred places in Christendom, attests to a great history and a formidable spiritual venture. A unique collection of artistic and architectural masterpieces lies within the boundaries of this small state. As the site of the tomb of St Peter and a pilgrimage centre, the Vatican is directly and materially linked with the history of Christianity. Furthermore, it is both an ideal and an exemplary creation of the Renaissance and of Baroque art. It exerted an underlying influence on the development of art from the sixteenth century.

The independent Vatican City State defined by the 1929 Lateran Treaty between the Holy See and Italy, has a territorial sovereignty of less than 0.5 km². However, this tiny enclave within Rome has, in the heritage of mankind, an importance which is inversely proportional to its area. The centre of Christianity since the time of Constantine in the fourth century and the seat of papal power, the Vatican is at once an important archaeological site of the Roman world, the pre-eminently holy city of Catholics and one of the major cultural reference points of both Christians and non-Christians.

Its prestigious past explains the development of an architectural and artistic ensemble of exceptional value. The churches and palaces rest on a substratum impregnated with history. At its centre is the Basilica of St Peter, with its double colonnade and a circular piazza in front and bordered by palaces and gardens. The basilica was first built in 315 over the tomb of St Peter the Apostle but its present-day appearance dates from the sixteenth century, when Pope Julius II inaugurated a massive artistic project for the refoundation of the entire basilica, along with the decoration of the Stanze Vaticane (the papal apartments) and the Sistine Chapel, and the construction of his own tomb. The result is the fruit of the combined genius of Bramante, Raphael, Michelangelo, Bernini and Maderna.

The Apostolic Palace or Vatican Palace is the result of a long series of construction campaigns in which successive popes, from the Middle Ages onwards rivalled each other in their munificence. It is the official residence of the Pope and houses the Vatican Museum, the Vatican Library and various chapels including the Sistine Chapel.

World Heritage site since

∙ 1978 ∙ 1979 ∙ 1980 ∙ 1981 ∙ 1982 ∙ 1983 ∙ **1984**

Works of Antoni Gaudí
Spain

Criteria – Human creative genius; Interchange of
values; Significance in human history

The works of the architect Antoni Gaudí
(1852–1926) represent outstanding examples
of early twentieth century residential and
public architecture. In particular, seven of his
properties in and around Barcelona testify to
his exceptional creative contribution to the
development of architecture and building
technology in the late nineteenth and early
twentieth centuries.

The seven buildings in the World Heritage
Site are Casa Vicens, Gaudí's work on the
Nativity façade and Crypt of La Sagrada
Familia, Casa Batlló, Casa Milà, Park Güell,
Palacio Güell and the crypt in Colonia Güell.

These monuments represent an eclectic
and very personal style which was given free
reign in the design of gardens, sculpture and
all decorative arts, as well as architecture.

Construction began on La Sagrada Familia in
1882 and continues to this day. It is expected to be
complete by 2026.

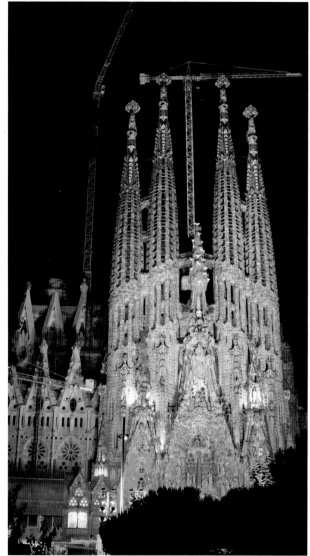

Gaudí's work exhibits an important
interchange of values closely
associated with the cultural and
artistic currents of his time, as
represented in El Modernisme
movement of Catalonia. It also
anticipated and influenced many of
the forms and techniques that were
relevant to the development of
modern construction in the
twentieth century.

World Heritage site since

• 1978 • 1979 • 1980 • 1981 • 1982 • 1983 • **1984**

Sun Temple, Konârak
India

Criteria – Human creative genius; Testimony to cultural tradition; Heritage associated with events of universal significance

On the shores of the Bay of Bengal, bathed in the rays of the rising sun, the temple at Konârak was one of the earliest centres of sun worship in India. Built around 1250, the entire temple was conceived as a representation of the Sun God Surya's chariot, with a set of spokes and elaborate carvings. Its twenty-four wheels are decorated with symbolic designs referring to the cycle of the seasons and the months, and it is led by a team of seven horses, six of which still exist. The temple is carefully oriented so as to permit the first rays of the Sun to strike its principal entry. It is one of the most famous Brahmin sanctuaries of Asia.

Legend has it that the temple was constructed by Samba, the son of Lord Krishna. Samba was afflicted by leprosy and after twelve years of penance he was cured by Surya, the Sun God, in whose honour he built this temple.

One of the twenty-four ornately carved stone wheels on the Sun Temple at Konârak.

▼

Yosemite National Park
USA

Criteria – Natural phenomena or beauty; Major stages of Earth's history

El Capitan is a 910 m ▶ rock formation predominantly carved out during the Sherwin Glaciation around one million years ago.

Yosemite National Park lies in the heart of California in an area of outstanding wilderness and great scenic beauty. With its hanging valleys, many waterfalls, cirque lakes, polished domes, moraines and U-shaped valleys, it provides an excellent overview of all kinds of granite relief fashioned by glaciation.

At 600–4,000 m, a great variety of flora and fauna can also be found here. The National Park, on the west slope of the central Sierra Nevada Mountains, represents practically all the different environments found within the Sierra Nevada, including sequoia groves, historic resources, evidence of Indian habitation, and domes, valleys, polished granites and other geological features that illustrate the formation of the mountain range.

Yosemite's natural beauty was the impetus for the implementation of the concept of the national park. Its archaeological features add to the area's cultural importance.

The variety of flora in the park is reflected in the existence of six distinct vegetation zones which are governed by altitude. There are 1,200 species of flowering plant along with various other ferns, bryophytes and lichens.

Port, Fortresses and Group of Monuments, Cartagena
Colombia

Criteria – Significance in human history; Heritage associated with events of universal significance

Cartagena, together with La Habana and San Juan de Puerto Rico, was one of the three most important ports in the West Indies. It is an outstanding example of the military architecture of the sixteenth–eighteenth centuries, the most extensive in the New World and one of the most complete. The fortifications, finally completed in the seventeenth century, made Cartagena an impregnable stronghold, which successfully resisted attack until 1697. Within the shelter of the formidable defences, the city continued to grow. The plan, characteristic of colonial foundations of the sixteenth century, illustrates a rigorous zoning system, divided into three quarters corresponding to the major social categories: San Pedro, with the cathedral and many Andalusian-style palaces; San Diego, where merchants and the middle class lived; and Gethsemani, the 'popular quarter'.

The quarter of San Pedro, where the nobles and the notables resided, still preserves monuments of high quality such as the cathedral, the Church and Convent of San Pedro Claver, the Church of Santo Domingo, and the building that once was the Monastery of San Diego.

World Heritage site since

· 1978 · 1979 · 1980 · 1981 · 1982 · 1983 · **1984**

Salonga National Park
Dem. Rep. of the Congo

Criteria – Natural phenomena or beauty;
Significant ecological and biological processes

Salonga is the largest tropical forest national park in the world. Situated at the heart of the central basin of the Congo river, the park is very isolated and accessible mainly by water. Equatorial forest covers most of the area, varying in composition according to the geomorphology. There are three types of landscape: low plateaus, river terraces and high plateaus. The total area of grassland is under 0.5 per cent of the park

area. The park is the habitat of many endangered species, the most important of which is the endemic dwarf chimpanzee, or bonobo. Other species include colobus monkeys, hippopotamus and leopard.

Rivers in the west of the north sector are large and meandering with marshy banks. In the higher east, valleys are deeper with cliffs up to 80 m high. The south sector includes the watershed between the basin of the Luilaka to the north and east, Likoro to the west, and Lukenje to the south.

Mana Pools National Park, Sapi and Chewore Safari Areas
Zimbabwe

Criteria – Natural phenomena or beauty;
Significant ecological and biological processes;
Significant natural habitat for biodiversity

On the banks of the Zambezi, great cliffs overhang the river and the floodplains. The Mana Pools are former channels of the Zambezi. With the Sapi and Chewore areas, they total some 6,766 km². The area contains the last remaining natural stretch of the Middle Zambezi and there is virtually no permanent human habitation. The area is home to a remarkable concentration of wild animals, including elephants, buffalo,

leopards and cheetahs. An important concentration of Nile crocodiles is also found there. Much of the Chewore is heavily dissected and the Mupata Gorge (some 30 km long) occurs along the northern border of this area. Above the Mupata Gorges the river is broad and sandy, flowing through numerous channels, sandbanks and islands.

Well-grassed miombo woodland dominates the mountainous escarpment and higher Chewore areas with small but significant riparian communities along the numerous streams. The valley floor is dominated by mopane woodlands or dry, highly deciduous thickets known as Jesse.

World Heritage site since

· 1978 · 1979 · 1980 · 1981 · 1982 · 1983 · **1984**

Statue of Liberty
USA

Criteria – Human creative genius; Heritage
associated with events of universal significance

The Statue of Liberty is a masterpiece of the
human creative spirit. Its construction in the
studios of Bartholdi in Paris represents one
of the greatest technical exploits of the
nineteenth century.

It welcomed immigrants at the entrance
to New York harbour, and so is directly
associated with an event of outstanding
historical significance: the populating of the
USA, the melting pot of disparate peoples in
the later nineteenth century. That the statue
was paid for by international subscription
and built in Europe by a French sculptor
only strengthens its symbolic significance.

Liberty was dedicated on 28 October 1886
and features a woman holding a book and a
torch. It stands on Liberty Island and was
designated a National Monument in 1924.
Ellis Island, the immigrants' former landing
place, became part of the Statue of Liberty
National Monument in 1965.

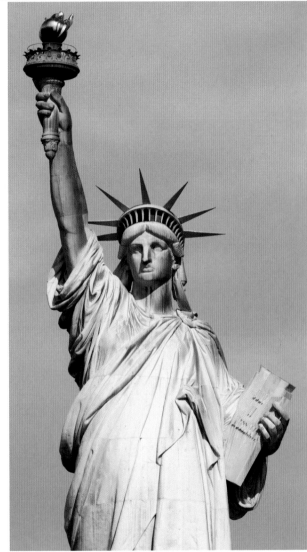

▲

This towering monument (46 m tall)
to liberty was a gift from France in
1886 to celebrate the centenary of
American independence – ten years
late. 'Liberty Enlightening the World',
symbolizing the ideals of Washington
and Lincoln, was extensively restored
for its centenary and the annual
celebration of American independence
on 4 July 1986.

World Heritage site since

• 1978 • 1979 • 1980 • 1981 • 1982 • 1983 • 1984

Iguazu National Park
Argentina

Criteria – Natural phenomena or beauty;
Significant natural habitat for biodiversity

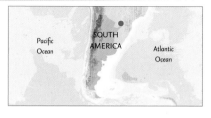

Iguazu Falls. ▶

The first inhabitants
in the area were the
Caingangues Indians.
This tribe was
dislodged by the
Tupi-Guaranies who
coined the name
Iguazu (Big Water).
The first European to
reach the Iguazu falls
was the Spanish
explorer Don Alvar
Nuñes Cabeza de
Vaca in 1541; some ten
years later Spanish
and Portuguese
colonization began.
There are at least two
sites of particular
archaeological
interest within the
national park.

One of the world's most spectacular
waterfalls, the Iguazu Falls, lies at the heart
of this vast, rich and diverse national park.
The waterfall is semicircular, some 80 m
high and 2,700 m in diameter and stands on
a basaltic line that spans the border between
Argentina and Brazil.

The site consists of the national park and
national reserves in Misiones Province,
northeastern Argentina. The Iguazu River
forms the northern boundary of both the
reserves and park, and also the southern
boundary of Iguaçu National Park World
Heritage site in Brazil.

The Iguazu Falls lie on the Argentina-
Brazil border and are made up of many
cascades that generate vast sprays of water
and produce one of the most magnificent
waterfalls in the world. The vegetation is
mostly subtropical wet forest rich in lianas
and epithytes, although the forests have less
species diversity when compared with
others in Brazil and parts of Paraguay.
Nonetheless, over 2,000 species of vascular
plant have been identified.

Vegetation around the falls is particularly
luxuriant due to the constant spray. The site
is particularly rich in bird life, with almost
half of Argentina's bird species found there.
The fauna are typical of the region and
include tapir, coatimundi, and tamandua.

Threatened mammals such as the jaguar,
ocelot and tiger-cat number among the
carnivores, and the giant anteater and
Brazilian otter are also found. Primates
include the black-capped capuchin and
black howler monkey. There are also small
populations of the endangered broad-nosed
cayman and the threatened Brazilian
merganser (sawbill duck).

World Heritage site since

• 1978 • 1979 • 1980 • 1981 • 1982 • 1983 • **1984**

Lake Malawi National Park
Malawi

Criteria – Natural phenomena or beauty;
Significant ecological and biological processes;
Significant natural habitat for biodiversity

Located at the southern end of the great expanse of Lake Malawi, with its deep, clear waters and mountain backdrop, the national park is home to many hundreds of fish species, nearly all endemic. Lake Malawi itself is the third deepest in the world and contains the largest number of fish species of any lake in the world. The park is rich in birdlife, including fish eagle, along the shoreline. Mammals include hippo, baboon, warthog and occasional elephant. The islands, especially Mumbo and Boadzulu, are important nesting areas for white-throated cormorant which number several thousand. Reptiles include crocodiles and abundant monitor lizards. The area's importance for the study of evolution is comparable to that of the Galápagos Islands.

Archaeological evidence points to a long period of human occupation with sites dating back to the Iron Age in the fourth century. The Cape Maclear area was one focal point in the ivory and slave trade era. More recently a Livingstone Mission was established there and the area was a stopover on the Cape to London flying boat service.

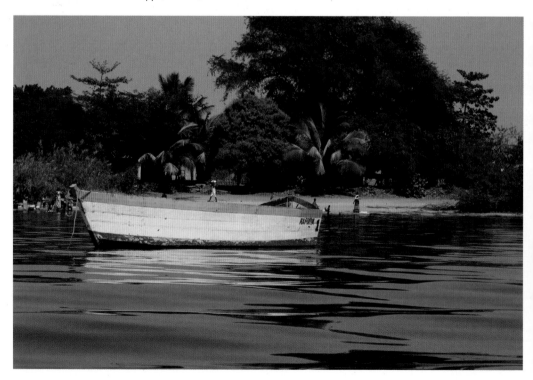

World Heritage site since

• 1978 • 1979 • 1980 • 1981 • 1982 • 1983 • 1984

Baalbek
Lebanon

Criteria – Human creative genius; Significance in human history

ASIA

Mediterranean Sea

AFRICA

Construction of the Great Court at Baalbek began during the reign of Trajan (98–117). It contained various religious buildings and altars and was surrounded by a splendid colonnade of 128 rose granite columns.

Baalbek, with its colossal structures, is a pre-eminent example of a sanctuary of the imperial Roman period. This Phoenician city, where a triad of deities was worshipped, was known as Heliopolis during the Hellenistic period. The arrival of the Romans in Phoenicia in 64 BC heralded the beginning of more than two centuries of monumental construction in which the Romanized triad of Heliopolis (Jupiter, Venus and Mercury) came to replace the

Phoenician triad (Baal-Shamash, Anta and Alyn). The first building work, that of the Temple of Jupiter, was begun during the reign of Emperor Augustus in the late first century BC and completed soon after AD 60 under Nero. The immense sanctuary of Jupiter Heliopolitanus, which attracted thousands of pilgrims, was lined by 104 massive granite columns imported from Aswan and held a temple surrounded by fifty additional columns.

The Temple of Jupiter, pictured below. Today, only six columns remain standing, the rest having been destroyed by earthquakes or taken to other sites.

▼

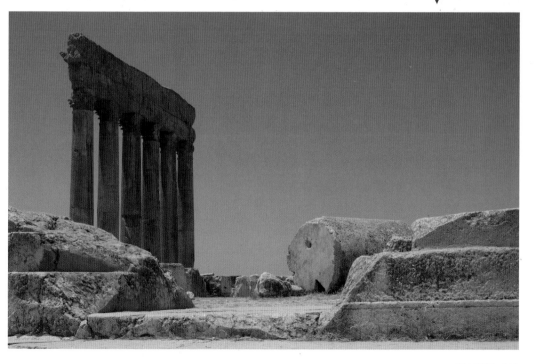

World Heritage site since

· 1978 · 1979 · 1980 · 1981 · 1982 · 1983 · 1984

Byblos
Lebanon

Criteria – Testimony to cultural tradition;
Significance in human history; Heritage
associated with events of universal significance

The ruins of many successive civilizations
are found at Byblos, one of the oldest
Phoenician cities. Inhabited since Neolithic
times, it developed into a highly structured
city, enclosed by a massive fortified wall.
This city, of which numerous traces still
exist, was burned around 2150 BC by the
invading Amorites: a thick layer of ash (in
some places 50 cm) seals off the original
levels. Approximately two centuries later,
the city was rebuilt with new temples.

Castle of the Crusaders, Byblos.
▼

A commercial city, Byblos was able to
accommodate successive dominations,
whether Assyrian, Babylonian, Achaemenid
or Greek. During the Roman period, its
commercial role declined, but the city
assumed an eminent religious function:
hordes of pilgrims crowded its temples,
which were constantly reconstructed and
embellished. Its decline began during the
Byzantine period and continued during the
Arab occupation after AD 636.

Towards the middle
of the Bronze Age, the
treasure of the nine
Royal Tombs of
Byblos attested to
the sophistication of
Phoenician culture:
an inscription in
Phoenician characters
is addressed to
eventual grave robbers,
and one may see in
this curse the proof
that writing, widely
disseminated, was no
longer the monopoly
of the scribes.

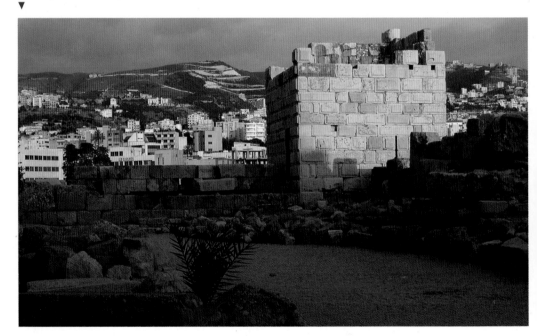

World Heritage site since

• 1978 • 1979 • 1980 • 1981 • 1982 • 1983 • 1984

Castles of Augustusburg and Falkenlust at Brühl
Germany
Criteria – Interchange of values; Significance in human history

The castle of Augustusburg and the hunting lodge of Falkenlust represent the first masterpieces of the Rococo style in Germany. For more than a century, they served as models for most of the princely courts and are outstanding examples of the large princely residences of the eighteenth century. The castle was the sumptuous residence of the prince-archbishops of Cologne and is a bold and successful revamping of a previous lacklustre construction. The beautiful decoration of the new grand summer apartments, with its delicate faïence tiles, is particularly striking. Falkenlust, a small rural folly, is a dazzling creation which, with the castle, is set in an idyllic garden landscape, with monumental ramps, walkways and beautifully designed flower beds on an impressive scale.

Augustusburg Castle is home to a true piece of creative genius, the staircase of Balthasar Neumann. This rapturous structure unites a lively movement of marble, stucco, jasper columns and caryatids, and culminates in an astonishing frescoed ceiling.

Monastery and Site of the Escurial, Madrid
Spain
Criteria – Human creative genius; Interchange of values; Heritage associated with events of universal significance

This royal monastery dedicated to St Lawrence is a unique artistic achievement. There is nothing in the project, in the form or in the design of this monument, which is not exceptional. Built on a remote and impressive site in Castile in the sixteenth century, it is said to resemble an inverted grid-iron, the instrument of the martyrdom of St Lawrence. The handle is represented by the Royal Palace, while four angle towers, 55 m high, represent the feet. Its outwardly austere architecture, a break with previous styles, had a considerable influence on Spanish architecture for more than half a century. In the last years of Philip II's reign it became the centre of the greatest political power of the time.

The spectaular retablo in the church of San Lorenzo is 30 m high and unites coloured marbles, paintings, gilding and large bronze statues.

World Heritage site since

· 1978 · 1979 · 1980 · 1981 · 1982 · 1983 · 1984

Canadian Rocky Mountain Parks
Canada

Criteria – Natural phenomena or beauty; Major stages of Earth's history

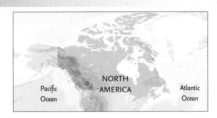

Athabasca Glacier.

Studded with mountain peaks, glaciers, lakes, waterfalls, canyons and limestone caves, the Canadian Rocky Mountain Parks form a spectacular mountain landscape. The Burgess Shale fossil site, well known for its fossil remains of soft-bodied marine animals, is also found there.

The Canadian Rocky Mountain Parks comprise seven parks in total: the contiguous national parks of Banff, Jasper, Kootenay and Yoho, and the Mount Robson, Mount Assiniboine and Hamber provincial parks.

The Canadian Rocky Mountains are oriented in a southeastern to northwestern direction along the continental divide which separates the orientation of rivers that flow to the east and to the west. It consists of the Western Ranges, the Main Ranges, the Front Ranges and the Foothills, all of which are represented within the parks. Active glaciers and ice fields still exist throughout the region, particularly in the Main Ranges. The most significant is the Columbia Ice Field, the largest in North America's subarctic interior.

The Rockies have been divided into three life zones or ecoregions: montane, subalpine and alpine. Montane vegetation occurs in major valley bottoms and on the foothills and lower sun-exposed mountain slopes, especially in the Front Ranges. Montane wetlands and meadows occupy areas by major rivers. Forest is generally found between 1,200 m and 1,800 m and typical species include Douglas fir, white spruce, aspen and poplar. The subalpine ecoregion occupies mountainsides between 1,800 m and 2,100 m, and valley bottoms of high elevations and is the most extensive ecoregion in the Rockies. The alpine ecoregion occurs above the timberline and is characterized by diminutive and hardy vegetation such as low-growing willow and dwarf birch, heath and sedge.

Fifty-six mammal species have been recorded. Characteristic species of alpine meadows include Rocky Mountain goat, bighorn sheep, northern pika and hoary marmot. Forest mammals include moose, mule deer, white-tailed deer, caribou, elk and red squirrel, while carnivores include grey wolf, grizzly bear, black bear, wolverine, lynx and cougar. Some 280 bird species have been noted, including northern three-toed woodpecker, white-tailed ptarmigan, grey jay, mountain bluebird, Clark's nutcracker, golden eagle, mountain chickadee and rock pipit. Other recorded fauna includes toad, frog, salamander and snake.

Covering 325 km², the massive Columbia Ice Field spans the east-west continental divide and straddles the boundary between Jasper and Banff National Parks. The Columbia Ice Fields of Jasper National Park are regarded as the hydrographic apex of North America and are the headwaters to three major river systems: the North Saskatchewan, the Athabasca and the Columbia.

Emerald Lake, Yoho National Park.

World Heritage site since

· 1978 · 1979 · 1980 · 1981 · 1982 · 1983 · **1984**

Chitwan National Park
Nepal

Criteria – Natural phenomena or beauty;
Significant ecological and biological processes;
Significant natural habitat for biodiversity

ASIA

Arabian
Sea

Bay of
Bengal

Chitwan National
Park is situated in
a river valley basin
along the flood plains
of the Rapti, Reu and
Narayani rivers. The
Narayani, also called
the Gandaki, is the
third-largest river in
Nepal. It originates
in the high Himalaya
and drains into the
Bay of Bengal.

At the foot of the Himalaya on the border between Nepal and India, Chitwan is one of the few remaining undisturbed vestiges of the 'Terai' region, which formerly extended over the foothills of India and Nepal. The park covers 932 km² of subtropical lowland. It has a particularly rich flora and fauna. One of the last populations (estimated at 400) of single-horned Asiatic rhinoceros lives in the park, which is also one of the last refuges of the Bengal tiger. Prior to its re-introduction to Royal Bardia National Park in 1986, the park also contained the last Nepalese population of the Indian rhinoceros. Other endangered mammals include leopard, wild dog and sloth bear. Over 350 bird species are reported and some 99 fish species inhabit the rivers and oxbow lakes. The threatened Indian python is also found within the park.

World Heritage site since

· 1978 · 1979 · 1980 · 1981 · 1982 · 1983 · **1984**

Tyre
Lebanon

Criteria – Testimony to cultural tradition;
Heritage associated with events of universal
significance

The great Phoenician city of Tyre ruled the
seas and founded prosperous colonies such
as Cadiz and Carthage. From the fifth
century BC, when Herodotus of
Halicarnassus visited it, Tyre was considered
one of the oldest metropolises in the world.
The city, which was constructed on an
impregnable island, succumbed in 332 BC to
the attack of Alexander of Macedonia, who
had blockaded the straits with a dyke before
his final assault. The original Greek city was
followed in 64 BC by a Roman city
constructed on this historically charged site.
Following the Crusades, the historic role of
the city declined. Almost totally destroyed
by the Mamelukes at the end of the
thirteenth century, it was only modestly
reconstructed in the eighteenth century.

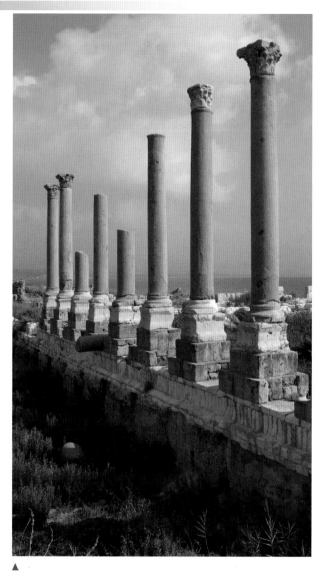

▲
The remains of ancient columns at Al Mina excavation site.

In the present souk (market),
archaeological remains include the
Roman city and the medieval
constructions of the Crusades. The
imposing ruins of the palaestra, the
thermae, and the arena still exist, as
do the remains of the cathedral built
in 1127 by the Venetians, along with
some of the walls of the castle
constructed during the Crusades.

Historic Centre of Córdoba
Spain

Criteria – Human creative genius; Interchange of values; Testimony to cultural tradition; Significance in human history

EUROPE

Atlantic Ocean

Mediterranean Sea

AFRICA

Mezquita, mosque-cathedral. ▶

Córdoba's historic centre, clustering round the mosque-cathedral, the Mezquita, preserves much of its medieval urban fabric with narrow, winding streets. The city's Roman past can be seen in the sixteen-span bridge that crosses the river Guadalquivir, the fine mosaics in the Alcázar and sections of the Roman wall. The gardens of the Alcázar are good examples of Moorish Andalusian garden design. The remains of the monumental Caliphal Baths are nearby. La Judería, the old Jewish quarter, best preserves the medieval street pattern.

Córdoba has one of the finest historical heritages of any city in the world. It was the capital of the extensive Moorish Caliphate of Córdoba, and one of the largest cities in the world by the tenth century, with innumerable palaces, public buildings and mosques that rivalled the splendours of Constantinople, Damascus and Baghdad. After the city's recapture by the Christian Spanish, a series of new defensive structures was built. Córdoba's extent and plan, its historical significance as a living expression of the different cultures that existed there, and its relationship with its river, the Guadalquivir, is a historical ensemble of extraordinary value.

Córdoba was a flourishing Carthaginian township when the Romans captured it in 206 BC. Recognising its strategic and commercial importance, they made it the capital of Hispania Inferior, fortified it and adorned it with fine buildings.

The city fell to successive invasions: first to the Visigoths in AD 550, then to the Moors from North Africa in 716. In 756 the Caliph of Damascus set up court at Córdoba and laid the foundations for an illustrious period of the city's history. He began building the Great Mosque on the site of a church that was itself originally a Roman temple. Córdoba became the centre of a caliphate

renowned for its artistic and intellectual predominance, but the kingdom collapsed after an eleventh-century civil war.

In 1236 Ferdinand III of Castile and Leon, captured the city. The mosque became the cathedral and new defensive structures were raised as befitted the status of a frontier town under constant threat from the Moors.

The Alcázar de los Reyes Cristianos dates from the early fourteenth century and was built as a royal residence. The Torre de la Calahorra formed part of a medieval fortress. Churches include San Jacinto (now the Palace of Congresses and Exhibitions); the Chapel of San Bartolomeo, Moorish in origin and now clearly Christian; and San Francisco and San Nicolás. There are important buildings from the sixteenth century: the Seminary of San Pelagio, Puerta del Puente, Casa Solariega de los Pàez de Castillo and Casa del Marqués de la Fuensanta del Valle, which illustrate the religious, military and architectural styles. From the eighteenth century come the civic buildings the Triunfos de San Rafael and Hospital del Cardenal Salazar.

Burgos Cathedral
Spain

Criteria – Interchange of values; Significance in
human history; Heritage associated with events
of universal significance

Begun in 1221 at the same time as the great
cathedrals of the Île-de-France and
completed in 1567, Santa María de Burgos
is a striking summary of the evolution of
Gothic architecture. The plan of the
cathedral is based on a Latin cross of
pleasing proportions. Initial work on the
cathedral was completed in 1293. After a
hiatus of nearly 200 years, work was
resumed in the mid-fifteenth century and
continued for more than 100 years. These
were embellishments of a profuse splendour
– including paintings, choir stalls, reredos,
tombs, cupolas (pictured far right), and
stained-glass windows – which have ensured
the status of this magnificent building. The
two-storeyed cloister that was completed
towards 1280 still fits within the framework
of 'French' High Gothic.

The three-storey
elevation, the vaulting,
and the tracery of
the windows are
closely related to
contemporary models
of the north of France.
The portals of the
transept (the Puerta del
Sarmental to the south
and the Puerta de la
Coronería to the north)
may also be compared
with the great sculpted
ensembles of the
French royal domain.

Alhambra, Generalife and Albayzín, Granada
Spain

Criteria – Human creative genius; Testimony to cultural tradition; Significance in human history

A view across the basin in the Patio de los Arrayanes (Myrtle Courtyard) looking towards the Hall of the Ambassadors, Alhambra Palace.

Unique artistic creations set on a hill above Granada, the Alhambra palace and fortress and the Generalife residence and gardens bear exceptional testimony to Muslim Spain and are exceptional examples of royal Arab residences of the medieval period. Standing on an adjacent hill is the residential district of the Albayzín, a rich repository of Moorish vernacular architecture into which traditional Andalusian architecture blends harmoniously. It survives as a remarkable example of a Spanish-Moorish town. During the early period of Moorish rule in Spain, power initially rested with the Caliphate of Córdoba until civil war ended its dominance in 1031. From then on, the Emirate of Granada grew steadily in importance and prosperity but the town did not become an important centre of Muslim Spain until 1238, when Muhammad ibn al Ahmar founded the present Alhambra.

The palace was completed in the fourteenth century. Organized around two rectangular courts, the Patio de los Arrayanes and the Patio de los Leones, it has many, highly-decorated rooms with marble columns, stalactite cupolas, stucco work, azulejos (ceramic tiles), precious wood, and paintings on leather, all competing with the delicacy of the natural decor: water, still and flowing in immense basins, narrow canals and fountains, including the spectacular fountain of the Patio de los Leones (Court of Lions).

The Alhambra (in Arabic 'the Red') incorporates palaces, guard rooms, patios and gardens as well as workshops, shops, baths and mosque (independently of the church of Santa María built in the sixteenth century on the site of the royal mosque). It is enclosed by a massive fortified wall with towers.

At a short distance to the east of the Alhambra, the enchantment is extended to the gardens of the Generalife, rural residence of the emirs who ruled this part of Spain in the thirteenth and fourteenth centuries. Here the relationship between the architectural and the natural has been reversed: gardens and water predominate over the pavilions, summerhouses and living quarters. The massive boxwood trees, rose, carnation and gillyflower bushes, and shrubs ranging from willow to cypress, comprise an absolute masterpiece of the art of horticulture by restoring the Koranic image of paradise to the believers.

Much of the Albayzín's significance lies in its medieval town plan, with narrow streets and small squares and the relatively modest Moorish and Andalusian houses that line them.

After the Reconquista, the Christian reconquest of Spain in 1492, the influx of a substantial Christian population into Granada brought new developments. Late Gothic or early Plateresque churches and monasteries harmonized with the existing architecture. However, the Albayzín still bears witness to its medieval Moorish origins as its urban fabric, architecture and main characteristics adapted successfully to new ways of living.

World Heritage site since

· 1978 · 1979 · 1980 · 1981 · 1982 · 1983 · 1984

Group of Monuments at Mahabalipuram
India

Criteria – Human creative genius; Interchange of values; Testimony to cultural tradition; Heritage associated with events of universal significance

These exceptional sanctuaries on the Coromandel coast, founded by the Pallava kings, were carved out of rock in the seventh and eighth centuries. The monuments may be subdivided into five categories: ratha temples in the form of processional chariots, cut into the rocks which emerge from the sand; mandapa, or rock sanctuaries, modelled as rooms covered with bas-reliefs; rock reliefs in the open air that illustrate a popular episode in the

iconography of Siva; temples built from cut stone, like the Temple of Rivage, with its high-stepped pyramidal tower and thousands of sculptures dedicated to the glory of Siva; and monolithic rathas, of one to three storeys, in a variety of architectural forms. In addition the Shore Temple represents the peak of Pallava architecture, although it has been eroded by seawater and air and the sculptures have become indistinct.

The rock reliefs tell the story of the Descent of the Ganges. Begged by King Baghirata, Siva ordered the river Ganges to descend to Earth and to nourish the world. The sculptors used the natural fissure in the rock to suggest this cosmic event to which a swarming crowd of gods, goddesses, mythical beings, wild animals and domestic animals bear witness.

▼

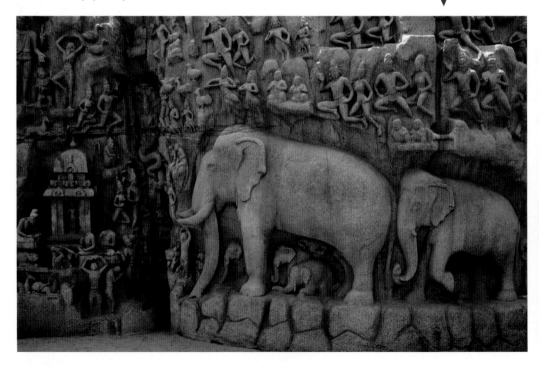

World Heritage site since

· 1978 · 1979 · 1980 · 1981 · 1982 · 1983 · 1984

Anjar
Lebanon

Criteria – Testimony to cultural tradition;
Significance in human history

ASIA

Mediterranean Sea

AFRICA

Public and private
buildings are laid out
according to a strict
plan: the principal
palace and mosque
in the southeast
quadrant; the
secondary palace and
baths in the northeast
and northwest
quadrants; and the
densely inhabited
southwest quadrant,
criss-crossed by a
network of streets.

The ruins of Anjar reveal a very regular
layout, reminiscent of the palace-cities of
ancient times, and are a unique testimony
to city planning under the Umayyads.
It was discovered when archaeological
explorations began in 1949 in the Beqaa.
On a site that had long been occupied, the
city of Anjar was founded at the beginning
of the eighth century by Caliph Walid I
(705–715). Re-used parts of earlier Greek,
Roman and early Christian buildings are
frequently found in the masonry of its walls.
It flourished for only 20–30 years before the
Abbasids overran the city and it fell into
disuse. At its peak, it housed more than 600
shops, Roman-style baths, two palaces and
a mosque. It takes its name from the Arabic
term ayn al-jaar (water from the rock),
referring to the streams that flow from the
nearby mountains.

World Heritage site since

• 1978 • 1979 • 1980 • 1981 • 1982 • 1983 • 1984 • **1985**

Historic District of Old Québec
Canada

Criteria – Significance in human history; Heritage associated with events of universal significance

Château Frontenac ▶
grand hotel overlooks
Québec's Lower City.

The city is an early example of urban heritage conservation as a result of action in the 1870s by the Governor General Lord Dufferin, who took a stand against the demolition of the fortifications which, from a strategic standpoint, had become useless. He simply had new gates to the city cut into them. From the beginning of the twentieth century, long before its listing as a historic monument in 1957, the fortified walls of Québec were maintained by Canadian government funds.

Québec is one of the finest examples of a fortified colonial city. It is the only North American city to have preserved its ramparts, together with the numerous bastions, gates and defensive works that surround the historic district.

The Upper City, built on a cliff and defended by walls with bastions, has remained the religious and administrative centre, with its churches, convents and other monuments like the Dauphine Redoubt, the Citadel and Château Frontenac (which can be seen at the top of the photo on the right). Together with the Lower City and its harbour and old quarters, it forms a coherent urban ensemble which is by far the most complete fortified colonial town in North America.

Québec illustrates one of the major stages in the population and growth of the Americas during the modern and contemporary period. When Samuel de Champlain founded Québec, the capital of New France in 1608, he chose the natural site of a steep plateau overlooking the St Laurent River. The old heart of the city was established on this promontory, Cap-aux-Diamants, which is protected by Fort St Louis.

Québec had an urban organization early on and a zoning system which stemmed from its various functions as a town, a fortified city and a harbour for trade from the North and Europe. Its cliff divided the city into two districts: business and naval district in the Lower City, and the administrative and religious centre in the Upper City.

The construction of a citadel at the far southeast end of Cap-aux-Diamants by the engineer Elias Durnford from 1819–31 and the expansion of the system of fortifications to cover the city's entire perimeter were in keeping with the original spatial organization of the city and gave Québec its current topographical features.

The oldest quarters are located in the Lower City around the Place Royale which, along with the Rue Notre Dame, is lined with old seventeenth- and eighteenth-century houses. In the Upper City the seventeenth-century convents and seminary still have some original elements. Of 700 old civil or religious buildings remaining, 2 per cent date to the seventeenth century, 9 per cent to the eighteenth and 43 per cent to the first half of the nineteenth century. The city took on its present aspect under the influence of the Baillairgés, a dynasty of architects who, for generations, imposed an interpretation of neoclassical style.

Historic Centre of Salvador de Bahia
Brazil

Criteria – Significance in human history; Heritage associated with events of universal significance

Salvador de Bahia, with Ouro Preto, is the colonial city par excellence in the Brazilian northeast. An eminent example of Renaissance town planning, the city has many outstanding monuments and Renaissance buildings. It was the first slave market in the New World and became a major point of convergence of European, African and American Indian cultures from the sixteenth to the eighteenth century.

Founded by the Portuguese, the city was the first colonial capital of Brazil from 1549 until the administration was transferred to Rio de Janeiro in 1763.

Commercial activity revolved around the port while the upper city, in the area of Bahia de Todos los Santos, was hilly and picturesque, with residential and administrative buildings. Its situation on a ridge parallel to the Atlantic coast also made it defensible against attack in the sixteenth and seventeenth centuries.

In addition to a number of major buildings of the seventeenth and eighteenth centuries, the historic centre of Salvador retains a host of sixteenth-century open spaces and Baroque palaces. There are streets characteristic of the colonial city, lined with bright, multicoloured houses, often decorated with high-quality stucco.

▼

World Heritage site since

· 1978 · 1979 · 1980 · 1981 · 1982 · 1983 · 1984 · **1985**

Old Town of Segovia and its Aqueduct
Spain

Criteria – Human creative genius; Testimony to cultural tradition; Significance in human history

The Roman Aqueduct of Segovia (pictured below), the symbol of the city, is a magnificent, double-tiered construction. Probably built around AD 50, it is the best known of Spain's remaining Roman aqueducts owing to its monumentality, its excellent state of conservation and its location in one of the most beautiful historic cities in the world.

The Roman hydraulic engineers brought the waters of the Río Frío in the Sierra de Guadarrama 18 km to Segovia via a canal with an average gradient of 1 per cent. The biggest natural obstacle they encountered was the valley of the Río Clamores at the end of the route. In order to reach the city they built an enormous stone aqueduct 813 m long, with four straight segments and two superimposed arcades borne by 128 pillars.

At the valley's lowest point, the aqueduct stands 28.5 m above the ground.

Other important monuments in the old city include the Alcázar, the castle begun around the eleventh century, and the stunning sixteenth-century Gothic cathedral, one of the last in Europe of the style.

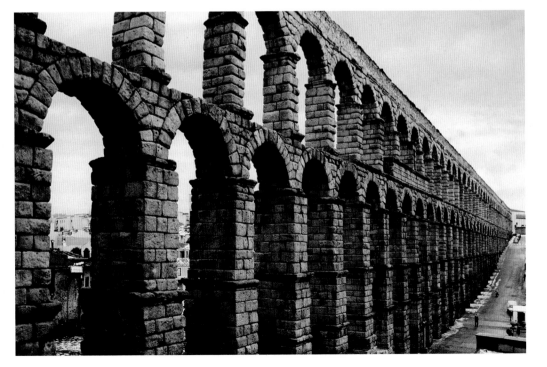

World Heritage site since

· 1978 • 1979 • 1980 • 1981 • 1982 • 1983 • 1984 • **1985**

Chavín (Archaeological site)
Peru
Criteria – Testimony to cultural tradition

The archaeological site of Chavín gave its name to the culture that developed between 1500 and 300 BC in this high valley of the Peruvian Andes. This former place of worship is one of the earliest and best-known pre-Columbian sites. Its appearance is striking, with the complex of terraces and squares, surrounded by structures of dressed stone, and the mainly zoomorphic ornamentation.

Chavín's location in a high valley of the Peruvian Andes at an altitude of 3,177 m didn't stop its architects and artists producing some remarkable structures. These include immense sculpted megaliths, one of which is more than 4 m in height.

◄

A feline head, one of the zoomorphic carvings at Chavín.

Painted Churches in the Troodos Region
Cyprus
Criteria – Interchange of values; Testimony to cultural tradition; Significance in human history

In the Troodos Mountains, in the heart of Cyprus, can be found one of the greatest concentrations of churches and monasteries of the Byzantine Empire, by which the island was annexed during the conquest of 965. The complex of ten monuments included on the World Heritage List, all richly decorated with murals, provides an overview of Byzantine and post-Byzantine painting in Cyprus. They range from small churches, whose rural architectural style is in stark contrast to their highly refined decoration, to monasteries such as that of St John Lampadistis. Among the most significant cycles is that of Panagia Phorbiotissa of Nikitari, which was painted in 1105–6, and that of Panagia tou Arakou in Lagoudera, which was executed during the last six months of 1192.

The Church of the Transfiguration of the Saviour (Ayia Sotira) in Palaichori has a steep-pitched wooden roof with flat hooked tiles. This type of roofing over a Byzantine church is not found elsewhere, making the wooden-roofed churches of Cyprus a unique group example of religious architecture.

World Heritage site since

· 1978 · 1979 · 1980 · 1981 · 1982 · 1983 · 1984 · **1985**

Santiago de Compostela (Old Town)
Spain

Criteria – Human creative genius; Interchange of values; Heritage associated with events of universal significance

The Old Town of Santiago de Compostela, with Romanesque, Gothic and Baroque buildings, is one of the world's most beautiful urban areas and one of the most famous pilgrimage sites in the Christian world. It became a symbol in the Spanish Christians' struggle against the Islamic Moors after its destruction by the Muslims at the end of the tenth century.

Santiago conserves a valuable historic centre worthy of one of Christianity's greatest holy cities. The oldest monuments are grouped around the tomb of St James and the cathedral, which is a masterpiece of Romanesque art. Civil and religious architectural elements from the Middle Ages and the Renaissance are also integrated into a high-quality urban fabric.

During the Romanesque and Baroque periods Santiago exerted a decisive influence on the development of architecture and art across the northern Iberian peninsula.

Santiago de Compostela is associated with pilgrimage, one of the major themes of the medieval centuries. From the shores of the North Sea and the Baltic, thousands carrying the pilgrims' scallop shell and staff walked to the Galician sanctuary along the paths of Santiago (St James) to the tomb of St James the Great.

The Cathedral at Santiago de Compostela.
▼

Petra
Jordan

Criteria – Human creative genius; Testimony to cultural tradition; Significance in human history

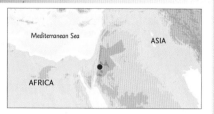

Petra is one of the world's most famous and spectacular archaeological sites, where ancient Eastern traditions blend with Hellenistic architecture. Situated between the Red Sea and the Dead Sea and half-built, half-carved in the rock, Petra was an important crossroads between Arabia, Egypt and Syria-Phoenicia.

Petra was first established around the sixth century BC by the Nabataean Arabs, a Semitic people who laid the foundations of a commercial empire that extended into Syria. In AD 106 the Roman Emperor Trajan annexed the Nabataean Kingdom as part of the province of Arabia. The many earthquakes that hit Petra triggered a slow decline for the city, which was not halted by its designation as an archepiscopal see. Muslim Arabs conquered the city in 636 but it remained distant from the pilgrim road to Mecca. The Crusaders constructed a fort there in the twelfth century and Petra returned to its ancient splendour, but soon they withdrew, leaving it to the local people until the early nineteenth century, when it was visited by the Swiss explorer Burckhardt.

Petra lies south of modern Amman on the edge of the mountainous desert of Wadi Araba, surrounded by towering hills of sandstone which gave the city some natural protection against invaders. It was for centuries the meeting point of the main routes used by camel caravans transporting spices between the Mediterranean and the Near East, Africa and India.

The Khazneh el Faroun, or the Treasury of the Pharaoh, is one of Petra's most famous sights: an imposing façade some 40 m tall, carved into the mountain rock like a half-finished sculpture. The Khazneh is the only rock-cut building in Petra with no Nabataean element and links exclusively with the Alexandrian world and Hellenistic artistic traditions. Behind the impressive façade, a large square room has been carved out of the rock of the cliff. Typically for the tombs in Petra, its interior is as plain as its exterior is intricate.

North from the Khazneh lies the massif of Jebel Khubtha. Three large structures (Royal Tombs) are carved into the rock face, which is known as the King's Wall: the Urn Tomb, the Corinthian Tomb and the Palace Tomb (Silk Tomb), named for the extraordinary chromatic effect of the rock.

The main entrance to ▶ Petra is through the Siq, a gorge formed by the Musa, which the Nabataeans blocked with a dam and channelled to carry drinking water to the city. The Siq narrows to little more than 5 m in width, twisting and turning through sheer walls towering hundreds of metres on either side. The Khazneh, or Treasury, stands at the end of the gorge.

Petra has notable Roman relics, including its first century AD theatre: carved almost entirely in the rock, it could hold more than 8,000 spectators.

World Heritage site since

· 1978 · 1979 · 1980 · 1981 · 1982 · 1983 · 1984 · **1985**

Huascarán National Park
Peru

Criteria – Natural phenomena or beauty; Major
stages of Earth's history

The Cordillera region
has for centuries been
a site for the
settlement of ethnic
groups, as witnessed
by ruins at Gekosh
and Chuchumpunta
and elsewhere. These
represent the largest
collection of such
remains in the world.

Huascarán National Park is located in the
Cordillera Blanca Range in the Peruvian
Andes. The park covers most of the
Cordillera Blanca, the highest tropical
mountain range in the world. It has twenty-
seven snow-capped peaks 6,000 m above
sea level, of which El Huascarán (6,768 m) is
the highest. The deep ravines watered by
numerous torrents, the glacial lakes and the
variety of the vegetation make it a site of
spectacular beauty. It is the home of such
species as the spectacled bear and the
Andean condor. Puma, mountain cat, white-
tailed deer and vicuna are other important
indigenous species, but all have been heavily
hunted in the past. The national park is
uninhabited, although there is some
grazing in the lowlands by native livestock
(llama and alpaca) under an agreement with
the local people.

The peak of El
Huascarán.
▼

Hatra
Iraq

Criteria – Interchange of values; Testimony to cultural tradition; Significance in human history; Heritage associated with events of universal significance

Hatra was a large fortified city under the influence of the Parthian Empire and capital of the first Arab Kingdom. It flourished as a major staging-post on the famous oriental Silk Road to become another of the great Arab cities like Palmyra in Syria, Petra in Jordan, and Baalbek in Lebanon. This Eastern monarchy was a source of concern for the Romans who sought unsuccessfully to destroy it. Hatra withstood invasions by the Romans in AD 116 and 198 thanks to its high, thick walls reinforced by towers. The remains of the city, especially the temples where Hellenistic and Roman architecture blend with Eastern decorative features, attest to the greatness of an entire facet of Assyro-Babylonian civilisation influenced by Greeks, Parthians, Romans and Arabs.

Hatra is a circular city, almost 2 km in diameter, with four fortified gates set in immense double walls. The external wall is an earthen bank; a wide ditch separates this from a stone wall. The perfect condition of the double wall in an untouched environment sets it aside as an outstanding example of this type of fortification.

Manas Wildlife Sanctuary
India

Criteria – Natural phenomena or beauty; Significant ecological and biological processes; Significant natural habitat for biodiversity

On a gentle slope in the foothills of the Himalaya, where wooded hills give way to alluvial grasslands and tropical forests, the Manas sanctuary is home to a great variety of wildlife. Named after the Goddess Manasa, the site is noted for its spectacular scenery, with a variety of habitat types that support a diverse fauna, making it the richest of all Indian wildlife areas. The park represents the core of an extensive tiger reserve that protects an important migratory wildlife resource along the West Bengal to Arunachal Pradesh and Bhutan borders. Its wetlands are of international importance. It is also the single most important site for the survival of pygmy hog, hispid hare and golden langur.

Over 450 species of bird have been recorded, including the threatened Bengal florican, great pied hornbill, wreathed hornbill and other hornbills. Uncommon waterfowl species include spot-billed pelican, lesser adjutant and greater adjutant.

Reptiles include the Assam roofed turtle, a variety of snakes, gharial and monitor lizard.

Keoladeo National Park
India

Criteria – Significant natural habitat for
biodiversity

This former duck-hunting reserve of the
Maharajas is one of the major wintering
areas for large numbers of aquatic birds
from Afghanistan, Turkmenistan, China and
Siberia. Some 364 species of bird, including
the rare Siberian crane, have been recorded
in the park, giving it a unique assemblage of
species. The park's location in the Gangetic
Plain makes it an unrivalled breeding site for
herons, storks and cormorants and an
important wintering ground for large
numbers of migrant ducks. An estimated
sixty-five million fish fry are carried into the
park's water impoundments by river
flooding every year during the monsoon
season, providing the food base for large
numbers of wading and fish-eating birds.
There are also many birds of prey including
the osprey, peregrine and various species
of eagle.

The area consists of
a flat patchwork of
marshes, artificially
created in the 1850s
and maintained ever
since by a system of
canals, sluices and
dykes. Large
predators are absent,
leopard having been
deliberately
exterminated by 1964,
but many species of
small carnivores
inhabit the park along
with primates such as
rhesus macaque.

Monuments of Oviedo and the Kingdom of the Asturias
Spain

Criteria – Human creative genius; Interchange of values; Significance in human history

In the ninth century the flame of Christianity was kept alive in the Iberian peninsula in the tiny Kingdom of the Asturias. Here an innovative pre-Romanesque architectural style was created that was to play a significant role in the development of the religious architecture of the peninsula. Its highest achievements can be seen in the churches of Santa María del Naranco, San Miguel de Lillo, Santa Cristina de Lena, the Cámara Santa and San Julián de los Prados, in and around the ancient capital city of Oviedo. These churches, which are basilical in layout and entirely vaulted, and which make use of columns instead of piers, have very rich decors combining influences from a variety of sources. Associated with them is the remarkable contemporary hydraulic engineering structure known as La Foncalada.

Santa María del Naranco is a former royal residence built on two levels. Excavations in 1930–4 revealed the existence of baths in one of the lower rooms. This rectangular palace was converted into a church between 905 and 1065.

▼

Medina of Marrakesh
Morocco

Criteria – Human creative genius; Interchange of values; Significance in human history; Traditional human settlement

Atlantic Ocean

Mediterranean Sea

AFRICA

The minaret of the Koutoubia Mosque. ▶

The legacy of Marrakesh's Saadian rulers can be seen in the ruins of the El Badi Palace and especially in the magnificent Saadian tombs. Elaborately decorated with delicate carvings, coloured tiles and Arabic script, these tombs of the city's rulers and wealthy were sealed by the Alawites and remained closed until 1917. Materials for their building came from great distances, such as the fine marble from Carrara which the writer Montaigne observed being cut in Tuscany 'for the king of Morocco in Berberia'.

Marrakesh, which gave its name to the Moroccan Empire, is the textbook example of a large Islamic capital in the Western world. With its maze of narrow streets, houses, souks (markets), traditional crafts and trade activities, and its medina, this ancient settlement is an outstanding example of a vibrant historic city.

Founded in 1070–2 by the Almoravids, Marrakesh became the true capital of these conquering nomads and a political, economic and cultural centre that was influential throughout the western Muslim world from North Africa to Andalusia. For the next two centuries, Marrakesh played a decisive role in the development of urban planning.

In Marrakesh, as in other North African cities, the medina is the oldest, walled part of the city. The original layout of Marrakesh's medina dates back to the Almoravid period from which there still remain various monumental vestiges. The medina walls were built in 1126–7 and it is believed the Almoravids planted the palm groves that still grow there, now covering a 1.3 km² area east of the city.

The Berber Almohads took Marrakesh in 1147, destroying many of their predecessors' buildings. The city nevertheless remained the capital and for two centuries under its Almohad rulers, Marrakesh experienced new and unprecedented prosperity.

The Almohads built the Koutoubia Mosque on Almoravid foundations. Its incomparable minaret (pictured on the right), a key monument of Muslim architecture, is one of the major features of the cityscape and the symbol of the city. They built new quarters, extended the city wall, fortified the Kasbah (fortress) which was an extension of the city to the south with its own ramparts and gates (Bab Agnaou, Bab Robb), its mosque, palace, market, hospital, parade ground and gardens. These leaders strengthened their control over their domains by planting crops and by civil engineering achievements such as the Tensift Bridge.

Although Marrakesh went into decline after the Almohads lost power in 1269, notable buildings, such as the Ben Salih Mosque and minaret, were still built. The rebirth of the capital under the Saadian rulers from 1510–1669 brought a new blossoming of the arts, and from the seventeenth century onwards Marrakesh's Alawite rulers also added to the town fabric, building a new mosque, madrasas, palaces and residences, all harmoniously integrated into the old town.

World Heritage site since

• 1978 • 1979 • 1980 • 1981 • 1982 • 1983 • 1984 • **1985**

Cave of Altamira and Paleolithic Cave Art of Northern Spain
Spain

Criteria – Human creative genius; Testimony to cultural tradition

Altamira, the 'Sistine Chapel of Prehistory', is a unique artistic achievement and bears exceptional testimony to the Magdalenian cultures of southern Europe around 15,500 years ago. Discovered by chance in 1869, the Cave of Altamira revealed the existence of two very rich archaeological levels. It was inhabited as early as the Aurignacian, the date of the first figurative representations depicted on its walls, around 18,500 years ago. It was at the start of the Magdalenian period that the largest room in the cavern was decorated. Under its vault there are superb paintings of bison, horses, deer and boars using a palette of colours consisting of only a small number of shades (ochre, reds and blacks). In 2008, seventeen decorated caves, representing the apogee of Paleolithic cave art that developed across Europe, from the Urals to the Iberian Peninusula, from 35,000 to 11,000 BC, were inscribed as an extension to the Altamira Cave site. With deep galleries, and isolated from external climatic influences, these caves are particularly well preserved.

The large animal images (the doe is 2.2 m long) are striking in their naturalism, and their specific features are scrupulously reproduced. They are also outstanding in the variety of fur and mane textures, which are extremely well rendered, and the variety of poses which make masterly use of the cave's surface and crevices that provide surprising trompe-l'œil effects.

Punic Town of Kerkuane and its Necropolis
Tunisia

Criteria – Testimony to cultural tradition

This Phoenician city was active for over 400 years and then abandoned during the First Punic War c. 250 BC. It was not rebuilt by the Romans and its remains constitute the only example of a Phoenicio-Punic city to have survived, offering a unique snapshot of Phoenician city life in the third century BC. Its port, ramparts, residential districts, shops, workshops, streets, squares, temples and necropolis remain as they were when the city was abandoned. The city was carefully laid out, with advanced use of hydraulics and high standards of hygiene. Houses were built to a standard plan: a single entrance and a corridor gave access to an interior courtyard with a well, a washbasin and a bath; around the courtyard were the reception rooms.

The necropolis of Arg el Ghazouani, located on a rocky hill less than 1 km northwest of the city, is the best conserved portion of the great Kerkuane necropolis whose tombs are scattered throughout the coastal hills at the extreme end of Cap Bon. In the protected area there are approximately 200 tombs, including 50 that have not been excavated.

World Heritage site since

• 1978 • 1979 • 1980 • 1981 • 1982 • 1983 • 1984 • **1985**

Quseir Amra
Jordan

Criteria – Human creative genius; Testimony to cultural tradition; Significance in human history

The murals consist of historical themes (royal figures who were defeated by the Umayyad caliphs), mythological representations (the muses of Poetry, Philosophy and History, with their names in Greek), a zodiac, hunting scenes and hammam scenes as well as some imaginary themes (such as animal musicians, and a hunter being chased by a lion).

Built in the early eighth century, this exceptionally well-preserved desert castle was both a fortress with a garrison and a residence of the Umayyad caliphs. The most outstanding features of this small pleasure-palace are the reception hall and the hammam (steam bath), whose walls and vaults are both richly decorated with figurative murals that reflect the secular art of the time. Quseir Amra was probably built under Walid I (705–15), although a more recent theory suggests the reign of Walid II (743–4). Of great interest is the remarkable architectural structure of the reception hall and also the existence of a very extensive bath complex, fed by an aqueduct, that resembles Roman baths with its three rooms: the changing-room (apodyterium), the warm bath (tepidarium) and the hot bath (caldarium), in addition to the service room.

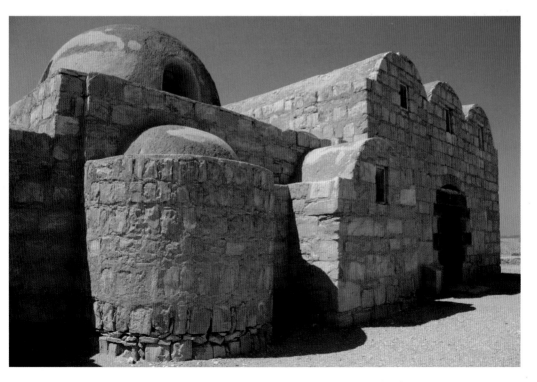

World Heritage site since

• 1978 • 1979 • 1980 • 1981 • 1982 • 1983 • 1984 • **1985**

Ruins of the Buddhist Vihara at Paharpur
Bangladesh

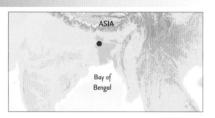

Criteria – *Human creative genius; Interchange of values; Heritage associated with events of universal significance*

Enclosed by thick walls up to 5 m high, this remarkable monastery is quadrangular, and has a colossal temple with a cross-shaped floor plan in the centre of the courtyard and with an elaborate gateway complex on the north.

Somapura Mahavira (Great Monastery) was a renowned intellectual centre until the twelfth century, epitomising the rise of Mahayana Buddhism in Bengal from the seventh century onwards. With its simple, harmonious lines and its profusion of carved decoration, this monastery-city represents a unique artistic as well as religious achievement. The monastery had cells for 177 monks, ranged around its central quadrangle. Its layout was perfectly adapted to its function and it influenced Buddhist architecture as far away as Cambodia. The wide range of excavated finds include terracotta plaques, images of different gods and goddesses, pottery, coins, inscriptions and ornamental bricks. The site is the most important and largest known monastery south of the Himalaya to have been excavated.

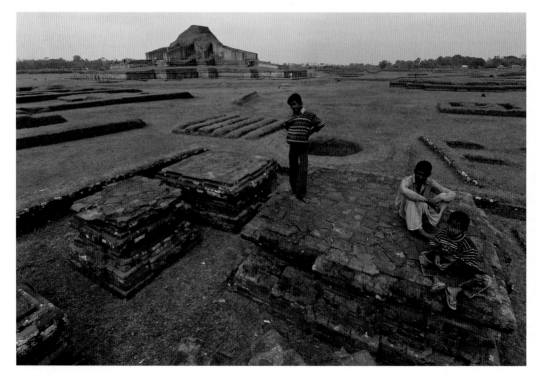

World Heritage site since

· 1978 · 1979 · 1980 · 1981 · 1982 · 1983 · 1984 · **1985**

Sanctuary of Bom Jesus do Congonhas
Brazil

Criteria – Human creative genius; Significance in human history

The wish of a Portuguese immigrant who had been miraculously cured of a crippling infirmity was the impetus for the construction of one of Christian art's most amazing groupings of monuments. Buried in the still luxuriant Brazilian highlands, the Sanctuary was completed in the 1770s after little more than sixty years. The Church of Bom Jesus is a simple construction in the tradition of the area. However, after the death of its founder, Feliciano Mendes, in

1765 it was given a sumptuous Rococo interior. Externally, the flight of steps, begun in 1770, was later decorated with twelve soapstone statues of the Prophets by Antônio Francisco Lisboa (Aleijadinho). In seven small chapels in the grounds are housed 'The Passos', seven Stations of the Cross, sculpted in wood by Aleijadinho. Christian art in Latin America reached its unquestioned zenith with these multicoloured groups.

In the eighteenth century, the region of Minas Gerais in Brazil was in its heyday – there were more than 30,000 gold prospectors in 1712. Moreover, the devotion of these pioneers was responsible for a remarkable blossoming of religious art, full of Baroque touches and influenced by Rococo invention.

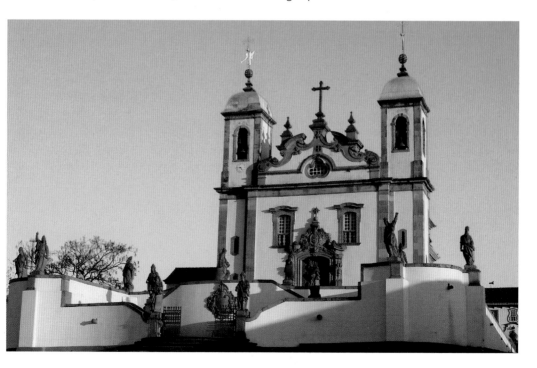

World Heritage site since

··· 1978 · 1979 · 1980 · 1981 · 1982 · 1983 · 1984 · **1985**

Kaziranga National Park
India

Criteria – Significant ecological and biological processes; Significant natural habitat for biodiversity

In the heart of Assam, this park is one of the last areas in eastern India undisturbed by human activity. It is inhabited by the world's largest populations of one-horned rhinoceroses and Indian elephants (pictured below) as well as many other mammals, including tigers, panthers and bears, and thousands of birds. The site is in the flood plains on the southern bank of the Brahmaputra River at the foot of the Mikir Hills. The riverine habitat consists primarily of tall, dense grasslands interspersed with open forests, streams and numerous small lakes (bheels). Over three-quarters of the area is submerged annually by the flood waters of the Brahmaputra. The park contains about fifteen species of India's threatened mammals. The numerous areas of water are rich reservoirs of food (including fish) and thousands of migratory birds, representing over 100 species, visit the park seasonally.

Other mammals include the capped langur, a small population of hoolock gibbon, Ganges dolphin, otter, swamp deer, hog deer and Indian muntjac. Birds of interest include grey pelican, black-necked stork, Pallas's fish eagle, Bengal florican, swamp partridge, grey peacock-pheasant, great pied hornbill and green imperial pigeon. The reptilian fauna include the water monitor, Indian python, common cobra and king cobra.

World Heritage site since

• 1978 • 1979 • 1980 • 1981 • 1982 • 1983 • 1984 • **1985**

Great Mosque and Hospital of Divriği
Turkey

Criteria – Human creative genius; Significance in human history

The Divriği ensemble presents a gripping contrast between the low, blind walls of its rectangular enclosure and the three immense gates which afford access to the hospital at the west and to the mosque at the north and west.

The Divriği mosque was founded in 1228-9 by Emir Ahmet Shah, along with a *marestan* (hospital for the insane) endowed by his wife. These two complementary monuments were built simultaneously by the same architect. Divriği is an outstanding example of Selçuk mosques in Anatolia, having neither a courtyard, colonnades, nor an uncovered ablutions basin, but which (due to the harshness of the climate) organises all religious functions in an enclosed area. The mosque has a single prayer room and is crowned by two cupolas. The highly sophisticated technique of vault construction, and a creative, exuberant type of decorative sculpture – particularly on the three doorways, in contrast to the unadorned walls of the interior – are the unique features of this masterpiece of Islamic architecture.

St Mary's Cathedral and St Michael's Church at Hildesheim
Germany

Criteria – Human creative genius; Interchange of values; Testimony to cultural tradition

The Church of St Michael and St Mary's Cathedral have an exemplary selection of interior decorative elements which beautifully express the spirit of Romanesque architecture. St Michael's famous bronze doors (c. 1015) retrace the events from the book of Genesis and the life of Christ, and the Bernward bronze column (c. 1020) depicts scenes from the New Testament.

The ancient Benedictine abbey church of St Michael, built between 1010 and 1022 by Bernward, Bishop of Hildesheim, is one of the key monuments of mediaeval art. It has a symmetrical plan with two apses that was characteristic of Ottonian Romanesque art in Old Saxony. In the nave, square impost pillars alternate in an original rhythm with cubic-capital columns to create a distinctive type of elevation. St Mary's Cathedral, rebuilt after the fire of 1046, still retains its original crypt, and was modelled after St Michael's. It has a similar nave arrangement, but its proportions are more slender. Notable treasures of the churches include the corona of light of Bishop Hezilon and the baptismal fonts of gold-plated bronze of Bishop Conrad.

World Heritage site since

• 1978 • 1979 • 1980 • 1981 • 1982 • 1983 • 1984 • **1985**

Historic Areas of Istanbul Turkey

Criteria – Human creative genius; Interchange of values; Testimony to cultural tradition; Significance in human history

The Blue Mosque, ▶ Istanbul.

The monuments of the city have greatly influenced the development of architecture, monumental arts and the organization of space, in both Europe and Asia for many centuries. Thus, the 6,650 m terrestrial wall of Byzantine Emperor Theodosius II, created in AD 447, was a leading reference for military architecture; St Sophia became a model for an entire family of churches and later mosques; and the mosaics of Constantinople's palaces and churches influenced Eastern and Western Christian art.

Istanbul was built at the crossroads of two continents and was successively the capital of three empires, the Eastern Roman empire, the Byzantine Empire and the Ottoman Empire. First as Byzantium, then as Constantinople and currently as Istanbul, the city has constantly been associated with major events in political, religious and artistic history in both Europe and Asia for two millennia. Masterpieces of the city's built heritage include the ancient Hippodrome of Constantine, the sixth-century Hagia Sophia and the sixteenth-century Süleymaniye Mosque, all now under threat from population pressure, industrial pollution and uncontrolled urbanization.

The World Heritage site covers four zones, illustrating the major phases of the city's history using its most prestigious monuments: the Archaeological Park, at the tip of the peninsula on which the western city stands; the Süleymaniye quarter; the Zeyrek quarter; and the zone of the ramparts.

The ancient city and the capital of the Eastern Roman Empire are both represented, by the Hippodrome of Constantine (dating from 324) in the Archaeological Park, by the aqueduct of Valens (378) in the Süleymaniye quarter, and

by the ramparts (begun in 413), located in the fourth zone.

The capital of the Byzantine Empire is highlighted by several major monuments. In the Archaeological Park are the churches of St Sophia and St Irene, built in the reign of Justinian (527–65). In the Zeyrek quarter is the ancient Pantocrator Monastery, founded under John II Comnenus (1118–43); in the zone of the ramparts there is the old church of the Holy Saviour in Chora (now the Kariye Camii) with its marvellous mosaics and fourteenth- and fifteenth-century paintings. Moreover, the current layout of the walls results from modifications performed in the seventh and twelfth centuries to include the quarter and the Palace of the Blachernes.

The capital of the Ottoman Empire is represented by its most important monuments architecturally: Topkapı Saray and the Blue Mosque in the archaeological zone; the Sehzade and Süleymaniye mosques in the Süleymaniye quarter; and the vernacular settlement vestiges of this quarter, in 525 listed and protected wooden houses.

World Heritage site since

• 1978 • 1979 • 1980 • 1981 • 1982 • 1983 • 1984 • **1985**

Historic Mosque City of Bagerhat
Bangladesh
Criteria – Significance in human history

ASIA

Bay of
Bengal

Formely known as Khalifatabad this historic city is an outstanding example of an architectural ensemble which illustrates a significant stage in human history. Situated in the suburbs of Bagerhat, at the meeting point of the Ganges and Brahmaputra rivers, this ancient city was founded by the Turkish general Ulugh Khan Jahan in the fifteenth century. The city had 360 mosques, public buildings, mausoleums, bridges, roads, water tanks and other public buildings, all built from baked brick. Shait Gumbad Mosque and Khan Jahan's Mausoleum are just two examples of these historic buildings. The quality of the infrastructures – the supply and evacuation of water, the cisterns and reservoirs, the roads and bridges – reveal a perfect mastery of the techniques of planning and a will towards spatial organisation.

This remarkable city had no sooner been created than it was swallowed up by the jungle, after its founder died in 1459. The density of Islamic religious monuments is explained by the piety of Khan Jahan, which is shown by the engraved inscription on his tomb. The lack of fortifications is attributable to the possibilities of retreat into the impenetrable swamps of the Sundarbans.

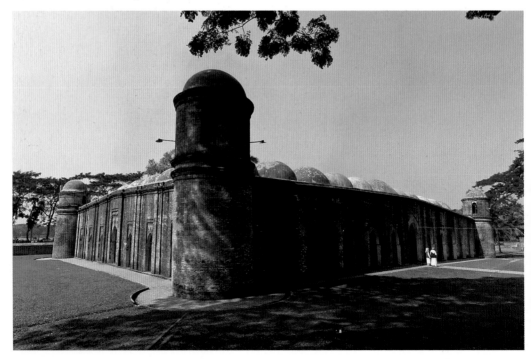

World Heritage site since

• 1978 • 1979 • 1980 • 1981 • 1982 • 1983 • 1984 • **1985**

Pont du Gard (Roman Aqueduct)
France

Criteria – Human creative genius; Testimony to cultural tradition; Significance in human history

The Pont du Gard was built shortly before the Christian era to carry an aqueduct across the Gardon River. The Roman architects and hydraulic engineers who designed this bridge, which stands almost 50 m high and is on three levels – the longest measuring 275 m – created a technical and artistic masterpiece. The first level, which was used as a bridge in the Middle Ages, consists of six semi-circular arches, the second level eleven, and the third level, at the top of which runs the water channel, has thirty-five. On the two lower levels large stone blocks, which can weigh up to 6 tonnes, were used while the upper level was constructed of small stone rubble. It is one of the most significant monuments of the early Imperial period, most likely built upon the initiative of Agrippa about 20 BC.

In order to meet the needs of the colony of Nemausus (Nîmes), springs were tapped near Uzès. To achieve an average gradient of 34 cm per 1,000 m, the 50 km aqueduct compensates for the topography by following a winding path. Near Remoulins it had to cross the deep valley of the Gardon, requiring the construction of this exceptional bridge. ▼

World Heritage site since

· 1978 · 1979 · 1980 · 1981 · 1982 · 1983 · 1984 · **1985**

Göreme National Park and the Rock Sites of Cappadocia
Turkey

Criteria – Human creative genius; Testimony to cultural tradition; Traditional human settlement; Natural phenomena or beauty

EUROPE
Black Sea
Mediterranean Sea
ASIA

In a spectacular landscape, entirely sculptured by erosion, the Göreme valley and its surroundings contain rock-hewn sanctuaries that provide unique evidence of Byzantine art in the post-iconoclastic period of the ninth century AD onwards. Dwellings, troglodyte villages and underground towns – the remains of a traditional human habitat dating back to the fourth century – can also be seen there.

In the ruin-like landscape of the Cappadocia plateau where natural erosion sculpted the rock into shapes eerily reminiscent of towers, spires, domes and pyramids, man has added to the workmanship of the elements by digging cells, churches and veritable subterranean cities which together make up one of the world's largest cave-dwelling complexes. The historical setting, the rock-hewn churches and the unusual eroded landforms combine to produce a mixed cultural and natural landscape of unusual appearance.

Although the area has been extensively used and modified by man for centuries, the resulting landscape is one of harmony and consideration of the intrinsic values of the natural landforms. Architectural styles are based on the local stone and the valley has changed little over time.

Although interesting from a geological and ethnological perspective, this phenomenal site excels especially for the incomparable beauty of the rupestral decor in the Christian sanctuaries whose features make Cappadocia one of the leading examples of post-iconoclast-period Byzantine art.

The first signs of monastic activity in Cappadocia are thought to date from the fourth century when, on the instructions of Basil the Great, Bishop of Caesarea (Kayseri), small, hermit communities began inhabiting the cells dug into the rock. Later, to resist Arab forays they began banding together into troglodyte villages or subterranean towns such as Kaymakli or Derinkuyu, which served as places of refuge.

Cappadocian monasticism was already well established in the iconoclast period (725–842), as illustrated by the decoration in many of the sanctuaries: a minimum of symbols, most often sculpted or tempera-painted crosses. But after 842 many rupestral churches were dug in Cappadocia and these were were richly decorated with brightly coloured figurative painting. Among them in the Göreme valley were Tokali Kilise and El Nazar Kilise in the tenth century, Barbara Kilise and Sakli Kilise in the eleventh century, and El Mali Kilise and Karanlik Kilise, created in the late twelfth and early thirteenth centuries.

The Göreme Valley is ▶ a spectacular example of the effects of wind and water erosion on soft volcanic tuff. Pillars, columns, towers, obelisks and needles reaching heights of 40 m are typical features of the landscape. The nearby Erciyas volcano is still active, with occasional minor eruptions.

Within these rock formations people have excavated a network of caves which served as refuges, residences, storage and places of worship dating from the fourth century. The surrounding landscape is agricultural with a number of small, scattered rural villages.

Royal Palaces of Abomey
Benin

Criteria – Testimony to cultural tradition;
Significance in human history

The West African Kingdom of Abomey (later Dahomey), founded in 1625 by the Fon people, developed into a powerful military and commercial empire. Under the twelve kings who succeeded one another from 1695 to 1900, the kingdom became one of the most powerful on the west coast of Africa. Until the late nineteenth century its primary source of wealth was from selling prisoners of war as slaves to European slave traders for transport across the Atlantic to the New World. Each of the twelve kings built a lavish palace on the royal grounds in Abomey, the capital city, all within the same cob-walled area. Still used regularly for rituals and royal ceremonies, the palace buildings both represent the past and continue its traditions.

The bas-relief decorations provide a unique history of this society that had no written records. They glorify each king and document the myths, customs and rituals of the Fon people whose kingdom this was. The walls show that the military might of the Abomey kingdom was based, in part, on companies of female warriors who matched their male counterparts in fierceness and courage.

Rock Art of Alta
Norway

Criteria – Testimony to cultural tradition

The petroglyphs of the Alta fjord in the province of Tromsø are among the leading rock art sites in the world. Close to the Arctic Circle, they are a valuable illustration of human activity between 4200 and 500 BC in the far North. The thousands of paintings and engravings are located at forty-five sites scattered over seven localities and show a definite chronological sequence. The position of the paintings and engravings with respect to sea level at different postglacial periods constitutes a relative dating element, which is corroborated by objective iconography data. According to the principle of reverse stratigraphy, the most ancient works are generally the highest, the most recent being close to the present sea level (the height difference is roughly 26 m).

The drawings represent northern wildlife, including reindeer, elk and bear, geese, cormorants and salmon. There are depictions of hunting, trapping and fishing, dancing and ceremonial acts. The climate warmed as time passed and the latest drawings show agricultural activities.

Old Town of Ávila with its Extra-Muros Churches
Spain

Criteria – Testimony to cultural tradition;
Significance in human history

Ávila is an outstanding example of a fortified city of the Middle Ages, the surrounding walls of which are fully intact (pictured below). The density of religious and secular monuments, both inside (intra) and outside (extra) the city walls (muros), makes it an urban ensemble of exceptional value. Founded in the eleventh century to protect the Spanish territories from the Moors, this 'City of Saints and Stones', the birthplace of St Teresa and the burial place of the Grand Inquisitor Torquemada, has kept its medieval austerity. The walls, which date back to 1090 (but mostly rebuilt during the twelfth century), have an average thickness of 3 m and are flanked by eighty-two semicircular towers, with nine gates of different periods. The cathedral, with its crenellated Romanesque choir linked to the curtain wall, is part of the system of fortifications.

The church of San Pedro Extra-Muros was begun in 1100. In its beautiful open atrium, royal receptions took place, and it was here that the Catholic kings in June 1475 and Emperor Charles I in May 1534 vowed to respect the city's charters.

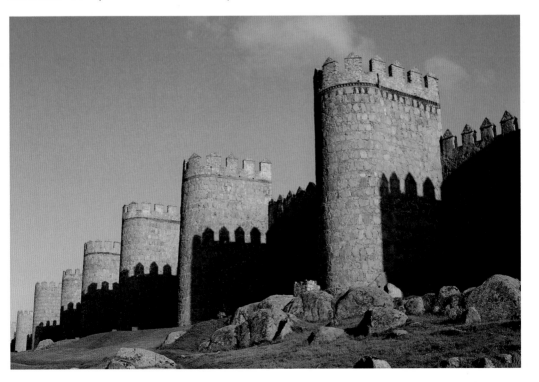

Thracian Tomb of Sveshtari
Bulgaria
Criteria – Human creative genius; Testimony to
cultural tradition

The discovery in 1982 of the Thracian tomb
of Sveshtari was one of the most spectacular
archaeological events of the twentieth
century. This third-century BC tomb reflects
the fundamental structural principles of
Thracian cult buildings. The tomb has a
unique architectural décor, with polychrome
half-human, half-plant caryatids and
painted murals. The ten female figures
carved in high relief on the walls of the

central chamber and the decoration of the
lunette in its vault are the only examples of
this type found so far in the Thracian lands.
The tomb consists of a corridor (dromos)
and three square chambers: antechamber,
lateral chamber, and main burial chamber
covered by a semi-cylindrical vault.

The tomb is an
exceptional testimony
to the culture of the
Getae, a Thracian
people living in the
north of Hemus,
who were in contact
with the Greek and
Hyperborean worlds,
according to ancient
geographers.

Rock-Art Sites of Tadrart
Acacus
Libya
Criteria – Testimony to cultural tradition

On the borders of Tassili N'Ajjer in Algeria,
also a World Heritage site, this rocky massif
has thousands of cave paintings reflecting
marked changes in fauna and flora, and
the different ways of life of the populations
that succeeded one another in this region
of the Sahara. The oldest images (12,000
BC) are outline engravings of large savanna
mammals such as elephant and rhinoceros.
Paintings of magic religious scenes and

representations of a humid landscape
appear alongside engravings around
8000 BC. The domesticated horse features
about 1500 BC in a semi-arid climate, while
the first centuries BC saw the intensification
of a desert environment. The dromedary
settled in the region at this time and
became the main subject of the last rock art
paintings.

As well as its
remarkable cave
paintings, Tadrart
Acacus boasts some
of the most
extraordinary
scenery in the world.
Its unique natural
wonders include
isolated towers
emerging from the
sand and eroded
into bizarre shapes,
petrified arches, vast
dunes, and canyons
carved by ancient
rivers.

Iguaçu National Park
Brazil

Criteria – Natural phenomena or beauty;
Significant natural habitat for biodiversity

The park shares with Iguazú National Park in Argentina one of the world's largest and most impressive waterfalls. The Iguaçu Falls span the border between Argentina and Brazil. At 80 m high and 2,700 m wide, the falls produce vast clouds of spray that encourage the growth of lush vegetation of which around 90 per cent is subtropical rainforest.

The park is home to many rare and endangered species of flora and fauna, among them the giant otter and the giant anteater.

Among the many other species recorded are La Plata otter, ocelot, jaguar, puma, margay, brocket deer, pampas deer, American tapir, black howler monkey, collared peccary, white-lipped peccary and urutu viper.

Noteworthy birds include great dusky swift, solitary tinamou, ornate hawk eagle, red-breasted toucan, glaucous macaw, vinaceous-breasted and red-spectacled parrots, white-tailed trogon and harpy eagle.

Vegetation is lush and abundant. The lower park has subtropical rainforest with tree ferns, lianas and epiphytes. The upper part is mainly humid subtropical deciduous forest and has stands of the Brazilian pine with two palms, the Assai palm and wild coconut palm, and the imbuya. These stands are limited to a small section in the north-east of the park.

World Heritage site since

• 1978 • 1979 • 1980 • 1981 • 1982 • 1983 • 1984 • 1985 • **1986**

Ancient City of Aleppo
Syrian Arab Republic

Criteria – Testimony to cultural tradition;
Significance in human history

The ancient city of Aleppo is one of the oldest continuously inhabited cities in the world. Located at the crossroads of trade routes between the Mediterranean and the East, it prospered from the third millennium BC. Successive occupiers – including Byzantines, Romans, Greeks, Crusaders and Arabs – have left their mark in the architecture and the city plan.

Aleppo is dominated by its huge medieval castle, the Citadel (pictured below), which stands on a partly artificial mound towering 50 m above the city. Although the structure dates from around the twelfth century, the hill on which it stands has been used for defensive purposes from around the third millennium BC.

The old city was surrounded by a defensive wall of which parts still exist along with seven of its fortified gates; Bab Qinnesrin is the most impressive remaining.

The souks or bazaars of Aleppo's old town are among the most famous in the Middle East. Enclosed by stone vaulted roofs, they twist for 7 km along narrow streets.

The Great Mosque was founded around AD 715 but little from that time remains: it was largely rebuilt around 1250 although its highest minaret dates from 1090.

◄
The Citadel of Aleppo.

World Heritage site since

· 1978 · 1979 · 1980 · 1981 · 1982 · 1983 · 1984 · 1985 · **1986**

Churches and Convents of Goa
India

Criteria – Interchange of values; Significance in human history; Heritage associated with events of universal significance

The churches and convents of Goa, the former capital of the Portuguese Indies – particularly the Church of Bom Jesus, which contains the tomb of St Francis-Xavier – illustrate the evangelization of Asia. These monuments were influential in spreading forms of Manueline, Mannerist and Baroque art in all the countries of Asia where missions were established.

The Sé Cathedral is a fine example of Renaissance architecture, with a Tuscan exterior, Corinthian columns, raised platform with steps leading to the entrance, and barrel-vault.

◄

The church of Bom Jesus.

Hattusha: the Hittite Capital
Turkey

Criteria – Human creative genius; Interchange of values; Testimony to cultural tradition; Significance in human history

Hattusha exerted a dominating influence upon the civilizations in the thirteenth century BC in Anatolia and northern Syria. The palaces, temples, trading quarters and necropolis of this political and religious metropolis provide a comprehensive picture of a capital city and bear unique testimony to the vanished Hittite civilization. The city's fortifications, along with the Lion Gate, the Royal Gate and the Yazılıkaya rupestral ensemble with its sculptured friezes,

represent unique artistic achievements as monuments. Inside the walls, the city is built on two levels. To the northwest is the lower town with its great temple, dedicated to the god of storms and the goddess of the Sun, Arinna. Thousands of cuneiform tablets were found in this area. To the south is the upper city with the royal residence of Büyükkale.

At its largest, the city spread over a sloping, uneven plateau, covering 2.1 km from north to south and 1.3 km from east to west. In the thirteenth century, the city was surrounded by a system of double walls forming a perimeter of roughly 8 km.

World Heritage site since

· 1978 · 1979 · 1980 · 1981 · 1982 · 1983 · 1984 · 1985 · **1986**

Chan Chan Archaeological Zone
Peru

Criteria – Human creative genius; Testimony to cultural tradition

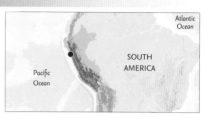

The planning of Chan Chan, largest city of pre-Hispanic America and a unique testimony to the disappeared Chimú kingdom, is a masterpiece of inhabited space and hierarchical construction. Chan Chan was the capital of the kingdom of Chimor which reached its zenith in the fifteenth century, shortly before its fall to the Chimús' great rivals, the Incas.

The planning of this huge, 6 km² city reflects a strict political and social strategy, illustrated by its division into nine 'palaces' –

autonomous units delineated by high, earthen walls. Each 'palace' was grouped around one or more squares and their buildings include temples, dwellings, storehouses, kitchens, orchards, gardens and funeral platforms.

Nearby lie four industrial sectors where the main activities appear to have been woodworking, weaving and precious-metal working. The remains of an irrigation system suggest another area used for farming.

An irrigation system channeled water from the Moche River to Chan Chan. It is difficult to imagine the fertility of this now-desert region during the height of the Chimú civilization.

Hatred of the Incas led the Chimú to welcome the Spanish conquistadores. In 1535 the Spanish founded a new capital at Trujillo, 5 km from Chan Chan which was abandoned.

Ironbridge Gorge
United Kingdom

Criteria – Human creative genius; Interchange of values; Significance in human history; Heritage associated with events of universal significance

Ironbridge, the site of the world's first cast-iron bridge, is known throughout the world as the symbol of the Industrial Revolution. In the blast furnace at nearby Coalbrookdale were developed the coke-based iron-production techniques that drove the eighteenth-century steel revolution. Coalbrookdale and Ironbridge exerted great influence on the development of industrial techniques and architecture, and the area provides a fascinating summary of the progress of the industrial age.

In the area there are five major areas of interest: Coalbrookdale, with Abraham Darby's coke-fired blast furnace; Ironbridge, which takes its name from the bridge built in 1779; Hay Brook valley with its open-air museum featuring extraction galleries and preserved blast furnaces; Jackfield, a former mining town; and Coalport with a porcelain museum in its former porcelain-production factory.

Ironbridge Gorge is a concentration of mining areas, foundries, factories and warehouses, coexisting with a network of paths, roads, canals and railways, as well as substantial remains of traditional landscape and housing, public buildings and infrastructure of the eighteenth and nineteenth centuries. These are well preserved and together comprise an excellent educational environment.

▼

World Heritage site since

· 1978 · 1979 · 1980 · 1981 · 1982 · 1983 · 1984 · 1985 · **1986**

Great Zimbabwe National Monument
Zimbabwe

Criteria – Human creative genius; Testimony to cultural tradition; Heritage associated with events of universal significance

The ruins of Great Zimbabwe – the capital of the Queen of Sheba, according to legend – are a unique testimony to the civilisation of the Shona people of the eleventh to fifteenth centuries. There are three main areas of the site. The Hill Ruins are the remains of a royal city, perched atop a large granite spur. The Great Enclosure below the hill dates from the fourteenth century and holds a series of brick-built living quarters. The Valley Ruins are a series of living ensembles surrounded by drystone masonry walls. Finds made in the inhabited areas have revealed vital information about the farming and pastoral activities of the inhabitants at the time of Great Zimbabwe's heyday and about earthenware and smithing craft activities.

The city of Great Zimbabwe has captured the imagination of travellers since the Middle Ages, and remains a powerful symbol of national identity today. It covers an area of nearly 0.8 km² and was an important trading centre with both European and Asian cultures. In the fourteenth century, it was the principal city of a major state extending over the gold-rich plateaus, with a population of more than 10,000.

Temple of Apollo Epicurius at Bassae
Greece

Criteria – Human creative genius; Interchange of values; Testimony to cultural tradition

This famous temple to the god of healing and the sun was built towards the middle of the fifth century BC in the lonely heights of the Arcadian mountains. The temple, which has the oldest Corinthian capital yet found, combines the Archaic style and the serenity of the Doric style with some daring architectural features. The decoration is notable, particularly on account of the different materials used: the walls and the bases of the columns are limestone, and the Ionic capitals and the Corinthian capital are in Doliana marble. The discovery of the Ionic frieze's twenty-two sculptured plates ultimately divested the site of these remarkable sculptures, which were transferred to the British Museum along with the Corinthian capital.

The temple was dedicated by the inhabitants of Phigalia to Apollo Epicurius, the god-healer who came to their aid when they were beset by plague. Its remoteness kept it undiscovered until 1765 when a French architect happened upon it.

World Heritage site since

· 1978 · 1979 · 1980 · 1981 · 1982 · 1983 · 1984 · 1985 · **1986**

St Kilda
United Kingdom

Criteria – Testimony to cultural tradition;
Traditional human settlement; Natural
phenomena or beauty; Significant ecological and
biological processes; Significant natural habitat
for biodiversity

The archipelago
comprises the islands
of Hirta, Dun, Soay
and Boreray and lies
in the Atlantic 66 km
west of the island of
Benbecula.

St Kilda is a remote volcanic archipelago
of exceptional natural beauty which
supports significant natural habitats. It is
unique in the very high bird densities that
occur in a relatively small area, conditioned
by the site's complex and different
ecological niches. Its cliffs are among the
highest in Europe and are home to large
colonies of endangered birds, especially
puffins and gannets. There is also a complex
ecological dynamic in the site's three marine

zones that is essential to the maintenance
of both marine and terrestrial biodiversity.

St Kilda bears the evidence of more than
2,000 years of human occupation in extreme
conditions. Human vestiges include built
structures and field systems, cleits (dry-stone
huts) and traditional Highland stone houses
(both pictured below) – the vulnerable
remains of a subsistence economy based on
the products of birds, agriculture and sheep
farming and reflecting age-old traditions.

The islanders of
St Kilda were
evacuated at their
own request by the
British government
in 1930 and the only
inhabitants now are
British government
Ministry of Defence
staff and a seasonal
nature warden.

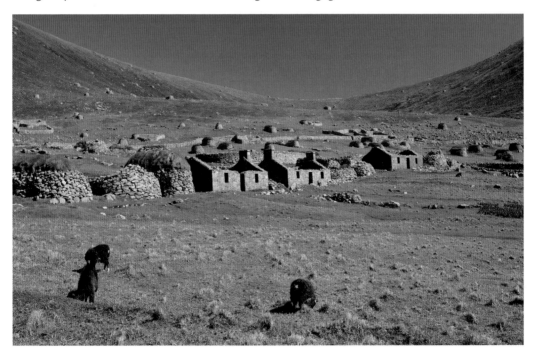

World Heritage site since

• 1978 • 1979 • 1980 • 1981 • 1982 • 1983 • 1984 • 1985 • 1986

Historic City of Toledo
Spain

Criteria – Human creative genius; Interchange of values; Testimony to cultural tradition; Significance in human history

Toledo is the repository of more than 2,000 years of history with architectural and artistic masterpieces that are the product of several civilizations and their three religions – Christianity, Judaism and Islam.

A centre of power for centuries, the city was successively a self-governing Roman municipium, the capital of the Visigothic Kingdom, a fortress of the Emirate of Córdoba, an outpost of the Christian kingdoms fighting the Moors and, in the sixteenth century, the temporary seat of supreme power under Holy Roman Emperor and King of Spain Charles V, who endowed it with the status of imperial and crowned city. During the Renaissance the city became one of the most important artistic centres in Spain.

Ironically, the irreversible economic and political decadence of Toledo after 1561, when Phillip II of Spain chose Madrid as his capital, miraculously spared this museum-city.

Each set of inhabitants left their mark on Toledo: Rome, with vestiges of the circus, aqueduct and sewer; the remains of Visigoth walls; the Islamic monuments of the Emirate of Córdoba; and remarkable churches and synagogues built after the reconquest of 1085. Furthermore, Toledo possesses a broad range of medieval structures – walls and fortified buildings, bridges, streets and houses.

The cathedral, pictured right, and the bridge, gates and Alcázar of Toledo, pictured below. ▼

World Heritage site since

• 1978 • 1979 • 1980 • 1981 • 1982 • 1983 • 1984 • 1985 • **1986**

Giant's Causeway and Causeway Coast
United Kingdom

Criteria – Natural phenomena or beauty; Major stages of Earth's history

Atlantic Ocean

North Sea

EUROPE

The site lies on the north coast of the County of Antrim, Northern Ireland, and includes the Causeway Coast, a 6 km stretch of extraordinary geological formations representing volcanic activity during the early Tertiary period some 50–60 million years ago. The most characteristic and unique feature of the site is the Giant's Causeway, a sea-level promontory of around 40,000 polygonal columns of basalt in perfect horizontal sections forming a pavement. The dramatic sight has inspired legends of giants striding over the sea to Scotland. The Giant's Causeway featured in the eighteenth-century geological controversies on the origins of basalts, and geological studies of these formations over the last 300 years have greatly contributed to the development of the earth sciences.

Other features of the Causeway Coast include the Giant's Organ (about sixty regular columns, 12 m high), the Chimney Tops (a number of columns separated from the cliffs by erosion), and Hamilton's Seat (a viewpoint).

Old City of Sana'a
Yemen

Criteria – Significance in human history; Traditional human settlement; Heritage associated with events of universal significance

Given official status in the second century BC when it was an outpost of the Yemenite kingdoms, Sana'a (Arabic for 'fortified place') was associated with all the major historical events that took place in Arabia Felix.

Situated in a mountain valley at an altitude of 2,200 m, Sana'a has been inhabited for more than 2,500 years and has been the capital of the Yemen since 1962. The Great Mosque is said to have been constructed while the Prophet Muhammad was still living, and in the seventh and eighth centuries the city became a major centre for the propagation of Islam. This religious and political heritage can be seen in the 103 mosques, 14 hammams (steam baths) and over 6,000 houses, all built before the eleventh century. Sana'a's many-storeyed tower-houses, built of rammed earth, add to the beauty of the site. The successive reconstructions of Sana'a under Ottoman domination, beginning in the sixteenth century, respected the proportions and balance of the medieval city while changing its appearance.

World Heritage site since

· 1978 • 1979 • 1980 • 1981 • 1982 • 1983 • 1984 • 1985 · **1986**

Durham Castle and Cathedral
United Kingdom

Criteria – Interchange of values; Significance in human history; Heritage associated with events of universal significance

Atlantic Ocean

North Sea

EUROPE

Located on a rocky promontory overlooking a bend in the river Wear, the monumental array constituted by the cathedral and its outbuildings to the south and by the castle to the north makes up one of the best-known cityscapes of medieval Europe. Durham Cathedral was built in the late-eleventh and early twelfth centuries to house the relics of St Cuthbert, evangelizer of Northumbria, and the Venerable Bede. It attests to the importance of the early

Benedictine monastic community and is the largest and finest example of Norman architecture in England. The innovative audacity of its vaulting foreshadowed Gothic architecture. Behind the cathedral stands the castle, an ancient Norman fortress which regularly faced the onslaught of Scottish troops. It later became the residence of the prince-bishops of Durham and in the nineteenth century was incorporated into Durham University.

The present castle is a veritable labyrinth of halls and galleries of different periods, and in its north wing it houses various vestiges of the Romanesque epoch, including the castral chapel, built in 1080.

World Heritage site since

• 1978 • 1979 • 1980 • 1981 • 1982 • 1983 • 1984 • 1985 • **1986**

Fatehpur Sikri
India

Criteria – Interchange of values; Testimony to
cultural tradition; Significance in human history

Built during the second half of the
sixteenth century by the Emperor Akbar,
Fatehpur Sikri – the City of Victory – was the
capital of the Mughal Empire for a mere
fourteen years. Constructed between 1571
and 1573, it was abandoned in 1585 when
Akbar went to fight against the Afghan
tribes and chose a new capital, Lahore.
Briefly, for three months in 1619, the city
resumed its role as the seat of the great
Mughal court when Jahangir sought
refuge there from the plague that
devastated Agra. The site was then finally
abandoned, until its archaeological
exploration in 1892. The complex of
monuments and temples in the city, all in
a uniform architectural style, includes one
of the largest mosques in India, the Jama
Masjid, able to accommodate some
10,000 of the faithful.

This capital without a
future was considerably
more than the fancy of
a sovereign during the
fourteen years of its
existence. Described by
the English traveller
Ralph Fitch in 1585 as
'considerably larger
than London and more
populous', it comprised
a series of palaces, public
buildings and mosques,
as well as living areas
for the court, the army,
servants of the king and
an entire population.

Walls of the fort at Fatehpur Sikri. ▼

World Heritage site since

• 1978 • 1979 • 1980 • 1981 • 1982 • 1983 • 1984 • 1985 • **1986**

Studley Royal Park including the Ruins of Fountains Abbey
United Kingdom

Criteria – *Human creative genius; Significance in human history*

The Fountains site in Yorkshire owes its originality to the fact that a strikingly beautiful landscape was constituted around the largest medieval ruins of the United Kingdom. Fountains Abbey was founded in 1132 by thirteen Cistercian monks from York, who were searching for an ideal of life in closer keeping with St Benedict's teachings. But by the time the monastic community was abolished by Henry VIII in 1530 it had become the richest abbey in the kingdom, owing to massive donations. These four centuries of prosperity are reflected in the utter magnitude of the ruins of the buildings. Essential to the ruins are the small Fountains Hall Castle, the landscaping, the gardens, the canal created by John Aislabie in the eighteenth century, the plantations and vistas of the nineteenth century, and Studley Royal Church.

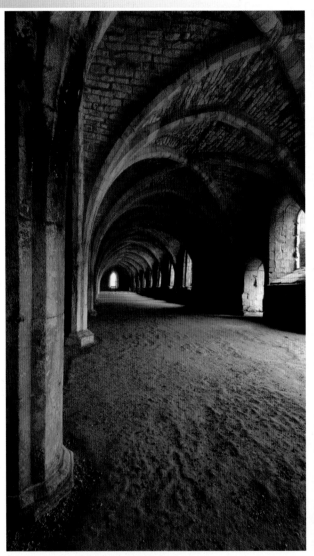

▲
Vaulted ceilings in the Cellarium at Fountains Abbey.

The nave of the abbey church is close to the pristine ideal of Cistercian austerity. However, the rich array of monastic buildings grouped together to the south testifies to the deep-seated changes occurring in a community which rapidly grew away from the pristine ideal owing to its land wealth and its spiritual influence.

World Heritage site since

• 1978 • 1979 • 1980 • 1981 • 1982 • 1983 • 1984 • 1985 • **1986**

Khajuraho Group of Monuments
India

Criteria – *Human creative genius; Testimony to cultural tradition*

The temples at Khajuraho were built during the Chandela dynasty, which reached its apogee between 950 and 1050. The Temple of Kandariya is decorated with a profusion of sculptures that are among the greatest masterpieces of Indian art. Of the eighty-five temples built, only about twenty remain; they fall into three distinct groups and belong to two different religions – Hinduism and Jainism. They strike a perfect balance between architecture and sculpture. Yasovarman (AD 954) built the temple of

Vishnu, now famous as Lakshmana temple; this ornate example proclaims the prestige of the Chandelas. The largest and grandest temple is the Kandariya Mahadeva, attributed to Ganda (1017–29). Greatly influenced by the Tantric school of thought, the Chandela kings promoted various Tantric doctrines through royal monuments, including temples. The sculptors of Khajuraho depicted all aspects of life, secular, spiritual and sexual.

The temples of Khajuraho comprise an elevated platform, on which rises the richly decorated building, the 'jangha', covered with sculpted panels. This is crowned by a series of bundled towers with curvilinear contours, the 'sikharas'. Each of these towers, which is characteristic of the temples in the Nagera style, symbolizes the 'cosmic mountain', Mount Kailasha.

◄

Vishwanath Temple at Khajuraho.

World Heritage site since

· 1978 · 1979 · 1980 · 1981 · 1982 · 1983 · 1984 · 1985 · **1986**

Garajonay National Park
Spain

Criteria – Natural phenomena or beauty;
Significant ecological and biological processes

Garajonay contains almost half of the remaining forest in the Canary Islands, including many species considered to be nationally threatened. The park's rich vegetation is maintained by mist, condensed water vapour and the island's numerous streams and springs.

Garajonay National Park is situated in the middle of the island of La Gomera in the Canary Islands archipelago. It consists of an eroded plateau and gently sloping central terrain with steep escarpments running to the park edges. Some 70 per cent of the park is covered by one of the world's largest continuous areas of laurisilva (laurel) forest, a habitat which has almost disappeared from southern Europe and North Africa due to long-term climatic changes. Over 450 floral species have been recorded, of which eighty-one are endemic to the archipelago, thirty-four are endemic to the island, and eight are restricted to the national park. A notable cultural heritage is the whistle language, developed by the local people to communicate over long distances.

Studenica Monastery
Serbia

Criteria – Human creative genius; Interchange of values; Significance in human history; Heritage associated with events of universal significance

Studenica was a central symbol for medieval Serbia – it was the necropolis of the ruling dynasty and the founding-place of the Serbian Orthodox church under St Sava, the youngest son of Stefan Nemanja.

The Studenica Monastery was established in the late twelfth century by Stefan Nemanja, founder of the medieval Serb state, shortly after his abdication. It is the largest and richest of Serbia's Orthodox monasteries. Its two principal monuments, the Church of the Virgin and the Church of the King, both built of white marble, enshrine priceless collections of thirteenth- and fourteenth-century Byzantine painting. The Church of the King houses a cycle of the Life of the Virgin Mary, which is among the leading works of this period. The murals in the Church of the Virgin are characterized by a new concept of space and a new expressiveness, and are an essential milestone in the history not only of Byzantine art, but also of Western art.

Roman Monuments, Cathedral of St Peter and Church of Our Lady in Trier
Germany

Criteria – Human creative genius; Testimony to cultural tradition; Significance in human history; Heritage associated with events of universal significance

Trier, which stands on the Moselle River, was a Roman colony from the first century AD and then became a great trading centre in the next century. It was one of the capitals of the Tetrarchy at the end of the third century, when it was known as the 'second Rome'. The number and quality of the surviving monuments are an outstanding testimony to Roman civilization. The original centre of the colonial town, for the most part built during the reign of Claudius (41–54), had extended so much by the mid-second century that a wall was built and a sandstone and basalt bridge was constructed over the Moselle. The reconstruction of the city was then undertaken by Constantine the Great after 306. The restored amphitheatre and thermae, the Circus maximus, and what remains of an immense imperial palace date from this time.

Some of the major monuments have had long use: for example, the Aula Palatina, where Constantine gave audiences, became the palace of the Frankish counts and then the great hall of the bishop's palace, while Constantine's two basilicas of 326, almost completely reconstructed between the eleventh and thirteenth centuries, became the Cathedral of St Peter and the Church of Our Lady.

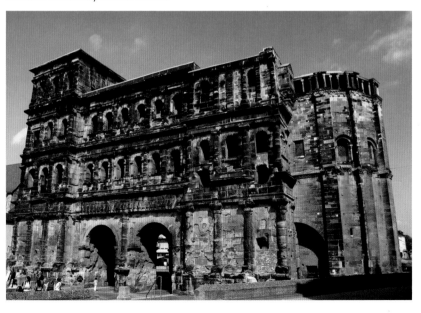

◄
The Porta Nigra viewed from the south (town) side. This was one of four Roman city gates in Trier.

World Heritage site since

· 1978 · 1979 · 1980 · 1981 · 1982 · 1983 · 1984 · 1985 · **1986**

Group of Monuments at Hampi
India

Criteria – Human creative genius; Testimony to cultural tradition; Significance in human history

In one of the interior courtyards of the temple of Vitthala can be found a stone monument of a chariot pulled by two small elephants, a favourite of tourists today as it was of travellers of the past.

The city of Hampi bears exceptional testimony to the vanished civilization of the Hindu kingdom of Vijayanagar, which reached its peak under Krishna Deva Raya (1509–30). Its fabulously rich princes built Dravidian temples and palaces which won the admiration of travellers between the fourteenth and sixteenth centuries. Conquered by the Deccan Muslim confederacy in 1565, the city was pillaged over a period of six months before being abandoned. Hampi, enriched by the cotton and the spice trade, was one of the most beautiful cities of the medieval world. The temples of Ramachandra (1513) and Hazara Rama (1520), with their sophisticated structures, may be counted among the most extraordinary buildings in India. Besides the temples, the impressive complex of civil, princely and public buildings (elephant stables, Queen's Bath, Lotus Mahal, bazaars, markets) are enclosed in the massive fortifications.

Ancient water pool and temple (background) at Krishna market, Hampi. ▼

World Heritage site since

• 1978 • 1979 • 1980 • 1981 • 1982 • 1983 • 1984 • 1985 • **1986**

Old Town of Cáceres
Spain

Criteria – Testimony to cultural tradition;
Significance in human history

When Spanish
adventurers returned
from America in the
sixteenth century,
new palaces were
constructed: Palacio
Godoy, built by a
newly-rich
conquistador and
Palacio de los Toledo-
Moctezuma, built in
the second half of the
sixteenth century for
the grandson of
Moctezuma II, the
Aztec ruler when Cortes
reached Mexico.

Cáceres is an outstanding example of
a feudal city that developed after the
conflicts between the Christians and Moors.
Its history is reflected in its architecture,
which is a blend of Roman, Islamic,
Northern Gothic and Italian Renaissance
styles. Originally a Roman city, the Islamic
Almohads built remarkable fortifications
which completely changed the appearance
of the Roman walls. Of the thirty or so
towers from the Muslim period, the Torre
del Bujaco is the most famous. The street
pattern, with winding backstreets that open
on to tiny squares, also dates from this
period. After the Reconquista, the city
became the stage for power struggles
between rival clans and fortified houses
dotted the landscape. In the fifteenth and
sixteenth centuries, noble pride was
demonstrated by adding richly decorated
coats of arms to the front of houses and by
building many defensive towers.

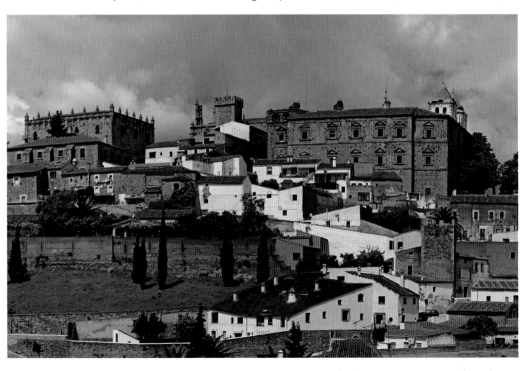

World Heritage site since

• 1978 • 1979 • 1980 • 1981 • 1982 • 1983 • 1984 • 1985 • **1986**

Stonehenge, Avebury and Associated Sites
United Kingdom

Criteria – Human creative genius; Interchange of values; Testimony to cultural tradition

Stonehenge and Avebury are among the most famous groups of megaliths in the world. Together with their associated sites, they represent a masterpiece of human creative genius of the Neolithic age.

The megalithic sites of Stonehenge and Avebury consist of circles of menhirs arranged in a pattern of obvious astronomical significance which is still being explored. However, a number of satellite sites make it possible to better understand the more famous sites by examining them in a broader context.

Stonehenge was built in several distinct phases from 3100–1100 BC and its size, height and perfection make it one of the most impressive megalithic monuments in the world. Its plan was based on a series of concentric circles and the menhirs used are huge: from the third phase of construction onwards, large lintels were placed upon the vertical blocks, thereby creating a type of bonded entablature. The Avenue, an earthwork cut into the chalk soil, runs straight into the northeast corner of Stonehenge.

Avebury lies about 30 km to the north of Stonehenge, and although less well known, it is nevertheless Europe's largest circular megalithic ensemble: its exterior circle

comprises some 100 menhirs. In all, 180 standing stones were put into place here before the beginning of the third millennium BC, as demonstrated by abundant ceramic samples found on the site.

There are four avenues at Avebury of which only the southern one, West Kennet Avenue, is still lined with megaliths; the avenues lead to the four cardinal points of the circle. West Kennet Avenue leads to the site of The Sanctuary at Overton Hill 2.5 km away. The Sanctuary was a series of concentric timber and stone circles; their purpose remains unknown.

There are several other Neolithic satellite sites around Avebury, including Silbury Hill, the largest known man-made earthen mound in Europe. As with The Sanctuary, its purpose is not known. Windmill Hill, a Neolithic causewayed enclosure, is 2 km northwest of Avebury and West Kennet chambered long barrow lies to the south.

Two different materials were used for the Stonehenge constructions: irregular sandstone blocks, known as sarsens, which were quarried in a plain near Salisbury; and bluestones, quarried about 200 km away in Pembrokeshire in Wales.

Although the ritual function of Stonehenge is not known in detail, the cosmic references of its structure appear essential. An old theory is that the site was a sanctuary for worship of the sun. Although there is no unanimous agreement among prehistorians on the subject, Stonehenge nevertheless attracts a folkloric gathering at dawn each Midsummer Day.

World Heritage site since

· 1978 · 1979 · 1980 · 1981 · 1982 · 1983 · 1984 · 1985 · **1986**

Mudéjar Architecture of Aragon
Spain
Criteria – Significance in human history

EUROPE

Atlantic
Ocean
Mediterranean Sea

AFRICA

Tower in Mudéjar
architectural style,
Teruel.
▼

Mudéjar art represents the fusion of two artistic traditions, Islamic and Christian, in the region of Aragon, after the Reconquista of the twelfth century. Present until the early seventeenth century, it is characterized by an extremely refined and inventive use of brick and glazed tiles, especially in the belfries, the most visible element of Mudéjar architecture. The towers of Teruel together form a coherent ensemble which is truly characteristic of Mudéjar art after the Reconquista. The architects of the Christian churches copied the structure and decoration of Almohad minarets, although giving them new functions right from the start. Another typical feature of Mudéjar architecture is found in the painted and decorated wooden ceilings (e.g. Santa María de Mediavilla) of Teruel. Mudéjar architecture is also found in monasteries, castles, and residential buildings.

Mudéjar art continued to predominate over Gothic, except in some minor areas in the south until, in the sixteenth seventeenth centuries the Mudéjars were forced to convert to Christianity, becoming 'new Christians' (Moriscos). This was followed by a period of intolerance, resulting in their expulsion in 1609–10, and the extinction of Mudéjar art.

World Heritage site since

· 1978 · 1979 · 1980 · 1981 · 1982 · 1983 · 1984 · 1985 · **1986**

Khami Ruins National Monument
Zimbabwe

Criteria – Testimony to cultural tradition;
Significance in human history

Khami, which developed after the capital of Great Zimbabwe had been abandoned in the mid-sixteenth century, is of great archaeological interest. It is scattered over more than 2 km, from Passage Ruin to North Ruin. Although located in an area where a human presence can be traced back roughly 100,000 years, the city grew between 1450 and 1650. As is the case in Great Zimbabwe, several sectors can be clearly differentiated in terms of use.

The chief's residence (mambo) is towards the north, on the Hill Ruins site, which is a hill, created largely of earth used to level the terraces, contained by bearing walls. Some highly significant imported goods have been found here: sixteenth century Rhineland stoneware, Ming porcelain pieces which date back to the seventeenth century, Portuguese imitations of Chinese porcelain and seventeenth century Spanish silverware.

The people of Khami lived in huts made from cob (a mixture of earth, sand and straw) surrounded by granite walls. The fences and walls are similar to later constructions at Great Zimbabwe. Worthy of note are the many decorative friezes, with chevron and chequered patterns, and the great number of narrow passageways and galleries.

Castles and Town Walls of King Edward in Gwynedd
United Kingdom

Criteria – Human creative genius; Testimony to cultural tradition; Significance in human history

The castles of Beaumaris and Harlech, largely the work of the greatest military engineer of the time, James of St George, and the fortified complexes of Caernarfon and Conwy are located in the former principality of Gwynedd, in north Wales. These extremely well-preserved monuments are examples of the colonization and defence works carried out throughout the reign of Edward I (1272–1307) and the military architecture of the time.

From 1283, Edward I undertook a castle-building programme of unprecedented scale. In twenty years, ten fortresses were built, not to mention those restored after being wrested from the enemy, creating a strategic and symbolic expression of English power.

◄

Caernarfon castle and battlements along the river Seiont in north Wales.

World Heritage site since

$\cdots\cdots\cdots\cdots\cdots\cdots\cdots\cdots\cdots\cdots$ 1978 • 1979 • 1980 • 1981 • 1982 • 1983 • 1984 • 1985 • **1986**

Historic Centre of Évora
Portugal

Criteria – Interchange of values; Significance in human history

University of The ▶
Holy Spirit in Évora.

Évora is the finest example of a city of the golden age of Portugal after the destruction of Lisbon by the earthquake of 1755. A museum-city whose roots go back to Roman times, it reached its apogee in the fifteenth century when it became the residence of the Portuguese kings. Its unique quality stems from the whitewashed houses decorated with azulejos (ceramic tiles) and wrought-iron balconies dating from the sixteenth to the eighteenth century. The cityscape of Évora demonstrates the influence exerted by Portuguese architecture in Brazil, in sites such as Salvador de Bahia.

Évora has been shaped by some twenty centuries of history, going back to pre-Roman Celtic times. The city fell under Roman domination, when it was called Liberalitas Julia; among other ruins, the Temple of Diana still stands in the town. During the Visigothic period, the Christian city occupied the area surrounded by the Roman wall, which was reworked. Under Moorish domination, which ended in 1165, further improvements were made to the original defensive system as seen in a fortified gate and the remains of the ancient Kasbah. Moreover, place names are indicative of the Maghreb population, which remained after the Reconquest in the La Mouraria quarter of the northeast.

There are a number of buildings from the medieval period, the best known of which is unquestionably the cathedral, begun in 1186 and essentially completed in the thirteenth to fourteenth centuries. It was in the fifteenth century, however, when the Portuguese kings began living in the city on an increasingly regular basis, that Évora's golden age began. Convents and royal palaces sprang up across the city. These splendid monuments, which were either entirely new buildings or else constructed within already existing establishments, are characterized by the Manueline style which survived in the major creations of the sixteenth century, such as the Palace of the Counts of Basto, built on the site of the Alcazar, and the Church of the Knights of Calatrava.

The sixteenth century was a time of major urban planning: the Agua da Prata aqueduct was built in 1537 and many fountains remain from that time. Évora's intellectual and religious influence was also strong: the Jesuits taught at the University of the Holy Spirit from 1553 until their expulsion in 1759, when the city's rapid decline began.

Évora's unique character derives from the coherence of the minor architecture of the sixteenth, seventeenth and eighteenth centuries. This finds its expression in the myriad low, whitewashed, tile-roofed houses, and in the terraces which line the narrow medieval streets of the old city centre and other areas. Wrought iron and azulejo decoration, splendid in the convents and palaces and charming in the most humble dwellings, strengthens the fundamental unity of a type of architecture which is perfectly adapted to the climate and the site.

World Heritage site since

• 1978 • 1979 • 1980 • 1981 • 1982 • 1983 • 1984 • 1985 • **1986**

Gondwana Rainforests of Australia
Australia

Criteria – Major stages of Earth's history;
Significant ecological and biological processes;
Significant natural habitat for biodiversity

This site, comprising approximately forty
separate reserves, is situated predominantly
along the Great Escarpment on Australia's
east coast. The outstanding geological
features displayed around shield volcanic
craters and the 200 rare and threatened
rainforest species are of international
significance for science and conservation.
The evolution of new species is encouraged
by the natural separation and isolation of
rainforest stands. The site includes the most
extensive areas of subtropical rainforest in
the world, large areas of warm temperate
rainforest and almost all of the Antarctic
beech cool temperate rainforest. Although
rainforests cover only about 0.3 per cent of
Australia, they contain about half of all
Australian plant families and about a third of
Australia's mammal and bird species. Many
plants and animals found here are locally
restricted to a few sites or occur in widely
separated populations.

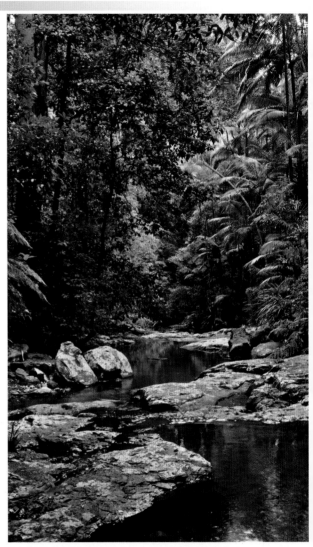

Rainforest near Protestors Falls, Nightcap National Park, ▲
New South Wales.

Few places on Earth contain so many
plants and animals whose ancestors
can be traced through the fossil
record to Gondwanan origins that
today remain relatively unchanged.
There is a concentration of primitive
plant families that shows a direct link
with the origin of flowering plants
over 100 million years ago, as well as
some of the oldest of the world's
ferns and conifers.

World Heritage site since

· 1978 · 1979 · 1980 · 1981 · 1982 · 1983 · 1984 · 1985 · **1986**

Škocjan Caves
Slovenia

Criteria – Natural phenomena or beauty; Major stages of Earth's history

This system of subterranean passages, fashioned by the Reka river, constitutes a dramatic example of large-scale karst drainage. An underground system of passages runs from the Reka's source to Timavo on the Gulf of Trieste in Italy. In places the surfaces of the galleries at several levels have collapsed and give the appearance of deep chasms. The river enters the Škocjan grotto through an underground passage 350 m long, reappearing at the bottom of a chasm 150 m deep and 300 m long, before disappearing into a passage 2 km long. There are five galleries and a canal. A gallery of stalactites and stalagmites leads to the surface. In total there are twenty-five cascades along the river.

The site, located in the Kras region (literally meaning 'karst'), is one of the most famous in the world for the study of karstic phenomena. The protected area extends over 2 km² and includes four deep and picturesque chasms, Sokolak in the south, Globocak in the west, and Lisicina and Sapen dol in the north.

Old Town of Ghadamès
Libya

Criteria – Traditional human settlement

The historic city of Ghadamès, known as 'the pearl of the desert,' is today a small oasis city situated next to a palm grove. It is one of the oldest pre-Saharan cities and an outstanding example of a traditional settlement. Its domestic architecture is characterized by a vertical division of functions: the ground floor was used to store supplies; then came another floor for the family, overhanging covered alleys that create what is almost an underground network of passageways; and at the top were open-air terraces reserved for the women. Roughly circular in layout, the city comprises a cluster of houses. The reinforced outer walls of the houses on the edge of the city form a fortified wall.

The unique layout of this unusual city cannot be perceived as a whole. Ground level passageways form arcades rather than actual streets, and are principally the reserve of the men. At the upper level, women socialize on connected terraces.

World Heritage site since

• 1978 • 1979 • 1980 • 1981 • 1982 • 1983 • 1984 • 1985 • 1986 • **1987**

Archaeological Site of Delphi Greece

Criteria – Human creative genius; Interchange of values; Testimony to cultural tradition; Significance in human history; Heritage associated with events of universal significance

EUROPE

Ionian Sea

Mediterranean Sea

Delphi Tholos. ▶

The development of the sanctuary and oracle began in the eighth century BC when the cult of Apollo was established. The sanctuary had strong religious and political influence across Greece.

The Pythian Games were reorganized and held here from the sixth century BC. At that time the sanctuary was enlarged and enriched with fine buildings, statues and other offerings.

During the Roman period Delphi's fortunes were mixed. As Christianity spread it lost its religious significance and was finally closed down by Emperor Theodosius I in AD 395.

The Pan-Hellenic sanctuary of Delphi, standing in a magnificent natural setting on Mount Parnassus, was the site of the Delphic Oracle through which the god Apollo spoke. Blending harmoniously with the superb landscape and charged with sacred meaning, Delphi in the sixth century BC was both the religious centre and symbol of unity of the ancient Greek world.

The modular elements of the Delphi site – terraces, temples and treasuries – combine to form a strong expression of its physical and moral values. There are several monuments; the following are among the most important.

Temple of Apollo: Dated to the fourth century BC, the temple was erected on the remains of an earlier, sixth-century temple. Inside was the seat of the Pythia, the priestess who presided over the Oracle and delivered the prophesies inspired by Apollo. Delphi was the most important oracle in the Greek world.

Altar of the Chians: The large altar of the sanctuary, in front of the temple, erected in the fifth century BC.

Treasury of the Athenians: A small building in Doric order, built by the Athenians at the end of the sixth century BC to house their offerings to Apollo.

Stoa of the Athenians: Built in the Ionic order, has seven fluted columns, each made from a single stone. According to an inscription, it was built by the Athenians after 478 BC to house the trophies taken in their naval victories over the Persians.

Theatre: Originally built in the fourth century BC, its visible ruins actually date from the Roman imperial period. The theatre was used mostly for the performances during the great festivals.

Stadium: Constructed in the fifth century BC and remodelled in the second century AD at the expense of Herodes Atticus. The Pan-Hellenic Pythian Games, one of the forerunners of the Olympic Games, took place in this stadium.

Tholos: A circular building in Doric order, built around 380 BC (pictured on the right). Although its function is unknown it must have been important, judging from the fine workmanship.

Polygonal Wall: Built after the destruction of the old temple of Apollo in 548 BC to support the terrace on which the new temple was to be erected. Many inscriptions, mostly manumissions of slaves, are carved into its stones.

World Heritage site since

• 1978 • 1979 • 1980 • 1981 • 1982 • 1983 • 1984 • 1985 • 1986 • **1987**

Hawaii Volcanoes National Park
USA

Criteria – Major stages of Earth's history

NORTH AMERICA

Pacific Ocean

Atlantic Ocean

The park extends from the volcanic sea-cliff headlands of the southern coast to the summit calderas of Kilauea, the world's most active volcano, and Mauna Loa. The latter is a massive, flat-domed shield volcano built by lava flow layers and is considered to be the best example of its type in the world, extending from 5,581 m below sea level to 4,170 m above.

Two of the most active volcanoes in the world, Mauna Loa (4,170 m) and Kilauea (1,250 m), tower over the Pacific Ocean at this site where volcanic eruptions have created a constantly changing landscape.

Climate varies with altitude from tropical humid to alpine desert and the park contains a high diversity of plant communities with striking life-form and physiognomic differences. There are twenty-three distinct vegetation types, grouped into five major ecosystems: subalpine, montane seasonal, montane rainforest, submontane seasonal and coastal lowlands.

Except for a single species of Hawaiian hoary bat, the park has no native mammals and most endemic birds are rare or endangered. Ranching and the introduction of species such as the pig, goat and mongoose have had serious biological consequences, including destruction of native ecosystems and widespread extinction of endemic species.

◄

Part of the volcanic shelf collapsed into the ocean five days after this photograph was taken in November 2005.

World Heritage site since

• 1978 • 1979 • 1980 • 1981 • 1982 • 1983 • 1984 • 1985 • 1986 • **1987**

Piazza del Duomo, Pisa
Italy

Criteria – Human creative genius; Interchange of values; Significance in human history; Heritage associated with events of universal significance

The world-famous monuments of the Piazza del Duomo are masterpieces of medieval architecture. The cathedral, its baptistry, its campanile – the Leaning Tower – and its walled cemetery, had a huge influence on monumental art in medieval Italy.

The huge marble-and-stone cathedral has been identified as the best example of Pisan Romanesque style. Work began in 1064 and was completed in the twelfth century. The cathedral is in the shape of a Latin cross, with five naves. Its Romanesque baptistry, with a pulpit by the sculptor Nicola Pisano, was completed in 1363. The cathedral's famous leaning bell tower began subsiding soon after construction began in 1173. War meant it remained unfinished until almost 200 years later.

The monumental cemetery was virtually destroyed by Allied bombing during the Second World War but has since been restored to its original state.

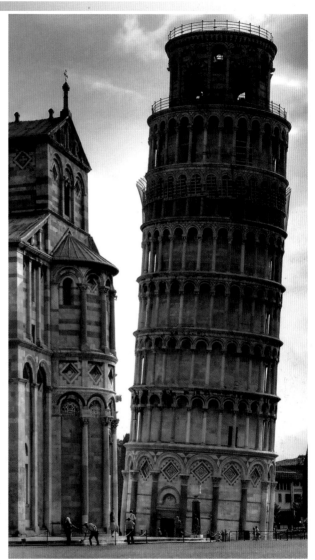

Cathedral and its campanile (the Leaning Tower). ▲

Pisa was an ancient port and one of Italy's four wealthy Maritime Republics, powerful trading city-states. Its enormous wealth meant the city flourished until commercial rivalry and war precipitated a decline in the late thirteenth century. In the cathedral hangs the bronze lamp of Possenti da Pietrasanta; its swinging was said to have inspired Galileo's discovery of the principle of isochronism.

World Heritage site since

· 1978 · 1979 · 1980 · 1981 · 1982 · 1983 · 1984 · 1985 · 1986 · **1987**

Cathedral, Alcázar and Archivo de Indias in Seville
Spain

Criteria – Human creative genius; Interchange of values; Testimony to cultural tradition; Heritage associated with events of universal significance

These three buildings in the heart of Seville together form a remarkable monumental complex. The cathedral and Alcázar date from the Reconquista, the recapture from the Moors of the Iberian peninsula, and reflect elements of the civilizations of the Berber Almohads and of Christian Andalusia. Begun in the late sixteenth century, the Casa Lonja was intended as a Trades Hall but by the 1790s it had become the Archivo General de Indias, housing

collections of documents of the Spanish overseas empire.

The cathedral, the largest Gothic cathedral in the world (pictured below), houses the tomb of Christopher Columbus. The Alcázar is a palatial fortress first built in 712 by the conquering Arabs. After the Spanish retook Seville in 1248 it became a Spanish royal residence.

The cathedral reflects a chequered history in its complex structure. The capitals of several columns in one area date from the time of the Visigoths; these represent the last vestiges of the original cathedral which Seville's Arab conquerors destroyed in 712. The Great Mosque they built in the twelfth century was itself built over, although the spectacular Giralda minaret remains.

View of the cathedral from the Giralda tower. ▼

World Heritage site since

· 1978 • 1979 • 1980 • 1981 • 1982 • 1983 • 1984 • 1985 • 1986 • **1987**

Sian Ka'an
Mexico

Criteria – Natural phenomena or beauty;
Significant natural habitat for biodiversity

This biosphere reserve on the east coast of the Yucatán peninsula contains tropical forests, mangroves, marshes and a large marine section intersected by a barrier reef. The complex hydrological system provides a habitat for a rich flora and a fauna comprising more than 300 species of birds and a large number of the region's characteristic terrestrial vertebrates.

Sian Ka'an lies on a partially emerged coastal limestone plain which forms part of the extensive barrier-reef system along Central America's east coast. The hydrological cycle is complex and the water table is permanently close to the surface although shallow limestone soils mean that there is little surface running water within the reserve.

There are an estimated 1,200 plant species. In the medium and low semi-deciduous forest, abundance of palm is a characteristic feature. Coastal dunes stretch along 64 km of the coast.

The area has 103 types of mammal including jaguar, puma, ocelot, margay and jaguarondi; Central American tapir and red brocket; spider monkey and howler monkey; kinkajou, collared anteater and Caribbean manatee. Some 339 bird and 42 amphibian and reptile species have been recorded as well as over 52 types of fish, which are abundant.

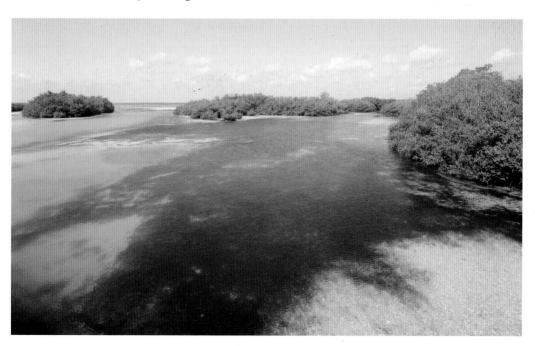

World Heritage site since

• 1978 • 1979 • 1980 • 1981 • 1982 • 1983 • 1984 • 1985 • 1986 • **1987**

Venice and its Lagoon
Italy

Criteria – Human creative genius; Interchange of values; Testimony to cultural tradition; Significance in human history; Traditional human settlement; Heritage associated with events of universal significance

Venice is a unique artistic achievement: built on 118 small islands, the city seems to float on the waters of the Venetian Lagoon. Venice possesses an incomparable series of architectural ensembles that collectively illustrate the longevity of its splendour.

Standing in this inland sea on a tiny archipelago at the very edge of the waves, Venice is one of the most extraordinary built-up areas of the Middle Ages. From Torcello in the north to Chioggia in the south, almost every small island had its own settlement. In the centre of the 50,000-km² lagoon, Venice stood as one of the greatest capitals in the medieval world.

In the fifth century AD, Venetian populations fleeing hostile invaders first found refuge on the sandy islands of Torcello, Iesolo and Malamocco. What had begun as temporary settlements gradually became permanent and the one-time refuge of land-dwelling peasants and fishermen grew into one of the world's foremost maritime powers.

Venetian power grew steadily from the twelfth to the fifteenth century. The independent city-state was one of the four Italian Maritime Republics and from its strategically crucial position at the head of the Adriatic Sea, Venice controlled the length of the eastern Mediterranean to the Ionian Sea. This control allowed Venice to dominate trade between Europe and the Byzantine Empire and the Near East, including the Crusader States. In 1204, led by its ruler, the Doge Enrico Dàndolo, Venice allied with the Crusaders to loot Constantinople. Among the abundant spoils brought back were the bronze horses that still stand over the entrance to St Mark's Cathedral.

With the development of overseas empires in the fifteenth century and the expansion of the Turkish Ottoman Empire into Byzantium, the balances of power on which Venice's wealth was built began to change, and the city's long decline began. It finally lost its independence to Napoleon in 1797, after which many of its palaces and notable buildings fell into disrepair.

The influence of Venice on the development of architecture and monumental arts has been considerable. The fabulous wealth that its trading empire brought is reflected in the scale and grandeur of its beautiful buildings and monuments. The city has been inspiration to some of the world's greatest artists, including Canaletto, Giorgione, Titian, Tintoretto and Veronese.

Part of the Grand Canal and one of the numerous side canals that dissect the city. ▶

The islands of the Comune of Venice are grouped around the historic city at its centre. Transport and communication in this necessarily car-free area is by water. Canals – such as the Giudecca Canal, St Mark's Canal and the Grand Canal – and the network of rii, or rivers, are the arteries of the city. In this unreal space where there is no notion of the concept of terra firma, masterpieces of one of the most extraordinary architectural museums on Earth have been accumulated for over 1,000 years.

World Heritage site since

• 1978 • 1979 • 1980 • 1981 • 1982 • 1983 • 1984 • 1985 • 1986 • **1987**

Blenheim Palace
United Kingdom

Criteria – Interchange of values; Significance in human history

Blenheim Palace and park illustrate the beginnings of the English Romantic movement, characterized by the eclecticism of its inspiration, its return to national sources and its love of nature. The influence of Blenheim on the architecture and the organization of space in the eighteenth and nineteenth centuries was greatly felt both in England and abroad.

Situated near Oxford, Blenheim Palace stands in an 8.5-km² romantic park created by the famous landscape gardener Lancelot 'Capability' Brown. It was presented by the English nation to John Churchill, first Duke of Marlborough, in recognition of his victory in 1704 over French and Bavarian troops at the Battle of Blenheim. Built by John Vanbrugh and Nicholas Hawksmoor between 1705 and 1722, it is a perfect example of an eighteenth-century princely dwelling.

Between 1764 and 1774 'Capability' Brown, one of the most famous English landscape gardeners, turned the classical park laid out by Vanbrugh into a wonderful artificial landscape by the creation of two lakes. In the later eighteenth century, Gothic or neo-Gothic style buildings were added.

The British Prime Minister Winston Churchill was born in the palace in 1874.

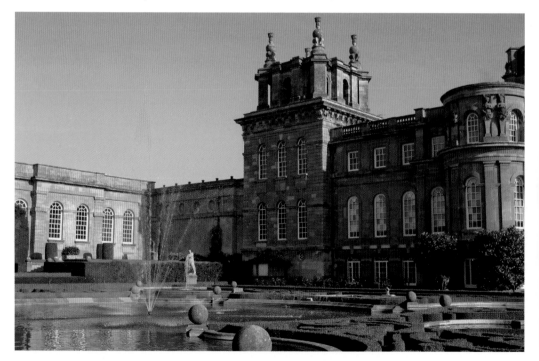

Sundarbans National Park
India

Criteria – Significant ecological and biological processes; Significant natural habitat for biodiversity

The Sundarbans covers 10,000 km² of land and water in the Ganges delta, more than half of it in India, the rest in Bangladesh . It contains the world's largest area of mangrove forests. A number of rare or endangered species live in the park, including tigers, aquatic mammals, birds and reptiles.

The Sundarban waterways now carry little freshwater as the outflow of the Ganges has shifted progressively eastwards since the seventeenth century. This is due to subsidence of the Bengal Basin and a gradual eastward tilting of the overlying crust. Waterways in the tiger reserve are maintained largely by the diurnal tidal flow.

Elephanta Caves
India

Criteria – Human creative genius; Testimony to cultural tradition

The 'City of Caves', consists of seven caves on an island in the Arabian Sea close to Mumbai. With their decorated temples and images from Hindu mythology, they bear a unique testimony to a civilisation that has disappeared and are one of the most striking collections of rock art in India. There are two groups of caves, dating from the sixth – eighth centuries AD. To the east, Stupa Hill (named after the small brick Buddhist monument at the top) contains two caves, one of which is unfinished, and several cisterns. To the west, the larger group consists of five rock-cut Hindu shrines. The main cave is universally famous for its huge high reliefs to the glory of Shiva, who is exalted in various forms and actions.

The island of Elephanta owes its name to the enormous stone elephant found there by Portuguese navigators. This elephant was cut into pieces, removed to Mumbai and somehow put together again. It is today the melancholy guardian of Victoria Gardens Zoo in Mumbai.

◄
Entrance to the secondary cave on Elephanta Island.

World Heritage site since

· 1978 · 1979 · 1980 · 1981 · 1982 · 1983 · 1984 · 1985 · 1986 · **1987**

Palace of Westminster and Westminster Abbey including Saint Margaret's Church
United Kingdom

Criteria – Human creative genius; Interchange of values; Significance in human history

The Palace of Westminster is the home of the Houses of Parliament and is an outstanding and complete example of neo-Gothic architecture. The site includes the medieval church of Saint Margaret and Westminster Abbey, where all England's sovereigns have been crowned since the eleventh century, and is of great historic and symbolic significance.

The construction of a new Palace of Westminster by Barry and Pugin began in 1835 after fire destroyed its predecessor. The seat of Parliament, which includes the House of Lords to the south of a central tower and the House of Commons to the north, illustrates in colossal proportions the grandeur of the constitutional monarchy and the principle of the bicameral system.

The site includes Westminster Abbey, a unique construction representing the successive phases of English Gothic architecture and, in the abbey grounds, the charming Perpendicular Gothic church of St Margaret. Rebuilt and remodelled since the fifteenth century, St Margaret's is the Anglican parish church of the House of Commons.

The new Palace of Westminster, with the magnificent interiors of the Royal Gallery, House of Lords, Central Lobby, House of Commons, library, and apartments is a vivid symbol of one of the oldest parliamentary institutions in the world. Its façade, situated along the river Thames, is 266m long; the Victoria Tower which holds three million archival documents is to the south, and the Clock Tower (Big Ben) to the north.

World Heritage site since

· 1978 • 1979 • 1980 • 1981 • 1982 • 1983 • 1984 • 1985 • 1986 • **1987**

Frontiers of the Roman Empire
United Kingdom and Germany

Criteria – Interchange of values; Testimony to cultural tradition; Significance in human history

The Roman Limes or frontier represents the border line of the Roman Empire at its greatest extent in the second century AD.

The two sections in Germany cover a length of 550 km from the northwest of the country to the Danube in the southeast. The 118 km-long Hadrian's Wall in northern England was built on the orders of the Emperor Hadrian around AD 122 at what were then the northernmost limits of the Roman province of Britannia. It is a striking example of the organization of a military zone and illustrates the defensive techniques and geopolitical strategies of ancient Rome.

The 60-km-long Antonine Wall, across central Scotland, was started by Emperor Antoninus Pius in AD 142 as a defence against the "barbarians" of the north and represents the most northerly frontier of the Roman Empire.

The remains of the limes today consist of vestiges of built walls, ditches, forts, fortresses, watchtowers and civilian settlements. Certain elements of the line have been excavated, some reconstructed and a few destroyed.

The Roman Empire stretched over 5,000 km from the Atlantic coast of Britain through Europe to the Black Sea, and from there to the Red Sea and across North Africa.

The physical remains of the limes – walls, earthworks, forts, watchtowers, settlements, and the hinterland dependent on the frontier – illustrate the complexities of Roman culture and its unifying character.

Hadrian's Wall, Northumberland, UK. ▼

Budapest, including the Banks of the Danube, the Buda Castle Quarter and Andrássy Avenue

Hungary

Criteria – Interchange of values; Significance in human history

EUROPE

Adriatic Sea

Black Sea

The Danube River at ► dusk with W.T. Clark's suspension bridge (foreground) and the Hungarian Houses of Parliament on the far riverbank.

Budapest is one of the world's outstanding urban landscapes and illustrates in its architecture the great periods in the history of the Hungarian capital. It has the remains of monuments from various periods, such as the Roman Fort of Contra Aquincum and the Gothic castle of Buda, which have had a considerable influence on the architecture.

Within the unified perspective of an immense urban panorama, the Danube is the dividing line between what were originally two cities: Buda on the spur on the right bank, and Pest in the plain on the left bank. Human occupation can be traced back to the Palaeolithic period, but the city's historic importance dates from the Roman period when it was part of Lower Pannonia, a border province of the Empire in the second century AD.

After the Hungarian invasion in the ninth century, Pest became the first medieval urban centre, only to be devastated by Mongol raids in 1241–2. A few years later Bela IV built the castle of Buda on the right bank and the inhabitants of Pest found shelter within its fortified outer walls. Buda Castle played an essential role in the diffusion of Gothic art in the Magyar region from the fourteenth century.

Buda's history became closely identified with that of the Hungarian monarchy and the city followed its changing fortunes. Two centuries of ascendancy from 1308 to the 1490s and beyond were ended when the Turks ransacked the city in 1526, precipitating its final fall in 1541. Recovery did not really begin again until the eighteenth century.

In the nineteenth century the city's role as capital was enhanced by the foundation of the Hungarian Academy (1830) and especially by the construction of the imposing neo-Gothic Parliament building (1884–1904). The parliament (pictured on the right) is an outstanding example of a great official building on a par with those of London, Munich, Vienna and Athens. It exemplifies the eclectic architecture of the nineteenth century while symbolizing the political function of the second capital of the Austro-Hungarian monarchy. Since 1849, W. T. Clark's suspension bridge over the Danube has symbolized the reunification of Buda and Pest, which did not become official until 1873. With this union, Budapest truly became the nation's capital.

With no attempts made at organized urban development since the Middle Ages, the Hungarian capital caught up in one great leap in respect of public services, transportation and city planning. The route of Andrássy Avenue cut straight through an unregulated suburban area, thereby radically transforming its urban structure. The Siemens and Halske companies built the first underground railway on the European continent there between 1893 and 1896, which in turn led to the construction of more city monuments.

World Heritage site since

• 1978 • 1979 • 1980 • 1981 • 1982 • 1983 • 1984 • 1985 • 1986 • **1987**

Great Living Chola Temples
India

Criteria – Interchange of values; Testimony to
cultural tradition

The great temple of
Thanjavur was built in
a few years, from
1003–10, during the
reign of the great king
Rajaraja (985–1014).
Richly endowed by the
sovereign, the
sanctuary had a
permanent staff of
several hundred
priests, 400 sacred
dancers and fifty-
seven musicians,
according to
inscriptions and
chronicles.

The Great Chola Temples of southern India
are an exceptional testimony to the
architecture and ideology of the Chola
Empire and the Tamil civilization in
southern India. The site includes three great
eleventh- and twelfth-century temples: the
Brihadisvara Temple at Thanjavur (Tanjore),
the Brihadisvara Temple at
Gangaikondacholisvaram and the
Airavatesvara Temple at Darasuram. The
Temple of Gangaikondacholisvaram, built

by Rajendra I, was completed in 1035.
Its 53m vimana sanctum tower has recessed
corners and a graceful upward curving
movement, contrasting with the straight
and severe tower at Thanjavur. The
Airavatesvara temple complex at
Darasuram, built by Rajaraja II, features a
24m vimana and a stone image of Shiva. The
temples testify to the brilliant achievements
of the Chola in architecture, sculpture,
painting and bronze casting.

The Temple of Gangai-
kondacholisvaram.
▼

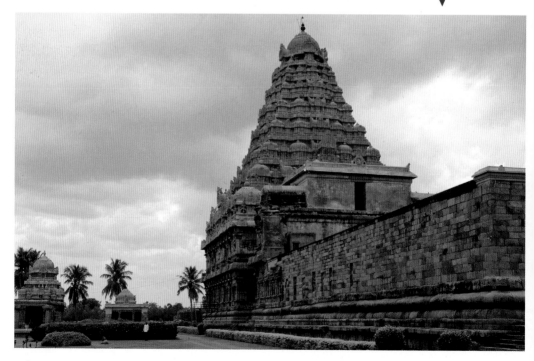

World Heritage site since

· 1978 · 1979 · 1980 · 1981 · 1982 · 1983 · 1984 · 1985 · 1986 · **1987**

Imperial Palaces of the Ming and Qing Dynasties in Beijing and Shenyang
China

Criteria – Human creative genius; Interchange of values; Testimony to cultural tradition; Significance in human history

The Imperial Palaces illustrate the grandeur of the imperial institution in China from the Qing dynasty to the earlier Ming and Yuan dynasties. Seat of supreme power for five centuries (1416–1911), the Forbidden City in Beijing, with its landscaped gardens and many magnificent buildings containing nearly 10,000 rooms, constitutes a priceless testimony to Chinese civilization. Lying to the north of Tiananmen Square, the Forbidden City (pictured below), was the Imperial Palace during the Ming and Qing dynasties. Now known as the Palace Museum, it is the world's largest palace complex. The Imperial Palace of the Qing Dynasty in Shenyang consists of 114 buildings constructed between 1625 and 1636. It contains an important library and offers invaluable historical testimony to the history of the Qing Dynasty and the cultural traditions of the Manchu and other tribes in the north of China.

The Forbidden City is an extremely formal place: it is almost symmetrical and hierarchically arranged so that all the important buildings run down the centre, north-south. In keeping with geomancy, the main gate is in the south and the northern side is 'protected' by the artificial Coal Hill.

▼

World Heritage site since

· 1978 · 1979 · 1980 · 1981 · 1982 · 1983 · 1984 · 1985 · 1986 · 1987

Kilimanjaro National Park
Tanzania
Criteria – Natural phenomena or beauty

The area around the mountain is quite heavily populated, principally by the Chagga people, and the northern and western slopes of the forest reserve surrounding the national park have eighteen medium-to-large forest villages. Although it is illegal, these people use the forest for many household and medicinal products, for fuelwood, small-scale farming, beekeeping, hunting, charcoal production and logging.

Some 12 per cent of the forest is plantation, some of which almost reaches down to the moorland.

At 5,895 m, the volcanic massif of Mount Kilimanjaro is the highest point in Africa. It stands in splendid isolation above the surrounding plains, encircled by mountain forest, its snowy peak looming over the savanna. Numerous mammals, many of them endangered, live in the park.

The national park and forest reserve occupy the upper part of Kilimanjaro adjacent to the Kenyan border. The national park comprises all the mountain above the timberline and six forest corridors stretching down through the montane forest belt. Kilimanjaro, one of the largest volcanoes in the world, last showed signs of major activity in the Pleistocene period (between 1.8 million and 10,000 years ago). It stands alone but is the largest of an east-west belt of volcanoes stretching across northern Tanzania. It has three main volcanic peaks of varying ages, Shira, Mawenzi and Kibo, and a number of smaller parasitic cones.

Kilimanjaro has five main vegetation zones: savanna bushland at 700–1,000 m (on the south slopes) 1,400–1,600 m (on the north slopes) and densely populated submontane agroforest on southern and southeastern slopes, the montane forest belt, subalpine moorland and alpine bogs. Above this is alpine desert.

The montane forest belt circles the mountain between 1,300 m (about 1,600 m on the drier north slopes) to 2,800 m. Forests above 2,700 m are within the national park. According to a 2001 study there are 2,500 plant species on the mountain, 1,600 of them on the southern slopes and 900 within the forest belt. There are 130 species of tree, with the greatest diversity being found between 1,800 and 2,000 m.

The whole mountain including the montane forest belt, part of which extends into the national park, is very rich in animal life: there are 140 mammals (eighty-seven forest species), including seven primates, twenty-five carnivores, twenty-five antelopes and twenty-four species of bat. Above the timberline at least seven of the larger mammal species have been recorded, although it is likely that many of these also use the lower montane forest habitat.

Although 179 highland bird species have been recorded on the mountain, species recorded in the upper zones are few in number. The white-necked raven is the most conspicuous bird species at higher altitudes.

Brasilia
Brazil

Criteria – Human creative genius; Significance in human history

Brasilia, a capital created ex nihilo in the centre of the country in 1956, was a landmark in the history of town planning. Urban planner Lucio Costa and architect Oscar Niemeyer intended that every element – from the layout of the residential and administrative districts (often compared to the shape of a bird in flight) to the symmetry of the buildings themselves – should be in harmony with the city's overall design. The curving north-south axis of the city forms a wide transportation artery, along which are situated the residential zones, each with its own commercial and leisure centres, green spaces, schools, churches, etc. The perpendicular east-west axis, known as the Monumental Axis, links the administrative sections of the new city and is where Niemeyer's most renowned edifices were built.

The 'pilot plan' that Costa drew up for Brasilia consisted of a cross formed by two bars intersecting at right angles. This figure was then adapted to the topography of the land and its orientation improved by curving the arms of one of the crossbars. Brasilia became the official capital of the country in 1960.

National cathedral and museum.
▼

Hanseatic City of Lübeck
Germany
Criteria – Significance in human history

North Sea

Baltic Sea

EUROPE

Lübeck – the former capital and Queen City of the Hanseatic League – was founded in the twelfth century and prospered until the sixteeenth century as the major trading centre for northern Europe. It has remained a centre for maritime commerce to this day, particularly with the Nordic countries. Despite the damage it suffered during the Second World War, the basic structure of the old city, consisting mainly of fifteenth- and sixteenth-century patrician residences,

public monuments, the famous Holstentor brick gate (pictured below), churches and salt storehouses, remains unaltered. The plan of Lübeck, with its blade-like outline determined by two parallel traffic routes, dates to the beginnings of the site. To the west lay the richest quarters with the trading houses and the homes of the merchants and to the east were small traders and artisans.

Almost 20 per cent of the city was destroyed during the Second World War, including the cathedral, the churches of St Peter and St Mary, and especially the Gründungsviertel, the hilltop quarter where the gabled houses of the rich merchants clustered. Selective reconstruction has permitted the replacement of the most important churches and monuments.

Holstentor brick gate. ▼

World Heritage site since

• 1978 • 1979 • 1980 • 1981 • 1982 • 1983 • 1984 • 1985 • 1986 • **1987**

Acropolis, Athens
Greece

Criteria – Human creative genius; Interchange
of values; Testimony to cultural tradition;
Significance in human history; Heritage
associated with events of universal significance

EUROPE

Ionian
Sea

Mediterranean Sea

The Acropolis of
Athens (**pictured right**)
and its monuments
are universal symbols
of the classical spirit
and civilization, and
form the greatest
architectural and
artistic complex of
Greek antiquity.

The Athenian Acropolis is the supreme
expression of the adaptation of architecture
to a natural site, a unique series of public
monuments built and conserved in one of
the densest spaces of the Mediterranean.
This grand composition of perfectly
balanced massive structures creates a
monumental landscape of unique beauty
consisting of a complete series of
masterpieces of the fifth century BC. The
monuments of the Acropolis have exerted
an exceptional influence, not only in
Graeco-Roman antiquity, a time in the
Mediterranean world when they were
considered exemplary models, but also in
contemporary times.

In the later fifth century BC, Athens
followed its victory against the Persians and
the establishment of democracy by taking a
leading position among the other city-states
of the ancient world. In the age that
followed, as philosophy and art flourished,
an exceptional group of artists put into
effect the ambitious plans of Athenian
statesman Pericles and, under the inspired
guidance of the sculptor Pheidias,
transformed the rocky hill of the Acropolis
into a unique monument of thought and
the arts.

The years from 447–406 BC saw the
successive building of the Parthenon

(pictured on the right), the main temple
dedicated to Athena; the Propylaea, the
monumental entrance to the Acropolis built
on the site of one of the entrances to the
citadel of the ancient kings; the temple of
Athena Nike; and the Erechtheion – the four
masterpieces of classical Greek art.

The sacred hill of Athens was protected
throughout the period of Roman
domination until the Herulian raid in AD 267.
Since then and despite long periods of
relative calm, the monuments and site have
been damaged many times.

The Byzantines converted the temples into
churches and removed their art treasures to
Constantinople. After the Byzantine Empire
fell in 1204, Athens was put into the hands of
Frankish lords who had little respect for its
ruins. When the Turks took the city in 1456, it
became a mosque and the Erechtheion was
the occasional harem of the Turkish
governor. In 1687 the siege of the Acropolis
by Venetian armies resulted in the explosion
of the Parthenon, used as the Turks' powder
magazine. Finally in the nineteenth century,
the British ambassador Lord Elgin pillaged
the marble sections which since 1815 have
been in the British Museum.

The Acropolis stands
on a rocky
promontory 156 m
above the Ilissos valley
and covers an area of
less than 30,000 m².
From the third
millennium BC it was
a fortress protecting
places of worship and
royal palaces.

The Acropolis is now
a testing ground for
innovative open-air
conservation
techniques aimed at
safeguarding the
marble sections which
are being affected by
pollution.

World Heritage site since

• 1978 • 1979 • 1980 • 1981 • 1982 • 1983 • 1984 • 1985 • 1986 • **1987**

Historic Centre of Mexico City and Xochimilco
Mexico

Criteria – Interchange of values; Testimony to cultural tradition; Significance in human history; Traditional human settlement

Mexico City was built in the sixteenth century by the Spanish on the ruins of Tenochtitlan, the old Aztec capital. It has the largest cathedral in the Americas and fine nineteenth- and twentieth-century buildings such as the Palacio de las Bellas Artes. Templo Mayor was one of the main Aztec temples in Tenochtitlan. Construction started in 1390 and it may have been rebuilt up to six times on top of the original until destroyed by the Spanish in 1521.

Xochimilco lies 28 km south of Mexico City. With its network of canals and artificial islands, it testifies to the efforts of the Aztec people to build a habitat in the midst of an unfavourable environment. Its characteristic urban and rural structures, built since the sixteenth century and during the colonial period, have been preserved in an exceptional manner.

The value of these two properties is unequalled. The historic centre of Mexico City includes the archaeological site of Templo Mayor with its remarkable array of colonial monuments and famous cathedral. The lakeside area of Xochimilco still features some chinampas, the floating gardens that the Spanish so admired.

Historic Centre of Puebla
Mexico

Criteria – Interchange of values; Significance in human history

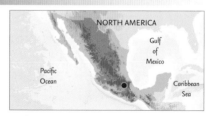

Puebla, which was founded ex nihilo in 1531, is situated about 100 km east of Mexico City, at the foot of the Popocatepetl volcano. It was the first city in central Mexico founded by the Spanish conquerors that was not built upon the ruins of a conquered Amerindian settlement. On 5 May 1862, it was in Puebla that General Zaragoza won the first significant victory over the French expeditionary corps. The city was subsequently renamed Puebla de Zaragoza in memory of this event of national

importance. It has preserved its great religious structures such as the sixteenth–seventeenth-century cathedral and fine buildings such as the old archbishop's palace, as well as a host of houses with walls covered in tiles (azulejos). The new aesthetic concepts resulting from the fusion of European and American styles were adopted locally and are peculiar to the Baroque district of Puebla.

The Historic Centre of Puebla comprises major religious buildings such as the Cathedral of Santo Domingo and the Jesuit Church, as well as superb palaces. Nineteenth-century transformations of the urban landscape have further endowed Puebla with high-quality public and private architecture.

World Heritage site since

• 1978 • 1979 • 1980 • 1981 • 1982 • 1983 • 1984 • 1985 • 1986 • **1987**

Chaco Culture
USA

Criteria – Testimony to cultural tradition

For over 2,000 years, Pueblo peoples occupied a vast region of the southwestern United States. Chaco Canyon is the area with the highest concentration of archaeological sites of the whole zone. Chaco society is characterized by an elaborate ground occupation system, which includes a constellation of towns surrounded by satellite villages and linked by a road network. The Chaco people combined pre-planned architectural designs, astronomical alignments, geometry, landscaping and engineering to create an ancient urban centre of spectacular public architecture. It became a major centre of ancestral Pueblo culture between 850 and 1250, and was a focus for ceremonials, trade and political activity for the prehistoric Four Corners area. In addition to the Chaco Culture National Historical Park, the World Heritage property includes the Aztec Ruins National Monument and several smaller Chaco sites.

Between the twelfth and thirteenth centuries the Chaco population died out and the pueblos were abandoned. After 1250, the people migrated from the area, moving south, east and west. The region remained practically uninhabited until the seventeenth century, when it was taken over by Navajo Indians.

◄
Pueblo village ruins, including a 'kiva' – an underground/partially underground chamber used by the men especially for ceremonies or councils.

Historic Centre of Oaxaca and Archaeological Site of Monte Albán
Mexico

Criteria – *Human creative genius; Interchange of values; Testimony to cultural tradition; Significance in human history*

NORTH AMERICA

Pacific Ocean

Caribbean Sea

Pre-Hispanic archaeological site of Monte Albán. ▶

The modern city of Oaxaca has retained its historic centre. The major religious monuments, the superb patrician town houses (including the house of conquistador Hernán Cortés) and whole streets lined with other dwellings combine to create a harmonious cityscape and reconstitute the image of a former colonial city whose monumental aspect has been kept intact.

Near Oaxaca is the birthplace of Benito Juárez, the first indigenous president of Mexico and a national hero. On his death in 1872, the city formally took the name of Oaxaca de Juárez.

Three distinct cultural properties stand in the Oaxaca valley: the historic centre of the city founded in 1529 by the Spanish; the pre-Hispanic archaeological site of Monte Albán; and the village of Cuilapan, where the Dominicans built a vast monastery in the mid-sixteenth century.

Monte Albán is an outstanding example of a pre-Columbian ceremonial centre. It stands in the middle zone of present-day Mexico which was subjected to influences from the north – first from Teotihuacan and later the Aztecs – and from the Maya from the south. With its pelota court, magnificent temples, tombs and bas-reliefs with hieroglyphic inscriptions, Monte Albán bears unique testimony to the successive civilizations occupying the region during the pre-Classic and Classic periods that stretched from around 1800 BC to AD 900. For more than a millennium it exerted considerable influence on the whole cultural area.

Among some 200 pre-Hispanic archaeological sites inventoried in the valley of Oaxaca, the Monte Albán complex best represents the singular evolution of a region inhabited by a succession of peoples: the Olmecs, Zapotecs and Mixtecs.

Monte Albán was literally carved out from a solid mountain, in various stages spanning 1,500 years. Man-made terraces and esplanades replaced the natural unevenness of the site with a whole new sacred topography of pyramids, and artificial knolls and mounds. The ensemble began to decline around 800 when the Mixtecs, descending from the mountains, threatened the Zapotecs living in the valley.

A short time before the arrival of the Spanish conquistadores, the Aztecs took control of the valley and founded the stronghold of Huaxyacac. This place name survived, when in 1521 the Spanish erected the fort of Antequera de Oaxaca on the same site.

Oaxaca is built on a grid pattern and is a good example of Spanish colonial town planning. Its monumental heritage is one of the richest and most coherent in the area that was known as New Spain. The solidity and volume of the city's buildings show that these architectural gems were adapted to the earthquake-prone region in which they were constructed.

The Cuilapan Convent, 10 km to the south, was founded in 1555. Its roofless, open-air church was never finished.

World Heritage site since

• 1978 • 1979 • 1980 • 1981 • 1982 • 1983 • 1984 • 1985 • 1986 • **1987**

Pre-Hispanic City of Teotihuacan
Mexico

Criteria – Human creative genius; Interchange of values; Testimony to cultural tradition; Significance in human history; Heritage associated with events of universal significance

The location of the first sanctuary, the Pyramid of the Sun (built on a cave discovered in 1971), was calculated on the position of the sun at its zenith, and astronomical calculations determined the organization of the space: the Avenue of the Dead was drawn out perpendicularly to the principal axis of the solar temple.

Located 48 km northeast of Mexico City, the holy city of Teotihuacan ('the place where the gods were created') is one of the oldest known archaeological sites in Mexico. Built between the first and seventh centuries AD, it is characterized by the vast size of its sacred monuments, which were laid out on geometric and symbolic principles. Lining the immense Avenue of the Dead, this unique group of monuments and places of worship (Pyramids of the Sun, the Moon and Quetzalcoatl, and Palaces of Quetzalmariposa, Jaguars, Yayahuala and others) constitutes an outstanding example of a pre-Columbian ceremonial centre. As one of the most powerful cultural centres in Mesoamerica, Teotihuacan extended its cultural and artistic influence throughout the region and beyond.

World Heritage site since

• 1978 • 1979 • 1980 • 1981 • 1982 • 1983 • 1984 • 1985 • 1986 • **1987**

City of Potosí
Bolivia

Criteria – Interchange of values; Significance in human history; Heritage associated with events of universal significance

Pacific
Ocean

Atlantic
Ocean

The 'Imperial City' of Potosí, which it became following the visit of Francisco de Toledo in 1572, exerted lasting influence on the development of architecture and monumental arts in the central region of the Andes by spreading the forms of a Baroque style incorporating Indian influence.

Potosí owes its importance to the discovery, between 1542 and 1545, of the New World's biggest silver lodes in the Cerro de Potosí, the mountain south of the city and which overlooks it. As a result it quickly became the world's largest industrial complex, with the extraction of silver ore relying on a series of hydraulic mills. The site consists of the industrial monuments of the Cerro Rico, where water is provided by an intricate system of aqueducts and artificial lakes; the colonial town with the Casa de la Moneda; the Church of San Lorenzo; several patrician houses; and the barrios mitayos, the areas where the workers lived. Production continued until the nineteenth century, slowing down only after the country's independence in 1825.

World Heritage site since

• 1978 • 1979 • 1980 • 1981 • 1982 • 1983 • 1984 • 1985 • 1986 • **1987**

City of Bath
United Kingdom

Criteria – Human creative genius; Interchange
of values; Significance in human history

Founded by the Romans as a thermal spa,
Bath has an exceptionally rich architectural
heritage which reflects the city's history
through several periods from its time as an
important Roman spa town.

The town grew around a temple the
Romans built between AD 60 and 70 on the
site of a geothermal spring. The mineral
spring was a shrine to the British goddess
Sulis, a local divinity whom the Romans
associated with Minerva, goddess of
wisdom and medicine. The Romans kept the
old reference in the name they gave the
town, Aquae Sulis (the waters of Sulis).

The spring yielded over 1,200,000 litres of
water daily at more than 46°C, and between
the first and fourth centuries the Romans
built a hot bath (calidarium), warm bath
(tepidarium) and cold bath (frigidarium)
together with all the standard equipment of
tepidaria, frigidaria and hypocausts, the
underfloor central-heating systems that
maintained the water temperature.

The town retained its importance after the
departure of the Romans in the fifth
century. In 1090 Bath succeeded Wells as
the seat of the see of Somerset and
consequently the church that had been Bath
Abbey became a cathedral. To match Bath's
new status, a new cathedral was begun and
new baths were also constructed. However,
the see returned to Wells and the cathedral
remained unfinished. In the sixteenth
century a rebuilt and remodelled church in
the Perpendicular Gothic style was finally
completed. The beautiful fan vaulting in the
nave was added as late as the nineteenth
century according, it is believed, to the
sixteenth century plans.

Medieval Bath grew wealthy on the wool
trade and the town became an important
centre of the wool industry. Although the
wool trade declined in the sixteenth and
seventeenth centuries, the city was by now
attracting wealthy visitors to take the waters.

In the eighteenth century Bath was
developed into an elegant and fashionable
spa town with neoclassical Palladian
buildings that blended harmoniously with
its Roman baths. The neoclassical style, scale
and grandeur of its public buildings (the
Rooms, the Pump Room, the Circus, and
especially, Royal Crescent) reflect the city's
confidence and ambitions during the reign
of George III.

A group of
exceptional figures
drove Bath's
eighteenth-century
rebirth, turning it into
a city where
architecture and
landscape combined
harmoniously for the
delight of enlightened
cure-takers.

Architect John Wood
planned the city's
Palladian architecture,
including the famous
Circus; his son John
oversaw the building
and also planned the
Assembly Rooms and
Royal Crescent.

Quarry-owner Ralph
Allen organized the
supply of the honey-
coloured, dressed
stone Wood needed
for his buildings.

As the city's Master of
Ceremonies, dandy
and gambler Beau
Nash masterminded
Bath's metamorphosis
into the most
fashionable resort in
England.

Pulteney Bridge which ▶
crosses the river Avon
in Bath. Constructed
in the eighteenth
century it is one of the
few bridges in the
world with shops built
into it on both sides.

World Heritage site since

• 1978 • 1979 • 1980 • 1981 • 1982 • 1983 • 1984 • 1985 • 1986 • **1987**

Nemrut Dağ
Turkey

Criteria – Human creative genius; Testimony to
cultural tradition; Significance in human history

The rulers of Commagene, a kingdom
founded north of Syria and the Euphrates,
left behind several breathtakingly beautiful
funerary sanctuaries. Nemrut Dağ, the most
impressive of all the tomb sites, is that of
Antiochos I of Commagene (69–34 BC). Its
landscaping is one of the most colossal
undertakings of the Hellenistic epoch.
Dominating the summit of Nemrut Dağ is a
conical tumulus of stone chips. This funerary
mound, whose interior layout remains
unknown, is surrounded by artificial terraces.
On the east terrace there is a row of five
colossal seated figures (7 m high)
representing deities, with a lion and an eagle
symmetrically positioned at either end. On
the north side, these stones are decorated
with relief sculptures representing the
Persian ancestors of Antiochos. On the
south side, his Macedonian ancestors
symmetrically face the others.

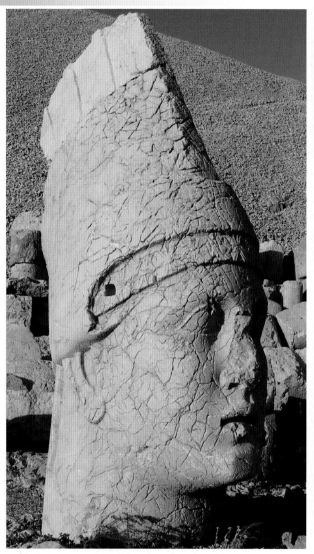

Head of Antiochus, Nemrut Dağ. ▲

When the empire of Alexander the
Great was breaking up, one of the
kingdoms that formed was
Commagene, which, from 162 BC to
AD 72, existed as a semi-independent
state, its sovereigns defending their
autonomy first against the Seleucids
and then against the Romans.
The monarchs of this dynasty bore
the Greek names of Antiochos or
Mithridates.

World Heritage site since

• 1978 • 1979 • 1980 • 1981 • 1982 • 1983 • 1984 • 1985 • 1986 • **1987**

Old Village of Hollókő and its Surroundings
Hungary
Criteria – Traditional human settlement

EUROPE

Adriatic
Sea

Black
Sea

A 1783 decree prohibiting the use of wood for building was ignored, and consequently the village was periodically devastated by fire. The last fire was in 1909 but the houses were rebuilt in the traditional style: half-timbered houses on a stone base with roughcast white-washed walls, enhanced by high wooden pillared galleries with balconies on the street side protected by overhanging porch roofs.
▼

Hollókő is an exceptional example of a traditional Central European culture that flourished before the agricultural revolution of the twentieth century. This village, which developed mainly during the seventeenth and eighteenth centuries, is a living example of rural life, using traditional farming and forestry techniques. Located about 100 km northeast of Budapest, Hollókő is a small community whose 126 houses and farm buildings, strip-field farming, orchards,

vineyards, meadows and woods cover 1.4 km². As was customary in the region, the first generation of inhabitants settled on either side of the main street. In this one-street village, subsequent generations built their houses at the back of the narrow family plots, thus progressively enlarging the built-up area. The barns were built apart from the village, on the edges of the fields, according to local Palocz custom.

The Great Wall
China

Criteria – Human creative genius; Interchange of values; Testimony to cultural tradition; Significance in human history; Heritage associated with events of universal significance

Known to the Chinese as the 'Long Wall of Ten Thousand Li', the formidable defensive structures built to ward off invasion is more commonly known as the Great Wall of China. At the end of its nineteen-century-long construction, the Great Wall was the world's largest military structure. Its historic and strategic importance is matched only by its architectural significance.

The building of defensive walls was a common strategy against potential invasion and several were built in China from the eighth century BC onwards. From 220 BC Qin Shi Huang, the first emperor of a unified China, undertook to restore and link the separate sections of the Great Wall which stretched from the region of the Ordos to Manchuria. These were to form the first cohesive defence system against invasions from the north, and by the first century BC, ongoing extensions meant the Wall spanned approximately 6,000 km between Dunhuang in the west and the Bohai Sea in the east.

After the downfall of the Han dynasty in AD 220, construction and maintenance works on the Great Wall were halted: China at that time enjoyed such great military power that the need for a defence policy was no longer felt.

It was the Ming emperors (1368–1644) who, after a long period of conflict that ended with the expulsion of the Mongols, revived the principles of Qin Shi Huang's defence policy and during these centuries 5,650 km of wall were built.

To defend the northern frontier, the Wall was divided into nine zhen, or military districts, and fortresses were built at strategically important points such as passes or fords. Passageways running along the top of the wall made it possible to move troops rapidly and for imperial couriers to travel.

The Great Wall of the Ming is a masterpiece, not only because of the ambition of the undertaking but also the perfection of its construction. The wall constitutes, on the vast scale of a continent, a perfect example of architecture integrated into the landscape.

This complex, diachronic cultural property is a unique example of a military architectural ensemble serving a single strategic purpose for 2,000 years. Its construction history illustrates advances in defence techniques and adaptation to changing political contexts.

The Wall's testimony to the civilizations of ancient China is illustrated as much by the earlier, tamped-earth sections in Gansu Province as by the famed masonry of the Ming period.

The purpose of the Great Wall was to protect China from military aggression and cultural ingression, and it remains an essential reference in Chinese literature.

World Heritage site since

• 1978 • 1979 • 1980 • 1981 • 1982 • 1983 • 1984 • 1985 • 1986 • **1987**

Manú National Park
Peru

Criteria – Significant ecological and biological processes; Significant natural habitat for biodiversity

The biological diversity found in the 15,000 km² Manú National Park exceeds that of any other place on Earth. The park is located on the eastern slopes of the Andes and on the Peruvian Amazon, and is situated within the Amazon River basin. It has successive tiers of vegetation rising from 150–4,200 m. The most widespread vegetation types are tropical lowland rainforest, tropical montane rainforest and puna vegetation (grasslands). Despite the high diversity of plant species, the flora of Manú is still poorly known. In the last ten years, 1,147 plant species have been identified within quite a small area, and it is likely many more species will be found. Some 850 species of birds have been identified and rare species, such as the giant otter and the giant armadillo, also find refuge there. Jaguars are often sighted.

The park is inhabited by at least four different native groups: the Machiguenga, the Mascho-Piro, the Yaminahua and the Amahuaca. The forest Indians are nomadic, mostly subsistent on some form of root-crop agriculture on alluvial soils along river banks and lakes, on hunting along water courses and inside the forest, on fishing and on the collection of turtle eggs.

Manú River, Manú National Park. ▲

World Heritage site since

· 1978 · 1979 · 1980 · 1981 · 1982 · 1983 · 1984 · 1985 · 1986 · **1987**

Mount Taishan
China

Criteria – Human creative genius; Interchange of values; Testimony to cultural tradition; Significance in human history; Traditional human settlement; Heritage associated with events of universal significance; Natural phenomena or beauty

Mount Taishan is one of the birthplaces of Chinese civilization, evidence of human activity dating back 400,000 years to the Palaeolithic Yiyuan Man. Cultural relics include memorial objects, ancient architectural complexes, stone sculptures and archaeological sites of outstanding importance. For over 3,000 years, Chinese emperors of various dynasties have made pilgrimages to Mount Taishan for sacrificial and other ceremonial purposes. Rock inscriptions, stone tablets and temples bear testimony to such visits. Renowned scholars, including Confucius whose home town, Qufu, is only 70 km away, have composed poetry and prose and left their calligraphy on the mountain. Mount Taishan was also an important centre of religious activity for both Buddhism and Taoism. The way in which this rich cultural heritage has been integrated with the natural landscape of the area is considered to be one of China's most precious legacies.

A Temple on Mount Taishan. ▲

The Spring and Autumn Period (770–476 BC) of the Zhou dynasty saw the emergence of two rival states in the area, Qi to the north and Lu to the south. The State of Qi built a 500 km wall as protection from possible invasion from the State of Chu. The ruins of this earliest of great walls in Chinese history are still evident.

World Heritage site since

· 1978 · 1979 · 1980 · 1981 · 1982 · 1983 · 1984 · 1985 · 1986 · **1987**

Mogao Caves
China

Criteria – Human creative genius; Interchange of values; Testimony to cultural tradition; Significance in human history; Traditional human settlement; Heritage associated with events of universal significance

Situated at a strategic point along the Silk Route, at the crossroads of trade as well as religious, cultural and intellectual influences, the 492 cells and cave sanctuaries in Mogao are famous for their statues and wall paintings, spanning 1,000 years of Buddhist art.

The group of caves at Mogao were still occupied by Buddhist monks until 1930, making this a fine example of a traditional monastic settlement as well as a unique artistic achievement.

◄

Entrance to the Mogao Caves.

Peking Man Site at Zhoukoudian
China

Criteria – Testimony to cultural tradition; Heritage associated with events of universal significance

Scientific work at the site, which lies 42 km southwest of Beijing, is still underway. So far, it has led to the discovery of the remains of Sinanthropus pekinensis, who lived in the Middle Pleistocene, along with various objects, and remains of Homo sapiens dating as far back as 18,000–11,000 BC.
The site is not only an exceptional reminder of the prehistorical human societies of the Asian continent, but also illustrates the process of evolution.

The discovery of hominid remains in the sediment of a cave in 1926 by the Chinese archaeologist Pei Wen Chung (Pei Wen Zhong) excited universal interest and overthrew the then-accepted chronology of the beginnings of human history.

◄

Part of the statue of the head of 'Peking Man' outside the entrance to the Peking Man Museum in Zhoukoudian.

World Heritage site since

· 1978 · 1979 · 1980 · 1981 · 1982 · 1983 · 1984 · 1985 · 1986 · **1987**

Pre-Hispanic City and National Park of Palenque
Mexico

Criteria – Human creative genius; Interchange of values; Testimony to cultural tradition; Significance in human history

The layout of the site is incredible. Artificial terracing changed the natural topography of the site, which is between the rugged foothills of the Chiapas and the lowlands, by creating a whole hierarchy of spaces where platforms and buildings are organized in harmonious balance.

A prime example of a Mayan sanctuary of the classical period, Palenque was at its height between AD 500 and 700, when its influence extended throughout the basin of the Usumacinta River. The elegance and craftsmanship of the buildings, as well as the lightness of the sculpted reliefs with their Mayan mythological themes, attest to the creative genius of this civilization. The dominant element in the central cleared area is the Palacio. Erected at different periods on an immense artificial knoll shaped like a truncated pyramid, the various buildings include a four-storey watchtower or astronomical observatory, unique in Mayan architecture. Even larger is the Temple of Inscriptions (pictured below), set atop a stepped pyramid located below the Palacio. Towards the end of the tenth century, coastal peoples from the Gulf of Mexico region invaded and caused its downfall and abandonment.

Temple of Inscriptions.
▼

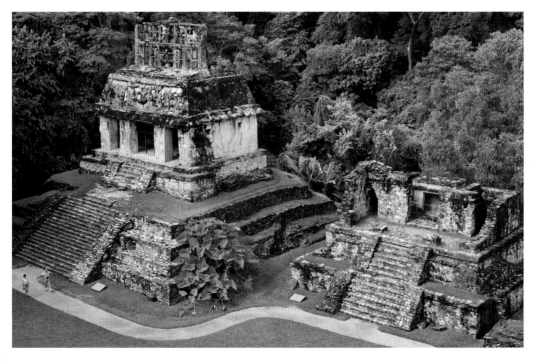

World Heritage site since

• 1978 • 1979 • 1980 • 1981 • 1982 • 1983 • 1984 • 1985 • 1986 • **1987**

Mausoleum of the First Qin Emperor
China

Criteria – Human creative genius; Testimony to cultural tradition; Significance in human history; Heritage associated with events of universal significance

While sinking a well ▶ in 1974, three local farmers came upon a pit containing lifesize terracotta statues of warriors. Excavations were begun immediately.

The mausoleum of Qin Shi Huang is the largest preserved in China and contains the famous army of terracotta warriors. It is a unique and stunning architectural ensemble whose layout echoes the urban plan of the capital, Xianyang. The site constitutes one of the most fabulous archaeological reserves in the world.

Qin Shi Huang, the first Emperor of China, arranged for his burial long before his accession. As king of Qin in 247 BC he selected a site at the foot of Mount Li. However, after his accession as emperor in 221 BC, work at his tomb took on extraordinary dimensions.

About 700,000 workers from every Chinese province worked unceasingly to construct a subterranean city within a gigantic mound. The resulting necropolis complex was a scale model of the emperor's palace, the empire and the Earth. Its treasures were safeguarded by automatically triggered weapons designed to kill tomb robbers and its principal craftsmen were walled up alive within the complex to prevent their betraying its secrets.

Qin died in 210 BC and is buried, surrounded by the famous terracotta warriors, at the centre of a complex designed to mirror the urban plan of the capital. The life-size terracotta figures are all different; with their horses, chariots and weapons, they are masterpieces of realism and of great historical interest. According to current estimates, the statue army of the Qin Shi Huang Mausoleum must have represented the exact number of the imperial guards. The emperor's tomb and much of the site remain unexcavated.

The mausoleum's superstructures have disappeared and there remains only a wooded knoll resembling a truncated pyramid on a 350-m-square base. The interior is built within a first square enclosure, with doors in the middle of each of four walls corresponding to the four cardinal points. This in turn is surrounded by a second rectangular enclosure running north to south.

Because of their exceptional technical and artistic qualities, the terracotta warriors and horses and the funerary carts in bronze are major works in the history of Chinese sculpture. The army of statues also bears unique testimony to military organization in China from the fifth to the third century BC, while the direct testimony of their weapons – lances, swords, axes, halberds, bows and arrows – is evident.

Three pits have so far been excavated. Pit 1 contained an army of almost 2,000 warriors, the infantry and cavalry corps standing in battle formation with archers protecting the flanks.

Two other pits to the north were found to contain similar items – 1,500 warriors, carts and horses in Pit 2, and sixty-eight officers and dignitaries and a cart with four horses in Pit 3.

World Heritage site since

· 1978 · 1979 · 1980 · 1981 · 1982 · 1983 · 1984 · 1985 · 1986 · **1987**

Gros Morne National Park
Canada

Criteria – Natural phenomena or beauty; Major stages of Earth's history

Typical species found in Gros Morne are fox, caribou, moose and arctic hare. Whales including minke, fin and pilot, and harbour seals are some of the more common marine mammals regularly sighted from the park.

Glaciated valley of Western Brook Pond.
▼

With spectacular scenery, outstanding geology and diverse ecology, Gros Morne, located on the western shore of the island of Newfoundland, provided the evidence that helped define the theory of plate tectonics. These exceptional geological formations are the remnants of an ancient continent and ocean from hundreds of millions of years ago and preserved within them is one of the best and most accessible examples of exposed ocean crust and mantle material.

A superb fossil assemblage illustrating the evolution of life from early Cambrian period through mid-Ordovician times is found in sedimentary rocks in the park. At Green Point the rocks and the fossils they contain have been designated by the International Union of Geologic Sciences as the world stratotype representing the boundary between Cambrian and Ordovician periods in the geological timescale.

More recent glacial action has exposed the park's bedrock for scientific study and resulted in the remarkable scenery of fjords, glacial valleys, and waterfalls from the alpine plateau of the Long Range Mountains to the Gulf of St. Lawrence coastal lowlands with its estuaries, beaches, sheer cliffs and dunes. These distinctly different landscapes provide a range of habitats for a wide variety of flora and fauna. The park contains more than thirty separate vegetation communities, is home to 60 per cent of the plants species that grow on the island, and is a significant breeding site for harlequin ducks, blackpoll warblers, common terns and artic terns.

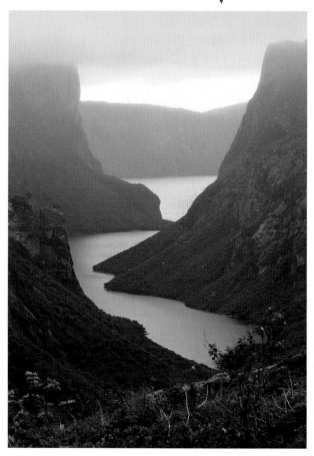

Bahla Fort
Oman
Criteria – Significance in human history

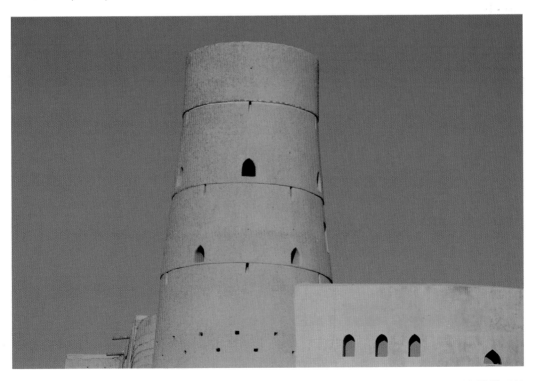

The Gulf

ASIA

Arabian Sea

Bahla Fort is an outstanding example of the military architecture of the Sultanate of Oman. The oasis of Bahla owed its prosperity to the Banu Nabhan who, from the mid-twelfth century to the end of the fifteenth century, imposed their rule on the other tribes. Only the ruins of what was a glorious past now remain. Built on a stone base, the adobe walls and towers of the immense fort probably include some

structural elements of the pre-Islamic period, but the major part dates from the time of the Banu Nabhan. At the foot of the fort lies the Friday Mosque with its beautiful sculpted mihrab (prayer niche) probably dating back to the fourteenth century. These monuments are inseparable from the small town of Bahla and its souk, palm grove and adobe ramparts surrounding the oasis.

The monuments of Bahla were in a critical state when it was inscribed on the World Heritage List. They had never been restored (thereby conserving a high degree of authenticity), and were not protected by any conservation measures. Major restoration work at the fort and Friday Mosque is now underway.

Monticello and the University of Virginia in Charlottesville
USA

Criteria – Human creative genius; Significance in human history; Heritage associated with events of universal significance

Thomas Jefferson, better known for his political career, designed Monticello (1769–1809), his plantation home, and his ideal 'academical village' (1817–26), which is still the heart of the University of Virginia. The integration of the building into the landscape, the originality of design, and the refined proportions and decor make Monticello (pictured below) an outstanding example of a neoclassical villa rustica, based on a Roman design, as elaborated by Andrea

Palladio (1508–80). The western façade is dominated by an octagonal dome. The University of Virginia is an unrivalled example of an Enlightenment institution. A half-scale copy of the Pantheon in Rome, which houses the library, dominates the academic village. The ten pavilions housing the professors of the ten schools that made up the university are connected by colonnades that give a feeling of unity to this space.

Thomas Jefferson, author of the American Declaration of Independence and third president of the United States, was also a talented architect. Jefferson's use of an architectural vocabulary based upon classical antiquity symbolizes both the aspirations of the new American republic as the inheritor of European tradition and the cultural experimentation that could be expected as the country matured.

World Heritage site since

• 1978 • 1979 • 1980 • 1981 • 1982 • 1983 • 1984 • 1985 • 1986 • **1987**

Ksar of Ait-Ben-Haddou
Morocco

Criteria – Significance in human history;
Traditional human settlement

An astonishing loft-fortress overlooks the mountain against which the ksar is located. The lofts (agadir or ighram) are not uncommon in Morocco, but their defensive character is not always as evident with a fortification system linking the loft with the village, conceived as the last bastion of resistance in the event of a siege.

Ait-Ben-Haddou is a striking example of a southern Moroccan ksar, a group of earthen buildings surrounded by high walls, that is a traditional pre-Saharan village community. Inside the defensive walls, which are reinforced by angle towers, each with a zigzag-shaped gate, houses crowd together. Some are modest, others resemble small urban castles with their high angle towers whose upper portion includes decorative motifs in clay brick. There are also public buildings and community areas: collective sheep pens and stables, lofts and silos, a market place, a meeting room for the assembly of family chiefs, a mosque and madrasas. Ait-Ben-Haddou is an extraordinary ensemble of buildings offering a complete panorama of pre-Saharan construction techniques using rammed and moulded earth, clay and brick.

World Heritage site since

• 1978 • 1979 • 1980 • 1981 • 1982 • 1983 • 1984 • 1985 • 1986 • **1987**

Uluru-Kata Tjuṯa National Park
Australia

Criteria – Traditional human settlement; Heritage associated with events of universal significance; Natural phenomena or beauty; Major stages of Earth's history

Uluru-Kata Tjuṯa National Park is included on the World Heritage List for both its natural and cultural values. Formerly called Ayers Rock – Mount Olga National Park, it is located in Australia's Red Centre. It lies in the traditional lands of the Western Desert Aboriginal people, locally known as Aṉangu. Aṉangu are part of one of the oldest human societies in the world.

The huge rock formations of Uluru and Kata Tjuṯa and the surrounding country are part of an important cultural landscape. For Aṉangu these features are physical evidence of the actions, artefacts and bodies of the ancestral beings (tjukuritja) who travelled the Earth in the creation time. These ancestors, who combined the attributes of humans and animals, journeyed across the landscape creating not only its features, but also Tjukurpa (the law) – the code of behaviour followed by Aṉangu today.

Uluru and the rock domes of Kata Tjuṯa dominate the vast red plain, dwarfing the desert oak and spinifex grass of central Australia. Uluru is composed of hard red sandstone, exposed as a result of the folding, faulting and erosion of the surrounding rock. It is 9.4 km in circumference and rises to a relatively flat top that is more than 340 m above the shallow, red sandy dunes around it. Rock art in the caves around its base provides further evidence of the enduring cultural traditions of Aṉangu.

The thirty-six steep-sided rock domes of Kata Tjuṯa, lying about 32 kilometres to the west of Uluru, are made up of gently dipping Mount Currie conglomerate. The undulating domes are interspersed with moisture-rich gullies and rocky valleys that are home to rare plants and desert animals. Like Uluru, Kata Tjuṯa's domes are the visible tips of huge rock slabs that extend far beneath the ground.

The park is home to twenty-one native mammals including the rare hairy-footed dunnart, the sandhill dunnart and the mulgara. More than 170 bird species, 73 species of reptile and at least 7 species of bat have been recorded in the park.

The Uluru monolith. ▶

The park's Aboriginal owners, Aṉangu, have cared for the landscape for thousands of years using traditional practices governed by Tjukurpa (the law). Aboriginal people learned how to patch burn the country from Tjukurpa, and this knowledge informs an active burning programme that is now a major ecological management tool in the park. Tjukurpa also teaches about the location and care of rock holes and other water sources.

World Heritage site since

· 1978 · 1979 · 1980 · 1981 · 1982 · 1983 · 1984 · 1985 · 1986 · **1987**

Group of Monuments at Pattadakal
India

Criteria – Testimony to cultural tradition; Significance in human history

Pattadakal, in Karnataka, represents the high point of an eclectic art which, in the seventh and eighth centuries under the Chalukya dynasty, achieved a harmonious blend of architectural forms from northern and southern India. An impressive series of nine Hindu temples, as well as a Jain sanctuary, can be seen there. One masterpiece from the group stands out – the Temple of Virupaksha, built c. 740 by Queen Lokamahadevi to commemorate her husband's victory over the kings from the South.

The evocative sanctuary ruins in the enclosure may be reached through monumental gates on the west and east sides. In the axis of the courtyard, before the temple, is a pavilion housing a black stone statue of Siva's sacred bull.

◄

Sangameshvara Temple at Pattadakal.

Dja Faunal Reserve
Cameroon

Criteria – Significant ecological and biological processes; Significant natural habitat for biodiversity

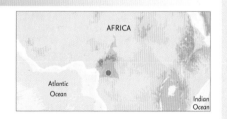

This is one of the largest and best-protected rainforests in Africa, with 90 per cent of its area left undisturbed. Almost completely surrounded by the Dja river, which forms a natural boundary, the reserve is located in a transition zone between the forests of southern Nigeria, southwest Cameroon and the Congo Basin. Except in the southeast, the relief is fairly flat and consists of a succession of round-topped hills. Cliffs in the south are associated with a section of

the river broken up by rapids and waterfalls. Although the area is poorly studied, it is known to have a wide range of primate species. Other mammals include elephant, buffalo, leopard, warthog and pangolin. Reptiles include python, lizard and two species of crocodile, both of which are threatened.

Vegetation in the reserve mainly comprises dense evergreen Congo rainforest, together with swamp vegetation and secondary forest around old villages (which were abandoned in 1946) and recently abandoned cocoa and coffee plantations. A population of pygmies lives in small sporadic encampments in the reserve, maintaining an essentially traditional lifestyle.

World Heritage site since

• 1978 • 1979 • 1980 • 1981 • 1982 • 1983 • 1984 • 1985 • 1986 • 1987 • **1988**

Mount Athos
Greece

Criteria – Human creative genius; Interchange of values; Significance in human history; Traditional human settlement; Heritage associated with events of universal significance; Natural phenomena or beauty

The transformation of a mountain into a sacred place made Mount Athos a unique artistic creation, combining the natural beauty of its site with the expanded forms of architectural creation. Moreover, the monasteries of Mount Athos are a veritable conservatory of masterpieces, including the wall paintings, portable icons, gold objects, embroideries and illuminated manuscripts which each monastery carefully preserves. Mount Athos is the spiritual centre of the Orthodox world, and has exerted a lasting influence both on it and on the development of religious architecture and monumental painting.

Mount Athos enjoyed an autonomous statute since Byzantine times (from the tenth century onwards). The 'Holy Mountain', which is forbidden to women and children, is also a recognized artistic site. Its monasteries had an influence as far afield as Russia, and its school of painting influenced the history of Orthodox art.

Athos is a self-governing monastic republic within Greece. It includes twenty monasteries, twelve sketes (convents), and about 700 houses, cells or hermitages. Over 1,000 monks live there, either in communities or alone, as well as in the 'desert' of Karoulia where cells cling to the cliff face rising steeply above the sea.

▼

World Heritage site since

· 1978 · 1979 · 1980 · 1981 · 1982 · 1983 · 1984 · 1985 · 1986 · 1987 · **1988**

Old Towns of Djenné
Mali

Criteria – Testimony to cultural tradition;
Significance in human history

Djenné-Djeno, along with Hambarketolo, Tonomba and Kaniana, bears exceptional witness to the pre-Islamic civilizations on the inland delta of the Niger. Djenné is an outstanding example of an architectural group of buildings illustrating a significant historic period. It has been defined both as 'the most beautiful city of Africa' and 'the typical African city'.

Inhabited since 250 BC, Djenné became a market centre and was an important link in the trans-Saharan gold trade. In the fifteenth and sixteenth centuries it was one of the centres for the propagation of Islam. Its traditional houses, of which nearly 2,000 have survived, are built on hillocks called toguère, as protection from the seasonal Niger floods.

Djenné, which spreads over several toguère, is bisected by a wide avenue. Its Market Place is dominated by the Great Mosque (see picture below). Traditional houses extend out from both sides of this thoroughfare over an ancient land parcel of approximately 2km². The main feature of the domestic architecture, influenced by that of Morocco, is its verticality.

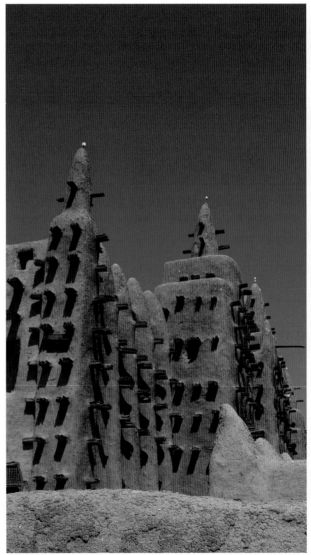

The Great Mosque of Djenné. ▶

World Heritage site since

• 1978 • 1979 • 1980 • 1981 • 1982 • 1983 • 1984 • 1985 • 1986 • 1987 • **1988**

Wet Tropics of Queensland
Australia

Criteria – Natural phenomena or beauty; Major stages of Earth's history; Significant ecological and biological processes; Significant natural habitat for biodiversity

The Wet Tropics of Queensland provides an unparalleled living record of the ecological and evolutionary processes that shaped the flora and fauna of Australia over the past 415 million years, first when it was part of the Pangaean landmass, then as the ancient continent Gondwana, and for the past 50 million years an island continent. During this period of evolution the processes of speciation, extinction and adaptation have been determined by history, particularly

continental drift and cycles of climatic change.

The site, which stretches along the northeast coast of Australia for some 450 km, from just south of Cooktown to just north of Townsville, is made up largely of tropical rainforests. This area offers a particularly extensive and varied array of plants, marsupials and song birds, along with many rare and endangered animals and plant species.

The rainforests, which make up about 80 per cent of the site, have more plant families with primitive characteristics than any other area on Earth.

The ancestry of Australia's unique marsupials and many of its other animals originated in rainforest ecosystems. The Wet Tropics of Queensland still contains many of their closest surviving members.

World Heritage site since

.... 1978 • 1979 • 1980 • 1981 • 1982 • 1983 • 1984 • 1985 • 1986 • 1987 • **1988**

Tower of London
United Kingdom

Criteria – Interchange of values; Significance in human history

The Tower of London is an imposing fortress with many layers of history. Built on the Thames by William the Conqueror to protect his London base and to assert his power over the newly conquered English, it became one of the symbols of royalty in England and is a major reference for the history of medieval military architecture.

The Tower is a complex of fortifications, courtyards and buildings extending over 73,000 m². There are many towers in the ensemble and the impressive White Tower, begun around 1078 and completed around nine years later, is the centrepiece. Although a royal residence for centuries, the White Tower was never intended as the main royal palace but rather as a stronghold, a notion reinforced by the formidable curtain walls, moats and ditches successive kings built around it.

The Crown Jewels are on display in the Tower of London.

The Water Gate entrance was nicknamed Traitors' Gate because prisoners were brought through it to the Tower. Queen Anne Boleyn, Thomas More, Queen Catherine Howard and Princess Elizabeth, later Elizabeth I, entered it as prisoners.

◀
The White Tower stands more than 27 m high and its walls are over 4.5 m thick at their base.

World Heritage site since

· 1978 · 1979 · 1980 · 1981 · 1982 · 1983 · 1984 · 1985 · 1986 · 1987 · **1988**

Manovo-Gounda St Floris National Park
Central African Republic

Criteria – Significant ecological and biological processes; Significant natural habitat for biodiversity

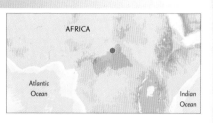

The importance of this park derives from its wealth of flora and fauna. Its vast savannas are home to a wide variety of species: black rhinoceroses, elephants, cheetahs, leopards, wild dogs, red-fronted gazelles and buffalo, while various types of waterfowl are to be found in the northern floodplains.

Some 320 species of bird have been identified in the park, with at least twenty-five species of raptor including bateleur and African fish eagle. There are large seasonal populations of pelican and marabou stork, and many waterbirds and shorebirds.

Paleochristian and Byzantine Monuments of Thessalonika
Greece

Criteria – Human creative genius; Interchange of values; Significance in human history

Founded in 315 BC, the provincial capital and sea port of Thessalonika was one of the first bases for the spread of Christianity. Among its Christian monuments are fine churches, some built on the Greek cross plan and others on the three-nave basilica plan. Constructed over a long period, from the fourth to the fifteenth century, they constitute a diachronic typological series, which had considerable influence in the Byzantine world. The mosaics of the rotunda, St Demetrius and St David are among the great masterpieces of early Christian art.

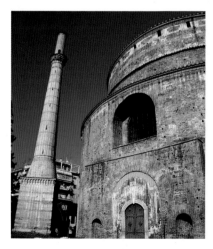

Cosmopolitan and prosperous, Thessalonika grew in commercial and strategic importance during the Roman period and was one of the first bases for the spread of Christianity. St Paul visited twice, in AD 50 and 56, founding a church there.

◄
The Rodonta Temple in Thessalonika.

World Heritage site since

· 1978 · 1979 · 1980 · 1981 · 1982 · 1983 · 1984 · 1985 · 1986 · 1987 · **1988**

Sacred City of Kandy
Sri Lanka

Criteria – Significance in human history;
Heritage associated with events of universal
significance

This sacred Buddhist site, popularly known
as the city of Senkadagalapura, was the last
capital of the Sinhala kings, whose
patronage enabled the Dinahala culture to
flourish for more than 2,500 years. It is also
the site of the Temple of the Tooth Relic,
the sacred tooth of the Buddha, which is
a famous pilgrimage site. The Temple of the
Tooth, the palatial complex, and the sacred
city of Kandy are directly associated with the
history of the spread of Buddhism. Kandy,
founded in the fourteenth century, forms the
southern tip of Sri Lanka's 'Cultural Triangle'.
It became the capital of the kingdom in 1592
and remained one of the bastions of
Sinhalese independence until the arrival of
the British in 1815. It is still the religious
capital of Buddhism and a sacred city for
millions of believers.

A Buddhist temple in Kandy. ▲

Enshrined in the Dalada Maligawa
is the relic of the tooth of Buddha.
The ceremonial high point each
year is the splendid ritual on the
feast of Esala Perahera, in which
one of the inner caskets used for
covering the tooth relic is taken in
a grand procession through the
streets of the city.

Sanctuary of Asklepios at Epidaurus

Greece

Criteria – Human creative genius; Interchange of values; Testimony to cultural tradition; Significance in human history; Heritage associated with events of universal significance

EUROPE

Ionian Sea

Mediterranean Sea

The temples and the hospital facilities influenced all the sanctuaries in the Hellenic and Roman world. The emergence of modern medicine in a sanctuary originally based on the miraculous healing of supposedly incurable patients is strikingly described in the engraved inscriptions on the remarkable stelae preserved in the museum at Epidaurus.

In a small valley in the Peloponnisos, the shrine of Asklepios, the god of medicine, developed in the sixth century BC out of a much earlier cult of Apollo Maleatas. The group of temples and the hospital facilities comprising the Sanctuary of Epidaurus bears exceptional testimony to the healing cults of the Hellenic and Roman worlds. The theatre, the temples of Artemis and Asklepios, the Tholos, the Enkoimeterion (where the sick awaited their cures) and the

Propylaea are exceptional examples of Hellenic architecture of the fourth century BC. In particular, the theatre, an architectural masterpiece by Polycletes the Younger of Argos, is famed for its setting and the perfection of its proportions and acoustics. Epidaurus continued to flourish during the Hellenistic period. Despite pillaging by Sulla in 87 BC and by Cilician pirates, the sanctuary prospered during the Roman period.

Theatre at Epidaurus.
▼

World Heritage site since

· 1978 · 1979 · 1980 · 1981 · 1982 · 1983 · 1984 · 1985 · 1986 · 1987 · **1988**

Sinharaja Forest Reserve
Sri Lanka

Criteria – Significant ecological and biological processes; Significant natural habitat for biodiversity

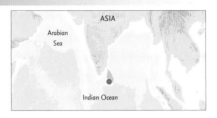

Sinharaja is Sri Lanka's last viable area of primary tropical rainforest. This narrow strip of undulating terrain consists of a series of ridges and valleys. Two main types of forest can be recognized: remnants of Dipterocarpus forest occur in valleys and on their lower slopes; secondary forest and scrub occur where the original forest cover has been removed by shifting cultivation and in other places the forest has been replaced by rubber and tea plantations.

Mesua-Doona forest is the climax vegetation in most of the reserve. More than 60 per cent of the trees are endemic and many of them are considered rare. There is much endemic wildlife, especially birds, and the reserve is also home to over 50 per cent of Sri Lanka's endemic species of mammals and butterflies, as well as many kinds of insects, reptiles and rare amphibians.

The Sinharaja region has long featured in the legends and lore of the people of Sri Lanka. Its name, literally meaning lion (sinha) king (raja), perhaps refers to the original 'king-sized or royal forest of the Sinhalese', a people of the legendary 'lion-race' of Sri Lanka, or to the home of a legendary lion of Sri Lanka.

A spider's web in morning sunlight in Sinharaja Rainforest.
▼

World Heritage site since

• 1978 • 1979 • 1980 • 1981 • 1982 • 1983 • 1984 • 1985 • 1986 • 1987 • **1988**

Medina of Sousse
Tunisia

Criteria – Testimony to cultural tradition;
Significance in human history; Traditional human
settlement

Sousse was an important commercial and
military port during the Aghlabid period in
the ninth century and is an outstanding
example of a town dating from the first
centuries of Islam. Among the earliest
buildings is the ribat, a combined fort and
religious building, that helped defend
Sousse against Byzantine fleets. In 821 its
fortifications were completed with a square
bastion and tower which served both as
a watchtower and as a minaret. Under the

Aghlabids, Sousse rapidly flourished:
significant monuments constructed in this
golden century included the mosque of
Bu Ftata, the first kasbah, and the Great
Mosque. By 859, the town walls neared
completion, and the limits of the medina
were broadly drawn. The surrounding
fortifications made the military function of
the ribat less vital and it reverted fully to its
religious function.

The 'ribat' of Sousse
housed a garrison of
the Defenders of the
Faith, the Mourabitin,
and the austere
architecture reflects its
dual military/
religious function.
A rectangular
enclosure is flanked
by towers and turrets,
with a single gate on
the south and an inner
courtyard rising over
two levels. It has a
mosque on the
southern side.

▼

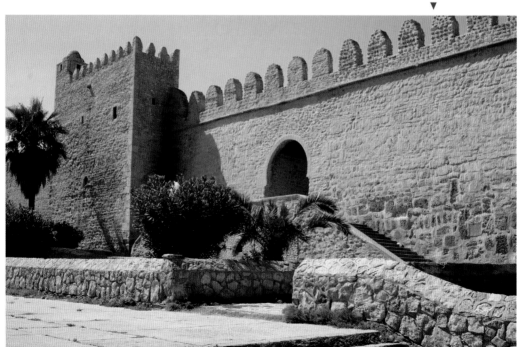

World Heritage site since

• 1978 • 1979 • 1980 • 1981 • 1982 • 1983 • 1984 • 1985 • 1986 • 1987 • **1988**

Historic Town of Guanajuato and Adjacent Mines
Mexico

NORTH AMERICA

Pacific Ocean

Caribbean Sea

Criteria – Human creative genius; Interchange of values; Significance in human history; Heritage associated with events of universal significance

Guanajuato is an outstanding example of an architectural ensemble that incorporates the industrial and economic aspects of a mining operation. Founded by the Spanish in the early sixteenth century, the town became the world's leading silver-extraction centre in the eighteenth century. This past can be seen in its 'subterranean streets' and the 'Boca del Inferno', a mineshaft that plunges a breathtaking 600 m. The town's beautiful Baroque and neoclassical buildings, built with the prosperity from the mines, have influenced buildings throughout central Mexico. The churches of La Compañía and La Valenciana are considered to be among the most beautiful examples of Baroque architecture in Central and South America. Guanajuato was also witness to events which changed the history of the country.

Spanish conquistadores first settled in the region in 1529, and in 1548 they discovered rich outcrops of silver at Guanaxhuata. To protect prospectors, miners and the new settlers, four fortified structures were erected at Marfil, Tepetapa, Santa Ana and Cerro del Cuarto; these settlements formed the nuclei of the later town of Guanajuato. Sprawling through a winding valley at an altitude of 2,084 m, Guanajuato differs from the other colonial towns in New Spain in that it was not laid out on the standard grid plan. Instead, the scattered areas grew together through the spontaneous urbanization of suitable sites on the rough, natural terrain.

Founded when the silver mines were opened, Guanajuato had a symbiotic relationship with them until the nineteenth century. Its growth, the layout of its streets, including the picturesque 'subterranean' streets through which its traffic runs, its plazas, and the construction of hospitals, churches, convents and palaces are all inextricably linked with the industrial history of the region which, with the decline of the Potosí mines in the eighteenth century, became the world's leading silver extraction centre.

The city played a part in the Mexican War of Independence of 1810–21: Miguel Hidalgo, the rebel leader, began his uprising in the state of Guanajuato of which the city is capital.

Tunnels from the silver mines under the town of Guanajuato. ▶

The splendour of the Baroque buildings of Guanajuato is directly linked to the wealth of the mines. The churches of La Compañía (1745–65) and above all La Valenciana (1765–88) are masterpieces of the Mexican Churrigueresque style. The church of La Vanenciana and the mansion of Casa Rul y Valenciana were financed by the most prosperous mines, but even the smaller mines also had churches, palaces or houses close by.

World Heritage site since

• 1978 • 1979 • 1980 • 1981 • 1982 • 1983 • 1984 • 1985 • 1986 • 1987 • **1988**

Old Town of Galle and its Fortifications
Sri Lanka

Criteria – Significance in human history

The Clock Tower at the Dutch Fort in Galle. ▲

Founded in the sixteenth century by the Portuguese, Galle reached the height of its development in the eighteenth century, before the arrival of the British. It is the best example of a fortified city built by Europeans in south and southeast Asia, showing the interaction between European architectural styles and south Asian traditions. This fortified city, protected by a sea wall finished in 1729, still exists, with few changes. It has an area of 0.52 km² inside the walls defended by fourteen bastions. The city was laid out on a regular grid pattern adapted to the configuration of the terrain: north-south peripheral streets are parallel to the ramparts and not to the central traffic axes. As befitted a fortified city, the Commandant's residence, the arsenal and the powder house were prominent features of the original layout.

The most salient feature of the architecture at Galle is the use of European models adapted to the geological, climatic, historical, and cultural conditions of Sri Lanka. In the structure of the ramparts, coral is frequently used along with granite.

Timbuktu
Mali
Criteria – Interchange of values; Significance in
human history; Traditional human settlement

Home of the prestigious Koranic Sankore
University and other madrasas, Timbuktu
was an important centre for the
dissemination of Islam throughout Africa in
the fifteenth and sixteenth centuries. Its
numerous schools were attended, it is said,
by some 25,000 students. Scholars,
engineers and architects from various
regions in Africa rubbed shoulders with wise
men and marabouts in this intellectual and
religious centre. Its three great mosques,

Djingareyber, Sankore and Sidi Yahia, recall
Timbuktu's golden age. Although
continuously restored, these monuments
are today under threat from desertification.
Apart from the mosques, the World
Heritage site comprises sixteen cemeteries
and mausolea, essential elements in a
religious system as, according to popular
belief, they constitute a rampart that shields
the city from all misfortune.

Timbuktu is thought
to have been founded
in the fifth century of
the Hegira by a group
of Imakcharen
Tuaregs who, having
wandered 250 km
south of their base,
established a
temporary camp
guarded by an old
woman, Buktu.
Gradually, Tim-Buktu
(the place of Buktu)
became a small
sedentary village at
the crossroads of
several trade routes.

Henderson Island
United Kingdom
Criteria – Natural phenomena or beauty;
Significant natural habitat for biodiversity

Henderson Island is a raised coral atoll
forming part of the Pitcairn Island group in
the South Pacific. It is one of the few atolls in
the world whose ecology has been
practically untouched by human presence.
Although it was colonized by Polynesians
between the twelfth and fifteenth centuries,
this period of settlement had little
ecological impact and the island has
remained uninhabited in modern times. Its
isolated location provides the ideal context

for studying the dynamics of insular
evolution and natural selection. The island is
arid with only one freshwater spring and has
a rugged topography beneath the dense
tangled vegetation. It is particularly notable
for the ten plant species and four land bird
species that are endemic to the island.

With no major
landmass within a
5,000 km radius,
Henderson Island's
remoteness and
inhospitable nature
have so far effectively
ensured its
conservation. As a
near pristine island
ecosystem, it is of
immense scientific
value.

World Heritage site since

· 1978 · 1979 · 1980 · 1981 · 1982 · 1983 · 1984 · 1985 · 1986 · 1987 · **1988**

Archaeological sites of Bat, Al-Khutm and Al-Ayn
Oman

Criteria – Testimony to cultural tradition;
Significance in human history

The zone encompassing the settlement and necropolises of Bat is the most complete and best-known site of the third millennium BC, bearing unique witness to the evolution of funeral practices during the first Bronze Age in the Oman peninsula. The settlement and necropolis zones of Bat form a coherent and representative group with two neighbouring contemporary archaeological sites: the tower of Al-Khutm, 2 km west of Bat, and the group of beehive tombs of Qubur Juhhal at Al-Ayn (pictured on the right), 22 km east-southeast of Bat. The twenty-one tombs from the third millennium, aligned on a rocky crest that stands out in the superb mountainous landscape of Jebel Misht to the north, are in a remarkable state of preservation.

Six of twenty-one beehive tombs of Qubur Juhhal at Al-Ayn. ▲

In the settlement zone there are five stone 'towers,' one of which has been entirely excavated. It has been determined that it was built between 2595 and 2465 BC.

From the tower can be distinguished to the east a series of rectangular houses with central courts and, to the north, a vast necropolis.

World Heritage site since

• 1978 • 1979 • 1980 • 1981 • 1982 • 1983 • 1984 • 1985 • 1986 • 1987 • **1988**

Trinidad and the Valley de los Ingenios
Cuba

Criteria – Significance in human history;
Traditional human settlement

Founded by the Spanish in the early sixteenth century in honour of the Holy Trinity, Trinidad is an outstanding example of a colonial city. Towards the end of the eighteenth century, the sugar industry was firmly established in the nearby Valle de Los Ingenios and Trinidad prospered; by 1796 it was the third-largest city in Cuba. The present city owes its charm to its eighteenth and nineteenth century buildings, such as

the Palacio Brunet and the Palacio Cantero. Valle de Los Ingenios is a living museum of the sugar industry, featuring seventy-five ruined sugar mills, summer mansions, barracks, and other facilities related to the field. The famous Manaca-Iznaga Tower, built in 1816, is 45 m high, and the tolling of its bells once marked the beginning and end of working hours on the sugar plantations.

Trinidad was one of the bridgeheads for the conquest of the American continent. It was the departure point for the expeditions led by Francisco Hernández de Córdova in 1517 and by Cortez in 1518.

Santisma Trinidad Church.
▼

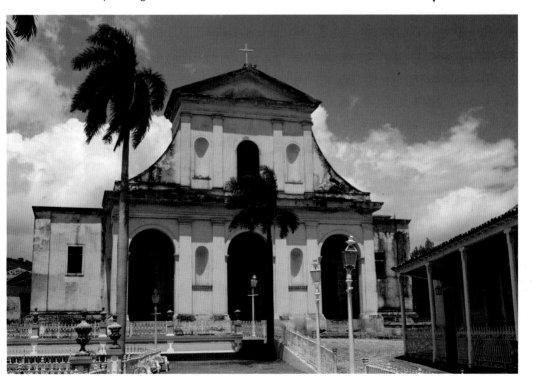

World Heritage site since

• 1978 • 1979 • 1980 • 1981 • 1982 • 1983 • 1984 • 1985 • 1986 • 1987 • **1988**

Medieval City of Rhodes
Greece

Criteria – Interchange of values; Significance in
human history; Traditional human settlement

Rhodes is an outstanding example of a
medieval defensive architectural ensemble.
The fortifications of Rhodes, long
considered impregnable, exerted an
influence throughout the eastern
Mediterranean basin in the later Middle
Ages. Within its walls, the old town of
Rhodes is an important example of
traditional human settlement characterized
by cultural assimilation.

From 1309–1523 Rhodes was in the
possession of the Order of St John of
Jerusalem, the Knights Hospitaller.
A military hospital order founded to care
for sick pilgrims in the Holy Land, the
Knights lost their last foothold in Palestine
in 1291 with the fall of Acre. In 1309 the
Order took Rhodes from the ailing
Byzantine Empire, rebuilding the town
and transforming it into a stronghold.

The medieval city is located in the Upper
Town (Collachium) within a wall 4 km long.
Built by the Knights, the town is one of the
most beautiful urban ensembles of the
Gothic period.

The Order was organized into seven
'Tongues', each having its own seat. The inns
of the Tongues of Italy, France, Spain and
Provence lined both sides of the principal
east-west axis, the famous Street of the

Knights, one of the finest testimonies to
Gothic urbanism.

The Knights' first hospice was replaced in
the late-fifteenth century by the Great
Hospital; today the building is used as the
archaeological museum. Northwest of the
Collachium are the Grand Masters' Palace
and St John's Church. At the eastern end of
the Street of the Knights, built against the
wall, is St Mary's Church which the Knights
transformed into a cathedral.

The Lower Town is almost as dense with
monuments as the Collachium. In 1522, with
a population of 5,000, it was replete with
churches, some of Byzantine construction.

Rhodes withstood two invasions in the
fifteenth century, firstly by Egyptians and
then by Turks. It fell in 1523 to the Ottoman
Sultan Suleiman the Magnificent who
arrived with a 100,000-strong army,
besieging Rhodes for six months.

After 1523 many of the buildings were
converted into Islamic mosques but the
influence of the Ottoman occupation is
seen particularly in combined vernacular
architecture, with decorative elements of
Ottoman origin. In the Lower Town, Gothic
architecture coexists with mosques, public
baths and other buildings from the
Ottoman period.

The Knights built up
the fortifications of
Rhodes over two
centuries. The
ramparts of the
medieval city, partially
erected on the
foundations of the
Byzantine enclosure,
were constantly
maintained and
remodelled between
the fourteenth and
sixteenth centuries.
Artillery firing posts
were the final features
to be added. In the
section of the Amboise
Gate which was built
on the northwestern
angle in 1512, the
curtain wall was 12 m
thick with a 4 m high
parapet pierced with
gun holes.

Historic Centre of Lima
Peru

Criteria – Significance in human history

Lima was founded in 1535. The city played a leading role in the history of the New World from 1542, when the Holy Roman Emperor Charles V established the Viceroyalty of Peru to govern most of Spanish South America. However, the creation of the viceroyalties of New Granada and of La Plata in the eighteenth century gradually ended Lima's power.

San Francisco Convent. ▼

Although severely damaged by earthquakes, this 'City of the Kings' was, until the mid-eighteenth century, the capital and most important city of the Spanish dominions in South America. The historic centre of Lima bears witness to the architecture and urban development of a Spanish colonial town of great political, economic, and cultural importance.

The historic monuments – religious or public buildings, such as the Torre Tagle Palace – which lie within the perimeter of the World Heritage site date from the seventeenth and eighteenth centuries and are typical examples of Hispano-American Baroque. The architecture of the other buildings is often of the same period and style with the result that, despite the addition of certain nineteenth century constructions such as Art Nouveau Casa Courret, the town's historic nucleus recalls Lima at the time of the Spanish Kingdom of Peru.

World Heritage site since

• 1978 • 1979 • 1980 • 1981 • 1982 • 1983 • 1984 • 1985 • 1986 • 1987 • **1988**

Canterbury Cathedral, St Augustine's Abbey and St Martin's Church
United Kingdom

Criteria – Human creative genius; Interchange of values; Heritage associated with events of universal significance

Canterbury, in Kent, has been the seat of the spiritual head of the Church of England for nearly five centuries. Three distinct cultural properties are on the World Heritage List: the modest St Martin's Church, the oldest church in England; the ruins of St Augustine's Abbey, which fell into disuse following the dissolution of the community by Henry VIII in 1538; and the superb Christ Church Cathedral, a breathtaking mixture of Romanesque and Perpendicular Gothic, where Archbishop Thomas Becket was murdered in 1170. The cathedral's beauty is enhanced by a set of exceptional stained glass windows which constitute the richest collection in the United Kingdom. These three monuments are milestones in the religious history of the regions of Great Britain before the Reformation.

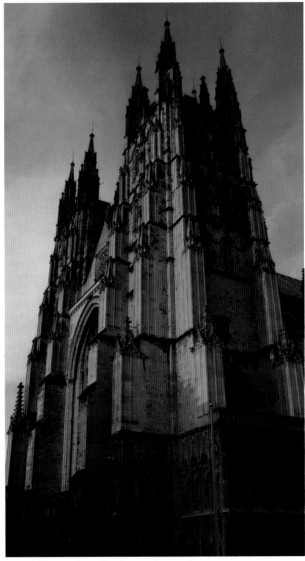

Christ Church Cathedral (Canterbury Cathedral). ▲

St Martin's Church, located outside the walls of Roman Durovernum, existed in 597 when the monk Augustine was sent from Rome by Gregory the Great to bring Christianity to the Saxon kingdom of Kent. It undoubtedly includes a Roman structure from the fourth century.

World Heritage site since

· 1978 · 1979 · 1980 · 1981 · 1982 · 1983 · 1984 · 1985 · 1986 · 1987 · **1988**

Old City of Salamanca
Spain

Criteria – *Human creative genius; Interchange
of values; Significance in human history*

Salamanca is one of the key centres of
a dynasty of architects, decorators and
sculptors from Catalonia, the Churriguera.
The Churrigueresque style also exerted
considerable influence in the eighteenth
century in the countries of Latin America.
However, the city owes its most essential
features to its university. The remarkable
group of buildings in the Gothic,
Renaissance and Baroque styles which, from
the fifteenth to the eighteenth centuries,

grew up around the institution that
proclaimed itself 'Mother of Virtues, of
Sciences and of the Arts'. The University had
already established itself by 1250 as one of
the best in Europe. The oldest university
building in Salamanca, now the Rectorate,
is the former Hospital del Estudio, built in
1413. The main university buildings,
Las Escuelas Mayores, are grouped around
a central patio and were built between
1415 and 1433.

Beginning with the
Roman bridge that
spans the Río Tormes
southwest of the city,
numerous witnesses
to the history of
Salamanca still stand:
the Old Cathedral
and San Marcos
(twelfth century); the
Salina and the
Monterrey palaces
(sixteenth century);
and the **Plaza Mayor
(pictured below)**, the
most sumptuous of
the Baroque squares
in Spain (eighteenth
century).

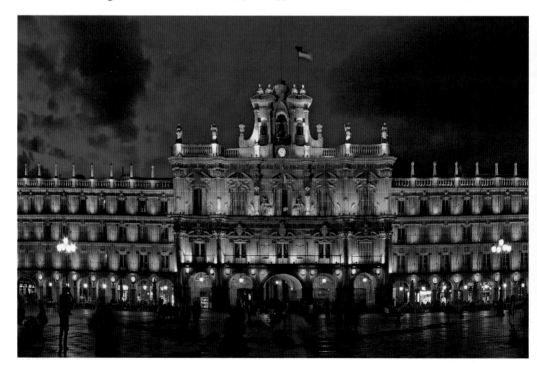

World Heritage site since

• 1978 • 1979 • 1980 • 1981 • 1982 • 1983 • 1984 • 1985 • 1986 • 1987 • **1988**

Hierapolis-Pamukkale
Turkey

Criteria – Testimony to cultural tradition;
Significance in human history; Natural
phenomena or beauty

Mineral-laden waters from hot springs at
Pamukkale (in Turkish, literally 'cotton
castle') have created an unreal landscape,
made up of mineral forests, petrified
waterfalls and a series of terraced pools.
At the end of the second century BC the
dynasty of the Attalids, the kings of
Pergamon, established the thermal spa of
Hierapolis here. The ruins of the baths,
temples and other Greek monuments can
be seen at the site. The Romans acquired full

control in 129 BC and it prospered as a
cosmopolitan city where Anatolians,
Graeco-Macedonians, Romans and Jews
intermingled. The hot springs also served
another purpose: the scouring and dyeing
of wool. According to Christian tradition,
Philip the Apostle converted it and was
crucified here by Domitian around the year 87.
Christian remains include the cathedral,
baptistery, churches and the martyrium of
St Philip.

The therapeutic
virtues of the waters
were exploited with
immense hot basins
and pools for
swimming.
Hydrotherapy was
accompanied by
religious practices,
which were developed
in relation to local cults.
The Temple of Apollo
was erected on a fault
from which noxious
vapours escaped.

Travertine pools and
terraces.

▼

World Heritage site since

• 1978 • 1979 • 1980 • 1981 • 1982 • 1983 • 1984 • 1985 • 1986 • 1987 • **1988**

Pre-Hispanic City of Chichen-Itza
Mexico

Criteria – Human creative genius; Interchange of values; Testimony to cultural tradition

NORTH AMERICA

Pacific Ocean

Caribbean Sea

Pyramid of Kukulcán, ▶ El Castillo.

The buildings of Chichen-Itza illustrate the fusion of the Mayan and Toltec traditions. Specific examples are the Caracol, a circular observatory, and the Pyramid of Kukulcán, El Castillo. Surrounding El Castillo are terraces where the major monumental complexes were built: on the northwest are the Great Ball Court, Skull Wall, Jaguar Temple and the House of Eagles; on the northeast the Temple of the Warriors, Group of the Thousand Columns, market and ball courts; and on the southwest the Tomb of the High Priest.

Chichen-Itza is the most important archaeological vestige of the Maya-Toltec civilization in Yucatán. Its monuments are among the undisputed masterpieces of Mesoamerican architecture because of the beauty of their proportions, the refinement of their construction and the splendour of their sculpted decorations. These monuments exerted an influence throughout the entire Yucatán cultural zone from the tenth to the fifteenth centuries.

Chichen-Itza is the northernmost of the major archaeological sites in Yucatán. Covering more than 3km², it is also one of the largest and richest in monuments. Above all, it is one of the most significant in historical terms because it illustrates two major periods in pre-Hispanic civilizations in the Mesoamerican zone.

The town was established during the Classic period around the early or mid-fifth century AD close to two natural cavities (cenotes or chenes) which facilitated the tapping of underground water. The town that grew up around the sector known as Chichen Viejo already boasted important monuments: the Building of the Nuns, Temple of the Panels and Temple of the Stag, constructed between the sixth and tenth centuries.

The second settlement of Chichen-Itza, and the most important for historians, corresponded to the migration of Toltec warriors from the Mexican plateau towards the south during the tenth century. The Toltec invaders subjugated the local population with a ferocity which even five centuries later the chronicles of the 'sacred books' of the Mayans spoke of. The Toltecs imposed the ritual of human sacrifice which until then was rarely, if at all, practised in the region.

Following the conquest of Yucatán a new style blending the Mayan and Toltec traditions developed, symbolizing the acculturation. Chichen-Itza is a clear illustration of this fusion.

This new architecture, known today as Maya-Yucatec, took from the old local structures the art of stereotomy used on walls and vaults while incorporating certain Toltec elements in the decorations.

After the thirteenth century no major monuments seem to have been constructed at Chichen-Itza and the city rapidly declined in the fifteenth century. In 1556 Bishop Diego de Landa visited the practically abandoned ruins and recorded the legends pertaining to the various monuments. The ruins were not excavated until 1841.

Meteora
Greece

Criteria – Human creative genius; Interchange of values; Significance in human history; Traditional human settlement; Natural phenomena or beauty

EUROPE

Ionian
Sea

Mediterranean Sea

Rising starkly above the Peneas valley in the Thessalian plain, the Meteora, or rock pinnacles, are enormous residual masses of sandstone and conglomerate. Hermits and ascetics probably began settling in this extraordinary area in the eleventh century. In the late-twelfth century a small church called the Panaghia Doupiani or 'Skete' was built at the foot of one of these 'heavenly columns', where monks had already taken up residence. During the fearsome time of political instability in fourteenth-century Thessaly, monasteries were systematically built on top of the inaccessible peaks and, towards the end of the fifteenth century, there were twenty-four of them. They continued to flourish until the seventeenth century. Today, only four monasteries – the Aghios Stephanos, the Aghia Trias, Varlaam and the Meteoron – still house religious communities.

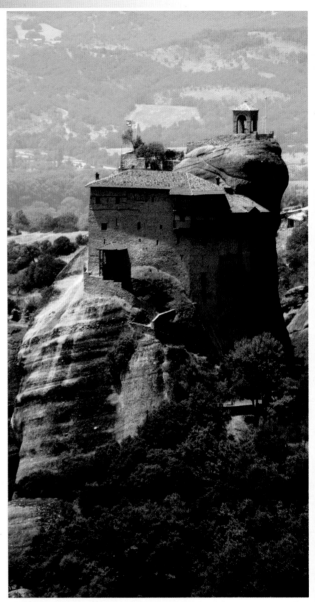

The holy monastery of Saint Nicholas Anapafsa. ▲

The sixteenth-century frescoes in the monasteries built on the Meteora mark a key stage in the development of post-Byzantine painting.

World Heritage site since

• 1978 • 1979 • 1980 • 1981 • 1982 • 1983 • 1984 • 1985 • 1986 • 1987 • **1988**

Nanda Devi and Valley of Flowers National Parks
India

Criteria – Natural phenomena or beauty;
Significant natural habitat for biodiversity

Nestled high in the west Himalaya, India's Valley of Flowers National Park is renowned for its meadows of endemic alpine flowers and outstanding natural beauty. This richly diverse area is also home to rare and endangered animals, including the Asiatic black bear, snow leopard, brown bear and blue sheep. The gentle landscape of the Valley of Flowers National Park complements the rugged mountain wilderness of Nanda Devi National Park. Together they encompass a unique transition zone between the mountain ranges of the Zanskar and Great Himalaya, praised by mountaineers and botanists for over a century and in Hindu mythology for much longer.

The area is a vast glacial basin, divided by a series of parallel, north-south oriented ridges which rise up to the encircling mountain rim. Nanda Devi West, India's second-highest mountain, lies on a short ridge projecting into the basin.

Xanthos-Letoon
Turkey

Criteria – Interchange of values; Testimony to cultural tradition

This site, which was the capital of Lycia, illustrates the blending of Lycian traditions and Hellenic influence, especially in its funerary art. The epigraphic inscriptions are crucial for our understanding of the history of the Lycian people and their Indo-European language.

The Lycians were one of the 'Sea Peoples' who invaded the Hittite Empire around 1200 BC. The Greek historian Herodotus, who lived in the fifth century BC, related that they came from Crete to take part in the Trojan War.

◄

Pillar tombs at Xanthos-Letoon, with the 'Harpy Tomb' on the right.

Strasbourg – Grande Île
France

Criteria – Human creative genius; Interchange of values; Significance in human history

Atlantic
Ocean
EUROPE

The cathedral, with its single spire, is the principal element of the World Heritage site. Goethe considered Notre-Dame de Strasbourg to be the Gothic cathedral par excellence and it had great influence on the development of Gothic sculpture and architecture in Germanic lands.

The Grande Île of Strasbourg is an outstanding example of a European medieval city and a unique ensemble of domestic architecture in the Rhine valley of the fifteenth and sixteenth centuries. Surrounded by two arms of the river Ill, the Grande Île (Large Island) is the historic centre of the Alsatian capital. Rising above the high-pitched roofs with multi-storeyed dormer windows, the cathedral and four ancient churches stand out on the skyline. Facing the south transept of the cathedral is the Palais Rohan, built by the Rohan family in 1732–42 as a residence for the cardinals, princes and bishops of the family. The tight network of streets contain public buildings such as the Hôtel de Ville (1585, today the Chamber of Commerce), inns, shops and workshops, as well as elegant town mansions.

World Heritage site since

• 1978 • 1979 • 1980 • 1981 • 1982 • 1983 • 1984 • 1985 • 1986 • 1987 • **1988**

Kairouan
Tunisia

Criteria – Human creative genius; Interchange of values; Testimony to cultural tradition; Traditional human settlement; Heritage associated with events of universal significance

Founded in 670, Kairouan flourished under the Aghlabid dynasty in the ninth century and bears exceptional witness to the civilization of the first centuries of Islam in north Africa. Its rich architectural heritage includes the Great Mosque, with its marble and porphyry columns, the ninth century Mosque of the Three Gates and the Basin of the Aghlabids, filled by water brought by an aqueduct. Kairouan is, moreover, one of the holy cities of Islam. The medina is surrounded by more than 3 km of walls with three gates: its skyline is punctuated by the minarets and the cupolas of its mosques and zawiyas (monasteries), and it has preserved its network of winding streets and courtyard houses. Very few small windows or arched doorways are cut in the exterior walls, but inner walls have larger openings that give on to central courtyards.

The first Islamic place of worship founded in the Maghreb only thirty-eight years after the death of the Prophet Muhammad, is the Zawiya of Sidi Sahab at Kairouan, where the remains of Abu Djama, one of Muhammad's companions, are kept.
▼

Archaeological Site of Olympia
Greece

Criteria – Human creative genius; Interchange of values; Testimony to cultural tradition; Significance in human history; Heritage associated with events of universal significance

Olympia bears exceptional testimony to the ancient civilizations of Peloponnisos. The site has been inhabited since prehistoric times. Religious centres of worship succeeded one another during the Hellenic period until, in the tenth century BC, Olympia became a centre for the worship of Zeus. Consecrated to Zeus, the Altis is a major sanctuary that includes the ruins of the two principal temples: the Temple of

Hera (sixth century BC) and the Temple of Zeus (fifth century BC). The sanctuary contained one of the highest concentrations of masterpieces of the ancient Mediterranean world, many of which have been lost. In addition, the site includes the remains of the sports stadia and other structures erected for the Olympic Games, which were held in Olympia every four years beginning in 776 BC.

The significance of the Olympic Games demonstrates the lofty ideals of Hellenic humanism: peaceful competition between free and equal men, whose only ambition is the symbolic reward of an olive wreath. Later, not only athletes but also orators, poets and musicians came to celebrate Zeus at the Games.

Remains of dozens of columns at Olympia.
▼

World Heritage site since

· 1978 · 1979 · 1980 · 1981 · 1982 · 1983 · 1984 · 1985 · 1986 · 1987 · 1988 · **1989**

Monastery of Alcobaça
Portugal

Criteria – Human creative genius; Significance in human history

The monastery is an outstanding example of a great Cistercian establishment with the church of Santa Maria d'Alcobaça, a masterpiece of Gothic Cistercian art, and a significant grouping of medieval monastic buildings (cloister and lavabo, chapter room, parlour, dormitory, the monks' room and the refectory). The monastery was given by King Alfonso I to the Cistercians after 1152 on the understanding that they would colonize and work the surrounding lands. In the thirteenth century, while the abbey church and beautiful monastic buildings were under construction, the abbey's intellectual and political influence had already spread throughout the western part of the Iberian Peninsula. The ultimate symbol of its privileged relationship with the Portuguese monarchy is found in the tombs of Dom Pedro and Doña Inés de Castro, dating from 1360, among the most beautiful of Gothic funerary sculptures.

Front entrance of the Monastery of Alcobaça. ▲

The tombs of Inés de Castro and Dom Pedro (Peter I) are the tangible sign of Peter I's rehabilitation of Inés, assassinated at Coimbra on the orders of his father, Alfonso IV. The quality of the sculpture is surpassed by the compelling symbolism of the iconography which evokes human destiny, death and the Christian hope of eternal life.

World Heritage site since

• 1978 • 1979 • 1980 • 1981 • 1982 • 1983 • 1984 • 1985 • 1986 • 1987 • 1988 • **1989**

Mosi-oa-Tunya / Victoria Falls
Zambia and Zimbabwe

Criteria – Natural phenomena or beauty; Major stages of Earth's history

The Victoria Falls are among the most spectacular waterfalls in the world. The Zambezi River, which is more than 2 km wide at this point, plunges noisily down a series of basalt gorges and raises an iridescent mist that can be seen more than 20 km away.

The falls and associated gorges are an outstanding example of river capture and the erosive forces of the water still continue to sculpture the hard basalts. The complex of conservation areas in Zimbabwe covers over 18,500km² excluding forest reserves. The Mosi-oa-Tunya/Victoria Falls National Park abuts Dambwa Forest Reserve in Zambia. The falls are the most significant feature of the park, and when the Zambezi is in full flood (usually February or March) they form the largest curtain of falling water in the world. During these months over 500 million litres of water per minute go over the falls, which are 1,708 m wide, and drop 99 m at Rainbow Falls in Zambia. At low water in November flow can be reduced to around 10 million litres per minute, and the river is divided into a series of braided channels that descend in many separate falls.

The predominant vegetation is mopane forest, with small areas of teak and miombo woodland and a narrow band of riverine forest along the Zambezi. The riverine 'rainforest' within the waterfall splash zone is of particular interest: a fragile ecosystem of discontinuous forest on sandy alluvium, dependent upon maintenance of abundant water and high humidity resulting from the spray plume. There are many tree species within this forest and also some herbaceous species.

Several herds of elephant live in Zambezi National Park, occasionally crossing to the islands and Zambian mainland during the dry season when water levels are low. Small herds of buffalo and wildebeest, as well as zebra, warthog, giraffe, bushpig and hippopotamus are frequently found above the falls. Vervet monkey and chacma baboon are common. Lion and leopard are occasionally seen. Taita falcon breed in the gorges, as do black stork, black eagle, peregrine falcon and augur buzzard.

Victoria Falls forms a geographical barrier between the distinct fish faunas of the upper and middle Zambezi River. Thirty-nine species of fish have been recorded from the waters below the falls.

Below the falls the Zambezi enters a series of gorges which represent locations successively occupied by the falls earlier in their history. Since the uplifting of the Makgadikgadi Pan area two million years ago, the river has been cutting through the basalt, exploiting fissures and forming a series of retreating gorges. Seven previous waterfalls occupied the seven gorges below the present falls, and Devil's Cataract in Zimbabwe is the starting point for a new waterfall that will eventually leave the present lip high above the river in the gorge below.

World Heritage site since

• 1978 • 1979 • 1980 • 1981 • 1982 • 1983 • 1984 • 1985 • 1986 • 1987 • 1988 • **1989**

Cliff of Bandiagara (Land of the Dogons)
Mali

Criteria – Traditional human settlement; Natural phenomena or beauty

The Bandiagara site is an outstanding landscape of cliffs and sandy plateaus and one of the main centres for the Dogon culture. The Dogon subsistence farmers did not arrive until the fifteenth and sixteenth centuries, yet the region is rich in unique architecture, from flat-roofed huts to tapering granaries capped with thatch, cliff cemeteries and communal meeting-places. Several age-old social traditions live on in the region, through masks, feasts, rituals, and ceremonies involving ancestor worship. The Dogon people also maintain a strong relationship with the environment with their use of curative and medicinal wild plants and the sacred associations with pale fox, jackal and crocodile. The geological, archaeological and ethnological interest, together with the landscape, make the Bandiagara plateau one of West Africa's most impressive sites.

The plateau of Bandiagara is covered in a typically Sudanian savanna vegetation, and a wide range of animal species is found in the region. The cliff and rock habitats support a diversity of species including fox-kestrel, Gabar goshawk, yellow-billed shrike, scarlet-chested sunbird, abundant cliff chats and rock doves.

Banc d'Arguin National Park
Mauritania

Criteria – Significant ecological and biological processes; Significant natural habitat for biodiversity

Banc d'Arguin is located on the Atlantic desert-coast of Mauritania, and the park provides a unique example of a transition zone between the Sahara and the Atlantic. It is a vast area of islands and coastline, with dunes of windblown Saharan sand, shallow coastal pools, mudflats and mangrove swamps. The contrast between the harsh desert environment and the biodiversity of the marine zone has resulted in a land- and seascape of outstanding natural significance. Shallow water vegetation comprises extensive seagrass beds and various seaweeds, offering a favourable habitat for fish. This in turn attracts huge numbers of birds to Banc d'Arguin, which hosts the largest concentration of wintering waders in the world and an extremely diversified community of nesting fish-eating birds.

The local people, the Imraguen or Amrig, relate many of their customs to the natural environment. Even their name literally means 'the ones who gather life'. Fishing techniques, unchanged since first recorded by fifteenth-century Portuguese explorers, include the unique symbiotic collaboration with wild dolphins to catch schools of grey mullet.

World Heritage site since

• 1978 • 1979 • 1980 • 1981 • 1982 • 1983 • 1984 • 1985 • 1986 • 1987 • 1988 • **1989**

Archaeological Site of Mystras
Greece

Criteria – Interchange of values; Testimony to cultural tradition; Significance in human history

Mystras was built around the fortress erected in 1249 on a hill overlooking Sparta by William of Villehardouin. For almost six centuries, Mystras had a troubled existence and was abandoned in 1832, leaving only the breathtaking medieval ruins, standing in a beautiful landscape. From 1262–1348, Mystras was the seat of the Byzantine military governor. The bishopric of Sparta was transferred to the new city: the

Metropolis, dedicated to St Demetrios, was built in 1264, and convents were built and richly decorated. From 1348–1460 Mystras became the capital of the Despotate of Morea. During this period, the zenith of Mystras, the cosmopolitan city was of great importance and its fall to the Turks on 30 May 1460 was seen as being almost equal in importance to the fall of Constantinople in 1453.

The beauty of the churches of Mystras, which, during the fourteenth-century Paleologus Renaissance, had been covered with dramatic frescoes, the renown of its libraries and the glory of its writers (including Georges Gemiste Plethon and Jean Bessarion who brought neo-Platonic humanism to Italy) gave substance to the legend of the 'Wonder of Morea'.

The medieval ruins of Mystras. ▼

World Heritage site since

• 1978 • 1979 • 1980 • 1981 • 1982 • 1983 • 1984 • 1985 • 1986 • 1987 • 1988 • **1989**

Buddhist Monuments at Sanchi
India

Criteria – Human creative genius; Interchange of values; Testimony to cultural tradition; Significance in human history; Heritage associated with events of universal significance

On a hill overlooking a plain, about 40 km from Bhopal, the site of Sanchi comprises a group of Buddhist monuments, monolithic pillars, palaces, temples and monasteries, all in different states of conservation and mainly dating back to the second and first centuries BC. It is the oldest Buddhist sanctuary in existence and was a major centre of Buddhism in India until the twelfth century AD. The principal monument at Sanchi, known as Stupa 1 (pictured on the right), consists of a gigantic mound of sandstone surrounded by sumptuous porticoes with stone railings. Its hemispherical dome measures 36 m in diameter and is 16 m high. It is particularly famous for the extraordinarily rich decorative work on the four monumental gateways that provide access.

When it was discovered in 1818, Sanchi had lain abandoned for 600 years and was overrun with vegetation. Gradually the hill was cleared, uncovering the ruins of about fifty monuments in one of the most remarkable archaeological complexes in India.

World Heritage site since

• 1978 • 1979 • 1980 • 1981 • 1982 • 1983 • 1984 • 1985 • 1986 • 1987 • 1988 • 1989 • **1990**

Monasteries of Daphni, Hosios Loukas and Nea Moni of Chios
Greece

Criteria – Human creative genius; Significance in human history

Although geographically distant from each other, these three monasteries belong to the same typological series and share the same aesthetic characteristics. The first is in Attica, near Athens, the second in Phocida near Delphi, and the third on an island in the Aegean Sea, near Asia Minor. The churches are built on a cross-in-square plan with a large dome supported by squinches defining an octagonal space. In the eleventh and twelfth centuries they were decorated with superb marble works as well as mosaics on a gold background, all characteristic of the 'second golden age of Byzantine art'.

The Monastery of Hosios Loukas has an immense central dome, 9 m in diameter, and is one of the most perfect creations of Byzantine architecture. The church is filled with iconographic treasures of a magnitude and coherence rarely equalled.

Colonial City of Santo Domingo
Dominican Republic

Criteria – Interchange of values; Significance in human history; Heritage associated with events of universal significance

After Christopher Columbus's arrival on the island of Hispaniola in 1492, Santo Domingo became the site of the first cathedral, hospital, customs house and university in the Americas. This Ciudad Colonial (Colonial City), founded in 1498, was laid out on a grid pattern that became the model for almost all town planners in the New World.

Among the Colonial City's most outstanding buildings is the cathedral, constructed between 1514 and 1542. It is the oldest in the Americas and one of the architectural wonders of the original town. The Ozama Fortress and Tower of Homage were built in 1503: this stone group is said to be the oldest formal military outpost still standing in the Americas. The Tower of Homage in the centre of the grounds is an impressive architectural structure that is medieval in style and design.

Bartholomew Columbus, brother of Christopher, founded the city in 1496 on the left bank of the Ozama River. In 1502 a tropical storm destroyed the city and the colony's new governor Nicolás de Ovando decided that it should be completely rebuilt on the site it presently occupies. Its town plan became the model for Spanish towns in the New World.

▼ Museum of the Royal Houses.

World Heritage site since

· 1978 · 1979 · 1980 · 1981 · 1982 · 1983 · 1984 · 1985 · 1986 · 1987 · 1988 · 1989 · **1990**

Historic Centre of Saint Petersburg and Related Groups of Monuments
Russian Federation

Criteria – Human creative genius; Interchange of values; Significance in human history; Heritage associated with events of universal significance

Winter Palace in St Petersburg. ▶

Known as the 'Venice of the North', with its numerous canals and hundreds of bridges, the city of St Petersburg on Russia's Baltic coast is the result of a vast urban project begun in 1703 under Peter the Great (1672–1725).

St Petersburg's architectural heritage reconciles the very different Baroque and pure neoclassical styles, as can be seen in the Admiralty, the Winter Palace, the Marble Palace and the Hermitage.

The metamorphosis of an inhospitable Baltic coastal area into a superb city where palaces, churches, convents and two-storey stone houses fit in to the urban designs of the Frenchman Alexandre Leblond, was completed in less than twenty years.

The building of Peter the Great's planned capital began in the eighteenth century on the backs of colossal forced labour of Russian soldiers, Swedish and Ottoman prisoners of war, and Finnish and Estonian workers. A network of canals, streets and quays was gradually built up until, by the reign of Catherine the Great (1729–96) at the end of the century, the urban landscape of St Petersburg took on its monumental splendour. An array of foreign architects rivalled one another with audaciousness and splendour in their designs of the

capital's huge palaces and convents and in imperial and princely suburban residences such as Petrodvorets, Lomonosov, Tsarskoie Selo (Pushkin), Pavlovsk and Gatchina.

The impetus of the eighteenth century continued into the nineteenth with astonishing monumental works. In the history of urbanism St Petersburg is probably the only example of a vast project that retained all its logic despite a rapid succession of styles that were reputed to be irreconcilable. Yet from the disparity of styles, an impression of timeless grandeur emerges in this distended historic centre where the greatness of the monuments is on a scale with a landscape free of any background, open to the sea, perpetually swept by sea breezes and criss-crossed by canals running beneath, it is said, more than 400 bridges.

The ensembles designed in St Petersburg and the surrounding area by several international architects exerted great influence in the eighteenth and nineteenth centuries on the development of architecture and monumental arts in Russia and Finland. The site links outstanding examples of Baroque imperial residences with the architectural ensemble of St Petersburg, the Baroque and neoclassical capital par excellence.

Under its previous name of Petrograd, the city was the starting place of the October Revolution of 1917 that brought the Bolsheviks to power in Russia. It was renamed Leningrad as part of the USSR. More than a million of its citizens died of starvation between 1941 and 1944 when the city was besieged for 872 days by the Nazis during the Second World War.

The city voted to readopt the name of St Petersburg (Sankt Peterburg) in 1991 after the fall of Communism.

World Heritage site since

·· • 1978 • 1979 • 1980 • 1981 • 1982 • 1983 • 1984 • 1985 • 1986 • 1987 • 1988 • 1989 • **1990**

Palaces and Parks of Potsdam and Berlin
Germany

Criteria – Human creative genius; Interchange of values; Significance in human history

King Frederick the Great of Prussia (1712–1786) transformed Potsdam from its previous status of garrison town into the 'Prussian Versailles' which was to be his main residence. Sanssouci, a name which reflects the king's desire for intimacy and simplicity, translates the theme of a rustic villa into the marble, mirrors and gold of a Rococo-style palace.

With 5 km² of parks and 150 buildings constructed between 1730 and 1916, Potsdam's complex of palaces and parks forms an artistic whole, whose eclectic nature reinforces its sense of uniqueness. This series of architectural and landscaping masterpieces was built progressively within a single space, illustrating opposing and reputedly irreconcilable styles, yet without detracting from the harmony of a general composition. The area extends into the district of Berlin-Zehlendorf, with the palaces and parks lining the banks of the river Havel and Lake Glienicke.

The World Heritage site covers two other ensembles that include parks, chateaux and buildings, in the middle of which stands the Marble Palace, the king's summer residence. In summer 1945 the Chateau of Cecilienhof at the northern end of the park was the site of the Potsdam Conference that decided the fate of postwar Germany.

Chinese Tea House in Sanssouci Park, Potsdam. ▼

World Heritage site since

• 1978 • 1979 • 1980 • 1981 • 1982 • 1983 • 1984 • 1985 • 1986 • 1987 • 1988 • 1989 • **1990**

Kiev: Saint-Sophia Cathedral and Related Monastic Buildings, Kiev-Pechersk Lavra
Ukraine

Criteria – Human creative genius; Interchange of values; Testimony to cultural tradition; Significance in human history

Designed to rival Hagia Sophia in Constantinople, Kiev's Saint-Sophia Cathedral symbolizes the 'new Constantinople', capital of the Christian principality of Kiev, which was created in the eleventh century. Devastated by the Mongols and the Tatars, Kiev-Pechersk Lavra was almost entirely rebuilt from the seventeenth century onwards. These were times of great prosperity, when pilgrims flocked to the site, and the grounds were filled with numerous Baroque monuments. The Clock Tower and the Refectory Church are two of the main landmarks in a monastic landscape totally transformed by the construction or the renovation of numerous churches. The spiritual and intellectual influence of Kiev-Pechersk Lavra contributed to the spread of Orthodox thought and the Orthodox faith in the Russian world from the seventeenth to the nineteenth centuries.

Today the major elements of the very old historic heritage are Trinity Church, whose twelfth-century structure is hidden by the extremely rich Baroque decor, and especially the catacombs, which include the Near Caves and the Far Caves, whose entrances are respectively at All Saints' Church and at the Church of the Conception of St Anna.

St Sophia Cathedral.
▼

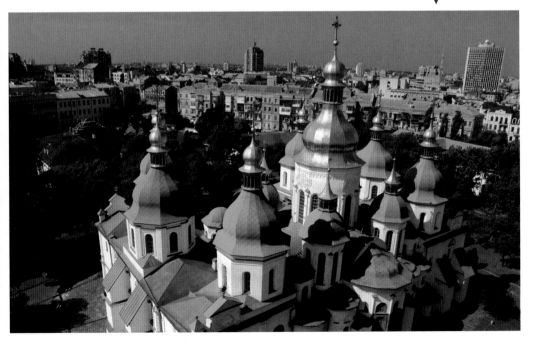

World Heritage site since

• 1978 • 1979 • 1980 • 1981 • 1982 • 1983 • 1984 • 1985 • 1986 • 1987 • 1988 • 1989 • **1990**

Jesuit Missions of the Chiquitos
Bolivia

Criteria – Significance in human history;
Traditional human settlement

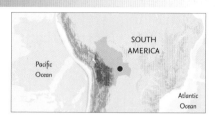

Sent by the Spanish Crown to assure the conquest of the Indias del Cielo, the Jesuit fathers arrived at the Viceroyalty of Peru in 1567 to bring Christianity to the indigenous communities. Between 1696 and 1760, six ensembles of *reducciones* (settlements of Christianised Indians inspired by the 'ideal cities' of the sixteenth-century philosophers) were founded by the Jesuits in a style that married Catholic architecture with local traditions. Unlike other Jesuit missions in

South America that were abandoned after 1767, the *reducciones* of the Chiquitos survived the expulsion of the Company of Jesus. The six that remain – San Francisco Javier, Concepción, Santa Ana, San Miguel, San Rafael and San José – make up a living heritage on the former territory of the Chiquitos.

The *reducciones* defined the urban model: houses were regularly spaced along three sides of a rectangular space, with the fourth reserved for the church, workshops and schools, and sometimes for the Casa de la Misericordia (almshouse), for widows and abandoned women.

Itchan Kala
Uzbekistan

Criteria – Testimony to cultural tradition;
Significance in human history; Traditional human settlement

Itchan Kala is the inner town protected by brick walls some 10 m high of the old Khiva oasis, which was the last resting-place of caravans before crossing the desert to Iran. Although few very old monuments still remain, it is a coherent and well-preserved example of the Muslim architecture of Central Asia. There are several outstanding structures such as the Djuma Mosque, the mausoleums and the *madrasas*, and the two magnificent palaces built at the beginning of the nineteenth century by Alla-Kulli-Khan.

Khiva oasis was the final halt for caravans before crossing the desert to Persia. The outstanding qualities of Itchan Kala derive not so much from the individual monuments as from the incomparable urban composition and harmony of the city.

◄
A view across the city from the city walls.

Tongariro National Park
New Zealand

Criteria – Heritage associated with beliefs;
Natural phenomena or beauty; Major stages of
Earth's history

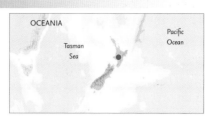

Tongariro National Park is situated on the central North Island volcanic plateau. The mountains at the heart of the park have cultural and religious significance for the Maori people and symbolize the spiritual links between this community and its environment. The park lies at the southern end of a discontinuous 2,500 km chain of volcanoes which extends northeast into the Pacific and contains active and extinct volcanoes. Glaciers are currently restricted to Mount Ruapehu, although all are now less than 1 km in length after several decades of retreat. Habitats are diverse, ranging from remnants of rainforest to practically barren ice fields. The vertebrate fauna is restricted mainly to birds, although native mammals are represented by short-tailed bat and long-tailed bat. More than fifty-six bird species have been recorded in the park, including the brown kiwi and North Island fern bird.

Horonuku te Heuheu Tukino, Paramount Chief of the Ngati Tuwharetoa Maori Tribe, gifted the peaks of Ruapehu, Ngauruhoe and Tongariro to the Crown in 1887. Known as the 'Sacred Gift', it was an invitation to Queen Victoria to stand alongside him to maintain trusteeship over their esteemed taonga (treasure).

Emerald Lake in Tongariro National Park.
▼

World Heritage site since

• 1978 • 1979 • 1980 • 1981 • 1982 • 1983 • 1984 • 1985 • 1986 • 1987 • 1988 • 1989 • **1990**

Kremlin and Red Square, Moscow
Russian Federation

Criteria – Human creative genius; Interchange of values; Significance in human history; Heritage associated with events of universal significance

St Basil's Cathedral. ▶

The citadel of the Kremlin has been inextricably linked to all the most important historical and political events in Russia since it was built between the fourteenth and seventeenth centuries.

Ever since the establishment of the Principality of Moscow in 1263 and the transfer to Moscow of the seat of the Metropolitan see in 1328, the Kremlin of Moscow was the centre of both temporal and spiritual power. Some of its original buildings border Cathedral Square while others, such as the Nativity of the Virgin (1393), were incorporated into the Great Palace when it was rebuilt.

The nucleus expanded northward with the palace of the Patriarchs and the Church of the Twelve Apostles, erected in the seventeenth century, and especially with the Arsenal of Peter the Great which fills the northwest angle of the boundary wall. The triangular palace of the Senate (today the seat of the Council of Ministers) was built by the architect Matvey Kazakov for Empress Catherine II in the northeast sector between the Arsenal and the monasteries of the Miracle and of the Ascension, two splendid structures that were razed in 1932. In the southeast sector Kazakov built for the empress another smaller palace, known as the Nicholas palace, also destroyed in 1932.

The Kremlin has been a major influence in Russian architecture as well as a model for the kremlins, or citadels, in the centre of other Russian cities, such as Pskov, Tula, Kazan and Smolensk.

Red Square, lying beneath the east wall, is closely associated with the Kremlin. At its south end is the famous onion-domed Cathedral of St Basil the Blessed (see photo on the right), one of the most beautiful monuments of Orthodox art. It was originally one of a pair of churches, the other being the Cathedral of Kazan, erected in the vast open area bordering the 'Goum' in 1633 by Prince Pozarsky to commemorate the victory over the Poles. It disappeared in the early 1930s along with several convents in the neighbouring area (Saviour-behind-the-Images, St Nicholas and Epiphany).

The Kremlin contains within its walls a unique series of architectural and artistic masterpieces. These include religious monuments of exceptional beauty such as the Church of the Annunciation, Cathedral of the Dormition, Church of the Archangel and the bell tower of Ivan Veliki; and palaces such as the Great Palace of the Kremlin, the yellow-and-white palace of the tsars which contains the Church of the Nativity of the Virgin, and the Teremnoi Palace.

World Heritage site since

· 1978 · 1979 · 1980 · 1981 · 1982 · 1983 · 1984 · 1985 · 1986 · 1987 · 1988 · 1989 · **1990**

Tsingy de Bemaraha Strict Nature Reserve
Madagascar

Criteria – Natural phenomena or beauty;
Significant natural habitat for biodiversity

This reserve lies 60–80 km inland from the west coast, north of the Manambolo river. It contains spectacular karstic landscapes and limestone uplands cut into impressive tsingy peaks (sharp-edged and very tall towers of limestone) and a 'forest' of limestone needles. The limestone karst is delimited to the east by abrupt cliffs which rise some 300–400 m above the Manambolo river, creating an impressive canyon. The western slopes rise more gently, and the whole western region of the reserve forms a plateau with rounded hillocks. To the north undulating hills alternate with limestone extrusions, whereas in the south extensive pinnacle formations make access extremely restricted. Vegetation is characteristic of the calcareous karst regions of western Madagascar, with dense, dry, deciduous forest, and extensive savannas and some mangrove swamps.

The fauna of the region has not been studied in any detail. The Tsingy is the only known location for the chameleon and the only protected area where the endemic nesomyine rodent occurs. Other notable threatened species include the goshawk and various species of lemur.

World Heritage site since

• 1978 • 1979 • 1980 • 1981 • 1982 • 1983 • 1984 • 1985 • 1986 • 1987 • 1988 • 1989 • **1990**

Delos
Greece

Criteria – Interchange of values; Testimony to
cultural tradition; Significance in human history;
Heritage associated with events of universal
significance

Delos bears unique witness to the
civilizations of the Aegean world from the
third millennium BC to the early Christian
era. According to Greek mythology, Apollo
was born on this tiny island in the Cyclades
and it became the major sanctuary
dedicated to him, attracting pilgrims from
all over Greece. It was a very important
cosmopolitan Mediterranean port. Today
the island's landscape consists solely of
exceptionally extensive and rich ruins

unearthed systematically since 1872. The
principal zones are the northeast coastal
plain (Sanctuary of Apollo, Agora of the
Compitaliasts, Agora of the Delians); the
Sacred Lake region (Agora of Theophrastos,
Agora of the Italians, the renowned Terrace
of the Lions); the Mount Kynthos area
(Terrace of the Sanctuaries of the Foreign
Gods, Heraion); and the theatre quarter,
whose poignant ruins have been overrun
by vegetation.

Delos' era of maritime
trade ended in 69 BC
with the sacking of
the island by
Athenodoros, and it
was then abandoned
in the sixth century.
It was turned into a
quarry site and the
columns of its
temples were
consumed in lime
kilns and the walls of
its houses left in ruins.

Terrace of the Lions.
▼

World Heritage site since

• 1978 • 1979 • 1980 • 1981 • 1982 • 1983 • 1984 • 1985 • 1986 • 1987 • 1988 • 1989 • 1990

Te Wahipounamu – South West New Zealand
New Zealand

Criteria – Natural phenomena or beauty; Major stages of Earth's history; Significant ecological and biological processes; Significant natural habitat for biodiversity

Aoraki (Mount Cook). ▶

As the least-modified region on mainland New Zealand, this is the core habitat for many indigenous animals and contains the country's largest population of forest birds. A few mountain valleys in Fiordland harbour the total wild population (about 170 birds) of the takahe, a large, flightless rail believed extinct until 'rediscovered' in 1948. Most of New Zealand's fur seals are found along the southwest coast. Virtually wiped out by sealing in the early 1800s, they currently number about 50,000.

Te Wahipounamu, situated in southwest New Zealand, comprises the least-disturbed tenth of New Zealand's landmass, with some 20,000 km² of temperate rainforest, 450 km of alpine communities, and a distinctive fauna. The park provides a habitat for rare and endangered species such as the kea, the world's only alpine parrot, and the takahe, a large, flightless bird. It also contains the best modern representation of the ancient flora and fauna of the original southern supercontinent of Gondwanaland, including Podocarpus species and genera of beech which cover two thirds of the park and can be over 800 years old, flightless kiwis, 'bush' moas and carnivorous Powelliphanta land snails.

The overwhelming mountainous character of the area results from tectonic movement between the Pacific and Indo-Australian plates over the last five million years. High local relief is the result of deep glacial excavation and glaciers are an important feature of the area, especially in the vicinity of Westland and Aoraki/Mount Cook national parks. There have also been substantial post-glacial changes, especially marked in south Westland and the Southern Alps. Erosion is rapid, especially west of the Main Divide. Intense gullying, serrated ridges, and major and minor rock falls are characteristic of this zone. However, glacial landforms are almost entirely intact in Fiordland.

The vegetation is notable for its diversity and essentially pristine condition. A floristically rich alpine vegetation of shrubs, tussocks and herbs extends around the summits of the mountains, from about 1,000 m to the permanent snowline. At warmer lower altitudes, the rainforest is dominated by dense stands of tall podocarps. The wetter, milder west is characterized by luxuriant rainforest and wetlands; the drier, more continental east has more open forest, shrublands and tussock grasslands. The most extensive and least modified natural freshwater wetlands in New Zealand are found in this area. Sizeable open wetlands, including high-fertility swamps and low-fertility peat bogs, are a particular feature of the south Westland coastal plain.

The best-known vegetation chronosequences are those on glacial landforms where the ages of outwash, terrace and higher piedmont surfaces are known. The most impressive landform chronosequence is found in the flights of marine terraces in southern Fiordland.

World Heritage site since

· 1978 · 1979 · 1980 · 1981 · 1982 · 1983 · 1984 · 1985 · 1986 · 1987 · 1988 · 1989 · **1990**

Kizhi Pogost
Russian Federation

Criteria – *Human creative genius; Significance in human history; Traditional human settlement*

The pogost of Kizhi (the Kizhi enclosure) is located on one of the many islands in Lake Onega, in Karelia. Two eighteenth-century wooden churches, and an octagonal clock tower, also in wood and built in 1862, can be seen there. These unusual constructions, in which carpenters created a bold visionary architecture, perpetuate an ancient model of parish space and are in harmony with the surrounding landscape.

Kizhi Pogost represents the adaptation of the Orthodox Church parish organization to the challenges posed by the immense distances and far-flung communities of northern Russia. Here, all the buildings needed in the parish's religious life were grouped in one place.

◄

Church of the Transfiguration.

Río Abiseo National Park
Peru

Criteria – *Testimony to cultural tradition; Natural phenomena or beauty; Significant ecological and biological processes; Significant natural habitat for biodiversity*

Río Abiseo National Park is an outstanding example of ongoing geological processes, biological evolution and man's interaction with the natural environment. The topography is mountainous, often with very steep slopes. The Río Abiseo soils are generally acidic and have never been disturbed by agriculture or timber extraction. The park was created in 1983 to protect the fauna and flora of the rainforests, which includes many rare and

important species. Jaguar, spectacled bear, jaguarundi and giant armadillo all thrive here, and the yellow-tailed woolly monkey, previously thought extinct, is found only in this area. Research undertaken since 1985 has already uncovered at altitudes of between 2,500 and 4,000 m, thirty-six previously unknown archaeological sites which give a good picture of pre-Inca society.

Río Abiseo is renowned for its pristine primary cloud forest and highland grasslands (paramo). Archaeological evidence from the park suggests that humans settled in the area from as early as 6000 BC.

World Heritage site since

· 1978 · 1979 · 1980 · 1981 · 1982 · 1983 · 1984 · 1985 · 1986 · 1987 · 1988 · 1989 · **1990**

Mount Huangshan
China

Criteria – Interchange of values; Natural phenomena or beauty; Significant natural habitat for biodiversity

Huangshan, known as 'the loveliest mountain of China', has been acclaimed in art and literature for much of Chinese history. Today it holds the same fascination for those who come on a pilgrimage to the mountain, which is renowned for its magnificent scenery made up of many granite peaks and strangely shaped rocks emerging out of a sea of clouds. It presents a beautiful spectacle, with ridges, gorges, forests, lakes and waterfalls. Many of the lakes having clear blue, turquoise or green waters, while in autumn many of the leaves turn a range of rich colours. The site supports a high diversity of plant and animal species, including some that are threatened. A number of trees are celebrated on account of their age, grotesque shape or precipitously perched position, including 1,000-year-old specimens of Huangshan pine, ginkgo and alpine juniper.

▲

Huangshan is considered to be a prime example of classic Chinese scenery, as typified in Chinese landscape paintings. On 17 June 747, during the Tang dynasty, an imperial order was issued to name it Huangshan (Yellow Mountain). Poets, scholars and artists were among the many visitors, and by the Yuan dynasty (1271–1368) sixty-four temples had been constructed there.

World Heritage site since

• 1978 • 1979 • 1980 • 1981 • 1982 • 1983 • 1984 • 1985 • 1986 • 1987 • 1988 • 1989 • **1990**

Historic Centre of San Gimignano
Italy

Criteria – Human creative genius; Testimony to cultural tradition; Significance in human history

San Gimignano bears exceptional testimony to the civilization of the Italian Middle Ages in that it groups together within a small area all the buildings typical of urban life: squares and streets, houses and palaces, wells and fountains. San Gimignano was a relay point on the Via Francigena for pilgrims journeying to and from Rome. The town was controlled by two major rival families and was the scene of incessant conflicts between the two clans. As symbols of their wealth and power, seventy-two tower houses were built, some as high as 50 m, of which fourteen have survived. Its walls and fortified houses form an unforgettable skyline, in the heart of the Etruscan landscape. The historic centre of San Gimignano contains a series of masterpieces of fourteenth- and fifteenth-century Italian art in their original architectural settings.

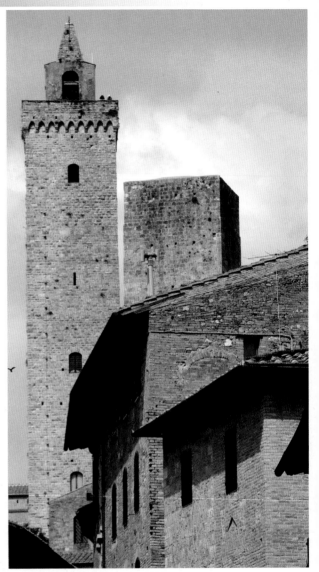

▲ One of the surviving tower houses in San Gimignano.

The frescoes by Memmo di Filippuccio, which the township commissioned in 1303 to decorate the chambers of the podestà in the Palazzo del Popolo, are among the most frequently reproduced documents used to illustrates daily life, down to its most domestic details, of the early fourteenth century.

Historic City of Ayutthaya
Thailand

Criteria – Testimony to cultural tradition

Ayutthaya bears excellent witness to the period of development of a true national Thai art. Founded around 1350, it was the second Siamese capital after Sukhothai and became one of the largest and wealthiest cities in the East. It was destroyed in the eighteenth century but its remains give an idea of its past splendour.

Initially, Ayutthayan art was characterized by a mixture of local traditions with strong influences from Sukhothai. It was only from the fifteenth century that a true national art was born, the product of diverse cultural influences. Traces of outside culture began to appear through its trade links with the West and once these new influences were assimilated, Siamese art entered a period of rich mannerism.

In 1765 the city fell into Burmese hands and was destroyed.

The city's characteristic architectural feature was the prang, a reliquary tower. The kings of Ayutthaya richly endowed the city with monasteries, such as Wat Mahathat in the fourteenth to seventeenth centuries, as well as the Royal Palace, Wang Luang, and gigantic Buddha statues.

One of the few undamaged buddhas remaining at Ayutthaya.
▼

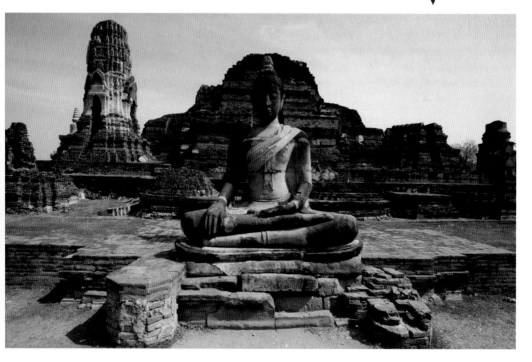

World Heritage site since

• 1978 • 1979 • 1980 • 1981 • 1982 • 1983 • 1984 • 1985 • 1986 • 1987 • 1988 • 1989 • 1990 • **1991**

Paris, Banks of the Seine
France

Criteria – Human creative genius; Interchange
of values; Significance in human history

Atlantic
Ocean

EUROPE

Masterpieces along
the Seine include
Notre Dame (pictured
right) and Sainte
Chapelle, Louvre,
Palais de l'Institut, Les
Invalides, Place de la
Concorde, École
Militaire,
La Monnaie, Eiffel
Tower (pictured below)
and Palais
de Chaillot.

The banks of the Seine are studded with
a succession of masterpieces. From the
Louvre to the Eiffel Tower, from the Place de
la Concorde to the Grand and Petit Palais,
the evolution of Paris and its history can be
seen from the river Seine. The Cathedral of
Notre Dame and the Sainte Chapelle are
architectural masterpieces while Baron
Haussmann's wide squares and boulevards
influenced late-nineteenth- and twentieth-
century town planning the world over.

Paris is a river town. Ever since the first
human settlements from prehistoric days
and the village of the Parisii tribes, the Seine
has played both a defensive and an
economic role. The present historic city,
which developed between the sixteenth,
and particularly, the seventeenth centuries
and the twentieth century, shows the
evolution of the relationship between the
river and the people: for defence, for
trading, for promenades, and so on.

The site and the river were gradually
brought under control in a series of
measures: the articulation of the two islets,
Île de la Cité and Île Saint-Louis, with the
bank; the creation of north–south
thoroughfares; installations along the river
course; construction of quays; and the
channelling of the river. Similarly, although

the city's defensive walls have disappeared,
traces of their existence can be seen in the
difference in size and spacing of the
buildings: these are closer together in the
Marais and the Île Saint-Louis, and more
open after the Louvre.

Beyond the Louvre are a number of major
classic constructions laid along three
perpendicular cross-river axes: Palais
Bourbon, Concorde and Madeleine; Les
Invalides and the Grand and Petit Palais;
and the Champ de Mars, École Militaire
and Palais de Chaillot. The ensemble must
be regarded as a geographical and historic
entity. It constitutes a remarkable example
of urban riverside architecture, where the
strata of history are harmoniously
superimposed.

Haussmann's urban plan, which marks
the western part of the city, inspired the
construction of the great cities of the
New World, particularly in Latin America.
The Eiffel Tower and the Palais de Chaillot
are living testimony of the great universal
exhibitions which were of such great
importance in the nineteenth and
twentieth centuries.

Some, such as Notre
Dame were definitive
references in the
spread of Gothic
construction, while
the Place de la
Concorde or the vista
at the Invalides
influenced the
development of
European capitals.
The Marais and Île
Saint-Louis have
coherent architectural
ensembles, with
significant examples
of seventeenth and
eighteenth century
Parisian construction:
Hôtel Lauzun and
Hôtel Lambert,
Quai Malaquais and
Quai Voltaire.

World Heritage site since

· 1978 · 1979 · 1980 · 1981 · 1982 · 1983 · 1984 · 1985 · 1986 · 1987 · 1988 · 1989 · 1990 · **1991**

Danube Delta
Romania

Criteria – Natural phenomena or beauty;
Significant natural habitat for biodiversity

EUROPE

Black Sea

The waters of the Danube, which flow into the Black Sea, form the second-largest of Europe's deltas. The reserve is vast in European terms with numerous freshwater lakes interconnected by narrow channels featuring huge expanses of aquatic vegetation. Although the Volga has a bigger delta area, with the greatest stretch of reedbeds in the world, the Danube Delta is the largest continuous marshland in Europe. The delta has been classified into twelve habitat types: aquatic, lakes covered with flooded reedbeds; 'plaur', flooded islets; flooded reeds and willows; riverine forest of willows and poplars; cane fields; sandy and muddy beaches; wet meadows; dry meadows; human settlements; sandy and rocky areas; steep banks; and forests on high ground.

Over 300 bird species have been recorded, of which over 176 breed, the most important being cormorant, pygmy cormorant, white pelican and Dalmatian pelican.

The Danube delta is a remarkable alluvial feature constituting critical habitat for migratory birds and other animals. It is the major remaining wetland on the flyway between central and Eastern Europe and the Mediterranean, Middle East and Africa.
▼

World Heritage site since

• 1978 • 1979 • 1980 • 1981 • 1982 • 1983 • 1984 • 1985 • 1986 • 1987 • 1988 • 1989 • 1990 • 1991

Golden Temple of Dambulla
Sri Lanka

Criteria – Human creative genius; Heritage associated with events of universal significance

A sacred pilgrimage site for twenty-two centuries, this cave monastery, with its five sanctuaries, is the largest and best-preserved cave-temple complex in Sri Lanka. The site was originally occupied by a Buddhist monastic establishment; remains of eighty rock-shelter residences established at that time have been identified. Most probably in the first century BC, the uppermost group of shelters on Dambulla's south face was transformed into shrines.

These transformations continued between the fifth and thirteenth centuries: cave-temples were extended into the sheltering rock, and brick walls constructed to screen the caves. By the end of the twelfth century, with the introduction of sculpture on the upper terrace, the caves assumed their present general form and layout. The Buddhist mural paintings covering an area of 2,100 m² are of particular importance, as are the 157 statues.

One of the site's distinguishing characteristics is the regular renewal of decorated surfaces over time. Conservation measures devoted to stripping back layers of later painting on wall surfaces or sculpture to reveal earlier images would be ignoring the worth of the ongoing tradition which has regularly ensured complete repainting of surfaces.

World Heritage site since

· 1978 · 1979 · 1980 · 1981 · 1982 · 1983 · 1984 · 1985 · 1986 · 1987 · 1988 · 1989 · 1990 · **1991**

Thungyai-Huai Kha Khaeng Wildlife Sanctuaries
Thailand

Criteria – Natural phenomena or beauty;
Significant ecological and biological processes;
Significant natural habitat for biodiversity

The site comprises two contiguous wildlife sanctuaries: Thung Yai and Huai Kha Khaeng, which cover more than 6,000 km² along Thailand's western international border with Myanmar (Burma). The sanctuaries contain examples of almost all the forest types of continental southeast Asia and are among the few areas in Asia large enough to support viable populations of large herbivores (300 elephants) and predators (e.g. tigers). They are home to a very diverse array of animals, including 77 per cent of the large mammals, 50 per cent of the large birds and 33 per cent of the land vertebrates to be found in this region. The reason for such exceptional diversity is partly due to its status as one of only two evergreen forest refuges during the driest periods of the Pleistocene glaciations.

At least thirty-four internationally threatened species are found within the confines of the two sanctuaries. It is also home to twenty-two species of woodpecker, more than any other park in the world.

World Heritage site since

• 1978 • 1979 • 1980 • 1981 • 1982 • 1983 • 1984 • 1985 • 1986 • 1987 • 1988 • 1989 • 1990 • **1991**

Island of Mozambique
Mozambique

Criteria – Significance in human history;
Heritage associated with events of universal
significance

The island of Mozambique bears important
witness to the establishment and
development of the Portuguese maritime
routes between western Europe and the
Indian subcontinent and thence all of Asia.
The towns and the fortifications on the
island, and on the smaller island of
St Laurent, are an outstanding example of
an architecture in which local traditions,
Portuguese influences, and to a somewhat
lesser extent Indian and Arab influences, are

all interwoven, producing a unified whole.

The incredible architectural unity of the
island derives from the uninterrupted use of
the same building techniques with the same
materials and the same decorative principles.

The island's patrimony also includes its
oldest extant fortress – St Sebastian, built
between 1558 and 1620 – other defensive
buildings and numerous religious buildings,
including many from the sixteenth century.

Portuguese
connections with
Mozambique began
in 1497 when Manuel I
of Portugal asked
Vasco da Gama to
establish a trade route
to India. The explorer
left in July 1497 and in
March 1498 reached
Mozambique where
he was welcomed by
the sultan who thought
the Portuguese were
Muslims. During his
second voyage he
occupied the territories
of Mozambique and
returned to Lisbon in
1503 laden with gold.

Main square of the town of Mozambique. ▼

Poblet Monastery
Spain

Criteria – Human creative genius; Significance in human history

EUROPE

Atlantic Ocean

Mediterranean Sea

AFRICA

Santa María of Poblet has served as one of the most majestic and austere Cistercian abbeys, as a massive military complex and as a royal residence and pantheon. North of the church is the great cloister with its fountain, chapter room, monks' dormitory, closed cloister, calefactory, refectory and kitchens. The former lay brothers' buildings are on the west and the infirmary to the north. The monastery also has a gatehouse,

guest house, abbot's and prior's lodgings and work buildings. As a fortress, its walls are an excellent example of fourteenth-century military architecture. Poblet is directly associated with the history of the royal houses of Barcelona, Aragon and Castile. Shortly after 1349 Peter IV had a sumptuous dynastic burial place built in the abbey church and part of the monastery was used as a royal residence.

Lying midway between Tarragona and Lérida, at the foot of the Sierra de Montsant, the Cistercian monastery founded in 1150 by the monks of Fontfroide was transformed into a stronghold in the fourteenth century by Peter IV 'the Ceremonious', King of Aragon, during the War of Castile.
▼

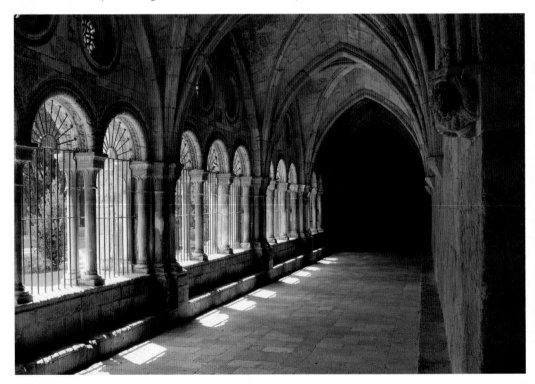

World Heritage site since

• 1978 • 1979 • 1980 • 1981 • 1982 • 1983 • 1984 • 1985 • 1986 • 1987 • 1988 • 1989 • 1990 • **1991**

Historic City of Sucre
Bolivia

Criteria – Significance in human history

Founded in the early sixteenth century, Sucre is an exceptional example of the blending of local architectural traditions with styles imported from Europe. There are many well-preserved sixteenth-century religious buildings, such as San Lázaro, San Francisco and Santo Domingo. The impressive Metropolitan Cathedral was begun in 1559 but not completely finished until 250 years later. In August 1825, the republic of Bolivia declared its independence and the city's name was changed in honour of Mariscal António José de Sucre, who fought against Spanish rule. The House of Freedom is one of Bolivia's most important historical monuments, and many key events that led to independence took place here. It was originally built in 1621 as part of the Convent of the Jesuits.

Sucre was founded as the city of La Plata in 1538. The first capital of Bolivia, its early wealth came from mining activities, but it soon also became a major cultural centre, being home to the Universidad de San Francisco, the Royal Academia Carolina and the seat of the Characas Audiencia, a forerunner of the present Supreme Court.

Aïr and Ténéré Natural Reserves
Niger

Criteria – Natural phenomena or beauty; Significant ecological and biological processes; Significant natural habitat for biodiversity

This is the second-largest protected area in Africa, covering some 77,000 km², though the area considered a protected sanctuary constitutes only one-sixth of the total area. It includes the volcanic rock mass of the Aïr, a small Sahelian pocket, isolated as regards its climate and flora and fauna, and situated in the Saharan desert of Ténéré. The reserves boast an outstanding variety of landscapes, plant species and wild animals.

The reserves harbour significant populations of the wild relatives of several important crop species: olive, millet and sorghum. Both Sudanese and Mediterranean flora are found above 1,000 m in the sheltered wetter localities in the massifs.

World Heritage site since

• 1978 • 1979 • 1980 • 1981 • 1982 • 1983 • 1984 • 1985 • 1986 • 1987 • 1988 • 1989 • 1990 • **1991**

Shark Bay, Western Australia
Australia

Criteria – Natural phenomena or beauty; Major stages of Earth's history; Significant ecological and biological processes; Significant natural habitat for biodiversity

At the most westerly point of the Australian continent, Shark Bay, with its islands and remarkable coastal scenery, is an area of major zoological importance, primarily due to its island habitats being isolated from the disturbances that have occurred elsewhere. The region has three exceptional natural features: its vast seagrass beds, which are the largest and richest in the world; its population of around 10,000 dugongs or 'sea cows'; and its stromatolites, colonies of

algae which form hard, dome-shaped deposits and are among the oldest forms of life on Earth. The stromatolites and microbial mats of Hamelin Pool in Shark Bay assist greatly in the understanding of the evolution of the Earth's biosphere. Shark Bay is also home to five species of endangered mammals and has a rich birdlife, with over 230 species, or 35 per cent of Australia's bird species, having been recorded.

The site is renowned for its marine fauna. In addition to its dugong population, humpback whales use the bay as a migratory staging post. Bottlenose dolphin and green turtle also occur in the bay, and endangered loggerhead turtle nest on the beaches. Large numbers of sharks and rays can also be observed.

Old Rauma
Finland

Criteria – Significance in human history; Traditional human settlement

Situated on the Gulf of Bothnia, Rauma is one of the oldest harbours in Finland. Built around a Franciscan monastery, where the mid-fifteenth-century Holy Cross Church still stands, it is an outstanding example of an old Nordic city constructed in wood. Although ravaged by fire in the late seventeenth century, it has preserved its ancient vernacular architectural heritage.

Old Rauma is the largest and one of the most beautiful historical wooden towns in the Nordic countries. The majority of the buildings in the old city have been sensitively restored as part of a comprehensive development plan.

World Heritage site since

• 1978 • 1979 • 1980 • 1981 • 1982 • 1983 • 1984 • 1985 • 1986 • 1987 • 1988 • 1989 • 1990 • **1991**

Historic Centre of Morelia
Mexico

Criteria – Interchange of values; Significance in human history; Heritage associated with events of universal significance

Built in the sixteenth century, Morelia is an outstanding example of urban planning, combining the ideas of the Spanish Renaissance with the Mesoamerican experience. In 1537 a Franciscan monastery was established near the Indian village of Guayangareo. In 1541, it became the new provincial capital, renamed Valladolid. Although fifty noble families settled here, as did many Europeans over the next few centuries, the population remained predominantly of Indian origin. Valladolid became a bishop's see in 1580. At the same time the College of St Nicholas Obispo (founded in 1540 at Patzcuaro), the oldest institution of higher learning in Mexico, transferred here. Well-adapted to its hilly site, streets still follow the original grid layout. More than 200 historic buildings, including twenty public buildings and twenty-one churches, all in the region's characteristic pink stone, reflect the town's architectural history.

As an intellectual centre Valladolid was among the principal towns in Mexico's fight for independence in the early nineteenth century. Two of the leading figures in the struggle were both priests: Miguel Hidalgo and José Maria Morelos. In honour of the latter, a native of Valladolid, the town's name was changed to Morelia in 1828.

Small courtyard plaza with fountain in the historic centre of Morelia. ▼

World Heritage site since

· 1978 • 1979 • 1980 • 1981 • 1982 • 1983 • 1984 • 1985 • 1986 • 1987 • 1988 • 1989 • 1990 • **1991**

Komodo National Park
Indonesia

Criteria – Natural phenomena or beauty;
Significant natural habitat for biodiversity

These volcanic islands in southern Indonesia, of which Komodo is the largest, are best known for the Komodo monitor, the world's largest living lizard, whose appearance and aggressive behaviour have led to them being called 'Komodo dragons' (see photo below). They exist nowhere else in the world and are of great interest to scientists studying the theory of evolution. Mammals include primates such as crab-eating macaque. Introduced species, such as wild boar, as well as feral domestic animals, form important prey species for the Komodo monitor. The seas around the islands are reported to be among the most productive in the world due to upwelling and a high degree of oxygenation resulting from strong tidal currents. The rugged hillsides of dry savanna and pockets of thorny green vegetation contrast starkly with the brilliant white sandy beaches and the blue waters surging over coral.

It is thought that the islands have long been settled due to their strategic importance and the existence of sheltered anchorages and supplies of fresh water on Komodo and Rinca. The evidence of early settlement is further supported by the recent discovery of Neolithic graves, artefacts and megaliths on Komodo Island.

Royal Domain of Drottningholm
Sweden

Criteria – Significance in human history

With its castle, its perfectly preserved theatre, its Chinese pavilion and gardens, the ensemble at Drottningholm is the finest example of an eighteenth-century north European royal residence inspired by the Palace of Versailles. The royal domain of Drottningholm (meaning 'Queen's Island') is located on Lake Mälaren, outside Stockholm, and the island's name acknowledges the closely interwoven history of the castle with the different queens of Sweden. The castle was begun in the seventeenth century but work on it continued throughout the eighteenth century. In 1922, when it once again became a royal residence, it was restored and a large part of the furnishings and decorations of the eighteenth century were returned.

The Chinese pavilion, built in 1769 to replace a wooden pavilion from 1753, is considered one of the most important examples of this type of structure conserved in Europe.

In the early twentieth century the theatre, built in 1766, was restored to its original appearance and refurbished with the original fittings, even the stage sets. It is a unique example of a European theatre of the eighteenth century that has conserved its original state. The sophisticated theatrical machinery is still fully intact, permitting quick changes of scene with the curtain up.

Drottningholm Castle. ▼

World Heritage site since

· 1978 · 1979 · 1980 · 1981 · 1982 · 1983 · 1984 · 1985 · 1986 · 1987 · 1988 · 1989 · 1990 · **1991**

Cathedral of Notre-Dame, Former Abbey of Saint-Rémi and Palace of Tau, Reims
France

Criteria – Human creative genius; Interchange of values; Heritage associated with events of universal significance

The outstanding handling of new architectural techniques in the thirteenth century and the harmonious marriage of sculptural decoration with architecture, made Notre-Dame in Reims a masterpiece of Gothic art. The perfection of the architecture and the sculptural ensemble of the cathedral were such that numerous edifices were influenced by it, particularly in regions of Germany. The former abbey still has its beautiful ninth century nave in which lie the remains of Archbishop Saint Rémi

(440–533) who baptized Clovis, the unifier and first King of the Franks. The former archepiscopal palace known as the Tau Palace, which played an important role in religious ceremonies, was almost entirely rebuilt in the seventeenth century.

The cathedral, the archepiscopal palace and the old Abbey of Saint-Rémi are directly linked to the history of the French monarchy, as the place of coronation of the kings of France.

The thirteenth century builders of Reims, perhaps conscious of erecting the cathedral for the coronation of the kings of France, enhanced its structural elements with greater lightness and made more openings in the walls to allow a maximum of light to filter through the stained glass and illuminate the sacred space within.

▼

World Heritage site since

• 1978 • 1979 • 1980 • 1981 • 1982 • 1983 • 1984 • 1985 • 1986 • 1987 • 1988 • 1989 • 1990 • **1991**

Prambanan Temple Compounds
Indonesia

Criteria – Human creative genius; Significance in human history

Dedicated to the three great Hindu divinities, Siva, Brahma and Vishnu, Prambanan Temple or Lorojonggrang (Slender Maiden) Temple, as it is known locally, is an outstanding example of Siva art in Indonesia.

Prambanan is a magnificent Hindu temple complex in Java, built in the ninth century and designed as three concentric squares. In all there are 224 temples in the entire complex. The inner square contains sixteen temples, the most significant being the imposing 47-m-high Siva temple flanked to the north by the Brahma temple and to the south by the Vishnu temple. Each temple is decorated with reliefs illustrating the Ramayana. There are also three smaller temples for the animals who serve them (Bull for Siva, Eagle for Brahma and Swan for Vishnu). The compound was deserted soon after it was completed, possibly owing to the eruption of nearby volcano, Mount Merapi. The neighbouring Buddhist complex at Sewu comprises a central temple surrounded by a multitude of minor temples and, surprisingly, shares many design attributes with Prambanan.

Prambanan Temple.
▼

World Heritage site since

• 1978 • 1979 • 1980 • 1981 • 1982 • 1983 • 1984 • 1985 • 1986 • 1987 • 1988 • 1989 • 1990 • **1991**

Serra da Capivara National Park
Brazil
Criteria – Testimony to cultural tradition

The park area has rich archaeological elements but is especially remarkable because of the rock art paintings that decorate its caves and shelters.

Many of the numerous rock shelters in the Serra da Capivara National Park are decorated with cave paintings, some more than 25,000 years old. They are an outstanding testimony to one of the oldest human communities of South America. The paintings' iconography reveals major aspects of the religious beliefs and practices of the area's ancient inhabitants. In total, over 300 archaeological sites have been found within the park. Certain geological formations and palaeofauna that included giant sloths, horses, camelids and early llamas indicate that the Ice Age environment was quite different from the existing semi-arid conditions. Fragments of broken wall found in the Pedra Furada shelter appear to be the oldest traces of rock art in South America; they have been dated to 26,000–22,000 BC.

Ujung Kulon National Park
Indonesia
Criteria – Natural phenomena or beauty;
Significant natural habitat for biodiversity

As a result of human and natural impact, the primary lowland rainforest (**pictured below**) that is the area's natural vegetation now covers only 50 per cent of the park. The single most notable event in this regard was the Krakatoa volcanic eruption of 1883.

This national park, located in the extreme southwest tip of Java on the Sunda shelf, includes the Ujung Kulon peninsula and several offshore islands and encompasses the nature reserve of Krakatoa. In addition to its natural beauty and geological interest – particularly for the study of inland volcanoes – it contains the largest remaining area of lowland rainforests in the Java plain. Several species of endangered plants and animals can be found there, the Javan rhinoceros being the most under threat.

World Heritage site since

· 1978 · 1979 · 1980 · 1981 · 1982 · 1983 · 1984 · 1985 · 1986 · 1987 · 1988 · 1989 · 1990 · **1991**

Historic Town of Sukhothai and Associated Historic Towns
Thailand

Criteria – Human creative genius; Testimony to cultural tradition

Sukhothai was the capital of the first Kingdom of Siam in the thirteenth and fourteenth centuries. The great civilization of Sukhothai absorbed numerous influences and ancient local traditions to create what is known as the 'Sukhothai style'. The historic town of Sukhothai has a number of fine monuments illustrating the beginnings of Thai architecture, including the monastery (wat) Mahathat, with its royal temple and its cemetery; Sra Si Wat, with its two stupas,

their graceful lines reflected in the water of the town's biggest reservoir; and an impressive prang (reliquary tower) from a somewhat later period. In addition it still has a large part of its fortifications. The associated towns of Si Satchanm, famous for its ceramics, and Kamohena Pet (wall of diamonds), significant for its strategic importance, are also included in the designation of the site.

Ramkhamhaeng (c. 1280–1318) was one of the most important Thai sovereigns, as he brought Sukhothai extensive territory through his military victories. He invented the Siamese alphabet (Khmer script), imposed strict observance of the Buddhist religion and instituted a military and social organization copied from his vanquished neighbours, the Khmers.

Sukhothai Buddha statue in Sukhothai.
▼

World Heritage site since

.... • 1978 • 1979 • 1980 • 1981 • 1982 • 1983 • 1984 • 1985 • 1986 • 1987 • 1988 • 1989 • 1990 • **1991**

Borobudur Temple Compounds
Indonesia

Criteria – Human creative genius; Interchange of values; Heritage associated with events of universal significance

One of the statues of ▶ Buddha and openwork 'stupas' on the circular terraces.

Borobudur is one of the greatest Buddhist monuments in the world. Founded by a king of the Saliendra dynasty, it was built to honour the glory of both the Buddha and its founder.

This harmonious temple complex was built on several levels around a hill which forms a natural centre. The first level above the base comprises five square terraces, graduated in size and forming the base of a pyramid. Above this level are three concentric circular platforms crowned by the main stupa (relic mound) to which stairways provide access. The base and balustrades enclosing the square terraces are decorated in reliefs sculpted in the stone. They illustrate the different phases of the soul's progression towards redemption and episodes from the life of Buddha. The circular terraces are decorated with seventy-two openwork stupas, each containing a statue of Buddha.

Stylistically the art of Borobudur is a tributary of Indian influences (Gupta and post-Gupta styles). The walls of Borobudur are sculptured in bas-reliefs, extending over a total length of 6 km. It has been hailed as the largest and most complete ensemble of Buddhist reliefs in the world, unsurpassed in artistic merit, each scene an individual masterpiece.

This colossal temple was built between AD 750 and 842, more than 300 years before Cambodia's Angkor Wat and 400 years before work had begun on the great European cathedrals. Little is known about its early history except that a huge army of workers toiled in the tropical heat to shift and carve the 60,000 m³ of stone. At the beginning of the eleventh century AD, because of the political situation in Central Java, divine monuments in that area, including the Borobudur Temple, became completely neglected and given over to decay. The sanctuary was exposed to volcanic eruption and other ravages of nature. The temple was not rediscovered until the nineteenth century. A first restoration campaign, supervised by Theodor van Erp, was undertaken shortly after the turn of the century. A second, more recent one (1973–82) was funded by UNESCO.

The name Borobudur is believed to have been derived from the Sanskrit words 'vihara Buddha uhr', meaning 'the Buddhist monastery on the hill'.

Borobudur temple is located in Muntilan, Magelang, about 42 km from Yogyakarta city.

It lay forgotten for centuries under a blanket of volcanic ash and vegetation. Its rediscovery in 1814 was due in large part to Thomas Stamford Raffles, the British Lieutenant-Governor of Java. The temple was fully unearthed in 1835.

World Heritage site since

• 1978 • 1979 • 1980 • 1981 • 1982 • 1983 • 1984 • 1985 • 1986 • 1987 • 1988 • 1989 • 1990 • **1991**

Fortress of Suomenlinna
Finland

Criteria – Significance in human history

Barents
Sea

Norwegian
Sea

Scandinavia

EUROPE

Located on islands off Helsinki, Suomenlinna is one of the largest maritime fortresses in the world. Built in the second half of the eighteenth century by Sweden, when Finland was part of the Swedish realm, the purpose was to link and fortify several islands so that entry into the city's harbour could be controlled. The work began in 1748 under the supervision of the Swedish Admiral Augustin Ehrensvärd, who adapted

Vauban's theories to the very special geographical features of Helsinki. By the time of his death in 1772, Ehrensvärd had produced the chain of forts, collectively called Sveaborg (Swedish Fortress), that were to protect the approaches to Helsinki. Following Finland's independence (1918), the name was changed to Suomenlinna (Fortress of Finland), and 6 km of walls and 190 buildings have been preserved.

Sveaborg was built to help Sweden counter the ambitions of Russia, whose principal military and naval base in the Gulf of Finland was Kronstadt, commissioned by Peter the Great to protect the city of St Petersburg. However, the fortress was occupied by the Russians after the war of 1808–9 (despite its reputation as being invulnerable).

Abbey and Altenmünster of Lorsch
Germany

Criteria – Testimony to cultural tradition;
Significance in human history

The religious complex of the ruined Lorsch Abbey with its 1,200-year-old Torhalle (gatehouse) and associated artworks comprises a rare architectural document of the Carolingian era with impressively preserved sculptures and paintings of that period. It gives architectural evidence of the awakening of the West to the spirit of the early and high Middle Ages under the first king and emperor, Charlemagne, and is a reminder of the past grandeur of an abbey founded around 760–4. The monastery's zenith was probably in 876 when, on the death of Louis II the German, it became the burial place for the Carolingian kings of Germany. The monastery flourished throughout the tenth century, but in 1090 was ravaged by fire.

During the Thirty Years' War, in 1620–1 the Spanish armies pillaged the monastic buildings, which had been in a state of abandon since the Reformation. Only the Torhalle, part of the Romanesque church, insignificant vestiges of the medieval monastery, and classical buildings dating from the period when the Electors of Mainz administered Lorsch, still survive today.

Kasbah of Algiers
Algeria

Criteria – Interchange of values; Traditional human settlement

The Kasbah of Algiers is a unique kind of medina, or Islamic city. It preserves very interesting traditional houses in which the ancestral Arab lifestyle and Muslim customs have blended with other architectural traditions. The Kasbah also contains the remains of the citadel, old mosques and Ottoman-style palaces. This tightly integrated urban structure is associated with a deep-rooted sense of community.

It stands in one of the finest coastal sites on the Mediterranean, overlooking the islands where a Phoenician trading-post was established in the fourth century BC. This unique natural site has helped define the city's characteristic winding streets and ancient alleys, while the wealth that its position helped create is reflected in the extreme richness of the interior decoration of the houses.

The first schemes for safeguarding the Algiers Kasbah were approved in the early 1970s. A sensitive redevelopment plan is currently under way, introducing modern comfort without upsetting the traditional urbanism and architecture and restoring the Kasbah's original functions: residential, commercial and cultural quarters.

World Heritage site since

· 1978 · 1979 · 1980 · 1981 · 1982 · 1983 · 1984 · 1985 · 1986 · 1987 · 1988 · 1989 · 1990 · 1991 · **1992**

Taos Pueblo
USA
Criteria – Significance in human history

Situated in the valley of a tributary of the Rio Grande, this adobe pueblo represents the culture of the Pueblo Indians of Arizona and New Mexico.

Taos is a remarkable example of a traditional, pre-Hispanic architectural ensemble that is unique to this region and shows the traditional method of adobe construction. The pueblo consists of two clusters of houses built from sun-dried mud brick. Rooms are stepped back so the roofs of lower units form terraces for those above. Access to upper units is by ladders through holes in the roof. The living quarters are on the top and outside, while the rooms deep within were used for grain storage. The roofs are made from cedar logs, their ends protruding through the walls; on the logs are mats of branches on which are laid grasses covered with a thick layer of mud and a finishing coat of adobe plaster. It is a massive system of construction and well suited to the rigours of the climate.

Taos comprises a group of dwellings and ceremonial centres: six kivas, rooms used for religious ceremonies, have been conserved.

The pueblo has largely become a seasonal habitat reserved for ceremonial functions and tourist attractions.

Jiuzhaigou Valley Scenic and Historic Interest Area
China
Criteria – Natural phenomena or beauty

The best-known features in the area are its lakes. Many of these, lying at the base of glacially formed valleys, are classic ribbon lakes which have been dammed naturally, for example behind rock falls from avalanches.

Stretching over 720 km² in the northern part of Sichuan Province, the jagged Jiuzhaigou valley reaches a height of more than 4,800 m, and comprises a series of diverse forest ecosystems. Its superb landscapes are particularly interesting for their series of narrow conic karst landforms and spectacular waterfalls. Some 140 bird species also inhabit the valley, as well as a number of endangered plant and animal species, including the giant panda and the Sichuan takin.

Bourges Cathedral
France

Criteria – Human creative genius; Significance in human history

The Cathedral of St Etienne of Bourges, built between the late twelfth and late thirteenth centuries, is one of the great masterpieces of Gothic art and attests to the power of Christianity in medieval France. The tympanum, sculptures and stained-glass windows are particularly striking. The cathedral was built to a simple but harmonious plan: it is basilical in form, with chapels surrounding the nave. The perspective of the side walls and the unity of the interior space are outstanding features of the building. The cathedral is still surrounded by the half-timbered houses of the medieval town and is essentially as it was when it was completed, both in form and materials, although many elements have been replaced over the centuries, as is the case with all Gothic cathedrals.

The tympanum of the central portal of the west façade bears a grandiose sculptural representation of the Last Judgement, in which Hell swarms with demons and creatures in the torments of despair. The sculptures on the north and south doors and the Last Judgement are notable examples of the art of the period.

▼ Stained glass window in the choir of the cathedral.

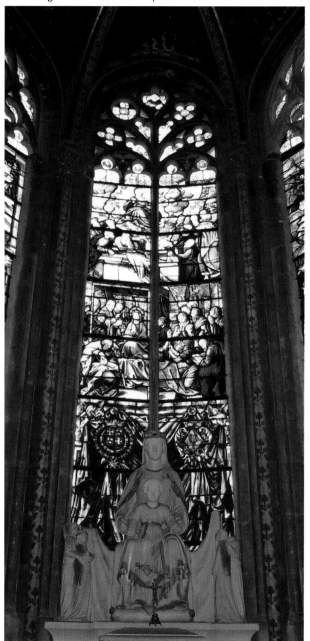

World Heritage site since

• 1978 • 1979 • 1980 • 1981 • 1982 • 1983 • 1984 • 1985 • 1986 • 1987 • 1988 • 1989 • 1990 • 1991 • **1992**

Wulingyuan Scenic and Historic Interest Area
China
Criteria – Natural phenomena or beauty

A spectacular area stretching over more than 260 km² in China's Hunan Province, the site is dominated by more than 3,000 narrow sandstone pillars and peaks, many over 200 m high. Between the peaks lie ravines and gorges with streams, pools and waterfalls. The site also contains a number of karst features, notably some forty caves, many of them with spectacular calcite deposits. There are two spectacular natural bridges: Xianrenqiao (Bridge of the Immortals) and Tianqiashengkong (Bridge Across the Sky), which at 357 m above the valley floor may be the highest natural bridge in the world. In addition to the striking beauty of the landscape, the region is also notable for being home to a number of endangered plant and animal species.

This beautiful area is a vital refuge for a number of animal species that are globally threatened with extinction. These include the Chinese giant salamander, Asiatic wild dog, Asiatic black bear, clouded leopard, leopard and Chinese water deer.

◄

Sandstone pillars and peaks in Wulingyuan Scenic and Historic Interest Area.

Old City of Zamość
Poland
Criteria – Significance in human history

Zamość was the personal creation of the Hetman (head of the army) Jan Zamysky, on his own lands. Located on the trade route linking western and northern Europe with the Black Sea, the town was conceived from the beginning as an economic centre based on trade. Modelled on Italian theories of the 'ideal city' and built by the Paduan architect Bernando Morando, Zamość is a perfect example of a late-sixteenth-century Renaissance town. To populate the city, Zamysky brought in merchants of various nationalities and displayed great religious tolerance to encourage people to settle there: they included Ruthenes (Slavs of the Orthodox Church), Turks, Armenians and Jews, among others. Moreover, he endowed the town with its own academy (1595), modelled on Italian cities.

Zamość escaped the destruction suffered by many other Polish towns during the Second World War, and retains its original layout and fortifications. It has a large number of buildings that blend Italian and central European architectural traditions, and is an outstanding example of Polish architecture and urbanism of the sixteenth and seventeenth centuries.

World Heritage site since

• 1978 • 1979 • 1980 • 1981 • 1982 • 1983 • 1984 • 1985 • 1986 • 1987 • 1988 • 1989 • 1990 • 1991 • **1992**

Historic Monuments of Novgorod and Surroundings
Russian Federation

Criteria – Interchange of values; Significance in human history; Heritage associated with events of universal significance

Situated on the ancient trade route between Central Asia and northern Europe, Novgorod was Russia's first capital in the ninth century. As an outstanding cultural and spiritual centre, birthplace of the national style of stone architecture and one of the oldest national schools of painting, the town of Novgorod influenced the development of Russian art as a whole throughout the Middle Ages. The broad range of monuments conserved in Novgorod makes it a veritable 'conservatory' of Russian architecture of the Middle Ages and later periods. Foremost amongst these are the Kremlin with its fifteenth-century fortifications, the church of St Sophia from the mid-eleventh century, the Church of the Transfiguration, decorated with frescoes at the end of the fourteenth century by Theophanes the Greek, and other monuments from the twelfth to nineteenth centuries.

▲ The church of St John the Baptist, Novgorod.

The most ancient Russian Old Church Slavonic manuscripts (eleventh century) were written at Novgorod, including an autonomous historiography (as early as the twelfth century) and, in particular, the first complete translation into Slavonic of the Old and New Testaments (late fifteenth century).

World Heritage site since

• 1978 • 1979 • 1980 • 1981 • 1982 • 1983 • 1984 • 1985 • 1986 • 1987 • 1988 • 1989 • 1990 • 1991 • **1992**

Historic Centre of Prague
Czech Republic

Criteria – Interchange of values; Significance in human history; Heritage associated with events of universal significance

The Charles Bridge and bridge tower on the Stare Město side of the river. Construction started in 1357 and finished in the early fifteenth century. Until 1841 it was the only bridge over the river Vltava. There are thirty seventeenth-century baroque-style statues lining the parapets of the bridge.

Prague is an urban architectural ensemble of outstanding quality, in terms of both its individual monuments and its townscape, and one that is deservedly world famous. The historic centre admirably illustrates the process of continuous urban growth from the Middle Ages to the present day. Its important role in the political, economic, social and cultural evolution of central Europe from the fourteenth century onwards and the richness of its architectural and artistic traditions made it a major model for urban development for much of central and eastern Europe.

The historic city of Prague comprises three separate cities: the Old Town (Stare Město), the Lesser Town (Malá Strana) and the New Town (Nove Město). Prague quickly became the capital of the Bohemian state after its founding on the banks of the Vltava in the ninth century. The twelfth century brought considerable expansion with the building of a monastery at Strahov and a new stone bridge across the river, which led to the growth of the Stare Město.

Growth continued in the mid-fourteenth century when the Nove Město was founded. Under Charles IV, the Holy Roman Emperor (1316–78), the city enjoyed a golden age as the imperial capital and became a major

centre of culture, attracting artists and architects from across Europe and notably Italy.

A disastrous fire in 1541 destroyed much of the settlement on the left bank of the Vltava, and in the rebuilding Renaissance styles predominated. Decline came at the end of the Thirty Years' War in 1648 and it was not until the end of the century that the city recovered, a period that saw the vigorous development of High Baroque. Urban development from 1880 onwards resulted in the demolition of many old buildings, notably in the Jewish Quarter on the right bank. However, the city benefited from the construction of a large number of outstanding buildings in contemporary style.

Prague is rich in monuments from all periods. Of particular importance are Prague Castle, the Cathedral of St Vitus, Hradčany Square, the Gothic Charles Bridge (pictured on the right), the Romanesque Rotunda of the Holy Rood, the Gothic arcaded houses round the Old Town Square, the High Gothic Minorite Church of St James in the Stare Město, and the late-nineteenth-century buildings and town plan of the Nove Město.

The role of Prague in the medieval development of Christianity in central Europe was outstanding, as was its formative influence in the evolution of towns. The city's political status attracted from all over Europe architects and artists who contributed to its wealth of treasures. Since the reign of Charles IV, Prague has also been the intellectual and cultural centre of the region, a status enhanced by the founding of Charles University in the fifteenth century, and the city is closely associated with such names as Wolfgang Amadeus Mozart and Franz Kafka.

World Heritage site since

• 1978 • 1979 • 1980 • 1981 • 1982 • 1983 • 1984 • 1985 • 1986 • 1987 • 1988 • 1989 • 1990 • 1991 • **1992**

Historic Centre of Český Krumlov
Czech Republic

Criteria – Significance in human history

Situated on the banks of the Vltava River, the town of Český Krumlov was built around a thirteenth-century castle with Gothic, Renaissance and Baroque elements. It is an outstanding example of a small central European medieval town whose architectural heritage has remained intact thanks to its peaceful evolution over more than five centuries. The wealth and importance of the town is reflected in the high quality of many of the burgher houses, as the presence of the seat of government led to Český Krumlov becoming an important craft and trade centre. There was also considerable ecclesiastical development, illustrated by the major fifteenth-century church of St Vitus and monasteries of various preaching and itinerant orders. There are two main historic areas: the Latrán area below the castle and the town proper on the opposite bank of the Vltava.

Other important historic buildings in the town are the Renaissance Jesuit College and Baroque seminary, the Town Hall (created by combining several burgher houses and embellishing them with a Renaissance façade), the remains of the fortifications, and the Renaissance armoury in Latrán.

Mines of Rammelsberg and Historic Town of Goslar and Upper Harz Water Management System

Germany

Criteria – Human creative genius; Interchange of values; Testimony to cultural tradition; Significance in human history

Situated near the Rammelsberg mines, Goslar held an important place in the Hanseatic League because of the rich Rammelsberg metallic ore deposits. It was the site of mining and metal production (silver, copper, lead, zinc and gold) from as early as the third century BC. From the tenth to the twelfth century it was one of the seats of the Holy Roman Empire of the German Nation. The town of Goslar grew up around the imperial residence. The revenues from mining, metal production, and trade financed the creation of the late medieval townscape of fortifications, churches, public buildings, and richly decorated mine-owners' residences which distinguish the present-day town. Mining and metallurgical operations continued at Rammelsberg until the last mine closed in 1988.

The Upper Harz mining water management system, which lies south of the mines, has been developed over a period of some 800 years to assist in the process of extracting ore for the production of non-ferrous metals. Constructed in the Middle Ages by Cistercian monks, and then developed on a vast scale from the end of the sixteenth century until the nineteenth century, it is made up of an extremely complex but perfectly coherent system of artificial ponds, small channels, tunnels and underground drains.

Goslar Market Square and Town Hall.
▼

World Heritage site since

• 1978 • 1979 • 1980 • 1981 • 1982 • 1983 • 1984 • 1985 • 1986 • 1987 • 1988 • 1989 • 1990 • 1991 • **1992**

Ban Chiang Archaeological Site
Thailand

Criteria – Testimony to cultural tradition

Ban Chiang was the centre of a remarkable phenomenon of human cultural, social, and technological evolution in the fifth millennium BC, which occurred independently in this area of southeast Asia and spread widely over the whole region. It is without question the most important prehistoric settlement so far discovered in southeast Asia. It presents the earliest evidence for true farming in the region and for the manufacture and use of metals: its long cultural sequence, size and economic status has no parallel in any other

contemporary site in the region. Although occupation ended at Ban Chiang in the third century AD, it was the principal settlement in this area of the Khorat plateau and has given its name to a distinctive archaeological culture.

In addition to farming and metal production, skills were developed in house construction and pottery manufacture. The equipment of burials and the presence of grave goods indicate both social complexity and prosperity.

◄

Artefacts on display at the Ban Chiang National Museum.

Pythagoreion and Heraion of Samos
Greece

Criteria – Interchange of values; Testimony to cultural tradition

Many civilizations have inhabited the small Aegean island of Samos since the third millennium BC. The remains of Pythagoreion, an ancient fortified port, can still be seen, as well as the Heraion or Temple of Hera. The fortifications round the ancient town date back to the classical period, with Hellenistic additions. Excavations have revealed much of the street plan of the city, together with its

aqueduct, sewage system, public buildings, sanctuaries and temples, agora, public baths, stadium and town houses. One of the most famous features is the Eupalineio, a tunnel running for 1,040 m through the mountainside to bring water to the city. The complex around the Heraion includes altars, smaller temples and statue bases, along with the remains of a fifth-century Christian basilica.

The Temple of Hera at Samos is fundamental to an understanding of classical architecture. The stylistic and structural innovations in each of its successive phases strongly influenced the design of temples and public buildings throughout the Greek world.

World Heritage site since

• 1978 • 1979 • 1980 • 1981 • 1982 • 1983 • 1984 • 1985 • 1986 • 1987 • 1988 • 1989 • 1990 • 1991 • **1992**

Butrint
Albania

Criteria – Testimony to cultural tradition

Inhabited since prehistoric times, Butrint has been the site of a Greek colony, a Roman city and an early Christian bishopric. It became an important trading city and reached its height in the fourth century BC. The fortifications date from the sixth century BC and the hill on which the acropolis stands is encircled by a wall built from huge stone blocks. The amphitheatre, from the third century BC, has stone banks of

seating, of which twenty-three rows have been preserved, while the theatre is situated at the foot of the acropolis, close by two temples, one of which is dedicated to Asklepios, the Greek god of medicine. Under Roman rule the city fell slowly into decay. Following a period of prosperity under Byzantine administration, it was abandoned in the late Middle Ages after marshes formed in the area.

Excavations started at the beginning of the twentieth century. The mud and vegetation that covered Butrint had protected it and the entire city was revealed almost intact. Many objects have been excavated – plates, vases, ceramic candlesticks – as well as sculptures, including the remarkable 'Goddess of Butrint' that embodies the Greek ideal of physical beauty.

World Heritage site since

• 1978 • 1979 • 1980 • 1981 • 1982 • 1983 • 1984 • 1985 • 1986 • 1987 • 1988 • 1989 • 1990 • 1991 • 1992

Angkor
Cambodia

Criteria – Human creative genius; Interchange of
values; Testimony to cultural tradition;
Significance in human history

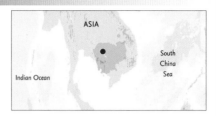

Angkor Wat Temple.

Khmer art, as
developed at Angkor,
had a profound
influence over much
of southeast Asia and
played a fundamental
role in its distinctive
evolution. Khmer
architecture evolved
largely from that of
the Indian
subcontinent, from
which it soon became
clearly distinct as it
developed its own
special characteristics;
some of these evolved
independently while
others were acquired
from neighbouring
cultural traditions.
The result was a new
artistic horizon in
oriental art and
architecture.

Angkor is one of the most important
archaeological sites in southeast Asia.
Stretching over some 400 km², Angkor
Archaeological Park contains the
magnificent remains of the different capitals
of the Khmer Empire, from the ninth to the
fifteenth century. It includes the famous
Temple of Angkor Wat (see photo on the
right) and the Bayon Temple with its
countless sculptural decorations at Angkor
Thom. In total, there are over a hundred
temples throughout the site.

In the early ninth century, Jayavarman II
united the two states that covered the
territory of modern Cambodia, laying the
foundations of the Khmer Empire that was
to be the major power in southeast Asia for
five centuries. Jayavarman's son
Yashovarman established Yashodapura
(later called Angkor), permanent capital of
the Khmer Empire until the fifteenth
century.

The first city had the fundamental
elements of a Khmer capital: a defensive
bank and ditch; a brick- or stone-built state
temple at the centre; and a wooden palace.
A large reservoir was another essential
feature of a Khmer capital and this, now
known as the Eastern Baray, was added a
decade later with a third temple built in its
centre.

In the 960s, Rajendravarman built a second
capital at Angkor; the state temple was
situated at Pre Rup. He also built the
Eastern Mebon temple on an artificial island
in the Eastern Baray, and the exquisite
temple of Banteay Srei. Rajendravarman's
son Jayavarman V abandoned Pre Rup in
favour of a new location with its state
temple at Ta Kev, which was consecrated
around 1000. Shortly afterwards he was
overthrown by Suryavarman I, who was
responsible for erecting the formidable
fortifications around his Royal Palace and
state temple, the Phimeanakas, and also for
the construction of the great Western Baray.
In 1050 his successor created a new and
more impressive state temple, the Baphuon.

The accession of Suryavarman II in 1113
brought the next great phase of building.
He was responsible for the greatest Khmer
monument, Angkor Wat, set within an
extensive enclosure and dedicated to
Vishnu.

A period of internal instabilty after
Suryavarman's death was ended in the 1180s
by Jayavarman VII who celebrated his
military success by creating yet another
capital at Angkor Thom and launching an
unprecedented building campaign. His
state temple was the towering Bayon,
dedicated to Buddha.

World Heritage site since

• 1978 • 1979 • 1980 • 1981 • 1982 • 1983 • 1984 • 1985 • 1986 • 1987 • 1988 • 1989 • 1990 • 1991 • **1992**

Historic Centre of Telč
Czech Republic

Criteria – Human creative genius; Significance in
human history

The later Middle Ages
in central Europe saw
the plantation of
planned settlement
and expansion into
areas of virgin forest.
Telč is an architectural
and artistic ensemble
of outstanding quality
and the best-
preserved surviving
example of such
settlements.

The houses in Telč, which stands on a
hilltop, were originally built of wood. After a
fire in the late fourteenth century, the town
was rebuilt in stone, surrounded by walls
and further strengthened by a network of
artificial ponds. The resulting town is an
outstanding example of Renaissance town
planning and architecture. Baroque
elements were introduced by the Jesuits,
who built a college (1651–65) and the Church
of the Name of Jesus (1666–7). At the same
time Baroque gables were added to the
façades of some of the houses in the
triangular marketplace; Rococo and
classical elements also followed in later
remodelling. The result is a public place
of great beauty as well as great cultural
importance, with a dazzling display of
architecture.

Cultural and Historic Ensemble of the Solovetsky Islands
Russian Federation

Criteria – Significance in human history

The Solovetsky archipelago comprises six
islands in the western part of the White Sea,
covering 300 km². They have been inhabited
since the fifth century BC and important
traces of a human presence from as far back
as the fifth millennium BC can be found
there. The archipelago has been the site of
fervent monastic activity since the fifteenth
century, and there are several churches
dating from the sixteenth to the nineteenth
century.

There are several
detached monasteries
at Solovetsky: four on
Solovetsky Island; the
early-seventeenth-
century Trinity
monastery on Anzer
Island; a sixteenth-
century complex on
Big Zayatsky Island;
and St Sergius
Monastery, founded
in the sixteenth
century on Big
Muksalma Island.

◀

The Solovetsky
Monastery.

World Heritage site since

• 1978 • 1979 • 1980 • 1981 • 1982 • 1983 • 1984 • 1985 • 1986 • 1987 • 1988 • 1989 • 1990 • 1991 • **1992**

Fraser Island
Australia

Criteria – Natural phenomena or beauty;
Significant ecological and biological processes;
Major stages of Earth's history

The earliest date for the occupation of Fraser Island is currently 1,500–2,000 years ago. The Badtjala and Kabi Kabi groups of Aboriginal people have cultural and other traditional affiliations with the area. European contact was sporadic and limited to explorers, escaped convicts and shipwreck survivors.

View from Indian Head, Fraser Island.
▼

Stretching over 120 km along the eastern coast of Queensland, Fraser Island is the largest sand island in the world. It is a place of exceptional beauty, with long white beaches flanked by strikingly coloured sand cliffs, tall rainforests and numerous freshwater lakes. The massive sand deposits provide a continuous record of climatic and sea level changes over the past 700,000 years. The highest dunes on the island reach up to 260 m above sea level. A surprising variety of vegetation types grow on the island, ranging from coastal heath to subtropical rainforests, with trees up to 50 m high. Birds are the most abundant form of animal life with over 230 species being recorded. It is a particularly important site for migratory wading birds. Few mammal species are present on the island. The most common are bats, particularly flying foxes.

El Tajin, Pre-Hispanic City
Mexico

Criteria – Testimony to cultural tradition;
Significance in human history

El Tajin, occupied from 800–1200, became the most important centre in northeast Mesoamerica after the fall of the Teotihuacan Empire. It has survived as an outstanding example of the grandeur and importance of the pre-Hispanic cultures of Mexico. Its cultural influence extended all along the Gulf of Mexico and penetrated into the Maya region and the high plateaus of central Mexico. Its architecture, which is unique in Mesoamerica, is characterized by elaborate columns of carved reliefs and key-pattern friezes. The 'Pyramid of the Niches' rises in six steps to a temple at the top, with each storey having rows of square niches. It is a masterpiece of ancient Mesoamerican architecture, which reveals the astronomical and symbolic significance of the building. The site was abandoned when the region came under the rule of the powerful Mexico-Tenochtitlan kingdom.

The artistic, architectural, and historical importance of El Tajin combines to make this a highly significant site. It has been extensively excavated in recent years and as a result it is probably better understood than many of the more famous pre-Hispanic sites in Mexico.

▼

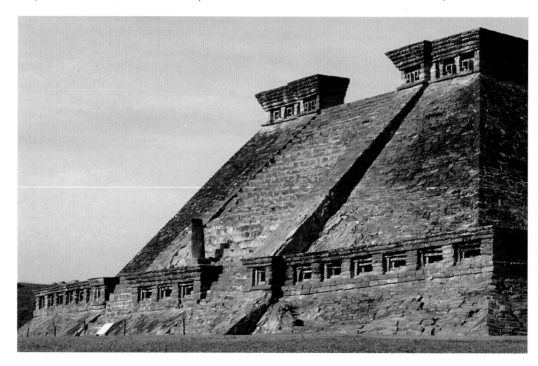

World Heritage site since

• 1978 • 1979 • 1980 • 1981 • 1982 • 1983 • 1984 • 1985 • 1986 • 1987 • 1988 • 1989 • 1990 • 1991 • 1992

Huanglong Scenic and Historic Interest Area
China
Criteria – Natural phenomena or beauty

ASIA

Pacific
Ocean

Situated in the northwest of Sichaun Province, the Huanglong valley boasts extensive areas of precipitous mountain scenery, snow-covered for much of the year. Xuebaoding, or Snow Mountain Peak, is permanently snow-covered and bears the easternmost glacier in China. Huanglong lies close to the intersection of four floral regions: Eastern Asia, Himalaya, and the subtropical and tropical zones of the Northern Hemisphere. In addition to its mountain landscape, diverse forest ecosystems can be found, as well as spectacular limestone formations, waterfalls and hot springs. The area also has a large number of endangered mammals including giant panda, golden snub-nosed monkey, brown bear, Asiatic black bear, leopard, Pallas' cat, Asiatic wild dog, Szechwan takin, mainland serow, common goral, argali and three species of deer.

The area has many spectacular steep-sided gorges and forested waterways. Calcite deposition has resulted in areas of travertine pools; algae and bacteria often proliferate, colouring the pools in deep shades from orange and yellow to green and blue.

▼

World Heritage site since

· 1978 · 1979 · 1980 · 1981 · 1982 · 1983 · 1984 · 1985 · 1986 · 1987 · 1988 · 1989 · 1990 · 1991 · **1992**

White Monuments of Vladimir and Suzdal
Russian Federation

Criteria – Human creative genius; Interchange of values; Significance in human history

The towns of Vladimir and Suzdal hold an important place in Russia's architectural history. Vladimir, founded in 1108, contains an important group of religious and secular monuments. The single-domed Cathedral of the Assumption (1158) contains frescoes by the master painters Andrei Rublev and Daniil Chernii (1408) to replace those destroyed by the Mongols in 1238. The Golden Gate (1164) formed part of the twelfth-century defences.

It is a cubic tower with a church dedicated to the Deposition of the Holy Robe on top. The exterior of the Cathedral of St Demetrius (1194–7) is noteworthy for over 1,000 stone carvings on the general theme of King David. Suzdal is dominated by the Cathedral of the Nativity, built in the thirteenth century and reconstructed in the sixteenth century, with its five-domed top and thirteenth-century Golden Doors.

The other buildings included within the site are the Princely Castle in Bogolyubovo, the Church of the Intercession in Vladimir, the Monastery of Our Saviour and St Euthymius in Suzdal and the Church of Sts Boris and Gleb, near Suzdal, the first church in Russia to be built from white limestone.

Church of the Intercession in Vladimir.
▼

Route of Santiago de Compostela
Spain

Criteria – Interchange of values; Significance in human history; Heritage associated with events of universal significance

EUROPE

Atlantic Ocean

Mediterranean Sea

AFRICA

This route from the border between France and Spain was – and still is – taken by pilgrims to Santiago de Compostela in Galicia. Some 1,800 buildings along the route, both religious and secular, are of great historic interest.

Pilgrimages were an essential part of western European spiritual and cultural life in the Middle Ages and the routes they took were equipped with facilities for the spiritual and physical well-being of pilgrims. The Route of St James of Compostela has

preserved the most complete material record in its ecclesiastical and secular buildings, settlements and civil-engineering structures.

The route played a fundamental role in encouraging cultural exchanges between the Iberian peninsula and the rest of Europe during the Middle Ages. It remains a testimony to the power of the Christian faith among people of all social classes and from all over Europe.

Two access routes into Spain from France enter at Roncesvalles (Valcarlos Pass) and Canfranc (Somport Pass) and merge west of Pamplona. The route passes through five autonomous communities and 166 towns and villages, and includes over 1,800 historic buildings. In many cases the modern road runs parallel to the ancient route. Thousands of pilgrims follow it on foot or bicycle every year.

World Heritage site since

· 1978 · 1979 · 1979 · 1980 · 1981 · 1982 · 1983 · 1984 · 1985 · 1986 · 1987 · 1988 · 1989 · 1990 · 1991 · 1992 · **1993**

Historic Town of Zabid
Yemen

Criteria – Interchange of values; Significance in human history; Heritage associated with events of universal significance

Zabid's domestic and military architecture and its urban plan make it an outstanding archaeological and historical site. Besides being the capital of Yemen from the thirteenth to the fifteenth century, the city played an important role in the Arab and Muslim world for many centuries because of its Islamic university.

Zabid has a remarkable network of streets and alleys, some as little as 2 m wide, which spreads over the town. Occasionally this labyrinth opens out into small squares, but the only large open space is that in front of the citadel.

◄
The Great Mosque of Zabid (also known as the Al-Asha'ir Mosque).

Coro and its Port
Venezuela

Criteria – Significance in human history; Traditional human settlement

With its earthen constructions unique to the Caribbean, Coro is the only surviving example of a rich fusion of local traditions with Spanish Mudéjar and Dutch architectural techniques. One of the first colonial towns founded in 1527, it has some 602 historic buildings.

Unlike other towns on this coast, even Coro's public buildings are of earthen construction, not stone. It has conserved its original layout and early urban landscape, presenting a remarkable record of the earliest years of Spanish colonization.

◄
La Casa de las Ventanas de Hierro (The House of the Iron Windows) which dates from 1765. Its Baroque doorway is 8m tall.

World Heritage site since

· 1978 · 1979 1979 · 1980 · 1981 · 1982 · 1983 · 1984 · 1985 · 1986 · 1987 · 1988 · 1989 · 1990 · 1991 · 1992 · **1993**

The Sassi and the Park of the Rupestrian Churches of Matera
Italy

Criteria – Testimony to cultural tradition; Significance in human history; Traditional human settlement

The Sassi of Matera and their park are the most outstanding, intact example of a rock-cut settlement in the Mediterranean region, perfectly adapted to its terrain and ecosystem.

Matera's development was due to its geological setting. A belt of soft tufa is located between 350 m and 400 m above the valley bed, and this also contains two natural depressions; it was here that the settlement grew up. The clay plateau above was reserved for agriculture and grazing livestock.

The Matera region has been inhabited since the Palaeolithic period, while later settlements illustrate a number of significant stages in human history. The harsh landscape fostered an independence of spirit which was resistant to successive waves of invaders after the Byzantine period. The area was also very attractive to monastic and utopian communities.

The earliest house form was a simple cave in the tufa with a closing wall formed from the excavated blocks. This developed into a vaulted room built out into the open space, making it available for adaptation and extension. Groups of dwellings around a common courtyard evolved into a vicinato (neighbourhood), with shared facilities such as a cistern.

▼

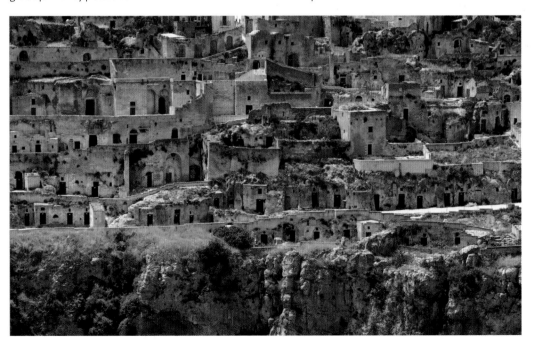

World Heritage site since

• 1978 • 1979 1979 • 1980 • 1981 • 1982 • 1983 • 1984 • 1985 • 1986 • 1987 • 1988 • 1989 • 1990 • 1991 • 1992 • **1993**

Yakushima
Japan

Criteria – Natural phenomena or beauty;
Significant ecological and biological processes

Located in the interior of Yaku Island, at the northern end of the Ryukyu archipelago, Yakushima exhibits a rich flora, with some 1,900 species and subspecies. Of these, ninety-four are endemic, mostly concentrated in the central high mountains. Yakushima is almost 2,000 m high and is the highest mountain in southern Japan. Several other peaks are over 1,800 m with mountain ridges over 1,000 m surrounding these central high peaks. Of great significance to the area is the presence of indigenous Japanese cedar, known colloquially as 'sugi', which can reach more than 1,000 years of age: specimens younger than 1,000 years are known as 'Kosugi'; older specimens, which may reach 3,000 years, are known as 'Yakusugi'. Traditionally, the Island Mountains have been considered to have a spiritual value and the 'Yakusugi' were revered as sacred trees.

The fauna of the island is diverse, with sixteen mammal species. Four mammal subspecies are endemic to the island and a further four are endemic to both Yaku Island and the neighbouring island of Tanegashima. Among the 150 bird species present, four, including Ryukyu robin and Japanese wood pigeon, have been designated as Natural Monuments.

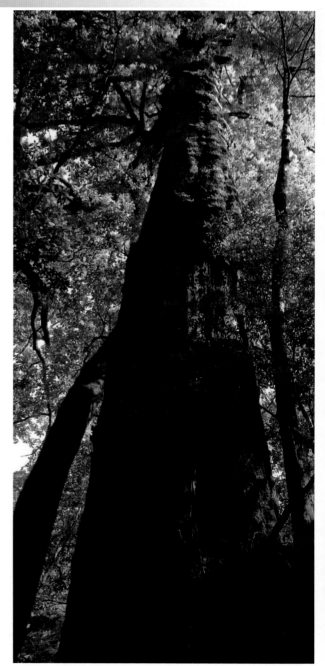

Brú na Bóinne – Archaeological Ensemble of the Bend of the Boyne
Ireland

Criteria – Human creative genius; Testimony to cultural tradition; Significance in human history

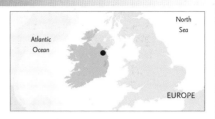

The three main prehistoric sites of the Brú na Bóinne Complex – Newgrange, Knowth and Dowth – are situated on the north bank of the river Boyne 50 km north of Dublin. These three great burial mounds are surrounded by about forty satellite passage-graves, creating a great prehistoric funerary landscape. The passage tomb complex in particular represents a spectacular survival of the embodiment of a set of ideas and beliefs of outstanding historical significance unequalled in its European counterparts. The site's ritual significance attracted later monuments, both in protohistory and in the Christian period. Its importance has been further enhanced by the fact that the river Boyne communicates both with the Celtic Sea and the heartland of Ireland, giving it considerable economic and political significance.

Nowhere else in the world is found the continuity of settlement and activity associated with a megalithic cemetery such as that which exists at Brú na Bóinne. The passage tomb complex represents a spectacular survival of the embodiment of a set of ideas and beliefs.

Whale Sanctuary of El Vizcaino
Mexico

Criteria – Significant natural habitat for biodiversity

Located in the central part of the peninsula of Baja California, the sanctuary contains some exceedingly interesting ecosystems. The coastal lagoons of Ojo de Liebre and San Ignacio are an exceptional reproduction and wintering site for grey whales as well as other mammals such as harbour seal, California sea lion, northern elephant seal and blue whale. The lagoons have a series of shallow, sandy bays and saltwater inlets as well as extensive mangroves, with dune communities, bushes and halophytic vegetation surrounding them. These rich ecosystems are important refuges for wintering wildfowl, and birds such as osprey and peregrine falcon also live within the site. The coastal zone is a vital habitat for approximately twenty threatened animal species, including four species of the endangered marine turtle.

As well as an abundance of wildlife, there are a number of prehistoric sites of importance on the peninsula. There are also petroglyphs, wall paintings and ancient ruined structures, together with evidence of the early colonisation from Europe.

World Heritage site since

• 1978 • 1979 1979 • 1980 • 1981 • 1982 • 1983 • 1984 • 1985 • 1986 • 1987 • 1988 • 1989 • 1990 • 1991 • 1992 • **1993**

Baroque Churches of the Philippines
Philippines

Criteria – Interchange of values; Significance in human history

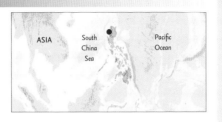

The churches are outstanding examples of the Philippine interpretation of the Baroque style and had an important influence on later church architecture in the region. They represent the fusion of European church design and construction with local materials and decorative motifs to form a new church-building tradition. The four churches, the first of which was built by the Spanish in the late sixteenth century, are located in Manila (San Agustín in Intramuros),

Santa Maria (Nuestra Señora de la Asuncion), Paoay (San Agustín) and Miag-ao (Santo Tomas de Villanueva). The sumptuous façade of the Church of Santo Tomas de Villanueva epitomizes the Filipino transfiguration of western decorative elements, with the figure of St Christopher on the pediment dressed in native clothes, carrying the Christ Child on his back, and holding on to a coconut palm for support.

Unlike other town churches in the Philippines, which conform to the Spanish tradition of siting them on the central plaza, the Church of Nuestra Señora de la Asuncion in Santa Maria with its convento are on a hill surrounded by a defensive wall.

◄ San Agustín in Intramuros Church, Manila.

World Heritage site since

· 1978 · 1979 1979 · 1980 · 1981 · 1982 · 1983 · 1984 · 1985 · 1986 · 1987 · 1988 · 1989 · 1990 · 1991 · 1992 · **1993**

Humayun's Tomb, Delhi
India

Criteria – Interchange of values; Significance in human history

Humayun had travelled widely in the Islamic world, notably in Persia and central Asia, and brought back ideas that were applied by the architect of his tomb. The tomb and its surrounding structures are substantially in their original state, and interventions in recent times have been minimal and of high quality.

This tomb is of particular cultural significance as it is the earliest surviving example of the Mughal scheme of the garden-tomb on the Indian subcontinent. The tomb of Humayun, second Mughal Emperor of India, was built by his widow in 1569–70, fourteen years after his death, at a cost of 1.5 million rupees. It was later used for the burial of various members of the ruling family and contains some 150 graves. It has aptly been described as the necropolis of the Mughal dynasty. The tomb itself is in the centre of a large garden, laid out in char baah (four-fold) style, with pools joined by channels. It inspired several major architectural innovations, culminating in the construction of the Taj Mahal a century later.

World Heritage site since

• 1978 • 1979 1979 • 1980 • 1981 • 1982 • 1983 • 1984 • 1985 • 1986 • 1987 • 1988 • 1989 • 1990 • 1991 • 1992 • **1993**

Birka and Hovgården
Sweden

Criteria – Testimony to cultural tradition;
Significance in human history

Birka-Hovgården is one of the most complete and undisturbed examples of a Viking trading settlement of the eighth–tenth centuries AD. It is also important as the site of the first Christian congregation in Sweden, founded in 831 by St Ansgar. The proto-town of Birka occupies much of the western part of the island of Björkö. The surface evidence is confined mostly to the ramparts of the hill fort, the long ramparts of the town wall, traces of harbours and stone jetties along the shore, and some 3,000 burial mounds and stone settings surrounding the main settlement. Its location on a small island has preserved the entire site from modern development and exploitation. Hovgården is situated on the neighbouring island of Adelsö.

There are no standing remains of the settlement at Birka itself, but its location is vividly indicated by the so-called 'Black Earth,' composed of layers of human occupation and the remains of wooden structures.

Villages with Fortified Churches in Transylvania
Romania

Criteria – Significance in human history

These Transylvanian villages with their fortified churches provide a vivid picture of the cultural landscape of southern Transylvania. The seven villages inscribed on the World Heritage List, founded by the Transylvanian Saxons, are characterized by a specific land-use system, settlement pattern and organization of the family farmstead that have been preserved since the late Middle Ages. They are dominated by their fortified churches, which illustrate building styles from the thirteenth to the sixteenth century.

Lacking the resources of the European nobility and rich merchants, who were able to fortify entire towns, the Transylvanian Saxons chose to create fortresses round their churches, enclosing storehouses within the enceintes to enable them to withstand long sieges.

◄
The Fortified Church in Viscri, Transylvania.

World Heritage site since

• 1978 • 1979 1979 • 1980 • 1981 • 1982 • 1983 • 1984 • 1985 • 1986 • 1987 • 1988 • 1989 • 1990 • 1991 • 1992 • **1993**

Historic Centre of Bukhara
Uzbekistan

Criteria – Interchange of values; Significance in human history; Heritage associated with events of universal significance

Before the Arab conquest, Bukhara was one of the largest cities of central Asia. It became a major cultural centre of the Caliphate of Baghdad in 709, and in 892 the capital of the independent Samanid Kingdom. A time of great economic growth came to an end with the sack of the city in 1220 by the Mongol horde of Genghis Khan.

▼

Bukhara, which is situated on the Silk Route, is more than 2,000 years old. It is the most complete example of a medieval city in Central Asia, with an urban fabric that has remained largely intact. Monuments of particular interest include the famous tomb of Ismail Samani, a masterpiece of tenth-century Muslim architecture, the decorated brick minaret of Poi-Kalyan from the eleventh century, the Magoki Mosque and the Chasma Ayub Shrine, along with a large number of seventeenth-century madrasas. The historic part of the city, which is in effect an open-air museum, combines the city's long history in a single ensemble. It should be stressed, however, that the real importance of Bukhara lies not in its individual buildings but rather in its overall level of urban planning and architecture.

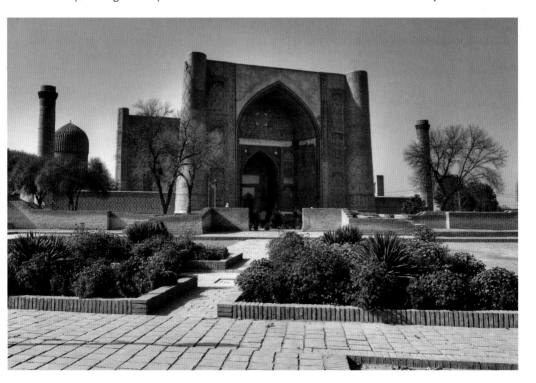

World Heritage site since

• 1978 • 1979 1979 • 1980 • 1981 • 1982 • 1983 • 1984 • 1985 • 1986 • 1987 • 1988 • 1989 • 1990 • 1991 • 1992 • 1993

Town of Bamberg
Germany

Criteria – Interchange of values; Significance in human history

The World Heritage site covers the three centres of settlement that coalesced when the town was founded. These are the Bergstadt, with the cathedral and its precincts; the Inselstadt, defined by the two-arms of the Regnitz River; and the Theuerstadt, a late medieval area of market gardens with scattered houses and large open spaces.

Bamberg is an outstanding and representative example of an early medieval town in central Europe, both in its plan and in its many surviving ecclesiastical and secular buildings. The town was laid out according to medieval planning rules as a cross, with the churches of St Michael, St Stephen, St Gangolf, and St Jacob at the four cardinal points. During its period of greatest prosperity, from the twelfth century onwards, the architecture of Bamberg strongly influenced urban construction in central Europe. This prosperity continued into the later Middle Ages, being helped by the fact that it was the starting point for shipping on the river Main, as well as a renowned cultural centre. In the late eighteenth century it was the centre of the Enlightenment in southern Germany, with eminent philosophers and writers such as Hegel and Hoffmann living there.

▼ Altes Rathaus (Old Town Hall) in Bamberg.

World Heritage site since

· 1978 • 1979 1979 • 1980 • 1981 • 1982 • 1983 • 1984 • 1985 • 1986 • 1987 • 1988 • 1989 • 1990 • 1991 • 1992 • **1993**

Jesuit Missions of La Santísima Trinidad de Paraná and Jesús de Tavarangue
Paraguay
Criteria – Significance in human history

The Spanish Crown granted the frontier zone of Paraguay to the Jesuits in 1609, and they created thirty *reducciones* (settlements) in the Rio de la Plata basin, each with its own mission. One of the Jesuits' objectives became the protection of the Indians against the abuses of the colonial *encomienda* system of tribute or labour, which reduced them to a condition of virtual slavery; at the same time they would be brought into the Christian Church and educated into a sedentary form of life. La Santísima Trinidad was the most ambitious of these missions and the capital of the Guayrá area. Designed by noted Jesuit architect Juan Bautista Primoli, it was constructed in stone in 1706 and has a fine dome and elaborate decoration.

La Santísima Trinidad, the best preserved of the three churches, is of great symbolic importance, because its decoration reflects the spirit of its conception, with its fusion of Christian and native artistic elements.

Maulbronn Monastery Complex
Germany
Criteria – Interchange of values; Significance in human history

Founded in 1147, the Cistercian Maulbronn Monastery is considered the most complete and best-preserved medieval monastic complex north of the Alps. The basic medieval layout and structure of the central complex is virtually complete. Only the monks' refectory and the lay brethren's dormitories have undergone transformations since the Reformation, in order to adapt them for use as a Protestant seminary. Surrounded by fortified walls, the main buildings were constructed between the twelfth and sixteenth centuries. The monastery's church, mainly in Transitional Gothic style, had a major influence in the spread of Gothic architecture over much of northern and central Europe. Its original wooden beams were replaced by Gothic vaulting in 1424, incorporating Romanesque traditions into the Cistercian requirements of austerity and renunciation.

The Cistercian Order was notable for its innovations in hydraulic engineering and at Maulbronn there exists an elaborate system of reservoirs, irrigation canals and drains to provide water for the community, for fish farming and for irrigating its farmland.

World Heritage site since

· 1978 · 1979 1979 · 1980 · 1981 · 1982 · 1983 · 1984 · 1985 · 1986 · 1987 · 1988 · 1989 · 1990 · 1991 · 1992 · **1993**

Engelsberg Ironworks
Sweden
Criteria – Significance in human history

Engelsberg is an outstanding example of an influential European industrial complex of the seventeenth–nineteenth centuries, with important technological remains and the associated administrative and residential buildings intact. It is the best preserved and most complete example of the type of iron-working estate that made Sweden the economic leader in this field for two centuries. Local peasants had been mining ore and smelting since the thirteenth century, but it was not until the introduction of the waterwheel to power the furnace and hammer bellows in the later Middle Ages that the iron industry began to significantly develop. The first bar-iron forge was operating at Engelsberg in the closing years of the sixteenth century, and by the mid-seventeenth century the scale of operations there was substantial.

Self-contained estates like Engelsberg comprised not only technical installations but also administrative and residential buildings for management and workers, including those who worked on the associated farm. This site's notable buildings include the master gardener's house, the brewery, stables, a coach-house, smiths' cottages and a monumental slagstone barn.

Monastery of Horezu
Romania
Criteria – Interchange of values

Founded in 1690 by the Cantacuzene Prince Constantine Brancovan, the monastery of Horezu in Wallachia is a masterpiece of the Brancovan style. It is laid out according to the precepts of the Athonite Order around the catholicon, which is enclosed by a wall and surrounded by a series of skites (daughter houses of the main monastery). The overall layout is symmetrical on an east-west axis, the skites forming a cruciform plan. The monastery is famous for its architectural purity and balance, the richness of its sculptural detail, the treatment of its religious compositions, its votive portraits and its painted decorative works. The school of mural and icon painting established at the monastery in the eighteenth century was famous throughout the Balkan region.

The church of Bolnica, which is a subgroup of the main monastery, was founded by Princess Maria, wife of Constantin Brancovan. It has an unusual mural, on the subject of the life of the good monk.

World Heritage site since

· 1978 · 1979 1979 · 1980 · 1981 · 1982 · 1983 · 1984 · 1985 · 1986 · 1987 · 1988 · 1989 · 1990 · 1991 · 1992 · **1993**

Himeji-jo
Japan

Criteria – Human creative genius; Significance in human history

Himeji-jo is the finest surviving example of early seventeenth-century Japanese castle architecture, comprising eighty-three buildings with highly developed systems of defence and ingenious protection devices dating from the beginning of the Shogun period. It is a masterpiece of construction in wood. The centre of the complex is the Tenshu-gun, consisting of a main keep and three subsidiary keeps, with connecting structures. This is surrounded by a system of watchtowers, gates and plastered earthen walls. Set on a low hill, it is visible from every part of the city. The main keep (Dai-Tenshu) has six interior storeys and a basement. The striking appearance of this great wooden structure with its white plastered walls is the source of the name by which it is often known, the Castle of the White Heron (Shirasagi-jo).

Many castles were built in Japan in the early years ▶
of the Shogun period. Most of these have
subsequently been demolished and others were
destroyed during the Second World War. Of the
handful that survives, Himeji-jo is the most
complete and unaltered, largely thanks to the efforts
of army officers after the Meiji restoration.

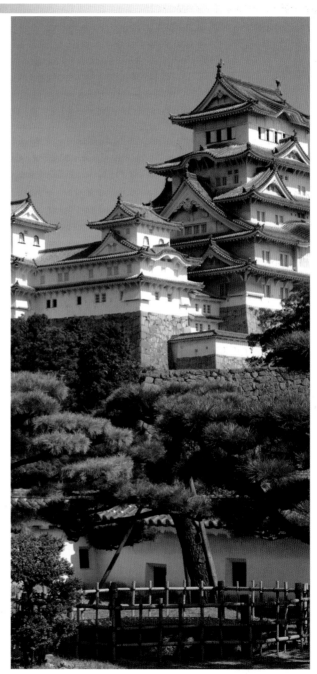

World Heritage site since

• 1978 • 1979 1979 • 1980 • 1981 • 1982 • 1983 • 1984 • 1985 • 1986 • 1987 • 1988 • 1989 • 1990 • 1991 • 1992 • **1993**

Churches of Moldavia
Romania

Criteria – Human creative genius; Significance in
human history

EUROPE

Black Sea

Mediterranean Sea

With their painted exterior walls, decorated
with fifteenth- and sixteenth-century
frescoes that are considered masterpieces of
Byzantine art, seven churches around
Suceava in northern Moldavia are unique in
Europe. Far from being merely wall
decorations, the paintings represent
complete cycles of religious murals on all
façades. Their outstanding composition,
elegant outline and harmonious colours
blend perfectly with the surrounding

landscape. At the Church of St George of
the former Voronet Monastery, founded by
Stephen the Great, the naos and sanctuary
were painted between 1488 and 1496 and the
narthex in 1552. The walls and the vault of
the exonarthex are covered by the 365
scenes of the Calendar of Saints. The
exterior murals depict traditional scenes and
the famous Last Judgement is on the
western wall.

A Christian tradition
of decorating the
exteriors of churches
was adopted and
extended in Moldavia.
It had its own specific
iconography,
dominated by certain
themes – the Church
hierarchy, the Last
Judgement and the
Tree of Jesse. The
Church of the
Suceviţa Monastery is
situated within the
fortified enclosure of
the Monastery and is
the only one to show a
representation of the
ladder of St John
Climacus.

Tubbataha Reefs Natural
Park
Philippines

Criteria – Natural phenomena or beauty;
Significant ecological and biological processes;
Significant natural habitat for biodiversity

ASIA   South   Pacific
        China   Ocean
        Sea

Celebes Sea

The Tubbataha Reefs Natural Park
comprises two atolls, North and South Reef,
separated by an 8 km channel, and the Jessie
Beazley Reef an emergent coral cay. The
North Reef is a large oblong-shaped
platform 2 km wide and completely
enclosing a sandy lagoon some 24 m deep.
The most prominent feature is the North
Islet which serves as
a nesting site for birds and marine turtles.
Steep and often perpendicular walls

extending to a depth of 100 m characterize
the seaward face of the reef. The South Reef
is a small triangular-shaped reef 1–2 km
wide. Like the North Reef, it consists of a
shallow platform enclosing a sandy lagoon.
South Islet is also used as a nesting site by
birds and marine turtles.

Tubbataha has a
diverse coral
assemblage, with
species representing
forty-six genera.
Forty-six bird species
have been recorded
and 379 species of fish.
Sightings of sharks
and rays are common.
There are no
permanent
inhabitants on the
reefs, other than
during the fishing
season, when
fishermen establish
temporary shelters.

World Heritage site since

• 1978 • 1979 1979 • 1980 • 1981 • 1982 • 1983 • 1984 • 1985 • 1986 • 1987 • 1988 • 1989 • 1990 • 1991 • 1992 • **1993**

Himeji-jo
Japan

Criteria – Human creative genius; Significance in human history

Himeji-jo is the finest surviving example of early seventeenth-century Japanese castle architecture, comprising eighty-three buildings with highly developed systems of defence and ingenious protection devices dating from the beginning of the Shogun period. It is a masterpiece of construction in wood. The centre of the complex is the Tenshu-gun, consisting of a main keep and three subsidiary keeps, with connecting structures. This is surrounded by a system of watchtowers, gates and plastered earthen walls. Set on a low hill, it is visible from every part of the city. The main keep (Dai-Tenshu) has six interior storeys and a basement. The striking appearance of this great wooden structure with its white plastered walls is the source of the name by which it is often known, the Castle of the White Heron (Shirasagi-jo).

Many castles were built in Japan in the early years ▶ of the Shogun period. Most of these have subsequently been demolished and others were destroyed during the Second World War. Of the handful that survives, Himeji-jo is the most complete and unaltered, largely thanks to the efforts of army officers after the Meiji restoration.

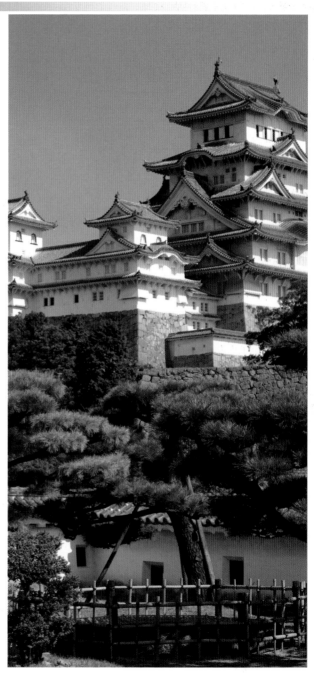

World Heritage site since

• 1978 • 1979 1979 • 1980 • 1981 • 1982 • 1983 • 1984 • 1985 • 1986 • 1987 • 1988 • 1989 • 1990 • 1991 • 1992 • **1993**

Archaeological Ensemble of Mérida
Spain

Criteria – Testimony to cultural tradition;
Significance in human history

The colony of Augusta Emerita, which became present-day Mérida in Estremadura, was founded in 25 BC at the end of the Spanish Campaign and was the capital of Lusitania. It is an excellent example of a provincial Roman capital during the empire and in the years afterwards. The main monuments in the World Heritage site are the Guadiana bridge (two sections of arches linked by a large pier); the amphitheatre, for 15,000 spectators; the classic Vitruvian theatre, set into a low hill and inaugurated under M. Agrippa; the Temple of Diana, probably from the early years of the first century AD; the alleged 'Arch of Trajan,' which may have been an entrance gate to the original town or, more likely, to the enceinte of the Temple of Diana; and the Circus, one of the largest in the Roman world.

The aqueducts and other elements of Roman water management are especially well preserved and complete. Apart from the aqueducts, the site includes three dams and various stretches of underground water channels. The Proserpina and Cornalvo dams, both still functioning, are the most remarkable surviving examples of Roman water management systems.

The Vitruvian Theatre in Mérida. ▼

World Heritage site since

· 1978 · 1979 1979 · 1980 · 1981 · 1982 · 1983 · 1984 · 1985 · 1986 · 1987 · 1988 · 1989 · 1990 · 1991 · 1992 · **1993**

Churches of Moldavia
Romania

Criteria – Human creative genius; Significance in human history

A Christian tradition of decorating the exteriors of churches was adopted and extended in Moldavia. It had its own specific iconography, dominated by certain themes – the Church hierarchy, the Last Judgement and the Tree of Jesse. The Church of the Suceviţa Monastery is situated within the fortified enclosure of the Monastery and is the only one to show a representation of the ladder of St John Climacus.

With their painted exterior walls, decorated with fifteenth- and sixteenth-century frescoes that are considered masterpieces of Byzantine art, seven churches around Suceava in northern Moldavia are unique in Europe. Far from being merely wall decorations, the paintings represent complete cycles of religious murals on all façades. Their outstanding composition, elegant outline and harmonious colours blend perfectly with the surrounding landscape. At the Church of St George of the former Voronet Monastery, founded by Stephen the Great, the naos and sanctuary were painted between 1488 and 1496 and the narthex in 1552. The walls and the vault of the exonarthex are covered by the 365 scenes of the Calendar of Saints. The exterior murals depict traditional scenes and the famous Last Judgement is on the western wall.

Tubbataha Reefs Natural Park
Philippines

Criteria – Natural phenomena or beauty; Significant ecological and biological processes; Significant natural habitat for biodiversity

Tubbataha has a diverse coral assemblage, with species representing forty-six genera. Forty-six bird species have been recorded and 379 species of fish. Sightings of sharks and rays are common. There are no permanent inhabitants on the reefs, other than during the fishing season, when fishermen establish temporary shelters.

The Tubbataha Reefs Natural Park comprises two atolls, North and South Reef, separated by an 8 km channel, and the Jessie Beazley Reef an emergent coral cay. The North Reef is a large oblong-shaped platform 2 km wide and completely enclosing a sandy lagoon some 24 m deep. The most prominent feature is the North Islet which serves as a nesting site for birds and marine turtles. Steep and often perpendicular walls extending to a depth of 100 m characterize the seaward face of the reef. The South Reef is a small triangular-shaped reef 1–2 km wide. Like the North Reef, it consists of a shallow platform enclosing a sandy lagoon. South Islet is also used as a nesting site by birds and marine turtles.

Complex of Hué Monuments
Vietnam

Criteria – Testimony to cultural tradition;
Significance in human history

Established as the capital of unified Viet Nam in 1802, Hué was not only the political but also the cultural and religious centre under the Nguyen dynasty until 1945. The integrity of the town layout and building design make it an exceptional specimen of late feudal urban planning. Four citadels or defended enclosures made up the city: Kinh Thanh (Capital City), for official administrative buildings; Hoang Thanh (Imperial City), for royal palaces and shrines; Tu Cam Thanh (Forbidden Purple City), for the royal residences; and Dai Noi (Inner City), defended by brick walls and a moat. A fifth fortress, Tran Hai Thanh, was constructed a little later to protect the capital against assault from the sea. The Perfume River, the main axis, divides the capital in two.

The new capital was planned in accordance with ancient oriental philosophy and Vietnamese tradition. The relationship between the five cardinal points (centre, west, east, north, south), five natural elements (earth, metal, wood, water, fire), and five basic colours (yellow, white, blue, black, red) underlies the conception of the city, and is reflected in the names of some important features.

Wall and gate of Tu Duc Tomb, Hué. ▼

World Heritage site since

· 1978 • 1979 1979 • 1980 • 1981 • 1982 • 1983 • 1984 • 1985 • 1986 • 1987 • 1988 • 1989 • 1990 • 1991 • 1992 • **1993**

Qutb Minar and its Monuments, Delhi
India

Criteria – Significance in human history

This important collection of Islamic buildings is dominated by the red sandstone tower of Qutb Minar, begun around 1202. In its present form it consists of five storeys, with each storey separated by balconies. The first three storeys are each decorated differently, the lowest being of alternating angular and rounded flutings, the second with rounded flutings alone, and the third with angular flutings alone. It is 72.5 m high, tapering from 14.32 m in diameter at its base to 2.75 m at its peak. The surrounding area contains funerary buildings, notably the magnificent Alai-Darwaza Gate, the masterpiece of Indo-Muslim art built in 1311, and two mosques, including the Quwwatu'l-Islam (Might of Islam), the oldest in northern India, built of materials reused from some twenty Brahman temples. This mosque consists of a courtyard, cloisters, and a prayer hall.

The Iron Pillar in the mosque compound is 7.02 m tall, 0.93 m of which is below ground. It bears a Sanskrit inscription from the fourth century AD. It is built up of many hundreds of small wrought-iron blooms welded together and is the largest known composite iron object from so early a period.

Ancient carved stone cloisters in Qutb Minar.
▼

World Heritage site since

• 1978 • 1979 1979 • 1980 • 1981 • 1982 • 1983 • 1984 • 1985 • 1986 • 1987 • 1988 • 1989 • 1990 • 1991 • 1992 • **1993**

Historic Town of Banská Štiavnica and the Technical Monuments in its Vicinity
Slovakia

Criteria – Significance in human history; Traditional human settlement

The old medieval mining centre of Banská Štiavnica blends into the surrounding landscape, which contains unique and historic evidence of mining and metallurgical activities. The fifteenth century was a time of immense prosperity: defences were built round the town, the parish church was rebuilt and fortified, and many new houses were built, some of which were, in the sixteenth century, converted into Renaissance 'palaces'. Technological progress continued, and in 1627 Banská

Štiavnica saw the first use of gunpowder in mining, an important breakthrough, and much work on the application of water power in deep mining and on ancillary processes was carried out, particularly in the eighteenth century. During this period, Banská Štiavnica became the most important centre for precious-metal mining in the Habsburg Empire, and many leading engineers and metallurgists from all over Europe were working in the town.

Banská Štiavnica is the oldest mining town in Slovakia; its town seal of 1275 is the earliest known bearing a mining emblem. It lies on the steep slopes of the Glanzenberg and Paradajz mountains. Its ore deposits have been exploited since the late Bronze Age, and a document of 1156 referred to it as the 'land of miners'.

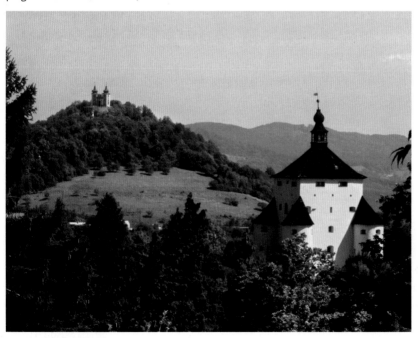

Nový Zámok (The New Castle), which was built in 1564–71 is located on a hill overlooking the town. It was originally a watch tower, but is now used as a museum.

World Heritage site since

• 1978 • 1979 1979 • 1980 • 1981 • 1982 • 1983 • 1984 • 1985 • 1986 • 1987 • 1988 • 1989 • 1990 • 1991 • 1992 • **1993**

Buddhist Monuments in the Horyu-ji Area

Japan

Criteria – Human creative genius; Interchange of values; Significance in human history; Heritage associated with events of universal significance

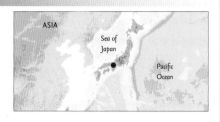

There are around forty-eight Buddhist monuments in the Horyu-ji Area, in Nara Prefecture. Several date from the late seventh or early eighth century, making them some of the oldest surviving wooden buildings in the world. These masterpieces of wooden architecture are important not only for the history of art, since they illustrate the adaptation of Chinese Buddhist architecture and layout to Japanese culture, but also for the history of religion, since their construction coincided

with the introduction of Buddhism to Japan from China by way of the Korean peninsula.

These temples, monasteries and associated buildings are the earliest Buddhist monuments in Japan, dating from shortly after the religion's introduction to the country in the mid-sixth century AD and they had a profound influence on Japanese religious architecture.

◄

A 'tsukubai' (water basin) in one of the Buddhist Temples in the Horyu-ji Area.

Shirakami-Sanchi

Japan

Criteria – Significant ecological and biological processes

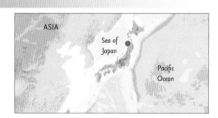

Situated in the mountains of northern Honshu, the area includes the last remaining virgin stand of Siebold's beech forest, which once covered the hills and mountain slopes of northern Japan. The protected area covers about one-third of the Shirakami Mountains which rise to just over 1,200 m and comprise a maze of steep-sided hills and deep valleys. The area is a

refuge for many typical Honshu flora and fauna. The eighty-seven bird species include golden eagle, which has a limited breeding record and is endangered in Japan. Three nesting pairs of black woodpecker, also endangered, are found in the core zone. Hodgson's hawk eagle, has also been recorded in the site as well as Japanese serow. Japanese black bear is common.

The area is a wilderness with no access trails or man-made facilities and its beech forest is virtually undisturbed. Wildlife is fully protected, apart from bears: the region's bear hunters, known as Matagi, use special hunting techniques and faith ceremonies.

World Heritage site since

• 1978 • 1979 1979 • 1980 • 1981 • 1982 • 1983 • 1984 • 1985 • 1986 • 1987 • 1988 • 1989 • 1990 • 1991 • 1992 • **1993**

Royal Monastery of Santa María de Guadalupe
Spain

Criteria – Significance in human history; Heritage associated with events of universal significance

The monastery overlooks a valley surrounded by high mountains and enhanced by abundant vegetation. Its famous statue of the Virgin became a powerful symbol of the Christianization of much of the New World.

The monastery is an outstanding repository of four centuries of Spanish religious architecture. It symbolizes two significant events in world history that occurred in 1492: the reconquest of the Iberian peninsula by the Catholic Kings, and Christopher Columbus' arrival in the Americas. The monastery was, and still remains, a centre of pilgrimage as well as a cultural centre of the highest order. Its hospitals and its medical school were renowned, as was its scriptorium and its library, containing a rich collection of documents. Many famous artists were attracted to Guadalupe, including Juan de Sevilla, Francisco de Zurbarán, Vicente Carducho and Luca Giordano. The harmony between the buildings and the works of art that it contains confers outstanding value upon the ensemble.

Joya de Cerén Archaeological Site
El Salvador

Criteria – Testimony to cultural tradition; Significance in human history

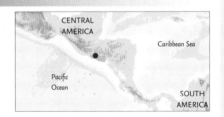

A warning earthquake apparently gave residents time to flee but the subsequent volcanic eruption was so sudden that everyday artefacts, from garden tools and bean-filled pots to sleeping mats and religious items, were found still in place around the buildings.

Joya de Cerén was a pre-Hispanic farming community that was buried under an eruption of the Laguna Caldera volcano c. AD 600. Because of the exceptional condition of the remains, they provide an insight into the daily lives of the Central American populations who worked the land at that time. Twelve structures have been excavated, including living quarters, storehouses, workshops, kitchens and a communal sauna. Cerén is thought to have been home to about 200 people, although no human remains have been found. The buildings are grouped into compounds that include structures for sleeping, storage, cooking and handicrafts. The specialised structures include a sweat house, a large communal building, and two which may have been used by specialists such as a shaman or a healer.

World Heritage site since

• • • • • • • • • • • • • • • • • • • 1978 • 1979 1979 • 1980 • 1981 • 1982 • 1983 • 1984 • 1985 • 1986 • 1987 • 1988 • 1989 • 1990 • 1991 • 1992 • **1993**

Levoča, Spišský Hrad and the Associated Cultural Monuments
Slovakia

Criteria – Significance in human history

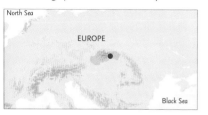

The historic town of Levoča was founded in the 13th and 14th centuries. Most of the site has been preserved and it includes the fourteenth century church of St James with its ten altars of the fifteenth and sixteenth centuries and a remarkable collection of polychrome works in the Late Gothic style.

Spišský Hrad (castle) and its three related sites contain one of the largest number of thirteenth-and fourteenth-century military, political and religious buildings in Eastern Europe. The castle stands on a dramatic hill rising out of the plain of western Slovakia.

The town of Spišské Podhradie was founded at the base of the castle mound. Its first church, destroyed in a Tatar raid, was rebuilt in 1258–73. The street pattern was laid out formally in the fourteenth century and extended in the fifteenth century. Following a fire, most of the houses were rebuilt in Renaissance style. Spišskà Kapitula, a unique fortified ecclesiastical complex of buildings, is based around the Cathedral of St Martin, which was started in 1285. Zehra is one of the earliest Slovak settlements in the region.

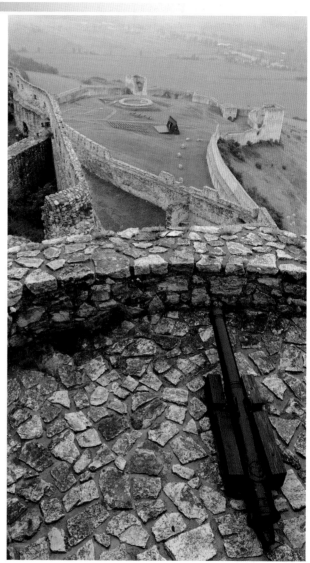

▲

The castle, one of the largest in Eastern Europe, is renowned for its Romanesque and Gothic architecture. It consists of the upper keep and its courtyard; two inner baileys with internal fortified access gates; the outer bailey, with the main entrance gate and remains of the garrison's quarters; and a large barbican area, now mostly ruined.

World Heritage site since

• 1978 • 1979 1979 • 1980 • 1981 • 1982 • 1983 • 1984 • 1985 • 1986 • 1987 • 1988 • 1989 • 1990 • 1991 • 1992 • **1993**

Vlkolínec
Slovakia

Criteria – Significance in human history;
Traditional human settlement

North Sea

EUROPE

Black Sea

Vlkolínec, situated in central Slovakia, is a remarkably intact settlement of forty-five vernacular buildings, providing a living example of a traditional central European village. It has preserved its ancient appearance with remarkable fidelity. Although most buildings date from the nineteenth century, Vlkolínec has retained its medieval layout. The characteristic houses of Vlkolínec are situated on the street frontages of narrow holdings, with

stables, smaller outbuildings, and barns ranged behind them. The houses are of a traditional timber construction with log walls on stone footings, the walls being coated with clay and whitewashed or painted blue. The parcels of land that surround Vlkolínec retain the elongated strip-shape characteristic of medieval land allotment over most of feudal Europe. Outside these lie areas of common land and forest.

The first recorded settlement at Vlkolínec was in the fourteenth century. A decree of 1630 suggests that its name derives from the important charge laid upon the villagers to maintain the wolf-pits in good order.

A typical Vlkolínec building.
▼

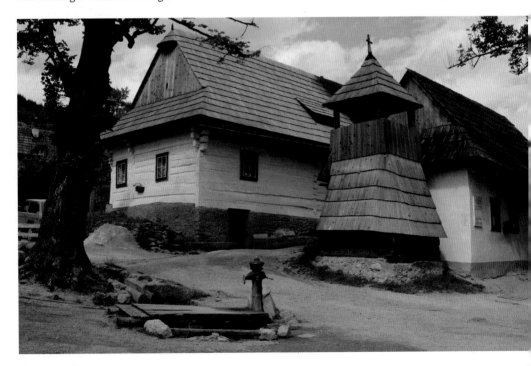

World Heritage site since

· 1978 · 1979 1979 · 1980 · 1981 · 1982 · 1983 · 1984 · 1985 · 1986 · 1987 · 1988 · 1989 · 1990 · 1991 · 1992 · **1993**

Historic Centre of Zacatecas
Mexico

Criteria – Interchange of values; Significance in human history

Founded in 1546 after the discovery of a rich silver lode, Zacatecas reached the height of its prosperity in the sixteenth and seventeenth centuries. Built on the steep slopes of a narrow valley, the town has breathtaking views and many important buildings. The cathedral, built between 1730 and 1760, dominates the centre of the town. It is a highly decorated Baroque structure with exceptional façades and other features

that reflect the absorption of indigenous ideas and techniques into Roman Catholic iconography. The Jesuit church of Santo Domingo has a quiet beauty which contrasts with the Baroque flamboyance of the college alongside it. Its massive dome and towers provide a counterpoint to the nearby cathedral. It now houses a new Fine Art Museum.

Zacatecas became the economic centre for the region, with a system of forts (presidios), villages and agricultural estates (haciendas) for defence and supply. It was also the base for colonization and the spread of Christianity further to the north; first the Convent of San Francisco and later the College of Guadalupe were responsible for establishing over seventy missions, as far north as Texas and California.

Rock Paintings of the Sierra de San Francisco
Mexico

Criteria – Human creative genius; Testimony to cultural tradition

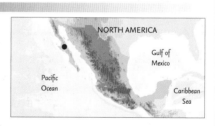

From c. 100 BC to AD 1300, the Sierra de San Francisco in the El Vizcaino reserve in Baja California was home to a people who have since disappeared but who left one of the most outstanding collections of rock paintings in the world. The paintings are remarkably well-preserved because of the dry climate and the inaccessibility of the site. Showing human figures and many

animal species, and illustrating the relationship between humans and their environment, they reveal a highly sophisticated culture. Their composition and size, as well as the precision of the outlines and the variety of colours, but especially the number of sites, make this an impressive testimony to a unique artistic tradition.

The prehistoric rock art of the region was first reported by the Jesuit Father Francisco Javier Clavijero in a publication in Rome in 1789 and some 400 sites have so far been registered.

World Heritage site since

• 1978 • 1979 1979 • 1980 • 1981 • 1982 • 1983 • 1984 • 1985 • 1986 • 1987 • 1988 • 1989 • 1990 • 1991 • 1992 • **1993**

Architectural Ensemble of the Trinity Sergius Lavra in Sergiev Posad

Russian Federation

Criteria – Interchange of values; Significance in human history

The Trinity Sergius Lavra is an outstanding and remarkably complete example of a working Orthodox monastery (lavra) of the fourteenth-eighteenth centuries and has exerted a profound influence on architecture in Russia. It was founded in the 1330s by St Sergius and fortified in 1540–60. Among its most important buildings are the Trinity Cathedral, completed in 1425, containing the renowned icon of 'The Trinity' by Rublev; The Church of the Holy Spirit (Dukhovskaya), a four-pillared church with three apses and a single dome built from white limestone; the Cathedral of the Assumption (see photo on the right), a towering structure echoing the Cathedral of the Assumption in the Moscow Kremlin; and the Belfry, which is the tallest building in the complex, begun in 1740 at the instigation of Catherine the Great. The monks' cells, two-storey stone buildings, were built up against the fortress walls in the sixteenth and seventeenth centuries.

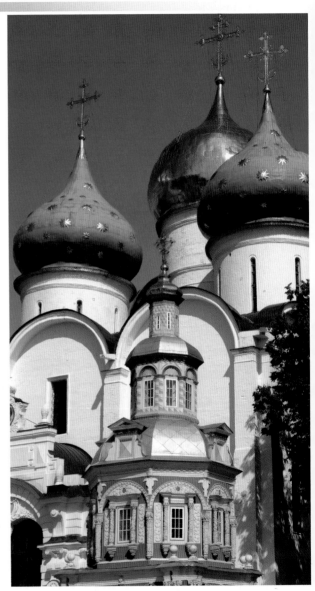

Cathedral of the Assumption. ▲

With Peter the Great's consolidation of power, a number of new buildings in the Baroque style were added to the monastery, including the refectory chamber with the Church of St Sergius; a stone palace for the Tsar (Chertogi); the Church over the Gates and the Chapel over the Well.

Vilnius Historic Centre
Lithuania

Criteria – Interchange of values; Significance in human history

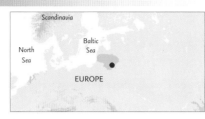

The Lithuanian capital Vilnius has had a profound influence on the cultural and architectural development of much of Eastern Europe. Despite invasions and partial destruction, it has preserved an impressive complex of Gothic, Renaissance, Baroque and classical buildings, as well as its medieval layout, and is an exceptional example of an Eastern European town that evolved organically over several centuries.

The conversion of Lithuania to Christianity in 1387 opened Vilnius to the Western world.

The town grew against the background of a series of major fires from the fifteenth to the eighteenth centuries. The notable churches that exist today date from the seventeenth century, but it was the successive reconstructions that gave the town many of its buildings of special character, including the cathedral, town hall and palaces. Many of the surviving earlier buildings were rebuilt or refurbished in the Baroque style.

The historic centre comprises the areas of the three castles (Upper, Lower and Curved) and the area that was encircled by the medieval wall. The plan is basically circular, radiating out from the original castle site. The street pattern is typically medieval, with small streets dividing it into irregular blocks, but with large squares inserted in later periods.

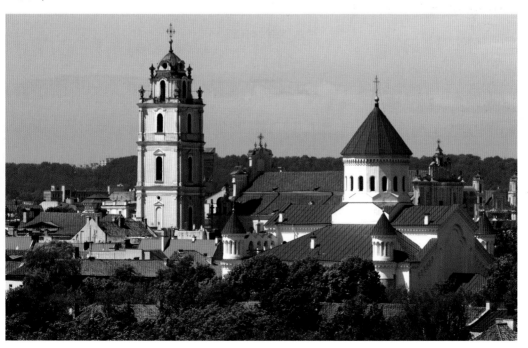

World Heritage site since

• 1978 • 1979 • 1980 • 1981 • 1982 • 1983 • 1984 • 1985 • 1986 • 1987 • 1988 • 1989 • 1990 • 1991 • 1992 • 1993 • **1994**

Bwindi Impenetrable National Park
Uganda

Criteria – Natural phenomena or beauty;
Significant natural habitat for biodiversity

Bwindi Park covers 320 km² and is known for its exceptional diversity of flora and fauna. Its forest gets the name 'impenetrable' from the dense cover of herbs, vines and shrubs inhabiting its valley floor. The forest is the most diverse in East Africa for tree species (more than 163) and ferns (more than 104). Sixteen species have only a very restricted distribution in southwest Uganda, and one species, Lovoa swynnertonii, is globally threatened.

Located in the Kigezi Highlands of southwest Uganda at the junction of the plain and mountain forests, Bwindi is characterized by steep hills and narrow valleys. The steepness of the slopes means that the soils are very susceptible to erosion in areas where trees are cleared. The park constitutes an important water catchment area, serving the surrounding densely populated agricultural land. Three major tributaries of the Ishasha River drain into Lake Edward to the north; and the Ndego, Kanyamwabo and Shongi rivers flow southwards towards Lake Mutanda.

Bwindi has one of the richest fauna communities in East Africa, including over 214 species of forest bird, 7 species of diurnal primate, 120 species of mammals and 202 species of butterfly. Highly significant is the presence of almost half of the world's population of mountain gorillas and many other endangered species.

The park is also an important locality for the conservation of Afromontane fauna, in particular those endemic to the mountains of the western rift valley. Overall, Bwindi contains nine globally threatened species: mountain gorilla, common chimpanzee, l'Hoest's monkey Cercopithecus l'hoesti, endangered species of African elephant, African green broadbill, Grauer's rush warbler, Chaplin's flycatcher, African giant swallowtail and cream-banded swallowtail. Buffalo were poached to extinction in the late 1960s, as were leopard more recently.

Although the wider Kigezi region may have been occupied from as early as 37,000 years ago, no archaeological sites are known inside the park. The earliest evidence of forest clearance dates back 4,800 years, most likely due to the presence of the Batwa hunter-gatherer people manipulating vegetation with fire. This is the earliest evidence for cultivation anywhere in tropical Africa.

Approximately 10,000 families, all Bantu, cultivate the land immediately surrounding the park. Commercial logging has never taken place in Bwindi due to the rugged terrain.

City of Luxembourg: its Old Quarters and Fortifications
Luxembourg
Criteria – Significance in human history

Luxembourg was one of Europe's greatest fortified sites from the sixteenth century until 1867. Its position made it a strategic and military prize and it was repeatedly reinforced by successive powers as it passed from one to another: the Holy Roman Emperors, the House of Burgundy, the Habsburgs, the French and Spanish kings, and the Prussians. Until their partial demolition, the fortifications were a fine example of military architecture spanning several centuries.

The old quarter extends westwards from the Bock promontory with its honeycomb of seventeenth- and eighteenth-century casemates. The Marché-aux-Poissons was the first open space in the town and the Church of Saint Michel, located there, originates from the tenth century. Notre Dame Cathedral is an outstanding example of Netherlands late-Gothic architecture, and the sixteenth-century Grand Ducal Palace stands at the heart of the old town.

Luxembourg's defences were such that it earned the nickname of the 'Gibraltar of the North'. However, the European powers agreed to the Grand Duchy's perpetual neutrality in the 1867 Treaty of London; this led to the demolition of the walls and fortifications and the transformation of its 1.8km² fortress into an open city.

The Stiechen Bridge.
▼

World Heritage site since

· 1978 · 1979 · 1980 · 1981 · 1982 · 1983 · 1984 · 1985 · 1986 · 1987 · 1988 · 1989 · 1990 · 1991 · 1992 · 1993 · **1994**

Historic Ensemble of the Potala Palace, Lhasa
China

Criteria – *Human creative genius; Significance in human history; Heritage associated with events of universal significance*

The Potala Palace, winter palace of the Dalai Lama since the seventh century, symbolizes Tibetan Buddhism and its central role in the traditional administration of Tibet. Also founded in the seventh century, the Jokhang Temple Monastery is an exceptional Buddhist religious complex. Norbulingka, the Dalai Lama's former summer palace, is a masterpiece of Tibetan art from the eighteenth century. The architectural beauty and originality of these sites, and their rich ornamentation and harmonious integration in a striking landscape, add to their historic and religious interest.

The Potala Palace complex, comprising the White and Red Palaces with their ancillary buildings, stands on Red Mountain in the Lhasa Valley at an altitude of 3,700 m. The White Palace holds the throne of the Dalai Lama and his personal apartments, while the Red Palace contains chapels and the stupa tombs of previous Dalai Lamas.

The Temple Monastery, in the centre of the old town of Lhasa, comprises an entrance porch, a courtyard and a Buddhist hall, surrounded by accommodation for monks, and storehouses. Norbulingka (treasure garden) is located on the bank of the Lhasa River about 2 km from the Potala Palace. The site consists of a large garden with palaces, halls and pavilions.

The Potala Palace.
▼

World Heritage site since

• 1978 • 1979 • 1980 • 1981 • 1982 • 1983 • 1984 • 1985 • 1986 • 1987 • 1988 • 1989 • 1990 • 1991 • 1992 • 1993 • **1994**

Los Katíos National Park
Colombia

Criteria – Significant ecological and biological processes; Significant natural habitat for biodiversity

Extending over 720 km² in northwestern Colombia, the park comprises two main regions: the mountains of the Serranía del Darién in the west, and in the east the floodplain of the Atrato River, the fastest-flowing river in the world. Lowland swamp forests cover approximately half of the park, while the remainder is lowland through to montane tropical rainforest. The wetlands of the Atrato floodplain are of special interest,

and cativo is one of the typical species of tree: it can reach 50 m. An exceptional biological diversity is found in the park, which is home to many threatened animal species and endemic plants. More than 450 species of bird have been recorded, along with some 550 species of vertebrate, excluding fish.

The region was previously inhabited by the Kuna, an indigenous group forced to migrate to Panama because of inter-tribal fighting with the Katío-Embera group, from which the park took its name.

Jelling Mounds, Runic Stones and Church
Denmark

Criteria – Testimony to cultural tradition

The Jelling complex, and especially the pagan burial mounds and the two runic stones, are outstanding examples of pagan Nordic culture. Jelling was a royal manor in the tenth century, during the reign of King Gorm and Queen Thyre. After the death of Thyre, her husband raised a stone in her memory and laid out a joint funerary monument consisting of two large mounds. On his death he was buried in the chamber of the north mound, which may already

have contained Thyre's remains. After bringing Denmark and Norway together and introducing Christianity into Denmark, their son Harald Bluetooth set up a stone between the two mounds proclaiming his achievements and built an impressive wooden church, in which the remains of his father were re-interred.

The present church was preceded by at least three churches built from wood, all of which were destroyed by fire. Mural paintings dating from around 1100 (and thus the earliest in Denmark) came to light on the walls of the chancel in 1874–5.

World Heritage site since

• 1978 • 1979 • 1980 • 1981 • 1982 • 1983 • 1984 • 1985 • 1986 • 1987 • 1988 • 1989 • 1990 • 1991 • 1992 • 1993 • **1994**

Church of the Ascension, Kolomenskoye
Russian Federation
Criteria – Interchange of values

The Church of the Ascension was built in 1532 on the imperial estate of Kolomenskoye, near Moscow, to celebrate the birth of the prince who was to become Tsar Ivan IV 'the Terrible'. As the first example of a traditional wooden tent-roofed church in stone and brick, it represents an imaginative and innovative advance in Russian Orthodox church design. Its ground plan is an equal-armed cross and it is unusual in that it has no apse. The interior of the church is small, as the walls are 3–4 m thick, but it is open to the top of the roof, 41 m above. The corners are decorated with pilasters which repeat, with some variations, the decoration of the exterior. With an overall height of 62 m and its very thick walls, the structure retains the elegance of its striking silhouette.

The so-called Italian (Alevisovsky) small brick, ▶ introduced by Italian architects at the end of the fifteenth century, was used for building the church. Carved details are in white limestone from Myachkovo, a suburb of Moscow.

World Heritage site since

· 1978 · 1979 · 1980 · 1981 · 1982 · 1983 · 1984 · 1985 · 1986 · 1987 · 1988 · 1989 · 1990 · 1991 · 1992 · 1993 · **1994**

City of Vicenza and the Palladian Villas of the Veneto
Italy

Criteria – Human creative genius; Interchange of values

EUROPE

Mediterranean Sea

Ionian
Sea

Founded in the second century BC in northern Italy, Vicenza prospered under Venetian rule from the early fifteenth to the end of the eighteenth centuries. But it was the advent of Andrea Palladio (1508–80) that gave Vicenza its enduring form. Palladio was profoundly influenced by his study of the surviving monuments of classical Rome. For Vicenza, he created both public (Basilica, Loggia del Capitaniato, Teatro Olimpico) and private buildings. A total of twenty-six

individual buildings or parts of buildings known to have been designed or reconstructed by Palladio make up the World Heritage site – twenty-three in the city itself and three villas in its immediate environs. Palladio's buildings had a decisive influence on the development of architecture and inspired a distinct architectural style known as Palladian, which spread to other European countries, as well as North America.

The ancient town plan is still recognizable in the modern town, Corso Palladio being the *decumanus maximus* and Contra Porti the *cardo maximus*. Among the surviving public buildings erected from the time of Augustus are the remains of the theatre, now incorporated into a more recent structure, and sections of the aqueduct to the north of the city.

The Villa Rotunda.
▼

World Heritage site since

• 1978 • 1979 • 1980 • 1981 • 1982 • 1983 • 1984 • 1985 • 1986 • 1987 • 1988 • 1989 • 1990 • 1991 • 1992 • 1993 • **1994**

Ancient Building Complex in the Wudang Mountains
China

Criteria – Human creative genius; Interchange of values; Heritage associated with events of universal significance

The palaces and temples which form the nucleus of this group of secular and religious buildings exemplify the architectural and artistic achievements of China's Yuan, Ming and Qing dynasties. Situated in the scenic valleys and on the slopes of the Wudang mountains in Hubei Province, the site, which was built as an organized complex during the Ming dynasty fourteenth–seventeenth centuries, contains Taoist buildings from as early as the seventh century. It represents the highest standards of Chinese art and architecture over a period of nearly 1,000 years.

Ming Emperor Zhu Di had, in the twelve years after his enthronement, 20,000 men working on construction in the Wudang Mountains. In that time they added nine palaces, nine temples, seventy-two cliff temples, thirty-six monasteries, and over one hundred stone bridges to the complex.

◀

Temple on Tianzhu Feng (Pillar of Heaven), Wudang Mountains.

Australian Fossil Mammal Sites (Riversleigh / Naracoorte)
Australia

Criteria – Major stages of Earth's history; Significant ecological and biological processes

These two sites are representative of the development of Australia's mammal fauna during the Cenozoic era (65 million years ago to the present).

The faunal assemblages of Riversleigh's fossil fields have profoundly altered understanding about Australia's Middle Cenozoic vertebrate diversity. They span a record of mammalian evolution over twenty million years, providing the first records for many distinctive groups of living mammals, as well as many other unique and now extinct Australian mammals such as 'marsupial lions'.

Naracoorte also opens a window into a significant period of the Earth's history on a continent dominated by marsupials. Its assemblage also spans the probable time of arrival of humans in Australia and thus is of additional value in helping to unravel the complex relationships between humans and their environment.

The Pleistocene fossil vertebrate deposits of Victoria Fossil Cave at Naracoorte are considered to be, in terms of both volume and diversity, Australia's largest and best preserved and one of the richest deposits in the world. Tens of thousands of specimens representing ninety-nine vertebrate species have been recovered, ranging in size from very small frogs to buffalo-sized marsupials.

World Heritage site since

• 1978 • 1979 • 1980 • 1981 • 1982 • 1983 • 1984 • 1985 • 1986 • 1987 • 1988 • 1989 • 1990 • 1991 • 1992 • 1993 • **1994**

Doñana National Park
Spain

Criteria – Natural phenomena or beauty;
Significant ecological and biological processes;
Significant natural habitat for biodiversity

In the context of a crowded and long-inhabited continent, Doñana National Park in Andalusia is one of the few national parks in Europe that can match the international significance met by parks in other parts of the world. The park is notable for the great diversity of its biotopes, especially lagoons, marshlands, fixed and mobile dunes, scrub woodland and maquis. It is home to five threatened bird species. It is one of the

largest heronries in the Mediterranean region and is the wintering site for more than 500,000 water fowl each year. In general the state of conservation of the park is satisfactory, but it does face numerous threats including agricultural development, tourism, poaching and over-grazing.

Doñana National Park has been a testing ground for conservation in Spain and has become very well known throughout Europe as a result of the controversies faced and the innovative management approaches that have been taken. As the main threats have been averted thus far and as restoration activities are under way, the future for the park looks encouraging.

Rwenzori Mountains National Park
Uganda

Criteria – Natural phenomena or beauty;
Significant natural habitat for biodiversity

Covering nearly 1,000 km² in western Uganda, the park comprises the main part of the Rwenzori mountain chain, which includes Africa's third highest peak, Mount Margherita (5,109 m). The region's glaciers, waterfalls and lakes make it one of Africa's most beautiful alpine areas. The park has many natural habitats of endangered species and a rich and unusual flora comprising, among other species, the giant heather.

There are several major vegetation zones

in the park: broken montane forest below 2,400 m; bamboo forest up to 3,000 m; a tree-heath zone of giant heathers up to 3,800 m; and Afro-alpine moorland up to 4,400 m. The park contains eighty-nine species of bird, four species of diurnal primate and fifteen species of butterfly. No people live within the park, although cultivation is evident in many places up to its border.

The highest reaches of the Rwenzori Mountains are covered by snowfields and glaciers which provide a permanent source of water for the surrounding areas.

In the east, the park is contiguous with Virunga National Park in the Democratic Republic of the Congo.

World Heritage site since

• 1978 • 1979 • 1980 • 1981 • 1982 • 1983 • 1984 • 1985 • 1986 • 1987 • 1988 • 1989 • 1990 • 1991 • 1992 • 1993 • **1994**

Canaima National Park
Venezuela

Criteria – Natural phenomena or beauty; Major
stages of Earth's history; Significant ecological
and biological processes; Significant natural
habitat for biodiversity

Canaima National Park extends over
30,000 km² in southeastern Venezuela
along the border between Guyana and
Brazil. Roughly 65 per cent of the park is
covered by table mountain (tepui) formations,
resulting in a unique landscape of great
geological interest. The sheer cliffs and
waterfalls, including the world's highest
waterfall (Angel Falls, 980 m), make this a
spectacular place. A main road from Ciudad
Bolívar runs along the eastern border of the
park, bisecting its southeast corner and
providing easy access for tourists. There are
no other metalled roads within the park, the
western section being accessible only by air.
The fauna is diverse: 118 mammal species,
550 birds, 72 reptiles and 55 amphibians have
been recorded. Canaima was established as
a national park in 1962 and its size was
doubled to the present area in 1975.

The forests and savanna of Canaima have been
occupied for 10,000 years by various groups of
Amerindians of the Carib family, collectively
known as the Pemon. Two archaeological sites,
containing various hand-fashioned stone tools
estimated to be 9,000 years old, have been found
in the park.

Angel Falls. ▲

World Heritage site since

· · · · · · · · · · · · · · · · · · 1978 · 1979 · 1980 · 1981 · 1982 · 1983 · 1984 · 1985 · 1986 · 1987 · 1988 · 1989 · 1990 · 1991 · 1992 · 1993 · **1994**

Earliest 16th-Century Monasteries on the Slopes of Popocatepetl
Mexico

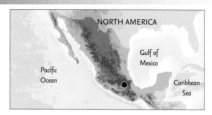

Criteria – Interchange of values; Significance in human history

These fourteen monasteries stand on the slopes of Popocatepetl, an active volcano, to the southeast of Mexico City. They are all built to a similar plan, with an atrium, church, and monastic buildings set around a small courtyard or patio. They are in an excellent state of conservation and are good examples of the architectural style adopted by the first missionaries – Franciscans, Dominicans and Augustinians – who converted the indigenous populations to Christianity in the early sixteenth century. Between 1525 and 1570 more than 100 monasteries were built in this region. By the end of the century over 300 had been established. In the late sixteenth century, many of the monasteries were taken over by the regular clergy and converted into parish churches.

These early monasteries represent an example of a new architectural concept in which open spaces are of renewed importance. They served as an important architectural model for a large number of smaller establishments known as 'missions' rather than monasteries. These were established as far away as the United States.

Rock Carvings in Tanum
Sweden

Criteria – Human creative genius; Testimony to cultural tradition; Significance in human history

The outstanding artistic qualities and vivid scenic compositions of Tanum's rock art make it a unique expression of Bronze Age existence. The elaborate motifs illustrate everyday life, warfare, cult, and religion. Some of the panels were obviously planned in advance. Northern Bohuslän is a land of granite bedrock, parts of which were scraped clean as the ice cap slowly moved northwards, leaving gently curved rock faces exposed. These were the 'canvases' selected by the Bronze Age artists, sited just above the shoreline of the period that began in 1500 BC, i.e. 25–29 m above today's sea level. There are at least 1,500 known rock-carving sites in northern Bohuslän, each with a number of images, but new examples are regularly coming to light as research continues.

The carvings vary from 1 mm deep to as much as 30 or 40 mm. It is suggested that the more deeply engraved figures were of greater symbolic significance and therefore required to be visible to larger gatherings of people.

World Heritage site since

• 1978 • 1979 • 1980 • 1981 • 1982 • 1983 • 1984 • 1985 • 1986 • 1987 • 1988 • 1989 • 1990 • 1991 • 1992 • 1993 • 1994

Temple and Cemetery of Confucius and the Kong Family Mansion in Qufu
China

Criteria – Human creative genius; Significance in human history; Heritage associated with events of universal significance

The temple, cemetery and family mansion of Confucius, the great philosopher, politician and educator of the sixth–fifth centuries BC, are located at Qufu in Shandong Province. Two years after his death, Confucius's house in Qufu was consecrated as a temple, within which were preserved his clothing, musical instruments, carriage and books. The temple was rebuilt in AD 153, and repaired and renovated several times in subsequent centuries. Today it comprises more than 100 buildings. The cemetery contains Confucius's tomb and the remains of more than 100,000 of his descendants. The small house of the Kong family developed into a gigantic aristocratic residence, of which 152 buildings with 480 rooms remain. The Qufu complex of monuments has retained its outstanding artistic and historic character due to the devotion of successive Chinese emperors over more than 2,000 years.

Over 1,000 stelae recording imperial donations and sacrifices from the Han dynasty onwards are preserved within the temple, along with outstanding examples of calligraphy and other forms of documentation, all priceless examples of Chinese art. There are many fine carved stones, among the most important being the Han stone reliefs (206 BC–AD 220).

World Heritage site since

• 1978 • 1979 • 1980 • 1981 • 1982 • 1983 • 1984 • 1985 • 1986 • 1987 • 1988 • 1989 • 1990 • 1991 • 1992 • 1993 • **1994**

Lines and Geoglyphs of Nasca and Pampas de Jumana
Peru

Criteria – Human creative genius; Testimony to cultural tradition; Significance in human history

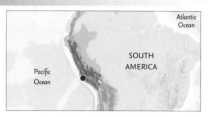

The geoglyphs of Nasca and the pampas of Jumana, which were scratched on the ground between 500 BC and AD 500, are among archaeology's greatest enigmas because of their quantity, nature, size and continuity. The geoglyphs depict living creatures, stylized plants and imaginary beings, as well as geometric figures several kilometres long. Their concentration and juxtaposition and cultural continuity demonstrate that this was an important and long-lasting activity. They are believed to have had ritual astronomical functions.

The Nasca geoglyphs are located in the arid Peruvian coastal plain 400 km south of Lima, and cover 450 km², both in the desert and in the Andean foothills. These are covered with ferruginous sand, and gravel which has acquired a dark patina from weathering. Removal of the gravel reveals the underlying lighter coloured stratum, which contrasts strongly with the darker gravels.

The geoglyphs fall ► generally into two categories. The first group is representational, depicting animals, birds, insects, plants, fantastic figures and even everyday objects.

The second group comprises the lines, generally straight and criss-crossing in all directions. Some stretch several kilometres and depict geometrical shapes. Others are so-called 'tracks' which appear to have been laid out to accommodate large numbers of people.

Skogskyrkogården
Sweden
Criteria – Interchange of values; Significance in human history

In 1912 an international architectural competition was held to create a new cemetery on the site of former gravel pits overgrown with pine trees. It was won by two young architects, Asplund and Lewerentz, whose design blended vegetation and architectural elements to create a landscape that is finely adapted to its function. Their sources were not 'high' architecture or landscape design but ancient and medieval Nordic burial archetypes. Nonetheless, skilful use was made of elements from Mediterranean antiquity, such as the Via Sepulchra at Pompeii. The intervention of footpaths, meandering freely through the woodland, is minimal. Graves are laid out without excessive alignment or regimentation among the natural forest. This dignified design has had a profound influence in many countries around the world.

The cemetery design stands out for its intense romantic naturalism, turning the untouched Nordic forest into the dominant experience. The evocation of raw Nordic wilderness constituted a radical departure in landscape architecture as well as cemetery layout in the early twentieth century.

Bagrati Cathedral and Gelati Monastery
Georgia
Criteria – Significance in human history

The construction of Bagrati Cathedral, named after Bagrat III, the first king of united Georgia, started at the end of the tenth century and was completed in the early years of the eleventh century. Although partly destroyed by the Turks in 1691, its ruins still lie in the centre of Kutaisi. Richly ornamented capitals and fragments of piers and vaulting are scattered throughout the interior. The Gelati Monastery, whose main buildings were erected between the twelfth and seventeenth centuries, is a well-preserved complex, with wonderful mosaics and wall paintings. The main church has an interior surmounted by a large dome which beautifully combines space and solemnity, with light streaming in from many windows. The cathedral and monastery epitomise the flowering of medieval architecture in Georgia.

Gelati was not simply a monastery – it was also a centre of science and education, and the Academy established there in the reign of David IV (1073–1125) was one of the most important centres of culture in ancient Georgia.

Mountain Resort and its Outlying Temples, Chengde
China

Criteria – Interchange of values; Significance in human history

The Mountain Resort, the Qing dynasty's summer palace, in Hebei Province, was built between 1703 and 1792. It is a vast complex of palaces and administrative and ceremonial buildings. Temples of various architectural styles and imperial gardens blend harmoniously into a landscape of lakes, pastureland and forests. In addition to its aesthetic interest, the Mountain Resort is a rare historic vestige of the final development of feudal society in China.

Each year the Emperor would bring his ministers, royal troops, family and concubines, to hunt at Mulan. To accommodate this entourage of several thousand people, twenty-one temporary palaces were built, among them the Mountain Resort and its Outlying Temples.

◄

Xumifosou Zhi Miao (Temple of Happiness and Longevity).

Petäjävesi Old Church
Finland

Criteria – Significance in human history

The Petäjävesi Evangelical Lutheran Old Church is a building of considerable global importance as an example of northern timber church architecture and of the skills of the peasant population. European architectural trends have influenced the external form and the ground plan of the church, but they have been applied masterfully to traditional log construction. The church combines the layout of a Renaissance central church conception and

older forms derived from Gothic groined ceilings. The church suffered a period of neglect between 1879 and the 1920s, which was actually a blessing in disguise. When restoration began the historical importance of the building had been recognised and only traditional techniques and materials were used. As a result the level of authenticity is exceptionally high.

This unique log church was built between 1763 and 1765 on a peninsula where Lakes Jamsa and Petäjävesi meet. The location was specifically chosen so that the congregation would be able to reach it by boat or over the ice in the winter.

World Heritage site since

• 1978 • 1979 • 1980 • 1981 • 1982 • 1983 • 1984 • 1985 • 1986 • 1987 • 1988 • 1989 • 1990 • 1991 • 1992 • 1993 • **1994**

Historical Monuments of Mtskheta
Georgia

Criteria – Testimony to cultural tradition; Significance in human history

The historic churches of Mtskheta, former capital of Georgia, are outstanding examples of medieval religious architecture in the Caucasus. They show the high level of art and culture in the vanished Kingdom of Georgia, which played an outstanding role in the medieval history of its region.

Mtskheta's fortunes had risen and fallen long before 1801, when Georgia became part of Russia. The town's strategic advantages brought settlement as early as the third millennium BC. The kingdom of Kartli-Iberia evolved from the collapse of Alexander's Greek Empire, and Mtskheta was its capital until the sixth century AD.

The Armaztsikhe (citadel and royal residence) was at the heart of the city and fortified quarters allocated to specialized trades clustered around it, making up 'Great Mtskheta'. Today its ruins stand with the remains of earlier monuments, including a temple and tomb on Bagineti Mountain.

Many of Mtskheta's early Christian monuments survive to the present day. They include the eleventh-century Svetitskhoveli Cathedral; the Mtskhetis Jvari (Church of the Holy Rood), the most sacred place in Georgia; and Samtavro (the Place of the Ruler), also built in the eleventh century, which contains the graves of Mirian, the first Georgian Christian king, and his wife.

Svetitskhoveli Cathedral
▼

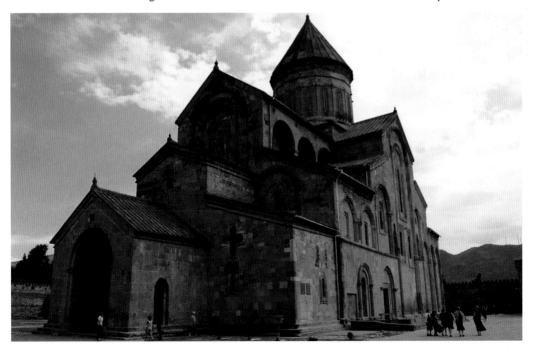

World Heritage site since

• 1978 • 1979 • 1980 • 1981 • 1982 • 1983 • 1984 • 1985 • 1986 • 1987 • 1988 • 1989 • 1990 • 1991 • 1992 • 1993 • **1994**

Historic Monuments of Ancient Kyoto (Kyoto, Uji and Otsu Cities)

Japan

Criteria – Interchange of values; Significance in human history

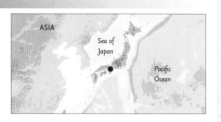

Kinkaku-ji, the 'Golden Pavilion', Kyoto.

Properties on the World Heritage site that date from the foundation of Heian-kyo in the late-eighth century are Karmwakeikauchi-jinja (Shinto shrine), Amomioya-jinja (Shinto shrine), Kyo-o-gokoku-ji To-ji (Buddhist temple), Kiyornim-dera (Buddhist temple), and Enryaku-ji (Buddhist temple); the two large Buddhist temples of Daigo-ji and Ninna-ji are representative of the early Heian period.

The Japanese government's introduction of the first ordinance for the protection of antiquities in 1871, and the Ancient Shrines and Temples Preservation Law of 1897, marked the beginning of the important protection and conservation programmes of modern Japan.

Built in AD 794 on the model of the capitals of ancient China, Kyoto was the imperial capital of Japan from its foundation until the mid-nineteenth century. As the centre of Japanese culture for more than 1,000 years, Kyoto illustrates the development of Japanese wooden architecture, particularly religious architecture, and the art of Japanese gardens, which has influenced landscape gardening the world over.

Both Chinese culture and Buddhism were having a profound influence on Japan when the capital moved to Kyoto, then named Heian-kyo, in AD 794. Aristocratic society clustered around the imperial court for the four centuries of the Heian period (794–1192). By the end of this period, however, the military samurai class was growing in power, and civil war started in 1185. It led to the establishment of a samurai military regime at Kamakum, although the imperial court remained at Kyoto. The Sekisui-in at Kozan-ji is the best example of the residential architecture of this period, which ended in 1332 with the establishment of the Muromachi Shogunate. This period saw the building of large temples of the Rinzai Zen sect, such as Temyu-ji, and the creation of Zen gardens, of which that at Saiho-ji is a representative example.

The Muromachi Shogunate reached its height at the end of the fourteenth century; this was reflected in buildings such as the villa of Shogun Ashikaga Yoshimitsu, which later became the Buddhist temple Rokuon-ji. Garden design was refined into pure art, as demonstrated by the garden of the abbot's residence at Ryoan-ji.

Much of Kyoto was destroyed in the Onin War (1467–77), but it was rebuilt by a new urban merchant class who replaced the aristocrats who had fled during the war. The centre of power moved to Edo (present-day Tokyo), and in Kyoto the strong castle of Ngo-jo was built at the heart of the city.

The political stability of the late sixteenth century saw a new spirit of confidence among both merchants and the military, reflected in the opulence and boldness of the architecture; the Sanpo-in residential complex and garden at Daigo-jo are examples of this. The following century saw Heian temples and shrines, such as Kiyomimdera, being restored in traditional style. During this period the supremacy of Kyoto as a centre of pilgrimage became established.

Ha Long Bay
Vietnam

Criteria – Natural phenomena or beauty; Major
stages of Earth's history

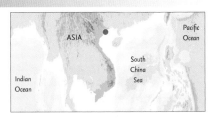

Ha Long Bay in the Gulf of Tonkin includes
some 1,600 islands and islets that form a
spectacular seascape of limestone pillars.
Because of their precipitous nature, most
of the islands are uninhabited. The site's
outstanding scenic beauty is complemented
by its great biological interest.

Ha Long Bay is known as a drowned karst
landscape due to the exceptional grouping
of its limestone karst features which have
been subject to repeated regression and
transgression of the sea over time. The
limestones of Ha Long Bay have been
eroded into a mature landscape of fengcong
(clusters of conical peaks) and fenglin
(isolated towers) karst features, modified by
sea invasion at a later stage.

The area provides a unique and extensive
reservoir of data for the future
understanding of geoclimatic history and
the nature of karst processes in a complex
environment.

The smaller islands
are 'fenglin' towers
50–100 m high. Many
have sheer faces on all
or most sides and
continue to evolve
through rock falls and
large slab failures.

A distinctive feature
of Ha Long Bay is the
abundance of lakes
and limestone caves
within the larger
limestone islands.
▼

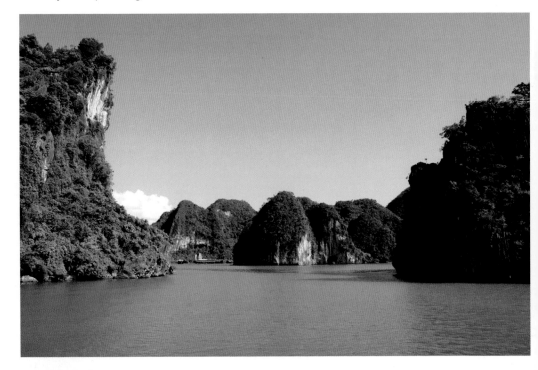

World Heritage site since

• 1978 • 1979 • 1980 • 1981 • 1982 • 1983 • 1984 • 1985 • 1986 • 1987 • 1988 • 1989 • 1990 • 1991 • 1992 • 1993 • **1994**

Collegiate Church, Castle, and Old Town of Quedlinburg
Germany
Criteria – Significance in human history

Quedlinburg, in the Land of Sachsen-Anhalt, was a capital of the East Franconian German Empire at the time of the Saxonian-Ottonian ruling dynasty. The importance of Quedlinburg rests on three main elements: the preservation of the medieval street pattern; the wealth of urban vernacular buildings, especially timber-framed houses of the sixteenth and seventeenth centuries; and the important Romanesque collegiate church of

St Servatius. The area comprises the historic town enclosed within the city walls, consisting of the old (tenth century) and new (twelfth century) towns, the Westendorf district with the collegiate church and the buildings of the imperial foundation, St Wipert's Church, and the Münzenberg, the hill on which a Benedictine monastery was founded in 946.

The original urban layout is remarkably well preserved. The town's nucleus is the castle hill, with its administrative and religious buildings, around which settlements of craftsmen and traders quickly grew to service the requirements of the rulers and their households.

Völklingen Ironworks
Germany
Criteria – Interchange of values; Significance in human history

The ironworks, which cover some 6,000 m², dominate the city of Völklingen. They are the only intact example, in the whole of western Europe and North America, of an integrated ironworks that was built and equipped in the nineteenth and twentieth centuries and has remained intact. Völklingen was the first ironworks in the world to use blast-furnace gas on a large scale to drive enormous blowers providing blast to the furnaces. By the end of the

nineteenth century Völklingen was one of Europe's most productive works and Germany's largest producer of steel beams. From the end of the Second World War until pig-iron production ceased in 1986, only minor modernisation and maintenance took place, giving the site the appearance of an ironworks of the 1930s.

The complex contains installations covering every stage in the pig-iron-production process, from raw-materials handling and processing equipment for coal and iron ore through to blast-furnace iron production. Historically the plant was a model for many other similar installations throughout the world.

World Heritage site since

• 1978 • 1979 • 1980 • 1981 • 1982 • 1983 • 1984 • 1985 • 1986 • 1987 • 1988 • 1989 • 1990 • 1991 • 1992 • 1993 • 1994

City of Safranbolu
Turkey

Criteria – Interchange of values; Significance in human history; Traditional human settlement

EUROPE

Black Sea

Mediterranean Sea

ASIA

Safranbolu is a typical Ottoman city that has survived to the present day. From the thirteenth century to the early twentieth century, Safranbolu was an important caravan station on the main east-west trade route. The Old Mosque, Old Bath and Süleyman Pasha Medrese were built in 1322. During its apogee in the seventeenth century, Safranbolu's architecture influenced urban development throughout much of the Ottoman Empire. Many buildings survive from this period, including the Cinci Inn with its sixty guest rooms (1640–8), Köprülü Mosque (1661) and Let Pasha Mosque (1796), as well as many stores, stables and baths. Following the advent of the railway in the early twentieth century, the town underwent a period of economic deprivation until the building of the Karabük steelworks, which provided a great deal of employment in the region.

Safranbolu consists of four distinct districts: the market place area of the inner city, known as Çukur (The Hole); the area of Kıranköy; Bağlar (The Vineyards); and an area of more recent settlement outside the historic area. The original Turkish settlement was located immediately south of the citadel and developed to the southeast.

Pilgrimage Church of St John of Nepomuk at Zelená Hora

Czech Republic

Criteria – Significance in human history

This pilgrimage church stands at Zelená Hora in Moravia. Constructed on a star-shaped plan, it is the most unusual work by the great architect Jan Blazej Santini, whose highly original Baroque and Neo-Gothic style displays great imagination and inventiveness. Work on the pilgrimage church began in 1719, three years before the formal canonization of John of Nepomuk. The construction of the main structure was completed by 1721.

The number five is dominant in the layout and proportions demonstrated by the five-pointed star shape for the church and the ten-pointed star for the surrounding cloisters that contain five chapels and five entrances.

The main impression given by the interior is its loftiness. The central space opens into five niches; of these, four are partitioned horizontally and the fifth, on the east, is filled by the main altar.

The church retains many of its original furnishings, which include the main altar, designed by Santini and representing the celebration of St John of Nepomuk in heaven; and the four side altars, also designed by Santini and depicting the four Evangelists.

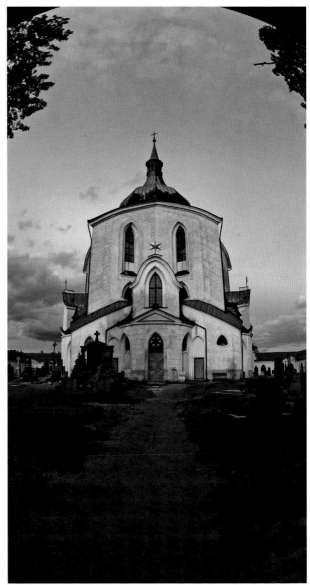

World Heritage site since

· 1978 · 1979 · 1980 · 1981 · 1982 · 1983 · 1984 · 1985 · 1986 · 1987 · 1988 · 1989 · 1990 · 1991 · 1992 · 1993 · 1994 · **1995**

Historic Centre of Avignon: Papal Palace, Episcopal Ensemble and Avignon Bridge
France

Criteria – Human creative genius; Interchange of values; Significance in human history

Avignon was the seat of the papacy in the fourteenth century and an exceptional group of monuments testify to the city's importance. The austere Gothic palace-fortress of the Palais des Papes dominates the historic centre that includes the Petit Palais, the Romanesque Cathedral of Notre-Dame-des-Doms and the remains of the twelfth-century Avignon Bridge.

In 1309 the Frenchman Bertrand de Got, who was declared Supreme Pontiff as Clement V, refused to go to Rome, choosing instead to install himself temporarily in the Dominican Convent at Avignon. The seat of the papacy did not return to Rome until 1417.

Clement's successor, John XXII (1316-34), moved to the former bishop's palace, which was converted into a papal palace. Benedict XII (1334–42) gradually demolished this building and replaced it with what is now known as the Old Palace, covering the northern part of the present site. It was Benedict's successor, Clement VI (1342–52), who was to complete the ensemble. Clement entrusted the interior decoration to the famous Italian painter Matteo Giovannetti. He also supervised the work of French and Italian painters within the palace.

In 1793 the French Revolutionary Convention decided to demolish this 'Bastille du Midi', but the massive building defied their efforts. Ownership passed to the town in 1810 and it was put at the disposal of the Minister of War who used it as a barracks until 1906, when it was returned to the town.

The Cathedral of Notre-Dame-des-Doms lies to the north of the Palais des Papes. The present building replaced the earlier group of episcopal buildings in the twelfth century.

The Petit Palais on the western side of the Place du Palais was built as a cardinal's residence. It was acquired by John XXII in 1336 to compensate the bishop for the demolition of his palace to allow the construction of the papal palace. The Petit Palais was continuously expanded in the fourteenth and fifteenth centuries.

Saint Bénézet Bridge, the Pont d'Avignon, is one of the most important medieval bridges in Europe. Originally built in the twelfth century, it spanned 900 m across the Rhône but suffered several collapses in the following centuries. It was not rebuilt after a flood in 1668 swept much of it away, and only four of its original twenty-two arches remain.

The Palais des Papes ▶ comprises two parts: to the north the Palais Vieux (Old Palace) of Benedict XII and to the south the Palais Neuf (New Palace) of Clement VI. The main courtyard is situated between the two palace buildings.

The palace also houses the pontiffs' private rooms, including robing rooms, bedrooms and studies.

The day room of Clement IV, the Chambre du Cerf, gives access to the Great Chapel of the Palais Neuf; its heavy vault is braced by a massive flying buttress that spans the neighbouring street.

Carlsbad Caverns National Park
USA

Criteria – Natural phenomena or beauty; Major stages of Earth's history

This karst landscape in New Mexico comprises eighty-one recognized caves that are outstanding not only for their size but also for the profusion, diversity and beauty of their mineral formations.

The park covers a segment of the Capitan Reef. An extensive cave system has developed within the reef as a result of sulphuric acid dissolution. Of the known caves, Carlsbad Cavern is the largest, and Lechuguilla Cave is the most extensive and decorated in the world.

The Capitan Reef complex dates back to the Permian period, some 225–280 million years ago. The exposed sections of this reef lying within the park are among the best preserved in the world accessible for scientific study.

The caves are noted for their migratory bat species. Various species of fungi and bacteria growing inside are of particular scientific and medical interest.

Carlsbad differs from the other existing World Heritage caves in its huge chambers, far larger than others, and for its decorative minerals. Since its initial exploration in 1985, Lechuguilla Cave has been strictly managed, allowing only closely monitored visits by researchers. This cave is noteworthy as an underground laboratory where geological processes can be studied in a virtually undisturbed environment.

Doll's Theatre, Big Room, Carlsbad Caverns National Park. ▼

World Heritage site since

· 1978 · 1979 · 1980 · 1981 · 1982 · 1983 · 1984 · 1985 · 1986 · 1987 · 1988 · 1989 · 1990 · 1991 · 1992 · 1993 · 1994 · **1995**

Cultural Landscape of Sintra
Portugal

Criteria – Interchange of values; Significance in human history; Traditional human settlement

The structures of Sintra and the Serra harmonize indigenous flora with a refined and cultivated landscape created by man as a result of literary and artistic influences.

The Royal Palace is the dominant architectural feature of Sintra. One of its most important features is the facing with tiles (azulejos), the finest example of this Mudejar technique on the Iberian Peninsula.

Pena Palace, Sintra.
▼

In the nineteenth century Sintra became the first centre of European Romantic architecture. Ferdinand II turned a ruined monastery into a castle, where this new sensitivity was displayed in the use of Gothic, Egyptian, Moorish and Renaissance elements, and in the creation of a park blending local and exotic species of trees. Other fine dwellings, built along the same lines in the surrounding mountains, created a unique combination of parks and gardens, which influenced the development of landscape architecture throughout Europe.

The Serra de Sintra, Ptolemy's 'Mountain of the Moon', encloses various significant parks and gardens. Although almost all the built heritage was destroyed in the 1755 earthquake, there are some outstanding court and military buildings, religious architecture and archaeological sites. These include the Royal Palace and the Palace of Ribafrias, Pena Palace, Quinta de Regaleira, the Town Hall and Trinity Convent.

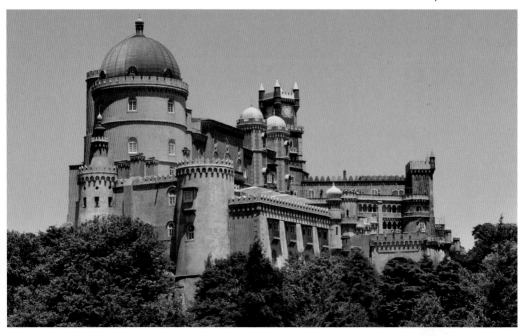

World Heritage site since

• 1978 • 1979 • 1980 • 1981 • 1982 • 1983 • 1984 • 1985 • 1986 • 1987 • 1988 • 1989 • 1990 • 1991 • 1992 • 1993 • 1994 • **1995**

Historic Centre of Naples
Italy

Criteria – Interchange of values; Significance in human history

EUROPE

Mediterranean Sea

Ionian Sea

Naples is one of the most ancient cities in Europe, whose contemporary urban fabric preserves the elements of its long and eventful history. Its street pattern, its wealth of historic buildings from many periods, and its setting on the Bay of Naples give it an unparalleled value and one that has had a profound influence in Europe and beyond.

Much of the significance of Naples is due to its urban fabric, which represents twenty-five centuries of growth. The street layout in the earliest parts of the city owes much to its classical origins.

Naples has retained the imprint of the successive cultures that emerged in Europe and the Mediterranean basin. This makes it a unique site, with a wealth of outstanding churches, such as Santa Chiara and San Lorenzo Maggiore, and monuments such as the Castel Nuovo.

Above ground, little survives of the Greek town founded in 470 BC, but important archaeological discoveries have been made since the Second World War. Three sections of the original Greek town walls are visible in the northwest. The surviving Roman remains, notably the large theatre, cemeteries and catacombs, are more substantial.

Castel Nuovo.
▼

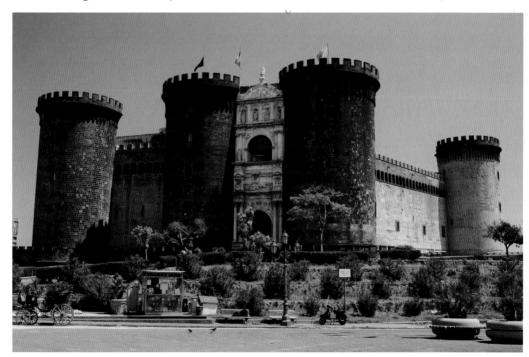

World Heritage site since

• 1978 • 1979 • 1980 • 1981 • 1982 • 1983 • 1984 • 1985 • 1986 • 1987 • 1988 • 1989 • 1990 • 1991 • 1992 • 1993 • 1994 • **1995**

Schokland and Surroundings
Netherlands

Criteria – Testimony to cultural tradition; Traditional human settlement

Schokland and its surroundings are outstanding examples of the prehistoric and historic occupation of a typical wetland, especially in relation to the reclamation and occupation of peat areas.

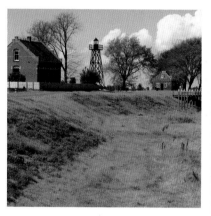

Schokland was a peninsula that by the fifteenth century had become an island. Occupied and then abandoned as the sea encroached, it had to be evacuated in 1859. But following the draining of the Zuider Zee, it has, since the 1940s, formed part of the land reclaimed from the sea. Schokland has vestiges of human habitation going back to prehistoric times. It symbolizes the heroic, age-old struggle of the people of the Netherlands against the encroachment of the sea.

Virgin Komi Forests
Russian Federation

Criteria – Natural phenomena or beauty; Significant ecological and biological processes

The forests form a haven for many threatened mammal species including wolf, otter, beaver, sable, wolverine and lynx. Flying squirrels, brown bears, elks and pine martens are also present.

The Virgin Komi Forests cover 32,800 km² of tundra and mountain landscape, and constitute one of the most extensive areas of virgin boreal forest remaining in Europe. The forest is dominated by lowlands in the west that rise to form the glaciated northern Ural mountains in the east. The vegetation of the lowlands comprises marshes and flood plain islands. Boreal forest extends from the marshes to the foothills of the Urals and is superseded by subalpine scrub woodlands, meadows, tundra and bedrock. This vast area of conifers, aspens, birches, peat bogs, rivers and natural lakes has been monitored and studied for over fifty years. It provides valuable evidence of the natural processes affecting biodiversity in the taiga.

World Heritage site since

• 1978 • 1979 • 1980 • 1981 • 1982 • 1983 • 1984 • 1985 • 1986 • 1987 • 1988 • 1989 • 1990 • 1991 • 1992 • 1993 • 1994 • **1995**

Waterton Glacier International Peace Park
Canada and USA

Criteria – Natural phenomena or beauty;
Significant ecological and biological processes

Waterton Lake in Canada.

The diverse habitats support a rich variety of mammals, birds, reptiles, amphibians, fish and invertebrates. These include an intact suite of predators including grey wolves, grizzly bears, cougars, lynx, fox, coyotes, fishers and wolverines.

Both parks strive to protect their shared ecosystem through cooperative management, not only between themselves, but also with other neighbours.

In 1932 Waterton Lakes National Park in Alberta, Canada, was joined with Glacier National Park in Montana, United States, to form the world's first International Peace Park. Situated on the border between the two countries and offering outstanding scenery, the combined park is exceptionally rich in plant and mammal species, and in prairie, forest, alpine and glacial features. Both parks feature long, narrow, glacial lakes and colourful, ancient rocks. The Peace Park celebrates the peace and goodwill existing along the world's longest undefended border, as well as a spirit of cooperation which is reflected in wildlife and vegetation management, search and rescue programmes, and joint interpretive programmes, brochures and exhibits.

The Waterton-Glacier stratigraphic record spans more than 1,600 million years of sedimentary and tectonic evolution. Local topography is dominated by the 2,500 m peaks of the Rocky Mountains, and the park is roughly split lengthwise by the Continental Divide. The dominant landforms are typical of mountain glaciation. The mountains were largely shaped by glacial erosion, whereas the rolling grasslands are a result of glacial deposition. The Peace Park's natural processes: fire, wind, flooding and glaciation continue to shape the landscape.

The region's climate also contributes to the richness of life found in the park. The area is influenced by two opposing systems, the Arctic Continental and the Pacific Maritime. The headwaters of three major continental watersheds are also protected within the boundaries of the Peace Park.

Five ecoregions are found within the Waterton-Glacier International Peace Park: alpine, subalpine, montane, foothills parkland, and grasslands. The alpine ecoregion is found above 2,100 m on the west slope and 1,800 m on the east. While it is not well vegetated, it has striking summer displays of wildflowers. Coniferous forest is typical of the cooler subalpine ecoregion, characterized by such species as lodgepole and ponderosa pine, subalpine fir and Englemann spruce. This 'snow forest' is the largest ecoregion in the Peace Park. The montane ecoregion occurs at low to mid elevations. It is a mix of dry grasslands and mixed poplar and coniferous forests. Douglas fir, white spruce and western larch are distinctive trees of this ecoregion. The foothills parkland ecoregion serves as a transition between prairie grasslands and the coniferous forest zone, and is mix of aspens and grasslands. Commonly known as bunchgrass prairie, a typical grass in this ecoregion is rough fescue.

World Heritage site since

• 1978 • 1979 • 1980 • 1981 • 1982 • 1983 • 1984 • 1985 • 1986 • 1987 • 1988 • 1989 • 1990 • 1991 • 1992 • 1993 • 1994 • **1995**

Roskilde Cathedral
Denmark

Criteria – Interchange of values; Significance in human history

Built in the twelfth and thirteenth centuries, this was Scandinavia's first Gothic cathedral to be constructed of brick and it encouraged the spread of this style throughout northern Europe. It has been the mausoleum of the Danish royal family since the fifteenth century. The original structure was Romanesque; however, when only the eastern half had been built, the plan was changed, the remainder to be under Gothic influence. The transept was located further back and the towers planned for the choir were moved to the west end. Work was virtually complete by around 1275, apart from the north tower, which was finished at the end of the fourteenth century. Porches and side chapels were added up to the end of the nineteenth century. The building thus provides a clear overview of the development of European religious architecture.

Many of the medieval furnishings of the cathedral disappeared at the Reformation, and more were sold at a notorious auction in 1806. The outstanding piece of what remains is the reredos, a masterpiece of Dutch religious art dating from around 1560. It is a triptych, probably from Antwerp, and bears scenes from the life of Christ.

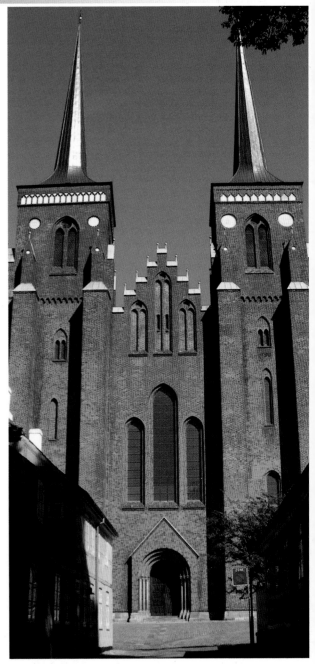

Ferrara, City of the Renaissance, and its Po Delta
Italy

Criteria – Interchange of values; Testimony to cultural tradition; Significance in human history; Traditional human settlement; Heritage associated with events of universal significance

EUROPE

Mediterranean Sea   Ionian Sea

Ferrara is an outstanding example of a planned Renaissance city which has retained its urban fabric virtually intact. Among the great Italian cities, it is the only one to have an original plan that is not derived from a Roman layout. It did not develop from a central area but rather on a linear axis, along the banks of the Po River, with longitudinal streets and many cross streets, around which the medieval city was organized.

Throughout the sixteenth century the city was planned with the aim of making it a future capital. Its evolution came to an end after the seventeenth century under papal administration, and the city did not undergo any extensions for almost three centuries. The developments in town planning expressed in Ferrara had a profound influence on urban design throughout the following centuries.

In the fifteenth and sixteenth centuries the city became an intellectual and artistic centre that attracted the greatest minds of the Italian Renaissance. Here, Piero della Francesca, Jacopo Bellini and Andrea Mantegna decorated the palaces of the House of Este, and the humanist concept of the 'ideal city' came to life in the neighbourhoods built by Biagio Rossetti in accordance with the new principles of perspective.

Castello Estense. ▼

World Heritage site since

• 1978 • 1979 • 1980 • 1981 • 1982 • 1983 • 1984 • 1985 • 1986 • 1987 • 1988 • 1989 • 1990 • 1991 • 1992 • 1993 • 1994 • **1995**

Rapa Nui National Park
Chile

Criteria – Human creative genius; Testimony to
cultural tradition; Traditional human settlement

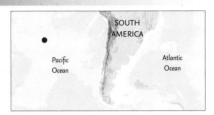

Ahu Tongariki, the
largest ahu on Rapa
Nui.

Several moai are still in
an uncompleted
condition in the
quarries, providing
valuable information
about their
manufacture. Some
have large cylindrical
pieces of red stone
known as pukao as
headdresses: these
are believed to denote
special ritual status.
There is a clear
stylistic evolution in
the form and size of
the moai, from the
earlier small, round-
headed and round-
eyed figures to the
best-known large,
elongated figures with
carefully carved
fingers, nostrils, long
ears and other
features.

Rapa Nui, the indigenous name of Easter
Island, bears witness to a unique cultural
phenomenon. A society that settled there
around AD 300 established a powerful and
original tradition of monumental sculpture
and architecture free from outside
influence. From the tenth to the sixteenth
centuries this society built shrines and
erected enormous stone figures known as
moai, creating an unrivalled cultural
landscape that continues to fascinate people
throughout the world.

The island was settled around AD 300 by
Polynesians, probably from the Marquesas,
who brought with them a wholly Stone Age
society. The high cultural level of this society
is best known by its moai and ceremonial
shrines (ahu); it is also noteworthy for a form
of pictographic writing (rongo rongo), so far
undeciphered. All the cultural elements in
Rapa Nui before the arrival of Europeans in
the eighteenth century indicate that there
were no other incoming groups.

Between the tenth and sixteenth centuries
the island community expanded steadily,
and settlements were set up along the
coastline. However, an economic and social
crisis in the sixteenth century, attributable to
over-population and environmental
deterioration, resulted in constant warfare
between two separate groups. The warrior
class that evolved gave rise to the Birdman
cult which superseded the statue-building
religion and toppled most of the moai and
ahu.

On Easter Sunday 1722 Jacob Roggeveen
of the Dutch East India Company chanced
upon the island and gave it its European
name. It was annexed to Chile in 1888.

Rapa Nui's most famous archaeological
features are the moai, believed to represent
sacred ancestors who watch over the
villages and ceremonial areas. They range
from 2 m to 20 m in height and are for the
most part carved from the scoria or
solidified lava, and lowered down the slopes
into previously dug holes.

The ahu vary considerably in size and form.
There are certain constant features: notably
a raised rectangular platform of large
worked stones filled with rubble; a ramp
often paved with rounded beach pebbles;
and a levelled area in front
of the platform. Some have moai on them,
and there are tombs in a number of the
ahu in which skeletal remains have been
discovered. The ahu are generally located
on the coast and orientated parallel to it.

World Heritage site since

· 1978 · 1979 · 1980 · 1981 · 1982 · 1983 · 1984 · 1985 · 1986 · 1987 · 1988 · 1989 · 1990 · 1991 · 1992 · 1993 · 1994 · **1995**

Caves of Aggtelek Karst and Slovak Karst
Hungary and Slovakia
Criteria – Major stages of Earth's history

The variety of formations and the fact that they are concentrated in a restricted area means that the 712 caves currently identified make up a typical temperate-zone karstic system. Because they display an extremely rare combination of tropical and glacial climatic effects, they make it possible to study geological history over tens of millions of years.

These caves are remarkable for having the world's highest stalagmite and an ice-filled abyss, which considering the territory's height above sea level, is a unique phenomenon for central Europe.

◄
Demänovská Cave of Freedom, Slovak Karst Caves.

Messel Pit Fossil Site
Germany
Criteria – Major stages of Earth's history

One of the world's four most significant fossil sites, Messel Pit gives the most complete view of the living environment of the Eocene, between 57 million and 36 million years ago. During this period of geological time, North America, Europe and Asia were in continuous land contact and the partial explanation of current distribution patterns is provided by the Eocene fossil record. Messel provides particularly rich information about the early stages of the evolution of mammals and includes exceptionally well-preserved mammal fossils, ranging from fully articulated skeletons to the contents of stomachs of animals of this period. Mammals were not the only component of the fauna – large quantities of birds, reptiles, fish, insects and plant remains all contribute to an extraordinary fossil assemblage.

The Eocene epoch was a remarkable period in the evolution of life on Earth, when mammals became firmly established in all the principal land ecosystems. They also reinvaded the seas, e.g. whales, and took to the air, e.g. bats.

Seokguram Grotto and Bulguksa Temple
Korea, Republic of

Criteria – *Human creative genius; Significance in human history*

Established in the eighth century on the slopes of Mount T'oham, the Seokguram Grotto consists of an antechamber, a corridor and a main rotunda. It is built from granite and features thirty-nine Buddhist engravings on the main wall and the principal sculpture of the Buddha in the centre. This monumental statue is posed in the bhumisparsha mudra position, the gesture with which the historical Buddha summoned the Earth as witness to his realization of Enlightenment. With the surrounding portrayals of gods,

Bodhisattvas and disciples, all realistically and delicately sculpted in high and low relief, it is considered a masterpiece of Buddhist art in the Far East. The Temple of Bulguksa, built in 774, and the Seokguram Grotto form a religious architectural complex of exceptional significance.

Multi-coloured lanterns decorate the Dabotap Pagoda, which is located in the Bulguksa Temple. The lanterns are to celebrate Buddha's birthday.
▼

The main Sakyamuni Buddha figure is 3.45 m high, and set on a lotus flower-shaped pedestal. The hair is tightly curled and there is a distinct usnisa, the protuberance on the top of the head symbolizing Supreme Wisdom. Beneath the broad forehead the eyebrows are shaped like crescent moons and the half-closed eyes gaze towards the Sea of Japan (East Sea).

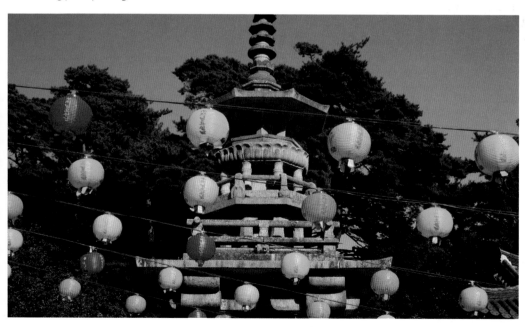

San Agustín Archeological Park
Colombia
Criteria – Testimony to cultural tradition

The principal archaeological monuments are Las Mesitas, containing artificial mounds, terraces, funerary structures and stone statues; the Fuente de Lavapatas, a religious monument carved in the stone bed of a stream; and the Bosque de Las Estatuas, where there are examples of stone statues from the whole region.

The wealth of megalithic statuary from the archaeological site in San Agustín Archeological Park bears vivid witness to the artistic creativity of the pre-Hispanic culture that flowered in the hostile tropical environment of the northern Andes from the first to the eighth centuries. During this period there was considerable social consolidation. The concentration of power in the hands of the chiefs made possible the production of gigantic works: hundreds of elaborate stone statues were carved, some in complex relief and large in size. Altogether some 300 enormous sculptures of gods, warriors and mythical beasts were created, in styles ranging from abstract to realist, and they make up the largest group of religious monuments in South America. The huge monumental platforms, terraces and mounds, and the temple-like architecture reflect a complex system of religious and magical beliefs.

Hanseatic Town of Visby
Sweden

Criteria – Significance in human history;
Traditional human settlement

A former Viking site on the island of Gotland, Visby was the main centre of the Hanseatic League in the Baltic from the twelfth to the fourteenth centuries. During this period, German merchants settled in the town, followed by Russian and Danish traders. Guild houses and churches were built, and the earlier small wooden buildings were replaced by large stone houses, built in parallel rows eastwards from the harbour.

As a result, Visby changed from a simple Gotland village into an impressive international town, enclosed by a strong defensive wall, and increasingly divorced from its rural hinterland. Its thirteenth-century ramparts and more than 200 buildings (warehouses and wealthy merchants' dwellings) from the same period make it the best-preserved fortified commercial city in northern Europe.

The best-preserved medieval warehouse is the Old Pharmacy on Strandgatan, with vaulted rooms on the ground and top floors, a latrine cellar, a medieval well, and original surrounds on doors and windows. Other notable buildings are von Lingen's House on St Hansgatan and a number of houses in the narrow streets running down to the harbour.

World Heritage site since

• 1978 • 1979 • 1980 • 1981 • 1982 • 1983 • 1984 • 1985 • 1986 • 1987 • 1988 • 1989 • 1990 • 1991 • 1992 • 1993 • 1994 • 1995

Historic Centre of Siena
Italy

Criteria – Human creative genius; Interchange of values; Significance in human history

EUROPE

Mediterranean Sea

Ionian Sea

Siena is the embodiment of a medieval city. Its character and quality are preserved to a remarkable degree, and its influence on art, architecture and town planning in the Middle Ages, both in Italy and elsewhere in Europe, was immense. The whole city of Siena, built around the Piazza del Campo, was devised as a work of art that blends into the surrounding landscape.

The historic centre is delimited by a 7-km fortification of ramparts dating from the fourteenth to the sixteenth centuries, the route of which follows the contours of the three hills on which the city stands. The walls, which have been enlarged on several occasions, also include part of the 25-km network of galleries (bottini), which evacuate the spring waters distributed by the public fountains. The main fountains, mostly from the thirteenth century, are veritable buildings in their own right and constructed like Gothic porticoes.

The historic centre developed along the Y-shaped segments defined by the three main arteries that meet at the Croce del Travaglio, adjoining the Piazza del Campo, and onto which the network of minor roads are grafted. Houses and palaces follow one another in rows along the main streets, creating a characteristic urban space with certain notable elements.

The Piazza del Campo, at the junction of three hills, is one of the most remarkable urban open spaces in Italy. Its formation coincides with the growth of the medieval city and the assertion of communal power. Financial and commercial activities were concentrated halfway along the Via Francigena, the entire lengths of the present-day Via dei Banchi Sopra and Via dei Banchi Sotto, and the market place proper was located in the Piazza del Campo, at that time divided in two sectors.

At the end of the twelfth century, the communal government decided to unite the two sectors to create a unique semicircular open space, and promulgated a series of ordinances that regulated not only commercial activities, but also the services and dimensions of the houses, in order to make the façades around the piazza uniform. Under the Medici who ruled Siena from the mid-sixteenth century, the piazza became the ideal setting for spectacular festivals and was opened up to the Palio, the famous horse race between teams from the different quarters of the city.

The Palazzo Pubblico, ▶ the focal point of the Piazza del Campo, was in all probability the model for the Gothic palaces of the great noble or mercantile families (Palazzo Tomei, Palazzo Buonsignore); these are characterized by an increase in breadth, the use of brick, large windows and the so-called 'Guelph' crenellation.

The highest point of the town is crowned by the Cathedral of Santa Maria. The lower part of its façade is the work of Giovanni Pisano. The cathedral's remarkable pavement and pulpit, which was carved by Nicolà Pisano, are extremely well-preserved.

World Heritage site since

• 1978 • 1979 • 1980 • 1981 • 1982 • 1983 • 1984 • 1985 • 1986 • 1987 • 1988 • 1989 • 1990 • 1991 • 1992 • 1993 • 1994 • **1995**

Historic Villages of Shirakawa-go and Gokayama
Japan

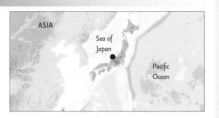

Criteria – Significance in human history; Traditional human settlement

Located in a mountainous region that was cut off from the rest of the world for a long period of time, these villages with their Gassho-style houses subsisted on the cultivation of mulberry trees and the rearing of silkworms. The large houses with their steeply pitched thatched roofs are the only examples of their kind in Japan. Despite economic upheavals, the villages of Ogimachi, Ainokura and Suganuma are outstanding examples of a traditional way of life perfectly adapted to the environment and people's social and economic circumstances.

The need for large, enclosed spaces to store mulberry leaves and for silkworm beds was important in the development of the area's characteristic gassho-style houses. Their steeply pitched roofs are also ideally designed to withstand the area's heavy snowfalls.

Haeinsa Temple Janggyeong Panjeon, the Depositories for the Tripitaka Koreana Woodblocks
Korea, Republic of

Criteria – Significance in human history; Heritage associated with events of universal significance

The Temple of Haeinsa, on Mount Kaya, is home to the Tripitaka Koreana, the most complete collection of Buddhist texts, engraved on 80,000 woodblocks between 1237 and 1248. The buildings of Janggyeong Panjeon date from the fifteenth century and were constructed to house the woodblocks which are also revered as exceptional works of art. As the oldest depository of the Tripitaka, they reveal an astonishing mastery of the invention and implementation of the conservation techniques used to preserve these woodblocks.

The Haeinsa Tripitaka woodblocks were carved in an appeal to the authority of the Buddha in the defence of Korea against Mongol invasions. They are recognized by Buddhist scholars around the world for their outstanding accuracy and superior quality.

Old Town Lunenburg
Canada

Criteria – Significance in human history;
Traditional human settlement

Lunenburg is the best surviving example of a planned British colonial settlement in North America. The Lunenburg plan (1753) incorporated all the principles of the 'model town': geometrically regular streets and blocks; the allocation of public spaces; an allowance for fortifications; and a distinction between urban and non-urban areas. Of these, all but the fortifications survive in present-day Lunenburg. The plan

consisted of six divisions of eight blocks each, each block being in turn subdivided into fourteen lots. Each settler was given a town lot and a larger 'garden lot' outside the town limits. The setting and layout of the town have changed minimally since 1753. Wood remains the principal construction material and traditional techniques have been maintained when restoration has been carried out on earlier buildings.

The pattern of construction of the residential buildings is repeated in the commercial and waterfront buildings, where wood predominates. The same applies to the churches: the second oldest Protestant church building in Canada, St John's Anglican Church, begun in 1754, is considered by experts to be an example of 'Carpenter Gothic' at its finest.

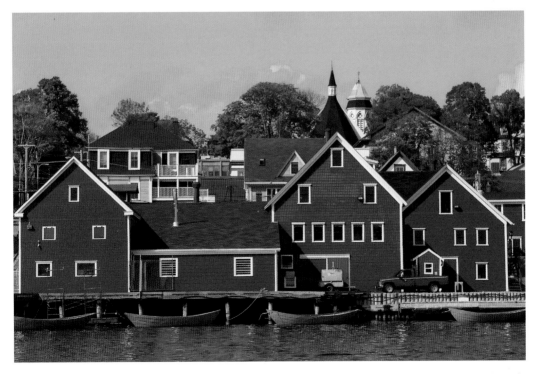

Town of Luang Prabang
Lao People's Democratic Republic

Criteria – Interchange of values; Significance in human history; Traditional human settlement

Luang Prabang is an outstanding example of the fusion of traditional Lao architecture and urban structures with European colonial building in the nineteenth and twentieth centuries. Its unique and remarkably well-preserved townscape illustrates a key stage in the blending of these two distinct cultural traditions. The political and religious centre of the town is situated on a peninsula formed by the Mekong River and its tributaries, and contains royal and noble residences, religious foundations and commercial buildings. The majority are built from wood (parts of the temples are in stone). The colonial element is characterized by one- or two-storey terraced houses built from brick. The monasteries generally consist of the religious buildings (shrine, chapel, library, stupa, stone post), and monastic buildings (communal buildings, cells, refectory).

The traditional Lao wooden houses are divided into two basic spaces: the private rooms and the public terraces. They are usually raised on wooden piles, giving a space beneath for working and for shelter, for both men and animals. Walling may be of planks or plaited bamboo on a wooden frame.

Wat Xieng Thong Temple in Luang Prabang.
▼

World Heritage site since

• 1978 • 1979 • 1980 • 1981 • 1982 • 1983 • 1984 • 1985 • 1986 • 1987 • 1988 • 1989 • 1990 • 1991 • 1992 • 1993 • 1994 • **1995**

Crespi d'Adda
Italy

Criteria – Significance in human history;
Traditional human settlement

The entire complex is laid out in a geometrically regular form and divided into two parts by the main road from Capriate. The factory, a single, compact block with medieval ornamentation, is on one side of the main road. The houses, constructed within a rectangular grid of roads in three lines, are on the opposite side.

Crespi d'Adda is an outstanding example of a late nineteenth-century 'company town' that survives remarkably intact, and part of which is still in industrial use. In 1878 Cristoforo Benigno Crespi, an enlightened textile manufacturer, built three-storey multi-family houses for his workers around his mill. When his son, Silvio Benigno Crespi, took over the management in 1889, he completed and modified the project. He turned away from the large multiple-occupancy blocks in favour of the single-family house with its own garden, which he saw as conducive to harmony, and a defence against industrial strife. In addition to small houses, a hydroelectric power station to supply the workers with free electricity; a clinic; public lavatories and wash houses; a consumer cooperative; a school and small theatre; a sports centre; houses for the local priest and doctor; and other common services were built.

World Heritage site since

• • • • • • • • • • • • • • • • • • 1978 • 1979 • 1980 • 1981 • 1982 • 1983 • 1984 • 1985 • 1986 • 1987 • 1988 • 1989 • 1990 • 1991 • 1992 • 1993 • 1994 • **1995**

Rice Terraces of the Philippine Cordilleras
Philippines

Criteria – Testimony to cultural tradition; Significance in human history; Traditional human settlement

The rice terraces of the Philippine Cordilleras are living cultural landscapes devoted to the production of one of the world's most important staple crops, rice. They preserve traditional techniques and forms, dating back many centuries, and still viable today. At the same time, they illustrate a remarkable degree of harmony between mankind and a natural environment of great aesthetic appeal, as well as demonstrating sustainable farming systems in mountainous terrain based on careful use of natural resources.

The rice terraces are the only monuments in the Philippines that show no evidence of having been influenced by colonial cultures. Owing to the difficult terrain, the Cordillera tribes are among the few peoples of the Philippines who have successfully resisted foreign domination and preserved their authentic tribal culture. The history of the terraces is intertwined with that of its people, their culture and traditional practices.

The Philippines culture, alone among southeast Asian cultures, is wholly wood-based and the terraces are the only form of stone construction from the pre-colonial period. Terracing began in the Cordilleras some 2,000 years ago, although scholars disagree about its original purpose.

However, it is evidence of a high level of knowledge of structural and hydraulic engineering among the terrace builders. The knowledge and practices involved in maintaining the terraces are transferred orally from generation to generation, without written records but supported by rituals.

Construction of the terraces demands great care and precision. An underground conduit is placed within the fill for drainage purposes. The groups of terraces blanket the mountainsides, following their contours. Above them, rising to the mountain tops, is a ring of private woods (muyong), intensively managed in conformity with traditional practices, which recognizes a total ecosystem and assures an adequate water supply to keep the terraces flooded. Water is equitably shared and no single terrace obstructs the flow on its way down to the next terrace. There is a complex system of communally maintained dams, sluices, channels and bamboo pipes, which drain into a stream at the bottom of the valley.

Villages are associated with groups of terraces, and consist of groups of single-family tribal dwellings which architecturally reproduce the people's spatial interpretation of their mountain environment.

Terraced rice fields are not uncommon in Asia, and the main differences between the Philippines terraces and those elsewhere are their higher altitudes (between 700 m and 1,500 m above sea level) and the steeper slopes. The high-altitude cultivation is based on the use of a special strain of rice which germinates under freezing conditions and grows chest-high, with non-shattering panicles, to facilitate harvesting on slopes that are too steep to permit the use of animals or machinery of any kind.

Jongmyo Shrine
Korea, Republic of

Criteria – Significance in human history

Jongmyo is the oldest and most authentic of the Confucian royal shrines to have been preserved. Dedicated to the forefathers of the Choson dynasty 1392–1910, the shrine has existed in its present form since the sixteenth century and houses tablets bearing the teachings of members of the former royal family. Ritual ceremonies linking music, song and dance still take place there, perpetuating a tradition that goes back to the fourteenth century. Jongmyo is situated in valleys and surrounded by low hills, with artificial additions created to reinforce the

balance of natural elements on the site as laid out in traditional geomancy. The complex is composed of three sets of buildings, each centred around an important shrine or other religious building.

T'aejo, founder of the kingdom, transferred the seat of government to Hanyang (present-day Seoul) in 1394 and ordered the building of Jongmyo. The spirit tablets of four generations of T'aejo's ancestors were later moved there; additional buildings were added later.

Gough and Inaccessible Islands
United Kingdom

Criteria – Natural phenomena or beauty; Significant natural habitat for biodiversity

The spectacular cliffs of Gough Island, towering above the remote South Atlantic, make it a strong contender for the title 'most important seabird colony in the world'. At least fifty-four bird species occur here, including 48 per cent of the world's population of the northern rockhopper penguin. Gough is also a major breeding site of the great shearwater with up to three million pairs breeding on the island. The

endangered wandering albatross *Diomedea dabbenena* is virtually restricted to Gough, with up to 2,000 breeding pairs. The last survivors of the southern giant petrel also breed on Gough, with only 100–150 pairs remaining. Inaccessible Island is almost as rich in wildlife, with two bird, eight plant and at least ten invertebrate species endemic to the island.

Gough Island's undisturbed nature makes it invaluable for biological research, which, with weather monitoring, is the only activity permitted on the island. Inaccessible Island is also largely pristine and is one of the few temperate oceanic islands without introduced mammals.

Kutná Hora: Historical Town Centre with the Church of St Barbara and the Cathedral of Our Lady at Sedlec
Czech Republic

Criteria – Interchange of values; Significance in human history

Kutná Hora, as a result of its silver mines, was one of the most important political and economic centres of Bohemia. Its medieval centre and churches influenced the architecture of central Europe. In the fourteenth century it became a royal city endowed with monuments that symbolized its prosperity: the Church of St Barbara, the Church of St James, the Stone House and the Gothic fountain. The interior of St Barbara's, a jewel of the late Gothic period, is decorated with medieval frescoes depicting the secular life of the medieval mining town of Kutná Hora. The Cistercian Cathedral of Our Lady at Sedlec was restored in line with the Baroque taste of the early eighteenth century. These masterpieces today form part of a well-preserved medieval urban fabric, with some particularly fine private dwellings.

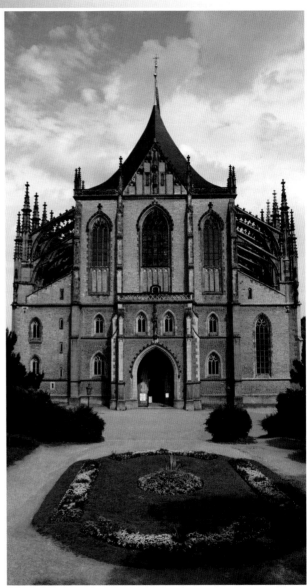

The Church of St Barbara. ▲

The town, built above the steep descent of the Vrchlice Creek, some 60 km east of Prague, prospered from the exploitation of the silver mines, which reached its peak in the fourteenth and fifteenth centuries, when the city became one of the richest in Europe.

World Heritage site since

· · · · · · · · · · · · · · · 1978 · 1979 · 1980 · 1981 · 1982 · 1983 · 1984 · 1985 · 1986 · 1987 · 1988 · 1989 · 1990 · 1991 · 1992 · 1993 · 1994 · **1995**

Old and New Towns of Edinburgh
United Kingdom
Criteria – Interchange of values; Significance in human history

Edinburgh Castle in ▶ the Old Town (right) and the eastern end of the New Town (below).

The Scottish capital since 1437, Edinburgh has two distinct areas: the Old Town, dominated by the medieval fortress of Edinburgh Castle; and the neoclassical New Town, whose development from the eighteenth century onwards had a far-reaching influence on European urban planning. The two areas are a remarkable blend of the urban phenomena of organic medieval growth and eighteenth- and nineteenth-century town planning. The successive planned extensions of the New Town and the high quality of the architecture set standards for Scotland and beyond.

Edinburgh Castle was built in the twelfth century on top of a crag-and-tail formation known as Castle Rock, and the main medieval High Street stood on the ridge of the 'tail' that ran downhill from the Castle to the city walls. Other streets, called closes or wynds, led off at right angles on either side. Regular wars with England meant that Edinburgh was well fortified and that building was concentrated largely inside the walls. The pressure on space and the steep fall-off in land on either side of the hill led to the development of multi-storey dwellings from the late medieval period onwards, with some streets effectively being built underground.

By the eighteenth century the town had become so crowded that the city authorities deemed it necessary to expand on the land to the north. A competition to design the new area was won in 1766 by a 26-year-old local architect, James Craig. His design for a formally organized grid of streets, considered to reflect the rational ideas of the Scottish Enlightenment in its order and in its neoclassical styling, was so successful that it was subsequently greatly extended. Part of the extension was Charlotte Square, designed by Robert Adam.

The linking of the Old and New Towns by road and bridge, and the construction of neoclassical buildings in both – such as Adam's design for the Old College of Edinburgh University – harmonized the two contrasting historic areas, giving the city its unique character.

The Chapel of St Margaret was the only part of Edinburgh Castle to survive destruction throughout centuries of wars and sieges. James VI of Scotland and I of England, son of Mary, Queen of Scots, was born in the Castle in 1556.

The Palace of Holyroodhouse, the scene of many events in Scottish history, was originally the guesthouse of Holyrood Abbey. It was transformed into a royal residence by King James IV (1473–1513) and is the official residence of the monarch in Scotland.

Historic Quarter of the City of Colonia del Sacramento
Uruguay
Criteria – Significance in human history

Colonia del Sacramento bears remarkable testimony in its layout and its buildings to the nature and objectives of European colonial settlement, particularly during the seminal period at the end of the seventeenth century. It also exercised an unquestioned influence on architectural development on either side of the Río de la Plata.

Founded by the Portuguese in 1680, Colonia del Sacramento was built on the extreme west side of a peninsula by the Río de la Plata. It illustrates the successful fusion of Portuguese, Spanish and Uruguayan styles. In 1704–5, during the War of the Spanish Succession, the town was razed to the ground by the Spanish. The Portuguese began reconstruction immediately and Sacramento became the powerhouse of material, commercial and cultural development in the colony. Its success had a decisive influence on the development of Buenos Aires and its region. The siege of 1777 saw Sacramento incorporated into the Spanish Empire. There are excellent examples of seventeenth to nineteenth-century buildings, ranging from elegant town houses to artisans dwellings, and the town has preserved its wide main streets, large squares, cobbled lanes and intimate open spaces.

World Heritage site since

· 1978 · 1979 · 1980 · 1981 · 1982 · 1983 · 1984 · 1985 · 1986 · 1987 · 1988 · 1989 · 1990 · 1991 · 1992 · 1993 · 1994 · **1995**

Historic Centre of Santa Cruz de Mompox
Colombia

Criteria – Significance in human history; Traditional human settlement

Founded in 1540 on the banks of the river Magdalena, Mompox played a key role in the Spanish colonisation of northern South America. The town was defined by the river, and initially grew only along the banks. Walls were built to protect it during periods of high water and, instead of a central square or plaza, it had three plazas in line, each with its own church, and corresponding with a former Indian settlement. The churches also

served as forts in the early years of the city. The historic centre has preserved the harmony and unity of the urban landscape. Most of the buildings are still used for their original purposes, providing an exceptional picture of what a Spanish colonial city was like.

Mompox grew along the banks of the river and was of great logistic and commercial importance: traffic between the port of Cartagena and the interior travelled along the rivers, while overland routes also converged upon the town.

National Archeological Park of Tierradentro
Colombia

Criteria – Testimony to cultural tradition

The hypogea (underground tombs) of Tierradentro are a unique testimony to the everyday life, ritual and burial customs of a stable but now vanished northern Andean pre-Hispanic society. In particular, their carved anthropomorphic representations and polychrome paintings are unique in America. Dating from the sixth to the tenth centuries, these huge burial chambers are up to 12 m wide. There is a symbolic symmetry between the houses of the living

above ground and the underground hypogea for the dead, created by a number of elegant elements. This conveys a pleasant aesthetic sensation and evokes a powerful image of the importance of a new stage into which the deceased has entered and the continuity between life and death, between the living and the ancestors.

Tierradentro is also remarkable for its stone statues. They are carved from stone of volcanic origin and represent standing human figures, with their upper limbs placed on their chests. Masculine figures have banded head-dresses, loincloths and various adornments whereas female figures wear turbans, sleeveless blouses and skirts.

Cologne Cathedral
Germany

Criteria – Human creative genius; Interchange of values; Significance in human history

North Sea

Baltic Sea

EUROPE

The cathedral is a High Gothic five-aisled basilica with a projecting transept and two-tower façade. The construction is totally unified. The western section changes in style but this is not perceptible in the overall building. Nineteenth-century work followed medieval forms and techniques faithfully. The original liturgical appointments of the choir include the high altar on a slab of black marble, carved-oak choir stalls (1308–11), painted choir screens (1332–40), fourteen statues on the pillars in the choir (1270–90) and the stained-glass windows, the largest extant cycle of fourteenth-century windows in Europe.

Cologne Cathedral, constructed over six centuries, is a masterpiece of Gothic architecture. Over the years, successive generations of builders were inspired by the same faith and a spirit of absolute fidelity to the original plans. The cathedral is powerful testimony to the strength and persistence of Christian belief in medieval and modern Europe.

The site of the cathedral is thought to have been first used for Christian worship as early as the fourth century AD. Following the Edict of Milan in 313, when the Emperors Constantine and Licinius proclaimed religious freedom in the Roman Empire, a Christian meeting house near the city walls was enlarged into a church. Alongside it were an atrium, a baptistry and a dwelling house, possibly for the bishop. This modest ensemble was greatly extended and enlarged in the following centuries. The result was an immense building, known by the thirteenth century as 'the mother and master of all churches in Germany'.

Despite its generous dimensions, this cathedral was found to be too small to accommodate the throngs of pilgrims who began to visit Cologne from 1164, when the Archbishop of Cologne brought back from Milan the relics of the Three Kings, the Magi who visited Jesus shortly after his birth.

The ambition of the Archbishop Engelbert of Cologne to make his cathedral into one of the most important in the Holy Roman Empire, and a fitting monument to house the sacred relics, led him to urge for the construction of an entirely new building. However, the archbishop was murdered in 1225 and work did not begin until 1248.

By 1560, much of the nave and the four side aisles had been completed, along with the main structure of the lofty south tower of the west end. Despite numerous efforts, the cathedral remained in an uncompleted state for several centuries. Work was delayed when the French seized Cologne in 1794, and only restarted in 1815 after the city passed to Prussia. The neoclassical architect Karl Friedrich Schinkel visited the cathedral in 1816 and sent his talented pupil Ernst Friedrich Zwirner there as cathedral architect. Work did not begin, however, until 1840. Building was finally completed in 1880, 632 years and 2 months after it first began in 1248.

World Heritage site since

• 1978 • 1979 • 1980 • 1981 • 1982 • 1983 • 1984 • 1985 • 1986 • 1987 • 1988 • 1989 • 1990 • 1991 • 1992 • 1993 • 1994 • 1995 • **1996**

Lake Baikal
Russian Federation

Criteria – Natural phenomena or beauty; Major stages of Earth's history; Significant ecological and biological processes; Significant natural habitat for biodiversity

More than twenty-five million years old and 1,700 m deep, 31,500 km² Lake Baikal in southeast Siberia is the oldest and deepest lake in the world. It contains 20 per cent of the world's total unfrozen freshwater reserves. Known as the 'Galápagos of Russia', its age and isolation have produced some of the world's richest and most unusual endemic freshwater floras and faunas, which are of exceptional value to evolutionary science, the most notable of which is the Baikal seal, a uniquely freshwater species.

The lake is also surrounded by a system of protected areas that have high scenic and other natural values.

The formation of the basin's geological structures took place during the Palaeozoic, Mesozoic and Cenozoic eras (from 540 million years ago to the present). Various tectonic forces are still ongoing, as evidenced in recent thermal vents in the depths of the lake.

The landscape surrounding the lake basin is exceptionally picturesque, with mountains, forests, tundra, lakes, islands and steppes.

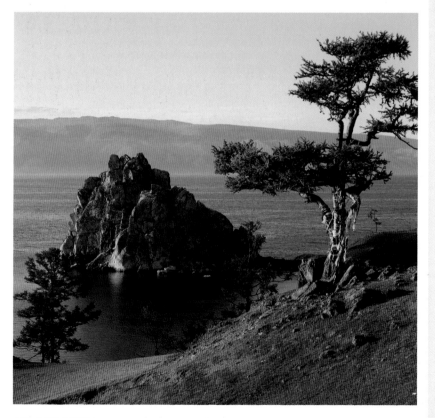

Hiroshima Peace Memorial (Genbaku Dome)

Japan

Criteria – Heritage associated with events of universal significance

The Hiroshima Peace Memorial is a stark symbol of the most destructive force ever created by humankind; it also expresses the hope for world peace and the ultimate elimination of nuclear weapons. The Hiroshima Prefectural Industrial Promotion Hall was the only structure left standing, albeit in skeletal form, in the area where the first atomic bomb exploded on the morning of 6 August 1945. It was preserved in that state when reconstruction of the city began, and became known as the Genbaku (Atomic Bomb) Dome. In 1966 Hiroshima City Council adopted a resolution that the dome should be preserved in perpetuity. The Peace Memorial Park, in which the dome is the principal landmark, was laid out between 1950 and 1964. Since 1952 the park has been the scene of the annual Hiroshima Peace Memorial Ceremony, held on 6 August.

The Hiroshima Prefectural Industrial Promotion Hall was a three-storey brick building with a five-storey central core topped by an elliptical dome. Located only 150 m from the hypocentre of the explosion, it was almost completely shattered and gutted. However, because the force of the blast came from directly above, the foundations of the core of the building under the dome remained standing.
▼

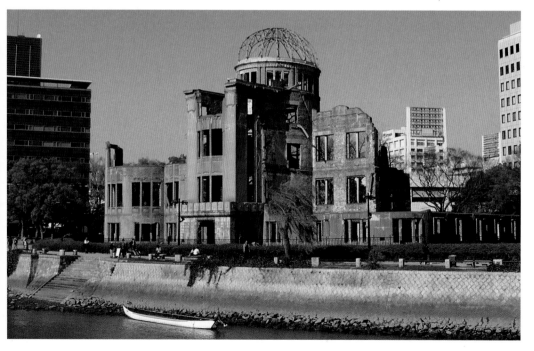

World Heritage site since

• • • • • • • • • • • • • • • • • 1978 • 1979 • 1980 • 1981 • 1982 • 1983 • 1984 • 1985 • 1986 • 1987 • 1988 • 1989 • 1990 • 1991 • 1992 • 1993 • 1994 • 1995 • **1996**

Ancient Ksour of Ouadane, Chinguetti, Tichitt and Oualata
Mauritania

Criteria – Testimony to cultural tradition; Significance in human history; Traditional human settlement

Founded in the eleventh and twelfth centuries to serve the caravans crossing the Sahara, these trading and religious centres became focal points of Islamic culture. Sited on the outskirts of a fertile valley or oasis, their original function was to provide religious instruction, and so they developed around mosques, accompanied by houses for teachers and students. Warehouses were built by traders to safeguard their goods, who needed accommodation for themselves, while inns were provided for those passing through on business. From these elements grew the characteristic form of settlement known as the ksar (plural ksour), with stone architecture and an urban form suited to extreme climatic conditions. Typically, houses with patios crowd along narrow streets around a mosque with a square minaret.

These four ancient cities are the only surviving places in Mauritania to have been inhabited since the Middle Ages. They illustrate a traditional way of life centred on the nomadic culture of the people of the western Sahara.

Okapi Wildlife Reserve
Dem. Rep. of the Congo

Criteria – Significant natural habitat for biodiversity

The Okapi Wildlife Reserve occupies about one-fifth of the Ituri forest in the northeast of the Democratic Republic of the Congo. The Congo River basin, of which the reserve and forest are a part, is one of the largest drainage systems in Africa. The reserve contains threatened species of primates and birds and about 5,000 of the estimated 30,000 okapi surviving in the wild. It also has some dramatic scenery, including waterfalls on the Ituri and Epulu rivers. The reserve is inhabited by traditional nomadic pygmy Mbuti and Efe hunters.

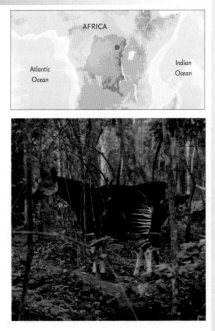

The Pygmy groups that today inhabit the Ituri forest excel in the use and identification of wild plants. Pygmies have a semi-nomadic hunter-gatherer lifestyle and when not hunting with traditional nets or archery, gather insects, fungi, fruits, seeds, plants and honey.

◀

Okapi in the Ituri forest.

World Heritage site since

• 1978 • 1979 • 1980 • 1981 • 1982 • 1983 • 1984 • 1985 • 1986 • 1987 • 1988 • 1989 • 1990 • 1991 • 1992 • 1993 • 1994 • 1995 • **1996**

Millenary Benedictine Abbey of Pannonhalma and its Natural Environment

Hungary

Criteria – Significance in human history; Heritage associated with events of universal significance

The landscape around the monastic site contains a natural oak forest, and a botanical garden, composed of forest trees and plants, and hedgerow and park species, both native and exotic.

Benedictine monks came in 996 to this sacred mountain in the former Roman province of Pannonia. They established the monastery as the eastern bridgehead of medieval European culture, a role it retained for 1,000 years, with only brief interruptions. The present church, of 1224, is the third on the site; it contains fragments of its predecessors. In 1472 the king took over the monastery and undertook extensive renovations. The present cloister and other buildings with a religious function were built, and the monastery was fortified. However, monastic life became difficult; the monastery was badly damaged by fire and largely abandoned in 1575, to be occupied by the Turks in 1594. The Benedictine community returned in 1638, and the Baroque elements of the monastery, such as the refectory, were added. Today the buildings still house a school and the monastic community.

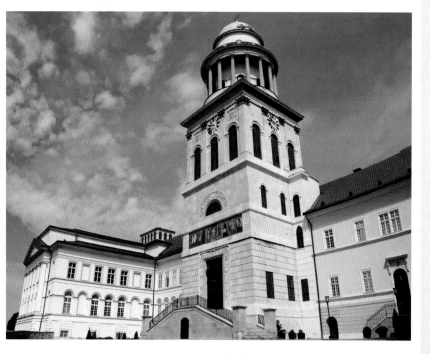

World Heritage site since

· · · · · · · · · · · · · · · 1978 · 1979 · 1980 · 1981 · 1982 · 1983 · 1984 · 1985 · 1986 · 1987 · 1988 · 1989 · 1990 · 1991 · 1992 · 1993 · 1994 · 1995 · **1996**

Canal du Midi
France

Criteria – Human creative genius; Interchange of values; Significance in human history; Heritage associated with events of universal significance

This 360-km network of navigable waterways linking the Mediterranean and the Atlantic through 328 structures – locks, aqueducts, bridges, tunnels, etc. – is one of the most remarkable feats of civil engineering of modern times. Built between 1667 and 1694, it paved the way for the Industrial Revolution. It was designed by Pierre-Paul Riquet, who was conscious that he was creating a symbol of the power of seventeenth-century France, as well as

a functional communication waterway. He made sure, therefore, that the quality of the architecture on the Canal was worthy of this role. The bridges, locks and associated structures were designed with monumental dignity and simplicity. He was also conscious of the impact of his work on the landscape, and took great pains to ensure that it harmonized with the landscape through which it passed.

One of the canal's most noteworthy features is the Saint-Ferréol dam on the Laudot River in the Montagne-Noire region. This is the largest project on the entire canal and the greatest work of civil engineering of its time.

Canal du Midi,
Toulouse.
▼

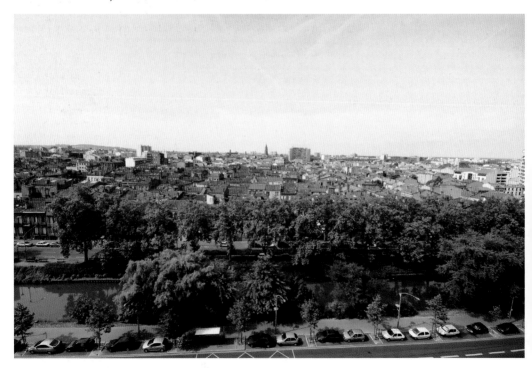

Mount Emei Scenic Area, including Leshan Giant Buddha Scenic Area
China

Criteria – Significance in human history; Heritage associated with events of universal significance; Significant natural habitat for biodiversity

The first Buddhist temple in China was built here in Sichuan Province in the first century AD in very beautiful surroundings atop Mount Emei. The addition of other temples turned the site into one of Buddhism's main holy places. Over the centuries, the cultural treasures grew in number. The most remarkable was the Giant Buddha of Leshan (pictured right), carved out of a hillside in the eighth century and looking down on the confluence of three rivers. At 71 m high, it is the largest Buddha in the world.

As one of the four holy lands of Chinese Buddhism, this site is of great historical importance. It's also a vital sanctuary for a many internationally threatened animal species, including lesser (red) panda, Asiatic black bear, and Asiatic golden cat.

Mount Emei is also notable for its very diverse vegetation, ranging from subtropical to sub-alpine pine forests. Some of the trees are more than 1,000 years old.

Upper Svaneti
Georgia

Criteria – Significance in human history; Traditional human settlement

Preserved by its long isolation, the Upper Svaneti region of the Caucasus has a characteristic landscape of small villages dominated by their church towers, set in a natural environment of gorges, alpine valleys and with a backdrop of snow-covered mountains. The unique tower-houses of the area served as dwellings, storehouses and defence posts against the invaders who plagued the region. The village of Chazhashi still has more than 200 of these very unusual buildings. The excellent natural conditions and the unity of architecture and landscape give this region an original quality of its own. The wealth of monumental and minor art (metal work, manuscript illustrations, textiles and embroidery, wood-carving, icon painting, vernacular architecture) is of great importance in the study of Georgia and the Caucasus.

The abundance of towers is the most notable feature of these settlements, especially in the frontier villages. Usually between three and five storeys high with walls that decrease in thickness as they rise, the towers have a slender, tapering profile.

World Heritage site since

• • • • • • • • • • • • • • • • • 1978 • 1979 • 1980 • 1981 • 1982 • 1983 • 1984 • 1985 • 1986 • 1987 • 1988 • 1989 • 1990 • 1991 • 1992 • 1993 • 1994 • 1995 • **1996**

Historic Centre of Oporto Portugal

Criteria – Significance in human history

The beautiful city of Oporto, built along the hillsides overlooking the mouth of the Douro River, is an exceptional urban landscape with a 2,000-year history.

The historic centre is of high aesthetic value, with evidence of urban development from the Roman, medieval and Almadas periods. The rich and varied civil architecture of the historic centre expresses the cultural values of succeeding periods –

Romanesque, Gothic, Renaissance, Baroque, neoclassical and modern.

The Romans named the town Portus, or port, and its continuous growth, linked to the sea, can be seen in the many and varied monuments, from the cathedral with its Romanesque choir, to the neoclassical Stock Exchange and the typically Portuguese Manueline-style Church of Santa Clara.

Oporto supported the expeditions of Henry the Navigator, the explorer prince born in the town in the fifteenth century.

In the eighteenth century English entrepreneurs invested in the vineyards of the Douro valley to supply port to the huge English market. Oporto benefited greatly as the shipping port for these wines, as the town's wealth of Baroque buildings demonstrates.

World Heritage site since

• 1978 • 1979 • 1980 • 1981 • 1982 • 1983 • 1984 • 1985 • 1986 • 1987 • 1988 • 1989 • 1990 • 1991 • 1992 • 1993 • 1994 • 1995 • **1996**

Belize Barrier Reef Reserve System
Belize

Criteria – Natural phenomena or beauty; Significant ecological and biological processes; Significant natural habitat for biodiversity

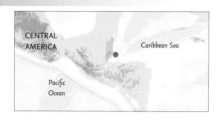

The coastal area of Belize is an outstanding natural system consisting of the largest barrier reef in the northern hemisphere, offshore atolls, several hundred sand cays, mangrove forests, coastal lagoons and estuaries. The system's seven sites illustrate the evolutionary history of reef development and are a significant habitat for threatened species, including marine turtles, manatees and the American marine crocodile.

The approximately 450 sand and mangrove cays confined within the barrier and atolls range in size from small, ephemeral sand spits to larger, permanent islands capable of sustaining human settlements.

A total of 178 terrestrial plants and 247 species of marine flora has been described from the area. There are over 500 species of fish, 65 scleritian corals, 45 hydroids and 350 molluscs in the area, plus a great diversity of sponges, marine worms and crustaceans.

The Belize submarine shelf and its barrier reef represent the world's second-largest reef system and the largest reef complex in the Atlantic-Caribbean area. Outside the barrier are three large atolls: Turneffe Islands, Lighthouse Reef and Glover's Reef. Between the mainland and the barrier reef is an extensive offshore lagoon which increases in width and depth from north to south.

World Heritage site since

• 1978 • 1979 • 1980 • 1981 • 1982 • 1983 • 1984 • 1985 • 1986 • 1987 • 1988 • 1989 • 1990 • 1991 • 1992 • 1993 • 1994 • 1995 • **1996**

Bauhaus and its Sites in Weimar and Dessau
Germany

Criteria – Interchange of values; Significance in human history; Heritage associated with events of universal significance

Between 1919 and 1933 the Bauhaus School, based first in Weimar and then in Dessau, revolutionized architectural and aesthetic concepts and practices. The buildings constructed and decorated by the school's professors Walter Gropius, Hannes Meyer, Laszlo Moholy-Nagy and Wassily Kandinsky launched the Modern Movement, which shaped much of the architecture of the twentieth century. The Weimar Bauhaus was obliged to close in 1925 for political reasons. Gropius found support for his cultural and political stance in Dessau, along with the opportunity to create a number of large-scale new buildings. These were situated on the outskirts of the town, and comprise the Bauhaus itself and the Masters' Houses (Meisterhäuser), which served as the residences of the Bauhaus directors and some of its distinguished teachers.

The Haus am Horn in Weimar was built to a design by Georg Muche in 1923 as a model building and exhibit, the first practical statement of the New Building Style. Annexes (a gatehouse, more rooms, a verandah, and a terrace) were added in 1925; however, the original appearance is unchanged. It is the only original Bauhaus building remaining in Weimar.

Lushan National Park
China

Criteria – Interchange of values; Testimony to cultural tradition; Significance in human history; Heritage associated with events of universal significance

Mount Lushan, in Jiangxi, is one of the spiritual centres of Chinese civilization. Buddhist and Taoist temples, along with landmarks of Confucianism, where the most eminent masters taught, blend effortlessly into a strikingly beautiful landscape. It is an area that has inspired philosophy and art, and into which high-quality cultural properties have been selectively and sensitively integrated up to recent times.

The mountains of Lushan have been the inspiration for some of the finest Chinese classical poetry.

Some 200 historic buildings are scattered over Lushan National Park. The most celebrated is the East Grove Temple complex at the foot of Xianglu Peak. Begun in AD 386, this ensemble was added to progressively over the centuries.

La Lonja de la Seda de Valencia
Spain
Criteria – Human creative genius; Significance in human history

La Lonja de la Seda de Valencia is an exceptional example of a secular building in late-Gothic style, which dramatically illustrates the power and wealth of one of the great Mediterranean mercantile cities. Built between 1482 and 1533, this group of buildings was originally used for trading in silk – hence its name, the Silk Exchange – and it has always been a centre for commerce. The land occupied by the Lonja is rectangular in plan. About half of the total area is covered by the main Sala de Contratación; the Tower (including the Chapel), the Consulado, and the large garden complete the ensemble. At the present time, it is still a major trading exchange, now dealing primarily in agricultural products.

The Sala de Contratación is a magnificent hall. The lofty interior is divided into three main aisles by five rows of slender spiral pillars from which spring the elegant vaulting of the roof. It is lit by soaring Gothic windows, the external frames of which, like the doors, are exuberantly ornamented, notably by a series of grotesque gargoyles.

W National Park of Niger
Niger
Criteria – Significant ecological and biological processes; Significant natural habitat for biodiversity

The 'W' National Park, named after the local configuration of the Niger River, is located in a transition zone between savanna and forest landscapes. W hosts important ecosystems that represent the interaction between natural resources and humans since Neolithic times. This interaction has produced characteristic landscapes and plant formations, and a rich biodiversity. The park is known for its large mammals, including aardvarks, baboons, buffalo, caracal, cheetahs, elephants, hippopotamuses, leopards, lions, serval and warthogs. The wetland area of the park is of international importance for the conservation of birds. A total of 454 plant species has been recorded, including two orchid species found only in Niger. More than seventy mammal and 350 bird species are found in the area.

Many of the park's bird species need large areas for their seasonal migrations. The fact that the park is contiguous to other protected areas in Burkina and Niger makes this area increasingly important to the survival of these species.

World Heritage site since

• • • • • • • • • • • • • • • • • • 1978 • 1979 • 1980 • 1981 • 1982 • 1983 • 1984 • 1985 • 1986 • 1987 • 1988 • 1989 • 1990 • 1991 • 1992 • 1993 • 1994 • 1995 • **1996**

Itsukushima Shinto Shrine
Japan

Criteria – Human creative genius; Interchange of values; Significance in human history; Heritage associated with events of universal significance

The island of Itsukushima, in the Seto inland sea, has been a holy place of Shintoism since the earliest times. The first shrine buildings here were probably erected in the sixth century. The present shrine dates from the twelfth century. The design of the buildings plays on the contrasts in colour and form between mountains and sea, and illustrates the Japanese concept of scenic beauty, which combines nature and human creativity. The architectural style of the north-facing Honsha buildings and the west-facing buildings of the Sessha Marodo-jinja, connected by the kairo (roofed corridor), was influenced by the aristocratic dwelling-house style of the Heian period. The frontal view of the buildings, with the mountain as a backdrop, is emphasized, and the entire area resembles a succession of folding screens.

Like many other Shinto shrines that included Buddhist buildings, Itsukushima-jinja lost many of them after the rejection of Buddhism with the Meiji Restoration of 1868. The few that survive in the surrounding hills are considered to be as indispensable to the history of Itsukushima-jinja as its Shinto monuments.

Verla Groundwood and Board Mill
Finland

Criteria – Significance in human history

The Verla Groundwood and Board Mill and its associated residential area is an outstanding, remarkably well-preserved example of the small-scale rural industrial settlements associated with pulp, paper and board production that flourished in northern Europe and North America in the nineteenth and early twentieth centuries. The Industrial Revolution that reached the Kymi river valley in the first half of the 1870s was one of the most dramatic phenomena in the economic history of Finland. Over a very short time dozens of steam sawmills, groundwood mills and board mills were established. The Kymi valley benefited in particular from the construction of timber-floating facilities, a dedicated railway, and the introduction of cooperative floating, enabling logs from the virgin forests of central Finland to be brought to the processing facilities.

Output at Verla gradually diminished throughout the twentieth century, until it was closed down on 18 July 1964, when the last of the old workers retired. The owners decided to preserve the entire complex intact as an industrial heritage museum, just as it had been when the last worker left.

Early Christian Monuments of Ravenna
Italy

Criteria – Human creative genius; Interchange of values; Testimony to cultural tradition; Significance in human history

EUROPE

Mediterranean Sea

Ionian Sea

Ravenna was the seat of the Roman Empire in the fifth century and then of Byzantine Italy until the eighth century. It has a unique collection of early Christian mosaics and monuments. All eight buildings – the Mausoleum of Galla Placidia, the Neonian Baptistery, the Basilica of Sant'Apollinare Nuovo, the Arian Baptistery, the Archiepiscopal Chapel, the Mausoleum of

Theodoric, the Church of San Vitale and the Basilica of Sant'Apollinare in Classe – were constructed in the fifth and sixth centuries. They show great artistic skill, including a wonderful blend of Graeco-Roman tradition, Christian iconography and oriental and Western styles.

Several of the buildings are unique: for example, the Neonian Baptistery is the finest and most complete example of an early-Christian baptistery; while the Mausoleum of Theodoric is the only surviving tomb of a barbarian king of this period.

◄
The mausoleum of Galla Placidia.

World Heritage site since

• 1978 • 1979 • 1980 • 1981 • 1982 • 1983 • 1984 • 1985 • 1986 • 1987 • 1988 • 1989 • 1990 • 1991 • 1992 • 1993 • 1994 • 1995 • 1996

Defence Line of Amsterdam
Netherlands

Criteria – Interchange of values; Significance in human history; Traditional human settlement

North Sea

EUROPE

From time immemorial, dykes, sluices and canals have been built in the Netherlands to drain the land. The Stelling van Amsterdam is of outstanding universal value because it elevated and integrated this activity into an extensive defence system which survives intact to this day.

Extending 135 km around the city of Amsterdam, this defence line built between 1883 and 1920 is a unique fortification using water. Since the sixteenth century, the people of the Netherlands have used their expert knowledge of hydraulic engineering for defence purposes. Earlier defensive lines were strengthened and co-ordinated into the Stelling, a system based on the intricate polder system of the western part of the

Netherlands. The centre of the country was protected by a network of forty-five armed forts, acting in concert with temporary flooding from polders and an intricate system of canals and locks. The sites of the forts are directly linked with the existing infrastructure of roads, waterways, dykes and settlements and the main defence line runs mainly along pre-existing dykes.

World Heritage site since

• 1978 • 1979 • 1980 • 1981 • 1982 • 1983 • 1984 • 1985 • 1986 • 1987 • 1988 • 1989 • 1990 • 1991 • 1992 • 1993 • 1994 • 1995 • 1996

Pre-Hispanic Town of Uxmal
Mexico

Criteria – Human creative genius; Interchange of values; Testimony to cultural tradition

NORTH AMERICA

Pacific Ocean

Caribbean Sea

The ruins of the ceremonial structures at Uxmal represent the pinnacle of late-Mayan art and architecture in their design, layout and ornamentation. And the complex of Uxmal and its three related towns of Kabáh, Labná and Sayil admirably demonstrate the social and economic structure of late-Mayan society. Uxmal, in Yucatán, was founded c. AD 700 and had some 25,000 inhabitants. The layout of the buildings, which date from between 700 and 1000, reveals a detailed knowledge of astronomy. The Pirámide del Adivino, as the Spaniards called it – or Pyramid of the Soothsayer – dominates the ceremonial centre, which has well-designed buildings decorated with a profusion of symbolic motifs and sculptures depicting Chaac, the god of rain.

By virtue of its size, the Pirámide del Adivino dominates the ensemble. It is made up of five superimposed elements, two of them reached by monumental stairways on either side of the structure. It is from the Late Classic period and brings together several artistic traditions, including that of the Toltec of Central Mexico.

▼

World Heritage site since

• • • • • • • • • • • • • • • • • • 1978 • 1979 • 1980 • 1981 • 1982 • 1983 • 1984 • 1985 • 1986 • 1987 • 1988 • 1989 • 1990 • 1991 • 1992 • 1993 • 1994 • 1995 • **1996**

Volcanoes of Kamchatka
Russian Federation

Criteria – Natural phenomena or beauty; Major stages of Earth's history; Significant ecological and biological processes; Significant natural habitat for biodiversity

ASIA   Pacific Ocean

An active crater on Mutnovsky Volcano, which is a complex of four superimposed stratovolcanoes.

The site, in the Russian Far East, comprises six distinct locations. One site is inland: Bystrinsky Nature Park, in the central mountainous spine of the Kamchatka Peninsula. The others, in coastal locations facing east towards the Bering Sea, are Koronotsky Nature Park; Nalychevo Nature Park; and the contiguous Southern Kamchatka Nature Park and Southern Kamchatka State Nature Reserve. Kluchevskoy Nature Park was added in 2001 as the sixth component of the site.

This is one of the most outstanding volcanic regions in the world, with a high density of active volcanoes, a variety of types and a wide range of related features. The six designated sites group together the majority of volcanic features of the Kamchatka peninsula. The interplay of active volcanoes and glaciers forms a dynamic landscape of great beauty, and the sites contain great species diversity, including the world's largest-known variety of salmonid fish, and exceptional concentrations of sea otter, brown bear and Steller's sea eagle.

The property represents the most pristine parts of the Kamchatka Peninsula and a remarkable collection of volcanic areas, characteristic of the Pacific Volcanic Ring. This is the surface expression of the subduction of the Pacific Ocean Continental Plate under the Eurasia Plate at a rate of 10 cm annually. There are more than 300 volcanoes in Kamchatka, twenty-nine of which are currently active, including caldera, strata-volcano, somma-volcano and mixed types. The largest in the site is Kronotskaya Sopka. In addition, there is a multitude of thermal and mineral springs, geysers and other phenomena of active volcanism.

Surrounded by sea, the peninsula enjoys a moist and relatively mild climate, which has lead to a lush vegetation cover. The vegetation includes mountain valley taiga forest of birch, larch and spruce; extensive stone-birch forest; riparian forest on alluvial soil of poplars, aspen, alder and willow; peat wetland and extensive coastal wetlands up to 50 km wide; and subalpine shrub and mountain tundra. The region also contains an especially diverse range of Palaearctic flora (including a number of nationally threatened species and at least sixteen endemic species).

The faunal complement is relatively low in diversity, with the Kamchatka Peninsula exhibiting some of the biogeographic qualities of an island. Nevertheless, some species are abundant, including bears, snow ram, northern deer, sable and wolverine, and there is a high level of endemism.

Noteworthy birds include Steller's sea eagle (the area has 50 per cent of world population), white-tailed eagle, gyrfalcon and peregrine falcon. There are numerous seabird colonies and a concentration of Aleutian tern nests.

Almost all rivers serve as spawning grounds for salmon, a key food-chain species for predatory birds and mammals. All eleven species of salmonid fish coexist in several of Kamchatka's rivers.

World Heritage site since

• • • • • • • • • • • • • • • • • • 1978 • 1979 • 1980 • 1981 • 1982 • 1983 • 1984 • 1985 • 1986 • 1987 • 1988 • 1989 • 1990 • 1991 • 1992 • 1993 • 1994 • 1995 • **1996**

Skellig Michael Monastery
Ireland

Criteria – Testimony to cultural tradition;
Significance in human history

There is a tradition that the monastery was founded by St Fionan in the seventh century. It was dedicated to St Michael somewhere between 950 and 1050 and this date fits in well with the architectural style of the oldest part of the existing church, known as St Michael's Church.

This monastic complex, perched since about the seventh century on the steep sides of the rocky island of Skellig Michael, some 12 km off the coast of southwest Ireland, illustrates the extremes of early Christian monasticism. Since the great remoteness of Skellig Michael has, until recently, discouraged visitors, the site is exceptionally well preserved. The principal monastic remains are situated on a sloping shelf on the ridge running north-south on the northeastern side of the island; the hermitage is on the steeper South Peak. The main monastic enclosure comprises a church, oratories, cells, a souterrain, and many crosses and cross-slabs. It was occupied continuously until the later twelfth century, when a general climatic deterioration led to increased storms in the seas around the island and forced the community to move to the mainland.

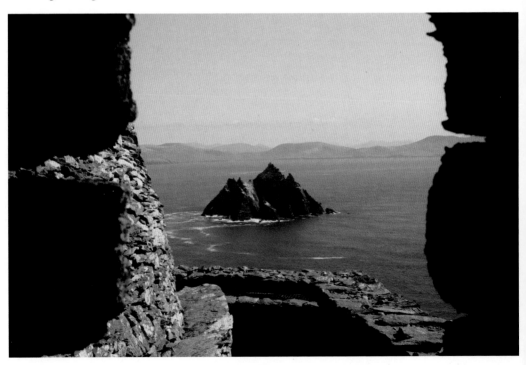

World Heritage site since

· 1978 · 1979 · 1980 · 1981 · 1982 · 1983 · 1984 · 1985 · 1986 · 1987 · 1988 · 1989 · 1990 · 1991 · 1992 · 1993 · 1994 · 1995 · **1996**

Lednice-Valtice Cultural Landscape
Czech Republic

Criteria – Human creative genius; Interchange
of values; Significance in human history

Between the seventeenth and twentieth
centuries, the ruling dukes of Liechtenstein
transformed their domains in southern
Moravia into a striking landscape that
married Baroque architecture with
countryside fashioned according to English
romantic principles of landscape
architecture. The realization of this
grandiose design began in the seventeenth
century with the creation of avenues
connecting Valtice with other parts of the
estate, and continued throughout the
eighteenth century, imposing order on

nature. The early years of the nineteenth
century saw the application of the English
concept of the designed park. The Chateau
of Valtice has medieval foundations, but it
underwent successive reconstructions in
Renaissance, Mannerist and, most
significantly, Baroque style. By contrast,
the Lednice Chateau (see photo below) is
not widely visible, having begun as a
Renaissance villa of around 1570, and then
progressively changed and reconstructed
to take account of Baroque, Classical and
Neo-Gothic fashions.

An important element
in the appearance of
the area is the very
wide range of native
and exotic tree species
and the planting
strategy adopted.
The greatest variety
is to be found in the
parklands which
cluster around the
two main residences
and along the banks
of the fishponds
between Lednice
and Valtice.

World Heritage site since

• 1978 • 1979 • 1980 • 1981 • 1982 • 1983 • 1984 • 1985 • 1986 • 1987 • 1988 • 1989 • 1990 • 1991 • 1992 • 1993 • 1994 • 1995 • **1996**

Historic City of Meknes

Morocco

Criteria – Significance in human history

The Historic City of Meknes provides an exceptionally well-preserved example of the urban fabric and monumental buildings of a seventeenth-century Maghreb capital city. Meknes was founded in the eleventh century by the Almoravids as a military settlement. Later, the founder of the Alawite dynasty, Moulay Ismail (1672–1727), made Meknes his capital city and carried out many reconstructions and additions, such as mosques, mausolea and gardens. But his main contribution was the creation of a new imperial city, built in the Hispano-Moorish style. It is impressive in both extent and construction, enclosed by high walls pierced by monumental gates, where the harmonious blending of the Islamic and European styles of the seventeenth-century Maghreb are still evident today. Within the walls are: the palace, with its enormous stables; a military academy; vast granaries; and water storage cisterns.

Some of the fondouks (inns) that cluster around the gates were devoted to specific crafts or trades: for example, the Fondouk Hanna dealt solely in henna, while the Jewish craftsmen worked at the Fondouk Lihoudi. Certain quarters were reserved for specific trades and activities.

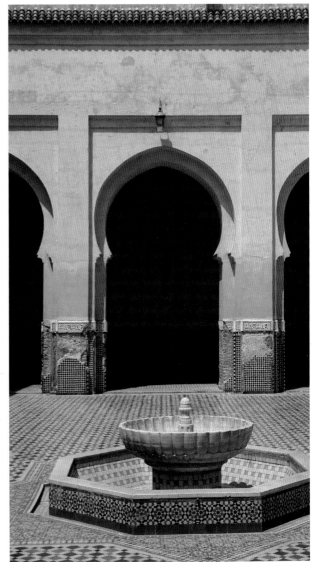

A traditional Moroccan palace in Meknes. ▶

Historic Centre of the City of Pienza
Italy

Criteria – Human creative genius; Interchange of values; Significance in human history

EUROPE

Mediterranean Sea

Ionian Sea

It was in this Tuscan town that Renaissance town-planning concepts were first put into practice after Pope Pius II decided, in 1459, to transform the look of his birthplace. He chose the architect Bernardo Rossellino, who applied the principles of his mentor, Leon Battista Alberti. This new vision of urban space was realized in the superb square known as Piazza Pio II and the buildings around it: the Piccolomini Palace,

the Borgia Palace and the cathedral, with its pure Renaissance exterior and an interior in the late-Gothic style of south German churches. Pius II's project also required the building of large houses for the cardinals in his retinue, and work on these began in 1463. Two structures with a social function, the hospital and the inn in front of the church of St Francis, were built on his orders.

The leading humanist Enea Silvio Piccolomini, elected Pope in 1458, was born in Corsignano, situated on a hill southeast of Siena. When he returned there after becoming Pope, he was struck by the extreme misery of its inhabitants, which inspired him to endow his birthplace with new buildings and a new name, and to make it his summer court.

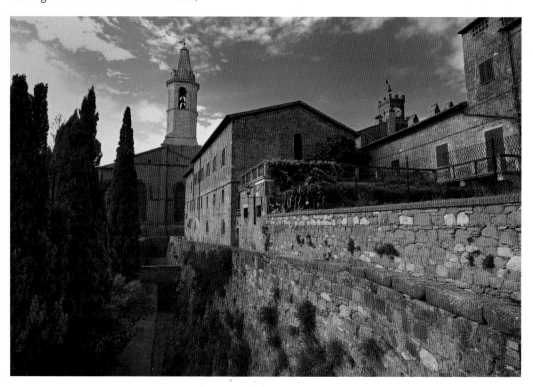

Historic Monuments Zone of Querétaro
Mexico

Criteria – Interchange of values; Significance in human history

The old colonial town of Querétaro is unusual in having retained the geometric street plan of the Spanish conquerors side by side with the twisting alleys of the Indian quarters. The Otomi, the Tarasco, the Chichimeca and the Spanish lived together peacefully in the town, which is notable for the many ornate civil and religious Baroque monuments from its golden age in the seventeenth and eighteenth centuries. Its first chapel

(La Cruz) was built on a small hillock at the eastern end of the valley. The Plaza de Armas, the seat of government, was arcaded on two sides, and surrounded by government buildings and residences of leading citizens. Many monastic orders established themselves and left behind outstanding Baroque buildings. The many non-religious buildings, again mostly Baroque, are enhanced by the pink stone of Querétaro.

Querétaro was the site of historic events: the peace treaty with the United States was concluded here in 1848, and in 1867 Emperor Maximilian was imprisoned and later executed after the defeat of his army. The National Constitution was signed on 5 February 1917 by all the revolutionary groups after two months of debate in the Teatro de la República.

World Heritage site since

• 1978 • 1979 • 1980 • 1981 • 1982 • 1983 • 1984 • 1985 • 1986 • 1987 • 1988 • 1989 • 1990 • 1991 • 1992 • 1993 • 1994 • 1995 • **1996**

Laponian Area
Sweden

Criteria – Testimony to cultural tradition; Traditional human settlement; Natural phenomena or beauty; Major stages of Earth's history; Significant ecological and biological processes

This area, which lies close to the Arctic Circle in northern Sweden, has been occupied continuously by the Saami people since prehistoric times. It is the largest area in the world with an ancestral way of life based on the seasonal movement of livestock (transhumance), the Saami spending the summer in the mountains and the winters in the coniferous forests to the east. There are no permanent settlements occupied throughout the year anywhere in this area. There are two landscape types: an eastern taiga area and a western mountainous landscape, with steep valleys and powerful rivers. Birch, low heath and alpine meadows are found below boulder fields, permanent snowfields and glaciers. The nomadic life based on herding of tame reindeer did not develop until the seventeenth and eighteenth centuries.

Researchers, working on large mammal predators and the white-tailed eagle, indicated that all populations seem to be healthy, with the exception of the wolverine. Also, there are more than 150 bird species and 100 bears, including wanderers, in the area.

A 'goahti' – traditional Saami shelter.
▼

World Heritage site since

• 1978 • 1979 • 1980 • 1981 • 1982 • 1983 • 1984 • 1985 • 1986 • 1987 • 1988 • 1989 • 1990 • 1991 • 1992 • 1993 • 1994 • 1995 • **1996**

Historic Centre of the City of Salzburg
Austria

Criteria – Interchange of values; Significance in human history; Heritage associated with events of universal significance

Salzburg is of outstanding value as an important example of a European ecclesiastical city-state. The city preserves to a remarkable degree its dramatic townscape, its historically significant urban fabric, and a large number of outstanding ecclesiastical and secular buildings developed from the Middle Ages through to the nineteenth century, when it was a city-state ruled by prince-archbishops. Its flamboyant Gothic art attracted many craftsmen and artists before the city became even better known through the work of the Italian architects Vincenzo Scamozzi and Santini Solari, to whom the historic centre owes much of its Baroque appearance. This meeting point of northern and southern Europe perhaps sparked the genius of Salzburg's most famous son, Wolfgang Amadeus Mozart, whose name has been associated with the city ever since.

Salzburg is rich in buildings from the Gothic period onwards, which combine to create a townscape of great individuality and beauty. The cathedral (St Rupert and St Virgil) is the pre-eminent ecclesiastical building and the spiritual city centre. The present structure dates from 1628 and is the work of Santini Solari, the court master builder. It replaced the former

cathedral, designed by Palladio's pupil Vincenzo Scamozzi, which burnt down in 1598. Solari's cathedral preserves many of Scamozzi's features. Mozart was christened in the cathedral in 1756 at one day old.

The Benedictine Abbey of St Peter, founded in the closing years of the seventh century, contains in its church the only High Romanesque structures in Salzburg, mostly dating from the early twelfth century. The main body of the church has undergone many modifications since then.

The Nonnberg Benedictine Nunnery is the oldest convent north of the Alps, founded around the same time as the Abbey of St Peter. The present massive complex, on the eastern peak of the Mönchberg, is a striking feature of the townscape, with its dominating church roof and Baroque dome.

The Hohensalzburg Fortress, on the steep rock fan overlooking the city, has been continually rebuilt and enlarged since its first foundation as a Roman fort through to the late seventeenth century, when it reached its present extent.

The Archbishop's Residence, begun in the early twelfth century, lies in the heart of the old town. The present layout dates to the major rebuilding carried out in the early seventeenth century.

There is a clear separatio visible on the ground an on the map, between the lands of the prince-archbishops and those of the burghers – t former is characterized b monumental buildings a open spaces, and the lat by small plots fronting o narrow streets, with the only open spaces provid by the three historic markets.

The city skyline is characterized by its profusion of spires and domes, and is dominated by the fortress of Hohensalzburg.

Salzburg cathedral.

Monasteries of Haghpat and Sanahin
Armenia

Criteria – Interchange of values; Significance in human history

These two Byzantine monasteries represent the highest flowering of Armenian religious architecture, which blends elements of Byzantine ecclesiastical architecture with vernacular architecture of the Caucasian region. The two monastic complexes were important centres of learning. Sanahin was renowned for its school of illuminators and calligraphers. It consists of a large group of buildings on the plateau above the Debet gorge, laid out on two rectangular axes, with

their façades facing west. The main church, built in the tenth century, is the Cathedral of the Redeemer. Construction of the main church of the large fortified monastic complex of Haghpat, dedicated to the Holy Cross, began in 966–7 and was completed in 991. The building is complete, apart from some eleventh- and twelfth-century restorations. The monastery also has a gavit, through which access is gained to the church, chapter house and library.

Armenia became independent at the end of the ninth century and Armenian art was revived when the kingdom was consolidated. The two monasteries of Haghpat and Sanahin date from this period, during the prosperity of the Kiurikian dynasty and the Zakarian Princes. They were important centres of learning, housing some 500 monks.

Bell tower of Haghpat Monastery. ▼

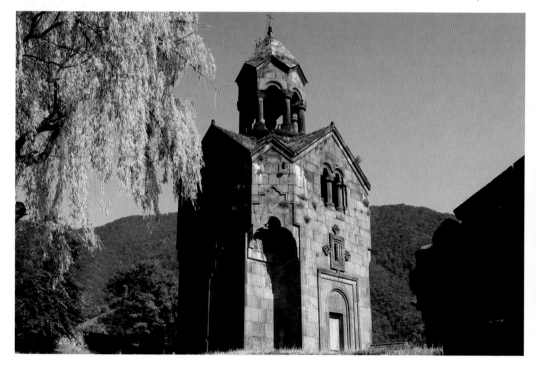

World Heritage site since

• • • • • • • • • • • • • • • 1978 • 1979 • 1980 • 1981 • 1982 • 1983 • 1984 • 1985 • 1986 • 1987 • 1988 • 1989 • 1990 • 1991 • 1992 • 1993 • 1994 • 1995 • **1996**

The Trulli of Alberobello
Italy

Criteria – Testimony to cultural tradition;
Significance in human history; Traditional human
settlement

Alberobello, the city of drystone dwellings
known as trulli, is an exceptional example of
vernacular architecture. Trulli, mostly dating
from before the end of the eighteenth
century, were constructed using roughly
worked limestone boulders and were built
directly on the underlying natural rock.
The walls that form the rectangular rooms
are pierced by small windows. Fireplaces,
ovens and alcoves are recessed into the
thickness of the walls. The stone roofs, which
are circular or oval, are not painted and
develop a patina of mosses and lichens; they
sometimes bear mythological or religious
symbols in white ash. By contrast, the walls
of the trulli must be whitewashed at regular
intervals. The Monti quarter contains
1,030 trulli. Its streets run downhill and
converge at the base of the hill. The Aja
Piccola quarter, with 590 trulli, is less
homogeneous than Monti.

Tradition has it that drystone
walling was imposed upon villagers
so their houses could be quickly
dismantled, either to dispossess
recalcitrant householders or to
avoid house tax (with the houses
being quickly reconstructed once
the tax collector departed).

Palace and Gardens of Schönbrunn
Austria

Criteria – Human creative genius; Significance in human history

Schönbrunn is a remarkable example of a Baroque royal palace that vividly illustrates the tastes, interests and aspirations of successive Habsburg monarchs. Apart from some minor nineteenth-century additions, the palace and its gardens were built in the eighteenth century. Schönbrunn was designed by the architects Johann Bernhard Fischer von Erlach and Nicolaus Pacassi and is full of outstanding examples of decorative art.

The vast Baroque gardens and their buildings testify to the imperial dimensions and functions of the palace; the courtyard provides access to the Palace Chapel and the Palace Theatre. The orangery on the east side of the main palace building was used by the Empress Maria Theresa to cultivate exotic plants, and the Schönbrunn zoo, founded in 1752 by her husband, is the oldest in the world.

The impressive Great Gallery is elaborately decorated with stucco ornamentation and ceiling frescoes symbolizing the Habsburg Empire, while the Ceremonial Hall is notable for its series of monumental paintings depicting events in the long reign of the Empress Maria Theresa.

World Heritage site since

• • • • • • • • • • • • • 1978 • 1979 • 1980 • 1981 • 1982 • 1983 • 1984 • 1985 • 1986 • 1987 • 1988 • 1989 • 1990 • 1991 • 1992 • 1993 • 1994 • 1995 • **1996**

Luther Memorials in Eisleben and Wittenberg
Germany

Criteria – Significance in human history; Heritage associated with events of universal significance

These places in Saxony-Anhalt are all associated with the lives of Martin Luther and his fellow-reformer Melanchthon. They include Melanchthon's house in Wittenberg, the houses in Eisleben where Luther was born in 1483 and died in 1546, his room in Wittenberg, the local church and the castle church where, on 31 October 1517, Luther posted his famous '95 Theses', thereby launching the Reformation and a

new era in the religious and political history of the Western world. Because of its symbolic importance, the famous bronze door on the north side of the church, where the Latin text of the 95 Theses is displayed, is only used on special occasions. The church houses the tombs of Luther and Melanchthon.

In 1525 Luther broke with his monastic vows and married the former nun, Katharina von Bora. His household in Wittenberg became the centre for reformists from all over Europe, and the family room that he created on the first floor was the setting for his 'table talks', which were later published.

Sangiran Early Man Site
Indonesia

Criteria – Testimony to cultural tradition; Heritage associated with events of universal significance

Sangiran is a key site for the understanding of human evolution. Excavations from 1936 to 1941 led to the discovery of the first hominid fossil at this site. Later, fifty early human fossils (Pithecanthropus erectus/Homo erectus) were found – half of all the world's known hominid fossils – together with numerous animal and floral fossils such as rhinoceros, elephant ivory, buffalo horn, deer horn and many others. Palaeolithic stone tools found at Ngebung include flakes, choppers and cleavers in chalcedony and jasper and, more

recently, bone tools. The site has also produced Neolithic axes. This evidence indicates that hominids have inhabited the area for at least 1.5 million years. Nowadays, the region is entirely devoted to peasant agriculture.

Ever since von Koenigswald found flake tools in the Ngebung village in 1934, the site has made an immense contribution to the study of evolution over the past million years by illustrating the evolution of Homo erectus. Homo erectus is important to the study of the early history of mankind before the emergence of the modern Homo sapiens.

◄

Display of fossil elephant ivory at Sangiran.

World Heritage site since

• • • • • • • • • • • • • 1978 • 1979 • 1980 • 1981 • 1982 • 1983 • 1984 • 1985 • 1986 • 1987 • 1988 • 1989 • 1990 • 1991 • 1992 • 1993 • 1994 • 1995 • **1996**

Archaeological Site of Aigai (modern name Vergina)
Greece

Criteria – Human creative genius; Testimony to cultural tradition

The city of Aigai, the ancient first capital of the Kingdom of Macedonia, was discovered in the nineteenth century near Vergina, in northern Greece. The most important building so far discovered is the monumental palace, located on a plateau directly below the acropolis. Sumptuously decorated, its large gallery commanded a view of the whole Macedonian plain. The site also has a necropolis which extends for over 3 km and contains over 300 grave-mounds, some as early as the eleventh century BC. One of the royal tombs in the Great Tumulus contained a solid gold casket with remains identified as those of Philip II. He conquered all the Greek cities, paving the way for his son Alexander and the expansion of the Hellenistic world.

As capital and site of the royal court, Aigai was the most important urban centre in the region from 800 to 400 BC. Philip II was assassinated in the theatre here in 336 BC and Alexander the Great proclaimed king.

Church Village of Gammelstad, Luleå
Sweden

Criteria – Interchange of values; Significance in human history; Traditional human settlement

Gammelstad, ('Old Town') at the head of the Gulf of Bothnia, is the best-preserved example of a 'church village', a unique kind of village formerly found throughout northern Scandinavia. The 424 wooden houses, huddled round the early fifteenth-century stone church, were used only on Sundays and at religious festivals to house worshippers from the surrounding countryside who could not return home the same day because of the distance and difficult travelling conditions. The doors, which face the street, are very varied in design, as are the window shutters. Most of the doors bear a pyramid device, a motif from pagan antiquity reinterpreted as a Christian symbol depicting an altar with a sacrificial fire. Gammelstad's church is the largest of its type in northern Scandinavia.

Luleå Gammelstad illustrates the adaptation of conventional urban design to the special geographical and climatic conditions of a hostile natural environment. The settlement has been shaped by people's religious and social needs rather than economic and geographical forces.

World Heritage site since

• 1978 • 1979 • 1980 • 1981 • 1982 • 1983 • 1984 • 1985 • 1986 • 1987 • 1988 • 1989 • 1990 • 1991 • 1992 • 1993 • 1994 • 1995 • **1996**

Historic Walled Town of Cuenca
Spain

Criteria – Interchange of values; Traditional human settlement

Built by the Moors in a defensive position at the heart of the Caliphate of Cordoba, Cuenca is an unusually well-preserved medieval fortified town. Conquered by the Castilians in the twelfth century, it became a royal town and bishopric. In the upper town some remains of the Moorish fortress still survive among the large aristocratic houses, monasteries, and churches from the medieval, Renaissance and Baroque periods. The twelfth-century cathedral, built on the site of the former Great Mosque, was the first Gothic cathedral in Spain. Most of its churches and monastic buildings were founded early in the town's history and underwent many additions over the following centuries. The importance of the upper town lies, however, not so much in its individual buildings, as in the townscape that they create, on the fortified site dominating the river valleys.

The private houses near the Episcopal Palace were built in the later medieval period on the spectacular steep bluffs overlooking the bend of the Huécar River. These famous 'casas colgadas' (hanging houses) were rebuilt in the sixteenth century in their present narrow, high form, with two or three rooms on each of three or more floors.

▼

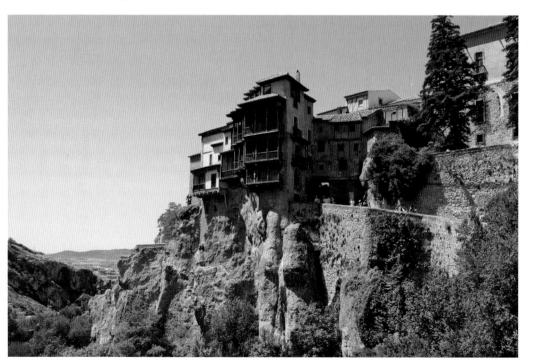

World Heritage site since

· 1978 · 1979 · 1980 · 1981 · 1982 · 1983 · 1984 · 1985 · 1986 · 1987 · 1988 · 1989 · 1990 · 1991 · 1992 · 1993 · 1994 · 1995 · **1996**

Castel del Monte
Italy

Criteria – Human creative genius; Interchange of values; Testimony to cultural tradition

When the Emperor Frederick II built this castle near Bari in the thirteenth century, he imbued it with symbolic significance, as reflected in its location and the mathematical and astronomical precision of its design. A unique masterpiece of medieval military architecture, Castel del Monte is a successful blend of elements from classical antiquity, the Islamic Orient and north European Cistercian Gothic. It is sited on a rocky peak that dominates the surrounding countryside and consists of a regular octagon surrounding a courtyard, with a tower, also octagonal, at each angle. The castle is of special interest because of the absence of features that are common to the overwhelming majority of military monuments of this period such as outer bailey, moat, stables, kitchen, storerooms and chapel.

The site offers a fittingly impressive monument to its originator, Frederick II. A polyglot, mathematician, astronomer and scientist, he also founded the University of Naples and brought social and economic stability to his people.

World Heritage site since

· 1978 · 1979 · 1980 · 1981 · 1982 · 1983 · 1984 · 1985 · 1986 · 1987 · 1988 · 1989 · 1990 · 1991 · 1992 · 1993 · 1994 · 1995 · 1996 · **1997**

Macquarie Island
Australia

Criteria – Natural phenomena or beauty; Major stages of Earth's history

Macquarie Island is an oceanic island in the Southern Ocean, lying 1,500 km southeast of Tasmania and approximately halfway between Australia and the Antarctic continent. The island, approximately 34-km long and 5.5-km wide, is the exposed crest of the undersea Macquarie Ridge, raised to its present position where the Indo-Australian tectonic plate meets the Pacific plate. It is a site of major geoconservation significance, being the only island in the world composed entirely of oceanic crust and rocks from the Earth's mantle 6 km below the ocean floor that are being actively exposed above sea-level. These unique exposures include excellent examples of pillow basalts and other extrusive rocks. Macquarie Island's beauty lies in its remote and windswept landscape of steep escarpments, lakes, dramatic changes in vegetation, and the vast congregations of wildlife around its dark, dramatic shores.

The breeding population of royal penguins is estimated at over 850,000 pairs – one of the greatest concentrations of sea birds in the world. The penguins share the island with elephant seals and four species of albatross. The surrounding Nature Reserve and Macquarie Island Marine Park contain one of the world's largest marine highly-protected zones, covering more than 160,000 km^2.

World Heritage site since

• • • • • • • • • • • • • • • • • • • 1978 • 1979 • 1980 • 1981 • 1982 • 1983 • 1984 • 1985 • 1986 • 1987 • 1988 • 1989 • 1990 • 1991 • 1992 • 1993 • 1994 • 1995 • 1996 • **1997**

Maritime Greenwich
United Kingdom

Criteria – Human creative genius; Interchange of values; Significance in human history; Heritage associated with events of universal significance

Atlantic Ocean

North Sea

EUROPE

The Old Royal Observatory is situated on the brow of Greenwich Hill and dominates the landscape. It houses an octagonal room which was used by the Royal Society for meetings and dinners, and this is surmounted by the famous time-ball, which indicates Greenwich Mean Time daily at 13.00.

▼

The ensemble of buildings at Greenwich, an outlying district of London, and the park in which they are set, symbolize English artistic and scientific endeavour in the seventeenth and eighteenth centuries. The focus of the ensemble is the Queen's House, the work of Inigo Jones, and the first true Renaissance building in Britain, and a striking departure from the architectural forms that preceded it. It was inspired by Italian style, and it was in its turn the direct inspiration for classical houses all over Britain. The Queen's House and its associated buildings have housed the National Maritime Museum since 1937. The complex that was until recently the Royal Naval College was designed by Christopher Wren and is the most outstanding group of Baroque buildings in Britain. Greenwich Royal Park contains the Old Royal Observatory, the work of Wren and the scientist Robert Hooke.

World Heritage site since

• • • • • • • • • • • • • • • 1978 • 1979 • 1980 • 1981 • 1982 • 1983 • 1984 • 1985 • 1986 • 1987 • 1988 • 1989 • 1990 • 1991 • 1992 • 1993 • 1994 • 1995 • 1996 • **1997**

Mount Kenya National Park/ Natural Forest
Kenya

Criteria – Natural phenomena or beauty; Significant ecological and biological processes

At 5,199 m, Mount Kenya is the second-highest peak in Africa. It is an ancient extinct volcano, and during its period of activity, around three million years ago, it is thought to have risen to 6,500 m. There are twelve remnant glaciers on the mountain, all receding rapidly, and four secondary peaks that sit at the head of the U-shaped glacial valleys. With its rugged glacier-clad summits and forested middle slopes, Mount Kenya is

one of the most impressive landscapes in East Africa. The evolution of its afro-alpine flora also provide an outstanding example of ecological processes. Mount Kenya is regarded as a holy mountain by all the communities (Kikuyu and Meru) living adjacent to it. They believe that their traditional God (Ngai) and his wife (Mumbi) live on the peak of the mountain and use it for their traditional rituals.

In the lower forest and bamboo zone, mammals include giant forest hog, white-tailed mongoose, elephant, black rhinoceros, and leopard (which have also been seen in the alpine zone). There have also been reported sightings of the golden cat.

Pyrénées – Mont Perdu
France and Spain

Criteria – Testimony to cultural tradition; Significance in human history; Traditional human settlement; Natural phenomena or beauty; Major stages of Earth's history

This outstanding mountain landscape, which spans the contemporary national borders of France and Spain, is centred around the peak of Mount Perdu, a calcareous massif that rises to 3,352 m. The site, with a total area of 306 km², includes two of Europe's largest and deepest canyons on the Spanish side and three major cirque walls on the more abrupt northern slopes within France, classic presentations of these geological landforms. The site is also a

pastoral landscape reflecting an agricultural way of life that was once widespread in the upland regions of Europe but now survives only in this part of the Pyrenees. Thus it provides exceptional insights into past European society through its landscape of villages, farms, fields, upland pastures and mountain roads.

The location of the Pyrenees between two seas, their geological structure and climatic asymmetries result in a rich mosaic of vegetation types. The site supports many valuable wildlife species including the marmot and the Spanish ibex, of which there are only three female individuals.

World Heritage site since

• • • • • • • • • • • • • • • • • • • 1978 • 1979 • 1980 • 1981 • 1982 • 1983 • 1984 • 1985 • 1986 • 1987 • 1988 • 1989 • 1990 • 1991 • 1992 • 1993 • 1994 • 1995 • 1996 • **1997**

Historic Centre (Old Town) of Tallinn
Estonia

Criteria – Interchange of values; Significance in human history

Tallinn is an exceptionally well-preserved example of a northern European medieval trading city. The origins of Tallinn date back to the thirteenth century, when a castle was built there by the crusading knights of the Teutonic Order. It developed into a major centre of the Hanseatic League, and its wealth is demonstrated by the opulence of the public buildings and the domestic architecture of the merchants' houses.

The lower town preserves to a remarkable extent the medieval urban fabric of narrow winding streets and fine public and burgher buildings. There are several medieval churches within the city walls. The restored Church of St Nicholas (Niguliste) and the Church of St Olaf (Oleviste) are both in typical basilical form, with lofty vaulting and a precise geometry of form, in what is recognized as the distinctive Tallinn School.

The most prominent feature of the town is the Toompea limestone hill. The western part is occupied by the castle, of which the tower known as Long Hermann, two bastions and the imposing walls survive on the western, northern and eastern sides.

The tower of St Olaf's church overlooks the Old Town.
▼

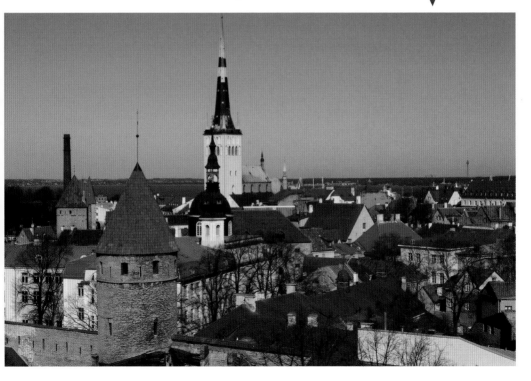

World Heritage site since

• • • • • • • • • • • • • • • • • 1978 • 1979 • 1980 • 1981 • 1982 • 1983 • 1984 • 1985 • 1986 • 1987 • 1988 • 1989 • 1990 • 1991 • 1992 • 1993 • 1994 • 1995 • 1996 • **1997**

Old Town of Lijiang
China

Criteria – Interchange of values; Significance in
human history; Traditional human settlement

The Old Town of Lijiang has retained a
historic townscape of high quality and
authenticity. Its architecture is noteworthy
for the blending of elements from several
cultures over many centuries. Lijiang, which
is perfectly adapted to its uneven
topography, also possesses an ancient
water-supply system of great complexity
and ingenuity that still functions effectively
today.

The old town is built on a mountain slope
running from northwest to southeast, facing
a deep river. The northern part was a
commercial district and the main streets
there radiate from the broad thoroughfare
known as Sifangjie, traditionally the
commercial and trading centre of northwest
Yunnan Province. On the west side of the
Sifangjie is the imposing three-storeyed
Kegongfang (Imperial Examination
Archway), flanked by the Western and
Central rivers.

A sluice on the Western River uses the
different levels of the two waterways to
wash the streets, which are paved with slabs
of a fine-grained red breccia. In this unique
form of municipal sanitation, water flows on
to the Shuangshi Bridge where it branches
into three tributaries which subdivide into a
network of channels and culverts to supply
every house in the town. Many springs and
wells in the town supplement the supply.

Such a complex system of watercourses
requires a large number of bridges and the
city has 354 altogether, of several types. It is
from these that Lijiang derives its name, the
'City of Bridges'.

The feature that most represents the
culture of the Naxi people who settled in the
area is the wealth of domestic dwellings in
the city. The basic timber-framed structure
developed into a unique architectural style
with the absorption of elements of Han and
Zang architecture. Most houses are two-
storeyed. The chuandoushi wooden frames
are walled with adobe on the ground floor
and planks on the upper floors; the walls
have stone foundation courses. Exteriors are
plastered and lime-washed, and there are
often brick panels at the corners. Roofs are
tiled and the houses have verandas.

Decoration of the houses is important,
with arches over gateways, screen walls,
external corridors, doors and windows,
courtyards and roof beams. Wooden
elements are elaborately carved with
domestic and cultural imagery – pottery,
musical instruments, flowers, birds, etc. –
and gate arches take several elegant forms.

The Lijiang Junmin
prefecture was
established in 1382.
Of the original
286 m-long complex
that was built to house
the administration,
only the Yizi Pavilion,
the Guagbi Tower and
a stone archway
remain.

The group known as
the Yuquan
architectural
structures in the
Heilongtan Park (Jade
Spring Park) dates
from the Ming and
Qing dynasties that
ruled from the
fourteenth century
onwards. Most
notable is the Wufeng
Tower (1601), moved
from the Fugue
Temple of which it
formed part; it is now
one of the major
historical sites in
Yunnan Province.

World Heritage site since

• • • • • • • • • • • • • • • • 1978 • 1979 • 1980 • 1981 • 1982 • 1983 • 1984 • 1985 • 1986 • 1987 • 1988 • 1989 • 1990 • 1991 • 1992 • 1993 • 1994 • 1995 • 1996 • **1997**

Lumbini, the Birthplace of the Lord Buddha
Nepal

Criteria – Testimony to cultural tradition; Heritage associated with events of universal significance

Siddhartha Gautama, the Lord Buddha, was born in 623 BC in the famous gardens of Lumbini, which soon became a place of pilgrimage. Among the pilgrims was the Indian emperor Ashoka, who erected one of his commemorative pillars there. The site is now being developed as a Buddhist pilgrimage centre, where the archaeological remains associated with the birth of the Lord Buddha form a central feature.

Lumbini is situated at the foothills of the Himalaya in modern Nepal. In the Buddha's time, Lumbini was a beautiful garden full of green and shady sal trees, and the site still retains its legendary charm and serenity.

The Sundarbans
Bangladesh

Criteria – Significant ecological and biological processes; Significant natural habitat for biodiversity

The Sundarbans mangrove forest, one of the largest such forests in the world at 1,400 km², lies on the delta of the Ganges, Brahmaputra and Meghna rivers on the Bay of Bengal. It is adjacent to the border of India's Sundarbans World Heritage site inscribed in 1987. The site is intersected by a complex network of tidal waterways, mudflats and small islands of salt-tolerant mangrove forests, and presents an excellent example of ongoing ecological processes. The area is known for its wide range of fauna, including 260 bird species, the

Bengal tiger and other threatened species such as the estuarine crocodile and the Indian python.

The Sundarbans is a uniquely dynamic landscape, shaped in turn by monsoon rains, flooding, delta formation, and tidal influence. The area also supports one of the largest populations of Royal Bengal Tiger with 350 individuals.

World Heritage site since

• • • • • • • • • • • • • • • • • 1978 • 1979 • 1980 • 1981 • 1982 • 1983 • 1984 • 1985 • 1986 • 1987 • 1988 • 1989 • 1990 • 1991 • 1992 • 1993 • 1994 • 1995 • 1996 • **1997**

Portovenere, Cinque Terre, and the Islands (Palmaria, Tino and Tinetto)
Italy

Criteria – Interchange of values; Significance in human history; Traditional human settlement

The eastern Ligurian coast between Cinque Terre and Portovenere is a site of outstanding scenic and cultural value. The area covers some 15 km of jagged, steep coastline, which the work of man over the centuries has transformed into an intensively terraced landscape, so as to be able to wrest from nature a few hectares of land suitable for agriculture, such as growing vines and olive trees. Most of these

cultivation terraces were built in the twelfth century. The human communities have adapted themselves to this inhospitable terrain by building compact settlements directly on the rock, with winding streets. The use of natural stone for footing gives these settlements their characteristic appearance. They are generally grouped round religious buildings or medieval castles.

The five villages of Cinque Terre date back to the later Middle Ages. Starting from the north, the first is the fortified centre of Monterosso al Mare; then come Vernazza, Corniglia, Manarola and Riomaggiore (pictured below). Off the coast at Portovenere are the three islands of Palmaria, Tino and Tinetto, noteworthy for the many remains of early monastic establishments that they contain.

Historic Fortified City of Carcassonne
France

Criteria – Interchange of values; Significance in human history

The historic city of Carcassonne is an outstanding example of a medieval fortified town, with its massive defences encircling the castle and its fine Gothic cathedral. A fortified settlement has existed on the hill where Carcassonne now stands since pre-Roman times. During the turbulent years of the late third and early fourth centuries, the town was protected by the construction of a defensive wall some 1,200 m long. The

twelfth-century count's castle was built over the western part of the Roman wall, and by the end of the thirteenth century the town had assumed its definitive appearance as a medieval fortress. Carcassonne is also of special importance because of the lengthy restoration campaign undertaken during the second half of the nineteenth century by Viollet-le-Duc, one of the founders of the modern science of conservation.

The exterior of the cathedral, like that of most southern French Gothic churches, has no flying buttresses, stability being assured by means of the interior vaulting. It contains some important sculpture, notably the thirteenth-century tomb of Bishop Radulph. The stained glass in the windows of the apse and the transept is of exceptionally high quality.

World Heritage site since

• • • • • • • • • • • • • • • • • • • 1978 • 1979 • 1980 • 1981 • 1982 • 1983 • 1984 • 1985 • 1986 • 1987 • 1988 • 1989 • 1990 • 1991 • 1992 • 1993 • 1994 • 1995 • 1996 • **1997**

Morne Trois Pitons National Park
Dominica

Criteria – Major stages of Earth's history; Significant natural habitat for biodiversity

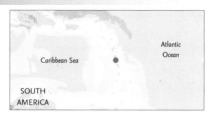

Caribbean Sea

Atlantic Ocean

SOUTH AMERICA

Luxuriant tropical forest blends with scenic volcanic features of great scientific interest in this national park, centred on the 1,342 m-high volcano known as Morne Trois Pitons. The landscape is characterized by volcanic piles with precipitous slopes and deeply incised valleys. The so-called Valley of Desolation (Grand Soufriere) contains fumaroles, hot springs, mud pots, sulphur vents and the Boiling Lake, which is the world's second largest of its kind. The valley is a large amphitheatre surrounded by mountains and consisting of at least three separate craters, where steam vents, small ponds and hot springs bubble up through the ground. Boiling Lake is surrounded by cliffs and is almost always covered by clouds of steam. The Morne Trois Pitons National Park covers nearly 70 km² and has the richest biodiversity of the Lesser Antilles.

Other outstanding features in the area include the Emerald Pool, fed by the Middleham Falls Stinking Hole, a lava tube in the middle of the forest; and the Boeri and Freshwater lakes. Freshwater Lake is the largest of Dominica's four freshwater lakes. Boeri Lake is located in the crater of an extinct volcano.

Middleham Falls which feeds the Emerald Pool.

▼

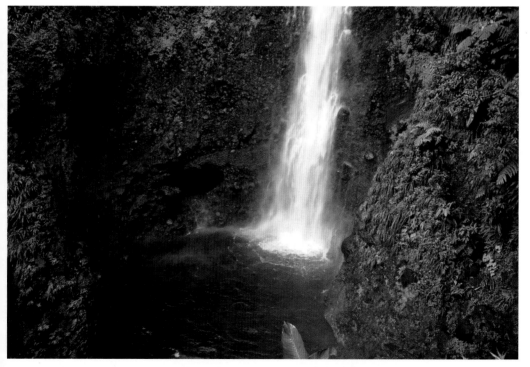

World Heritage site since

• • • • • • • • • • • • • • • • • 1978 • 1979 • 1980 • 1981 • 1982 • 1983 • 1984 • 1985 • 1986 • 1987 • 1988 • 1989 • 1990 • 1991 • 1992 • 1993 • 1994 • 1995 • 1996 • **1997**

Cocos Island National Park
Costa Rica

Criteria – Significant ecological and biological processes; Significant natural habitat for biodiversity

Cocos Island National Park, located 550 km off the Pacific coast of Costa Rica, is the only island in the tropical eastern Pacific with a tropical rainforest. Its position as the first point of contact with the northern equatorial counter-current, and the myriad interactions between the island and the surrounding marine ecosystem, make the area an ideal laboratory for the study of biological processes. The underwater world of the National Park has become famous due to the

attraction it holds for divers, who rate it as one of the best places in the world to view large pelagic species such as sharks, rays, tuna and dolphins. Like other oceanic islands, Isla del Coco presents an impoverished flora compared to that of the continent, but has a high number of endemic species (at least seventy species of vascular plant). The vegetation is exuberant and owes its lushness to the heavy rainfalls and rugged relief, which favours condensation.

The island has been known to mariners and cartographers since the first half of the sixteenth century. However, its position was vaguely indicated and therefore could only be located by experienced sailors. Fishermen, pirates, commercial sailors and scientific expeditions arrived at the island searching for fresh water and shelter.

Episcopal Complex of the Euphrasian Basilica in the Historic Centre of Poreč
Croatia

Criteria – Interchange of values; testimony to cultural tradition; significance in human history

The group of religious monuments in Poreč, where Christianity was established as early as the fourth century, constitutes the most complete surviving complex of its type. The basilica, atrium, baptistery and episcopal palace are outstanding examples of religious architecture, while the basilica itself combines classical and Byzantine elements. Erected by Bishop Euphrasia, all these buildings were richly ornamented

with mosaics, alabaster, marble, mother-of-pearl and stucco, in the lavish tradition of the Byzantine 'Golden Age' during the reign of Justinian. Later additions to the complex were the Kanonika (Canon's House) of 1257, the sixteenth-century bell tower, and some minor buildings such as the sacristy (fifteenth century) and two chapels (seventeenth and nineteenth centuries respectively).

The Episcopal Complex is an integral part of the historic centre of Poreč, which has preserved to a considerable extent its Roman street pattern, dating from the time when the town was part of the province of Histria.

World Heritage site since

• • • • • • • • • • • • • • • • • • • 1978 • 1979 • 1980 • 1981 • 1982 • 1983 • 1984 • 1985 • 1986 • 1987 • 1988 • 1989 • 1990 • 1991 • 1992 • 1993 • 1994 • 1995 • 1996 • **1997**

Lake Turkana National Parks
Kenya

Criteria – Major stages of Earth's history;
Significant natural habitat for biodiversity

The area around Lake Turkana is mostly semi-desert, with open plains flanked by volcanic formations including Mount Sibiloi, the site of the remains of a petrified forest possibly seven million years old. The most saline of Africa's large lakes, Turkana is an outstanding laboratory for the study of plant and animal communities. The three National Parks are major breeding grounds for the Nile crocodile, hippopotamus and a variety of venomous snakes. Mammals include Burchell's and Grevy's zebras, Grant's gazelle, Beisa oryx, hartebeest, topi, lesser kudu, lion and cheetah. More than 350 species of aquatic and terrestrial bird have been recorded in Lake Turkana, and it serves as a stopover for migrant birds such as warblers, wagtails and little stints.

Extensive palaeontological finds in the parks have contributed more to the understanding of palaeo-environments than any other site on the continent. These include evidence of the existence of a relatively intelligent hominid two million years ago. Human fossils include the remains of Australopithecus robustus, Homo habilis, Homo erectus and Homo sapiens.

World Heritage site since

• • • • • • • • • • • • • • • • • 1978 • 1979 • 1980 • 1981 • 1982 • 1983 • 1984 • 1985 • 1986 • 1987 • 1988 • 1989 • 1990 • 1991 • 1992 • 1993 • 1994 • 1995 • 1996 • **1997**

Classical Gardens of Suzhou
China

Criteria – Human creative genius; Interchange of values; Testimony to cultural tradition; Significance in human history; Traditional human settlement

Chinese gardens have certain elements in common governing their positioning, layout, scenery, planting, contents and philosophy. The end result is one in which art, nature, and ideas are integrated perfectly to create ensembles of great beauty and harmony.

Located on the lower Yangtze River, Suzhou is spanned by numerous waterways and its streets retain their traditional beauty. Marco Polo called the city 'Venice of the Orient' when he visited in the thirteenth century. The city's many gardens were created by retired bureaucrats and politicians of the Ming and Qing Dynasties.

Classical Chinese garden design, which seeks to recreate natural landscapes in miniature, is nowhere better illustrated than in the nine gardens in the historic city of Suzhou. They are generally acknowledged to be masterpieces of the genre. Dating from the eleventh to the nineteenth centuries, the gardens reflect in their meticulous design the profound metaphysical importance of natural beauty in Chinese culture.

The Canglang Pavilion was built in the early eleventh century. It is reached across a zigzag stone bridge from which the mountains, covered with old trees and bamboo, suddenly become visible.

The Lion Forest Garden was created in 1342 as the Budhi Orthodox Monastery but was detached from the temple in the seventeenth century. It features a series of man-made mountains and an artificial waterfall on steep cliffs.

The sixteenth-century Garden of Cultivation is typical, both in layout and in the design of its buildings, of the classical Ming dynasty garden. A pond takes up a quarter of its area.

The Couple's Garden Retreat dates from the eighteenth century. The East Garden is dominated by a mountain rising from a pool flanked by buildings. The more subdued

West Garden has limestone hills pierced by interlinking caves.

In the Retreat and Reflection Garden, the central feature is the pool, surrounded by elegant buildings and the double-tiered Celestial Bridge.

The Mountain Villa with Embracing Beauty dates from the sixteenth century. It is intensively detailed, with peaks rising to 7 m, dells, paths, caves, stone houses, ravines, precipices and cliff.

The Humble Administrator's Garden has been the site of the residence of Suzhou notables since the second century AD and is one of China's most famous gardens. Its central section is a re-creation of the scenery of the Lower Yangtze.

The Lingering Garden dates from the sixteenth century. It features mountain and lake scenery encircled by buildings and visited by means of a narrow, winding path which gives unexpected views of great beauty.

The Garden of the Master of the Nets is entered from the south through a gateway flanked by enormous carved blocks of stone, designating the owner's court rank. The layout of buildings and gardens is extremely subtle, so that a small area gives the impression of great size and variety.

World Heritage site since

• • • • • • • • • • • • • • • • • • 1978 • 1979 • 1980 • 1981 • 1982 • 1983 • 1984 • 1985 • 1986 • 1987 • 1988 • 1989 • 1990 • 1991 • 1992 • 1993 • 1994 • 1995 • 1996 • **1997**

Cathedral, Torre Civica and Piazza Grande, Modena
Italy

Criteria – Human creative genius; Interchange of values; Testimony to cultural tradition; Significance in human history

The magnificent twelfth-century cathedral at Modena, the work of two great artists Lanfranco and Wiligelmo, is a supreme example of early Romanesque art. With its piazza and soaring bell tower, the Modena complex exemplifies an architectural complex where religious and civic values are combined. The cathedral was also a large sculpture workshop, brilliantly illustrated by Wiligelmo, particularly in the façade, which is a veritable corpus of the sculptor's work. The Maestri Campionesi – architects and sculptors commissioned to maintain the building from the second half of the twelfth century onwards – made various alterations and improvements to the building. Only minor changes have been made to the Piazza Grande: its quadrangular shape has been preserved and it has been lined on its northern side by the flank of the cathedral.

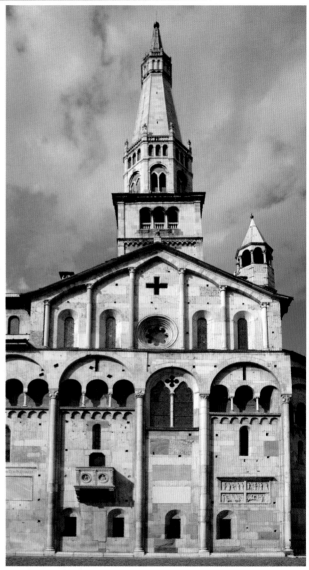

▲

The Torre Civica, whose tall silhouette is a landmark to travellers approaching the town, is closely linked to the cathedral by two arches. This monumental tower, built from the same materials as the cathedral, consists of six floors emphasized by small blind arcades lit by simple openings, and then by two- and three-light windows on the upper floors.

World Heritage site since

• • • • • • • • • • • • • • • • • 1978 • 1979 • 1980 • 1981 • 1982 • 1983 • 1984 • 1985 • 1986 • 1987 • 1988 • 1989 • 1990 • 1991 • 1992 • 1993 • 1994 • 1995 • 1996 • **1997**

Changdeokgung Palace Complex
Korea, Republic of

Criteria – Interchange of values; Testimony to cultural tradition; Significance in human history

In the early fifteenth century, the Emperor T'aejong ordered the construction of a new palace, which he named Changdeokgung (Palace of Illustrious Virtue). A Bureau of Palace Construction was set up to create the complex in accordance with traditional design principles. These included the palace in front, the market behind, three gates and three courts (administrative court, royal residence court and official audience court). The compound was divided into two parts: the main palace buildings and the Piwon (royal secret garden). The result is an exceptional example of Far Eastern palace architecture and design, in which the buildings are integrated into and harmonized with the natural setting. Changdeokgung Palace had a great influence on the development of Korean architecture, and garden and landscape planning for many centuries.

The garden was landscaped with a series of terraces planted with lawns, flowering trees, flowers, a lotus pool, and pavilions set against a wooded background. There are over 26,000 specimens of 100 indigenous trees in the garden, along with 23,000 planted specimens of 15 imported species.

World Heritage site since

• • • • • • • • • • • • • • • • • • 1978 • 1979 • 1980 • 1981 • 1982 • 1983 • 1984 • 1985 • 1986 • 1987 • 1988 • 1989 • 1990 • 1991 • 1992 • 1993 • 1994 • 1995 • 1996 • **1997**

Medina of Tétouan (formerly known as Titawin)
Morocco

Criteria – Interchange of values; Significance in human history; Traditional human settlement

Tétouan was of particular importance in the Islamic period, from the eighth century onwards, since it served as the main point of contact between Morocco and Andalusia. After the Reconquest, the town was rebuilt by Andalusian refugees who had been expelled by the Spanish. This is well illustrated by its art and architecture, which reveal clear Andalusian influence. Although one of the smallest of the Moroccan medinas, Tétouan is unquestionably the most complete and it has been largely untouched by subsequent outside influences.

Tétouan is mentioned by a number of Arab writers of the tenth–twelfth centuries. However it wasn't until the fortifications were rebuilt in the mid-eighteenth century that the medina assumed its current distinctive 'figure-of-eight' configuration.

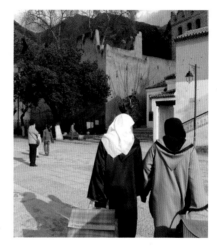

◄
Main Square, Tétouan.

Heard and McDonald Islands
Australia

Criteria – Major stages of Earth's history; Significant ecological and biological processes

Heard and McDonald Islands are located in the Southern Ocean, approximately 1,700 km from the Antarctic continent and over 4,100 km southwest of Perth. As the only volcanically active subantarctic islands they 'open a window into the Earth', thus providing the opportunity to observe ongoing geomorphic processes. Permanent snow and ice cover about 70 per cent of

Heard Island, and its relatively fast-flowing glaciers respond quickly to changes in climate. The distinctive conservation value of Heard and McDonald Islands – one of the world's rare pristine island ecosystems – lies in the absence of introduced plants and animals, making them especially valuable for scientific reference purposes.

Lying in a remote and stormy part of the globe, Heard and McDonald Islands were unknown to humanity until the nineteenth century. Driving westerly winds create unique weather patterns including spectacular cloud formations and rapid changes in precipitation.

World Heritage site since

• • • • • • • • • • • • • • • 1978 • 1979 • 1980 • 1981 • 1982 • 1983 • 1984 • 1985 • 1986 • 1987 • 1988 • 1989 • 1990 • 1991 • 1992 • 1993 • 1994 • 1995 • 1996 • **1997**

Mill Network at Kinderdijk-Elshout
Netherlands

Criteria – *Human creative genius; Interchange of values; Significance in human history*

North Sea

EUROPE

The Kinderdijk-Elshout mill network bears powerful testimony to the outstanding contribution made by the people of the Netherlands to the technology of handling water. The site illustrates all the typical features associated with this technology – dykes, reservoirs, pumping stations, administrative buildings and a series of beautifully preserved windmills. At one time, there were more than 150 such mills in the

Alblasserwaard and Vijfheerenlanden area; this had dropped to seventy-eight in the 1870s, but today the total is only twenty-eight. The World Heritage Site contains nineteen of these mills, mostly dating from the mid-eighteenth century. Although they went out of use in the late 1940s, all nineteen are still maintained in operating condition, functioning as fall-back mills in case of failure of the modern equipment.

Most of the mills are so-called bonnet mills, in which only the top section revolves with the wind. Built from brick or wood, they have large sails that come within 30 cm of the ground, hence their name, 'ground sailers'.
▼

World Heritage site since

• • • • • • • • • • • • • • • • • • 1978 • 1979 • 1980 • 1981 • 1982 • 1983 • 1984 • 1985 • 1986 • 1987 • 1988 • 1989 • 1990 • 1991 • 1992 • 1993 • 1994 • 1995 • 1996 • **1997**

Archaeological Areas of Pompei, Herculaneum and Torre Annunziata
Italy

Criteria – Testimony to cultural tradition; Significance in human history; Traditional human settlement

Part of Pompei. ▶

Pompei was founded by the southern Italian Osci (Opicians) in the sixth century BC, while Herculaneum was said to have been founded by Hercules. They fell to the Romans in 89 BC.

Both towns came to an abrupt and catastrophic end on 24 August AD 79. The area had recently been shaken by an earthquake and reconstruction work was still in progress when Vesuvius erupted with tremendous violence. Pompei was buried under a thick layer of volcanic ash and stone and Herculaneum disappeared under a pyroclastic flow of volcanic mud.

The remains of the towns of Pompei and Herculaneum, buried by the eruption of Vesuvius on 24 August AD 79, provide a complete and vivid picture of society and daily life at a specific moment in the past that is without parallel anywhere in the world.

When Vesuvius erupted it engulfed the two flourishing Roman towns and many wealthy villas in the area. Since the mid eighteenth century these have been progressively excavated and made accessible to the public. The vast expanse of the commercial town of Pompei contrasts with the smaller but better-preserved remains of the holiday resort of Herculaneum, while the superb wall paintings of the Villa Oplontis at Torre Annunziata give a vivid impression of the opulent lifestyle enjoyed by the wealthier citizens of the Early Roman Empire.

The main forum of Pompei is flanked by the foundations of several imposing public buildings including the Capitolium (temple), Basilica (courthouse) and public baths. Pompei is renowned for its domestic buildings, ranged along well-paved streets. The earliest type is the atrium house of which the House of the Surgeon, entirely inward looking with a courtyard at its centre, is a good example. The exceptional Villa dei

Misteri (House of the Mysteries) takes its name from the wall paintings in the triclinium (dining room) that depict the initiation rites ('mysteries') of the cult of Dionysus.

A special characteristic of Pompei is its wealth of graffiti. An election was imminent at the time of the eruption and many slogans were scrawled on walls along with other graffiti of a more personal, often scurrilous, nature.

Much less of Herculaneum, built on a promontory overlooking the Bay of Naples, has been uncovered, partly because of the depth to which it was buried. However, the nature of its covering is such that the buildings are better preserved than those of Pompei.

There are several impressive public buildings, and the houses are also remarkable for their extent and decoration. Those fronting on the sea, such as the House of the Deer, have large courtyards and rich decoration. The town is noteworthy for the completeness of its shops, still containing fittings such as enormous wine jars. Of great importance in both towns are the artistic styles represented by sculptures, mosaics and, above all, wall paintings.

World Heritage site since

• • • • • • • • • • • • • • • • • 1978 • 1979 • 1980 • 1981 • 1982 • 1983 • 1984 • 1985 • 1986 • 1987 • 1988 • 1989 • 1990 • 1991 • 1992 • 1993 • 1994 • 1995 • 1996 • 1997

Medieval Town of Toruń
Poland

Criteria – Interchange of values; Significance in human history

Toruń is a small historic trading city that preserves to a remarkable extent its original street pattern and outstanding early buildings. The town owes its origins to the Teutonic Order, which built a castle there in the mid-thirteenth century as a base for the conquest and colonization of Prussia. It soon developed a commercial role as part of the Hanseatic League. In the Old and New Towns, the many imposing public and private buildings from the fourteenth and fifteenth centuries, among them the house of Copernicus, are striking evidence of Toruń's importance. The Old Town, which forms the western part of the complex, is laid out around its central Market Place. The New Town developed from 1264, to the north of the castle and the east of the Old Town, into a centre for crafts and industry.

The Old Town was fortified progressively between 1250 and 1300 with a double wall strengthened by bastions. These fortifications were reconstructed in 1420–49 and partly dismantled in the nineteenth century, but most of the southern sector, with gates and towers facing the river, survives intact.

Toruń Town Hall.
▼

Eighteenth-Century Royal Palace at Caserta with the Park, the Aqueduct of Vanvitelli, and the San Leucio Complex

Italy

Criteria – Human creative genius; Interchange of values; Testimony to cultural tradition; Significance in human history

The monumental complex at Caserta, while cast in the same mould as other eighteenth-century royal palaces, is exceptional for the broad sweep of its design. The King of Naples decided in 1750 to build a new royal palace to rival the Palace of Versailles. He employed Luigi Vanvitelli, then engaged in the restoration of St Peter's in Rome. The Royal Palace is rectangular in plan, with four large interior courtyards and contains 1,200 rooms and thirty-four staircases. The main axis of the park is punctuated by a series of Baroque fountains and stretches of water. This magnificent perspective terminates in the Great Fountain, where water cascades down from a height of 150 m. The works at San Leucio, designed to produce silk, are also of outstanding interest because of the idealistic principles underlying its original conception and management.

A waterfall, which is a copy of one at Versailles, in the grounds of the Palace of Caserta. ▲

In 1778 the king decided to begin the production of silk at San Leucio, and the industrial complex included a school, accommodation for teachers, silkworm rooms, and facilities for spinning and dyeing the silk. His regulations of 1789 laid down piecework rates of pay, abolished dowries and prescribed similar clothing for all the workers.

World Heritage site since

• • • • • • • • • • • • • 1978 • 1979 • 1980 • 1981 • 1982 • 1983 • 1984 • 1985 • 1986 • 1987 • 1988 • 1989 • 1990 • 1991 • 1992 • 1993 • 1994 • 1995 • 1996 • **1997**

Palau de la Música Catalana and Hospital de Sant Pau, Barcelona
Spain

Criteria – Human creative genius; Interchange of values; Significance in human history

These two monuments are among the finest contributions to Barcelona's architecture by the Catalan art nouveau architect Lluis Doménech i Montaner. The Palau de la Música Catalana is an exuberant steel-framed structure, full of light and space and decorated by many of the leading designers of the day. Construction began in 1905 and was completed three years later. The Hospital de Sant Pau is equally bold

in its design and decoration, while at the same time perfectly adapted to the needs of the sick. Work began in 1901 and was not finally completed until 1930. The hospital is of immense architectural importance because it is the largest hospital complex in Modernist style.

The Hospital de Sant Pau is an outstanding vindication of its creator's maxim that beauty has therapeutic value. For Doménech i Montaner it was essential to give sick people a feeling of well-being and beauty, which would contribute to an early convalescence.

Historic Area of Willemstad, Inner City and Harbour, Curaçao
Netherlands

Criteria – Interchange of values; Significance in human history; Traditional human settlement

The people of the Netherlands established a trading settlement at a fine natural harbour on the Caribbean island of Curaçao in 1634. The town developed continuously over the following centuries. The modern town consists of several distinct historic districts whose architecture reflects not only European urban-planning concepts but also styles from the Netherlands and from the Spanish and Portuguese colonial towns with which Willemstad engaged in trade.

Willemstad stands out for the diversity of its four historic districts, separated by a natural harbour. Each has its own unique urban morphology, while sharing a distinctive 'tropicalized' Dutch architecture.

World Heritage site since

• • • • • • • • • • • • • • • • • • • 1978 • 1979 • 1980 • 1981 • 1982 • 1983 • 1984 • 1985 • 1986 • 1987 • 1988 • 1989 • 1990 • 1991 • 1992 • 1993 • 1994 • 1995 • 1996 • **1997**

Archaeological Site of Panamá Viejo and Historic District of Panamá

Panama

Criteria – Interchange of values; Significance in human history; Heritage associated with events of universal significance

The archaeological site of Panamá Viejo is the site of the oldest European town on the American mainland, founded in 1519 by the conquistador Pedrarías Dávila. It soon became a commercial and administrative centre, as well as an important port and the seat of a Royal Tribunal. Only the climate, being considered unhealthy, prevented the development of the town to the size and importance of Guatemala or Bogotá. The old town was destroyed by fire in 1672, and a new town (the 'Historic District' of Panamá), 8 km to the southwest, replaced it a year later, and the site was abandoned and never rebuilt; it is now a public park where the impressive ruins of the cathedral, churches, water installations, town hall and private houses are preserved.

Cathedral at Panamá Viejo. ▲

The 'Historic District' of Panamá has preserved its original street plan, its architecture and an unusual mixture of Spanish, French and early American styles.

The Salón Bolívar was the venue for the unsuccessful attempt made by Simón Bolívar, El Libertador, in 1826 to establish a Pan-American congress.

PANAMÁ VIEJO 529

World Heritage site since

• 1978 • 1979 • 1980 • 1981 • 1982 • 1983 • 1984 • 1985 • 1986 • 1987 • 1988 • 1989 • 1990 • 1991 • 1992 • 1993 • 1994 • 1995 • 1996 • **1997**

Dougga / Thugga
Tunisia

Criteria – Interchange of values; Testimony to cultural tradition

Before the Roman annexation of Numidia in 46 BC, the town of Thugga, built on an elevated site overlooking a fertile plain, was the capital of an important Libyco-Punic state. It flourished under Roman and Byzantine rule, but declined in the Islamic period. Its impressive ruins include temples and sanctuaries, a forum, public baths, a theatre, an amphitheatre, a circus, a market, fountains, private houses, shops and mausoleums. The small rectangular forum, which is surrounded by a marble colonnade, is crossed by part of the later Byzantine fortifications. On one side of it is the *capitolium*, dedicated to Jupiter, Juno and Minerva, and one of the finest buildings of its type in North Africa. One of the most significant monuments in Thugga is the Libyco-Punic mausoleum in the southern part of the town. This is the only major monument of Punic architecture still surviving in Tunisia.

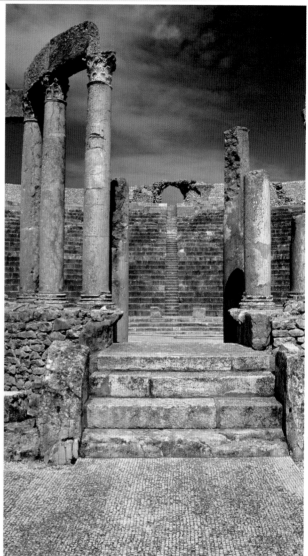

Entrance to the theatre. ▲

The important collection of over 2,000 Libyan, Punic, Greek and Roman inscriptions from Thugga has made a decisive contribution to the deciphering of the Libyan language; also to knowledge of the social and municipal life of the Numidians, and Roman colonial policy and municipal organization in its provinces.

Hallstatt-Dachstein / Salzkammergut Cultural Landscape
Austria

Criteria – Testimony to cultural tradition;
Significance in human history

Human activity in the magnificent natural landscape of the Salzkammergut began in prehistoric times, with the salt deposits being exploited as early as the second millennium BC. This resource formed the basis of the area's prosperity up to the middle of the twentieth century, a prosperity that is reflected in the fine architecture of the town of Hallstatt. The name of the medieval town, first recorded in a deed of

1305, is derived from the West German hal (salt) and the Old High German stat (settlement). The site also includes the Dachstein Mountains, rising to some 3,000 m, which form the highest of the karst massifs in the northern limestone Alps. They are notable for the large number of caves they contain, the longest being the Hirlatzhöhle (96 km).

The typical Hallstatt house is tall and narrow, making maximum use of the restricted space and the steep topography. The lower storeys are constructed in stone, with barrel vaulting supporting timber-framed upper storeys, as is customary in Alpine regions. Only a few preserve the original flat saddleback roofs covered with wooden planks or shingles.

World Heritage site since

• • • • • • • • • • • • • • • • • • 1978 • 1979 • 1980 • 1981 • 1982 • 1983 • 1984 • 1985 • 1986 • 1987 • 1988 • 1989 • 1990 • 1991 • 1992 • 1993 • 1994 • 1995 • 1996 • **1997**

Botanical Garden (Orto Botanico), Padua
Italy
Criteria – Interchange of values; Testimony to cultural tradition

The Botanical Garden of Padua is the original of all botanical gardens throughout the world. It was created in 1545 and still preserves its original layout: a circular central plot, symbolizing the world, surrounded by a ring of water, representing the ocean. Various additions have been made in the intervening centuries – a pumping installation to supply ten fountains in the seventeenth century, four monumental entrances in 1704, and new masonry greenhouses in the late eighteenth and early nineteenth centuries. An arboretum, an English garden with winding paths, and a small hillock (belvedere) were also added around this time. The garden has traditionally collected and grown particularly rare plants, which have then been introduced into the rest of Europe. Currently there are over 6,000 species grown here.

The Botanical Garden also houses two important collections. The library contains more than 50,000 volumes and manuscripts of immense historical and bibliographic importance. The herbarium is the second most extensive in Italy.

Rohtas Fort
Pakistan
Criteria – Interchange of values; Significance in human history

Following his defeat of the Mughal emperor Humayun in 1541, Sher Shah Suri built a strong fortified complex at Rohtas, a strategic site in the north of what is now Pakistan. It was never taken by force and has survived intact to the present day. The main fortifications consist of the massive walls, which extend for more than 4 km; they are lined with bastions and pierced by monumental gateways. Rohtas Fort, also called Qila Rohtas, is an exceptional example of early Muslim military architecture in Central and South Asia.

Rohtas is a complex of defensive works surrounding a small hill alongside the Kahan River. Its stone walls vary according to the terrain, with heights ranging from 10.05 m to 18.28 m and a thickness of up to 12.5 m.

◄

Section of the fortifications of Rohtas Fort.

Historic City of Trogir
Croatia

Criteria – Interchange of values; Significance in human history

Trogir is a remarkable example of urban continuity. The street plan of this island settlement dates back to the Hellenistic period and it was embellished by successive rulers with many fine public and domestic buildings and fortifications. Its beautiful Romanesque churches are complemented by the outstanding Renaissance and Baroque buildings from the period of Venetian rule after 1420. The ancient town of Tragurion (island of goats) was founded as a trading settlement by Greek colonists in the third century BC. The town flourished in the Roman period. Between the thirteenth and fifteenth centuries much new building took place, including the cathedral and the Camerlengo fortress and the reconstruction of the fortifications. Throughout the town, and in particular round the ramparts, are the palaces of leading families. Many of these rise directly from the foundations of late Classical or Romanesque buildings.

The plan of contemporary Trogir reflects the Hellenistic layout in the location, dimensions and shapes of its residential blocks. The two ancient main streets, the cardo and the decumanus, are still in use, and paving from the forum has been located by excavation at their intersection.

World Heritage site since

• 1978 • 1979 • 1980 • 1981 • 1982 • 1983 • 1984 • 1985 • 1986 • 1987 • 1988 • 1989 • 1990 • 1991 • 1992 • 1993 • 1994 • 1995 • 1996 • **1997**

Hospicio Cabañas, Guadalajara
Mexico

Criteria – Human creative genius; Interchange of values; Testimony to cultural tradition; Significance in human history

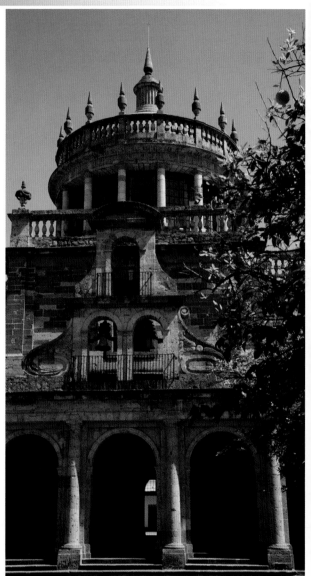

The Hospicio Cabañas was built at the beginning of the nineteenth century by the Bishop of Guadalajara, Juan Ruiz de Cabañas, to provide care and shelter for the disadvantaged – orphans, old people, the handicapped and chronic invalids. This remarkable complex, which incorporates several unusual features designed specifically to meet the needs of its occupants, was created by Manuel Tolsá. The entire complex is laid out on a rectangular plan: all the buildings, which are single storey, except the chapel and the kitchen, are ranged round twenty-three courtyards. The great majority of these are arcaded on at least two sides. In the 1930s, the chapel was decorated with a superb series of murals, now considered some of the masterpieces of Mexican art. They are the work of José Clemente Orozco, one of the greatest Mexican muralists of the period.

The growth of the Mexican muralist movement was a demonstration of national cohesion and identity. In the 1930s, Orozco was commissioned by the government to paint the murals in the chapel of the Hospicio Cabañas. They represented the multi-ethnic character of Mexican society and the allegory of the Man of Fire, which are among his finest works.

World Heritage site since

• • • • • • • • • • • • • • • • • • 1978 • 1979 • 1980 • 1981 • 1982 • 1983 • 1984 • 1985 • 1986 • 1987 • 1988 • 1989 • 1990 • 1991 • 1992 • 1993 • 1994 • 1995 • 1996 • **1997**

Las Médulas
Spain

Criteria – Human creative genius; Interchange of values; Testimony to cultural tradition; Significance in human history

Las Médulas gold-mining area is an outstanding example of innovative Roman technology, based on hydraulic power, in which all the elements of the ancient landscape, both industrial and domestic, have survived. The Archaeological Zone of Las Médulas (ZAM) comprises the mines themselves and also large areas where the tailings resulting from the process were deposited. Within the area there are dams

used to collect the vast amounts of water needed for the mining process and the intricate canals by means of which the water was conveyed to the mines. Human settlement is represented by villages, of both the indigenous inhabitants and the imperial administrative and support personnel (including army units).

Unlike the situation in other imperial gold-mining areas such as Wales, the workers at Las Médulas were free men, not slaves. Their settlements stand alongside, yet are clearly distinguishable from those which housed the imperial officials and their staff.

San Millán Yuso and Suso Monasteries
Spain

Criteria – Interchange of values; Significance in human history; Heritage associated with events of universal significance

The monastic community founded by St Millán in the mid-sixth century became a place of pilgrimage. A fine Romanesque church built in honour of the holy man still stands at the site of Suso. The monastery consists of a series of hermits' caves, a church, and an entrance porch or narthex. The caves, originally used by the monks, are cut into the southern slope of the mountain. It was here that the first literature was produced in Castilian, and from which one

of the most widely spoken languages in the world today is derived. In the early sixteenth century the community was housed in the fine new monastery of Yuso, below the older complex; it is still a thriving community today.

The Codex Aemilianensis 60 was written in the Suso scriptorium in the ninth and tenth centuries by a monk who added Castilian and Basque marginal notes, with a prayer in Castilian: this is the first known example of written Spanish.

Hwaseong Fortress
Korea, Republic of

Criteria – Interchange of values; Testimony to cultural tradition

Parts of the Fortress were destroyed or damaged during the Japanese occupation and the Korean War, but the availability of the original Archives on the Construction of Hwaseong Fortress has made it possible for the Fortress to be restored to its original form. Work began in 1964, and has continued since that time.

Hwaseong Fortress had a great influence on the development of Korean architecture and is a landmark in the history of military architecture. When the Choson emperor Chongjo moved his father's tomb to Suwon at the end of the eighteenth century, he surrounded it with strong defensive works, laid out according to the precepts of an influential military architect of the period, who brought together the latest developments from both East and West.

Building was completed between 1794 and 1796. The massive walls, extending for nearly 6 km, still survive. They follow the topography of the land. There were originally forty-eight defensive features along the length of the walls – four gates, floodgates, observation towers, command posts, multiple-arrow launcher towers, firearms bastions, angle towers, secret gates, beacon towers, bastions and bunkers – and most of these survive intact.

Historic Centre of São Luís
Brazil

Criteria – Testimony to cultural tradition;
Significance in human history; Traditional human
settlement

The late seventeenth-century core of this historic town, founded by the French in 1612, and occupied by the Dutch before coming under Portuguese rule, has preserved the original rectangular street plan in its entirety. Due to a period of economic stagnation in the early twentieth century, an exceptional number of fine historic buildings have survived, making this an outstanding example of an Iberian colonial town. Private houses were built round courtyards, and the most outstanding examples have tiled roofs; façades adorned with Portuguese azulejos (painted ceramic tiles) or painted, ornamented cornices; tall, narrow window bays with decorated surrounds; and balconies with forged or cast-iron railings. The floors are of dressed stone. Features relating to the tropical climate include raised piers and shuttered verandas on the inside. There are some 4,000 buildings within the Historic Centre.

In addition to the private houses that make up the greater proportion of the town's stock of historic buildings, there are a number of public buildings from the nineteenth and early twentieth centuries, which are largely neoclassical in style.

World Heritage site since

• • • • • • • • • • • • • • • 1978 • 1979 • 1980 • 1981 • 1982 • 1983 • 1984 • 1985 • 1986 • 1987 • 1988 • 1989 • 1990 • 1991 • 1992 • 1993 • 1994 • 1995 • 1996 • **1997**

Costiera Amalfitana
Italy

Criteria – Interchange of values; Significance in human history; Traditional human settlement

The layout of the settlements on the Costiera Amalfitana shows an eastern influence, with closely-spaced houses climbing steep hillsides and connected by a maze of alleys and stairs. A distinctive Arab-Sicilian architecture originated and developed in Amalfi.

Intensively settled in the sixth century, Amalfi quickly became a maritime trading power, enjoying a near-monopoly in the Tyrrhenian Sea. Wood, iron, weapons, wine and fruit were traded in eastern markets for spices, perfumes, pearls, jewels, textiles and carpets to sell in the West. However, Amalfi was eclipsed by the power of Pisa in the twelfth century.

Costiera Amalfitana (Amalfi Coast) is an outstanding example of a Mediterranean landscape and an area of great physical beauty and natural diversity. It has been intensively settled by communities since the early Middle Ages and has a number of towns, such as Amalfi and Ravello, with significant architectural and artistic works. Rural areas show the versatility of the inhabitants in adapting their use of the land to the diverse terrain, which ranges from terraced vineyards and orchards on lower slopes to wide upland pastures.

The site covers 112 km² in the Province of Salerno. Its exceptional cultural and natural scenic values are a result of its dramatic topography and historical evolution. The area's natural boundary is the southern slope of the peninsula formed by the Lattari hills. It consists of four main stretches of coast (Amalfi, Atrani, Reginna Maior, Reginna Minor), some minor ones (Positano, Praiano, Certaria, Hercle), with mountain villages and hamlets behind and above them.

The towns and villages of Costiera Amalfitana are characterized by their architectural monuments, such as the Torre Saracena at Cetara; the Romanesque Cathedral of Amalfi and its 'Cloister of Paradise', with their strong oriental influences; the Church of San Salvatore de' Bireto at Atrani; and Ravello with its fine cathedral and the superb Villa Rufolo.

There is an immense diversity of landscapes, ranging from coastal settlements through intensively cultivated lower slopes and large areas of open pastoral land to dramatic high mountains. In addition, there are micro-landscapes of great scientific interest resulting from topographical and climatic variations, and striking natural formations in the limestone karst at both sea level and above.

Inland, the steep slopes rising from the coast are covered with terraces banked with drystone walling and used for the cultivation of citrus and other fruits, olives, vines and vegetables. Further inland, the hillsides are given over to dairy farming, which has ancient roots in the area, based on sheep, goats, cattle and buffalo. In some parts of the Costiera the natural landscape survives intact, with little, if any, human intervention. It supports the traditional Mediterranean flora of myrtle, lentisk, broom and euphorbia. Elsewhere there are stands of trees such as holm oak, alder, beech and chestnut. Other zones shelter pantropical ferns, butterwort, dwarf palms and endemic carnivorous species.

World Heritage site since

• • • • • • • • • • • • • • • 1978 • 1979 • 1980 • 1981 • 1982 • 1983 • 1984 • 1985 • 1986 • 1987 • 1988 • 1989 • 1990 • 1991 • 1992 • 1993 • 1994 • 1995 • 1996 • **1997**

Ancient City of Ping Yao
China

Criteria – Interchange of values; Testimony to
cultural tradition; Significance in human history

Prosperity derived
from trade and
banking meant that,
in addition to public
buildings and
temples, shops and
monuments, Ping Yao
was endowed with
high-quality, well-built
private houses; these
have largely survived.

The Ancient City of Ping Yao is an
outstanding example of a Han Chinese city
of the Ming and Qing dynasties
(fourteenth–twentieth centuries) that has
retained all its features to an exceptional
degree. It offers a remarkably complete
picture of cultural, social, economic and
religious development during one of the
most seminal periods of Chinese history. In
1370, during the reign of the Ming Emperor

Hong Wu, the city was fortified with a
massive new defensive wall and the internal
layout was greatly altered, reflecting the
strict rules of Han planning. The circuit of
walls measures 6 km in length, the precise
dimension for a city of this grade according
to Han prescriptions. There are six fortified
gates and seventy-two massive bastions
along its length.

World Heritage site since

• • • • • • • • • • • • • • • 1978 • 1979 • 1980 • 1981 • 1982 • 1983 • 1984 • 1985 • 1986 • 1987 • 1988 • 1989 • 1990 • 1991 • 1992 • 1993 • 1994 • 1995 • 1996 • **1997**

Residences of the Royal House of Savoy
Italy

Criteria – Human creative genius; Interchange of values; Significance in human history; Traditional human settlement

When Emmanuel-Philibert, Duke of Savoy, moved his capital to the small fortified medieval town of Turin in 1562, he began a vast series of building projects, continued in Baroque style by his successors, to demonstrate the power of the ruling house. This outstanding complex of buildings was designed and embellished by the leading architects and artists of the time. It radiates into the surrounding countryside from the Royal Palace (Palazzo Reale) in the centre of

Turin to include many country residences and hunting lodges. The brick Palazzo Reale, late seventeenth century in its present form, was built around a courtyard, with porticoes opening behind onto landscaped gardens. It formed the focus of a 'Command Centre', linked to many buildings, including the Palazzo Chiablese on the Piazza Reale, and buildings on the Piazza Castello (former State Secretariats and the Palazzo Madama).

Guarino Guarini gave his personal touch to Turin's Baroque architecture with the Palazzo Carignano (1679–85), one of the most attractive and impressive seventeenth century-Italian palaces. He placed an oval rotunda in the middle of the main façade, giving it an undulating appearance.

The recently restored ballroom of the Royal Palace (Palazzo Reale).
▼

Archaeological Area of Agrigento
Italy

Criteria – Human creative genius; Interchange of values; Testimony to cultural tradition; Significance in human history

EUROPE

Mediterranean Sea   Ionian Sea

The Valley of the Temples covers most of the built-up part of the ancient city and its public monuments. It is closed by the ridge running parallel to the sea that was assigned, in antiquity, the role of a sacred area.

The area between the acropolis and the temples was laid out in the early fifth century BC.

Agrigento was one of the greatest cities of the ancient Mediterranean world and it has been exceptionally well preserved. Its great row of Doric temples is one of the most outstanding monuments of Greek art. Founded as a Greek colony in the sixth century BC, it reached its height during the rule of the tyrant Thero (488–473). The most substantial remains are from this time. The Temple of Olympian Zeus, of which only the foundations and main altar survive, was one of the largest of all Greek temples. The so-called Temple of Concord is the most impressive surviving Doric temple in the Greek world after the Parthenon in Athens. In addition, there are large excavated areas of the residential Hellenistic and Roman Agrigento, and extensive ancient cemeteries with tombs and monuments from the pagan and Christian periods.

Temple of Hera (Juno) in Agrigento.
▼

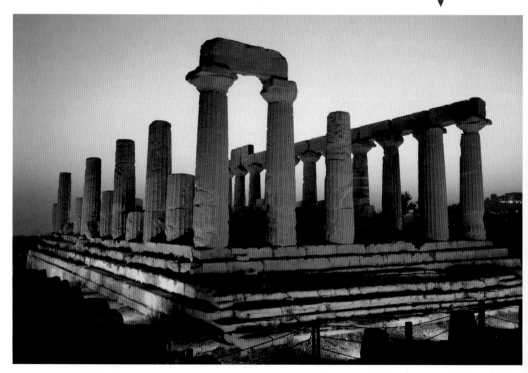

World Heritage site since

• • • • • • • • • • • • • • 1978 • 1979 • 1980 • 1981 • 1982 • 1983 • 1984 • 1985 • 1986 • 1987 • 1988 • 1989 • 1990 • 1991 • 1992 • 1993 • 1994 • 1995 • 1996 • **1997**

Archaeological Site of Volubilis

Morocco

Criteria – Interchange of values; Testimony to cultural tradition; Significance in human history; Heritage associated with events of universal significance

Atlantic Ocean

Mediterranean Sea

AFRICA

The Mauritanian capital, founded in the third century BC, became an important outpost of the Roman Empire after AD 40 and is an exceptionally well-preserved example of a colonial town on the fringes of the Roman Empire. During the Roman period, a town wall, with eight monumental gates, and a new monumental centre including a capitol, basilica and baths, were constructed. The triumphal arch of Caracalla, which spans the decumanus

maximus, marks the boundary between the Punic-Hellenistic town and the extension in the Roman period to the northeast. At the beginning of the reign of Diocletian, in 285, the Romans abruptly abandoned the region, for reasons that remain obscure, and Volubilis entered its 'dark age'. Volubilis was later briefly to become the capital of Idris I, founder of the Idrisid dynasty, who is buried at nearby Moulay Idris.

The buildings of Volubilis are for the most part constructed using the grey-blue limestone quarried nearby on the Zerhoun massif. They are notable for the large number of mosaic floors still in situ. Although they do not attain the artistic level of other North African mosaics, they are lively and varied in form and subject matter.

The triumphal arch of Caracalla.
▼

World Heritage site since

• • • • • • • • • • • • • • • 1978 • 1979 • 1980 • 1981 • 1982 • 1983 • 1984 • 1985 • 1986 • 1987 • 1988 • 1989 • 1990 • 1991 • 1992 • 1993 • 1994 • 1995 • 1996 • **1997**

Historic Centre of Riga
Latvia

Criteria – Human creative genius; Interchange of values

Riga was independent from 1221 and in 1282 it formed an alliance with Lübeck and Visby to become a member of the Hanseatic League. By the fifteenth century Riga was a typical Hanseatic town, with winding streets and densely-packed houses, a large central market and strong fortifications.

In the sixteenth century the city became embroiled in struggles between Russia, Poland and Sweden. Finally in 1710, it fell to the Russian army, remaining part of the Tsarist Russian Empire until the creation of the first Republic of Latvia in 1918.

The Historic Centre of Riga, while retaining its medieval and later urban fabric relatively intact, is of outstanding value by virtue of the quality and the quantity of its Jugendstil, or German Art Nouveau architecture, unparalleled anywhere in the world, and its nineteenth-century architecture in wood. It has exerted a considerable influence within the Baltic cultural area on subsequent developments in architecture.

Riga was a major centre of the powerful Hanseatic League of north European and Baltic traders, deriving its prosperity in the thirteenth to the fifteenth centuries from the trade with central and eastern Europe. The urban fabric of its medieval centre reflects this prosperity, though most of the earliest buildings were destroyed by fire or war. Riga became an important economic centre in the nineteenth century, when the suburbs surrounding the medieval town were laid out, first with imposing wooden buildings in neoclassical style and then in Jugendstil. These three districts comprise the historic centre of the city.

Few medieval houses are still intact; of these one of the most interesting is the House of the Three Brothers, an impeccably restored group from the fifteenth century. The late-seventeenth-century Reutem's House and Dammnstem's House are more

monumental buildings, notable for their interior decorations and fittings and for their impressive façades.

The boulevards are lined with many important public buildings from the nineteenth and early twentieth centuries; they include the National Theatre and the Museum of Latvian Art. The creation of the boulevards coincided with the reign of eclecticism in Europe, and this movement is abundantly represented. Eclecticism allowed architects to produce many flights of fancy, well-illustrated by the House of the Cat on Meistaru Street. The suburbs that developed so rapidly at this time are notable for both their wooden buildings in the classical Russian style and the extraordinary quality of the new buildings.

However, it was Jugendstil, which reached Riga via Finland at the end of the nineteenth century, that provided the suburban area with its most noteworthy feature. There are countless examples, perhaps the most outstanding of which are the works of Mikhail Eisenstein in Alberta Street and Elizabeth Street. National Romanticism evolved into Jugendstil in Latvia, again on the Finnish model. There are some striking examples of this movement in Alberta Street and Brivibas Street.

House of the Blackheads, Riga.

World Heritage site since

• • • • • • • • • • • • • • 1978 • 1979 • 1980 • 1981 • 1982 • 1983 • 1984 • 1985 • 1986 • 1987 • 1988 • 1989 • 1990 • 1991 • 1992 • 1993 • 1994 • 1995 • 1996 • **1997**

Villa Romana del Casale
Italy

Criteria – Human creative genius; Interchange of values; Testimony to cultural tradition

Villa del Casale at Piazza Armerina is the supreme example of a luxury Roman villa. The area that has been excavated, which is only part of the full establishment and covers about 4,000 m², may be divided into four zones or groups of rooms, all of them decorated with floor mosaics of superlative quality. The first is the monumental entrance, which opens into a courtyard, onto which faces the elaborate baths complex. Next comes the impressive main peristyle with its monumental fountain in the centre. To the south is the third group, around the elliptical peristyle. The fourth group lies to the east of the main peristyle, linked by the long Corridor of the Great Hunting Scene.

The mosaics are the glory of the Villa del Casale. Among the more famous are those depicting the capture of wild animals in Africa, and a group of sportswomen dressed in costumes remarkably similar to modern bikinis.

Su Nuraxi di Barumini
Italy

Criteria – Human creative genius; Testimony to cultural tradition; Significance in human history

During the late second millennium BC in the Bronze Age, a special type of defensive structure known as nuraghi, for which no parallel exists anywhere else in the world, developed on the island of Sardinia. The complex consists of circular defensive towers in the form of truncated cones built of dressed stone, with corbel-vaulted internal chambers. The complex at Barumini, which was extended and reinforced in the first half of the first millennium under Carthaginian pressure, is the finest and most complete example of this remarkable form of prehistoric architecture.

Some time in the seventh century BC, Su Nuraxi was sacked by the Carthaginians and the defensive works were neglected. However, it continued as a settlement, the houses being rebuilt in a different style. With the Roman conquest of the island in the second century BC most of the nuraghi went out of use. However, excavations have shown that there were people living at Su Nuraxi until the third century BC.

The central defensive structures are thought to have been built by families or clans. As Sardinian society evolved there was a tendency for more isolated towers to attract additional structures, and villages of small, circular-plan houses developed around some strongpoints.

World Heritage site since

• • • • • • • • • • • • • • • • • • 1978 • 1979 • 1980 • 1981 • 1982 • 1983 • 1984 • 1985 • 1986 • 1987 • 1988 • 1989 • 1990 • 1991 • 1992 • 1993 • 1994 • 1995 • 1996 • **1997**

Castle of the Teutonic Order in Malbork
Poland

Criteria – Interchange of values; Testimony to cultural tradition; Significance in human history

The immense brick castle at Malbork, started by the Teutonic Order after 1270, greatly influenced Gothic buildings in a wide region of northeast Europe. The importance of Malbork increased greatly after 1309, when the seat of the Grand Master of the Order was moved here from Venice. The original Fore Castle was adapted as his residence and administrative headquarters, the impressive Palace of the Grand Masters being built in its southwest corner. The Great Refectory was built to the north of the palace; the north side of the Middle Castle was closed by a wing, housing the hospital and the residence of the commander, and the chapel in the High Castle was enlarged. The whole complex is surrounded by an intricate system of defensive works, including massive walls and bastions, wet and dry moats and ditches, earthen ramparts and ponds.

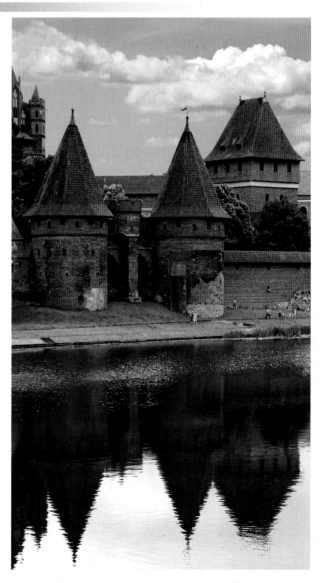

The castle fell into decay at the end of the eighteenth century, but was meticulously restored in the nineteenth and early twentieth centuries. Many of the conservation techniques now accepted as standard evolved here. Following severe damage in the Second World War it was once again restored, using the detailed documentation prepared by earlier conservators.

San Pedro de la Roca Castle, Santiago de Cuba
Cuba

Criteria – Significance in human history; Traditional human settlement

The Castle of San Pedro de la Roca and its associated defensive works are the largest and most comprehensive example of the principles of Renaissance military engineering, adapted to the requirements of European colonial powers, in the Caribbean. Commercial and political rivalries in the Caribbean region in the seventeenth century resulted in the construction of this massive series of fortifications on a rocky promontory, to protect the important port of Santiago. This intricate complex of forts, magazines, bastions and batteries underwent little change from the late nineteenth century, when it went out of use, until the 1960s, when restoration work began. It is one of three fortresses designed by the famous father and son military architects, Bautista and Juan Bautista Antonelli.

The castle stands on a promontory with steep cliffs rising over 20 m. The terrain is such that its various elements could be built in a series of terraces above one another and linked by a series of stairways.

Historic Monuments Zone of Tlacotalpan
Mexico

Criteria – Interchange of values; Significance in human history

Tlacotalpan, a Spanish colonial river port on the Gulf coast of Mexico, was founded in the mid-sixteenth century. It has preserved its original urban fabric to a remarkable degree, with wide streets, colonnaded houses in a profusion of styles and colours, and many mature trees in the public open spaces and private gardens. Although it was established in the sixteenth century, it was not until 1821 that Tlacotalpan experienced any economic expansion. It became the port for the products of Oaxaca and Puebla destined for Veracruz and beyond to New Orleans, Havana and Bordeaux. By 1855 its fleet had grown to eighteen steamers and one large sailing ship, used to transport timber, tobacco, cotton, grain, sugar, brandy, leather, salt meat, crocodiles, heron feathers, furniture and soap.

The architecture and 'chequerboard' town plan of Tlacotalpan represent a unique fusion of Spanish and Caribbean traditions of exceptional importance and quality.

Classical Weimar
Germany

Criteria – Testimony to cultural tradition; Heritage associated with events of universal significance

North Sea

Baltic Sea

EUROPE

In the late-eighteenth and early nineteenth centuries the small Thuringian town of Weimar witnessed a remarkable cultural flowering. Enlightened ducal patronage attracted many of the leading German writers and artists to the town, including Johann Sebastian Bach, Johann Wolfgang Goethe, Friedrich Schiller and Franz Liszt, making it the cultural centre of the Europe of the day. This development is reflected in the high quality of many of the buildings

and parks in the surrounding area. The World Heritage site comprises twelve separate buildings or ensembles, including Goethe's House, Schiller's House, Belvedere Palace (see picture below), and the Dowager's Palace, which was the centre of intellectual life at the height of classical Weimar. The site also includes the Princes' Tomb and the Historic Cemetery, constructed in 1823, where Schiller and Goethe are both buried.

Goethe's House, a Baroque town house built in 1707–9, underwent a number of alterations during his occupancy. The original interior furnishings are preserved in a number of rooms. Schiller's House is a simple late-Baroque house built in 1777, incorporating part of a sixteenth century outbuilding (the Mint). Most of the rooms are furnished as they were during the lifetime of the poet.

Archaeological Site of Troy
Turkey

Criteria – Interchange of values; Testimony to
cultural tradition; Heritage associated with
events of universal significance

The Greek and Roman
cities at Troy are
represented above all
by the sanctuary
complex. Roman urban
organization is
reflected by two major
public buildings on
the edge of the agora.
Pictured below, the
odeion (concert hall) has
the traditional
horseshoe-shaped
plan and tiers of seats
made from limestone
blocks. The nearby
bouleuterion (council
house) is smaller but
similar in plan.

Troy, with its 4,000 years of history, is one of
the most famous archaeological sites in the
world. The first excavations at the site were
undertaken by Heinrich Schliemann, who
carried out seven major campaigns between
1868 and 1890. The extensive remains
uncovered by Schliemann are the most
significant demonstration of the first
contact between the civilizations of Anatolia
and the Mediterranean world. Moreover,
the siege of Troy by Spartan and Achaean
warriors from Greece in the thirteenth or
twelfth century BC, immortalized by Homer
in The Iliad, has inspired great creative artists
throughout the world ever since. Troy II
and Troy VI in particular are characteristic
examples of the ancient city, with a majestic
fortified citadel enclosing palaces and
administrative buildings, surrounded by
an extensive lower town, also fortified.

World Heritage site since

• • • • • • • • • • • • • • 1978 • 1979 • 1980 • 1981 • 1982 • 1983 • 1984 • 1985 • 1986 • 1987 • 1988 • 1989 • 1990 • 1991 • 1992 • 1993 • 1994 • 1995 • 1996 • 1997 • **1998**

Semmering Railway
Austria

Criteria – Interchange of values; Significance in human history

The Semmering Railway, built over 41 km of high mountains between 1848 and 1854, is one of the greatest feats of civil engineering from this pioneering phase of railway building. The high standard of the tunnels, viaducts and other works has ensured the continuous use of the line up to the present day. It runs through a spectacular mountain landscape. There are many fine buildings designed for leisure activities along the way, built when the area was opened up due to the advent of the railway.

The Semmering pass itself is well known for the 'summer architecture' of the villas and hotels that were built for Viennese society between Gloggnitz and the small market town of Schottwien in picturesque locations. It became one of the first artificially laid out Alpine resorts in the decades following the opening of the railway line.

◀

Kalte Rinne viaduct.

Holašovice Historical Village Reservation
Czech Republic

Criteria – Interchange of values; Significance in human history

Situated in the heart of South Bohemia, Holašovice is an exceptionally complete and well-preserved example of a traditional central European village. It has a large number of outstanding eighteenth- and nineteenth-century vernacular buildings in a style known as South Bohemian Folk Baroque, and preserves a ground plan dating from the Middle Ages. The village consists at the present time of 120 buildings

arranged round an elongated village square, with a small chapel and cross on it, and some more recent buildings on the outskirts. The historical reservation consists of the original village as surveyed in 1827, which includes twenty-three protected farmsteads along with their attached farm buildings and gardens. The farmsteads are all built with their gable-ends facing the square.

In addition to the farmsteads, there are several farm labourers' cottages that are much smaller and simpler in design. The village smithy and the smith's house are located in the middle of the village square. The other architectural feature in the village square is the small Chapel of St John of Nepomuk.

World Heritage site since

• • • • • • • • • • • • • • 1978 • 1979 • 1980 • 1981 • 1982 • 1983 • 1984 • 1985 • 1986 • 1987 • 1988 • 1989 • 1990 • 1991 • 1992 • 1993 • 1994 • 1995 • 1996 • 1997 • **1998**

Summer Palace and Imperial Garden in Beijing
China

Criteria – Human creative genius; Interchange of values; Testimony to cultural tradition

The Imperial Garden and Summer Palace in Beijing – first built in 1750, largely destroyed in the Second Opium War of 1860, and restored in 1886 – is a masterpiece of Chinese garden design. The natural landscape of hills and open water is combined with artificial features such as pavilions, halls, palaces, temples and bridges to form a harmonious ensemble of outstanding aesthetic value. The site covers an area of almost 3km², three-quarters of

which is covered by water. The main framework is supplied by the Hill of Longevity and Kunming Lake, complemented by man-made features. It is designed on a grandiose scale, commensurate with its role as an imperial garden. It is divided into three areas, each with its particular function: political and administrative activities, residence, and recreation and sightseeing. It became a public park in 1924.

The political area is reached by means of the monumental East Palace Gate. The central feature is the Hall of Benevolence and Longevity, an imposing structure with its own courtyard garden. This area connects directly with the residential area, which is made up of three complexes of buildings.

The Seventeen-Arch Bridge.
▼

World Heritage site since

• • • • • • • • • • • • • • 1978 • 1979 • 1980 • 1981 • 1982 • 1983 • 1984 • 1985 • 1986 • 1987 • 1988 • 1989 • 1990 • 1991 • 1992 • 1993 • 1994 • 1995 • 1996 • 1997 • **1998**

Naval Port of Karlskrona
Sweden

Criteria – Interchange of values; Significance in human history

Karlskrona is an outstanding example of a late-seventeenth-century European planned naval city. It was founded in 1680 when Sweden was a major power whose territory included modern Finland, Estonia, Latvia, and parts of north Germany. The plan of Karlskrona integrates strategic imperatives with the classical ideal. The Baroque layout with wide main streets radiating out from a central square lined with majestic public buildings is clearly discernible in the present-day town. The centre of the town is Stortorget (Great Square), at the highest point of the island of Trossö where the two main churches of the town, both dating from the first half of the eighteenth century, Rådhuset (the City Hall) from the same period, and later public buildings such as the Concert Hall, the City Library, and the Post Office, are located.

The naval harbour is to the south of the town, from which it was originally separated by an impressive enclosure wall, only small sections of which survive.

To the south of the Parade Ground is Gamle Varvet (the Old Shipyard). This is made up of a number of fine buildings dating mainly from the late-eighteenth century.

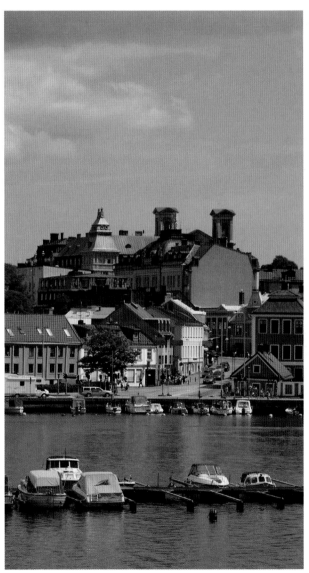

World Heritage site since

• • • • • • • • • • • • • 1978 • 1979 • 1980 • 1981 • 1982 • 1983 • 1984 • 1985 • 1986 • 1987 • 1988 • 1989 • 1990 • 1991 • 1992 • 1993 • 1994 • 1995 • 1996 • 1997 • **1998**

The Four Lifts on the Canal du Centre and their Environs, La Louvière and Le Roeulx (Hainault)

Belgium

Criteria – Testimony to cultural tradition; Significance in human history

These ingenious lifts consist essentially of two mobile compartments, each supported by a single hydraulic press. When one compartment is at the level of the upper bay, the other is at the lower level. As the first descends, the other rises.

The four hydraulic boat-lifts on this short stretch of the Canal du Centre represent the apogee of the application of engineering technology to the construction of canals. Of the eight hydraulic boat-lifts built around the end of the nineteenth century, the only ones in the world which still exist in their original working condition are these four. Together with the canal itself and its associated structures, they constitute a remarkably well-preserved and complete example of a late nineteenth-century industrial landscape. Lift No. 1 at Houdeng-Gœgnies was completed in 1888. The others were built thirteen years later and incorporate a number of modifications to the basic design, though the operating principle remains the same.

Choirokoitia

Cyprus

Criteria – Interchange of values; Testimony to cultural tradition; Significance in human history

Among the site's most noteworthy finds are the anthropomorphic figurines in stone (and one in clay), which point to the existence at this early period of elaborate spiritual beliefs.

The Neolithic settlement of Choirokoitia, occupied from the seventh to the fourth millennia BC, is one of the most important prehistoric sites in the eastern Mediterranean. The earliest occupation, consisting of circular houses built from mud-brick and stone with flat roofs, was on the eastern side of the hill. It was protected by natural slopes on three sides and a massive wall barring access from the west. A second defensive wall was erected to protect a later extension of the village. The finds from excavations at the site have thrown much light on the evolution of human society in this key region, and since only part of the site has been excavated, it forms an exceptional archaeological reserve for future study.

World Heritage site since

• • • • • • • • • • • • • 1978 • 1979 • 1980 • 1981 • 1982 • 1983 • 1984 • 1985 • 1986 • 1987 • 1988 • 1989 • 1990 • 1991 • 1992 • 1993 • 1994 • 1995 • 1996 • 1997 • **1998**

La Grand-Place, Brussels
Belgium
Criteria – Interchange of values; Significance in human history

La Grand-Place in Brussels is a remarkably homogeneous body of public and private buildings, dating mainly from the late-seventeenth century. The architecture provides a vivid illustration of the level of social and cultural life of the period in this important political and commercial centre. The earliest written reference to the Nedermarckt (Lower Market), as it was originally known, dates from 1174; the present name came into use in the last

quarter of the eighteenth century. The rectangular outline of today's Grand-Place has developed over the centuries as a result of successive enlargements and other modifications, and did not take on its definitive form until after 1695, when it was restored to its original layout and appearance following bombardment by the French. It has, however, always had seven streets running into it.

The Hôtel de Ville (City Hall), which covers most of the south side of the Grand-Place, consists of a group of buildings around a rectangular internal courtyard. The part facing on to the square is from the fifteenth century, consisting of two L-shaped buildings. The entire façade is decorated with statues dating from the nineteenth century.
▼

World Heritage site since

• • • • • • • • • • • • • 1978 • 1979 • 1980 • 1981 • 1982 • 1983 • 1984 • 1985 • 1986 • 1987 • 1988 • 1989 • 1990 • 1991 • 1992 • 1993 • 1994 • 1995 • 1996 • 1997 • **1998**

New Zealand Sub-Antarctic Islands
New Zealand

Criteria – Significant ecological and biological processes; Significant natural habitat for biodiversity

The New Zealand Sub-Antarctic Islands consist of five island groups – the Snares, Bounty Islands, Antipodes Islands, Auckland Islands and Campbell Island – located southeast of New Zealand. With the exception of the Bounty Islands, the remaining islands together with neighbouring Macquarie Island constitute a Centre of Plant Diversity and have the richest flora of all the sub-antarctic islands. They are particularly notable for the large number and diversity of pelagic seabirds and penguins that nest there. There are 126 bird species in total, including forty seabirds, of which five breed nowhere else in the world. The islands support major populations of ten of the world's twenty-four species of albatross. It is a critical breeding site for the southern right whale and 95 per cent of the world's population of New Zealand sea lion breed here.

The islands lie on the shallow continental shelf and three of the groups are eroded remnants of Pliocene volcanoes. Rivers are short with precipitous streams. Quaternary glaciers have left shallow cirques, moraines and fjords on some islands. Cool equable temperatures, strong westerly winds, a few hours of sunshine and high humidity prevail.

Fuerte de Samaipata
Bolivia

Criteria – Interchange of values; Testimony to cultural tradition

The archaeological site of Samaipata consists of two parts: the hill with its many rock carvings, believed to have been the ceremonial centre of the old town in the fourteenth–sixteenth centuries, and the area to the south of the hill, which formed the administrative and residential district. The hill is divided naturally into a higher part, known as El Mirador, and a lower, where the carvings are located. The huge sculptured rock, dominating the town below, is a unique testimony to pre-Hispanic traditions and has no parallel anywhere in the Americas. The site is known to have been occupied by people belonging to the Mojocoyas culture as early as AD 300 and it was at this time that work began on the shaping of the rock.

The site was occupied in the fourteenth century by the Incas, who made it a provincial capital. This is confirmed by the features that have been discovered by excavation – a large central plaza with monumental public buildings around it and terracing of the neighbouring hillsides for agriculture – which are characteristic of this type of Inca settlement.

World Heritage site since

• • • • • • • • • • • • • • 1978 • 1979 • 1980 • 1981 • 1982 • 1983 • 1984 • 1985 • 1986 • 1987 • 1988 • 1989 • 1990 • 1991 • 1992 • 1993 • 1994 • 1995 • 1996 • 1997 • **1998**

Golden Mountains of Altai
Russian Federation

Criteria – Significant natural habitat for
biodiversity

The Altai mountains in southern Siberia form
the major mountain range in the western
Siberia biogeographic region and provide
the source of its greatest rivers – the Ob and
the Irtysh. Three separate areas are inscribed:
Altaisky Zapovednik and a buffer zone around
Lake Teletskoye; Katunsky Zapovednik and
a buffer zone around Mount Belukha; and
the Ukok Quiet Zone on the Ukok plateau.
The total area covers 16,115 km². The region
represents the most complete sequence of

altitudinal vegetation zones in central Siberia,
from steppe, forest-steppe, mixed forest,
subalpine vegetation to alpine vegetation.
The site is also an important habitat for
endangered animal species such as the
snow leopard.

The area's few human
inhabitants have
co-existed with nature
for millennia and have
a strong affinity with
the natural
environment. Indeed,
the region's important
biodiversity is
probably due to
millennia of grazing as
well as natural factors.

Routes of Santiago de Compostela in France
France

Criteria – Interchange of values; Significance in
human history; Heritage associated with events
of universal significance

Santiago de Compostela was the supreme
goal for countless thousands of pious
pilgrims who converged there from all over
Europe throughout the Middle Ages.
To reach Spain pilgrims had to pass through
France, and the group of important historical
monuments included in this site marks out
the four routes by which they did so.

A number of bridges
on the routes are
known as 'pilgrims'
bridges', and that over
the Borade at Saint-
Chély-d'Aubrac even
has the figure of a
pilgrim carved on it.
Of special importance
is the Pont du Diable
over the Hérault at
Aniane, one of the
oldest medieval
bridges in France.

◄
The fourteenth century
fortified 'pilgrims'
bridge' at Cahors.

World Heritage site since

• • • • • • • • • • • • • • 1978 • 1979 • 1980 • 1981 • 1982 • 1983 • 1984 • 1985 • 1986 • 1987 • 1988 • 1989 • 1990 • 1991 • 1992 • 1993 • 1994 • 1995 • 1996 • 1997 • **1998**

Cilento and Vallo di Diano National Park with the Archeological sites of Paestum and Velia, and the Certosa di Padula
Italy

Criteria – Testimony to cultural tradition; Significance in human history

The Cilento is an outstanding cultural landscape. The dramatic groups of sanctuaries and settlements along its three east-west mountain ridges vividly represent the area's historical evolution: it was a major route not only for trade, but also for cultural and political interaction during the prehistoric and medieval periods. The Cilento was also the boundary between the Greek colonies of Magna Graecia and the indigenous Etruscan and Lucanian peoples. The remains of two major cities from classical times, Paestum and Velia, are found there. Of the monastic properties, the most impressive is the Certosa di San Lorenzo at Padula in the Vallo di Diano. Construction began in 1306, but in its present form it is essentially Baroque, built in the seventeenth and eighteenth centuries.

At Paestum, the Greek city of Poseidonia, a number of exceptional public buildings have been revealed, the most outstanding of which are the three great temples of Hera, Ceres and Poseidon. Less survives of Velia Elea, although its notable Porta Rosa is the oldest and most complete example of a Greek arched town gate.

East Rennell
Solomon Islands

Criteria – Significant ecological and biological processes

East Rennell makes up the southern third of Rennell Island, the southernmost island in the Solomon Island group in the western Pacific. Rennell, 86 km long by 15 km wide, is the largest raised coral atoll in the world. The site includes approximately 370 km² and a marine area extending 5.6 km to sea. A major feature of the island is Lake Tegano, which was the former lagoon on the atoll. The lake, the largest in the insular Pacific (155 km²), is brackish and contains many rugged limestone islands and endemic species. Rennell is mostly covered with dense forest, with a canopy averaging 20 m in height. Combined with the strong climatic effects of frequent cyclones, the site is a true natural laboratory for scientific study. The site is under customary land ownership and management.

Rennell was formed by the uplift of corals which formed on an undersea ridge and then were subject to faulting. The landform is a typical jagged and eroded limestone karst rising to 200 m.

World Heritage site since

• • • • • • • • • • • • • • • • 1978 • 1979 • 1980 • 1981 • 1982 • 1983 • 1984 • 1985 • 1986 • 1987 • 1988 • 1989 • 1990 • 1991 • 1992 • 1993 • 1994 • 1995 • 1996 • 1997 • **1998**

Temple of Heaven: an Imperial Sacrificial Altar in Beijing
China

Criteria – Human creative genius; Interchange of values; Testimony to cultural tradition

The Temple of Heaven is a masterpiece of architecture and landscape design which symbolizes the relationship between Earth and Heaven that stands at the heart of Chinese cosmogony, and also the special role played by the emperors within that relationship. The Altar of Heaven and Earth was completed in 1420. The central building was a large rectangular sacrificial hall, where sacrifices were offered to Heaven and Earth, with the Fasting Palace to the southwest. In the ninth year of the reign of Emperor Jiajing (1530) the decision was taken to offer separate sacrifices to Heaven and to Earth, and so the Circular Mound Altar was built to the south of the main hall, for sacrifices to Heaven. The Altar of Heaven and Earth was renamed the Temple of Heaven.

The area occupied by the Temple of Heaven is almost square, the two southern corners being right-angled and those on the north rounded. This symbolizes the ancient Chinese belief that Heaven is round and the Earth square. The main Temple of Heaven, the Circular Mound, repeats the symbolism of the walls, as the central round feature (Heaven) is inside a square enclosure (Earth).

Historic Monuments of Ancient Nara

Japan

Criteria – Interchange of values; Testimony to cultural tradition; Significance in human history; Heritage associated with events of universal significance

Nara was the capital of Japan from 710–84. A great city, based on Chinese examples, was laid out, with palaces, Buddhist temples, Shinto shrines and public buildings, all central to the development of Japanese architecture. The palace, occupying 1.2 km², comprised the official buildings, notably the Daigokuden (imperial audience hall) and Chōdō-in (state halls), and the imperial residence (Dairi). The main Buddhist temples were the Tōdai-ji, with its monumental wooden Kondō (Great Buddha Hall), the Kōfuku-ji, the Gangō-ji (the first Buddhist temple in Japan) and the Tōshōdai-ji, which still retains two buildings from the Nara period, the Kondō and the Kōdō (originally a state assembly hall from the imperial palace). After 784, Nara was abandoned and the palace became paddy fields (now being excavated and reconstructed), while most of the temples and shrines survived intact.

The buildings of the Kasuga-Taisha Shinto shrine have been restored and reconstructed on many occasions following decay and destruction. The natural environment is an integral element of Shinto shrines. At Kasuga-Taisha this is provided by Kasugayama, which has been preserved as a sacred forest, where there has been no human intervention beyond the provision of footpaths for pilgrims.

Tōdai-ji Temple.
▼

World Heritage site since

• • • • • • • • • • • • • 1978 • 1979 • 1980 • 1981 • 1982 • 1983 • 1984 • 1985 • 1986 • 1987 • 1988 • 1989 • 1990 • 1991 • 1992 • 1993 • 1994 • 1995 • 1996 • 1997 • **1998**

Historic Site of Lyons
France
Criteria – Interchange of values; Significance in human history

Lyons bears exceptional testimony to the continuity of urban settlement over more than two millennia on a site of great commercial and strategic significance, at the confluence of the rivers Rhône and Saône. The city was founded by the Romans in the first century BC. Notable ruins, including a large theatre of the early first century AD, capable of seating some 10,000 spectators, remain on the Fourvière hill. By the mid-fifteenth century it was one of the mostly heavily populated cities in Europe: overpopulation and the risk of epidemics led to a planned expansion starting in the mid-sixteenth century. The resulting urban fabric, visible today, contains areas of medieval streets and of eighteenth- and nineteenth-century town planning alongside one another. The city has a very rich stock of private houses from the thirteenth century onwards and many fine public buildings.

Lyons was founded by the Romans as the capital of the Three Gauls. The amphitheatre on Croix-Rousse hill was built around 19 BC to accompany the altar dedicated to Rome and Augustus; it was here that the Council of the Three Gauls met each August.

Bellecour Square with a statue of Louis XIV in the foreground and Fourvière Hill in the background.
▼

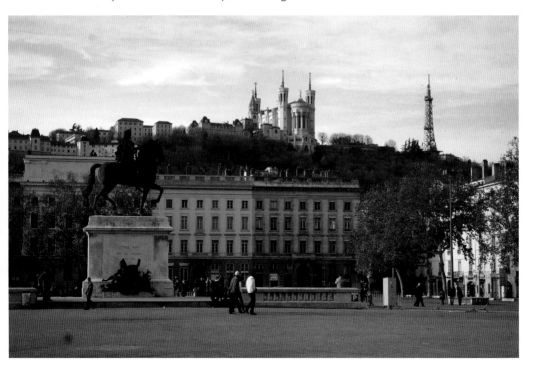

Rock Art of the Mediterranean Basin on the Iberian Peninsula
Spain
Criteria – Testimony to cultural tradition

There are more than 700 sites of late prehistoric rock art on the Mediterranean seaboard of the Iberian Peninsula, making this the largest such collection in Europe. Scenes of domestic daily life show groups of people sitting and talking, people walking together, seated hunters, and the butchering of animals among other activities. The representations of the human figure provide information on clothing and personal ornament, such as different hairstyles, bracelets, arm-rings and necklaces, and mark the beginnings of social inequality. Funerary rites are shown in the form of recumbent corpses and ritual scenes. Scenes illustrate the mythologies of these prehistoric societies: sorcerers in strange costumes are common, as are figures combining human characteristics with those of fauna (deer, bulls, birds).

The eastern Spanish rock art presents the first narrations in European prehistory and provides an exceptional picture of human life in a seminal period of cultural evolution. Hunting activities are most frequently represented and include hunting by groups and details of animal traps. The earliest depictions of combats and executions appear in the form of archers shooting at their victims.

Flemish Béguinages
Belgium
Criteria – Interchange of values; Testimony to cultural tradition; Significance in human history

The Béguines were women who dedicated their lives to God without retiring from the world. In the thirteenth century they founded the béguinages, enclosed communities designed to meet their spiritual and material needs. The Flemish béguinages are architectural ensembles composed of houses, churches, ancillary buildings and green spaces, with a layout of either urban or rural origin and built in styles specific to the Flemish cultural region. They are a fascinating reminder of the tradition of the Béguines that developed in northwestern Europe in the Middle Ages.

The Béguines were free to come and go in society and to withdraw from the community at will. Largely urban-based, they took houses near the hospitals and leper hospitals and devoted themselves to prayer, labour and caring for the sick.

◀
Little Béguinage of Gent.

World Heritage site since

• • • • • • • • • • • • • • 1978 • 1979 • 1980 • 1981 • 1982 • 1983 • 1984 • 1985 • 1986 • 1987 • 1988 • 1989 • 1990 • 1991 • 1992 • 1993 • 1994 • 1995 • 1996 • 1997 • **1998**

Archaeological Zone of Paquimé, Casas Grandes
Mexico

Criteria – Testimony to cultural tradition; Significance in human history

The archaeological site is located at the foot of the Sierra Madre Occidental range near the headwaters of the Casas Grandes River. It is estimated to contain the remains of some 2,000 rooms in clusters of living rooms, workshops, stores and patios. An estimated 10,000 people lived here at the height of its prosperity in the fourteenth–fifteenth centuries.

Paquimé, Casas Grandes, which reached its apogee in the fourteenth and fifteenth centuries, played a key role in trade and cultural contacts between the Pueblo culture of the southwestern United States and northern Mexico and the more advanced civilizations of Mesoamerica. The extensive remains, only part of which have been excavated, are clear evidence of the vitality of a culture which was perfectly adapted to its physical and economic environment.

The predominant building material is unfired clay (adobe). The presence of features such as platform mounds, ball courts, a sophisticated water-distribution system, and specialized storage buildings for exotic products such as macaws and turkeys, shell and copper artefacts, indicates influence from Mesoamerica.

Prehistoric Rock-Art Sites in the Côa Valley and Siega Verde
Portugal and Spain

Criteria – Human creative genius; Testimony to cultural tradition

The species represented include aurochs, horses, red deer, ibex and fish, but there are no domestic animals such as sheep or chickens, which were absent from the Iberian Peninsula at that time. One unique convention is the use of single bodies with two or three heads, in an attempt to convey a sense of movement.

This exceptional concentration of rock carvings, mostly from the Upper Palaeolithic (22,000–10,000 BC), is the most outstanding example of early human artistic activity in this form anywhere in the world. In the Côa Valley, Portugal, the carvings occur in three clusters. Furthest south is the small group of granite rock-shelter sites at Faia. Some 8 km further downstream is the cluster on either side of the river at Quinta da Barca and Penascosa, where the rock is schist. Finally, there is a cluster starting at Ribeira de Piscos

and continuing down the Côa to its confluence with the Douro. Not all the Côa material is Upper Palaeolithic, however: certain panels are of later date, from the Neolithic to the early modern period, while many have been drawn over or reused (palimpsests). Siega Verde, Spain, hosts 645 rock engravings on an imprpessive cliff. Most are of animals, although some schematic and geometric figures have been identified.

World Heritage site since

• • • • • • • • • • • • • 1978 • 1979 • 1980 • 1981 • 1982 • 1983 • 1984 • 1985 • 1986 • 1987 • 1988 • 1989 • 1990 • 1991 • 1992 • 1993 • 1994 • 1995 • 1996 • 1997 • **1998**

L'viv – the Ensemble of the Historic Centre
Ukraine

Criteria – Interchange of values; Traditional human settlement

The city of L'viv, founded in the late-Middle Ages, was a flourishing administrative, religious and commercial centre for several centuries. In its urban fabric and its architecture, it is an outstanding example of the fusion of the architectural and artistic traditions of Eastern Europe with those of Italy and Germany. The medieval urban topography has been preserved virtually intact; in particular, there is evidence of the different ethnic communities who lived

there – Ukrainian, Armenian, Jewish, German, Polish, Italian, Hungarian – along with many fine Baroque and later buildings. The heart of the city is the High Castle and the surrounding area, which developed in the later Middle Ages.

Only the castle mound and five churches still survive. The Seredmistia (Middle Town) preserves intact its original layout, an exceptional example of town planning in Eastern Europe at that time.

Among the notable features of the city is the Rynok Square with a tower at its centre, and around it fine houses in Renaissance, Baroque, and Empire style, many of them retaining their original medieval layout. There are fountains with figures from classical mythology at each corner of the square, dating from 1793.

World Heritage site since

• • • • • • • • • • • • 1978 • 1979 • 1980 • 1981 • 1982 • 1983 • 1984 • 1985 • 1986 • 1987 • 1988 • 1989 • 1990 • 1991 • 1992 • 1993 • 1994 • 1995 • 1996 • 1997 • **1998**

Archaeological Area and the Patriarchal Basilica of Aquileia
Italy

Criteria – Testimony to cultural tradition; Significance in human history; Heritage associated with events of universal significance

Aquileia in Friuli-Venezia Giulia, one of the largest and wealthiest cities of the Early Roman Empire, was destroyed by Attila in the mid-fifth century. Most of it still lies unexcavated beneath the fields, and as such it constitutes the greatest archaeological reserve of its kind. Excavations have revealed part of the forum and its Roman basilica, the Republican macellum, one of the sets of baths, and two luxurious residential complexes. Outside the late city walls, a cemetery with some impressive funerary monuments, the amphitheatre and the circus have been revealed. The most striking remains of the Roman city are those of the port installations, a row of warehouses and quays stretching along the bank of the river.

The dominant feature of Aquileia is the basilica. The original basilica was virtually destroyed by the Huns in AD 452. However, a striking feature dates from that time: its huge fourth-century mosaic, rediscovered 100 years ago. Its subjects include a sea scene with twelve fishermen, representing the Apostles.

Gardens and Castle at Kroměříž
Czech Republic

Criteria – Interchange of values; Significance in human history

Kroměříž stands on the site of an earlier ford across the river Morava, at the foot of the Chriby mountain range which dominates the central part of Moravia. The Gardens and Castle at Kroměříž are an exceptionally complete and well-preserved example of a princely residence and its associated landscape of the seventeenth and eighteenth centuries. The ensemble, and in particular the pleasure garden, played a significant role in the development of Baroque garden and palace design in central Europe. The pleasure garden, in the southwestern part of the historic centre of Kroměříž, is a formal garden in the Italian style, entered by an arcaded gallery which contains many statues and busts. Cast iron for the garden's elegant bridges came from the archiepiscopal foundry.

The castle is linked to the garden through spacious ground-floor rooms with grottoes opening out. Within the garden are several important architectural features, including a semi-circular colonnade in classical style built in 1846 to house sculptures from Pompei.

World Heritage site since

• • • • • • • • • • • • • • • 1978 • 1979 • 1980 • 1981 • 1982 • 1983 • 1984 • 1985 • 1986 • 1987 • 1988 • 1989 • 1990 • 1991 • 1992 • 1993 • 1994 • 1995 • 1996 • 1997 • **1998**

Ir. D.F. Woudagemaal (D.F. Wouda Steam Pumping Station)
Netherlands

Criteria - Human creative genius; Interchange of values; Significance in human history

The Dutch landscape has been created by battling against water and much of the country would be flooded if it had not been protected over the centuries by daily control and management of the sea and rivers (*waterstaat*).

For centuries, windmills were used to discharge excess water in the Netherlands. The first steam pump was built in 1825 and the construction of steam-driven pumping stations reached its peak between 1870 and 1885; very few new ones were built after 1900. There were about 700 in operation between 1900 and 1910. Extreme flooding in 1894 led to a decision to reclaim the Lauwerszee and drain the southwestern part of Friesland province. The Wouda Pumping Station at Lemmer, opened in 1920, was the key to this operation. It is the largest steam-pumping station ever built and is still in operation. It represents the high point of the contribution made by Netherlands engineers and architects in protecting their people and land against the natural forces of water.

World Heritage site since

• • • • • • • • • • • • • 1978 • 1979 • 1980 • 1981 • 1982 • 1983 • 1984 • 1985 • 1986 • 1987 • 1988 • 1989 • 1990 • 1991 • 1992 • 1993 • 1994 • 1995 • 1996 • 1997 • **1998**

Historic Centre of Urbino
Italy
Criteria – Interchange of values; Significance in human history

The great artist Raphael was born in Urbino, in a small fourteenth-century building with a charming interior courtyard. What was probably the artist's first important work, a Madonna and Child, is in the first-floor room where he was born in 1483.

During its short cultural pre-eminence in the fifteenth century, the hill-town of Urbino attracted some of the most outstanding humanist scholars and artists of the Renaissance, who created an exceptional urban setting whose influence spread far into Europe. In the mid-fifteenth century Federico II da Montefeltro, who ruled the city and duchy of Urbino, undertook a radical rebuilding campaign in the city. The walls were rebuilt according to the designs of Leonardo da Vinci. The new Ducal Palace, by Luciano Laurana and Francesco di Giorgio Martini, was inserted into the urban fabric with the minimum of disturbance, incorporating existing medieval structures. Along with the adjacent cathedral, the palace became the model for new buildings in the Renaissance style. Owing to Urbino's economic and cultural stagnation from the sixteenth century onwards, it has preserved much of its Renaissance appearance.

University and Historic Precinct of Alcalá de Henares
Spain

Criteria – Interchange of values; Significance in human history; Heritage associated with events of universal significance

The Complutense Polyglot Bible (1514–7) illustrates the type of work that began in Alcalá: a masterpiece of typography, it established the bases of modern linguistic analysis as well as the accepted structure for dictionaries. This work was supported by that of Antonio de Nebrija, author of the first European grammar of a Romance language, published in 1492.

Founded by Cardinal Jiménez de Cisneros in the early sixteenth century, Alcalá de Henares was the world's first planned university city. Cisneros took over a partly abandoned medieval town and converted it into a city whose function was solely that of a university. This included the creation of houses to lodge professors and students. The little Chapel of St Justus was rebuilt as a church and given the title 'Magistral'. More centres of learning were added progressively: there were eventually to be twenty-five Colegios Menores, while eight large monasteries were also colleges of the university. Its primary objective was to provide administrators for the Church and for the Spanish Empire, training over 12,000 students in the sixteenth century. From the mid-seventeenth century, the number of students declined, and in 1836 the university was transferred to Madrid.

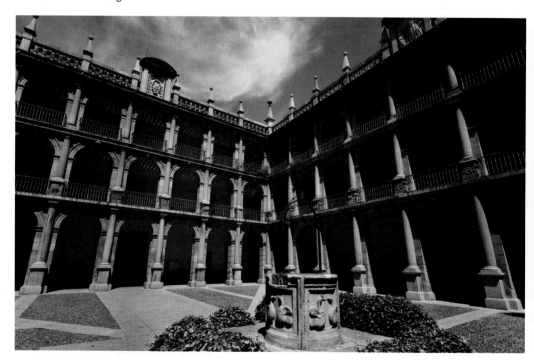

Ouadi Qadisha (the Holy Valley) and the Forest of the Cedars of God (Horsh Arz el-Rab)
Lebanon

Criteria – Testimony to cultural tradition;
Significance in human history

The Qadisha valley is one of the most important early Christian monastic settlements in the world. Its monasteries, many of which are of a great age, stand in dramatic positions in a rugged landscape. Nearby are the remains of the great forest of cedars of Lebanon, highly prized in antiquity for the construction of great religious buildings.

The deep Qadisha Valley is located at the foot of Mount al-Makmal. Its slopes form natural ramparts and their steep cliffs contain rock-cut chapels and hermitages, often surrounded by terraces made by the hermits for growing grain, grapes and olives.

◄

Forest of cedars, Bsharre.

Robben Island
South Africa

Criteria – Testimony to cultural tradition;
Heritage associated with events of universal significance

Robben Island, 7km off the coast from Cape Town, was used at various times between the seventeenth and twentieth centuries as a prison, a hospital for socially unacceptable groups and a military base.
Its buildings, particularly those of the late twentieth century such as the maximum security prison for political prisoners, witnessed the triumph of democracy and freedom over oppression and racism.

The most celebrated of Robben Island's prisoners was Nelson Mandela, who was incarcerated there for some twenty years. The last political prisoners left the island in 1991 and the prison closed down finally in 1996; since that time it has been developed as a museum.

◄

Prison buildings, Robben Island.

World Heritage site since

• • • • • • • • • • 1978 • 1979 • 1980 • 1981 • 1982 • 1983 • 1984 • 1985 • 1986 • 1987 • 1988 • 1989 • 1990 • 1991 • 1992 • 1993 • 1994 • 1995 • 1996 • 1997 • 1998 • **1999**

Heart of Neolithic Orkney
United Kingdom

Criteria – Human creative genius; Interchange of values; Testimony to cultural tradition; Significance in human history

The Neolithic monuments of Orkney bear unique or exceptional testimony to an important indigenous cultural tradition which flourished for between 500 and 1,000 years but disappeared by about 2000 BC. They are an outstanding example of a type of architectural ensemble and archaeological landscape which illustrates a significant stage of human history, during which the first large ceremonial monuments were built. They are testimony to the cultural achievements of the Neolithic peoples of northern Europe during the period 3000–2000 BC.

The monuments consist of Maes Howe, a large chambered tomb; the Stones of Stenness and the Ring of Brodgar, two ceremonial stone circles; and Skara Brae, a settlement. There are also a number of unexcavated burial, ceremonial and settlement sites. The group constitutes a major prehistoric cultural landscape which gives a graphic depiction of life in this remote archipelago in the far north of Scotland some 5,000 years ago.

Maes Howe is a Neolithic masterpiece, an exceptionally early architectural accomplishment. With its almost classical strength and simplicity it is a unique survivor from 5,000 years ago. It is an expression of genius within a group of people whose other tombs were claustrophobic chambers in smaller mounds.

Passage graves such as Maes Howe were large structures, made from stones erected to form a passage leading from the outer edge of the mound to the chamber containing the remains of the dead. The general orientation of these structures demonstrates their builders' knowledge in respect to seasonal movements.

Stenness is a unique and early expression of the ritual customs of the people who buried their dead in tombs like Maes Howe and lived in settlements like Skara Brae. The Ring of Brodgar is the finest known truly circular late-Neolithic or early Bronze Age stone ring.

Skara Brae has particularly rich surviving remains. It displays remarkable preservation of stone-built furniture and a fine range of ritual and domestic artefacts, which together demonstrate with exceptional completeness the domestic, ritual and burial practices of a now-vanished culture.

When it was built 5,000 years ago, the settlement of Skara Brae was further from the sea than it is now. The settlement was abandoned some 600 years after its construction and most of the houses were emptied of their contents.

In the mid-nineteenth century the remains of Skara Brae were revealed when the overlying sand dune was swept away by a violent storm. Some clearance work took place in 1913, and in 1924 a protective breakwater was built.

Part of the Ring of Brodgar in Orkney at sunset.

World Heritage site since

• • • • • • • • • • 1978 • 1979 • 1980 • 1981 • 1982 • 1983 • 1984 • 1985 • 1986 • 1987 • 1988 • 1989 • 1990 • 1991 • 1992 • 1993 • 1994 • 1995 • 1996 • 1997 • 1998 • **1999**

Ibiza, Biodiversity and Culture

Spain

Criteria – Interchange of values; Testimony to cultural tradition; Significance in human history; Significant ecological and biological processes; Significant natural habitat for biodiversity

Ibiza provides an excellent example of the interaction between marine and coastal ecosystems. The dense prairies of oceanic Posidonia (seagrass), an important endemic species found only in the Mediterranean basin, contain and support a diversity of marine life. The island also preserves considerable evidence of its long history. The archaeological sites at Sa Caleta settlement and Puig des Molins necropolis testify to the important role played by the island in the Mediterranean economy, particularly during the Phoenician-Carthaginian period. In 1235, Ibiza town was dominated by Christians, who built the Catalan castle, visible from the inside of the present building, the medieval fortifications, and the Gothic cathedral. The fortified Upper Town, Alta Vila, is an outstanding example of Renaissance military architecture; it had a profound influence on the development of fortifications in the Spanish settlements of the New World.

The Phoenician-Punic cemetery of Puig des Molins is situated in the southwest of the Upper Town. At the beginning of the sixth century BC, the ashes of the dead were placed in a natural grotto after cremation. Later, shafts and funerary chambers were dug, and sarcophagi were lowered through shafts into family sepulchres.

The cathedral and Old Town of Ibiza .
▼

World Heritage site since

• • • • • • • • • • 1978 • 1979 • 1980 • 1981 • 1982 • 1983 • 1984 • 1985 • 1986 • 1987 • 1988 • 1989 • 1990 • 1991 • 1992 • 1993 • 1994 • 1995 • 1996 • 1997 • 1998 • **1999**

State Historical and Cultural Park 'Ancient Merv'
Turkmenistan

Criteria – Interchange of values; Testimony to cultural tradition

The fifteenth century walls and moat of the city and citadel are of exceptional interest in that they represent the remarkable continuous record of the evolution of military architecture from the fifth century BC to the fifteenth–sixteenth centuries AD.

The cities of the vast Merv oasis exerted considerable influence over the cultures of Central Asia and Iran for four millennia. The oasis formed part of the Great Seljuk Empire, which had its capital here. This was one of the principal cities of its time, and its famous libraries attracted scholars from all over the Islamic world. It also had a pronounced influence in the development of architecture, architectural decoration, science and culture. Merv is the oldest and best-preserved of the oasis-cities along the Silk Route in Central Asia. A number of monuments are still visible, particularly from the last two millennia. These include the central Beni Makhan mosque and its cistern, the Buddhist stupa and monastery, and the 'Oval Building' in the northwest quarter.

Great Kyz Kala, Merv.
▼

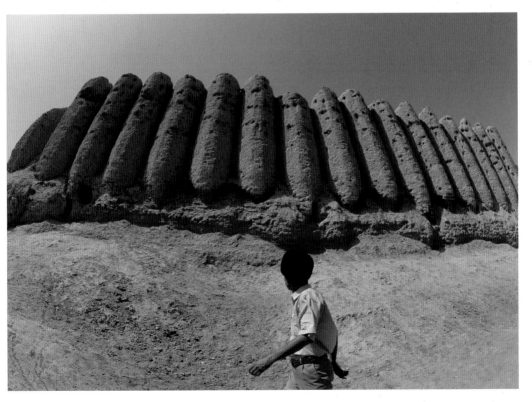

Archaeological Sites of Mycenae and Tiryns

Greece

Criteria – Human creative genius; Interchange of values; Testimony to cultural tradition; Significance in human history; Heritage associated with events of universal significance

The archaeological sites of Mycenae and Tiryns are the imposing ruins of the two greatest cities of the Mycenaean civilization, which dominated the eastern Mediterranean world from the fifteenth to the twelfth centuries BC and played a vital role in the development of classical Greek culture. These two cities are indissolubly linked to the Homeric epics, the Iliad and the Odyssey, which have influenced European art and literature for more than three millennia. The Palace at Mycenae was constructed on the summit of the hill and surrounded by massive cyclopean walls in three stages (c. 1350, 1250 and 1225 BC respectively). A series of tholos (beehive-shaped tombs) were also built on the slopes of the hill: the Tomb of Aegisthos (c. 1500 BC), the Lion Tholos Tomb (c. 1350 BC), the Tomb of Clytemnestra (c. 1220 BC).

As at Mycenae, the earliest human occupation known at Tiryns is from the Neolithic period. The oldest architectural remains, on the Upper Citadel, are from the early Bronze Age (c. 3000 BC). A new fortified palace complex was constructed in the fourteenth century BC, the defences were extended in the early thirteenth century BC, and the Lower Citadel was also fortified.

Lion Gate at Mycenae.
▼

World Heritage site since

• • • • • • • • • 1978 • 1979 • 1980 • 1981 • 1982 • 1983 • 1984 • 1985 • 1986 • 1987 • 1988 • 1989 • 1990 • 1991 • 1992 • 1993 • 1994 • 1995 • 1996 • 1997 • 1998 • **1999**

Belfries of Belgium and France
Belgium and France

Criteria – Interchange of values; Significance in human history

Belfries are outstanding representatives of civic and public architecture in Europe. Twenty-three belfries in the north of France and the belfry of Gembloux in Belgium were inscribed on the World Heritage list as a group, an extension to the thirty-two Belgian belfries inscribed in 1999 as 'Belfries of Flanders and Wallonia'. Built between the eleventh and seventeenth centuries, invariably in an urban setting, the belfries are potent symbols of the transition from feudalism to mercantile urban society. While Italian, German and English towns mainly chose to build town halls, in part of northwestern Europe greater emphasis was placed on building belfries. Compared with the keep symbol of the seigneurs and the bell-tower symbol of the Church, the belfry symbolizes the power of the aldermen. Over the centuries, they came to represent the influence and wealth of the towns.

Most of the belfries cover the periods of the fourteenth–fifteenth and sixteenth–seventeenth centuries, thereby illustrating the transition in style from Norman Gothic to later Gothic, which then mingles with Renaissance and Baroque forms. In the fourteenth and fifteenth centuries, the belfries abandoned the model of the keep in favour of finer, taller towers, such as those of Dendermonde, Lier and Aalst.

iSimangaliso Wetland Park
South Africa

Criteria – Natural phenomena or beauty; Significant ecological and biological processes; Significant natural habitat for biodiversity

The ongoing fluvial, marine and aeolian processes in the site have produced a variety of landforms, including coral reefs, long sandy beaches, coastal dunes, lake systems, swamps, and extensive reed and papyrus wetlands. The interplay of the park's environmental heterogeneity with major floods and coastal storms, and a transitional geographic location between subtropical and tropical Africa, has resulted in exceptional species diversity and ongoing speciation. The mosaic of landforms and habitat types creates superlative scenic vistas. The site contains critical habitat for a range of species from Africa's marine, wetland and savanna environments.

iSimangaliso Wetland Park (previously known as Greater St Lucia Wetland Park) is the largest and most diverse estuarine system in Africa. It is the only area with coral reefs and has a high number of threatened species, including rhino, hippo and leopard.

World Heritage site since

• • • • • • • • • • • 1978 • 1979 • 1980 • 1981 • 1982 • 1983 • 1984 • 1985 • 1986 • 1987 • 1988 • 1989 • 1990 • 1991 • 1992 • 1993 • 1994 • 1995 • 1996 • 1997 • 1998 • **1999**

Mountain Railways of India
India

Criteria – Interchange of values; Significance in human history

This site includes three railways, all still fully operational. The Darjeeling Himalayan Railway, opened in 1881, was the first example of a hill passenger railway, its design applying bold and ingenious engineering solutions to the problem of establishing an effective rail link across mountainous terrain. The construction of the Nilgiri Mountain Railway, a 46-km-long metre-gauge single-track railway in Tamil Nadu State was first proposed in 1854, but due to the difficulty of the mountainous location the work only started in 1891 and was completed in 1908. This railway, scaling

an elevation of 326 m to 2,203 m, represented the latest technology of the time. The Kalka Shimla Railway, a 96-km-long, single track working rail link was built in the mid-19th century to provide a service to the highland town of Shimla.

The three Mountain Railways of India are outstanding examples of the interchange of values on developments in technology. The Darjeeling Himalayan Railway helped the area become one of the main tea-growing areas in India and is still the most outstanding example of a hill passenger railway.

◄

The 'Himalayan Bird' or 'Toy Train' on the Darjeeling Himalayan Railway at Dali Monastery.

Historic Centre of Santa Ana de los Ríos de Cuenca
Ecuador

Criteria – Interchange of values; Significance in human history; Traditional human settlement

Santa Ana de los Ríos de Cuenca is set in a valley surrounded by the Andean mountains in the south of Ecuador. This inland colonial town (entroterra), now the country's third city, was founded in 1557 on the rigorous planning guidelines issued thirty years earlier by the Spanish king Charles V. Cuenca still observes the formal orthogonal town plan that it has respected for 400 years.

One of the region's agricultural and administrative centres, it has been a melting pot for local and immigrant populations. Cuenca's architecture, much of which dates from the eighteenth century, was 'modernized' in the economic prosperity of the nineteenth century as the city became a major exporter of quinine, straw hats and other products.

Despite the growth that came with its prosperity, the Andean mountain chains have allowed Cuenca to maintain close contact with its natural environment. The Urban Development Plan of 1982 also helped safeguard the image of the town.

World Heritage site since

• • • • • • • • • • 1978 • 1979 • 1980 • 1981 • 1982 • 1983 • 1984 • 1985 • 1986 • 1987 • 1988 • 1989 • 1990 • 1991 • 1992 • 1993 • 1994 • 1995 • 1996 • 1997 • 1998 • **1999**

Historic Fortified Town of Campeche
Mexico

Criteria – Interchange of values; Significance in human history

Campeche is a typical example of a harbour town from the Spanish colonial period in the New World. The historic centre has kept its outer walls and system of fortifications, designed to defend this Caribbean port against attacks from the sea. A chequerboard plan was chosen for the town, with a Plaza Mayor facing the sea and surrounded by government and religious edifices. The area of historic monuments is spread over 1.8 km², including 0.5 km² surrounded by walls, with the town stretching out on each side, following the configuration of the coast. The protected group of buildings consists of two subgroups: one with a high density of buildings of great heritage value, and another, which is not so dense or valuable but which forms a transitional and protective zone.

Among almost 1,000 buildings of historic value are the Cathedral of the Immaculate Conception, several churches, the Toro theatre and the municipal archives. The system of fortifications includes the redoubts of San José and San Miguel, and the batteries of San Lucas, San Matiás and San Luís.

A colourful street in Campeche. ▼

Museumsinsel (Museum Island), Berlin
Germany
Criteria – Interchange of values; Significance in human history

The museum as a social phenomenon owes its origins to the Age of Enlightenment in the eighteenth century. The five museums, built between 1824 and 1930 on the Museumsinsel, a small island in the river Spree, are the realization of a visionary project and show the evolution of approaches to museum design. The project began when the Altes Museum was built to the designs of Karl Friedrich Schinkel in 1824–8. A plan to develop the part of the island behind this museum was drawn up by the court architect, Friedrich August Stüler in 1841, followed by the building of the Neues Museum (1843–7). In 1866 the Nationalgalerie was built and in 1897–1904 the Kaiser-Friedrich-Museum (now the Bodemuseum). Stüler's plan was completed in 1909–30 with the construction of Alfred Messel's Pergamonmuseum.

Bodemuseum
▼

The three-winged Pergamonmuseum was built to exhibit the greatly expanded collections of antiquities resulting from German excavations at Pergamon and other Greek sites in Asia Minor as well as those from Mesopotamia formerly housed in the Vorderasiatisches Museum. It rises directly from the river Spree, like the Bodemuseum, with which it is harmonized in scale and proportions.

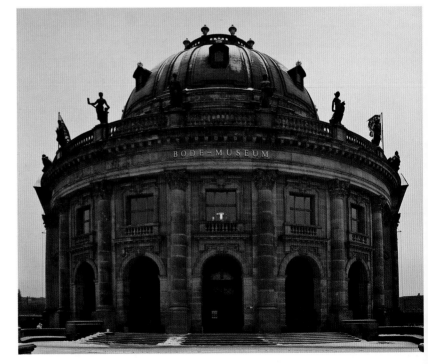

World Heritage site since

• • • • • • • • • • • • 1978 • 1979 • 1980 • 1981 • 1982 • 1983 • 1984 • 1985 • 1986 • 1987 • 1988 • 1989 • 1990 • 1991 • 1992 • 1993 • 1994 • 1995 • 1996 • 1997 • 1998 • **1999**

My Son Sanctuary
Vietnam

Criteria – Interchange of values; Testimony to cultural tradition

Between the fourth and thirteenth centuries a unique culture which owed its spiritual origins to Indian Hinduism developed on the coast of contemporary Vietnam. This is graphically illustrated by the remains of a series of impressive tower-temples located in a dramatic site that was the religious and political capital of the Champa Kingdom for most of its existence.

The ruins of My Son vividly illustrate the importance of the Champa Kingdom to the political and cultural history of Southeast Asia. A unique expression of cultural interchange, it marks the introduction of the Hindu architecture of the Indian subcontinent into the area.

◄
My Son sanctuary at Tra Kieu.

Discovery Coast Atlantic Forest Reserves
Brazil

Criteria – Significant ecological and biological processes; Significant natural habitat for biodiversity

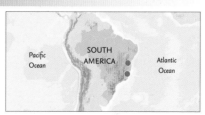

The Discovery Coast Atlantic Forest Reserves, in the states of Bahia and Espírito Santo, consist of eight separate protected areas containing 1,120 km² of Atlantic forest and associated shrub (restingas). The rainforests of Brazil's Atlantic coast are the world's richest in terms of biodiversity. The site contains a distinct range of species with a high level of endemism and reveals a pattern of evolution that is not only of great scientific interest but is also of importance for conservation.

The rainforests of southern Bahia and northern Espirito Santo have the world's highest density of tree species and perhaps the largest number of trees of Pau Brasil (brazil wood) left on Earth.

World Heritage site since

• • • • • • • • • • 1978 • 1979 • 1980 • 1981 • 1982 • 1983 • 1984 • 1985 • 1986 • 1987 • 1988 • 1989 • 1990 • 1991 • 1992 • 1993 • 1994 • 1995 • 1996 • 1997 • 1998 • **1999**

Droogmakerij de Beemster (Beemster Polder)
Netherlands

Criteria – Human creative genius; Interchange of values; Significance in human history

The innovative landscape of the Beemster Polder had a profound impact on reclamation projects in Europe and beyond. Its creation advanced the interrelationship between humankind and water at a crucial period of social and economic expansion.

The Netherlands owes its existence to reclaimed land like the Beemster Polder. If no dykes had been constructed and if there were no drainage of excess water, 65 per cent of the modern country would be under water. The seventeenth-century Beemster Polder is the oldest area of reclaimed land in the country and one of the most remarkable. It has preserved intact its well-ordered landscape of fields, roads, canals, dykes and settlements, laid out in accordance with classical planning principles. Draining large areas like Beemster was made possible by the dramatic improvement in pumping technology using windmills driving waterwheels. Pumps were later converted to steam power, then diesel in the twentieth century. Now drainage is carried out by a fully automated electric pumping station.

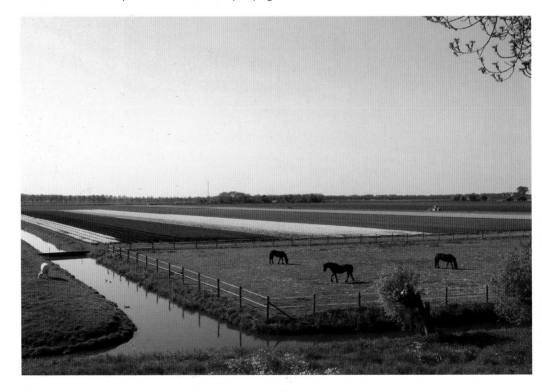

World Heritage site since

• • • • • • • • • • • 1978 • 1979 • 1980 • 1981 • 1982 • 1983 • 1984 • 1985 • 1986 • 1987 • 1988 • 1989 • 1990 • 1991 • 1992 • 1993 • 1994 • 1995 • 1996 • 1997 • 1998 • **1999**

Wooden Churches of Maramureș
Romania

Criteria – Significance in human history

EUROPE

Black Sea

Mediterranean
Sea

The churches of the Maramureș region are outstanding examples of vernacular religious wooden architecture resulting from the interchange of Orthodox religious traditions with Gothic influence. The eight churches of Maramureș are based on traditional timber architecture and stand on bases of stone blocks and pebble fillings. These narrow, high, timber constructions, characterized by their tall, slim clock towers at the western end of the building, show a high level of artistic maturity and craft skills. They are: the Church of the Presentation of the Virgin to the Temple (Bârsana); the Church of Saint Nicholas (Budești); the Church of the Pious Paraskeva (Desești); the Church of the Nativity of the Mother of God (Ieud-Deal); the Church of the Holy Archangels (Plopiș); the Church of the Holy Paraskeva (Poienile Izei); the Church of the Holy Archangels (Rogoz); and the Church of the Holy Archangels (Șurdești).

The Church of the Holy Paraskeva in Poienile Izei is one of the oldest of the wooden churches of Maramureș (1604), and reveals two phases in the development of such buildings. The first can be seen in the lower part of the walls, with a sanctuary based on a square plan. In the eighteenth century the walls were raised and the interior was decorated with paintings.

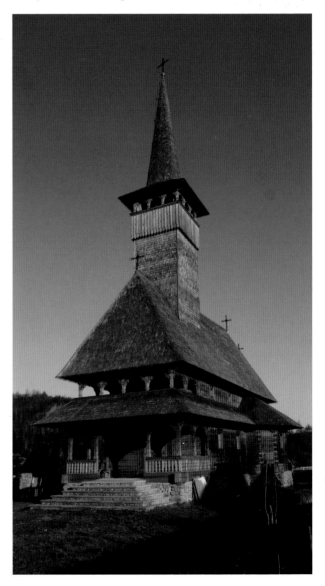

Typical wooden church of the Maramureș region. ▶

World Heritage site since

· · · · · · · · · · · 1978 · 1979 · 1980 · 1981 · 1982 · 1983 · 1984 · 1985 · 1986 · 1987 · 1988 · 1989 · 1990 · 1991 · 1992 · 1993 · 1994 · 1995 · 1996 · 1997 · 1998 · **1999**

Historic Town of Vigan
Philippines

Criteria – Interchange of values; Significance in
human history

Vigan's layout conforms closely to the traditional Spanish chequerboard plan. What makes it unique amongst colonial towns, however, is the blending of the Latin tradition with strong Chinese, Ilocano and Filipino influences.

The town is located in the delta of the Abra River, off the coastal plain of the China Sea, close to the north-east tip of the island of Luzon. The present-day municipality is divided into nine urban districts and thirty rural villages. Almost half the total area is still in use for agriculture. The Historic Core Zone is defined on two sides by the Govantes and Mestizo rivers.

Established in the sixteenth century, Vigan is the best-preserved example of a planned Spanish colonial town in Asia. Its architecture reflects the coming together of cultural elements from elsewhere in the Philippines, from China and from Europe, resulting in a culture and townscape that have no parallel anywhere in east and southeast Asia.

The Mestizo River was central to the development of the town in the sixteenth–nineteenth centuries: large sea-going vessels could berth in the delta and small craft communicated with the interior. It is no longer navigable owing to silting, and so the town is no longer on an island. As the major commercial centre for the region, Vigan traded directly with China. It also supplied goods for shipment to Mexico, and thence onwards to Europe. This trade resulted in constant exchanges of peoples and cultures between the Ilocanos, Filipinos, Chinese, Spanish, and (in the twentieth century) North Americans.

◄

St Paul's
Metropolitan
Cathedral, Vigan.

World Heritage site since

• • • • • • • • • • 1978 • 1979 • 1980 • 1981 • 1982 • 1983 • 1984 • 1985 • 1986 • 1987 • 1988 • 1989 • 1990 • 1991 • 1992 • 1993 • 1994 • 1995 • 1996 • 1997 • 1998 • **1999**

Desembarco del Granma National Park
Cuba

Criteria – Natural phenomena or beauty; Major stages of Earth's history

The park is situated in and around Cabo Cruz and includes the world's largest and best-preserved systems of marine terraces (both above and below sea level) on calcareous rock, as well as some of the most pristine and impressive coastal cliffs bordering the western Atlantic. It contains examples of most ecosystems present in the region, including the coral reef of Cabo Cruz, seagrass beds and mangroves and old submarine terraces up to 30 m deep. The area is one of the most important centres of plant diversity and endemism in Cuba. It has a remarkable archaeological value as it was the original settlement of groups that belonged to the Taina Culture, to which the local population has strong genetic and spiritual links. Many events related to the Cuban Revolution also took place in the area of Cabo Cruz.

A total of 512 species of plants exist in the site, of which around 60 per cent are endemic. There are also 13 species of mammal, 110 of birds, 44 of reptiles and 7 of amphibians. Several species are of conservation concern including the Caribbean manatee and blue-headed quail-dove.

Hortobágy National Park – the Puszta
Hungary

Criteria – Significance in human history; Traditional human settlement

The cultural landscape of the Hortobágy Puszta consists of a vast area of plains and wetlands in eastern Hungary. Traditional forms of land use, such as the grazing of domestic animals, have been present in this pastoral society for more than two millennia. The oldest surviving structures on the plains are the thirteenth-century stone bridges (including Nine Arch Bridge at Hortobágy, the longest stone bridge in Hungary), and the csárdas which were provincial inns built in the eighteenth and nineteenth centuries to provide food and lodging for travellers. The typical *csárda* consists of two buildings facing one another, both single-storeyed and thatched or, occasionally, roofed with shingles or tiles. These contained a tavern, guest rooms and provision for horses and carriages.

The Hortobágy National Park, the first national park in Hungary, preserves intact and visible the evidence of its traditional use over more than 2,000 years, representing the harmonious interaction between human beings and nature.

World Heritage site since

• • • • • • • • • • • 1978 • 1979 • 1980 • 1981 • 1982 • 1983 • 1984 • 1985 • 1986 • 1987 • 1988 • 1989 • 1990 • 1991 • 1992 • 1993 • 1994 • 1995 • 1996 • 1997 • 1998 • **1999**

Dazu Rock Carvings
China

Criteria – Human creative genius; Interchange of values; Testimony to cultural tradition

The Dazu carvings represent the pinnacle of Chinese rock art for their high aesthetic quality and their diversity of style and subject matter. Carvings in the steep hillsides of Dazu County date back to AD 650, in the early years of the Tang dynasty, but the main period began in the late ninth century continuing for over 400 years. There are seventy-five protected sites containing some 50,000 statues. Tantric

Buddhism from India and the Chinese Taoist and Confucian beliefs came together here to create a highly original and influential manifestation of spiritual harmony. They are remarkable for their subject matter, both secular and religious, and the light that they shed on everyday life in China during this period.

In one area, at Beishan, there are 264 niches with statues, one intaglio painting, and eight inscribed pillars. In all there are over 10,000 carvings, more than half of which represent Tantric Buddhism.

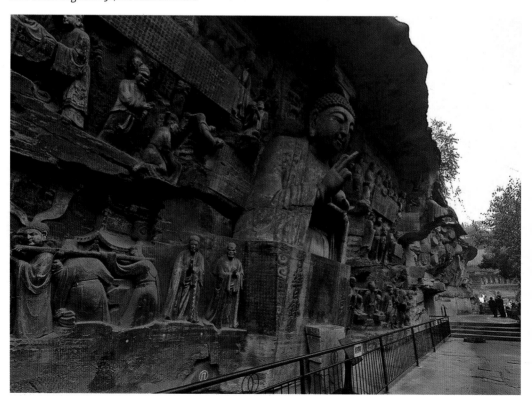

World Heritage site since

• • • • • • • • • • • 1978 • 1979 • 1980 • 1981 • 1982 • 1983 • 1984 • 1985 • 1986 • 1987 • 1988 • 1989 • 1990 • 1991 • 1992 • 1993 • 1994 • 1995 • 1996 • 1997 • 1998 • **1999**

City of Graz – Historic Centre and Schloss Eggenberg
Austria
Criteria – Interchange of values; Significance in human history

The historic centre of the city of Graz reflects artistic and architectural movements originating from the Germanic region, the Balkans, and the Mediterranean, for which it served as a crossroads for centuries. Among the hundreds of buildings of great historic and architectural interest are the Mausoleum of Emperor Ferdinand II, started in 1614, whose façade reflects the transition from the Renaissance to the Baroque style, and the Seminary (former Jesuit College), started in 1572, which illustrates the severe Renaissance architecture adopted by the order when it was first established in the German province. Schloss Eggenberg, about 3 km west, was built shortly after 1625. It is exceptionally well preserved bearing witness, through its architecture and external decoration, to the influence of the late Italian Renaissance and the Baroque period.

Frederick III built the present cathedral in late-Gothic style (1438–64) alongside a Romanesque church dedicated to St Aegidius. Following the transfer of the bishopric from Seckau to Graz, the church of St Aegidius, used for 200 years as a centre for the Counter-Reformation, became the cathedral of the new diocese in 1786.

World Heritage site since

• • • • • • • • • • • 1978 • 1979 • 1980 • 1981 • 1982 • 1983 • 1984 • 1985 • 1986 • 1987 • 1988 • 1989 • 1990 • 1991 • 1992 • 1993 • 1994 • 1995 • 1996 • 1997 • 1998 • **1999**

Hoi An Ancient Town
Vietnam

Criteria – Interchange of values; Traditional
human settlement

Hoi An Ancient Town is an exceptionally
well-preserved example of a southeast Asian
trading port dating from the fifteenth to the
nineteenth centuries. Its buildings and
street plan reflect the influences, both
indigenous and foreign, that combined to
produce this unique site. Most of the
buildings are in the traditional architectural
style of the nineteenth and twentieth
centuries. They are aligned along narrow

lanes and include many religious buildings,
such as pagodas, temples, meeting houses,
etc. The rise of other ports on the coast of
Vietnam, in particular Da Nang, and the
silting of Hoi An's harbour, led to its final
eclipse. As a result of this economic
stagnation, it has preserved its early
appearance in a remarkably intact state, the
only town in the country to have done so.

The pagodas are almost
all from the nineteenth
century, although
inscriptions show them
to have been founded
in the seventeenth and
eighteenth centuries.
They conform to a
square layout and
decoration is largely
confined to the
elaborate roofs. In the
case of the larger
examples, they
constituted nuclei of
associated buildings
with religious and
secular functions.

The harbour of Hoi An. ▼

World Heritage site since

• • • • • • • • • • 1978 • 1979 • 1980 • 1981 • 1982 • 1983 • 1984 • 1985 • 1986 • 1987 • 1988 • 1989 • 1990 • 1991 • 1992 • 1993 • 1994 • 1995 • 1996 • 1997 • 1998 • **1999**

Sukur Cultural Landscape
Nigeria

Criteria – Testimony to cultural tradition; Traditional human settlement; Heritage associated with events of universal significance

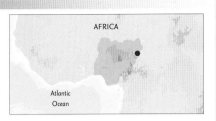

The Sukur Cultural Landscape, with the Palace of the Hidi Chief on a hill dominating the villages below, is a remarkably intact expression of a society and its spiritual and material culture. Situated on a plateau in northeastern Nigeria, the area has been occupied for centuries. There are a number of shrines and altars, particularly in and around the Hidi Palace. Complex social relationships can also be observed in the disposition of the cemeteries located in the surrounding hills, while the remains of many disused iron-smelting furnaces illustrate an elaborate economic pattern of production and distribution. Of considerable social and economic importance are the subterranean wells, surmounted by conical stone structures and surrounded by an enclosure wall.

The landscape of the Sukur plateau is characterized by extensive terracing, of a type known elsewhere in Nigeria. While primarily intended to provide level areas for agriculture, the terraces are also invested with a spiritual significance, as shown by the sacred trees, entrances and ritual sites within them.

San Cristóbal de La Laguna
Spain

Criteria – Interchange of values; Significance in human history

San Cristóbal de La Laguna, in the Canary Islands, has two nuclei: the original, unplanned Upper Town; and the Lower Town, the first ideal unfortified 'city-territory'. In 1502, a regular town plan based on Leonardo da Vinci's model for Imola was drawn up by the Captain General for the area. Wide major streets linked the public open spaces and formed the grid on which smaller streets were superimposed. The resulting Lower Town expanded rapidly, attracting the island's ruling classes, and monastic communities began building. A piped water supply was installed at the expense of the Town Council in 1521, and the first public buildings were constructed. A number of fine churches and public and private buildings dating from the sixteenth to the eighteenth centuries still exist.

San Cristóbal de La Laguna was founded in 1497 and was the first non-fortified Spanish colonial town; as such, its layout was the model for many colonial towns in the Americas.

Litomyšl Castle
Czech Republic

Criteria – Interchange of values; Significance in human history

Litomyšl Castle is an outstanding and immaculately preserved example of the arcade castle, a type of building first developed in Italy and modified in the Czech lands to create an evolved form of special architectural quality. It illustrates in an exceptional way the aristocratic residences of central Europe in the Renaissance and their subsequent development under the influence of new artistic movements. Its design and decoration are particularly fine, including the later High Baroque features added in the eighteenth century. It preserves intact the range of ancillary buildings associated with an aristocratic residence of this type, of which the most interesting is the Brewery. Originally constructed as a counterpart to the castle, it stylishly blends elements of High Baroque and neoclassicism.

One of the castle's most striking interior features is its late-eighteenth-century neoclassical theatre. Constructed entirely of wood, it seats 150 in nine loggias and a lower floor. Its original painted decoration, stage decorations and stage machinery have survived intact.

Historic Centre of the Town of Diamantina
Brazil

Criteria – Interchange of values; Significance in human history

Diamantina, a colonial village set like a jewel in a necklace of inhospitable rocky mountains, recalls the exploits of diamond prospectors in the eighteenth century and testifies to the triumph of human cultural and artistic endeavour over the environment. Inspired by the model of a Portuguese medieval town, the colonisers transposed some of the architectural features of their home country to their adopted land while still respecting the continuity of the first settlement.

The architecture is of Baroque inspiration, like most other mining villages in Brazil. Its streets are paved in a uniquely picturesque style and the *casario*, a regular alignment of eighteenth- and nineteenth-century semi-detached houses, has brightly coloured façades on a white ground, displaying some affiliations with the Portuguese Mannerist architecture.

The town has several architectural curiosities, including the Old Market Hall constructed in 1835 and recently restored; the Passadiço, a covered footbridge in blue and white wood; and the *chafariz* of the Rua Direita, near the cathedral, a sculpted fountain which guarantees that whoever drinks from it will return to Diamantina.

Wartburg Castle
Germany

Criteria – Testimony to cultural tradition; Heritage associated with events of universal significance

Wartburg Castle is an outstanding monument of the feudal period in central Europe. It is rich in cultural associations, most notably its role as the place of exile of Martin Luther, who composed his German translation of the New Testament here. In the midst of the forest, the castle occupies a rocky spur that looks down over the city of Eisenach. The castle is reached from the northern end of the spur, by a tower with a drawbridge, followed by a number of outbuildings which form an outer courtyard. Next follows the lower courtyard, the main features of which are the keep and the palace, onto which the Knights' Baths back. The South Tower marks the farther end of the spur. The centre of the lower courtyard is occupied by a cistern. The outworks are now partially buried or in ruins.

After the Napoleonic wars, a national sentiment emerged which revelled in the image of ancient Germany as symbolized by Wartburg Castle. On the initiative of the Grand Duke of Saxony, the site was completely renovated: the palace was rebuilt from its ruins, the curtain wall restored and the remainder of the buildings reconstructed.

World Heritage site since

• • • • • • • • • • 1978 • 1979 • 1980 • 1981 • 1982 • 1983 • 1984 • 1985 • 1986 • 1987 • 1988 • 1989 • 1990 • 1991 • 1992 • 1993 • 1994 • 1995 • 1996 • 1997 • 1998 • **1999**

Península Valdés
Argentina

Criteria – Significant natural habitat for biodiversity

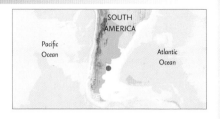

Península Valdés, in the Argentinean province of Chubut, is a 4,000 km² promontory, protruding 100 km eastwards into the South Atlantic. The 400-km shoreline includes a series of gulfs, rocky cliffs, shallow bays and lagoons with extensive mudflats, sandy and pebble beaches, coastal sand dunes and small islands. The Ameghino Isthmus, which links the peninsula to the rest of South America, has an average width of only 11 km; with the Golfo San José to the north and the Golfo Nuevo to the south, the area has an island quality.

It is a site of global significance for the conservation of marine mammals and the shores and waters around the peninsula are an important habitat for them. An important breeding population of southern right whales uses the protected waters for mating and calving and every year over 1,500 whales visit the peninsula. The stable population of orcas in this area have developed a unique hunting strategy to adapt to local coastal conditions. The southern elephant seal has its most northerly colony here. It reaches peak numbers of over 1,000 individuals and this is the only colony in the world reported to be on the increase. The southern sea lion also breeds here in large numbers. In addition, thirty-three other species of

marine mammals are found in the area.

Terrestrial mammals are abundant, with thirty-three species being reported. Large herds of guanaco can be seen throughout the peninsula. Other species include the Patagonian mara, also known as the Patagonian hare, and the red fox, both of which are endangered in other parts of the country.

Península Valdés has a high diversity of birds. There are 181 species present, of which sixty-six are migratory, including the Antarctic pigeon which is considered vulnerable. The peninsula's intertidal mudflats and coastal lagoons are important staging sites for migratory shorebirds. Most numerous is the Magellanic penguin with almost 40,000 active nests distributed among five different colonies.

The local population of orcas at Península Valdés has used the beaches of Valdés to develop a unique and spectacular form of shallow-water hunting. The orcas swim quickly towards the shore, chasing sea lions or young elephant seals into the surf where they then grab the prey in their jaws. The orcas often beach themselves in the process. Adult orcas have been seen teaching their young how to hunt in this way, sometimes repeatedly pulling their prey off the beach for youngsters to catch.

The tail (fluke) of a submerging right whale just off the coast of Península Valdés.

World Heritage site since

• • • • • • • • • • • • 1978 • 1979 • 1980 • 1981 • 1982 • 1983 • 1984 • 1985 • 1986 • 1987 • 1988 • 1989 • 1990 • 1991 • 1992 • 1993 • 1994 • 1995 • 1996 • 1997 • 1998 • **1999**

Historic Centre of Sighişoara
Romania

Criteria – Testimony to cultural tradition;
Traditional human settlement

Founded in the thirteenth century by German craftsmen and merchants, Sighişoara is a fine example of a small, fortified medieval town which played an important strategic and commercial role on the fringes of central Europe. Its historic centre is composed of the fortified citadel on a steeply sloping plateau and the lower town with its woody slopes below. Apart from nineteenth-century settlements, it has kept its original medieval urban character and its network of narrow streets. Many of the houses still have a barrel-vaulted basement, workshops on the ground floor, and the living rooms on the upper floors. The citadel plateau is enclosed by a wall, and nine of the original fourteen towers still stand. The imposing Clock Tower dominates the three squares of the historic centre and protects the stairway connecting the upper town and the lower town.

Notable among the monuments in the historic centre of Sighişoara is the Church of St Nicholas, typical of the Gothic architecture of Transylvania. Perched on the hill, it can be reached by a staircase of 175 steps. The decorative sculpture on the façade reflects Central European influences.

Fossil Hominid Sites of South Africa
South Africa

Criteria – Testimony to cultural tradition; Heritage associated with events of universal significance

The Sterkfontein area contains a large and scientifically significant group of sites that throw light on the earliest ancestors of humanity. They constitute a vast reserve of scientific data linked to the history of the most ancient periods of humanity.

The Taung Skull Fossil Site, part of the extension to the site inscribed in 1999, is the place where, in 1924, the celebrated Taung Skull – a specimen of the species Australopithecus africanus – was found. Makapan Valley, also in the site, features in its many archaeological caves traces of human occupation and evolution dating back some 3.3 million years. The area contains essential elements that define the origin and evolution of humanity. Fossils found there have enabled the identification of several specimens of early hominids, more particularly of Paranthropus, dating back between 4.5 million and 2.5 million years, as well as evidence of the domestication of fire 1.8 million to 1 million years ago.

Viñales Valley
Cuba

Criteria – Significance in human history

Viñales Valley supplies tobacco for the manufacture of the country's famous cigars. Traditional production methods, including animal traction, are still used after recent experiments showed that mechanical methods lower the quality of the tobacco.

The Viñales Valley is encircled by mountains and its landscape is interspersed with dramatic rocky outcrops. Traditional techniques are still in use for agricultural production, particularly of tobacco. The quality of this cultural landscape is enhanced by the vernacular architecture of its farms and villages, where a rich multi-ethnic society survives, illustrating the cultural development of the islands of the Caribbean, and of Cuba.

Kalwaria Zebrzydowska: the Mannerist Architectural and Park Landscape Complex and Pilgrimage Park
Poland

Criteria – Interchange of values; Significance in human history

The layout of Kalwaria Zebrzydowska was based on the landscape of Jerusalem at the time of Christ. This used a system of measurement that allowed the urban features of Jerusalem to be reproduced symbolically on the natural landscape.

Kalwaria Zebrzydowska is a breathtaking cultural landscape of great spiritual significance. The Counter-Reformation in the late-sixteenth century led to a flowering in the creation of calvaries in Europe. Mikolaj Zebrzydowski, the Voivod of Cracow, had already completed a private hermitage on this site when he was persuaded by Bernardine (Cistercian) monks to enlarge his original design. Building work on the new calvary started in 1600, eventually covering an extensive landscape complex with many chapels, linked in form and theme to those in Jerusalem. It was conceived as being for the use not only of the local inhabitants but also of believers from elsewhere in Poland and neighbouring countries. Remarkably, its layout has remained virtually unchanged since its conception and it remains to this day a sacred place of pilgrimage.

The Monastery of Kalwaria Zebrzydowska.
▼

World Heritage site since

• • • • • • • • • 1978 • 1979 • 1980 • 1981 • 1982 • 1983 • 1984 • 1985 • 1986 • 1987 • 1988 • 1989 • 1990 • 1991 • 1992 • 1993 • 1994 • 1995 • 1996 • 1997 • 1998 • **1999**

Villa Adriana (Tivoli)
Italy

Criteria – Human creative genius; Interchange of values; Testimony to cultural tradition

The Golden Square is one of the most impressive buildings in the complex: the vast peristyle is surrounded by a two-aisled portico with alternate columns in cipollino marble and Egyptian granite.

The Villa Adriana at Tivoli, near Rome, is a masterpiece that uniquely brings together the highest expressions of the material cultures of the ancient Mediterranean world. Its complex of classical buildings was created in the second century AD by the Roman emperor Hadrian. It was a symbol of a power that was gradually becoming absolute and which distanced itself from the capital. After Hadrian's death in 138,

his successors preferred Rome as their permanent residence, but the villa continued to be enlarged and further embellished. Study of the villa's monuments played a crucial role in the rediscovery of the elements of classical architecture by the architects of the Renaissance and the Baroque period. It also profoundly influenced many nineteenth- and twentieth-century architects and designers.

The Maritime Theatre at Villa Adriana.
▼

World Heritage site since

• • • • • • • • • • • 1978 • 1979 • 1980 • 1981 • 1982 • 1983 • 1984 • 1985 • 1986 • 1987 • 1988 • 1989 • 1990 • 1991 • 1992 • 1993 • 1994 • 1995 • 1996 • 1997 • 1998 • **1999**

Brimstone Hill Fortress National Park
Saint Kitts and Nevis

Criteria – Testimony to cultural tradition; Significance in human history

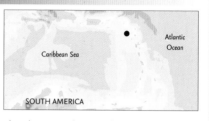

Brimstone Hill Fortress National Park is an outstandingly well-preserved example of seventeenth- and eighteenth-century military architecture in a Caribbean context. Designed by the British and built by African slave labour, the fortress is testimony to European colonial expansion, the African slave trade and the emergence of new societies in the Caribbean. The heart of the fortress is Fort George, the massive masonry structure on one of the twin peaks that dominate the complex and still in an excellent state of repair. It is the earliest surviving British example of the type of fortification known as the 'polygonal system', and one of the finest examples known anywhere in the world. The fortress was abandoned as a result of British defence cuts in 1853. The wooden buildings were auctioned and dismantled and masonry buildings were plundered for their cut stone.

On entering the fortress, the first structure is the Barrier Redoubt. Next comes the North-West Work, which incorporates the stout Magazine Bastion with its associated water catchments and cistern. This is linked to the South-East Work, the main feature of which is the Orillon Bastion. A prominent feature here is the bombproof Ordnance Storehouse.

Area de Conservación Guanacaste
Costa Rica

Criteria – Significant ecological and biological processes; Significant natural habitat for biodiversity

Guanacaste is located in northwestern Costa Rica. It stretches 105 km from the Pacific, across the Pacific coastal lowlands, over three high volcanoes and down into the Atlantic coastal lowlands. It includes the Guanacaste Cordillera and surrounding flatlands and coastal areas. It contains important natural habitats for the conservation of biological diversity, including the best dry-forest habitats from Central America to northern Mexico and key habitats for endangered or rare plant and animal species. The marine area includes various near-shore islands and islets (mostly uninhabited), open ocean marine zones, beaches, rocky coasts, and approximately 20 km of sea turtle nesting beaches and a high diversity of wetland ecosystems (thirty-seven wetlands). The wetland forests are considered to be among the most pristine in Central America and worldwide.

Guanacaste's beaches are of global importance for the protection of Olive ridley sea turtles and leatherback sea turtles, both endangered. The Naranjo and Nancite beaches alone host over 250,000 turtles during the breeding and mating season.

World Heritage site since

• • • • • • • • • • 1978 • 1979 • 1980 • 1981 • 1982 • 1983 • 1984 • 1985 • 1986 • 1987 • 1988 • 1989 • 1990 • 1991 • 1992 • 1993 • 1994 • 1995 • 1996 • 1997 • 1998 • **1999**

Dacian Fortresses of the Orastie Mountains
Romania

Criteria – Interchange of values; Testimony to cultural tradition; Significance in human history

The circular sanctuary at Sarmizegetusa Regia. ▼

Built in the first centuries BC and AD under Dacian rule, these fortresses show an unusual fusion of military and religious architectural techniques and concepts from the classical world and the late-European Iron Age. The Dacians inhabited the central and western part of the region between the Carpathians and the Danube. It was a typical Iron Age culture, practising agriculture, stock-raising, fishing and metal-working, as well as trade with the Graeco-Roman world. These six defensive works, which formed the nucleus of the Dacian Kingdom, were conquered by the Romans at the beginning of the second century AD. Their extensive and well-preserved remains stand in spectacular natural surroundings and give a dramatic picture of a vigorous and innovative civilization.

The system developed by the Dacians to defend their capital, Sarmizegetusa Regia, was composed of three distinct fortified elements: sites on dominant physical features, fortresses, and linear defences.

World Heritage site since

• • • • • • • • • • 1978 • 1979 • 1980 • 1981 • 1982 • 1983 • 1984 • 1985 • 1986 • 1987 • 1988 • 1989 • 1990 • 1991 • 1992 • 1993 • 1994 • 1995 • 1996 • 1997 • 1998 • **1999**

Mount Wuyi
China

Criteria – Testimony to cultural tradition;
Heritage associated with events of universal
significance; Natural phenomena or beauty;
Significant natural habitat for biodiversity

Mount Wuyi is the most outstanding area for
biodiversity conservation in southeast China.
It contains what is probably the largest and
best preserved areas of humid subtropical
forest in the world, and is a refuge for a large
number of ancient, relict species, many of
them endemic to China. The riverine landscape
of the Nine Bend River (lower gorge) is also
of exceptional scenic quality in its
juxtaposition of smooth rock cliffs with clear,
deep water. Its serene beauty is complemented
by numerous temples and monasteries,
many now in ruins. These provided the
setting for the development and spread of
neo-Confucianism, a doctrine that played
a dominant role in the countries of eastern
and southeastern Asia for many centuries
and influenced philosophy and government
over much of the world.

Mount Wuyi has
received international
recognition for its
high diversity and
large numbers of rare
and unusual fauna.

Endangered species
include Chinese tiger,
clouded leopard, black
muntjac and Chinese
giant salamander.

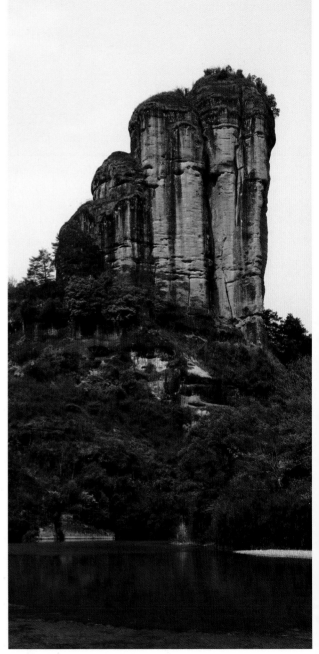

World Heritage site since

• • • • • • • • • 1978 • 1979 • 1980 • 1981 • 1982 • 1983 • 1984 • 1985 • 1986 • 1987 • 1988 • 1989 • 1990 • 1991 • 1992 • 1993 • 1994 • 1995 • 1996 • 1997 • 1998 • **1999**

Bronze Age Burial Site of Sammallahdenmäki
Finland

Criteria – Testimony to cultural tradition; Significance in human history

The Sammallahdenmäki cemetery includes thirty-three burial cairns and is the largest and best cairn site in all Finland. It provides a unique insight into the funerary practices and social and religious structures of northern Europe more than three millennia ago. Of the cairns, twenty-eight can be securely dated to the early Bronze Age. They lie along the crest and upper slopes of a 700-m-long ridge, and are disposed in several distinct clusters. The structures were built using granite boulders quarried from the cliff face or collected from the site itself. They can be classified into several different groups according to their shapes and sizes: small low round cairns, large mound-like cairns, and round walled cairns. They enclose cists made from stone slabs.

The site is associated with sun worship rituals, a cult that spread from Scandinavia over the entire region. At the time the hill of Sammallahdenmäki was completely bare of trees and was probably chosen for its unimpeded view of the sea and its openness to the sun in all directions.

Miguasha National Park
Canada

Criteria – Major stages of Earth's history

The palaeontological site of Miguasha Park, in southeastern Quebec on the southern coast of the Gaspé peninsula, is considered to be the world's most outstanding illustration of the Devonian Period known as the 'Age of Fishes'. Dating from 380 million years ago, the Upper Devonian Escuminac Formation represented here contains five of the six fossil fish groups associated with this period. Its paramount importance is due to it having the greatest number and best-preserved fossil specimens of the lobe-finned fishes that gave rise to the first four-legged, air-breathing terrestrial vertebrates – the tetrapods.

The site is characterized not only by the number of its fossil specimens but also by their exceptional condition, which allows further study: for example, of soft body parts represented in gill imprints, digestive traces and cartilaginous elements of skeleton.

World Heritage site since

• • • • • • • • • • 1978 • 1979 • 1980 • 1981 • 1982 • 1983 • 1984 • 1985 • 1986 • 1987 • 1988 • 1989 • 1990 • 1991 • 1992 • 1993 • 1994 • 1995 • 1996 • 1997 • 1998 • **1999**

Jurisdiction of Saint-Emilion
France

Criteria – Testimony to cultural tradition;
Significance in human history

The Jurisdiction of Saint-Emilion is an outstanding example of a historic vineyard landscape that has survived intact and remains active to the present day. Viticulture was introduced to this fertile region by the Roman emperor Augustus. He created the province of Aquitania in 27 BC and established the first vineyards by grafting new varieties of grape on the Vitis biturica that grew naturally in the region. This industry intensified in the Middle Ages when the Saint-Emilion area benefited from its location on the pilgrimage route to Santiago de Compostela. Many churches, monasteries and hospices were built there from the eleventh century onwards. It was granted the special status of a 'jurisdiction' during the period of English rule in the twelfth century.

In the eighteenth century the quality of the wines from the region was recognized as exceptional. Saint-Emilion has also been noteworthy for its innovations, such as the establishment of the first wine syndicate in 1884 and the first cooperative cellars in the Gironde in 1932.

World Heritage site since

• • • • • • • • • • 1978 • 1979 • 1980 • 1981 • 1982 • 1983 • 1984 • 1985 • 1986 • 1987 • 1988 • 1989 • 1990 • 1991 • 1992 • 1993 • 1994 • 1995 • 1996 • 1997 • 1998 • **1999**

Western Caucasus
Russian Federation

Criteria – Significant ecological and biological processes; Significant natural habitat for biodiversity

The Western Caucasus, extending over 2,750 km² of the extreme western end of the Caucasus mountains and located 50 km northeast of the Black Sea, is one of the few large mountain areas of Europe that has not experienced significant human impact. Its subalpine and alpine pastures have only been grazed by wild animals, and its extensive tracts of undisturbed mountain forests, extending from the lowlands to the subalpine zone, are unique in Europe. The site has a great diversity of ecosystems, with important endemic plants and wildlife, and is the place of origin and reintroduction of the mountain subspecies of the European bison.

The lack of human disturbance in this area has allowed ecological processes to continue naturally over the millennia. This offers exceptional opportunities for studying both competitive interactions between grazing animals and predator/prey interactions.

Puerto-Princesa Subterranean River National Park
Philippines

Criteria – Natural phenomena or beauty; Significant natural habitat for biodiversity

This park features a spectacular limestone karst landscape with an underground river. One of the river's distinguishing features is that it emerges directly into the sea, and its lower portion is subject to tidal influences. The area also represents a significant habitat for biodiversity conservation. The site contains a full 'mountain-to-sea' ecosystem and has some of the most important forests in Asia.

The spectacular karst landscape has both surface karst features and an extensive 8.2-km-long underground river system – one of the most unique of its type in the world, with chambers up to 120 m wide and 60 m high.

World Heritage site since

• • • • • • • • • • • • 1978 • 1979 • 1980 • 1981 • 1982 • 1983 • 1984 • 1985 • 1986 • 1987 • 1988 • 1989 • 1990 • 1991 • 1992 • 1993 • 1994 • 1995 • 1996 • 1997 • 1998 • **1999**

Laurisilva of Madeira
Portugal

Criteria – *Significant ecological and biological processes; Significant natural habitat for biodiversity*

The laurel forest's ancient trees in the valley bottoms, waterfalls and cliffs provide spectacular scenery and have great ecological value. By collecting and retaining moisture they help protect the micro-climate and maintain water supplies.

The Laurisilva of Madeira is an outstanding relict of a virtually extinct flora of great interest. Fossil evidence shows that laurisilva flora once covered much of southern Europe in the Tertiary era, 15–40 million years ago, but this vegetation is now confined to the Azores, Madeira and the Canary Islands. The laurisilva on Madeira is the largest area surviving, with approximately 150 km² within the 270 km² Madeira Nature Reserve, and is in very good condition, with around 90 per cent believed to be primary forest. The laurisilva of Madeira is notable for its biological diversity with at least sixty-six vascular plant species endemic to the island and many endemic animal species such as the Madeiran long-toed pigeon.

World Heritage site since

• • • • • • • • • •1978 • 1979 • 1980 • 1981 • 1982 • 1983 • 1984 • 1985 • 1986 • 1987 • 1988 • 1989 • 1990 • 1991 • 1992 • 1993 • 1994 • 1995 • 1996 • 1997 • 1998 • 1999

Historic Centre (Chorá) with the Monastery of Saint John 'the Theologian' and the Cave of the Apocalypse on the Island of Pátmos

Greece

Criteria – Testimony to cultural tradition; Significance in human history; Heritage associated with events of universal significance

The small island of Pátmos in the Dodecanese is reputed to be where St John the Theologian wrote both his Gospel and the Apocalypse, two of Christianity's most sacred works.

The Monastery of Hagios Ioannis Theologos (Saint John the Theologian) and the Cave of the Apocalypse was founded in the late-tenth century on the island of Pátmos, the northernmost island of the Dodecanese group. Together with the associated medieval settlement of Chorá, the monastery constitutes an exceptional example of a traditional Greek Orthodox pilgrimage centre of outstanding architectural interest. The town of Chorá is one of the few settlements in Greece that have evolved uninterruptedly since the twelfth century. There are few other places in the world where religious ceremonies that date back to the early Christian times are still being practised unchanged.

The Monastery of Saint John 'the Theologian'.

▼

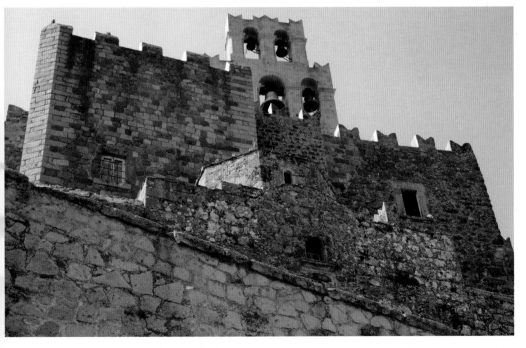

World Heritage site since

• • • • • • • • • • 1978 • 1979 • 1980 • 1981 • 1982 • 1983 • 1984 • 1985 • 1986 • 1987 • 1988 • 1989 • 1990 • 1991 • 1992 • 1993 • 1994 • 1995 • 1996 • 1997 • 1998 • **1999**

Lorentz National Park
Indonesia

Criteria – Major stages of Earth's history; Significant ecological and biological processes; Significant natural habitat for biodiversity

Lorentz National Park, 25,000 km²,is the largest protected area in southeast Asia. It is the only protected area in the world to incorporate a continuous, intact transect from snowcap to tropical marine environment, including extensive lowland wetlands. Located at the meeting-point of two colliding continental plates, the area has a complex geology with ongoing mountain formation as well as major sculpting by glaciation. The area also contains fossil sites which provide evidence of the evolution of life on New Guinea, a high level of endemism and the highest level of biodiversity in the region.

The park has two very distinct zones: the swampy lowlands and the high mountain area of the central cordillera. This zone is one of only three equatorial regions of sufficiently high altitude to retain permanent ice.

Shrines and Temples of Nikko
Japan

Criteria – Human creative genius; Significance in human history; Heritage associated with events of universal significance

The shrines and temples of Nikko, together with their natural surroundings, have for centuries been a sacred site known for its architectural and decorative masterpieces. They are closely associated with the history of the Tokugawa Shoguns.

The shrines and temples and their environment are associated with the Shinto perception of the relationship of man with nature, in which mountains and forests have a sacred meaning. This religious practice is still very much alive today.

◄
The Tashogu Temple at Nikko.

Archaeological Monuments Zone of Xochicalco
Mexico

Criteria – Testimony to cultural tradition;
Significance in human history

Xochicalco is an exceptionally well-preserved and complete example of a fortified political, religious and commercial centre from the Epiclassic period of Mesoamerica. Its architecture and art represent the fusion of cultural elements from different parts of Mesoamerica, from the troubled period of 650–900 that followed the break-up of the great Mesoamerican states such as Teotihuacan,

Monte Albán, Palenque and Tikal. The intensive cultural regrouping that followed the breakdown of these earlier political structures fuelled the city's growth. The city was built on a series of natural hills. The highest of these was the core of the settlement, with many public buildings, but evidence of occupation has been found on six of the lower hills surrounding it.

The scale of the city's engineering work is substantial. Terracing and massive retaining walls have created a series of open spaces defined by platforms and pyramidal structures. They are linked by a complex system of staircases, terraces and ramps to create a main north-south communication axis through the city.

World Heritage site since

• • • • • • • • • • 1978 • 1979 • 1980 • 1981 • 1982 • 1983 • 1984 • 1985 • 1986 • 1987 • 1988 • 1989 • 1990 • 1991 • 1992 • 1993 • 1994 • 1995 • 1996 • 1997 • 1998 • **1999**

Atlantic Forest South-East Reserves
Brazil

Criteria – Natural phenomena or beauty;
Significant ecological and biological processes;
Significant natural habitat for biodiversity

The twenty-five reserves that make up this site contain some of the best and most extensive examples of the remaining Atlantic forests in Brazil and display the biological wealth and evolutionary history of the one of the world's richest and most endangered habitats. From mountains covered by dense forests down to wetlands, and to coastal islands with isolated mountains and dunes, the area comprises a rich natural environment of great scenic beauty. Partially isolated since the Ice Age, the Atlantic forests have evolved into a complex ecosystem with exceptionally high endemism (70 per cent of the tree species, 85 per cent of the primates and 39 per cent of the mammals). More than 450 tree species per hectare can be found in some areas, indicating that the diversity of woody plants in the region is larger than in the Amazon rainforest.

The reserves contain a highly diverse fauna with several species of conservation concern. There are some 120 species of mammals, including jaguar (pictured below), ocelot, bush dog, La Plata otter, twenty species of bat and various species of endangered primate, notably muriqui and brown howler monkey. The newly discovered black-faced lion tamarin is endemic to the area.

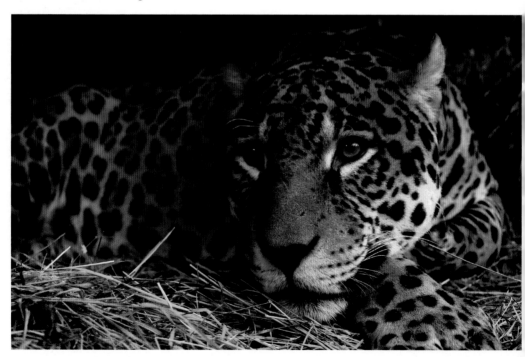

World Heritage site since

• • • • • • • • • • 1978 • 1979 • 1980 • 1981 • 1982 • 1983 • 1984 • 1985 • 1986 • 1987 • 1988 • 1989 • 1990 • 1991 • 1992 • 1993 • 1994 • 1995 • 1996 • 1997 • 1998 • **1999**

Cueva de las Manos, Río Pinturas
Argentina

Criteria – Testimony to cultural tradition

The Cueva de las Manos, Río Pinturas, contains an exceptional assemblage of cave art, executed between 13,000 and 9,500 years ago. It takes its name 'Cave of the Hands' from the stencilled outlines of human hands in the cave, but there are also many depictions of animals, such as guanacos, which are still common in the region, as well as hunting scenes. The people who were responsible for the paintings may have been the ancestors of the historic hunter-gatherer communities of Patagonia found by European settlers in the nineteenth century.

The hunting scenes in the caves depict animals and human figures interacting in a dynamic and naturalistic manner. Different hunting strategies are depicted, with animals being surrounded, ambushed or attacked by hunters using bolas, weighted throwing weapons.

World Heritage site since

• • • • • • 1978 • 1979 • 1980 • 1981 • 1982 • 1983 • 1984 • 1985 • 1986 • 1987 • 1988 • 1989 • 1990 • 1991 • 1992 • 1993 • 1994 • 1995 • 1996 • 1997 • 1998 • 1999 • **2000**

Walled City of Baku with the Shirvanshah's Palace and Maiden Tower
Azerbaijan

Criteria – Significance in human history

Built on a site inhabited since the Palaeolithic period, the Walled City of Baku reveals evidence of Zoroastrian, Sasanian, Arabic, Persian, Shirvani, Ottoman, and Russian presence in cultural continuity. The Inner City (Icheri Sheher) has preserved much of its twelfth-century defensive walls. The twelfth-century Maiden Tower (Giz Galasy) is built over earlier structures dating from the seventh to sixth centuries BC, and the fifteenth-century Shirvanshahs' Palace is one of the pearls of Azerbaijan's architecture.

The Maiden Tower is a unique monument of Azerbaijan architecture rising to eight storeys. This astonishing cylindrical structure was built in two periods, with the bottom three storeys built as early as the seventh or sixth centuries BC as an astronomical observatory or fire temple.

◄
Maiden Tower.

World Heritage site since

• • • • • • 1978 • 1979 • 1980 • 1981 • 1982 • 1983 • 1984 • 1985 • 1986 • 1987 • 1988 • 1989 • 1990 • 1991 • 1992 • 1993 • 1994 • 1995 • 1996 • 1997 • 1998 • 1999 • **2000**

Kronborg Castle
Denmark
Criteria – Significance in human history

North
Sea

Baltic
Sea

EUROPE

Located on a strategically important site commanding the Sund – the stretch of water between Denmark and Sweden – the royal castle of Kronborg at Helsingør is of immense symbolic value to the Danish people. Work began on the construction of this outstanding Renaissance castle in 1574. In 1629 Kronborg was devastated by fire, only the walls being left standing. Christian IV immediately commissioned the restoration of the castle, largely returning it to its original appearance. Under Frederik III and Christian V large fortifications were built, the outer defensive works were considerably enlarged under Frederik IV, and the castle itself underwent substantial restoration and alteration. In 1785 it passed to the military and has remained intact to the present day. It is world-renowned as Elsinore, the setting of Shakespeare's Hamlet.

In its original form the Banqueting Hall had a magnificently carved and gilded ceiling and its walls were hung with tapestries. Only fourteen of the tapestries, prepared for the north wall and depicting Danish kings, have survived; of these, seven are on display at Kronborg, the remainder being in the National Museum in Copenhagen.

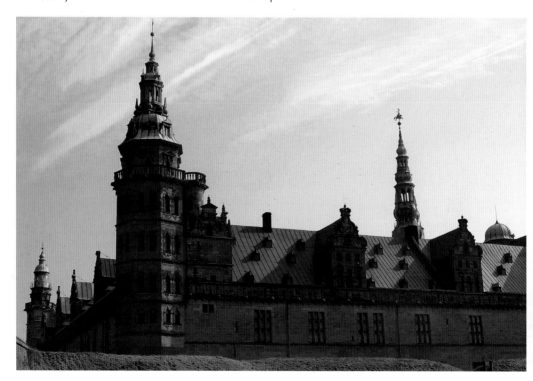

World Heritage site since

• • • • • • 1978 • 1979 • 1980 • 1981 • 1982 • 1983 • 1984 • 1985 • 1986 • 1987 • 1988 • 1989 • 1990 • 1991 • 1992 • 1993 • 1994 • 1995 • 1996 • 1997 • 1998 • 1999 • **2000**

Greater Blue Mountains Area
Australia

Criteria – *Significant ecological and biological processes; Significant natural habitat for biodiversity*

The Greater Blue Mountains consists of a mostly forested landscape on a sandstone plateau that commences about 60 kms west of central Sydney. The property is made up of eight protected areas: the Blue Mountains, Wollemi, Yengo, Nattai, Kanangra-Boyd, Gardens of Stone and Thirlmere Lakes National Parks, and the Jenolan Caves Karst Conservation Reserve. The plateau has enabled the survival of a rich diversity of plant and animal life by providing a refuge from climatic changes during recent geological history. It is particularly noted for its wide representation of eucalypt communities, ranging from wet and dry sclerophyll forests to mallee heathlands, and for the diversity of species of eucalypts. There are 101 species of eucalypt (over fourteen per cent of the global total) in the Greater Blue Mountains, twelve of which are believed to occur only in the Sydney sandstone region.

The Greater Blue Mountains also contains ancient, relict species of global significance. The most famous of these is the recently discovered Wollemi pine, a 'living fossil' dating back to the age of the dinosaurs. Thought to have been extinct for millions of years, the few surviving trees of this ancient species are known only from three small populations located in remote gorges within the Area.

Wollondilly Lookout, Nattai National Park. ▼

World Heritage site since

• • • • • • 1978 • 1979 • 1980 • 1981 • 1982 • 1983 • 1984 • 1985 • 1986 • 1987 • 1988 • 1989 • 1990 • 1991 • 1992 • 1993 • 1994 • 1995 • 1996 • 1997 • 1998 • 1999 • **2000**

Garden Kingdom of Dessau-Wörlitz
Germany
Criteria – Interchange of values; Significance in human history

The Garden Kingdom of Dessau-Wörlitz is an outstanding example of the application of the philosophical principles of the Age of the Enlightenment to the design of a landscape that integrates art, education and economy in a harmonious whole. The first essays in grand landscape design began in 1683 with the plan for Oranienbaum, which unified town, palace, and park. The resulting complete Baroque ensemble, with obvious

Dutch connections deriving from its designer, Cornelis Ryckwaert, has survived to this day. Further developments on these lines took place around 1700 with the reclamation of marshy areas along the river Elbe and the creation of planned villages and farmsteads. The final major stage of design was the work done by Prince Leopold III Friedrich Franz over the entire principality.

Prince Leopold III Friedrich Franz (1740–1817) developed existing landscape designs into something far more remarkable. By the time he died, virtually the entire principality had become a unified garden whose characteristic features have been preserved.

Three Castles, Defensive Wall and Ramparts of the Market-Town of Bellinzone
Switzerland
Criteria – Significance in human history

The Bellinzone site consists of a group of fortifications grouped around the castle of Castelgrande, which stands on a rocky peak looking out over the entire Ticino valley. Running from the castle, a series of fortified walls protect the ancient town and block the passage through the valley. A second castle, Montebello, forms an integral part of the fortifications; a third but separate castle, Sasso Corbaro, was built on an isolated rocky promontory southeast of the other fortifications.

The Bellinzone ensemble is the sole remaining example in the entire Alpine region of medieval military architecture.

◄
The towers of the castle of Castelgrande.

World Heritage site since

• • • • • • 1978 • 1979 • 1980 • 1981 • 1982 • 1983 • 1984 • 1985 • 1986 • 1987 • 1988 • 1989 • 1990 • 1991 • 1992 • 1993 • 1994 • 1995 • 1996 • 1997 • 1998 • 1999 • **2000**

Maloti-Drakensberg Park
Lesotho and South Africa

Criteria – Human creative genius; Testimony to
cultural tradition; Natural phenomena or beauty;
Significant natural habitat for biodiversity

Drakensberg Park, or uKhahlamba Park,
is the largest protected area on The Great
Escarpment of the southern African
subcontinent. It comprises a northern and a
significantly larger southern section. There
is considerable variation in topography,
including vast basalt and sandstone
cliffs, deep valleys, intervening spurs and
extensive plateau areas. Among a total
of 2,153 species of plant, there are a large
number of internationally and nationally
threatened species. The fauna includes
48 mammal, 296 bird, 48 reptile,

26 amphibian and 8 fish species. This
spectacular natural site also contains many
caves and rock-shelters with the largest and
most concentrated group of paintings in
Africa south of the Sahara, made by the San
people over a period of 4,000 years.
In 2013 Lesotho's Sehlabathebe National
Park was inscribed as an extension to the
existing site. The 6,550 hectare addition
consists of a spectacularly beautiful
watershed area that hosts flora and fauna
of scientific importance.

The vegetation in the
park is influenced by
topography and the
effects of climate,
soil, geology, slope,
drainage and fire. It
is altitudinally zoned,
forming three belts
coinciding with the
main topographical
features: the river
valley system, the
spurs and the summit
plateau.

The Giant's Castle
Game Reserve in the
central region of the
Drakensberg Park.
▼

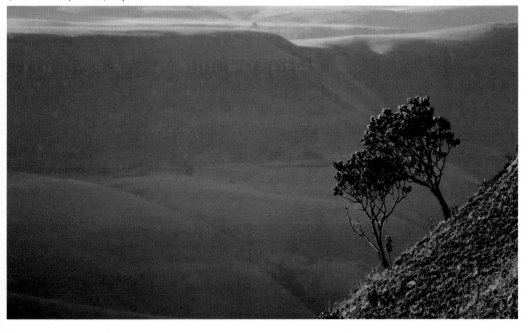

World Heritage site since

• • • • • 1978 • 1979 • 1980 • 1981 • 1982 • 1983 • 1984 • 1985 • 1986 • 1987 • 1988 • 1989 • 1990 • 1991 • 1992 • 1993 • 1994 • 1995 • 1996 • 1997 • 1998 • 1999 • **2000**

Stone Town of Zanzibar
Tanzania

Criteria – Interchange of values; Testimony to cultural tradition; Heritage associated with events of universal significance

The restored old dispensary, now the Stone Town Cultural Centre.

The Stone Town of Zanzibar is a fine example of the Swahili coastal trading towns of east Africa. It retains its urban fabric and townscape virtually intact and contains many fine buildings that reflect its culture, which has brought together and homogenized disparate elements of the cultures of Africa, Arabia, India and Europe over more than a millennium.

For many centuries there was intense trading activity between Asia and Africa, and this is illustrated admirably by the architecture and urban structure of the Stone Town. Zanzibar also has great symbolic importance in the history of slavery because it was one of the main slave-trading ports in east Africa and a key location in the Arab slave trade.

Zanzibar was one of a loose confederation of small coastal city states known as the Zenj bar (Black Empire) which operated in the eighth–tenth centuries; the name derives from the Perso-Arabic word meaning 'the coast of the blacks'. Arab settlers were present in Zanzibar by the tenth century.

The Portuguese established a presence in the region at the end of the fifteenth century, using it as a base for exploration, but they were expelled by Omani Arabs in the seventeenth century. The Arabs formed Zanzibar's ruling elite until the twentieth century.

The Omanis traded in spices, ivory and slaves, and the city became the largest slave-trade port in east Africa: in the nineteenth century, an estimated 50,000 slaves a year were passing through Zanzibar. As a consequence the city's rulers and merchants grew very rich and embellished the Stone Town, the oldest part of the city, with palaces and fine mansions. Its characteristic Swahili architecture was overwhelmed by the Omanis' style of massively built multi-storey blocks in mortared coral and with flat roofs. The Minaret Mosque dates from this period. Another architectural component came from India with the addition of wide verandas.

Modern urban development began during the reign of Sultan Barghash (1870–88). His most notable contribution to the Stone Town architecture was the House of Wonders, but his greatest legacy was the provision of piped water to the town. The final phase of architectural development came in 1890 when Zanzibar became a British protectorate. The British imported colonial architecture while also introducing features derived from the Islamic architecture of Istanbul and Morocco.

The historical evolution of the Stone Town is illustrated by its street pattern, one of narrow, winding streets resulting from the unplanned building of houses and shops. There are few public open spaces as many of the houses have their own enclosed spaces. The principal construction material is coralline-rag stone set in a thick, lime mortar and then plastered and lime-washed.

The vernacular architecture of the Stone Town is preponderantly of two-storey buildings with long, narrow rooms around an open courtyard, reached through a narrow corridor.

World Heritage site since

• • • • • • 1978 • 1979 • 1980 • 1981 • 1982 • 1983 • 1984 • 1985 • 1986 • 1987 • 1988 • 1989 • 1990 • 1991 • 1992 • 1993 • 1994 • 1995 • 1996 • 1997 • 1998 • 1999 • **2000**

Land of Frankincense
Oman

Criteria – Testimony to cultural tradition;
Significance in human history

This group of archaeological sites in Oman represents the production and distribution of frankincense, one of the most important luxury items of trade in antiquity, from the Mediterranean and Red Sea regions to Mesopotamia, India and China. They constitute outstanding testimony to the civilization that flourished in southern Arabia from the Neolithic to the late Islamic periods. The Oasis of Shishr and the entrepôts of Khor Rori and Al-Baleed are excellent examples of medieval fortified settlements in the Persian Gulf region and were important sites on the frankincense trade routes. The sources of ancient frankincense can be identified with the three areas in the Dhofar region in which the frankincense tree is still to be found, and are represented by the Frankincense Park of Wadi Dawkah.

The port of Sumhuram/Khor Rori was founded at the end of the first century to control the trade in Dhofar incense. Indian seamen who had brought cotton cloth, corn and oil in exchange for incense overwintered there, waiting for the favourable monsoon winds to take them home.

Monumental gate, Khor Rori.
▼

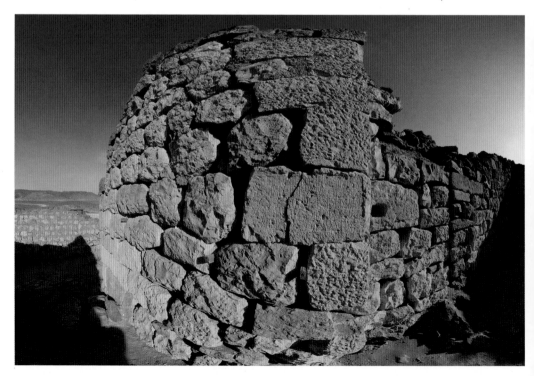

World Heritage site since

• • • • • 1978 • 1979 • 1980 • 1981 • 1982 • 1983 • 1984 • 1985 • 1986 • 1987 • 1988 • 1989 • 1990 • 1991 • 1992 • 1993 • 1994 • 1995 • 1996 • 1997 • 1998 • 1999 • **2000**

Curonian Spit
Lithuania and Russian Federation

Criteria – Traditional human settlement

EUROPE

ASIA

Pacific
Ocean

Human habitation of this elongated sand dune peninsula, 98 km long and 0.4–4 km wide, dates back to prehistoric times. Throughout this period it has been threatened by the natural forces of wind and waves. Its survival to the present day has been made possible only as a result of ceaseless human efforts to combat the erosion of the Spit, dramatically illustrated by continuing stabilization and reforestation

projects. The most significant element of the Spit's cultural heritage is represented by the old fishing settlements. The earliest of these were buried in sand when the woodland cover was removed. Those that have survived are all along the coast of the lagoon. At the end of the nineteenth century more elaborate buildings – lighthouses, churches, schools and villas – began to be erected alongside the simpler vernacular houses.

The surviving buildings of cultural significance are the houses of fishermen built during the nineteenth century. In their original form they were built from wood and thatched with reeds. A homestead consisted of two or three buildings: a dwelling house, a cattle shed, and a smokehouse for curing fish.

Sand dunes on the Curonian Spit.
▼

World Heritage site since

• • • • • 1978 • 1979 • 1980 • 1981 • 1982 • 1983 • 1984 • 1985 • 1986 • 1987 • 1988 • 1989 • 1990 • 1991 • 1992 • 1993 • 1994 • 1995 • 1996 • 1997 • 1998 • 1999 • **2000**

Imperial Tombs of the Ming and Qing Dynasties
China

Criteria – Human creative genius; Interchange of values; Testimony to cultural tradition; Significance in human history; Heritage associated with events of universal significance

The Imperial Tombs of the Ming and Qing Dynasties are seven groups of tombs in five provinces of eastern China. The tombs, designed in keeping with the Chinese principles of geomancy, provide outstanding evidence of Chinese beliefs and traditions from the fourteenth century onwards. The sites are characterized by the attempt to achieve harmony between the natural environment and the buildings.

A plain or broad valley was chosen, with the perspective of a mountain range to the north, against which the tombs would be built, with a lower elevation to the south. The site had to be framed on the east and west by chains of hills, and feature at least one waterway. A main access road several kilometres in length, known as the Way of the Spirits, led to the site.

The western Qing tomb contains fourteen imperial tombs and two building complexes: the Yongfu Tibetan Buddhist temple and the temporary palace where the imperial family resided when it came to honour its ancestors. The site of eastern Qing tombs contains fifteen mausolea in which 161 bodies were buried – emperors, empresses, concubines and princesses.

Western Qing tomb. ▼

World Heritage site since

• • • • • • 1978 • 1979 • 1980 • 1981 • 1982 • 1983 • 1984 • 1985 • 1986 • 1987 • 1988 • 1989 • 1990 • 1991 • 1992 • 1993 • 1994 • 1995 • 1996 • 1997 • 1998 • 1999 • **2000**

Historical Centre of the City of Arequipa
Peru

Criteria – Human creative genius; Significance in human history

The Historical Centre of Arequipa, built in a form of soft volcanic rock called sillar, represents a masterly integration of European and native building styles. This combination of influences is illustrated by the city's robust walls, archways and vaults, courtyards and open spaces, and the intricate Baroque decoration of its façades. The World Heritage site consists of forty-nine original blocks of the Spanish layout and twenty-four blocks from the colonial period and the nineteenth century. The core of the historic town is the Plaza de Armas (Plaza Mayor) with its mid-nineteenth-century cathedral, the most important neoclassical religious building in the country. At one corner of the Plaza are the church and cloisters of La Compañia, the most representative ensemble of the Baroque mestizo period at the end of the eighteenth century.

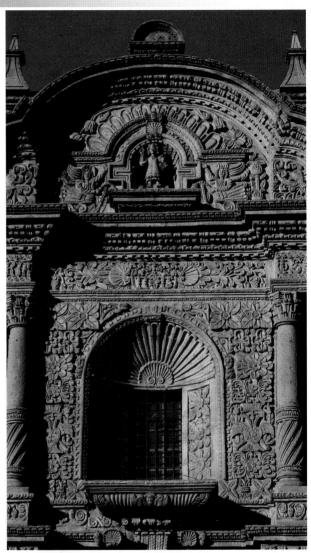

Façade of Iglesias de los Jesuitas, Arequipa. ▲

The merit of Arequipa architecture is also evident in the profusion of its casonas, characteristic well-proportioned vernacular houses. The Historical Centre contains some 500 casonas, of which over 250 are listed for protection. The heavy structures have been enhanced with ornamental designs in large thick rounded frames or deep protrusions and sculptures on flat surfaces.

World Heritage site since

• • • • • • 1978 • 1979 • 1980 • 1981 • 1982 • 1983 • 1984 • 1985 • 1986 • 1987 • 1988 • 1989 • 1990 • 1991 • 1992 • 1993 • 1994 • 1995 • 1996 • 1997 • 1998 • 1999 • **2000**

City of Verona
Italy

Criteria – Interchange of values; Significance in human history

EUROPE

Ionian Sea

Mediterranean Sea

The historic city of Verona was founded in the first century BC. It prospered under the rule of the Scaliger family in the thirteenth and fourteenth centuries and as part of the Republic of Venice from the fifteenth to eighteenth centuries. Verona has preserved a remarkable number of monuments from antiquity, and from the medieval and Renaissance periods. The core of the city consists of the Roman town in the loop of the Adige River, where the remains include city gates, the theatre and the Amphitheatre Arena, the second-largest after the Colosseum in Rome. The heart of Verona is the ensemble consisting of the Piazza delle Erbe and the Piazza dei Signori with their historic buildings, including the Palazzo del Comune, Palazzo del Governo, Loggia del Consiglio, Arche Scaligere and Domus Nova.

The cathedral (Duomo) was first built in the sixth century but rebuilt in the twelfth century after an earthquake. The façade, completed in the fourteenth century, is in Verona marble and has bas-reliefs representing sacred and profane episodes of different types. There is a fine twelfth-century cloister with arcades on double colonnades.

The Duomo and Adige River, Verona.
▼

World Heritage site since

• • • • • •1978 • 1979 • 1980 • 1981 • 1982 • 1983 • 1984 • 1985 • 1986 • 1987 • 1988 • 1989 • 1990 • 1991 • 1992 • 1993 • 1994 • 1995 • 1996 • 1997 • 1998 • 1999 • 2000

Ruins of León Viejo
Nicaragua

Criteria – Testimony to cultural tradition;
Significance in human history

León Viejo is one of the oldest Spanish colonial settlements in the Americas. The town was founded in 1524 by Francisco Hernández de Córdoba, who was sent from Panamá to conquer the Pacific zone northwards to Tezoatega (now the village of El Viejo). It developed, like many colonial towns in Latin America, round a central plaza, on the extreme northeast shore of what was to be called the Lake of León.

The town reached its peak of development around 1545, although it was still relatively small, with its Spanish population not exceeding some two hundred. The town was laid out on a grid pattern and excavations have uncovered remains of the Cathedral, the Convent of La Merced and the Royal Foundry.

The murder of Bishop Antonio de Valdivieso in 1550 seemed to mark a turning point in its fortunes: it was widely believed to have put a curse on the town, which suffered from both natural and economic disasters in the years that followed.

An eruption of the nearby volcano, Momotombo, in 1578, combined with raging inflation drove the richer inhabitants away. By 1603 there were only ten houses remaining. The final blow came on 11 January 1610, when a severe earthquake destroyed what was still standing, and the decision was taken to move the city to a site near the village of Subtiava.

Early Christian Necropolis of Pécs (Sopianae)
Hungary

Criteria – Testimony to cultural tradition;
Significance in human history

In the fourth century, a remarkable series of decorated tombs were constructed in the cemetery of the Roman provincial town of Sopianae, modern Pécs. The World Heritage site consists of sixteen funerary monuments which are important both structurally and architecturally, since they were built as underground burial chambers with memorial chapels above the ground. The tombs are important also in artistic terms, since they are richly decorated with

Christian-themed murals of outstanding quality. One of the most remarkable is Burial chamber I (Peter-Paul) which is cut into the slope of the Mecsek hills. Discovered in 1782, this late fourth-century chamber consists of an above-ground chapel, the subterranean burial chamber proper with fine religious wall paintings, and a small vestibule leading to the burial chamber.

The burial chambers illustrate the unique early Christian sepulchral art and architecture of the northern and western Roman provinces. One of the most exceptional chambers has a niche carved above the sarcophagus with a painting of a wine pitcher and glass, symbolising the thirst of the soul journeying to the netherworld.

World Heritage site since

• • • • • • 1978 • 1979 • 1980 • 1981 • 1982 • 1983 • 1984 • 1985 • 1986 • 1987 • 1988 • 1989 • 1990 • 1991 • 1992 • 1993 • 1994 • 1995 • 1996 • 1997 • 1998 • 1999 • 2000

Churches of Chiloé
Chile

Criteria – Interchange of values; Testimony to cultural tradition

The most typical feature of these buildings is the tower façade, on the side facing the esplanade, made up of an entrance portico, the gable wall or pediment, and the tower itself. Most are of two or three storeys, with hexagonal or octagonal drums to reduce wind resistance.

The Churches of Chiloé are outstanding examples of the successful fusion of European and indigenous cultural traditions to produce a unique form of wooden architecture. The mestizo culture, resulting from Jesuit missionary activities in the seventeenth and eighteenth centuries, has survived intact in the Chiloé archipelago, and achieves its highest expression in these wooden churches. By the end of the nineteenth century over 100 churches had been built; between fifty and sixty survive to the present day, and fourteen of these constitute the World Heritage site: Achao (Quinchao); Quinchao; Castro; Rilán (Castro); Nercón (Castro); Aldachildo (Puqueldón); Ichuac (Puqueldón); Detif (Puqueldón); Vilipulli (Chonchi); Chonchi; Tenaún (Quemchi); Colo (Quemchi); San Juan (Dalcahue); and Dalcahue. The traditional Chiloé churches are located near the shore, facing an esplanade.

Blaenavon Industrial Landscape
United Kingdom

Criteria – Testimony to cultural tradition; Significance in human history

Big Pit, the last substantial working colliery at Blaenavon, closed in 1980. Big Pit is now a museum of coal mining of international significance, and one of only two mining museums in the United Kingdom where visitors can be taken underground.

The area around Blaenavon is evidence of the pre-eminence of south Wales as the world's major producer of iron and coal in the nineteenth century. All the necessary elements can still be seen – coal and ore mines, quarries, a primitive railway system, furnaces, workers' homes, and the social infrastructure of the community. During the 1840s and 1850s, as population numbers increased with the influx of migrant workers, the scattered housing of the workers and the associated school, church and chapels were complemented by the evolution of a town with a variety of urban functions. There were three principal clusters of buildings in the area, one around the ironworks, one along the east-west axis, now King Street, and the other around St Peter's Church.

World Heritage site since

• • • • • 1978 • 1979 • 1980 • 1981 • 1982 • 1983 • 1984 • 1985 • 1986 • 1987 • 1988 • 1989 • 1990 • 1991 • 1992 • 1993 • 1994 • 1995 • 1996 • 1997 • 1998 • 1999 • **2000**

Historic Town of St George and Related Fortifications, Bermuda
United Kingdom
Criteria – Significance in human history

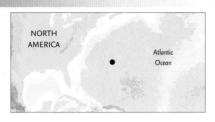

The historic town of St George is an outstanding example of a fortified colonial town dating from the early seventeenth century. It is the oldest English town in the New World. St George was a garrison town from its earliest days, and military installations developed on its eastern side. The first of many barracks were built on Barrack Hill in 1780, followed by other buildings such as hospitals and a chapel.

These were constructed in standard British military style but using local materials. The town's fortifications graphically illustrate the development of English military engineering from the seventeenth to the twentieth centuries, being adapted to take account of the development of artillery over this period. The fortifications continued to serve until the coastal defence came to an end in 1956.

The architecture of Bermuda has changed little since the end of the seventeenth century. The simple, well-proportioned houses, of one or two storeys, have roofs of stone slabs painted white. Some of the houses, such as Bridge House, the Hunter Building, or Whitehall, are impressive mansions, dating from the nineteenth century and embellished with imposing balconies and verandas.

Archaeological Ensemble of Tárraco
Spain
Criteria – Interchange of values; Testimony to cultural tradition

Tárraco, modern-day Tarragona, was a major administrative and mercantile city in Roman Spain and the centre of the Imperial cult for all the Iberian provinces. It was endowed with many fine buildings, and parts of these have been revealed in a series of exceptional excavations. Although most of the remains are fragmentary, many preserved beneath more recent buildings, they present a vivid picture of the grandeur of this Roman provincial capital.

The Roman town was sited on a hill with the seat of the provincial government at its crest and on two terraces created below. The town is rich in important buried remains, including some buildings that are completely preserved.

◀

The Roman Circus.

World Heritage site since

• • • • • 1978 • 1979 • 1980 • 1981 • 1982 • 1983 • 1984 • 1985 • 1986 • 1987 • 1988 • 1989 • 1990 • 1991 • 1992 • 1993 • 1994 • 1995 • 1996 • 1997 • 1998 • 1999 • **2000**

The Loire Valley between Sully-sur-Loire and Chalonnes

France

Criteria – Human creative genius; Interchange of values; Significance in human history

Château de Chambord.

The Loire basin occupies a huge area in central and western France stretching from the southern part of the Massif Central to an Atlantic coast estuary. Along the Loire, between Orléans and Angers, the valley is characterized by low cliffs of tufa and limestone. The valley has a long history of periodic catastrophic flooding, carefully recorded as stone-cut water levels at numerous places along its route, and even today its inhabitants live under perennial threat of severe inundation. Much contemporary river management is orientated to minimizing that risk.

The Loire Valley is an outstanding cultural landscape of great beauty, containing historic towns and villages, the great architectural monuments of the chateaux and cultivated lands formed by two millennia of interaction between their population and the physical environment, primarily the river Loire itself. It is noteworthy for the quality of its architectural heritage, in its historic towns such as Blois, Chinon, Orléans, Saumur and Tours, but in particular in its world-famous castles, such as the Château de Chambord (see photo on the right).

For most of its length within the World Heritage site, the Loire is confined by dykes. Its banks are punctuated at intervals of only a few kilometres by a series of villages, small towns and cities. Land use is varied, from urban density through intense horticulture to vineyards (some reliant on flooding) and hunting forest.

Roman impact on the landscape was massive, and it still strongly influences settlement location, urban form and road communications. The Loire was one of the most important arteries for communications and trade in Gaul. In the late Roman period around 372, St Martin, Bishop of Tours, founded an abbey at Marmoutier and this served as the model

for other monastic settlements in the Loire Valley in the centuries that followed.

The sanctuary at Tours was an early pilgrimage centre and the area's many monasteries served as focal points for settlement in the Middle Ages, as did local fortified settlements.

The Loire Valley was a frontier zone during the Hundred Years' War (1337–1453) and the scene of many confrontations between the French and English. Castles were rebuilt and extended to become massive fortresses, the forerunners of the chateaux of today. The ever-present danger to Paris from the English resulted in the royal court spending long periods at Tours. With the end of the war the valley proved an ideal place for humanism and the Renaissance to take root in France: this involved the dismantling of fortresses and their reconstruction as palaces for pleasure and recreation.

The seventeenth–eighteenth centuries saw the development of a secular commercial economy based on industry and trade. The romantic representation of the valley in the nineteenth century by writers and painters led to the Loire becoming a magnet for tourists, first from France, then Europe and the rest of the world.

World Heritage site since

• • • • • • 1978 • 1979 • 1980 • 1981 • 1982 • 1983 • 1984 • 1985 • 1986 • 1987 • 1988 • 1989 • 1990 • 1991 • 1992 • 1993 • 1994 • 1995 • 1996 • 1997 • 1998 • 1999 • **2000**

Central Amazon Conservation Complex
Brazil

Criteria – *Significant ecological and biological processes; Significant natural habitat for biodiversity*

The Central Amazon Conservation Complex makes up the largest protected area in the Amazon Basin (over 60,000 km²) and is one of the planet's richest regions in terms of biodiversity. The site is made up of Jaú National Park, Demonstration area of Mamairauá Sustainable Development Reserve, Amanã Sustainable Development Reserve and the Anavilhanas Ecological Station. It includes an important sample of annually flooded (*várzea*) ecosystems, igapó forests, lakes and channels, which take the form of a constantly evolving aquatic mosaic that is home to the largest array of electric fish in the world. Numerous species of conservation concern live within the park, including jaguar, giant otter, Amazonian manatee, South American river turtle and black cayman. The Complex contains approximately 60 per cent of the species of fish reported to exist within the Negro River watershed, and 60 per cent of the birds recorded from the central Amazon.

The site contains the nine-tier waterfall of the Carabinani River and also includes a significant proportion of the black-water drainage system, the headwaters of which are located primarily in the Guiana Shield. Its dark colour results from organic acids released into the water through the decomposition of organic matter and the lack of terrestrial sediments.

The Amazon Basin from space.
▼

Isole Eolie (Aeolian Islands)
Italy

Criteria – Major stages of Earth's history

The Isole Eolie (Aeolian Islands) are located off the northern coast of Sicily and provide an outstanding record of volcanic island-building and volcanic phenomena. The group consists of seven islands (Lipari, Vulcano, Salina, Stromboli, Filicudi, Alicudi and Panarea) and five small islets (Basiluzzo, Dattilo, Lisca Nera, Bottaro and Lisca Bianca) in the vicinity of Panarea. Studied since at least the eighteenth century, the islands have provided the science of

vulcanology with examples of two types of eruption (Vulcanian and Strombolian). A total of 900 plant species have been recorded in the Aeolian Islands, including four endemic species. About forty bird species have been recorded, including ten under the Sicilian Red List of threatened bird species. The islands are also important for migrant bird species, and are an 'Important Bird Area' for congregatory species identified by Birdlife International.

Panarea is the smallest of the islands. It has a remarkable variety of differing environments in comparison with the other islands, especially in terms of flora, and is a fascinating site for naturalists. Stromboli is the only island in the archipelago that has permanent volcanic activity.

Stromboli.
▼

Island of Saint-Louis
Senegal

Criteria – Interchange of values; Significance in human history

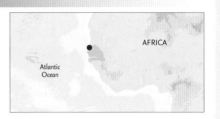

Founded as a French colonial settlement in the seventeenth century, Saint-Louis was urbanized in the mid-nineteenth century. It was the capital of Senegal from 1872 to 1957 and played an important cultural and economic role in the whole of West Africa. The island consists of a North quarter and a South quarter, with the Place Faidherbe in the centre. It is situated in a magnificent lagoon formed by the two arms of the Senegal River. The regular town plan, the system of quays, and the characteristic colonial architecture give Saint-Louis its distinctive appearance. The main historic buildings include the ancient fort, now the Governor's Palace, which marks the centre of the island. Situated next to it is the cathedral, completed in 1828.

In 1957, Saint-Louis ceased being capital of Senegal. This meant the departure of the French garrison and their families and the closure of offices and shops, with a drastic reduction in the French population. At present the city has revived its economy, based on fishing, agriculture and tourism.

Gochang, Hwasun and Ganghwa Dolmen Sites
Korea, Republic of

Criteria – Testimony to cultural tradition

The Gochang, Hwasun and Ganghwa sites contain the highest density and greatest variety of dolmens in the Republic of Korea, and indeed of any country. Dolmens are found in western China and the coastal areas of the Yellow Sea basin. They arrived in the Korean Peninsula with the Bronze Age and usually consist of two or more undressed stone slabs supporting a huge capstone. They were simple burial chambers, erected over the bodies or bones of Neolithic and Bronze Age worthies. The cemeteries at Gochang, Hwasun and Ganghwa contain many hundreds of excellent examples, preserving important evidence of how the stones were quarried, transported and raised and of how dolmen types changed during the second and first millennia BC in northeast Asia.

The dolmens would originally have been covered by earth mounds (barrows), but these gradually disappeared as a result of weathering and animal action. They may also have been platforms on which corpses were exposed to permit excarnation to take place, leaving bones for burial in collective or family tombs.

◄ Ganghwa dolmen.

World Heritage site since

• • • • • • 1978 • 1979 • 1980 • 1981 • 1982 • 1983 • 1984 • 1985 • 1986 • 1987 • 1988 • 1989 • 1990 • 1991 • 1992 • 1993 • 1994 • 1995 • 1996 • 1997 • 1998 • 1999 • 2000

The Cathedral of St James in Šibenik
Croatia

Criteria – Human creative genius; Interchange of values; Significance in human history

EUROPE

Adriatic Sea

Tyrrhenian Sea

The Cathedral of St James in Šibenik (built 1431–1535) bears witness to the considerable exchanges in the field of monumental arts between northern Italy, Dalmatia and Tuscany in the fifteenth and sixteenth centuries. The three architects who succeeded one another in the construction of the Cathedral – Francesco di Giacomo, Georgius Mathei Dalmaticus and Niccolò di Giovanni Fiorentino – developed a structure built entirely from stone, using unique construction methods for the vaulting and the dome of the cathedral. There is a close correspondence between the interior and exterior forms of the building. The decorative elements of the cathedral, such as a remarkable frieze containing seventy-one sculptured faces of men, women, and children, also illustrate the successful fusion of Gothic and Renaissance art.

The roofing of the aisles, as well as that of the apses and the dome, is made from stone 'tiles'. These roofing tiles are laid side by side with their horizontal edges overlapping, and the joints are made by the perfect fit. On the dome the tiles are held in place by stone wedges fitted with great precision.

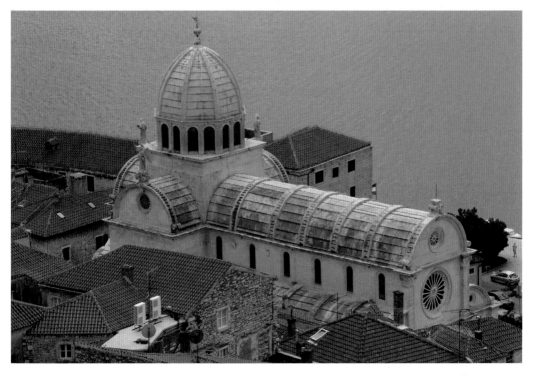

World Heritage site since

• • • • • •1978 • 1979 • 1980 • 1981 • 1982 • 1983 • 1984 • 1985 • 1986 • 1987 • 1988 • 1989 • 1990 • 1991 • 1992 • 1993 • 1994 • 1995 • 1996 • 1997 • 1998 • 1999 • **2000**

Ischigualasto / Talampaya Natural Parks

Argentina

Criteria – Major stages of Earth's history

Talampaya National Park and the contiguous Ischigualasto Provincial Park straddle the border between the provinces of San Juan and La Rioja in northwestern Argentina. The site constitutes almost the entire sedimentary basin known as the Ischigualasto-Villa Union Triassic basin. It was formed by layers of continental sediments deposited by rivers, lakes and swamps over the entire Triassic period (245–208 million years ago). The sediments

contain fossils of a wide range of plants and animals including the ancestors of mammals and dinosaurs. They constitute the world's most complete continental fossil record known from the Triassic, revealing the evolution of vertebrates as well as the environments they lived in during this period. Some fifty-six genera of fossil vertebrates have been recorded from the area, including fish, amphibians, and a great variety of reptiles.

Six geologic formations make up the Triassic basin, the earliest of which are the Talampaya and Tarjados formations, red sandstone that forms the impressive cliffs of the Talampaya National Park. The remaining formations are composed of lake beds, swamps, river channels and flood plain deposits. These formations contain the abundant vertebrate and flora fossils.

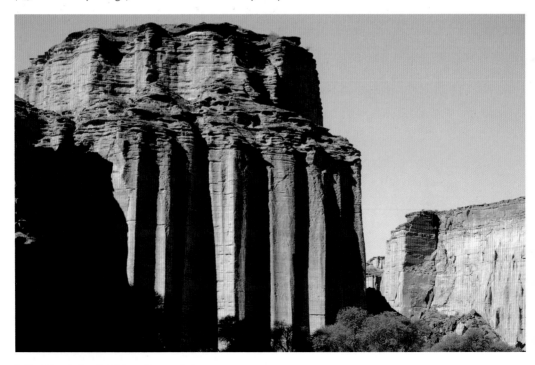

Historic Centre of Shakhrisyabz
Uzbekistan

Criteria – Testimony to cultural tradition;
Significance in human history

The historic centre of Shakhrisyabz contains a collection of exceptional monuments and ancient quarters which bear witness to the city's secular development, and particularly to the period of its apogee during the Timurid rule of the fifteenth–sixteenth centuries. The site consists of a number of monuments, including the grandiose Ak-Sarai Palace, begun in 1380; the Dorus Saodat complex, housing the royal mausoleum and religious areas; and the eighteenth-century Chor-su bazaar and baths. The dimensions of the magnificent Ak-Sarai Palace , known as the 'White Palace,' can be deduced from the size of the gate-towers, traces of which still survive: two towers each 50 m in height, and an arch with a span of 22 m.

The Dorus Saodat complex was designed as a place of burial for the ruling family and contained, in addition to the tombs themselves, a prayer hall, a mosque, and accommodation for the religious community and pilgrims. The main façade was faced with white marble. The tomb of Timur, also of white marble, is a masterpiece of the architecture of this period.

The two gate towers of Ak-Sarai Palace. ▼

World Heritage site since

• • • • • • 1978 • 1979 • 1980 • 1981 • 1982 • 1983 • 1984 • 1985 • 1986 • 1987 • 1988 • 1989 • 1990 • 1991 • 1992 • 1993 • 1994 • 1995 • 1996 • 1997 • 1998 • 1999 • 2000

High Coast / Kvarken Archipelago
Finland and Sweden
Criteria – Major stages of Earth's history

Displacement of settlements by land uplift has created a relict cultural landscape: Stone Age remains from 5000 BC are 150 m above sea level, while those of the Bronze and Iron Ages are at 30 m and 15 m respectively.

The High Coast, Sweden, and the Kvarken Archipelago, Finland, are situated in the Gulf of Bothnia, a northern extension of the Baltic Sea. The 5,600 islands of the Kvarken Archipelago feature unusual ridged washboard moraines, 'De Greer moraines', formed by the melting of the continental ice sheet, 10,000 to 24,000 years ago. The Archipelago is continuously rising from the sea in a process of rapid glacio-isostatic uplift, whereby the land, previously pressed down under the weight of a glacier, lifts at rates that are among the highest in the world. As a consequence islands appear and unite, peninsulas expand, and lakes evolve from bays and develop into marshes and peat fens. The High Coast has also been largely shaped by the combined processes of glaciation, glacial retreat and the emergence of new land from the sea. Since the last retreat of the ice from the High Coast 9,600 years ago, the uplift has been in the order of 285 m which is the highest known 'rebound'. The site affords outstanding opportunities for the understanding of the important processes that formed the glaciated and land uplift areas of the Earth's surface.

Monastery of Geghard and the Upper Azat Valley
Armenia
Criteria – Interchange of values

The monastery, founded in the fourth century and later rebuilt, was famous for its relics, most notably the spear that wounded Jesus on the Cross, and for relics of the Apostles Andrew and John.

The monastery of Geghard contains a number of churches and tombs, most of them cut into the rock, which illustrate the very peak of Armenian medieval architecture. The complex of medieval buildings is set into a landscape of great natural beauty, surrounded by towering cliffs at the entrance to the Azat Valley.

World Heritage site since

• • • • • • 1978 • 1979 • 1980 • 1981 • 1982 • 1983 • 1984 • 1985 • 1986 • 1987 • 1988 • 1989 • 1990 • 1991 • 1992 • 1993 • 1994 • 1995 • 1996 • 1997 • 1998 • 1999 • 2000

Kinabalu Park
Malaysia

Criteria – Significant ecological and biological processes; Significant natural habitat for biodiversity

Kinabalu Park is dominated by Mount Kinabalu (4,095 m), the highest mountain between the Himalaya and New Guinea. It has a wide range of habitats, from rich tropical lowland and hill rainforest to tropical mountain forest, sub-alpine forest and scrub on the higher elevations. It has been designated as a 'Centre of Plant Diversity for Southeast Asia' and is exceptionally rich in species, with examples of flora from the Himalaya, China, Australia and Malaysia. Wildlife is also diverse with ninety species of lowland mammal and twenty-two others found in the montane zone. Four species of primate occur and 326 bird species have been recorded. Half of all Borneo's bird, mammal and amphibian species – and two-thirds of its reptiles – are represented in the park, including many rare and endangered species.

The park has between 5,000–6,000 vascular plant species, 1,000 of which are orchids. Rafflesia, a rare parasitic plant, is also found. The mountain flora has diverse 'living fossils' such as the celery pine and the trig-oak, the evolutionary link between oaks and beeches.

Summit of Mount Kinabalu.
▼

World Heritage site since

• • • • • 1978 • 1979 • 1980 • 1981 • 1982 • 1983 • 1984 • 1985 • 1986 • 1987 • 1988 • 1989 • 1990 • 1991 • 1992 • 1993 • 1994 • 1995 • 1996 • 1997 • 1998 • 1999 • **2000**

Assisi, the Basilica of San Francesco and Other Franciscan Sites
Italy

Criteria – Human creative genius; Interchange of values; Testimony to cultural tradition; Significance in human history; Heritage associated with events of universal significance

EUROPE

Mediterranean Sea

Ionian Sea

Basilica of San Francesco. ▶

The Eremo delle Carceri on Mount Subasio were originally a series of caves where Francis and his companions came to pray. A small convent was later built on the site.

San Damiano is a monastic complex, essential for the understanding of the religious awakening of Francis; it was also Clare's convent and the place of her death.

Santa Maria degli Angeli is a sixteenth-century Renaissance church, built to protect the original chapel of Porziuncola, from where Francis sent his order to their mission and the place where he died.

The medieval hill town of Assisi is the birthplace of Saint Francis. It is a unique example of continuity of a city-sanctuary from its Umbrian-Roman and medieval origins to the present, represented in the cultural landscape, the religious ensembles and traditional land use. The town's medieval art masterpieces have made it a fundamental reference point for Italian and European art and architecture. It is also closely associated with the work of the Franciscan Order whose message has contributed significantly to developments in spirituality, art and architecture in the world.

Assisi stands on the hill of Asio at the foot of Mount Subasio. The most important event in its history was the life and work of Francis of Assisi (1182–1226), who initiated the Franciscan Order. His companion Clare, also later canonized, founded the sister order to the Franciscans, the Order of St Clare. After the canonization of Francis in 1228 it was decided to build a monumental church in his honour. This construction was followed by the Basilica of Santa Chiara to honour St Clare.

The Basilica of San Francesco is an outstanding example of an architectural ensemble that has significantly influenced the development of art and architecture.

Its construction began in 1228. The lower basilica is entered through an exquisite Gothic portal, its interior completely covered with frescoes. The upper basilica, entered through a loggia, has a magnificent east front in white limestone, with a large rose window in the centre. The interior walls are decorated with a series of paintings by Giotto and Cimabue relating to the faith and life of the saint.

The Cathedral of San Rufino probably dates from the eighth century; it was rebuilt around 1036 as a cathedral. The west front is a masterpiece of Umbrian Romanesque architecture, connected with the cathedral and the church of San Pietro of Spoleto.

The construction of the Basilica of Santa Chiara started in 1257. The structure is characterized by three flying buttresses and the interior is painted with a cycle of frescoes by several artists, illustrating the legend of St Clare.

Originally built outside the city walls, the Benedictine abbey of San Pietro is recorded from 1029; in the mid-twelfth century it adopted the Cluniac reform and it passed later to the Cistercians.

World Heritage site since

• • • • • • 1978 • 1979 • 1980 • 1981 • 1982 • 1983 • 1984 • 1985 • 1986 • 1987 • 1988 • 1989 • 1990 • 1991 • 1992 • 1993 • 1994 • 1995 • 1996 • 1997 • 1998 • 1999 • **2000**

Tiwanaku: Spiritual and Political Centre of the Tiwanaku Culture
Bolivia

Criteria – Testimony to cultural tradition;
Significance in human history

The ruins of Tiwanaku bear striking witness to the power of the empire that played a unique role in the development of the Andean pre-Hispanic civilization. The buildings are exceptional examples of the ceremonial and public architecture and art of one of the most important manifestations of the civilizations of the region. Tiwanaku began as a small settlement around 1200 BC. It was self-sufficient, with a non-irrigated form of farming based on frost-resistant crops, essential at this high altitude, producing tubers such as potatoes, oca and cereals, notably quinoa. In more sheltered locations near Lake Titicaca, maize and peaches were also cultivated. The inhabitants lived in rectangular adobe houses that were linked by paved streets. Following the introduction of copper metallurgy and improved irrigation, Tiwanaku's influence grew, reaching its apogee between 500 and 900 when it dominated a large area of the southern Andes and beyond.

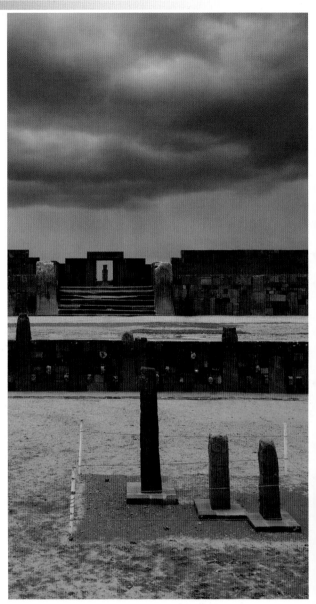

The most imposing monument at Tiwanaku is the temple of Akapana. Originally a pyramid with seven superimposed platforms, its retaining walls rose to a height of over 18 m and were clad in distinctive blue stone.

World Heritage site since

• • • • • 1978 • 1979 • 1980 • 1981 • 1982 • 1983 • 1984 • 1985 • 1986 • 1987 • 1988 • 1989 • 1990 • 1991 • 1992 • 1993 • 1994 • 1995 • 1996 • 1997 • 1998 • 1999 • **2000**

Mir Castle Complex
Belarus

Criteria – Interchange of values; Significance in human history

The Mir Castle complex vividly symbolizes the history of Belarus and, as such, it is one of the major national symbols of the country. It lies in a fertile region in the geographical centre of Europe, at the crossroads of the most important trade routes, and was, at the same time, at the epicentre of crucial European and global military conflicts between neighbouring powers with different religious and cultural traditions. The construction of this castle, in the Gothic style, began at the end of the

fifteenth century. It was subsequently extended and reconstructed, first in the Renaissance and then in the Baroque style. After being abandoned for nearly a century and suffering severe damage during the Napoleonic period, the castle was restored at the end of the nineteenth century, with the addition of a number of other elements and the landscaping of the surrounding area as a park. Its present form is graphic testimony to its often turbulent history.

The Mir Castle complex is situated on the bank of a small lake at the confluence of the Miryanka River and a small tributary. Its impressive fortified walls feature four exterior corner towers rising to five storeys and a six-storey external gate tower.
▼

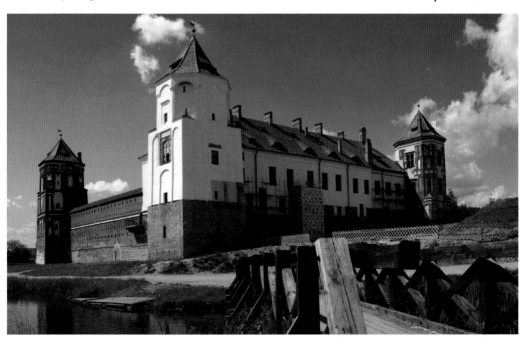

World Heritage site since

• • • • • • 1978 • 1979 • 1980 • 1981 • 1982 • 1983 • 1984 • 1985 • 1986 • 1987 • 1988 • 1989 • 1990 • 1991 • 1992 • 1993 • 1994 • 1995 • 1996 • 1997 • 1998 • 1999 • **2000**

Rietveld Schröderhuis (Rietveld Schröder House)
Netherlands

Criteria – Human creative genius; Interchange of values

The Rietveld Schröder House in Utrecht was commissioned by Ms Truus Schröder-Schräder, designed by the architect Gerrit Thomas Rietveld, and built in 1924. This small family house, with its interior, the flexible spatial arrangement, and the visual and formal qualities, was a manifesto of the ideals of the De Stijl group of artists and architects in the Netherlands in the 1920s, and has since been considered one of the icons of the Modern Movement in architecture.

The design and building of the house took place simultaneously. The owner and architect commissioned a full photographic documentation of the architecture to ensure that the new approach of the De Stijl group was presented to reflect their intended ideas.

Noel Kempff Mercado National Park
Bolivia

Criteria – Significant ecological and biological processes; Significant natural habitat for biodiversity

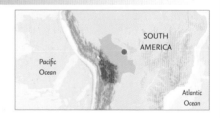

The National Park is one of the largest (15,230 km²) and most intact parks in the Amazon Basin. With an altitudinal range from 200 m to nearly 1,000 m, it is the site of a rich mosaic of habitat types from Cerrado savanna and forest to upland evergreen Amazonian forest. Located on the border with Brazil, the site includes a large section of the Huanchaca Plateau and surrounding lowlands. Several rivers have their sources on the plateau and form spectacular waterfalls. The park boasts an evolutionary history dating back over a billion years to the Precambrian period. An estimated 4,000 species of flora, as well as over 600 bird species and viable populations of many globally endangered or threatened vertebrate species, live in the park.

The park has five distinct ecosystems and its outstanding habitat diversity favours the existence of a wide range of wildlife. More than 130 species of animals live in the park including many of the rare mammals of Bolivia such as river otters and jaguars.

World Heritage site since

• • • • • • 1978 • 1979 • 1980 • 1981 • 1982 • 1983 • 1984 • 1985 • 1986 • 1987 • 1988 • 1989 • 1990 • 1991 • 1992 • 1993 • 1994 • 1995 • 1996 • 1997 • 1998 • 1999 • **2000**

Holy Trinity Column in Olomouc
Czech Republic

Criteria – Human creative genius; Significance in human history

The Olomouc Holy Trinity Column is one of the most exceptional examples of the apogee of central European Baroque artistic expression. In the reconstruction (1648–1650) following the Thirty Years' War the city of Olomouc took on a new appearance. Many impressive public and private buildings were constructed in a local variant of the prevailing style, which became known as 'Olomouc Baroque'. The most characteristic expression of this style was a group of monuments (columns and fountains), of which the Holy Trinity Column is the crowning glory. Erected in the early years of the eighteenth century and rising to a height of 35 m, it is decorated with many fine religious sculptures, including the work of the distinguished Moravian artist Ondrej Zahner.

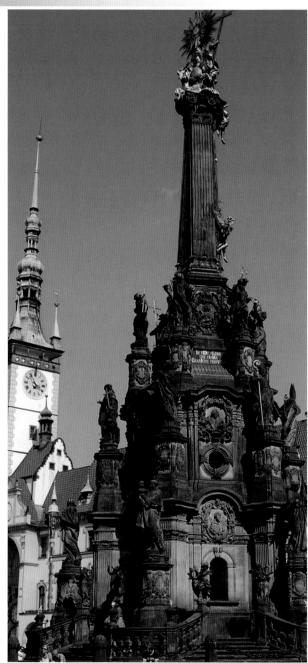

The Column forms a triumphal stone statement of the creeds of both Christianity and of citizenship. Faith and religious tradition are harmoniously combined with the idea of the city – its traditions, protection and civil administration. ▶

World Heritage site since

• • • • • •1978 • 1979 • 1980 • 1981 • 1982 • 1983 • 1984 • 1985 • 1986 • 1987 • 1988 • 1989 • 1990 • 1991 • 1992 • 1993 • 1994 • 1995 • 1996 • 1997 • 1998 • 1999 • 2000

Gunung Mulu National Park
Malaysia

Criteria – Natural phenomena or beauty; Major stages of Earth's history; Significant ecological and biological processes; Significant natural habitat for biodiversity

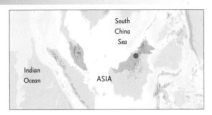

Gunung Mulu National Park on the island of Borneo protects an exceptional range of natural phenomena. The 529 km² park contains 17 vegetation zones, exhibiting some 3,500 species of vascular plants, 80 species of mammal and 270 species of bird (including 24 Borneon endemics). The park is considered to be one of the richest sites in the world for palms with 109 species of 20 genera identified. The park is dominated by Gunung Mulu, a 2,377-m-high sandstone pinnacle. Another outstanding karst feature is the 'pinnacles', 50-m-high sharp blades of rock that project through the rainforest canopy. The site also has a high concentration of large cave passages which provide a major wildlife spectacle of cave swiftlets and bats. Three million wrinkled-lipped freetail bats inhabit one cave alone.

The park is important for its karst features. There are at least 295 km of explored caves, estimated to be at least 2–3 million years old. Sarawak Chamber, which is 600 m by 415 m and 80 m high, is the largest known cave chamber in the world.

King's Chamber in Wind Cave in Gunung Mulu National Park.
▼

World Heritage site since

• • • • • • 1978 • 1979 • 1980 • 1981 • 1982 • 1983 • 1984 • 1985 • 1986 • 1987 • 1988 • 1989 • 1990 • 1991 • 1992 • 1993 • 1994 • 1995 • 1996 • 1997 • 1998 • 1999 • **2000**

Palmeral of Elche
Spain

Criteria – Interchange of values; Traditional
human settlement

The Palmeral (a landscape of date palm
groves) of Elche was laid out towards the
end of the tenth century AD, when the
Muslim city of Elche was also erected. Much
of the Iberian peninsula was Arab at this time
and the Palmeral represents a unique
transference of Arab agricultural practices to
the European continent. Cultivation of date
palms in Elche is known at least since Iberian
times, dating from around the fifth
century BC, but the Arabs introduced more
systematic practices, including an elaborate
irrigation system which is still functioning.
Arab geographers and European travellers
throughout history have testified to this
exceptional example of progressive
landscaping.

Palms form an
essential component of
the culture of Elche,
manifesting their
influence on society in
many ways, including
the processions on
Palm Sunday, the
Night of the Kings
and on the town's coat
of arms. ▶

World Heritage site since

• • • • • • 1978 • 1979 • 1980 • 1981 • 1982 • 1983 • 1984 • 1985 • 1986 • 1987 • 1988 • 1989 • 1990 • 1991 • 1992 • 1993 • 1994 • 1995 • 1996 • 1997 • 1998 • 1999 • **2000**

Agricultural Landscape of Southern Öland
Sweden

Criteria – Significance in human history;
Traditional human settlement

The interaction between man and the natural environment in the south of Öland, an island in the Baltic sea, is of unique universal value. Human beings have lived here for some five thousand years and adapted their way of life to the physical constraints of the island. As a consequence, the landscape is unique, with abundant evidence of continuous human settlement from prehistoric times to the present day.

Land use has not changed significantly since then, with arable farming and animal husbandry still remaining the principal economic activity. The southern part of the island is dominated by Stora Alvaret, one of the largest limestone pavements in Europe. Its medieval pattern of villages and field systems is still clearly visible, a very rare occurrence in northern Europe.

The prosperity of the island, due in no small measure to its situation on the main trading route through the Kalmar Sound, is reflected in the imposing stone churches built in the twelfth century, such as those at Hulterstad and Resmö. They were fortified as defence against attacks from marauders.

Monastic Island of Reichenau
Germany

Criteria – Testimony to cultural tradition;
Significance in human history; Heritage
associated with events of universal significance

The island of Reichenau on Lake Constance preserves the traces of the Benedictine monastery, founded in 724, which exercised remarkable spiritual, intellectual and artistic influence. The churches of St Mary and St Marcus, St Peter and St Paul, and St George, mainly built between the ninth and eleventh centuries, provide a panorama of early medieval monastic architecture in central Europe. Their wall paintings bear witness to impressive artistic activity.

The Monastery of Reichenau was a highly significant artistic centre in tenth- and eleventh-century Europe, as illustrated by its monumental wall paintings and illuminations, and it became a famous centre for teaching and creativity in literature, science, and the arts.

◄
Church of St George in Reichenau.

Wachau Cultural Landscape
Austria

Criteria – Interchange of values; Significance in human history

Several impressive castles dominate the towns and the Danube valley, and there are many architecturally and artistically significant ecclesiastical buildings spread throughout both townscape and landscape.

The Wachau, a stretch of the Danube valley between Melk and Krems, is an outstanding example of a riverine landscape bordered by mountains in which material evidence of its long historical evolution has survived to a remarkable degree. The architecture, the human settlements, and the agricultural use of the land in the Wachau vividly illustrate a basically medieval landscape which has evolved organically and harmoniously over time. Clearance of the natural forest cover by man began in the Neolithic period, although radical changes in the landscape did not take place until around 800, when the Bavarian and Salzburg monasteries began to cultivate the slopes of the Wachau, creating the present-day landscape pattern of vine terraces.

Vineyards near Spitz in Wachau.
▼

Gyeongju Historic Areas
Korea, Republic of

Criteria – Interchange of values; Testimony to
cultural tradition

The Korean peninsula
was ruled for almost
1,000 years by the
Shilla dynasty, and the
sites and monuments
in and around their
capital, Kyongju, bear
outstanding
testimony to their
cultural
achievements.

The Gyeongju Historic Areas contain a
remarkable concentration of outstanding
examples of Korean Buddhist art, in the
form of sculptures, reliefs, pagodas, and the
remains of temples and palaces from the
flowering, in particular between the seventh
and tenth centuries, of this unique form of
artistic expression. There are three major
areas ('belts') at Gyeongju. Mount Namsan
Belt has a large number of prehistoric and
historic remains. Wolsong Belt is home to
the ruined palace site of Wolsong, the
Kyerim woodland (which legend identifies
as the birthplace of the founder of the
Kyongju Kim clan), and the Ch'omsongdae
Observatory. Tumuli Park Belt consists of
three groups of royal tombs. Excavations
here have produced rich grave-goods of
gold, glass and fine ceramics.

Buddha relief
carved in rock on
Mount Namsan.
▼

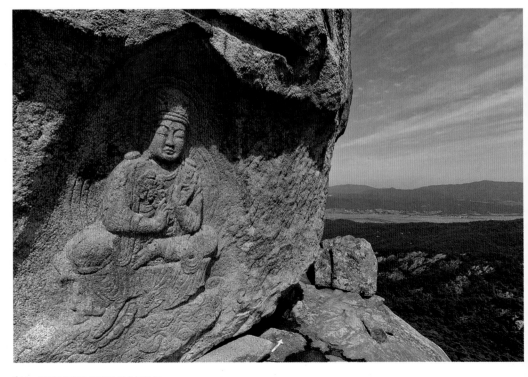

World Heritage site since

• • • • • • 1978 • 1979 • 1980 • 1981 • 1982 • 1983 • 1984 • 1985 • 1986 • 1987 • 1988 • 1989 • 1990 • 1991 • 1992 • 1993 • 1994 • 1995 • 1996 • 1997 • 1998 • 1999 • **2000**

Gusuku Sites and Related Properties of the Kingdom of Ryukyu

Japan

Criteria – Interchange of values; Testimony to cultural tradition; Heritage associated with events of universal significance

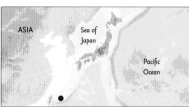

For several centuries the Ryukyu Islands served as a centre of economic and cultural interchange between southeast Asia, China, Korea and Japan, and this is vividly demonstrated by the surviving monuments. In the tenth–twelfth centuries, Ryukyuan farming communities began to enclose their villages with simple stone walls for protection. From the twelfth century onwards powerful groups known

as aji began to emerge. They enlarged the defences of their settlements, converting them into fortresses and adopting the term gusuku to describe these formidable castles. The ruins of the castles, on imposing elevated sites, are evidence for the social structure over much of that period, while the sacred sites provide testimony to the survival of an ancient form of religion.

The Stone Gate of the Sonohyan Shrine was erected in 1519 by Shô Shin. It was the guardian shrine of the Ryukyu Kingdom, where prayers were offered for peace and security at annual ritual ceremonies, and represents the unique style of Ryukyu stone architecture.

Ensemble of the Ferrapontov Monastery

Russian Federation

Criteria – Human creative genius; Significance in human history

The Ferrapontov Monastery, in the Vologda region of northern Russia, is an exceptionally well-preserved and complete example of a Russian Orthodox monastic complex of the fifteenth–seventeenth centuries, a period of great significance in the development of the unified Russian state and its culture. There are six major elements in the complex. The Cathedral of the Nativity of the Virgin (1490) is the earliest and the nucleus; its interior is

graced by the magnificent wall paintings of Dionisy, the greatest Russian artist of the end of the fifteenth century. This was followed by the Church of the Annunciation, the Treasury Chamber and ancillary buildings. In the seventeenth century the Gate Church, the Church of St Martinian and the bell tower were added.

In the nineteenth century a diminished area of the complex was enclosed by a brick wall. It reopened as a convent for nuns in 1904, but this was closed in 1924. It currently serves as the museum of the frescoes of Dionisy, opened in the first half of the twentieth century, but greatly enlarged and improved since 1975.

World Heritage site since

• • • • • • 1978 • 1979 • 1980 • 1981 • 1982 • 1983 • 1984 • 1985 • 1986 • 1987 • 1988 • 1989 • 1990 • 1991 • 1992 • 1993 • 1994 • 1995 • 1996 • 1997 • 1998 • 1999 • 2000

Ciudad Universitaria de Caracas
Venezuela

Criteria – Human creative genius; Significance in human history

The City University of Caracas is an outstanding example, and one of the best in the world, of the modern urban, architectural and artistic concepts of the early twentieth century. Built to the design of the architect Carlos Raúl Villanueva between 1940 and 1960, the university campus integrates the large number of buildings and functions into a clearly articulated ensemble which is at the same time protected from light and heat. It includes masterpieces of modern architecture and visual arts, such as the Aula Magna with the 'Clouds' of Alexander Calder, the Olympic Stadium, and the Covered Plaza. Villanueva's project is characterized by the application of modern technology, the audacity of the forms, and the use of bare concrete structures, conceived as sculptures.

The architecture of the university involves the use of spatial elements that have been extracted from Venezuelan colonial architecture, such as bright colours, latticed windows for ventilation and internal gardens of copious tropical vegetation.

Catalan Romanesque Churches of the Vall de Boí
Spain

Criteria – Testimony to cultural tradition; Significance in human history

The narrow Vall de Boí is screened by the high peaks of the Beciberri/Punta Alta massif, in the high Pyrenees. Its picturesque small villages are set amid woodland and meadows. Each village in the valley contains a Romanesque church, and is surrounded by a pattern of enclosed fields. There are extensive seasonally-used grazing lands on the higher slopes. The churches of the Vall de Boí are an especially pure and consistent example of Romanesque art in a virtually untouched rural setting. In the Middle Ages there was an influx of culture and money from outside the area. Most of the churches in the valley were built then, at the instigation of a single family, at the same time as historical Catalonia was being created.

The Arab invasion of the Iberian Peninsula never penetrated the valleys of the high Pyrenees, but they were exposed to outside cultural influences, particularly in the eleventh century from Lombardy, a noted centre of Romanesque architecture.

World Heritage site since

• • • • • 1978 • 1979 • 1980 • 1981 • 1982 • 1983 • 1984 • 1985 • 1986 • 1987 • 1988 • 1989 • 1990 • 1991 • 1992 • 1993 • 1994 • 1995 • 1996 • 1997 • 1998 • 1999 • 2000

Bardejov Town Conservation Reserve
Slovakia

Criteria – Testimony to cultural tradition;
Significance in human history

The fortified town of Bardejov provides exceptionally well-preserved evidence of the economic and social structure of trading towns in medieval central Europe. The plan, buildings and fortifications of the town illustrate the typical urban complex that developed in central Europe in the Middle Ages at major points along the great trade routes of the period. Bardejov is situated on a floodplain terrace of the Topl'a River, in northeastern Slovakia in the hills of the Beskyd Mountains. From the first quarter of the eighteenth century, Slovaks and Hassidic Jews came into Bardejov in large numbers, and among other remarkable features is the town's small Jewish quarter. Centred around the Great Synagogue, a fine building constructed in 1725–1747, the complex also contains ritual baths, a kosher slaughterhouse and a meeting building, now a school.

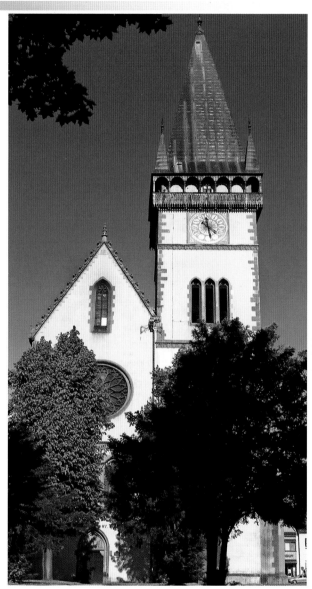

The town centre is dominated by the rectangular main square, closed on three sides by forty-six burgher houses with typical narrow frontages. On the fourth side is the parish church of St Egidius (**pictured** *above*), together with the town school.

World Heritage site since

• • • • • • 1978 • 1979 • 1980 • 1981 • 1982 • 1983 • 1984 • 1985 • 1986 • 1987 • 1988 • 1989 • 1990 • 1991 • 1992 • 1993 • 1994 • 1995 • 1996 • 1997 • 1998 • 1999 • **2000**

Historic and Architectural Complex of the Kazan Kremlin
Russian Federation

Criteria – Interchange of values; Testimony to cultural tradition; Significance in human history

Built on an ancient site, the Kazan Kremlin consists of an outstanding group of historic buildings dating from the sixteenth to nineteenth centuries. It is exceptional testimony of the Kazan Khanate and is the only surviving Tatar fortress with traces of the original town-planning conception. It is, furthermore, an excellent example of a synthesis of Tatar and Russian influences in architecture, integrating different cultures (Bulgar, Golden Horde, Tatar, Italian and Russian), as well as showing the impact of Islam and Christianity. It was conquered by Ivan the Terrible in 1552 and became the Christian See of the Volga Land, and is still an important place of pilgrimage.

The oldest building within the Kazan Kremlin complex is the sixteenth-century Annunciation Cathedral, constructed of local light sandstone.

The tower of the ▶ Kazan Kremlin.

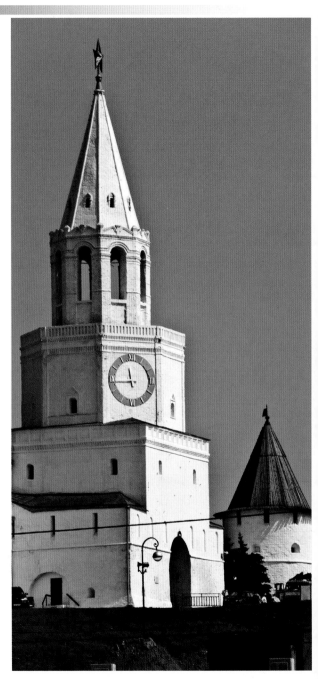

World Heritage site since

• • • • • • 1978 • 1979 • 1980 • 1981 • 1982 • 1983 • 1984 • 1985 • 1986 • 1987 • 1988 • 1989 • 1990 • 1991 • 1992 • 1993 • 1994 • 1995 • 1996 • 1997 • 1998 • 1999 • **2000**

Archaeological Site of Atapuerca
Spain
Criteria – Testimony to cultural tradition; Traditional human settlement

The caves of the Sierra de Atapuerca provide unique testimony of the origin and evolution both of the existing human civilisation and of other cultures that have disappeared. The rich fossil record ranges from the earliest human beings in Europe, living nearly one million years ago, right up to remains of modern man. They represent an exceptional reserve of data, the scientific study of which provides priceless

information about the appearance and the way of life of these remote human ancestors. The Galería del Silex site contains more than fifty painted and engraved panels with geometrical motifs, hunting scenes, and anthropomorphic and zoomorphic figures. Excavation has revealed human remains (largely young adults and children) and ceramic fragments, identified as being related to sacrificial activities.

The evolutionary line or lines from the African ancestors of modern man are documented in the Sierra de Atapuerca. The earliest human fossil remains in Europe, dating from around 800,000 years ago, were found in the Gran Dolina site here.

Jesuit Block and Estancias of Córdoba
Argentina
Criteria – Interchange of values; Significance in human history

The Jesuit Block in Córdoba, heart of the former Jesuit Province of Paraguay, contains the core buildings of the Jesuit system: the university, the church and residence of the Society of Jesus, and the college. Along with the five estancias, or farming estates, they are exceptional examples of the fusion of European and indigenous cultures during a seminal period in South America. The university is arranged round a central open space (originally a botanical garden), and

constructed in stone and brick, with spacious colonnades around the courtyard. The Society of Jesus Church is a massive domed structure with two squat towers at the west end. The interior is richly decorated, the retablo of the main altar and the pulpit being outstanding examples of Baroque.

Córdoba itself, established by Jerónimo Luis de Cabrera in 1573, was laid out on the standard Spanish colonial chequerboard pattern. In common with other religious orders, the Jesuits were allocated one of the seventy blocks of the original city.

World Heritage site since

• • • • • 1978 • 1979 • 1980 • 1981 • 1982 • 1983 • 1984 • 1985 • 1986 • 1987 • 1988 • 1989 • 1990 • 1991 • 1992 • 1993 • 1994 • 1995 • 1996 • 1997 • 1998 • 1999 • **2000**

Mount Qingcheng and the Dujiangyan Irrigation System
China

ASIA

Pacific
Ocean

Criteria – Interchange of values; Significance in human history; Heritage associated with events of universal significance

Construction of the Dujiangyan irrigation system began in the third century BC. This system still controls the waters of the Minjiang River and distributes it to the fertile farmland of the Chengdu plains. Mount Qingcheng was the birthplace of Taoism, which is celebrated in a series of ancient temples.

In AD 142 the philosopher Zhang Daoling founded the doctrine of Taoism on Mount Qingcheng. During the Jin dynasty (265–420) several Taoist temples were built on the mountain and the teachings of Taoism were disseminated widely from here throughout China.

◄
The Dujiangyan irrigation system crossing the Minjiang River.

Major Town Houses of the Architect Victor Horta (Brussels)
Belgium

North Sea

EUROPE

Bay of Biscay

Criteria – Human creative genius; Interchange of values; Significance in human history

The four major town houses – Hôtel Tassel, Hôtel Solvay, Hôtel van Eetvelde, and Maison and Atelier Horta – located in Brussels and designed by the architect Victor Horta, one of the earliest initiators of Art Nouveau, are some of the most remarkable pioneering works of architecture of the end of the nineteenth century. The stylistic revolution represented by these works is characterised by their open plan, the diffusion of light, and the brilliant joining of the curved lines of decoration with the structure of the building.

The Horta buildings brilliantly illustrate the transition from the nineteenth to the twentieth centuries in art, thought and society. Of the four houses, the Hôtel Solvay is the best preserved, with its interior intact and its utilities in functional order.

◄
Hôtel van Eetvelde.

World Heritage site since

• • • • • 1978 • 1979 • 1980 • 1981 • 1982 • 1983 • 1984 • 1985 • 1986 • 1987 • 1988 • 1989 • 1990 • 1991 • 1992 • 1993 • 1994 • 1995 • 1996 • 1997 • 1998 • 1999 • **2000**

Roman Walls of Lugo
Spain
Criteria – Significance in human history

The walls of Lugo were built in the later part of the third century to defend the Roman town of Lucus. The entire circuit survives intact and is the finest example of late Roman fortifications in western Europe. Despite the strength of its fortifications, Lugo was unable to resist the Suevi when they swept into the Iberian peninsula in the early fifth century and destroyed the town by fire. They were to be dislodged in turn by the Visigoths, who captured the town in 457 and settled it once again. The irresistible Moorish invasion of Spain saw Lugo overwhelmed and sacked in 714, but it was recaptured for Christendom by Alfonso I of Asturias in 755 and restored by Bishop Odarius. The town was to be ravaged once again in 968 by the Normans, on their way to the Mediterranean, and it was not restored until the following century.

Of the original interval towers, forty-six have survived intact, and there are a further thirty-nine that are wholly or partly dismantled. There are ten gates: five ancient and five recent. One of the best preserved is the Miñá Gate, which still has its original vaulted arch set between two towers, in characteristic Roman form.

Archaeological Landscape of the First Coffee Plantations in the South-East of Cuba
Cuba
Criteria – Testimony to cultural tradition; Significance in human history

The production of coffee in eastern Cuba during the nineteenth and early twentieth centuries resulted in the creation of a unique cultural landscape, illustrating a significant stage in the development of this form of agriculture. The site consists of the remains of 171 coffee plantations on the rugged slopes of the Sierra Maestra. The traditional plantation consists of a number of basic elements: at its centre is the residence of the owner, surrounded by much more modest accommodation for the slaves, both domestic and agricultural. The main industrial element was the terraced drying floor (secadero), on which the coffee beans were steeped in water in preparation for processing. The secaderos are recognizable as large sunken areas surrounded by low walls and linked with cisterns or water channels.

In the late nineteenth century, coffee production began in other parts of Latin America, such as Brazil, Colombia and Costa Rica. New techniques were introduced, based on developed agricultural systems. The early plantations in eastern Cuba found themselves unable to compete in the growing world markets and they gradually closed down.

World Heritage site since

• • • • • • 1978 • 1979 • 1980 • 1981 • 1982 • 1983 • 1984 • 1985 • 1986 • 1987 • 1988 • 1989 • 1990 • 1991 • 1992 • 1993 • 1994 • 1995 • 1996 • 1997 • 1998 • 1999 • **2000**

Historic Centre of Brugge
Belgium

Criteria – Interchange of values; Significance in human history; Heritage associated with events of universal significance

Brugge (Bruges) is an outstanding example of a medieval settlement that has maintained its historic fabric as it evolved over the centuries, and where original Gothic constructions form part of the town's identity. As one of Europe's commercial and cultural capitals, Brugge developed cultural links to different parts of the world. It is closely associated with the school of Flemish Primitive painting.

Archaeological excavations show evidence of human presence in the area of Brugge from the Iron Age and the Gallo-Roman period. It was the military and administrative centre of the region and commercial links with Scandinavia started at that time. The name of Brugge is first mentioned in the ninth century and is documented in Carolingian coins bearing the name Bruggia. At this time it was part of a defence system against the Normans, and the first fortification existed in 851 at the site of the present-day Bourg. The settlement developed gradually and it became a harbour and commercial centre with European connections.

The Brugge fair was established in 1200 and contacts with Britain were the first to develop, particularly in the wool trade. The city's growing prosperity was reflected in the construction of public buildings such

as the imposing belfry in the Grand Place, and Brugge was quickly established as an economic capital of Europe. Under Philippe le Bon (1419–67), the Duke of Burgundy, who set up his court in Brugge, the city became a centre of court life, of Flemish art, of miniature painting, and printing. Owing to the presence of Italians it soon became a centre of humanism and the Renaissance.

From the late fifteenth century Brugge gradually entered a period of stagnation. The Flemish regions were integrated into the Habsburg Empire, and the discovery of America displaced economic interests from the Atlantic to the Mediterranean. However, from 1600 to 1800, as a result of the construction of canal systems, Brugge re-established its maritime connection, albeit at a modest level. From 1815 to 1830 Brugge was part of the United Kingdom of the Netherlands and since 1830 has been part of Belgium. During the nineteenth century a colony of English aristocrats influenced the cultural life of the city and contributed to a renewed interest in the artistic heritage of Brugge and the restoration of historic buildings.

Brugge Belfry. ▶

The most important of Brugge's squares are the Burg and the Grand Place. For 1,000 years the Burg square has symbolized the alliance of religious and civic authorities. The Grand Place is the site of the halls, the belfry and the Waterhalle, symbolizing municipal autonomy.

From the Middle Ages the architecture of Brugge has been characterized by brick Gothic, particularly the style of construction known as *travée brugeoise*. Maintained until the seventeenth century, this type of construction was also the main inspiration for nineteenth-century restorations.

World Heritage site since

• • • • • 1978 • 1979 • 1980 • 1981 • 1982 • 1983 • 1984 • 1985 • 1986 • 1987 • 1988 • 1989 • 1990 • 1991 • 1992 • 1993 • 1994 • 1995 • 1996 • 1997 • 1998 • 1999 • **2000**

Neolithic Flint Mines at Spiennes (Mons)
Belgium

Criteria – Human creative genius; Testimony to cultural tradition; Significance in human history

Underground flint mining began around the mid-fifth millennium BC and carried on for centuries. The remains of the mines show the gradual development of technology by prehistoric man to extract a material essential for the production of tools and implements.

The Neolithic flint mines at Spiennes, covering more than 1 km², are the largest and earliest concentration of ancient mines in Europe. They are also remarkable for the diversity of technological solutions used for extraction and for the fact that they are directly linked to a settlement of the same period. Currently the site appears on the surface as a large area of meadows and fields strewn with millions of scraps of worked flint. Underground the site is an immense network of galleries linked to the surface by vertical shafts dug by Neolithic man. Many of the mines have never been excavated and those which are open to the public are in their original condition, with the exception of some modern shoring and props.

World Heritage site since

• • • • • •1978 • 1979 • 1980 • 1981 • 1982 • 1983 • 1984 • 1985 • 1986 • 1987 • 1988 • 1989 • 1990 • 1991 • 1992 • 1993 • 1994 • 1995 • 1996 • 1997 • 1998 • 1999 • **2000**

Ancient Villages in Southern Anhui – Xidi and Hongcun
China

Criteria – Interchange of values; Significance in human history; Traditional human settlement

Hongcun (**pictured below**) retains many of its fine buildings and its exceptional water system. The open watercourse runs through the village and forms two ponds, one in the centre (Moon Pond) and the other to the south of the village (South Lake).

The traditional non-urban settlements of China, which have to a very large extent disappeared during the twentieth century, are exceptionally well preserved in the villages of Xidi and Hongcun. The two villages are graphic illustrations of a type of human settlement created during a feudal period and based on a prosperous trading economy. In their buildings and their street patterns, they reflect the socio-economic structure of a long-lived settled period of Chinese history. The streets are all paved with granite and the buildings, which are widely spaced, are timber-framed with brick walls and elegantly carved decoration.

World Heritage site since

• • • • • • 1978 • 1979 • 1980 • 1981 • 1982 • 1983 • 1984 • 1985 • 1986 • 1987 • 1988 • 1989 • 1990 • 1991 • 1992 • 1993 • 1994 • 1995 • 1996 • 1997 • 1998 • 1999 • **2000**

Longmen Grottoes
China

Criteria – Human creative genius; Interchange of values; Testimony to cultural tradition

ASIA

Pacific
Ocean

In total 2,345 niches or grottoes have been recorded on the two sides of the river at Longmen. They house more than 100,000 Buddhist statues, about 2,500 stelae and inscriptions, and over 60 Buddhist pagodas.

The grottoes and niches of Longmen contain the largest and most impressive collection of Chinese art of the late Northern Wei and Tang dynasties. These works, entirely devoted to the Buddhist religion, represent the high point of Chinese stone carving. This perfection of a long-established art form was to play a highly significant role in the cultural evolution of this region of Asia. Work began on the

Longmen Grottoes in 493, when Emperor Xiaowen of the Northern Wei dynasty moved his capital to Luoyang, and was to continue for the next four centuries. The group of giant statues in Fengxiansi Cave is most fully representative of this phase of Chinese art at Longmen; they are generally acknowledged to be artistic masterpieces of truly global significance.

Boddhisatvas in the main grotto.
▼

World Heritage site since

• • • • • • 1978 • 1979 • 1980 • 1981 • 1982 • 1983 • 1984 • 1985 • 1986 • 1987 • 1988 • 1989 • 1990 • 1991 • 1992 • 1993 • 1994 • 1995 • 1996 • 1997 • 1998 • 1999 • **2000**

Notre-Dame Cathedral in Tournai
Belgium

Criteria – Interchange of values; Significance in human history

The Cathedral of Notre-Dame in Tournai was built in the first half of the twelfth century. The cathedral lies at the heart of the old town, not far from the left bank of the river Escaut. In architectural terms, it is the product of three design periods that can still easily be distinguished: the Romanesque nave is of extraordinary dimensions with a wealth of sculpture on its capitals; the choir, rebuilt in the thirteenth century, is in the pure Gothic style; these are linked by a transept in a transitional style featuring an impressive group of five bell towers. The cathedral's front is decorated with

sculptures dating from different periods (fourteenth, sixteenth and seventeenth centuries) depicting Old Testament scenes, episodes from the city's history, and saints.

The cathedral bears witness to an exchange of architectural influence between the Île de France, the Rhineland and Normandy in the short period at the start of the twelfth century that preceded the flowering of Gothic architecture.

Cathedral and Churches of Echmiatsin and the Archaeological Site of Zvartnots
Armenia

Criteria – Interchange of values; Testimony to cultural tradition

The cathedral and churches of Echmiatsin and the archaeological remains at Zvartnots graphically illustrate the evolution and development of the Armenian central-domed cross-hall type of church, which exerted a profound influence on architectural and artistic development in the region.

The Cathedral of Holy Echmiatsin, built in 301–3, is Armenia's most ancient Christian place of worship. Together with the other religious buildings and archaeological remains in Echmiatsin and Zvartnots, it bears witness to the founding of Christianity in the country.

◀

Ruins of the temple at Zvartnots.

World Heritage site since

• • • • • 1978 • 1979 • 1980 • 1981 • 1982 • 1983 • 1984 • 1985 • 1986 • 1987 • 1988 • 1989 • 1990 • 1991 • 1992 • 1993 • 1994 • 1995 • 1996 • 1997 • 1998 • 1999 • 2000

Pantanal Conservation Area
Brazil

Criteria – Natural phenomena or beauty;
Significant ecological and biological processes;
Significant natural habitat for biodiversity

The Pantanal Conservation Complex consists of a cluster of four protected areas located in western central Brazil at the southwest corner of the state of Mato Grosso. The site represents 1.3 per cent of Brazil's Pantanal region, one of the world's largest freshwater wetland ecosystems. The headwaters of the region's two major river systems, the Cuiabá and the Paraguay Rivers, are located here, and the abundance and diversity of its vegetation and animal life are spectacular.

The Pantanal is an immense alluvial plain. Its landscape encompasses a variety of ecological subregions, including river corridors, gallery forests, perennial wetlands and lakes, seasonally inundated grasslands and terrestrial forests.

Surrounded by mountain ridges and plains, the region presents a flat landscape with a small inclination which follows a north-south, east-west direction. The main source of water for the Pantanal is the Cuiabá River. The water spreads out and covers broad expanses, seeking a natural outlet, which lies hundreds of kilometres downstream at the confluence of the river and the Atlantic Ocean. Hydrological studies indicate the presence of a network of underground streams and a degree of subsurface water movement.

The vegetation is located in an area of transition between the dry savanna (cerrado) of central Brazil and the semi-deciduous forest of the south and southeast. The wide range of interacting habitat types produces a remarkable plant diversity.

The fauna of the Pantanal is extremely varied and includes 80 species of mammal, 650 bird, 50 reptile and 400 fish types. Dense populations of species of conservation concern live in the region; these include jaguar, marsh deer, giant anteater and giant otter.

The Pantanal is a sanctuary for birds with many species occurring in large numbers. It is one of the most important breeding grounds for typical wetland birds such as Jabiru stork, as well as several other species of heron, ibis and duck, which are found in enormous flocks.

The Pantanal Conservation Complex consists of a cluster of four protected areas: Pantanal Matogrossense National Park, Dorochê Private Reserve, Acurizal Private Reserve and Penha Private Reserve, with a total area of 1,878 km².

The area is home to twenty-six recorded parrot species including the hyacinth macaw (pictured right), the world's largest parrot. A large proportion of the remnant wild population of this species, now endangered, inhabit the region. Habitat destruction and capture for the pet trade are two factors that, in combination, have led to the risk of extinction.

World Heritage site since

• • • • • 1978 • 1979 • 1980 • 1981 • 1982 • 1983 • 1984 • 1985 • 1986 • 1987 • 1988 • 1989 • 1990 • 1991 • 1992 • 1993 • 1994 • 1995 • 1996 • 1997 • 1998 • 1999 • **2000**

Central Suriname Nature Reserve
Suriname

Criteria – Significant ecological and biological processes; Significant natural habitat for biodiversity

The Central Suriname Nature Reserve comprises 16,000 km² of primary tropical forest of west-central Suriname. It protects the upper watershed of the Coppename River and the headwaters of the Lucie, Oost, Zuid, Saramacca and Gran rivers and covers a range of topography and ecosystems of notable conservation value due to its pristine state. Its montane and lowland forests contain a high diversity of plant life with more than 5,000 vascular plant species collected to date. The Reserve's animals are typical of the region and include the jaguar, giant armadillo, giant river otter, tapir, sloths, eight species of primates and 400 bird species such as harpy eagle, Guianan cock-of-the-rock, and scarlet

Large parts of the Guiana Shield and Amazon regions are being rapidly transformed by logging, hunting, mining and settlement, but the reserve remains inaccessible, largely unaffected and unthreatened by human activity.

◄

White-faced saki, one of the eight primate species found in the Reserve.

World Heritage site since

• • 1978 • 1979 • 1980 • 1981 • 1982 • 1983 • 1984 • 1985 • 1986 • 1987 • 1988 • 1989 • 1990 • 1991 • 1992 • 1993 • 1994 • 1995 • 1996 • 1997 • 1998 • 1999 • 2000 • **2001**

Aranjuez Cultural Landscape
Spain

Criteria – Interchange of values; Significance in human history

The Aranjuez cultural landscape is an entity of complex relationships: between nature and human activity, between sinuous watercourses and geometric landscape design, between the rural and the urban, between forest landscape and the delicately modulated architecture of its palatial buildings. Three hundred years of royal attention to the development and care of this landscape have seen it express an evolution of concepts from humanism and political centralization, to characteristics such as those found in its eighteenth-century French-style Baroque garden, to the urban lifestyle which developed alongside the sciences of plant acclimatization and stock-breeding during the Age of Enlightenment.

The site incorporates a planned town, large gardens, vegetable gardens and orchards, lagoons, rivers and waterworks, woods and moors. The whole area appears as a green oasis in an otherwise dry, brown and fairly barren sierra-type landscape.

World Heritage site since

• • 1978 • 1979 • 1980 • 1981 • 1982 • 1983 • 1984 • 1985 • 1986 • 1987 • 1988 • 1989 • 1990 • 1991 • 1992 • 1993 • 1994 • 1995 • 1996 • 1997 • 1998 • 1999 • 2000 • **2001**

New Lanark
United Kingdom

Criteria – Interchange of values; Significance in human history; Heritage associated with events of universal significance

New Lanark is a small eighteenth-century village set in a sublime Scottish landscape where the philanthropist and idealist Robert Owen moulded a model industrial community in the early nineteenth century. The first cotton mill at New Lanark went into production in 1786 and Owen began to remodel the village around 1809. The imposing mill buildings, the spacious and well-designed workers' housing, and the dignified educational institute and school all testify to Owen's humanism.

The theme throughout is one of good proportion, good masonry, and simplicity of detail. The success of New Lanark inspired other benevolent industrialists to follow Owen's example and had a profound influence on social developments throughout the nineteenth century and beyond in matters such as progressive education, factory reform, humane working practices, international cooperation, and the concept of the garden city.

Robert Owen's idealistic vision of a society without crime, poverty, and misery had a wide appeal in the years following the Napoleonic Wars. He left New Lanark in 1828, after which new buildings were constructed, and others demolished or destroyed by fire, but the appearance of the village today remains very close to that of its heyday.

World Heritage site since

• • 1978 • 1979 • 1980 • 1981 • 1982 • 1983 • 1984 • 1985 • 1986 • 1987 • 1988 • 1989 • 1990 • 1991 • 1992 • 1993 • 1994 • 1995 • 1996 • 1997 • 1998 • 1999 • 2000 • **2001**

Swiss Alps Jungfrau-Aletsch
Switzerland

Criteria – Natural phenomena or beauty; Major stages of Earth's history; Significant ecological and biological processes

EUROPE

Atlantic Ocean

Mediterranean Sea

Adriatic Sea

The Aletsch Glacier. ▶

Fauna in the region is typical of the Alps, with a wide variety of species including ibex, lynx, red deer, roe deer, chamois and marmot as well as several reptiles and amphibians. A representative range of alpine birds also occurs in the area, including golden eagle, kestrel, chough, ptarmigan, black grouse, snow finch, wallcreeper, lammergeier, pygmy owl and various woodpecker species.

The Jungfrau-Aletsch region is the most glaciated part of the Alps, containing Europe's largest glacier and a range of classic glacial features. It provides an outstanding geological record of the uplift and compression that formed the High Alps. The diversity of flora and wildlife is represented in a range of Alpine and sub-Alpine habitats and plant colonization in the wake of retreating glaciers and provides an outstanding example of plant succession.

The geology of the site derives from the 'Helvetic nappe' (a large body of rock that was thrust over younger rock in Europe during the Miocene epoch). The folding and over-thrusting of rock layers during the formation of the Alps have produced very complex rock formations that have since been exposed by glacial activity. The physiography of the area is characterized by steep north-facing slopes and relatively gentle southern ones.

The area's scenic and aesthetic appeal is one of the most dramatic in the Alps. The impressive northern wall of the site with the panorama of the Eiger, Mönch and Jungfrau mountains provides a classic view of the north face of the High Alps - a view that has played an important role in European art and literature. Nine peaks in the region are

higher than 4,000 m. Classic examples of glacial phenomena in the area include U-shaped valleys, valley glaciers, cirques, horn peaks and moraines. The Aletsch Glacier is the largest and longest glacier in western Eurasia in terms of area (128 km²), length (23 km) and depth (900 m).

Vegetation and fauna vary by slope, aspect and elevation. There is a marked difference in vegetation between the northern and southern slopes. On the north side, forests at lower elevations consist of broadleaved species such as beech, ash, alder, elm and birch. The south side is too dry for beech, which is replaced by Scots pine. On the northern side, the subalpine zone is dominated by Norway spruce with mountain ash, silver birch and stone pine and, on the southern side, by more continental species such as European larch. Above the timberline are extensive areas of rhododendron scrub, alpine grassland and tundra vegetation and, on the dry southern slopes, steppe grassland.

World Heritage site since

• • 1978 • 1979 • 1980 • 1981 • 1982 • 1983 • 1984 • 1985 • 1986 • 1987 • 1988 • 1989 • 1990 • 1991 • 1992 • 1993 • 1994 • 1995 • 1996 • 1997 • 1998 • 1999 • 2000 • **2001**

Alto Douro Wine Region
Portugal

Criteria – Testimony to cultural tradition;
Significance in human history; Traditional human
settlement

The Alto Douro Region has been producing
wine for some 2,000 years. Since the
eighteenth century, its main product, port
wine, has been world-famous. This long
tradition of viticulture has produced a
cultural landscape of outstanding beauty
that reflects its technological, social and
economic evolution. The landscape in the
Demarcated Region of the Douro is formed
by steep hills and boxed-in valleys that
flatten out into plateaux above 400 m.
The most dominant feature of the landscape
is the terraced vineyards that blanket the
countryside. Throughout the centuries,
row upon row of terraces have been built
according to different techniques. The
earliest were narrow, irregular terraces
buttressed by walls of stone that were
regularly taken down and rebuilt. The long
lines of continuous, regularly-shaped
terraces date mainly from the end of the
nineteenth century.

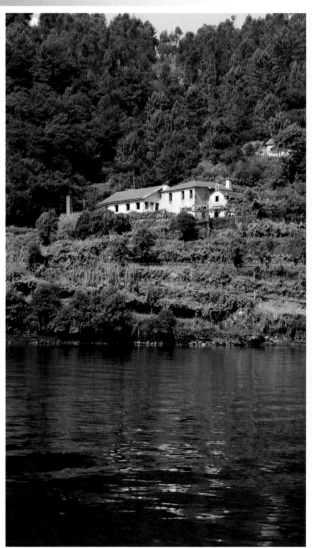

Vineyard by the river Douro. ▲

The more recent terracing
techniques, the *patamares*, have
greatly altered the appearance
of the landscape. Large plots of
slightly sloping earth-banked
land were laid out to facilitate

mechanization of the vineyard.
Trials of other systems are
continuing with a view to finding
alternatives to the *patamares* and
to minimize the impact of the new
methods on the landscape.

World Heritage site since

• • 1978 • 1979 • 1980 • 1981 • 1982 • 1983 • 1984 • 1985 • 1986 • 1987 • 1988 • 1989 • 1990 • 1991 • 1992 • 1993 • 1994 • 1995 • 1996 • 1997 • 1998 • 1999 • 2000 • **2001**

Tombs of Buganda Kings at Kasubi
Uganda

Criteria – Human creative genius; Testimony to cultural tradition; Significance in human history; Heritage associated with events of universal significance

The Tombs of Buganda Kings at Kasubi constitute a site embracing almost 0.3 km² of hillside within Kampala district. Most of the site is agricultural, farmed by traditional methods. At its core on the hilltop is the former palace of the Kabakas of Buganda, built in 1882 and converted into the royal burial ground in 1884. Four royal tombs now lie within the Muzibu Azaala Mpanga, the main building, which is circular and surmounted by a dome. It is a major example of an architectural achievement in organic materials, principally wood, thatch, reed, wattle and daub. The site's main significance lies, however, in its intangible values of belief, spirituality, continuity and identity.

◄ The Muzibu Azaala Mpanga.

The spatial organization of the Tombs represents the best extant example of a Baganda palace/ architectural ensemble. It reflects technical achievements developed over many centuries and is the most active religious place in the kingdom.

The Royal Hill of Ambohimanga
Madagascar

Criteria – Testimony to cultural tradition; Significance in human history; Heritage associated with events of universal significance

The Royal Hill of Ambohimanga is the most significant symbol of the cultural identity of the people of Madagascar. Its traditional design, materials and layout are representative of the social and political structure of Malagasy society from at least the sixteenth century. The site consists of a royal city and burial site and an ensemble of sacred places (wood, spring, lake, public meeting place). Fortifications protected the royal city in an arrangement of banks, ditches, and fourteen stone gateways. The site is associated with strong feelings of national identity, and has maintained its spiritual and sacred character both in ritual practice and in the popular imagination for the past 500 years. It remains a place of worship for pilgrims from Madagascar and elsewhere.

In 1897 the remains of royalty were transferred to Antananarivo by the French authorities in a failed attempt to erase the holiness of the site and the nationalistic legitimacy attached to it. The tombs were demolished and military buildings erected for the garrison on the site.

World Heritage site since

• • 1978 • 1979 • 1980 • 1981 • 1982 • 1983 • 1984 • 1985 • 1986 • 1987 • 1988 • 1989 • 1990 • 1991 • 1992 • 1993 • 1994 • 1995 • 1996 • 1997 • 1998 • 1999 • 2000 • **2001**

Central Sikhote-Alin
Russian Federation
Criteria – Significant natural habitat for biodiversity

The Sikhote-Alin protected areas are considered to contain the greatest plant and animal diversity on the northwestern Pacific coastline. Many of the plants, such as ginseng and Siberian ginseng, are of medicinal value and are important to the indigenous people.

The Sikhote-Alin mountain range contains one the richest and most unusual temperate forests in the world. The unique combination of its severe climatic characteristics, physical isolation, and traditional resource use by the indigenous peoples has meant that 80–90 per cent of the region's vegetation still remains as dense temperate forest and taiga. Alpine tundra, coastal shrublands, meadows and bogs account for the rest of the area. In this mixed zone between taiga and subtropics, southern species such as the tiger and Himalayan bear cohabit with northern species such as the brown bear and lynx. The site stretches from the peaks of Sikhote-Alin to the Sea of Japan and is important for the survival of many endangered species such as the Amur tiger.

Fertö/Neusiedlersee
Cultural Landscape
Austria and Hungary
Criteria – Traditional human settlement

Several eighteenth- and nineteenth-century palaces add to the area's considerable cultural interest. These include the Fertöd Esterházy Palace, the most important eighteenth-century palace of Hungary, built on the model of Versailles. Between 1769 and 1790 Josef Haydn's compositions were first heard here.

The Fertö/Neusiedler Lake and its surroundings are an outstanding example of a traditional human settlement and land use representative of a culture. The lake lies between the Alps, 70 km distant, and the lowlands in the territory of two states, Austria and Hungary. It has been the meeting place of different cultures for eight millennia, and this is graphically demonstrated by its varied landscape. The present character of the landscape is the result of ancient land-use forms based on stockraising and viticulture to an extent not found in other European lake areas. The remarkable rural architecture of the villages surrounding the lake is typified by the historic centre of the medieval free town of Rust, which perfectly symbolises a united society of townspeople and farmers.

World Heritage site since

• • 1978 • 1979 • 1980 • 1981 • 1982 • 1983 • 1984 • 1985 • 1986 • 1987 • 1988 • 1989 • 1990 • 1991 • 1992 • 1993 • 1994 • 1995 • 1996 • 1997 • 1998 • 1999 • 2000 • **2001**

Saltaire
United Kingdom

Criteria – Interchange of values; Significance in human history

Saltaire in west Yorkshire is a well-preserved industrial village of the second half of the nineteenth century. Its textile mills, public buildings and workers' housing are built in a harmonious style of high architectural quality, giving a vivid impression of Victorian philanthropic paternalism. Saltaire represents an important stage in the development of modern town planning and had a major influence on the 'garden city' movement. When Titus Salt, a wealthy businessman, became mayor of Bradford in

1848, he committed himself to reducing the town's pollution problems. Work on the mill began in 1851 and it was opened in 1853. Salt's new village eventually had over 800 dwellings in wide streets, with a large dining hall and kitchens, baths and wash houses, almshouse for retired workers, hospital and dispensary, educational institute and church, and ample recreational land and allotments.

The houses, built between 1854 and 1868, are fine examples of nineteenth-century hierarchical workers' homes. Each was equipped with its own water and gas supply and an outside lavatory. They vary in size from 'two-up two-down' terraces to much larger managers' houses with gardens.

Saltaire Mill and the river Aire.
▼

World Heritage site since

• • 1978 • 1979 • 1980 • 1981 • 1982 • 1983 • 1984 • 1985 • 1986 • 1987 • 1988 • 1989 • 1990 • 1991 • 1992 • 1993 • 1994 • 1995 • 1996 • 1997 • 1998 • 1999 • 2000 • **2001**

Medina of Essaouira (formerly Mogador)
Morocco

Criteria – Interchange of values; Significance in human history

Essaouira is an outstanding and well-preserved example of a late-eighteenth-century European fortified seaport town translated to a North African context. Since its foundation, it has been a major international trading seaport, linking Morocco and its Saharan hinterland with Europe and the rest of the world. As Morocco increasingly opened up to the rest of the world in the later seventeenth century, the old town needed to expand and a new plan was laid out by a French architect. The town has retained its European appearance to a substantial extent, and is a leading example of building inspired by European architecture – a town unique by virtue of its design.

In the medina of Essaouira a symbiosis was achieved between building techniques from Morocco and elsewhere that gave birth to some unique architectural masterpieces: the Sqalas (fortifications) of the port and of the medina, the Bab Marrakesh bastion, the water gate, mosques, synagogues and churches.

The Sqala du Port, Essaouira.
▼

World Heritage site since

• • 1978 • 1979 • 1980 • 1981 • 1982 • 1983 • 1984 • 1985 • 1986 • 1987 • 1988 • 1989 • 1990 • 1991 • 1992 • 1993 • 1994 • 1995 • 1996 • 1997 • 1998 • 1999 • 2000 • **2001**

Mining Area of the Great Copper Mountain in Falun

Sweden

Criteria – Interchange of values; Testimony to cultural tradition; Traditional human settlement

The Great Copper Mountain (Stora Kopparberget) is the oldest and most important mine working in Sweden and one of the world's most remarkable industrial monuments. Mining here began as early as the ninth century and came to an end in the closing years of the twentieth century. By the seventeenth century, Falun was producing 70 per cent of the world's copper and was the mainstay of Sweden's economy,

enabling it to become one of the leading European powers. The seventeenth-century planned town, with its many fine historic buildings, together with the industrial and domestic remains of a number of settlements spread over a wide area of the Dalarna region, provide a vivid picture of what was for centuries one of the world's most important mining areas.

The Great Copper Mountain was a corporate operation in which free miners owned shares in proportion to their interests in copper smelters. It is often referred to as 'the oldest company in the world.'

Zollverein Coal Mine Industrial Complex in Essen

Germany

Criteria – Interchange of values; Testimony to cultural tradition

The Zollverein industrial complex in Land Nordrhein-Westfalen consists of the complete infrastructure of a historical coal-mining site, with some twentieth-century buildings of outstanding architectural merit. It constitutes remarkable material evidence of the evolution and decline of an essential industry over the past 150 years. Mining began in the mid-nineteenth century at a depth of some 120 m and finished at 1,200 m. By the end of mining the underground roadways extended over

120 km; they were accessed by twelve shafts, opened up progressively between 1847 and 1932. The methods of mining evolved as technology developed from hand picks to mechanized coal cutting. Elements of the original pits, the central coking plant, railway lines, associated buildings and housing all survive today.

Zollverein is an exceptional industrial monument: its buildings are outstanding examples of the application of Modern Movement design concepts to wholly industrial architecture. Of particular note are the imposing administrative building (1906), the director's villa (1898), and the mine officials' residence (1878).

World Heritage site since

• • 1978 • 1979 • 1980 • 1981 • 1982 • 1983 • 1984 • 1985 • 1986 • 1987 • 1988 • 1989 • 1990 • 1991 • 1992 • 1993 • 1994 • 1995 • 1996 • 1997 • 1998 • 1999 • 2000 • **2001**

Brazilian Atlantic Islands: Fernando de Noronha and Atol das Rocas Reserves
Brazil

Criteria – Natural phenomena or beauty; Significant ecological and biological processes; Significant natural habitat for biodiversity

Peaks of the Southern Atlantic submarine ridge form the Fernando de Noronha Archipelago and Rocas Atoll off the coast of Brazil. They represent a large proportion of the island surface of the South Atlantic and their rich waters are extremely important for the breeding and feeding of tuna, shark, turtle and marine mammals. The islands are home to the largest concentration of tropical seabirds in the western Atlantic. Baia de Golfinhos has an exceptional population of resident dolphin and at low tide the Rocas Atoll provides a spectacular seascape of lagoons and tidal pools teeming with fish.

There are less than ten oceanic islands in the South Atlantic, and the Fernando de Noronha Archipelago and Rocas Atoll represent more than 50 per cent of such islands' surface area. Consequently, they are important for the biodiversity of the South Atlantic basin.

Tsodilo
Botswana

Criteria – Human creative genius; Testimony to cultural tradition; Heritage associated with events of universal significance

With one of the highest concentrations of rock art in the world, Tsodilo has been called the 'Louvre of the Desert'. For many thousands of years these rocky outcrops in the hostile landscape of the Kalahari Desert have been visited and settled by humans, who have left rich traces of their presence in the form of outstanding rock art. Over 4,500 paintings are preserved in an area of only 10 km². The archaeological record of the area gives a chronological account of human activities and environmental changes over at least 100,000 years.

The outcrops had immense symbolic and religious significance for the human communities who survived here, being respected as a place of worship frequented by ancestral spirits. Some of the art is thought to be more than 2,000 years old. Geometric art is regarded as about 1,000 years old while the pictures with cattle date from the animals' introduction to Tsodilo after the sixth century AD.

World Heritage site since

• • 1978 • 1979 • 1980 • 1981 • 1982 • 1983 • 1984 • 1985 • 1986 • 1987 • 1988 • 1989 • 1990 • 1991 • 1992 • 1993 • 1994 • 1995 • 1996 • 1997 • 1998 • 1999 • 2000 • **2001**

Provins, Town of Medieval Fairs
France

Criteria – Interchange of values; Significance in human history

At the beginning of the second millennium AD, Provins was one of several towns in the territory of the Counts of Champagne that became the venues for great annual trading fairs linking northern Europe with the Mediterranean world. The entire town developed in relation to the fairs, either directly serving the fair functions or being indirectly related as an outcome. Of the four towns where medieval fairs were held in the

reign of the Counts of Champagne, Provins is the only one to retain its original medieval fabric. There are two large buildings: the so-called 'Tour de César' or the Big Tower, a stone structure, dating initially from the twelfth-century, and consisting of three large spaces one above the other, covered with a seventeenth-century conical roof; and the Romanesque-Gothic church of Saint-Quiriace.

A characteristic of all the ancient buildings in Provins, whether for mixed or for commercial use, is their system of vaulted cellars, dating from the twelfth to the fourteenth centuries. These are either entirely underground (Upper Town) or partly built-up above ground (Lower Town), and all open out to the street by means of a large door to which access is gained by a wide stone staircase.

World Heritage site since

• • 1978 • 1979 • 1980 • 1981 • 1982 • 1983 • 1984 • 1985 • 1986 • 1987 • 1988 • 1989 • 1990 • 1991 • 1992 • 1993 • 1994 • 1995 • 1996 • 1997 • 1998 • 1999 • 2000 • **2001**

Samarkand – Crossroad of Cultures
Uzbekistan

Criteria – Human creative genius; Interchange of values; Significance in human history

Located on the crossroads of the great trade routes that traversed central Asia, the historic town of Samarkand illustrates in its art, architecture and urban structure the most important stages of central Asian cultural and political history from the thirteenth century to the present day. Founded in the seventh century BC as ancient Afrasiab, the city emerged as a major centre through the efforts of Timur the Lame (Tamerlane, c. 1336–1405). It was rebuilt on its present site, southwest of Afrasiab, and became the capital of Timur's powerful state and the repository of the material riches from conquered territories that extended from central Asia to Persia, Afghanistan, and India. The major monuments include the Registan Mosque and madrasas (see photo below), Bibi-Khanum Mosque, the Shakhi-Zinda compound and the Gur-Emir ensemble, as well as Ulugh-Beg's Observatory.

In 1868 the Russians conquered Samarkand, making it a provincial capital (1887) and thus reviving its economy. They constructed schools, churches, and hospitals, and the western part of Samarkand was redeveloped according to current town planning ideas. This period, however, also led to the destruction of the city walls and gates, as well as several monuments.

Registan Mosque.
▼

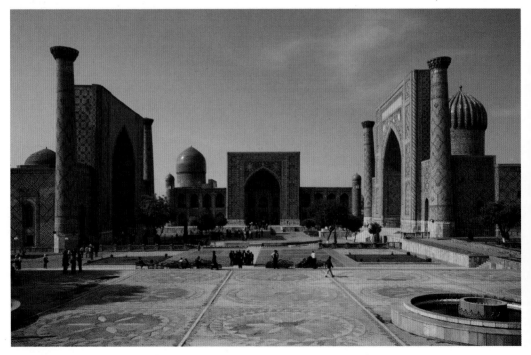

World Heritage site since

• • 1978 • 1979 • 1980 • 1981 • 1982 • 1983 • 1984 • 1985 • 1986 • 1987 • 1988 • 1989 • 1990 • 1991 • 1992 • 1993 • 1994 • 1995 • 1996 • 1997 • 1998 • 1999 • 2000 • **2001**

Dorset and East Devon Coast
United Kingdom

Criteria – Major stages of Earth's history

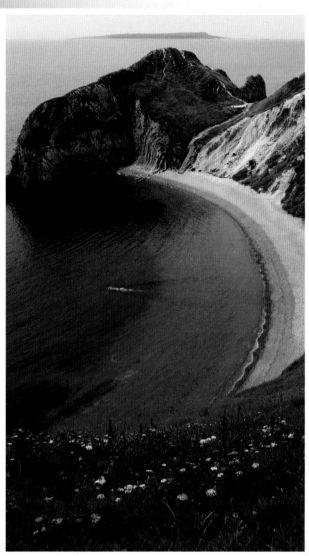

Man o' War Beach in Dorset. ▲

Located on the south coast of England, the property comprises eight sections along 155 km of coast. The property has a combination of geological, palaeontological and geomorphological features. These include a variety of fossils, a beach renowned for its pebbles, and textbook examples of common coastal features such as sea stacks and sea caves. The area has been studied for more than 300 years and has contributed to the development of earth sciences in the United Kingdom. The site includes a near-continuous sequence of Triassic, Jurassic and Cretaceous rock exposures, representing much of the Mesozoic era (251–66 million years ago) or approximately 185 million years of the Earth's history. A large number of vertebrate, invertebrate and plant fossils have been discovered. Among the finds are fossil dinosaur footprints, flying reptiles and marine reptiles.

Well-preserved remains of a late-Jurassic fossil forest are exposed on the Isle of Portland and the Purbeck coast. Chesil Beach, stretching from West Bay to Portland, is famous for the volume, type and grading of its pebbles. The Fleet Lagoon is one of the most important saline lagoons in Europe.

World Heritage site since

• • 1978 • 1979 • 1980 • 1981 • 1982 • 1983 • 1984 • 1985 • 1986 • 1987 • 1988 • 1989 • 1990 • 1991 • 1992 • 1993 • 1994 • 1995 • 1996 • 1997 • 1998 • 1999 • 2000 • 2001

Alejandro de Humboldt National Park
Cuba

Criteria – Significant ecological and biological processes; Significant natural habitat for biodiversity

The park, in southeastern Cuba, includes a complex system of mountains, tablelands, coastal plains, bays and coral reefs. It is the least explored natural area on the island and has locations where the plant life has not yet been assessed.

Complex geology and varied topography have given rise to a diversity of ecosystems and species unmatched in the insular Caribbean and created one of the most biologically diverse tropical island sites on Earth. Many of the underlying rocks are toxic to plants so species have had to adapt to survive in these hostile conditions. This unique process of evolution has resulted in the development of many new species and the park is one of the most important sites in the Western Hemisphere for the conservation of endemic flora. Endemism of vertebrates and invertebrates is also very high.

Yungang Grottoes
China

Criteria – Human creative genius; Interchange of values; Testimony to cultural tradition; Significance in human history

By AD 525 the initial project, sponsored by the court, was mostly completed, but low-ranking officials and monks continued to dig more caves and carve statues. During the Liao dynasty, wooden shelters were built in front of the caves, turning the grottoes into temple buildings, such as the Ten Famous Temples.

The Yungang Grottoes, in Datong city, Shanxi Province, with their 252 caves and 51,000 statues, represent the outstanding achievement of Buddhist cave art in China in the fifth and sixth centuries. The grottoes of the early period (AD 460–5) are composed of five main caves, dug under the direction of the monk Tan Yao and named after him. They have a U-shaped plan and arched roof and each cave has a door and a window. The central images occupy the major part of the caves, while on the outer walls 1,000 Buddhist statues are carved. The Yungang Grottoes also include four groups of twin caves and one group of triple caves; the site extends as much as 1 km east-west.

World Heritage site since

• • 1978 • 1979 • 1980 • 1981 • 1982 • 1983 • 1984 • 1985 • 1986 • 1987 • 1988 • 1989 • 1990 • 1991 • 1992 • 1993 • 1994 • 1995 • 1996 • 1997 • 1998 • 1999 • 2000 • **2001**

Villa d'Este, Tivoli
Italy

Criteria – Human creative genius; Interchange of values; Testimony to cultural tradition; Significance in human history; Heritage associated with events of universal significance

The gardens of the Villa d'Este had a profound influence on the development of garden design throughout Europe. They are among the earliest and finest of the *giardini delle meraviglie* and symbolize the flowering of Renaissance culture. The ensemble, composed of the palace and gardens, forms an irregular quadrilateral and covers an area of about 45,000 m². The plan of the villa is irregular because the architect was obliged to make use of certain parts of the previous monastic building. On the garden side the architecture of the palace is very simple: a long main body of three storeys, marked by bands, rows of windows, side pavilions and an elegant loggia. The lower level is decorated with the Fountain of Leda. The main rooms of the villa are arranged in rows on two floors and open on to the magnificent garden.

One of the villa's many outstanding features is the Alley of the Hundred Fountains, the waters from which cross the entire garden. There is also the innovative and striking design of the jets of the large cascade which were activated whenever unsuspecting people walked under the arcades. The garden also features its own artificial mountain, with three alcoves holding statues, and a water organ.

The Neptune Fountain (foreground) and the Organ Fountain (background). ▼

World Heritage site since

• • 1978 • 1979 • 1980 • 1981 • 1982 • 1983 • 1984 • 1985 • 1986 • 1987 • 1988 • 1989 • 1990 • 1991 • 1992 • 1993 • 1994 • 1995 • 1996 • 1997 • 1998 • 1999 • 2000 • 2001

Historic Centre of the Town of Goiás
Brazil

Criteria – Interchange of values; Significance in human history

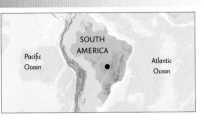

In its layout and architecture the historic town of Goiás is an outstanding example of a European town admirably adapted to the climatic, geographical and cultural constraints of central South America. It represents the evolution of a form of urban structure and architecture characteristic of the colonial settlement of South America, making full use of local materials and techniques and conserving its exceptional setting. The urban layout is an example of the organic development of a mining town, adapted to the conditions of the site. Although modest, both public and private architecture form a harmonious whole, thanks to the coherent use of local materials and vernacular techniques.

In 1748, Goiás' gold wealth meant it was chosen as the headquarters of a new subdistrict, and its first governor transformed the modest village into a small capital. Its townscape has not been subject to any major changes in modern times, making Goiás a remarkably well-preserved example of a mining town of the eighteenth and nineteenth centuries, including its natural environment, which has remained intact.

World Heritage site since

• • 1978 • 1979 • 1980 • 1981 • 1982 • 1983 • 1984 • 1985 • 1986 • 1987 • 1988 • 1989 • 1990 • 1991 • 1992 • 1993 • 1994 • 1995 • 1996 • 1997 • 1998 • 1999 • 2000 • **2001**

Churches of Peace in Jawor and Swidnica
Poland

Criteria – Testimony to cultural tradition; Significance in human history; Heritage associated with events of universal significance

The churches in Jawor and Swidnica differ in the character of their floor plans. Both have three aisles, and both terminate in a polygonal east end, but whereas in Jawor the eastern end is still a true chancel, in Swidnica it functions as a sacristy.

The Churches of Peace in Jawor and Swidnica, the largest timber-framed religious buildings in Europe, were built in former Silesia in the mid-seventeenth century, at a time of religious strife following the Peace of Westphalia. They are monuments not just to the skill of their designers, but also to the religious tolerance shown by the Catholic Habsburg Emperor towards Protestant communities in Silesia after the Thirty Years' War. In most of the province Protestants were persecuted but, through the agency of the Lutheran king of Sweden, the Emperor allowed the erection of three Lutheran churches, of which two survive. As a result of conditions imposed by the Emperor, the builders had to employ pioneering constructional techniques of a scale and complexity unknown in wooden architecture.

Derwent Valley Mills
United Kingdom

Criteria – Interchange of values; Significance in human history

Richard Arkwright developed the village of Cromford to attract the families of the mainly child workforce that he needed. Weavers lived in his houses, the parents weaving calico on their topmost floors and children working in the spinning mills.

The Derwent Valley in central England contains a series of eighteenth- and nineteenth-century cotton mills and an industrial landscape of high historical and technological interest. The modern factory system was effectively born here, when new types of building were erected to house the latest technology for spinning cotton developed by Richard Arkwright. This was large-scale industrial production in a hitherto rural landscape, and the need to provide housing and other facilities for workers and managers resulted in the creation of the first industrial towns. The workers' housing associated with this and the other mills remains intact and illustrates the socio-economic development of the area.

The complete heritage site is a continuous strip, 24 km long, from Matlock Bath to the centre of Derby.

World Heritage site since

· · 1978 · 1979 · 1980 · 1981 · 1982 · 1983 · 1984 · 1985 · 1986 · 1987 · 1988 · 1989 · 1990 · 1991 · 1992 · 1993 · 1994 · 1995 · 1996 · 1997 · 1998 · 1999 · 2000 · **2001**

Masada
Israel

Criteria – Testimony to cultural tradition;
Significance in human history; Heritage
associated with events of universal significance

Aerial view of
Masada, with one of
the Roman camps in
the foreground.

Masada is a rugged natural fortress of
majestic beauty set in the Judaean Desert
overlooking the Dead Sea. It is a symbol of
the ancient kingdom of Israel, its violent
destruction and the last stand of Jewish
patriots against the Roman army at the end
of the First Jewish-Roman War in AD 73.
The camps, fortifications and attack ramp
that encircle the monument constitute the
most complete Roman siege works
surviving to the present day.

The towering hill of Masada overlooks
a natural landscape of savage beauty. To the
west lie the hills and terraces of the Judaean
Desert; to the east is a wildly broken terrain,
running down to the brilliant colours of the
Dead Sea. A giant scarp stretches south to
the horizon and Masada forms part of this.

Masada was built as a palace complex in
the classic style of the early Roman Empire
by King Herod the Great of Judaea, who
ruled from 37–4 BC. The Northern Palace, in
its present form, dates from the main phase
of building in the late first century BC. It was
built on three slightly modified natural rock
terraces. The upper level was mainly
residential while imposing colonnaded
reception halls were situated on the two
lower levels. The lower reception level is the
best preserved of the three.

The nucleus of the Western Palace
comprised a courtyard surrounded by
bedrooms and reception rooms; two
extensive service wings were added in the
main phase of building. Its size, layout and
opulent decoration – mosaic floors and
walls of white plaster painted to imitate
marble panels – suggest that this was the
ceremonial palace, while the Northern
Palace was the private palace for the king
and his family.

The massive defensive wall, built in the
final phase, was 1,290 m long with twenty-
seven towers and about seventy rooms on
its inner side. Three gates pierce the wall:
the Western Gate, the Southern Gate, and
the Snake Path Gate (the eastern gate).
A fourth gate - the Water Gate - provided
access to the Northern Section; this
however was not integrated into the
casement wall. Water was delivered, during
the winter floods in the wadis to the west,
through a network of dams and channels to
the cisterns dug into the rock of Masada.

Most of the buildings on the hilltop were
occupied by around 1,000 people who lived
there in the Zealot period of the first
century AD.

There is a network of
eight Roman military
camps around
Masada. Most striking
are the hundreds of
contubernia (messing
units), consisting of
walls of stones
1–1.5 m high on which
the soldiers erected
their leather tents.
The great ramp used
for the final assault
on Masada was built
from soil and stones
braced by an armature
of timber beams.

The remains of a fifth-
century Byzantine
church also stands on
the summit. The floor
was originally covered
with mosaic but much
of this was removed
to the Louvre in the
nineteenth century.

World Heritage site since

• • 1978 • 1979 • 1980 • 1981 • 1982 • 1983 • 1984 • 1985 • 1986 • 1987 • 1988 • 1989 • 1990 • 1991 • 1992 • 1993 • 1994 • 1995 • 1996 • 1997 • 1998 • 1999 • 2000 • **2001**

Historic Centre of Vienna
Austria

Criteria – Interchange of values; Significance in human history; Heritage associated with events of universal significance

Vienna developed from early Celtic and Roman settlements into a Medieval and Baroque city, the capital of the Austro-Hungarian Empire. The historic centre of Vienna is rich in architectural ensembles, including Baroque castles and gardens, as well as the late-nineteenth-century Ringstrasse lined with grand buildings, monuments and parks. The property consists of the medieval core (based on the Roman settlement), the principal Baroque ensembles with their axes, and the

Gründerzeit constructions from the beginning of the modern period. The inner city contains a number of medieval historic buildings, including the Schottenkloster, the oldest monastery in Austria, and the churches of Maria am Gestade (one of the main Gothic structures), Michaelerkirche, Minoritenkirche and Minoritenkloster, from the thirteenth century. St Stephen's Cathedral dates from the fourteenth and fifteenth centuries.

Several historic buildings are now associated with the important Viennese residence of personalities such as Mozart, Beethoven, Schubert and others, when the city played an essential role as a leading European musical centre, from the great age of Viennese classicism through to the early part of the twentieth century.

The Rathaus (City Hall) of Vienna.
▼

World Heritage site since

• • 1978 • 1979 • 1980 • 1981 • 1982 • 1983 • 1984 • 1985 • 1986 • 1987 • 1988 • 1989 • 1990 • 1991 • 1992 • 1993 • 1994 • 1995 • 1996 • 1997 • 1998 • 1999 • 2000 • **2001**

Vat Phou and Associated Ancient Settlements within the Champasak Cultural Landscape
Lao People's Dem. Republic

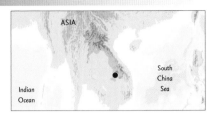

Criteria – Testimony to cultural tradition;
Significance in human history; Heritage
associated with events of universal significance

The Temple Complex of Vat Phou bears exceptional testimony to the cultures of southeast Asia, and in particular to the Khmer Empire, which dominated the region in the tenth–fourteenth centuries. It is an outstanding example of the integration of symbolic landscape of great spiritual significance to its natural surroundings. The origins of the site lie before AD 600, at least at the city of Shrestrapura, where

archaeological research has produced evidence of pre-Angkorian times (until c. AD 900). The development of the site as a whole, however, was intimately bound up with the origin, development and zenith of the Khmer Empire between the seventh and twelfth centuries. Two planned cities on the banks of the Mekong River are also part of the site, as well as Phou Kao mountain.

Vat Phou was shaped to express the Hindu vision of the relationship between nature and humanity, using an axis from mountain top to river bank to lay out a geometric pattern of temples, shrines and waterworks extending over some 10 km.
▼

Old City of Acre
Israel

Criteria – Interchange of values; Testimony to
cultural tradition; Traditional human settlement

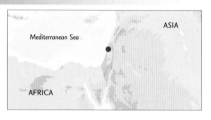

Acre is an exceptional port-historic town
that preserves the substantial remains of the
medieval Crusader buildings beneath the
existing Ottoman fortified town which dates
from the eighteenth and nineteenth
centuries. The remains of the Crusader
town, dating from 1104–1291, lie almost
intact, both above and below today's street
level, providing an exceptional picture of the
layout and structures of the capital of the
medieval Crusader kingdom of Jerusalem.

During the two centuries of Crusader rule,
Acre symbolized, better than any other city,
the interchange between eastern and
western cultures. New neighbourhoods
such as Monmizar to the north were built
and Acre was given a new double city wall.
What remains today is a remarkable mixture
of cultural elements from every period of
Acre's eventful history between the eleventh
and twentieth centuries.

Destroyed in the
sixteenth century,
Acre was a deserted
ghost town until
reconstruction began
in the mid-eighteenth
century, under Daher
El Amar and later El
Jazar, who rebuilt the
port and fortifications.
Enjoying renewed
economic expansion
in the nineteenth
century, wealthy
merchants settled
there, building grand
mansions in the eastern
neoclassical style.

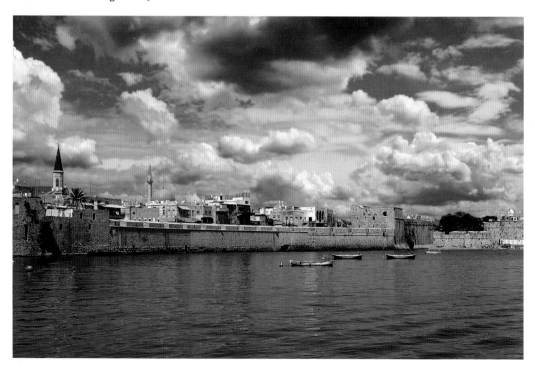

World Heritage site since

• • 1978 • 1979 • 1980 • 1981 • 1982 • 1983 • 1984 • 1985 • 1986 • 1987 • 1988 • 1989 • 1990 • 1991 • 1992 • 1993 • 1994 • 1995 • 1996 • 1997 • 1998 • 1999 • 2000 • **2001**

Cerrado Protected Areas: Chapada dos Veadeiros and Emas National Parks
Brazil

Criteria – Significant ecological and biological processes; Significant natural habitat for biodiversity

The two sites included in the designated area contain flora and fauna and key habitats that characterize the Cerrado – one of the world's oldest and most diverse tropical ecosystems. For millennia, these sites have served as refuge for several species during periods of climate change and will be vital for maintaining the biodiversity of the Cerrado region during future climate fluctuations.

Comprising the Chapada dos Veadeiros and the Emas National Parks the area is home to many threatened and endemic species, while mammals include giant anteater, giant armadillo, maned wolf, jaguar and pampas deer.

◄
Wild giant anteater.

Tugendhat Villa in Brno
Czech Republic

Criteria – Interchange of values; Significance in human history

The Tugendhat Villa in Brno is a masterpiece of the Modern Movement in architecture in Europe in the 1920s. Its particular value lies in the way the German architect Mies van der Rohe (1886–1969) applied the radical new concepts of the movement to the design of residential buildings and made extensive use of modern industrial capabilities. The architect designed original furniture specifically for this house, such as the steel and leather Tugendhat chair.

The back wall of the living area is made from beautiful onyx, brought from the Atlas Mountains and processed on site. The mechanical equipment designed and built for the house was also exceptional, including electrically operated large steel-frame windows, central heating and an air-conditioning system with a regulated fine-spray humidifying chamber.

The house lost most of its original furniture and suffered some damage after it was taken over by the German State in 1939. The Tugendhat Villa Fund was established in 1993 and a scientific restoration of the building took place.

World Heritage site since

• • 1978 • 1979 • 1980 • 1981 • 1982 • 1983 • 1984 • 1985 • 1986 • 1987 • 1988 • 1989 • 1990 • 1991 • 1992 • 1993 • 1994 • 1995 • 1996 • 1997 • 1998 • 1999 • 2000 • **2001**

Historic Centre of Guimarães
Portugal

Criteria – Interchange of values; Testimony to
cultural tradition; Significance in human history

The historic town of Guimarães is associated
with the emergence of Portuguese national
identity in the twelfth century. It is an
exceptionally well-preserved town illustrating
the evolution of particular building types
from the medieval settlement to the
present-day city. The historic centre is
formed by a large number of stone
constructions (950–1498). The period from
Renaissance to neoclassicism is characterized
by noble houses and the development of

civic facilities, city squares, etc. The residential
buildings make use of two construction
techniques, a half-timbered one (taipa de
rodízio) dating from before the sixteenth
century, and another from the nineteenth
century (taipa de fasquio) that uses timber
alone. Despite some changes during the
modern period, the town has maintained
its medieval urban layout.

Guimarães is of
particular significance
by virtue of the fact
that the specialized
building techniques
developed there in
the Middle Ages
were transmitted to
Portuguese colonies
in Africa and the
New World, becoming
their characteristic
feature.

Lamu Old Town
Kenya

Criteria – Interchange of values; Significance in
human history; Heritage associated with events
of universal significance

Lamu Old Town is the oldest and best-
preserved Swahili settlement in east Africa,
retaining its traditional functions. Built in
coral stone and mangrove timber, the town
is characterized by the simplicity of
structural forms enriched by such features
as inner courtyards, verandas, and
elaborately carved wooden doors. Lamu has
hosted major Muslim religious festivals
since the nineteenth century, and has
become a significant centre for the study of
Islamic and Swahili cultures.

The architecture and
urban structure of
Lamu graphically
demonstrate the
cultural influences
that have come
together there over
several centuries from
Europe, Arabia and
India, utilizing
traditional Swahili
techniques to produce
a distinct culture.

World Heritage site since

• 1979 • 1980 • 1981 • 1982 • 1983 • 1984 • 1985 • 1986 • 1987 • 1988 • 1989 • 1990 • 1991 • 1992 • 1993 • 1994 • 1995 • 1996 • 1997 • 1998 • 1999 • 2000 • 2001 • **2002**

Minaret and Archaeological Remains of Jam
Afghanistan

Criteria – Interchange of values; Testimony to cultural tradition; Significance in human history

The Minaret of Jam is a graceful, soaring structure, dating back to the twelfth century, believed to have been built to commemorate a major victory of the sultans of the Ghurid dynasty. Rising to 65 m from a 9-m-diameter octagonal base, its four tapering cylindrical shafts are constructed of fired brick bonded with lime mortar. The exterior of the minaret is completely covered with geometric decoration in relief laid over the plain structural bricks. The first cylinder is the most decorated: it is divided into eight vertical segments, matching those of the base. Each vertical zone has a narrow band of inscriptions running in an unbroken line around each panel. It is an outstanding example of Islamic architecture and ornamentation in this region and played a significant role in their further dissemination.

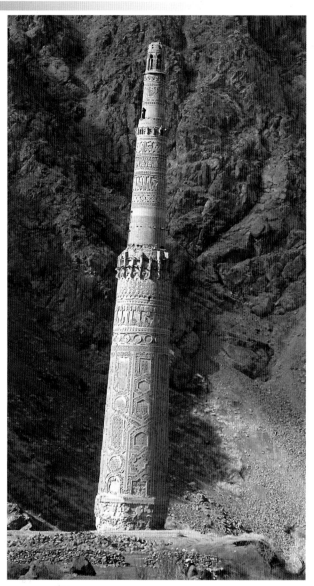

The remains of castles and towers of the Ghurid settlement are to be found on the opposite bank of the Hari River, north of the minaret and high on the cliff. There are also the remains of fortifications visible to the east of the minaret, suggesting that the minaret was surrounded not by a settlement but by a military camp.

World Heritage site since

• 1979 • 1980 • 1981 • 1982 • 1983 • 1984 • 1985 • 1986 • 1987 • 1988 • 1989 • 1990 • 1991 • 1992 • 1993 • 1994 • 1995 • 1996 • 1997 • 1998 • 1999 • 2000 • 2001 • **2002**

Upper Middle Rhine Valley
Germany

Criteria – Interchange of values; Significance in human history; Traditional human settlement

The Rhine Valley at ▶
Oberwesel.

As one of the most important transport routes in Europe, the Middle Rhine Valley has facilitated the exchange of culture between the Mediterranean region and the north for two millennia. It is an outstanding organic cultural landscape and an excellent example of an evolving traditional way of life and means of communication in a narrow river valley. The terracing of its steep slopes in particular has shaped the landscape. However, this form of land use is under threat from today's socio-economic pressures.

The 65-km-stretch of the Middle Rhine Valley, with its castles, historic towns, and vineyards, graphically illustrates the long history of human involvement with a dramatic and varied natural landscape. It is intimately associated with history and legend, and for centuries has exercised a powerful influence on writers, artists and composers.

The river breaks through the Rhenish Slate Mountains, connecting the broad floodplain of the Oberrheingraben with the lowland basin of the Lower Rhine. At the 5-km-long Bingen Gate the Rhine enters the upper canyon stretch of the river; here, the vineyards of the Rüdesheimer Berg are among the best in the Rheingau. In the 15-km-long Bacharach valley, the small town of Lorch is lined with terraced vineyards, while Bacharach contains many timber-framed houses and retains its medieval appearance. Kaub and its environs contain a number of monuments, including the town wall, the Pfalzgrafenstein castle and terraced vineyards created in the Middle Ages. Oberwesel has preserved some fine early houses, two Gothic churches, the medieval Schönburg castle, and the town wall.

The valley landscape begins to change at Oberwesel with the transition from soft clay-slates to hard sandstone. The result is a series of narrows, the most famous of which is the Lorelei. This stretch of river was once hazardous for shipping and is reputed to be the place where the fabulous treasure of the Niebelungs lies hidden. On the right bank of the river is St Goarshausen, with its castle of Neu-Katzenelnbogen. The design of the fortress of Burg Reichenberg suggests that it may have been inspired by Crusader fortresses in Syria and Palestine. Bad Salzig on the left bank marks the beginning of the section of horseshoe-shaped bends known as the Boppard Loops.

Boppard originated as a Roman way-station and fort. Beyond is Osterspai which has merged into one town with Niederspay. Together they contain more timber-framed houses than anywhere else on the Middle Rhine. On the left bank, Rhens is where the German Emperors were enthroned after their election and coronation.

The fortress of Marksburg, the only surviving medieval fortification on the Middle Rhine, towers above Braubach. The castle of Stolzenfels was restored in 1835 by the Prussians, while at Koblenz is the New Castle, the first and most important classicist building in the Rhineland.

World Heritage site since

• 1979 • 1980 • 1981 • 1982 • 1983 • 1984 • 1985 • 1986 • 1987 • 1988 • 1989 • 1990 • 1991 • 1992 • 1993 • 1994 • 1995 • 1996 • 1997 • 1998 • 1999 • 2000 • 2001 • **2002**

Tokaj Wine Region Historic Cultural Landscape
Hungary

Criteria – Testimony to cultural tradition;
Traditional human settlement

The cultural landscape of Tokaj graphically demonstrates the long tradition of wine production in this region of low hills and river valleys. The intricate pattern of vineyards, farms, villages, and small towns, with their historic networks of deep wine cellars, illustrates every facet of the production of the famous Tokaj wines. The name 'Tokaj' is derived from an Armenian word for grape that came into the Hungarian language as early as the tenth century, thus giving a date for the creation of the settlement. It was during the Ottoman period that the Tokaji Aszu, for which the region became world famous, was first produced. Legend has it that fears of Turkish raiders delayed the harvest until the grapes had shrivelled and botrytis infection had set in, thereby creating the 'noble rot' (pourriture noble) for which the wine is renowned.

The most characteristic structures in Tokaj are the wine cellars. There are two basic types: the vaulted and the excavated. Of special interest are the multi-level labyrinthine cellars with unsystematic floor plans. The most famous is the cellar network in the Ungvari district of Satoraljaujhely, the result of interconnecting no fewer than twenty-seven cellars at different levels.

The town of Tokaj.
▼

World Heritage site since

• 1979 • 1980 • 1981 • 1982 • 1983 • 1984 • 1985 • 1986 • 1987 • 1988 • 1989 • 1990 • 1991 • 1992 • 1993 • 1994 • 1995 • 1996 • 1997 • 1998 • 1999 • 2000 • 2001 • **2002**

Ancient Maya City of Calakmul, Campeche

Mexico

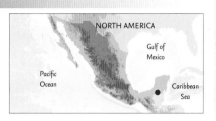

Criteria – Human creative genius; Interchange of values; Testimony to cultural tradition; Significance in human history

The archaeological site is set deep in the tropical forest of the Tierras Bajas of southern Mexico, within the Calakmul Biosphere Reserve, which was created in 1989 and is the largest in Mexico. Calakmul has a very well-preserved series of monuments representative of Maya architectural, artistic and urban development. These imposing structures and the intervening large public spaces create a vivid picture of life in an ancient Maya capital. The site is one of the most ancient in the region: buildings in the site's central zone indicate continuous occupation over some twelve centuries, and analysis of the complex iconography of a frieze shows that this antedates similar structures from Uaxactún and El Mirador, which were hitherto believed to be the oldest in the area.

Calakmul is especially noteworthy for the large number (120 to date) of *stelae* that have been found on the site. These are vital in establishing the history of the ancient city and in throwing light on the ancient Maya culture. The decorative sculpture and reliefs on the *stelae* are artistically of a high order. Two exceptional massive circular carved stones are particularly renowned for their quality and rarity in the Mayan context.

Historic Inner City of Paramaribo

Suriname

Criteria – Interchange of values; Significance in human history

Paramaribo is a former Dutch colonial town from the seventeenth and eighteenth centuries located on the northern coast of tropical South America. The original and highly characteristic street plan of the historic centre remains intact. Its buildings illustrate the gradual fusion of Dutch architectural influence with traditional local techniques and materials. The layout of the Inner City consists of a main axis stretching northwest behind Fort Zeelandia (the group of public buildings here is the central ensemble in the town plan), with streets crossing at right angles. To the north of Fort Zeelandia is the large public park known as the Garden of Palms. The wide streets and the public open spaces are tree-lined, giving a serene and spacious townscape.

The larger public buildings, such as Fort Zeelandia, the Presidential Palace, the Ministry of Finance, the Reformed Church, and the Roman Catholic cathedral, were built from stone and brick in traditional Dutch style. Increasingly however, over time, they incorporated native elements. Thus, the ground floor of the Presidential Palace is of stone but its upper storeys are of wood.

World Heritage site since

• 1979 • 1980 • 1981 • 1982 • 1983 • 1984 • 1985 • 1986 • 1987 • 1988 • 1989 • 1990 • 1991 • 1992 • 1993 • 1994 • 1995 • 1996 • 1997 • 1998 • 1999 • 2000 • 2001 • **2002**

St Catherine Area
Egypt

Criteria – Human creative genius; Testimony to
cultural tradition; Significance in human history;
Heritage associated with events of universal
significance

The Orthodox Monastery of St Catherine
stands at the foot of Mount Horeb, of the
Old Testament, where Moses received the
Tablets of the Law. The entire area is sacred
to three world religions: Christianity, Islam,
and Judaism. Ascetic monasticism in remote
areas prevailed in the early Christian church
and resulted in the establishment of
monastic communities in such places.
St Catherine's Monastery is one of the
earliest of these, and the oldest to have
survived intact, having been used for its

initial function without interruption since
the sixth century. Its walls and buildings are
very significant in the study of Byzantine
architecture and the monastery houses
outstanding collections of early Christian
manuscripts and icons.

The Christian
communities of
St Catherine's
Monastery have
always maintained
close relations with
Islam. In 623 a
document signed by
the Prophet himself
exempted the monks
of St Catherine's from
military service and
tax and called upon
Muslims to give them
every help. As a
reciprocal gesture the
monastic community
permitted the
conversion of a chapel,
within the walled
enceinte, to a mosque.

Mahabodhi Temple
Complex at Bodh Gaya
India

Criteria – Human creative genius; Interchange of
values; Testimony to cultural tradition; Significance
in human history; Heritage associated with events
of universal significance

The Mahabodhi Temple Complex is one of
the four holy sites related to the life of the
Lord Buddha (566–486 BC) as the place
where, in 531 BC, he attained the supreme
and perfect insight while seated under the
Bodhi Tree. It provides exceptional records
for the events associated with his life and for
subsequent worship, particularly since
Emperor Asoka made a pilgrimage to this

spot around 260 BC and built the first temple
at the site of the Bodhi Tree. The present
temple dates from the fifth or sixth
centuries and is one of the earliest Buddhist
temples built entirely in brick still standing
in India.

The most important
of the sacred places is
the giant Bodhi Tree
(ficus religiosa). This
tree is to the west of
the main temple and
is supposed to be a
direct descendant of
the original Bodhi
Tree under which the
Buddha spent his First
Week and where he
had his enlightenment.

World Heritage site since

• 1979 • 1980 • 1981 • 1982 • 1983 • 1984 • 1985 • 1986 • 1987 • 1988 • 1989 • 1990 • 1991 • 1992 • 1993 • 1994 • 1995 • 1996 • 1997 • 1998 • 1999 • 2000 • 2001 • 2002

Historic Centres of Stralsund and Wismar
Germany
Criteria – Interchange of values; Significance in human history

The medieval towns of Stralsund and Wismar, on the Baltic coast of northern Germany, were major trading centres of the Hanseatic League in the fourteenth and fifteenth centuries. In the seventeenth and eighteenth centuries they became Swedish administrative and defensive centres for the German territories.

Stralsund led the way in developing a particular form of construction, an independent architectural language

identified as Sundische Gothik. The fourteenth-century town hall is the most eloquent expression of this style. Building activities continued throughout the Renaissance and several civic constructions reflect the architectural forms of the Renaissance, Baroque and neoclassical periods while respecting the original medieval rhythm. The sumptuous Wismar Fürstenhof is a good example of these remarkable buildings.

Wismar was originally surrounded by moats, but these were filled on the landward side. The medieval port on the north side has been largely preserved. Stralsund was built on an island slightly oval in shape. The overall form and silhouette of the town have been particularly well preserved as a result.

Late Baroque Towns of the Val di Noto (South-Eastern Sicily)
Italy
Criteria – Human creative genius; Interchange of values; Significance in human history; Traditional human settlement

The eight towns in southeastern Sicily– Caltagirone, Militello Val di Catania, Catania, Modica, Noto, Palazzolo, Ragusa and Scicli– were all rebuilt after 1693 on or beside towns existing at the time of the earthquake in that year. They represent a considerable collective undertaking, successfully carried out at a high level of architectural and artistic achievement.

This group of Sicilian towns represents the culmination and final flowering of Baroque art in Europe and depicts distinctive innovations in town planning and urban building. The exceptional quality and homogeneity of the art and architecture in the Val di Noto towns is a direct result of rebuilding after the 1693 earthquake.

◀

Baroque church in Modica.

World Heritage site since

• 1980 • 1981 • 1982 • 1983 • 1984 • 1985 • 1986 • 1987 • 1988 • 1989 • 1990 • 1991 • 1992 • 1993 • 1994 • 1995 • 1996 • 1997 • 1998 • 1999 • 2000 • 2001 • 2002 • 2003

Takht-e Soleyman
Islamic Republic of Iran

Criteria – Human creative genius; Interchange of values; Testimony to cultural tradition; Significance in human history; Heritage associated with events of universal significance

The archaeological site of Takht-e Soleyman, in northwestern Iran, is situated in a valley set in a volcanic mountain region. The site includes the principal Zoroastrian sanctuary partly rebuilt in the Ilkhanid Mongol period (thirteenth century) as well as a temple of the Sassanian period (sixth and seventh centuries) dedicated to Anahita. The composition and the architectural elements created there by the Sassanians

have exerted a strong influence not only in the development of religious architecture in the Islamic period, but also in other cultures. The ensemble represents an outstanding example of a Zoroastrian sanctuary integrated with Sassanian palatial architecture, and is a unique testimony to the Zoroastrian fire and water cult that lasted for more than two-and-a-half millennia.

Takht-e Soleyman is an outstanding ensemble of royal architecture. The archaeological heritage of the site is further enriched by the Sassanian town, which is still to be excavated.

Azar Goshnab Fire Temple at Takht-e Soleyman.
▼

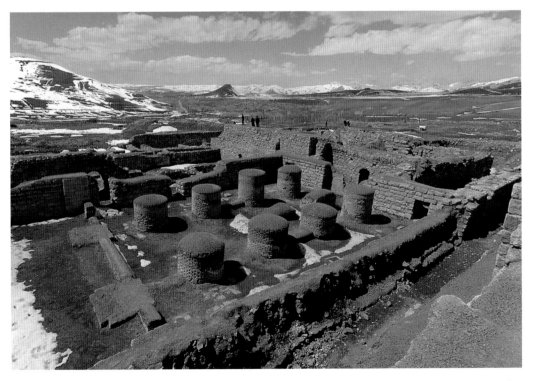

World Heritage site since

• 1980 • 1981 • 1982 • 1983 • 1984 • 1985 • 1986 • 1987 • 1988 • 1989 • 1990 • 1991 • 1992 • 1993 • 1994 • 1995 • 1996 • 1997 • 1998 • 1999 • 2000 • 2001 • 2002 • **2003**

Royal Botanic Gardens, Kew
United Kingdom

Criteria – Interchange of values; Testimony to cultural tradition; Significance in human history

Since their creation in 1759, the Royal Botanic Gardens of Kew have made a significant contribution to the study of plant diversity, and this is reflected in the richness of the collections housed there. The first botanic garden at Kew was originally for medicinal plants. Later, internationally renowned architects such as William Chambers and 'Capability' Brown not only created many new edifices, but also remodelled the earlier Baroque gardens to make a pastoral landscape in the English style, establishing a fashion that then spread throughout Europe. The landscape garden designed by William Nesfield – and the iron and glass structure, the Palm House, at its centre – is one of the outstanding features of Kew. As the number of visitors increased, the scientific collections were enriched and glasshouses and spaces were altered to house living plant collections.

The Palm House. ▲

Kew's exceptional living collections exemplify the European tradition of collecting and cultivating exotic plants for aesthetic, scientific and economic purposes. This tradition has also led to recording and monitoring of the very rich local biodiversity for over 120 years, including an outstanding range of birds, insects, lichens and fungi; some of the latter have proved to be new to science.

World Heritage site since

• 1980 • 1981 • 1982 • 1983 • 1984 • 1985 • 1986 • 1987 • 1988 • 1989 • 1990 • 1991 • 1992 • 1993 • 1994 • 1995 • 1996 • 1997 • 1998 • 1999 • 2000 • 2001 • 2002 • 2003

Mapungubwe Cultural Landscape
South Africa

Criteria – Interchange of values; Testimony to cultural tradition; Significance in human history; Traditional human settlement

Mapungubwe is set hard against the northern border of South Africa, joining Zimbabwe and Botswana. It is an open, expansive savanna landscape at the confluence of the Limpopo and Shashe rivers. Mapungubwe developed into the largest kingdom in the sub-continent before it was abandoned in the fourteenth

century. What survives are the almost untouched remains of the palace sites and also the entire settlement area dependent upon them, as well as two earlier capital sites. The whole presents an unrivalled picture of the development of social and political structures over some 400 years.

At its height, Mapungubwe was the largest and wealthiest kingdom in southern Africa through its trade of rich natural resources with Arabia, India and China. Its dominance and prosperity were ended by drastic climatic cooling in the fourteenth century.

Uvs Nuur Basin
Mongolia and Russian Federation

Criteria – Significant ecological and biological processes; Significant natural habitat for biodiversity

The Uvs Nuur Basin covers 10,689 km² and is the northernmost of the enclosed basins of central Asia. It takes its name from Uvs Nuur, a large, shallow and very saline lake, important for migrating birds, waterfowl and seabirds. The site is made up of twelve protected areas representing the major biomes of eastern Eurasia. The steppe ecosystem supports a rich diversity of birds and the desert is home to a number of rare gerbil, jerboas and the marbled polecat. The mountains are an important refuge for the globally endangered snow leopard, mountain sheep (argali) and the Asiatic ibex.

Uvs is the 'sea' of western Mongolia; it is frequented by a range of seabirds, even though the nearest ocean is 3,000 km away. The Uvs Nuur basin has an extraordinary temperature range; the lowest winter temperature in western Mongolia (-58 °C) has been recorded here but summer temperatures can rise to 40 °C.

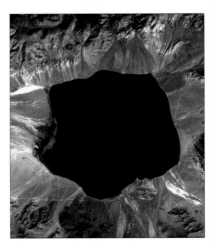

◀
Uvs Nuur from space.

World Heritage site since

• 1980 • 1981 • 1982 • 1983 • 1984 • 1985 • 1986 • 1987 • 1988 • 1989 • 1990 • 1991 • 1992 • 1993 • 1994 • 1995 • 1996 • 1997 • 1998 • 1999 • 2000 • 2001 • 2002 • **2003**

The White City of Tel-Aviv – The Modern Movement
Israel

Criteria – Interchange of values; Significance in human history

Tel Aviv was founded in 1909 and developed as a metropolitan city under the British Mandate in Palestine. The White City was constructed from the early 1930s until the 1950s, based on the urban plan by Sir Patrick Geddes, reflecting modern organic planning principles. The buildings were designed by architects who were trained in Europe where they practised their profession before immigrating. They created an outstanding architectural ensemble of the Modern Movement in a new cultural context.

Tel Aviv was conceived as a 'garden city', and its buildings reflect influences from the Bauhaus, Le Corbusier and Erich Mendelsohn adapted for local conditions. The large glazed surfaces of European buildings, for example, are reduced to relatively small, strip window openings, more suitable for the hot climate.

◀

Hotel Cinema is a renovated cinema built in the international style.

Rock Shelters of Bhimbetka
India

Criteria – Testimony to cultural tradition; Traditional human settlement

The Rock Shelters of Bhimbetka are in the foothills of the Vindhyan Mountains on the southern edge of the central Indian plateau. Within massive sandstone outcrops, above comparatively dense forest, are five clusters of natural rock shelters, displaying paintings that appear to date from the Mesolithic Period right through to the historical period. The cultural traditions of the inhabitants of the twenty-one villages adjacent to the site bear a strong resemblance to those represented in the rock paintings.

Bhimbetka reflects a long interaction between the people and the landscape. It is closely associated with a hunter-gatherer economy, as demonstrated both in the rock art and in the relics of this tradition in the local Adivasi villages nearby.

World Heritage site since

• 1980 • 1981 • 1982 • 1983 • 1984 • 1985 • 1986 • 1987 • 1988 • 1989 • 1990 • 1991 • 1992 • 1993 • 1994 • 1995 • 1996 • 1997 • 1998 • 1999 • 2000 • 2001 • 2002 • **2003**

Sacri Monti of Piedmont and Lombardy
Italy

Criteria – Interchange of values; Significance in human history

The phenomenon of Sacri Monti was conceived with the intention of creating, in Europe, places of prayer and devotion intended as alternatives to the Holy Places in Jerusalem and the Holy Land, to which access for pilgrims was difficult.

The nine Sacri Monti (Sacred Mountains) of northern Italy are groups of chapels and other architectural features created mostly in the late sixteenth and seventeenth centuries and dedicated to different aspects of the Christian faith. In addition to their symbolic spiritual value, they are skilfully integrated into the surrounding natural landscape of hills, forests and lakes. They also house much important artistic material in the form of wall paintings and statuary. The earliest Sacro Monte is the 'New Jerusalem' of Varallo. Work began in the last decade of the fifteenth century to construct a series of chapels on a rocky pass overlooking the small town of Varallo. The chapels contain statues and frescoes illustrating various sites of biblical significance.

Gebel Barkal and the Sites of the Napatan Region
Sudan

Criteria – Human creative genius; Interchange of values; Testimony to cultural tradition; Significance in human history; Heritage associated with events of universal significance

Many differences exist between these pyramids and their more famous Egyptian models. Unlike the larger Egyptian pyramids, which were built to enclose and hide the burial chamber, the Napatan ones are commemorative monuments to the deceased, buried in a hypogeum underneath. In front of the pyramid a small temple was built for offerings.

Gebel Barkal and the other sites bear exceptional testimony to the Napatan, Meroïtic and Kushite civilizations that existed along the Nile between 900 BC and AD 600. The Amun temple at Gebel Barkal is a main centre of what was once an almost universal religion and, together with the other sites, represents the revival of Egyptian religious values. Tombs, with and without pyramids, temples, living complexes and palaces, are spread throughout the 60 km site. Many of the temples are beautifully decorated and have carved hieroglyphic inscriptions. The largest temples are still considered by the local people as sacred places. There are thirty explored tombs, accessible by stairs, but Gebel Barkal still has vast archaeological areas that have neither been excavated nor studied.

World Heritage site since

• 1980 • 1981 • 1982 • 1983 • 1984 • 1985 • 1986 • 1987 • 1988 • 1989 • 1990 • 1991 • 1992 • 1993 • 1994 • 1995 • 1996 • 1997 • 1998 • 1999 • 2000 • 2001 • 2002 • 2003

Historic Quarter of the Seaport City of Valparaíso
Chile

Criteria – Testimony to cultural tradition

The colonial city of Valparaíso, the second largest in Chile, presents an excellent example of late-nineteenth-century urban and architectural development in Latin America. The geography of Valparaíso consists of a bay, a narrow coastal plain and a series of hills. In this natural amphitheatre-like setting, the city is characterized by a vernacular urban fabric adapted to the hillsides that are dotted with a great variety of church spires. The architecture of La Matríz Church (1842), Valparaíso's founding church, although rebuilt four times after destruction by pirates and earthquakes, is typical of the transition between colonial and republican styles. It is surrounded by late-nineteenth-century buildings, typical of the seaport architecture.

To ease movement up and down its steep hillsides, Valparaíso used to have as many as thirty elevators. The oldest of these, the Concepción Elevator, was inaugurated in 1883. Generally, they have two wooden or metal cars, moving simultaneously in opposite directions. They are mounted on a platform to which the wheels are attached.

Matobo Hills
Zimbabwe

Criteria – Testimony to cultural tradition; Traditional human settlement; Heritage associated with events of universal significance

The Matobo Hills have one of the highest concentrations of rock art in southern Africa. The rich evidence from archaeology and from the rock paintings at Matobo provide a detailed picture of foraging societies in the Stone Age and the agricultural societies that replaced them. The area exhibits a profusion of distinctive rock landforms rising above the granite shield that covers much of Zimbabwe. These boulders, cliff faces and natural caves feature an outstanding collection of rock paintings. The earlier paintings, dating back at least 13,000 years, are naturalistic interpretations of people, animals and trees. They are associated with hunting and gathering and are mostly executed using a red ochre pigment. The later paintings, associated with farming communities, used white pigment from kaolin or quartz.

Much of the art is impressionistic in that the figures have distorted bodily proportions to convey a sense of movement, or a large size to convey importance. In many sites there are layers of paintings superimposed one on top of the other. Images in the later paintings also appear to display a complex cosmology linked to religious beliefs.

World Heritage site since

• 1980 • 1981 • 1982 • 1983 • 1984 • 1985 • 1986 • 1987 • 1988 • 1989 • 1990 • 1991 • 1992 • 1993 • 1994 • 1995 • 1996 • 1997 • 1998 • 1999 • 2000 • 2001 • 2002 • **2003**

Ashur (Qal'at Sherqat)
Iraq

Criteria – Testimony to cultural tradition;
Significance in human history

The ancient city of Ashur is located on the Tigris River in northern Mesopotamia in a specific geo-ecological zone, at the borderline between rain-fed and irrigation agriculture. The city dates back to the third millennium BC. From the fourteenth to the ninth centuries BC it was the first capital of the Assyrian Empire, a city-state and trading platform of international importance. It also served as the religious capital of the Assyrians, associated with the god Ashur. The city was

destroyed by the Babylonians, but revived during the Parthian period in the first and second centuries AD.

The excavated remains of Ashur provide an outstanding record of the evolution of building practice from the Sumerian and Akkadian period through to the Assyrian empire. Artistic objects from the city are on display in the major museums of the world.

Renaissance Monumental Ensembles of Úbeda and Baeza
Spain

Criteria – Interchange of values; Significance in human history

The central areas of Úbeda and Baeza constitute outstanding early examples of Renaissance civic architecture and urban planning in Spain in the early sixteenth century. The two small towns, some 10 km apart, are located between the regions of Castile and Andalusia. Being on the frontier of the two regions, they have assumed a character of contrasts, which is reflected in the urban fabric that is of Arabic and Andalusian origin along with more northern

influences. Both towns prospered for a time in the sixteenth century and have survived until the present day. The urban functions of the towns are distributed so that Baeza's public, ecclesiastic and educational buildings complement Úbeda's aristocratic and palace buildings to form a Renaissance urban scheme of high architectural quality.

In its general character Baeza resembles Úbeda, with its spontaneously grown urban layout and the winding narrow streets. The most representative buildings of Baeza are situated in an axis starting from the Plaza de Santa María and running through the steep Cuesta de San Felipe down to the Cañuelo Gate.

World Heritage site since

• 1980 • 1981 • 1982 • 1983 • 1984 • 1985 • 1986 • 1987 • 1988 • 1989 • 1990 • 1991 • 1992 • 1993 • 1994 • 1995 • 1996 • 1997 • 1998 • 1999 • 2000 • 2001 • 2002 • **2003**

Citadel, Ancient City and Fortress Buildings of Derbent
Russian Federation

Criteria – Testimony to cultural tradition;
Significance in human history

The ancient city of Derbent has been crucial for the control of the north-south passage on the western side of the Caspian Sea since the first millennium BC. The defences built by the Sassanians in the fifth century AD were in continuous use by the Persian, Arabic, Mongol and Timurid governments for some fifteen centuries. The Defence Walls extend some 3.6 km from the Caspian Sea up to the citadel on the mountain.

There are two parallel walls (north and south) 300–400 m from each other. The city was built between these walls. The wall then continues over the mountains 40 km to the west, as well as extending 500 m into the sea, to protect the harbour. The site was strategically important until the nineteenth century.

The city's location forms a natural pass – the Caspian Gates – between the Caucasian foothills and the sea, so for centuries it was in a position to control traffic between Europe and the Middle East.

Kunta Kinteh Island and Related Sites
The Gambia

Criteria – Testimony to cultural tradition;
Heritage associated with events of universal significance

Kunta Kinteh Island and the related sites on the Gambia River provide exceptional testimony to the different facets of the African-European encounter, from the fifteenth to the twentieth centuries. The river formed the first trade route into the interior of Africa and became an early corridor for the slave trade. The property consists of seven separate sites, all of which were directly associated with the slave trade: the whole of Kunta Kinteh

Island, the remains of a Portuguese chapel and a colonial warehouse in the village of Albreda, the Maurel Frères Building in the village of Juffureh, the remains of the small Portuguese settlement of San Domingo, as well as Fort Bullen and the Six-Gun Battery.

The original structures on Kunta Kinteh Island comprise the fort, the slave house, the governor's kitchen, the blacksmith's shop and a store, all now in ruins. The fort is situated in the middle of this low island and is vulnerable to flooding by the tidal waters.

World Heritage site since

• 1980 • 1981 • 1982 • 1983 • 1984 • 1985 • 1986 • 1987 • 1988 • 1989 • 1990 • 1991 • 1992 • 1993 • 1994 • 1995 • 1996 • 1997 • 1998 • 1999 • 2000 • 2001 • 2002 • 2003

Purnululu National Park
Australia

Criteria – Natural phenomena or beauty;
Major stages of Earth's history

The 2,397 km² Purnululu National Park is located in the Kimberley region in the far north of the state of Western Australia. It is particularly notable for the Bungle Bungle Range, one of the most extensive and impressive occurrences of sandstone tower karst in the world. Devonian-age quartz sandstone has been eroded over a period of twenty million years into a series of beehive-shaped towers or cones amid sheer-sided gorges 100–200 m deep. The towers' surfaces are distinctly marked by regular horizontal bands of dark-grey cyanobacterial crust single-celled photosynthetic organisms. These outstanding examples of cone karst owe their existence and uniqueness to several interacting geological, biological, erosional and climatic phenomena.

The park comprises four major ecosystems: the Bungle Bungle Mountain Range, a deeply dissected plateau that dominates the centre of the park; wide sand plains surrounding the Bungle Bungles; the Ord River valley to the east and south of the park; and limestone ridges and ranges to the west and north of the park.

Sandstone tower karst in the Bungle Bungle Range. ▼

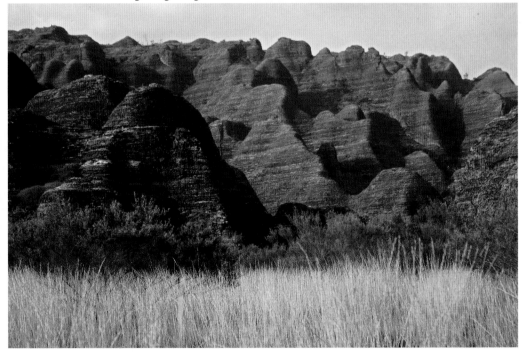

World Heritage site since

• 1980 • 1981 • 1982 • 1983 • 1984 • 1985 • 1986 • 1987 • 1988 • 1989 • 1990 • 1991 • 1992 • 1993 • 1994 • 1995 • 1996 • 1997 • 1998 • 1999 • 2000 • 2001 • 2002 • **2003**

Three Parallel Rivers of Yunnan Protected Areas China

Criteria – Natural phenomena or beauty; Major stages of Earth's history; Significant ecological and biological processes; Significant natural habitat for biodiversity

The Protected Areas within the boundaries of the Three Parallel Rivers National Park comprise a 17,000-km² site that features sections of the upper reaches of three of the great rivers of Asia: the Yangtze (Jinsha), the Mekong and the Salween. The rivers run roughly parallel, north to south for over 300 km, through steep gorges which, in places, are 3,000 m deep and bordered by glaciated peaks more than 6,000 m high. The site is an epicentre of Chinese biodiversity. It is also one of the richest temperate regions of the world in terms of biodiversity.

Three Parallel Rivers of Yunnan Protected Areas is situated in the mountainous northwest of Yunnan Province in south-central China. The site consists of fifteen protected areas in eight geographical clusters and extends 310 km from north to south and 180 km from east to west.

The World Heritage site lies over four parallel mountain ranges that reach in excess of 4,000 m above sea level. The ranges are part of the Hengduan Mountains which have been corrugated and uplifted by the pressures of crustal folding.

The land area encompassed by Three Parallel Rivers of Yunnan Protected Areas is one of the world's least-disturbed temperate ecological areas, an epicentre of Chinese endemic species and a natural gene pool of great richness. It supports the richest diversity of higher plants of China, owing to its altitudinal range and its position in a climatic corridor between north and south. It includes the equivalents of seven climatic zones: southern, central and northern subtropical zones, with dry hot valleys; warm, cool and cold temperate zones; and cold zones.

Owing to its function as a refuge during the last Ice Age and its location near the boundaries of three major biogeographic realms (east Asia, southeast Asia and the Tibetan plateau), the park has twenty-two vegetation subtypes and 6,000 plant species. The fauna is a complex mosaic of Palaearctic, oriental and endemic species adapted to almost all the inland climates from southern subtropical to frigid. The area is believed to support over 25 per cent of China's animal species, many being relict and endangered.

Snow-capped Baimang Snow Mountain between the Yangtze and Mekong rivers.

The site is dominated by a composite orogenic belt that shows the signs of powerful crustal movements. Notable is the compression of the Eurasian plate edge by the underlying Indian plate. The resulting squeeze created vast thrust nappes, violent shearing and uplift into high mountains, through which pre-existing rivers continue to cut, resulting in the area's characteristic extreme vertical relief.

Alpine landscapes and their evolution are represented in the eastern mountains, where plateaus and valleys are covered with meadows, waterfalls, streams and hundreds of lakes left by glacial erosion.

World Heritage site since

• 1980 • 1981 • 1982 • 1983 • 1984 • 1985 • 1986 • 1987 • 1988 • 1989 • 1990 • 1991 • 1992 • 1993 • 1994 • 1995 • 1996 • 1997 • 1998 • 1999 • 2000 • 2001 • 2002 • **2003**

Wooden Churches of Southern Małopolska Poland

Criteria – Testimony to cultural tradition;
Significance in human history

North
Sea

Baltic
Sea

EUROPE

The wooden churches of southern Małopolska represent outstanding examples of medieval church-building traditions in Roman Catholic culture. Built using the horizontal log technique, common in eastern and northern Europe since the Middle Ages, these churches offered an alternative to the stone structures erected in urban centres. Churches have been of particular significance in the development of Polish wooden architecture, and an essential element of settlement structures, both as landmarks and as ideological symbols. They were an outward sign of the cultural identity of communities, reflecting the artistic and social aspirations of their patrons and creators. The six sites in southern Małopolska represent different aspects of these developments.

The Church of Archangel Michael of Szalowa, built in 1736–1756, differs from the others because of its architectural form, although the same construction techniques were used. The church has a nave and two aisles, and is built in basilica form. The extremely rich polychrome decoration and fittings date from the eighteenth century.

The Church of St Philip and St James the Apostles (Sekowa). ▼

World Heritage site since

• 1980 • 1981 • 1982 • 1983 • 1984 • 1985 • 1986 • 1987 • 1988 • 1989 • 1990 • 1991 • 1992 • 1993 • 1994 • 1995 • 1996 • 1997 • 1998 • 1999 • 2000 • 2001 • 2002 • **2003**

Franciscan Missions in the Sierra Gorda of Querétaro
Mexico

Criteria – Interchange of values; Testimony to cultural tradition

The five Franciscan missions of Sierra Gorda were built during the last phase of the conversion to Christianity of the interior of Mexico in the mid-eighteenth century and became an important reference for the continuation of the evangelisation of California, Arizona and Texas. Each mission had to erect the church, find the natives, subdue them, and then group them in huts around the church. The missionaries had to learn the native language, supply the population with food, teach them how to behave, and only then evangelise them. The richly decorated church façades are of special interest as they represent an example of the joint creative efforts of the missionaries and the native Indios. The rural settlements that grew around the missions have retained their vernacular character.

The architecture of the missions follows a similar pattern and generally includes an atrium, sacramental doorway, open chapel, processional chapels and a cloister. All five missions share similar elements in relation to their environment, the town and the religious buildings.

Cultural Landscape and Archaeological Remains of the Bamiyan Valley
Afghanistan

Criteria – Human creative genius; Interchange of values; Testimony to cultural tradition; Significance in human history; Heritage associated with events of universal significance

The cultural landscape and archaeological remains of the Bamiyan Valley represent the artistic and religious developments which, from the first to the thirteenth centuries, characterized ancient Bakhtria, integrating various cultural influences into the Gandhara school of Buddhist art. The area contains numerous Buddhist monastic ensembles and sanctuaries, as well as fortified edifices from the Islamic period. The site is also testimony to the tragic destruction by the Taliban of the two standing Buddha statues in March 2001.

The Bamiyan Valley is a high pass (2,500 m) that formed one of the branches of the Silk Road. Its beautiful landscape is associated with legendary figures which contributed to its development as a major religious and cultural centre.

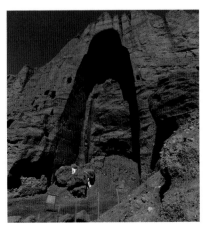

◄

One of the Buddha statues destroyed in 2001.

World Heritage site since

• 1980 • 1981 • 1982 • 1983 • 1984 • 1985 • 1986 • 1987 • 1988 • 1989 • 1990 • 1991 • 1992 • 1993 • 1994 • 1995 • 1996 • 1997 • 1998 • 1999 • 2000 • 2001 • 2002 • **2003**

Monte San Giorgio
Italy and Switzerland

Criteria – Major stages of Earth's history

The pyramid-shaped, wooded mountain 1,096 m above sea level, to the south of Lake Lugano, is regarded as the best fossil record of marine life from the Triassic Period, 245–230 million years ago. The sequence records life in a tropical lagoon environment, sheltered and partially separated from the open sea by an offshore reef. Diverse marine life flourished within this lagoon, including reptiles, fish, bivalves, ammonites, echinoderms and crustaceans. The site was extended in 2010 to the Italian

side of the border with its exceptionally important Triassic marine fossil record.

Fossils from the mountain have been known to science for over 150 years. The vertebrate material includes particularly spectacular specimens, with articulated skeletons up to 6 m in length. The site's record of marine life during a critical period in vertebrate evolution on Earth provides a global reference point for comparative studies of evolution.

◀

Monte San Giorgio on Lake Lugano.

Jewish Quarter and St Procopius' Basilica in Třebíč
Czech Republic

Criteria – Interchange of values; Testimony to cultural tradition

The ensemble of the Jewish Quarter, the old Jewish cemetery and the Basilica of St Procopius in Třebíč, are reminders of the co-existence of Jewish and Christian cultures from the Middle Ages to the twentieth century. The Jewish Quarter bears outstanding testimony to the different aspects of the life of this community. The area has preserved all essential social functions, including synagogues and

schools, as well as a leather factory. St Procopius' Basilica is situated in a good position on the hill with a view over the whole of Třebíč. Built in the thirteenth century as a monastic church, it is a mixture of Romanesque and early Gothic styles and presents a remarkable example of the influence of western European architectural heritage in this region.

The Jewish Quarter rises up the hillside from the river to which its two main streets are linked by small mediaeval alleys; some of these run through the houses. All the Jewish residents were deported during the Second World War.

World Heritage site since

• 1980 • 1981 • 1982 • 1983 • 1984 • 1985 • 1986 • 1987 • 1988 • 1989 • 1990 • 1991 • 1992 • 1993 • 1994 • 1995 • 1996 • 1997 • 1998 • 1999 • 2000 • 2001 • 2002 • 2003

Quebrada de Humahuaca
Argentina

Criteria – Interchange of values; Significance in human history; Traditional human settlement

Quebrada de Humahuaca follows the line of a major cultural route, the Camino Inca, along the spectacular valley of the Rio Grande, from its source in the cold High Andean desert plateau to its confluence with the Rio Leone some 150 km to the south. The valley shows substantial evidence of its use as a major trade route over the past 10,000 years. Scattered along the valley are extensive remains of successive settlements whose inhabitants created and used these linear routes. It features visible traces of prehistoric hunter-gatherer communities, of the Inca Empire (fifteenth–sixteenth centuries) and of the fight for independence in the sixteenth and twentieth centuries.

Of particular note are the extensive remains of stone-walled agricultural terraced fields at Coctaca, thought to have originated around 1,500 years ago and still in use today. The field system makes a dramatic impact on the landscape that is unrivalled in South America.

Seven Colours Mountain in Quebrada de Humahuaca.
▼

World Heritage site since

• 1980 • 1981 • 1982 • 1983 • 1984 • 1985 • 1986 • 1987 • 1988 • 1989 • 1990 • 1991 • 1992 • 1993 • 1994 • 1995 • 1996 • 1997 • 1998 • 1999 • 2000 • 2001 • 2002 • **2003**

Phong Nha-Ke Bang National Park
Vietnam
Criteria – Major stages of Earth's history

The karst formation of Phong Nha-Ke Bang National Park has evolved since the Palaeozoic era, some 400 million years ago, and is the oldest major karst area in Asia. Subject to massive tectonic changes, the park's karst landscape is extremely complex with many geomorphic features of considerable significance. The vast area, extending to the border with the Lao People's Democratic Republic, contains spectacular formations including 65 km of caves and underground rivers. The Phong Nha Cave is the most famous in the system, with a currently surveyed length of 44.5 km. Its entrance is part of an underground river and tour boats can penetrate inside to a distance of 1,500 m. Other extensive caves include the Vom cave and the Hang Khe Rhy cave.

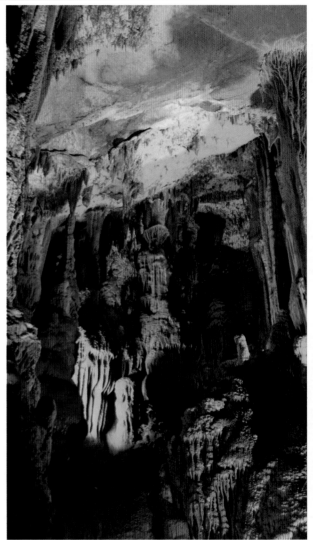

Stalactites and pillar formations in Phong Nha-Ke Bang National Park. ▲

Some 92 per cent of the park is covered by tropical forest. A total of 568 vertebrate species have been recorded in the site, comprising 113 mammals, 81 reptiles and amphibians, 302 birds and 72 fish.

The site is particularly rich in primates, with ten species and subspecies forming 45 per cent of the total number of species in Vietnam.

Mausoleum of Khoja Ahmed Yasawi
Kazakhstan

Criteria – Human creative genius; Testimony to cultural tradition; Significance in human history

The Mausoleum of Khoja Ahmed Yasawi, a distinguished Sufi master of the twelfth century, is situated in the city of Turkestan (Yasi) in southern Kazakhstan. The mausoleum is in the area of the former citadel, in the northeastern part of the ancient town, now an open archaeological site. To the south is a nature protection area; on the other sides the modern city of Turkestan surrounds the site.

The mausoleum was built at the time of Timur (Tamerlane), from 1389 to 1405. In this partly unfinished building, Persian master builders experimented with architectural and structural solutions later used in the construction of Samarkand, the capital of the Timurid Empire. Today it is one of the largest and best-preserved constructions of the Timurid period.

The Mausoleum's Main Hall is covered with a conic-spherical dome which is the largest in central Asia (18.2 m in diameter). The building also features a mosque, which is the only room where fragments of the original wall paintings are preserved.

Liverpool – Maritime Mercantile City
United Kingdom

Criteria – Interchange of values; Testimony to cultural tradition; Significance in human history

Six areas in the historic centre and docklands of the maritime mercantile city of Liverpool bear witness to the development of one of the world's major trading centres in the eighteenth and nineteenth centuries. Liverpool played an important role in the growth of the British Empire and became the major port for the mass movement of people, e.g. slaves, and emigrants from northern Europe to America. Liverpool was a pioneer in the development of modern

dock technology, transport systems and port management. It features a great number of significant commercial, civic and public buildings.

The site stretches along the waterfront from Albert Dock to Pier Head and Stanley Dock and takes in the historic, commercial and cultural districts of the city centre.

World Heritage site since

• 1981 • 1982 • 1983 • 1984 • 1985 • 1986 • 1987 • 1988 • 1989 • 1990 • 1991 • 1992 • 1993 • 1994 • 1995 • 1996 • 1997 • 1998 • 1999 • 2000 • 2001 • 2002 • 2003 • **2004**

Ilulissat Icefjord
Greenland (Denmark)

Criteria – Natural phenomena or beauty; Major
stages of Earth's history

NORTH
AMERICA

Atlantic
Ocean

EUROPE

Located on the west coast of Greenland,
250 km north of the Arctic Circle, Ilulissat
Icefjord (402 km²) is the sea mouth of
Sermeq Kujalleq, one of the few glaciers
through which the Greenland icecap
reaches the sea. Sermeq Kujalleq is one of
the fastest moving (19 m per day) and most
active glaciers in the world. It annually
calves over 35 km³ of ice, i.e. 10 per cent of
the production of all Greenland calf ice and
more than any other glacier outside
Antarctica. Studied for over 250 years, it has
helped to develop our understanding of
climate change and icecap glaciology. The
combination of a huge ice-sheet and the
dramatic sounds of a fast-moving glacial
ice-stream calving into a fjord covered by
icebergs makes for a dramatic and awe-
inspiring natural phenomenon.

Norsemen inhabited
southwest Greenland
between AD 985 and
1450. During the
sixteenth–eighteenth
centuries explorers,
followed by whalers,
inhabited the area. The
World Heritage area
includes the archaeo-
logically valuable sites
of Sermermuit,
abandoned in 1850, and
Qajaa on the south side
of the fjord, abandoned
earlier. The early settlers
summered in tents but
used stone and turf
hovels in winter.

◄

Ilulissat Icefjord as
seen from space.

World Heritage site since

• 1981 • 1982 • 1983 • 1984 • 1985 • 1986 • 1987 • 1988 • 1989 • 1990 • 1991 • 1992 • 1993 • 1994 • 1995 • 1996 • 1997 • 1998 • 1999 • 2000 • 2001 • 2002 • 2003 • 2004

Þingvellir National Park
Iceland

Criteria – Testimony to cultural tradition;
Heritage associated with events of universal
significance

Greenland

Atlantic
Ocean

Scandinavia

EUROPE

The Althing and its
hinterland, Þingvellir
National Park,
represent a unique
reflection of medieval
Norse/Germanic
culture which
persisted from its
foundation in AD 980
until the eighteenth
century.

Þingvellir (Thingvellir) is the National Park
where the Althing – an open-air assembly,
which represented the whole of Iceland –
was established in 930 and continued to
meet until 1798. Over two weeks a year, the
assembly set laws – seen as a covenant
between free men – and settled disputes.
The Althing has deep historical and
symbolic associations for the people of
Iceland. The property includes the Þingvellir

National Park and the remains of the
Althing itself: fragments of around fifty
booths built from turf and stone. Remains
from the tenth century are thought to be
buried underground. The site also includes
remains of agricultural use from the
eighteenth and nineteenth centuries. The
park shows evidence of the way the
landscape was husbanded over 1,000 years.

Þingvellir Church
▼

World Heritage site since

• 1981 • 1982 • 1983 • 1984 • 1985 • 1986 • 1987 • 1988 • 1989 • 1990 • 1991 • 1992 • 1993 • 1994 • 1995 • 1996 • 1997 • 1998 • 1999 • 2000 • 2001 • 2002 • 2003 • **2004**

Bam and its Cultural Landscape
Islamic Republic of Iran

Criteria – Interchange of values; Testimony to cultural tradition; Significance in human history; Traditional human settlement

Bam is an outstanding expression of the interaction of man and nature in a desert environment. The civilisation depended on a strict social system with precise tasks and responsibilities, which have been maintained in use until the present.

The Citadel, Bam, before the earthquake in 2003.
▼

Bam is situated in a desert environment on the southern edge of the Iranian high plateau. The origins of Bam can be traced back to the Achaemenid period, sixth to fourth centuries BC. Its heyday was from the seventh to eleventh centuries, being at the crossroads of important trade routes and known for the production of silk and cotton garments. The existence of life in the oasis was based on the underground irrigation canals, the qanāts, of which Bam has preserved some of the earliest evidence in Iran. Arg-e Bam is the most representative example of a fortified medieval town built in vernacular technique using mud layers (Chineh).

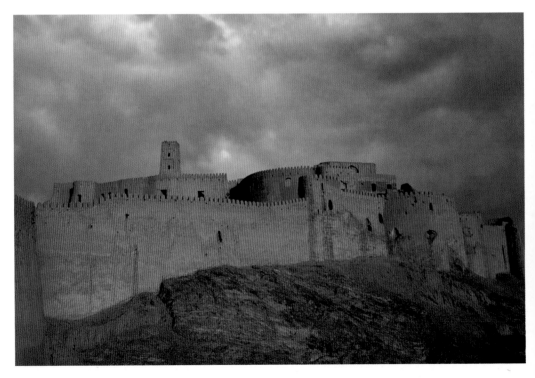

World Heritage site since

• 1981 • 1982 • 1983 • 1984 • 1985 • 1986 • 1987 • 1988 • 1989 • 1990 • 1991 • 1992 • 1993 • 1994 • 1995 • 1996 • 1997 • 1998 • 1999 • 2000 • 2001 • 2002 • 2003 • **2004**

Pitons Management Area
Saint Lucia

Criteria – Natural phenomena or beauty; Major stages of Earth's history

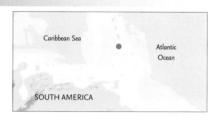

At least 148 plant species have been recorded on Gros Piton and 97 on Petit Piton. Among these are several endemic or rare plants, including eight rare species of tree. Some bird species, including five endemics, are known from Gros Piton, along with indigenous rodents, opossum, bats, reptiles and amphibians.

Dominating the mountainous landscape of St Lucia are the Pitons, two steep-sided volcanic spires rising side by side from the sea. Gros Piton (770 m) is 3 km in diameter at its base, and Petit Piton (743 m) is 1 km in diameter and linked to the former by the Piton Mitan ridge. The Pitons are part of a volcanic complex, known to geologists as the Soufrière Volcanic Centre, which is the remnant of one, or more, huge collapsed stratovolcano. The Marine Management Area is a coastal strip 11 km long and about 1 km wide. The coral reefs, which cover almost 60 per cent of the marine area, are healthy and diverse. The area is a multiple-use management system where agriculture, artisan fishing, human settlement (1,500 residents) and tourism (four large hotel developments) were present at the time of inscription.

World Heritage site since

• 1981 • 1982 • 1983 • 1984 • 1985 • 1986 • 1987 • 1988 • 1989 • 1990 • 1991 • 1992 • 1993 • 1994 • 1995 • 1996 • 1997 • 1998 • 1999 • 2000 • 2001 • 2002 • 2003 • **2004**

Tropical Rainforest Heritage of Sumatra
Indonesia

Criteria – Natural phenomena or beauty;
Significant ecological and biological processes;
Significant natural habitat for biodiversity

The 25,000 km² Tropical Rainforest Heritage of Sumatra comprises three widely-separated national parks along the Bukit Barisan mountain range: Gunung Leuser National Park, Kerinci Seblat National Park and Bukit Barisan Selatan National Park. The site holds the greatest potential for long-term conservation of the distinctive biodiversity of Sumatra, including many endangered species. The protected area is home to an estimated 10,000 plant species, including 17 endemic genera; more than 200 mammal species; and some 580 bird species, of which 465 are resident and 21 are endemic. Of the mammal species, twenty-two are Asian, not found elsewhere in the archipelago, and fifteen are confined to the Indonesian region, including the endemic Sumatran orang-utan. The site also provides biogeographic evidence of the evolution of the island.

Kerinci Seblat National Park contains the magnificent, active volcano Gunung Kerinci – at 3,805 m, the highest peak in Sumatra and the highest volcano in Indonesia. Nearby Gunung Tujuh has an outstandingly beautiful crater lake at 1,996 m.

A Sumatran orang-utan.
▼

World Heritage site since

• 1981 • 1982 • 1983 • 1984 • 1985 • 1986 • 1987 • 1988 • 1989 • 1990 • 1991 • 1992 • 1993 • 1994 • 1995 • 1996 • 1997 • 1998 • 1999 • 2000 • 2001 • 2002 • 2003 • 2004

Um er-Rasas (Kastrom Mefa'a)
Jordan

Criteria – Human creative genius; Significance in human history; Heritage associated with events of universal significance

Most of this archaeological site, which started as a Roman military camp and grew to become a town from the fifth century onwards, has not been excavated. It contains remains from the Roman, Byzantine and Early Muslim periods, the end of the third to ninth centuries AD, and a fortified Roman military camp. The site also has sixteen churches, some with well-preserved mosaic floors. Particularly noteworthy is the mosaic floor of the Church of St Stephen. Two square towers are probably the only remains of the practice, well known in this part of the world, of the stylites (ascetic monks who spent time in isolation atop a column or tower). Um er-Rasas is surrounded by, and dotted with, remains of ancient agricultural cultivation in an arid area.

The mosaic floor of the church of St Stephen shows an incredible representation of towns in Palestine, Jordan and Egypt, including their identification. Its artistic and technical qualities justify describing Um er-Rasas as a masterpiece of human creative genius.

Southern area of Um er-Rasas.
▼

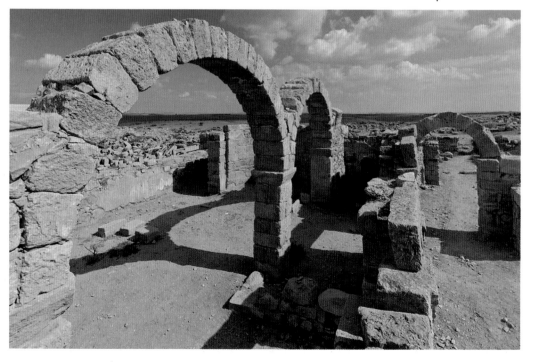

World Heritage site since

• 1981 • 1982 • 1983 • 1984 • 1985 • 1986 • 1987 • 1988 • 1989 • 1990 • 1991 • 1992 • 1993 • 1994 • 1995 • 1996 • 1997 • 1998 • 1999 • 2000 • 2001 • 2002 • 2003 • **2004**

Pasargadae
Islamic Republic of Iran

Criteria – Human creative genius; Interchange
of values; Testimony to cultural tradition;
Significance in human history

The Mausoleum of
Cyrus the Great was
built from white
limestone around
540–530 BC. In the
medieval period, the
monument was
thought to be the
tomb of Solomon's
mother, and a
mosque, which was in
use until the
fourteenth century,
was built around it.

Pasargadae was the first dynastic capital of
the Achaemenid Empire, founded by Cyrus
the Great in Pars, homeland of the Persians,
in the sixth century BC. Its palaces, gardens
and the mausoleum of Cyrus are
outstanding examples of the first phase
of royal Achaemenid art and architecture.
Particularly noteworthy remains in the
1.6 km² site include: the Mausoleum of
Cyrus the Great (pictured below); Tall-e Takht,
a fortified terrace; and a royal ensemble of
gatehouse, audience hall and residential
palace, originally located within a garden
ensemble (the so-called 'Four Gardens').
Pasargadae was the capital of the first great
multicultural empire in western Asia.
Spanning the eastern Mediterranean and
Egypt to the Indus River, it is considered
to be the first empire that respected the
cultural diversity of its different peoples.

World Heritage site since

• 1981 • 1982 • 1983 • 1984 • 1985 • 1986 • 1987 • 1988 • 1989 • 1990 • 1991 • 1992 • 1993 • 1994 • 1995 • 1996 • 1997 • 1998 • 1999 • 2000 • 2001 • 2002 • 2003 • **2004**

Complex of Koguryo Tombs
Korea, Democratic People's Republic of

Criteria – Human creative genius; Interchange of values; Testimony to cultural tradition; Significance in human history

The special burial customs of the Koguryo culture had an important influence on other cultures in the region, including those in Japan.

The property includes several group and individual tombs – totalling about thirty – from the later period of the Koguryo Kingdom. This was one of the strongest kingdoms in northeast China and the northern half of the Korean peninsula between the third century BC and seventh century AD. The tombs, many with beautiful wall paintings, are almost the only remains of this culture. Only about ninety out of more than 10,000 Koguryo tombs discovered in China and Korea, so far, have wall paintings. Almost half of these tombs are located on this site and they are thought to have been made for the burial of kings, members of the royal family and the aristocracy. These paintings offer a unique testimony to daily life of this period.

Kernavė Archaeological Site (Cultural Reserve of Kernavė)
Lithuania

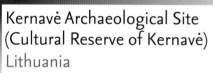

Criteria – Testimony to cultural tradition; Significance in human history

The burial ground of the complex was situated outside the town in the Kriveikiškis hill fort. Funeral customs, as well as the discovered cerecloths, reflect not only the traditions of the last pagan state in Europe, but also attest to the influence of neighbouring Christian countries.

The Kernavė Archaeological site, about 35 km northwest of Vilnius in eastern Lithuania, represents an exceptional testimony to some ten millennia of human settlements in this region. Situated in the valley of the river Neris, the site is a complex ensemble of archaeological properties, encompassing the town of Kernavė, forts, some unfortified settlements, burial sites and other archaeological, historical and cultural monuments from the late Palaeolithic Period to the Middle Ages. The site of 2 km² has preserved the traces of ancient land-use, as well as remains of five impressive hill forts, part of an exceptionally large defence system. Kernavė was an important feudal town in the Middle Ages. The town was destroyed by the Teutonic Order in the late fourteenth century, however the site remained in use until modern times.

◄ Hill forts in Kernavė.

World Heritage site since

• 1981 • 1982 • 1983 • 1984 • 1985 • 1986 • 1987 • 1988 • 1989 • 1990 • 1991 • 1992 • 1993 • 1994 • 1995 • 1996 • 1997 • 1998 • 1999 • 2000 • 2001 • 2002 • 2003 • 2004

Vegaøyan – the Vega Archipelago
Norway
Criteria – Traditional human settlement

A cluster of dozens of islands centred on Vega, just south of the Arctic Circle, forms a cultural landscape of 1,037 km², of which only 69 km² is land. The islands bear testimony to a distinctive frugal way of life based on fishing and the harvesting of the down of eider ducks, in an inhospitable environment. There are fishing villages, quays, warehouses, eider houses built for eider ducks to nest in, farming landscapes, lighthouses and beacons. There is evidence of human settlement from the Stone Age onwards. By the ninth century, the islands had become an important centre for the supply of down, which appears to have accounted for around a third of the islanders' income. The Vega Archipelago reflects the way fishermen/farmers have, over the past 1,500 years, maintained a sustainable living and also the contribution of women to eiderdown harvesting.

The fishing and hunting of marine animals has taken place in this area since the ice retreated around 10,000 years ago. The type of fishing varied throughout the year. Although today there are fewer active fishermen than 100 years ago, this unique culture is still preserved by some.

Natural System of Wrangel Island Reserve
Russian Federation
Criteria – Significant ecological and biological processes; Significant natural habitat for biodiversity

Located well above the Arctic Circle, the site includes the mountainous 7,608 km² Wrangel Island, 11 km² Herald Island and surrounding waters. Wrangel was not glaciated during the Quaternary Ice Age, resulting in exceptionally high levels of biodiversity for this region. The island boasts the world's largest population of Pacific walrus and the highest density of ancestral polar bear dens. It is a major feeding ground for the grey whale migrating from Mexico and the northernmost nesting ground for 100 migratory bird species, many endangered. Currently, 417 species and subspecies of vascular plants have been identified on the island, double that of any other Arctic tundra territory of comparable size and more than any other Arctic island. Some species are derivative of widespread continental forms, others are the result of recent hybridization, and twenty-three are endemic.

There is evidence of a Neolithic camp of Palaeo-Eskimo hunters from around 3,400 years ago in Krassin Bay on the south coast. Their prey included woolly mammoth and pygmy woolly mammoth, which lived on the island until 3,700 years ago.

World Heritage site since

• 1981 • 1982 • 1983 • 1984 • 1985 • 1986 • 1987 • 1988 • 1989 • 1990 • 1991 • 1992 • 1993 • 1994 • 1995 • 1996 • 1997 • 1998 • 1999 • 2000 • 2001 • 2002 • 2003 • 2004

Portuguese City of Mazagan (El Jadida)
Morocco

Criteria – Interchange of values; Significance in human history

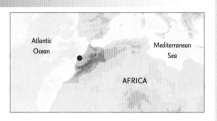

The Portuguese city of Mazagan – one of the early settlements of the Portuguese explorers in west Africa on the route to India – is an outstanding example of the interchange of influences between European and Moroccan cultures. Now part of the city of El Jadida, 90 km southwest of Casablanca, Mazagan was built as a fortified colony in the early sixteenth century. It was taken over by the Moroccans in 1769. The fortification, with its bastions and ramparts, is an early example of Renaissance military design. The surviving Portuguese buildings include the cistern and the Church of the Assumption. The nineteenth-century mosque, in front of the Church of the Assumption, delimits the urban square, the Praça Terreiro, which opens towards the entrance of the city. The minaret is an adaptation of the old Torre de Rebate, originally part of the cistern.

At the present time the fortification has four bastions: the Angel Bastion in the east, St Sebastian in the north, St Antoine in the west, and the Holy Ghost Bastion in the south. The fifth, the Governor's Bastion at the main entrance, is in ruins, having been destroyed by the Portuguese in 1769. The fort originally had three gates.

Medieval Monuments in Kosovo
Serbia

Criteria – Interchange of values; Testimony to cultural tradition; Significance in human history

The religious edifices of the site reflect the high points of the Byzantine-Romanesque ecclesiastical culture, with its distinct style of wall painting, which developed in the Balkans between the thirteenth and seventeenth centuries. The Dečani Monastery was built in the mid-fourteenth century for the Serbian king Stefan Dečanski and is also his mausoleum. The Patriarchate of Peć Monastery is a group of four domed churches featuring a series of wall paintings. The thirteenth-century frescoes of the Church of Holy Apostles are painted in a unique, monumental style. Early fourteenth-century frescoes in the Church of the Holy Virgin of Ljevisa represent the appearance of the new so-called Palaiologian Renaissance style, combining the influences of the eastern Orthodox Byzantine and the western Romanesque traditions. The style played a decisive role in subsequent Balkan art.

The main church of the Dečani Monastery has an exceptionally rich treasury with about sixty exceptional icons from the fourteenth to seventeenth centuries and many other precious objects.

World Heritage site since

• 1981 • 1982 • 1983 • 1984 • 1985 • 1986 • 1987 • 1988 • 1989 • 1990 • 1991 • 1992 • 1993 • 1994 • 1995 • 1996 • 1997 • 1998 • 1999 • 2000 • 2001 • 2002 • 2003 • **2004**

Royal Exhibition Building and Carlton Gardens
Australia

Criteria – Interchange of values

The aesthetic significance of the Carlton Gardens lies in its representation of the nineteenth-century Gardenesque style. This includes parterre garden beds, significant avenues including the southern carriage drive and Grande Allée, the path system, clusters of trees, two small lakes and three fountains.

The Royal Exhibition Building, in its original setting of the Carlton Gardens, is the only substantially intact example in the world of a Great Hall from a major international exhibition. The building and gardens were designed for the great exhibitions of 1880 and 1888 in Melbourne. The building is constructed of brick and timber, steel and slate. It combines elements from the Byzantine, Romanesque, Lombardic and Italian Renaissance styles. The property is typical of the international exhibition movement, which aimed to showcase technological innovation, and boasts many of the important features that made the expositions so dramatic, including a dome, a great hall, giant entry portals and complementary gardens and viewing areas. Unlike the structures at many international exhibitions, the building was conceived as a permanent construction that would have a future role in the cultural activities of the growing city of Melbourne.

World Heritage site since

• 1981 • 1982 • 1983 • 1984 • 1985 • 1986 • 1987 • 1988 • 1989 • 1990 • 1991 • 1992 • 1993 • 1994 • 1995 • 1996 • 1997 • 1998 • 1999 • 2000 • 2001 • 2002 • 2003 • 2004

Orkhon Valley Cultural Landscape
Mongolia

Criteria – Interchange of values; Testimony to cultural tradition; Significance in human history

The 1,220-km² Orkhon Valley Cultural Landscape encompasses an extensive area of pastureland on both banks of the Orkhon River and includes numerous archaeological remains dating back to the sixth century. The site also includes Kharkhorum, the thirteenth- and fourteenth-century capital of Chingis (Genghis) Khan's vast Empire. Collectively the remains in the site reflect the symbiotic links between nomadic, pastoral societies and their administrative and religious centres, and the importance of the Orkhon valley in the history of central Asia. The grassland is still grazed by Mongolian nomadic pastoralists.

In Mongolia, nomadic pastoralism is revered and glorified as the heart of Mongolian culture, and in the Orkhon Valley Cultural Landscape the links between such nomadic pastoralism and its associated settlements can be seen clearly.

Muskauer Park / Park Muzakowski
Germany and Poland

Criteria – Human creative genius; Significance in human history

A landscaped park of 5.6 km² astride the Neisse River and the border between Poland and Germany, Muskauer Park was created by Prince Hermann von Pückler-Muskau from 1815 to 1844. Blending seamlessly with the surrounding farmed landscape, the park pioneered new approaches to landscape design and influenced the development of landscape architecture in Europe and America. Designed as a 'painting with plants', it did not seek to evoke classical landscapes, paradise, or some lost perfection, instead using local plants to enhance the inherent qualities of the existing landscape. This integrated landscape extends into the town of Muskau with green passages that formed urban parks framing areas for development. The town thus became a design component in a utopian landscape. The site also features a reconstructed castle, bridges and an arboretum.

The site is the centre of a landscape park which extended around Muskau and into the countryside. After the Second World War the Neisse became the international border, leaving 3.5 km² of the park within Poland and 2.1 km² in Germany.

World Heritage site since

• 1981 • 1982 • 1983 • 1984 • 1985 • 1986 • 1987 • 1988 • 1989 • 1990 • 1991 • 1992 • 1993 • 1994 • 1995 • 1996 • 1997 • 1998 • 1999 • 2000 • 2001 • 2002 • 2003 • **2004**

Cape Floral Region Protected Areas
South Africa

Criteria – Significant ecological and biological processes; Significant natural habitat for biodiversity

Fynbos, Afrikaans for ▶ 'fine bush' is the natural, primarily evergreen, shrubland vegetation of the Cape Floral region.

Eight protected areas covering 5,530 km² make up the Cape Floral Region, one of the richest areas for plants in the world. It represents less than 0.5 per cent of the area of Africa but is home to nearly 20 per cent of the continent's flora. The site displays outstanding ecological and biological processes associated with the fynbos (fine bush) vegetation which is unique to the Cape Floral Region. The outstanding diversity, density and endemism of the flora are among the highest anywhere in the world. Unique plant-reproductive strategies, adaptive to fire, patterns of seed dispersal by insects and patterns of endemism and adaptive radiation found in the flora, are of outstanding value to science.

The region is located in the southwest corner of South Africa in Cape Province. Elevations range from 2,077 m in the Groot Winterhoek to sea level in the De Hoop Nature Reserve. A great part of the area is characterized by rugged mountain passes, rivers, rapids, cascades and pools.

The area has been designated as one of the World Centres of Plant Diversity. It has 44 per cent of the subcontinental flora of 20,367 species, including endemic and subendemic families and threatened species. The Cape Peninsula contains almost half of these species, with 25 per cent of the

flora of the whole region. The richness is due to the wide variety of macrohabitats and microhabitat mosaics resulting from the range of elevations, soils and climatic conditions, including the co-existence of winter-rainfall species with summer-rainfall species from further east.

Eight centres of endemism have been distinguished in the Cape Floral Region. The distinctive flora of the area, comprising 80 per cent of its richness, is the fynbos, fine-leaved vegetation adapted to both the Mediterranean type of climate and to periodic fires, and defined by the location or dominant species. Plant variety is based on soil types that range from predominantly coarse, sandy, acidic, nutrient-poor soils, to alkaline marine sands and slightly richer alluvials. There are pockets of evergreen forest in fire-protected gorges and on deeper soils; in the east are valley thickets and succulent thickets, which are less fire-dependent, and in the drier north, low succulent Karoo shrubland.

Characteristics of the Cape Floral Region that are of global scientific interest are the responses of its plants to fire; seed dispersal by ants and termites; the high level (83 per cent) of plant pollination by insects (mainly beetles and flies); and its links to the ancient continent of Gondwanaland, which allowed reconstruction of the flora's ancient connections.

Some of the species actually require fire for germination. Pollination and nutrient-cycling by termites are notable and the region also has a very high number of plants that are pollinated by birds and mammals.

World Heritage site since

• 1981 • 1982 • 1983 • 1984 • 1985 • 1986 • 1987 • 1988 • 1989 • 1990 • 1991 • 1992 • 1993 • 1994 • 1995 • 1996 • 1997 • 1998 • 1999 • 2000 • 2001 • 2002 • 2003 • 2004

Luis Barragán House and Studio
Mexico

Criteria – Human creative genius; Interchange of values

NORTH AMERICA
Gulf of Mexico
Pacific Ocean
Caribbean Sea

Built in 1948, the House and Studio of architect Luis Barragán in the suburbs of Mexico City represents an outstanding example of the architect's creative work in the post-Second World War period. The concrete building, totalling 1,161 m², consists of a ground floor and two upper storeys, as well as a small private garden.

Barragán's work integrated modern and traditional artistic and vernacular currents and elements into a new synthesis, which has been greatly influential, especially in the contemporary design of gardens, plazas and landscapes.

Luis Barragán began work on the house for a client but in 1948 decided to take the house for himself. The plans were gradually developed over the construction period and the house remained his studio and residence until his death.

Capital Cities and Tombs of the Ancient Koguryo Kingdom
China

Criteria – Human creative genius; Interchange of values; Testimony to cultural tradition; Significance in human history; Traditional human settlement

ASIA
Pacific Ocean

The site includes archaeological remains of three cities – Wunu Mountain City, Guonei City and Wandu Mountain City – and forty tombs. Fourteen tombs are imperial and twenty-six are of nobles. All belong to the Koguryo culture, named after the dynasty that ruled over parts of northern China and the northern half of the Korean Peninsula from 277 BC to AD 668. Wunu Mountain City is only partly excavated. Guonei City, within the modern city of Ji'an, played the role of a 'supporting capital' after

the main Koguryo capital moved to Pyongyang (in present day Democratic People's Republic of Korea). Wandu Mountain City, one of the capitals of the Koguryo Kingdom, contains many vestiges including a large palace and thirty-seven tombs. Some of the tombs show great ingenuity in their elaborate ceilings, which were designed to roof wide spaces without columns and carry the heavy load of a stone or earth tumulus mound placed above them.

The site represents exceptional testimony to the vanished Koguryo civilization. The capital cities are early examples of mountain cities and were later imitated by neighbouring cultures. Conversely, the Koguryo cities and tombs also show evidence of strong impact from other cultures.

World Heritage site since

• 1981 • 1982 • 1983 • 1984 • 1985 • 1986 • 1987 • 1988 • 1989 • 1990 • 1991 • 1992 • 1993 • 1994 • 1995 • 1996 • 1997 • 1998 • 1999 • 2000 • 2001 • 2002 • 2003 • **2004**

Chhatrapati Shivaji Terminus (formerly Victoria Terminus)
India

Criteria – Interchange of values; Significance in human history

The Chhatrapati Shivaji Terminus, formerly known as Victoria Terminus Station, in Mumbai (Bombay), is an outstanding example of Victorian Gothic Revival architecture in India. British architects worked closely with Indian craftsmen on the building to include local architectural traditions. The resulting structure, with its remarkable stone dome, turrets, pointed arches and eccentric ground plan is close to traditional Indian palace architecture, making it an outstanding example of the meeting of two cultures. The unique new style of the building soon came to symbolize Bombay as the 'Gothic City' and major international mercantile port of India.

The main structure is built from a judicious blend of Indian sandstone and limestone, while high-quality Italian marble was used for the key decorative elements. The main interiors are lavishly decorated: the ground floor of the North Wing, known as the Star Chamber, which is still the booking office, is embellished with Italian marble and polished Indian blue stone.

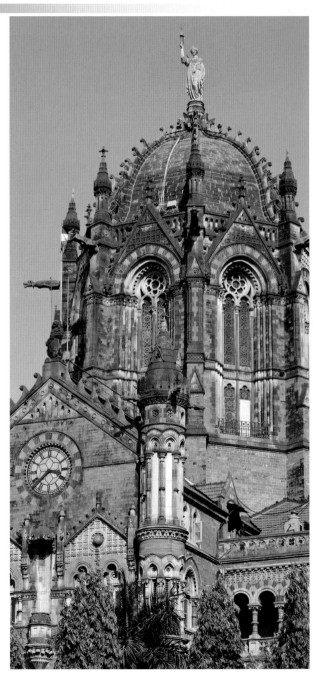

World Heritage site since

• 1981 • 1982 • 1983 • 1984 • 1985 • 1986 • 1987 • 1988 • 1989 • 1990 • 1991 • 1992 • 1993 • 1994 • 1995 • 1996 • 1997 • 1998 • 1999 • 2000 • 2001 • 2002 • 2003 • **2004**

Val d'Orcia
Italy

Criteria – Significance in human history;
Heritage associated with events of universal
significance

EUROPE

Mediterranean Sea

Ionian
Sea

The World Heritage
site is significant in
that the large
farmhouses assume
a dominant position
in the landscape and
are enriched by
prominent
architectural elements
such as loggias,
belvederes, porches
and avenues of trees
bordering the
approach roads.

Val d'Orcia is an exceptional reflection
of the way the landscape was rewritten in
Renaissance times to reflect the ideals of
good governance and to create an
aesthetically pleasing picture. The landscape
is 25 km from Siena's centre and was, in
effect, colonized by the city's merchants in
the fourteenth and fifteenth centuries. They
aimed to create an area of efficient

agricultural units that was also pleasing to
the eye. The landscape that resulted was one
of careful and conscious planning and
design and led to the beginning of the
concept of 'landscape' as a man-made
creation. The landscape's distinctive
aesthetics of fortified settlements on conical
hills rising out of flat chalk plains have
inspired many important artists.

World Heritage site since

• 1981 • 1982 • 1983 • 1984 • 1985 • 1986 • 1987 • 1988 • 1989 • 1990 • 1991 • 1992 • 1993 • 1994 • 1995 • 1996 • 1997 • 1998 • 1999 • 2000 • 2001 • 2002 • 2003 • **2004**

Varberg Radio Station
Sweden
Criteria – Interchange of values; Significance in human history

Varberg Radio Station was in regular service until the 1960s. It has been partly open to the public since 1997 although some equipment is still used by the Swedish Navy.

The Varberg Radio Station at Grimeton in southern Sweden built 1922–4 is an exceptionally well-preserved monument to early wireless transatlantic communication. It consists of the transmitter equipment, including the aerial system of six 127-m-high steel towers. Although no longer in regular use, the equipment has been maintained in operating condition. The 1.1 km² site comprises buildings housing the original Alexanderson transmitter, including the towers with their antennae, short-wave transmitters with their antennae, and a residential area with staff housing. The architect Carl Åkerblad designed the main buildings in the neoclassical style and the structural engineer Henrik Kreüger was responsible for the antenna towers, the tallest built structures in Sweden at that time. The site is an outstanding example of the development of telecommunications and is the only surviving example of a major transmitting station based on pre-electronic technology.

Tomb of Askia
Mali
Criteria – Interchange of values; Testimony to cultural tradition; Significance in human history

The dramatic 17-m pyramidal structure of the Tomb of Askia was built by Askia Mohamed, the Emperor of Songhai, in 1495 in his capital Gao. It bears testimony to the power and riches of the empire that flourished in the fifteenth and sixteenth centuries through its control of the trans-Saharan trade, notably in salt and gold. It is also a fine example of the monumental mud-building traditions of the Sahel.

The tomb's builder, Askia Mohamed, was founder of the Askia dynasty. It is said that on passing through Egypt on his way to Mecca, Askia Mohamed was impressed by the pyramids and decided to construct a pyramidal tomb for himself.

World Heritage site since

• 1981 • 1982 • 1983 • 1984 • 1985 • 1986 • 1987 • 1988 • 1989 • 1990 • 1991 • 1992 • 1993 • 1994 • 1995 • 1996 • 1997 • 1998 • 1999 • 2000 • 2001 • 2002 • 2003 • **2004**

Koutammakou, the Land of the Batammariba
Togo

Criteria – Traditional human settlement; Heritage associated with events of universal significance

The Koutammakou landscape in northeastern Togo, which extends into neighbouring Benin, is home to the Batammariba whose remarkable mud tower-houses, Takienta, have come to be seen as a symbol of Togo. In this landscape, nature is strongly associated with the rituals and beliefs of society. The 500 km² cultural landscape is remarkable due to the architecture of its tower-houses which are a reflection of social structure; its farmland

and forest; and the associations between people and landscape. Many of the buildings are two-storeys high and those with granaries feature an almost spherical form above a cylindrical base. Some of the buildings have flat roofs, others have conical thatched roofs. They are grouped in villages, which also include ceremonial spaces, springs, rocks and sites reserved for initiation ceremonies.

Whether hand-modelled or built from mud brick, the variety of architectural forms in West Africa illustrates the many ways in which the simple elements of earth and water are brought together to create works of striking artistic sophistication and interest.

Sacred Sites and Pilgrimage Routes in the Kii Mountain Range
Japan

Criteria – Interchange of values; Testimony to cultural tradition; Significance in human history; Heritage associated with events of universal significance

Set in the dense forests of the Kii Mountains, south of Osaka and overlooking the Pacific Ocean, these three sacred sites – Yoshino and Omine, Kumano Sanzan, Koyasan – linked by pilgrimage routes to the ancient capital cities of Nara and Kyoto, reflect the fusion of Shinto, rooted in the ancient tradition of nature worship in Japan, and Buddhism, which was introduced from China and the Korean Peninsula. The sites (5 km²) and their surrounding forest

landscape reflect a persistent and extraordinarily well-documented tradition of sacred mountains over 1,200 years. The area, with its abundance of streams, rivers and waterfalls, is still part of the living culture of Japan and is much visited for ritual purposes and hiking, with up to fifteen million visitors annually. Each of the three sites contains shrines, some of which were founded as early as the ninth century.

The shrines contain both buildings and objects, such as temples and statues, as well as such revered natural elements as trees and waterfalls. The journey to the shrines over arduous mountain routes was intended as part of the religious experience.

World Heritage site since

• 1981 • 1982 • 1983 • 1984 • 1985 • 1986 • 1987 • 1988 • 1989 • 1990 • 1991 • 1992 • 1993 • 1994 • 1995 • 1996 • 1997 • 1998 • 1999 • 2000 • 2001 • 2002 • 2003 • **2004**

Town Hall and Roland on the Marketplace of Bremen
Germany

Criteria – Testimony to cultural tradition; Significance in human history; Heritage associated with events of universal significance

Bremen is in northwestern Germany, on the river Weser. The medieval town was oblong, limited by the river on the south side and by the moat of the ancient defence system on the north side. The Town Hall and Roland statue are an outstanding ensemble representing civic autonomy and market freedom, as developed in the Holy Roman Empire. The old town hall was built in the

Gothic style in the early fifteenth century, after Bremen joined the Hanseatic League. The building was expertly renovated in the so-called Weser Renaissance style in the early seventeenth century. A new town hall was built next to the old one in the early twentieth century as part of an ensemble that survived bombardment during the Second World War.

The stone statue of Roland (a legendary figure in medieval Europe) is about 5.5 m tall, and it was initially erected in 1404, replacing an earlier wooden statue. It is considered the oldest Roland statue still in place in Germany and symbolizes the rights and privileges of the free and imperial city of Bremen.
▼

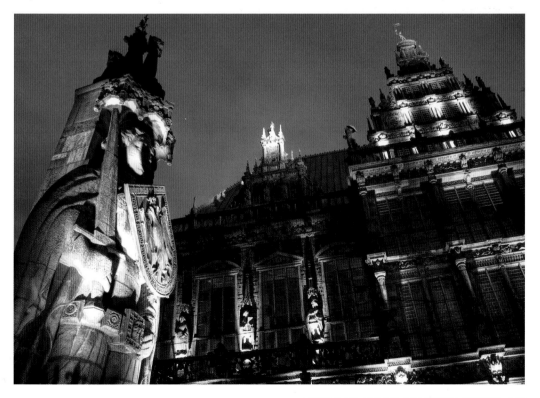

World Heritage site since

• 1981 • 1982 • 1983 • 1984 • 1985 • 1986 • 1987 • 1988 • 1989 • 1990 • 1991 • 1992 • 1993 • 1994 • 1995 • 1996 • 1997 • 1998 • 1999 • 2000 • 2001 • 2002 • 2003 • **2004**

Ensemble of the Novodevichy Convent
Russian Federation

Criteria – Human creative genius; Significance in human history; Heritage associated with events of universal significance

EUROPE

ASIA

Pacific Ocean

The convent was founded by Grand Duke Vasily III in the 1520s to mark the liberation of Smolensk and its return to the Russian State in 1514. It was dedicated to the Icon of the Mother God of Smolensk 'Hodigitria', the highest shrine of Russian orthodoxy.

The Novodevichy Convent is an exceptionally well-preserved monastic complex in southwest Moscow. It provides an example of the highest accomplishments of seventeenth century Moscow Baroque architecture, with rich interiors and an important collection of paintings and artefacts. Enclosed by a high masonry wall with twelve towers and surrounded by a park, the convent formed part of a chain of monastic ensembles that were integrated into the defence system of the city. It was directly associated with the political, cultural and religious history of Russia, and closely linked to the Moscow Kremlin. It was used by women of the Tsar's family and the aristocracy, and members of the Tsar's family and entourage were buried in its cemetery.

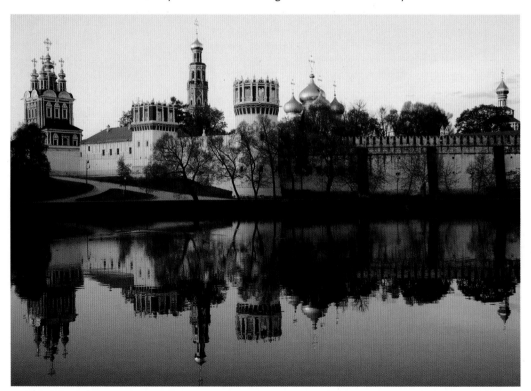

World Heritage site since

• 1981 • 1982 • 1983 • 1984 • 1985 • 1986 • 1987 • 1988 • 1989 • 1990 • 1991 • 1992 • 1993 • 1994 • 1995 • 1996 • 1997 • 1998 • 1999 • 2000 • 2001 • 2002 • 2003 • **2004**

Petroglyphs within the Archaeological Landscape of Tamgaly
Kazakhstan
Criteria – Testimony to cultural tradition

The petroglyphs have been dated to five distinct phases from Middle Bronze Age (fourteenth century BC) to the Modern Period, most recently in the twentieth century. The most exceptional engravings are the earliest and include solar deities and zoomorphic beings.

Set around the lush Tamgaly Gorge, amidst the vast, arid Chu-Ili mountains, is a remarkable concentration of some 5,000 petroglyphs (rock carvings) dating from the second half of the second millennium BC to the beginning of the twentieth century. Distributed among forty-eight complexes with associated settlements and burial grounds, they are testimonies to the husbandry, social organization and rituals of pastoral peoples. Human settlements in the site are often multilayered and show occupation through the ages. A huge number of ancient tombs are also to be found including stone enclosures with boxes and cists (middle and late Bronze Age), and mounds (kurgans) of stone and earth (early Iron Age to the present). The central canyon contains the densest concentration of engravings and what are believed to be altars, suggesting that these places were used for sacrificial offerings.

Etruscan Necropolises of Cerveteri and Tarquinia
Italy
Criteria – Human creative genius; Testimony to cultural tradition; Significance in human history

The tombs are a unique testimony to the vanished culture of the Etruscans and represent extraordinary evidence of what objects by themselves cannot show: depictions of daily life, ceremonies and mythology as well as the artistic abilities of their creators.

These two large Etruscan cemeteries reflect different types of burial practices from the ninth to first centuries BC, and bear witness to the achievements of Etruscan culture, which over nine centuries developed the earliest urban civilization in the northern Mediterranean. Some of the tombs are monumental, cut in rock and topped by impressive tumuli (burial mounds). Many feature carvings on their walls, others have wall paintings of outstanding quality. The necropolis near Cerveteri, known as Banditaccia, contains thousands of tombs organized in a city-like plan, with streets, small squares and neighbourhoods. These provide the only surviving evidence of Etruscan residential architecture. The necropolis of Tarquinia, also known as Monterozzi, contains 6,000 graves cut in the rock. It is famous for its 200 painted tombs, the earliest of which date from the seventh century BC.

World Heritage site since

• 1981 • 1982 • 1983 • 1984 • 1985 • 1986 • 1987 • 1988 • 1989 • 1990 • 1991 • 1992 • 1993 • 1994 • 1995 • 1996 • 1997 • 1998 • 1999 • 2000 • 2001 • 2002 • 2003 • **2004**

Champaner-Pavagadh Archaeological Park
India

Criteria – Testimony to cultural tradition; Significance in human history; Traditional human settlement; Heritage associated with events of universal significance

ASIA

Indian Ocean

The Champaner-Pavagadh Archaeological Park represents a perfect blend of Hindu and Muslim architecture, and is the only complete and unchanged Islamic pre-Mughal city. It boasts a high concentration of largely unexcavated archaeological, historic and living cultural heritage properties cradled in an impressive landscape. The Great Mosque (Jami Masjid) was a model for later mosque architecture in India and the site also includes fortifications, palaces, religious buildings, residential precincts, agricultural structures and water installations, from the eighth–fourteenth centuries. The Kalikamata Temple on top of Pavagadh Hill is considered to be an important shrine, attracting large numbers of pilgrims throughout the year.

Water installations are integral and important to the culture and design of Champaner. Different kinds of wells are known in the whole area, many of which are still in use. During the fifteenth century the water system was used for pleasure and aesthetic purposes as well as for daily use. Some houses had running water and many of the gardens and pavilions were decorated with water channels.

Ruins of one of the mosques at Champaner-Pavagadh Archaeological Park. ▼

World Heritage site since

• 1981 • 1982 • 1983 • 1984 • 1985 • 1986 • 1987 • 1988 • 1989 • 1990 • 1991 • 1992 • 1993 • 1994 • 1995 • 1996 • 1997 • 1998 • 1999 • 2000 • 2001 • 2002 • 2003 • 2004

Landscape of the Pico Island Vineyard Culture
Portugal

Criteria – Testimony to cultural tradition;
Traditional human settlement

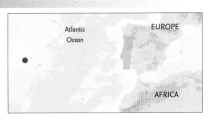

Pico is the second largest of the nine islands of the Azores and was uninhabited until the mid-fifteenth century.
Pico Mountain (a stratovolcano) dominates the island, reaching a height of 2,351 m above sea level.

The Pico Island landscape reflects a unique response to viticulture on a small volcanic island and is the best remaining area of a once much more widespread practice. The extraordinarily beautiful man-made landscape of small, stone-walled fields is testimony to generations of small-scale farmers who, in a hostile environment, created a sustainable living and a much prized wine. The walls were built to protect the thousands of small, contiguous, rectangular plots (currais) from wind and seawater. The resourcefulness and artistry of the inhabitants is also evident in the island's manor houses, wine-cellars, wells, churches and ports.

Madriu-Perafita-Claror Valley
Andorra

Criteria – Traditional human settlement

The cultural landscape of Madriu-Perafita-Claror Valley offers a microcosmic perspective of the way people have harvested the resources of the high Pyrenees over millennia. Its dramatic glacial landscapes of craggy cliffs and glaciers, with high open pastures and steep wooded valleys, covers an area of 42.5 km², 9 per cent of the total area of the principality. It reflects past changes in climate, economic fortune and social systems, as well as the persistence of pastoralism and a strong mountain culture, notably the survival of a communal land-ownership system dating back to the thirteenth century. The site features houses, notably summer settlements, terraced fields, stone tracks and evidence of iron smelting.

The valley has maintained its structures of organization and management since medieval times, surviving as a living witness to the history of Andorra, the culture of the men of the mountains and their coexistence with an extraordinary natural environment.

Historic Centres of Berat and Gjirokastra
Albania

Criteria – Testimony to cultural tradition; Significance in human history

The historic towns of Gjirokastra and Berat, in the Drinos River valley in southern Albania, are rare examples of well-preserved towns of an architectural character typical of the Ottoman period. The thirteenth-century citadel of Gjirokastra provides the focal point of the town with its typical tower houses (Turkish kule). Characteristic of the Balkan region, Gjirokastra contains a series of outstanding examples of kule, a type of building that crystallized in the seventeenth century. But Gjirokastra also features some more elaborate examples from the early nineteenth century. The kule has a tall basement, a first floor for use in the cold season, and a second floor for the warm season. Interiors feature rich decorative details and painted floral patterns, particularly in the zones reserved for the reception of visitors. The town also retains a bazaar, an eighteenth-century mosque and two churches of the same period.

Berat, which was inscribed as a World Heritage Site in 2008 features a kala, or castle, most of which was built in the thirteenth century. The citadel area contains many thirteenth-century Byzantine churches and several mosques of the Ottoman era.

World Heritage site since

• 1982 • 1983 • 1984 • 1985 • 1986 • 1987 • 1988 • 1989 • 1990 • 1991 • 1992 • 1993 • 1994 • 1995 • 1996 • 1997 • 1998 • 1999 • 2000 • 2001 • 2002 • 2003 • 2004 • **2005**

Islands and Protected Areas of the Gulf of California

Mexico

Criteria – Natural phenomena or beauty;
Significant ecological and biological processes;
Significant natural habitat for biodiversity

The site comprises 244 islands, islets and coastal areas located in the Gulf of California in northwestern Mexico. The Sea of Cortez and its islands have been called a natural laboratory for the investigation of speciation. Moreover, almost all major oceanographic processes are present in the property, giving it extraordinary importance. The site is one of striking natural beauty characterized by rugged islands with high cliffs and sandy beaches. It is home to 695 vascular plant species, more than in any other marine and insular property on the World Heritage List. Equally exceptional is the number of fish species: 891, of which 90 are endemic. The site, moreover, contains 39 per cent of the world's total number of species of marine mammals and a third of the world's marine cetacean species.

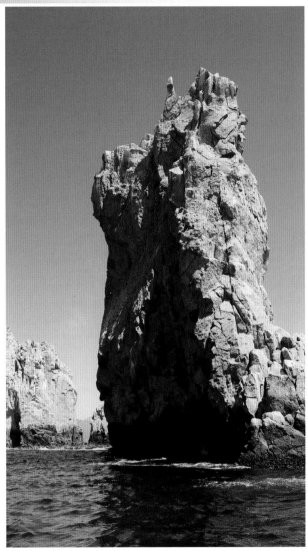

Rock formation near Cabo San Lucas at the southern tip of the Baja ▲
California peninsula.

The site is unique in that, in a very short distance, there are simultaneously 'bridge islands' (accessible by land) and 'oceanic islands' (accessible by sea and air).

The diversity and abundance of the marine life and the high water transparency make this a diver's paradise.

World Heritage site since

• 1982 • 1983 • 1984 • 1985 • 1986 • 1987 • 1988 • 1989 • 1990 • 1991 • 1992 • 1993 • 1994 • 1995 • 1996 • 1997 • 1998 • 1999 • 2000 • 2001 • 2002 • 2003 • 2004 • **2005**

Old Bridge Area of the Old City of Mostar
Bosnia and Herzegovina

Criteria – Heritage associated with events of universal significance

Mostar has long ► been known for its old Turkish houses and Old Bridge, Stari Most. In the conflict of the 1990s, however, most of the historic town and the Old Bridge, designed by the renowned architect Sinan (1489–1588), was destroyed. The Old Bridge was recently rebuilt and many of the buildings in the Old Town have been restored or rebuilt with the contribution of an international scientific committee established by UNESCO.

The Old Bridge area of Mostar, with its medieval, Ottoman, Mediterranean and Western European architectural features, is an outstanding example of a multicultural urban settlement. The Old Bridge and Old City of Mostar, reconstructed after conflict in 1990, is a symbol of reconciliation, international co-operation and of the coexistence of diverse cultural, ethnic and religious communities.

The historic town of Mostar spans a deep valley of the Neretva River. The area has been settled since prehistoric times and there is evidence of Roman occupation. Little is known of its medieval period, although Christian churches were established in the fifth–sixth centuries. The name of Mostar is first mentioned in 1474; its name came from the bridge-keepers (mostari) of the wooden bridge that crossed from the market town on the left bank of the river. Mostar's key position on the trade route between the Adriatic and mineral-rich central Bosnia led to the settlement's growth across the river. It became the leading town in Herzegovina and, after invasion by the Ottomans in 1468, the centre of Turkish rule in the area.

Mostar was an Ottoman frontier town and fortifications were built up in the sixteenth century; the bridge was also rebuilt in

stone. Religious and public buildings were constructed in a religious complex on the left bank, while private and commercial buildings, organized in distinct quarters, were also built. Several Ottoman inns survive, along with other buildings from this period, such as fountains and schools. Surviving late-Ottoman houses demonstrate the component features of this form of architecture – a hall, a residential upper storey, a paved courtyard and a verandah on one or two storeys.

Some early trading and craft buildings are still extant, notably low shops in wood or stone, stone storehouses and a group of former tanneries around an open courtyard. A number of elements of the early fortifications are visible. The Hercegusa Tower dates from the medieval period, whereas the Ottoman defences are represented by the Halebinovka and Tara Towers, the watchtowers over the ends of the Old Bridge and a stretch of the ramparts.

The city became part of Austro-Hungary in 1878 and all the administrative buildings of that period have neoclassical and Secessionist features. The nineteenth-century houses and commercial buildings are also predominantly neoclassical.

World Heritage site since

• 1982 • 1983 • 1984 • 1985 • 1986 • 1987 • 1988 • 1989 • 1990 • 1991 • 1992 • 1993 • 1994 • 1995 • 1996 • 1997 • 1998 • 1999 • 2000 • 2001 • 2002 • 2003 • 2004 • **2005**

Humberstone and Santa Laura Saltpeter Works
Chile

Criteria – Interchange of values; Testimony to cultural tradition; Significance in human history

Pacific Ocean

SOUTH AMERICA

Atlantic Ocean

The saltpetre industry was a huge cultural exchange complex where ideas were quickly absorbed and exploited. The two works are outstanding representations of this process.

Humberstone and Santa Laura works contain over 200 former saltpetre works where workers from Chile, Peru and Bolivia lived in company towns and forged a distinctive communal pampinos culture. That culture is manifest in their rich language, creativity, and solidarity, and, above all, in their pioneering struggle for social justice, which had a profound impact on social history. Situated in the remote Chilean Altiplano (high plains), near one of the driest deserts on Earth, the Atacama, thousands of pampinos lived and worked in this hostile environment for over sixty years, from 1880, to process the largest deposit of saltpetre in the world, producing the fertilizer sodium nitrate that was to transform agricultural lands in North and South America, and in Europe, and produce great wealth for Chile.

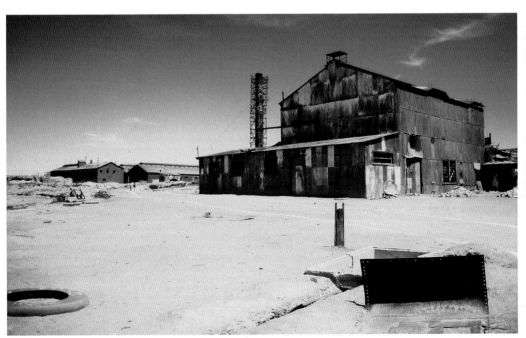

Historic Centre of Macao
China

Criteria – Interchange of values; Testimony to cultural tradition; Significance in human history; Heritage associated with events of universal significance

The World Heritage site of Macao consists of the Macao peninsula and the two islands of Taipa and Coloane. Macao, a port of strategic importance in the development of international trade, was under Portuguese administration from the mid-sixteenth century until 1999, when it came under Chinese sovereignty. The first core zone consists of the central area of the historic settlement of Macao. It includes a series of urban spaces and buildings representing the integration of Portuguese and Chinese

elements along the city's primary urban route, Rua Direita, which leads from the ancient Chinese harbour in the south to the old Christian city in the north. The second core zone consists of the Guia Fortress, located on the Guia Hill and incorporating Guia Chapel (1622) and Guia Lighthouse (1885), the oldest lighthouse in the South China seas.

Leal Senado Square (pictured below) is the main public square of the town. Close by there is the Cathedral Square with the Cathedral Church (rebuilt in 1850). Further north is St Dominic's Square with St Dominic's Church (founded in 1587), along with the old Chinese bazaar area and the Sam Kai Vui Kun Temple.

World Heritage site since

• 1982 • 1983 • 1984 • 1985 • 1986 • 1987 • 1988 • 1989 • 1990 • 1991 • 1992 • 1993 • 1994 • 1995 • 1996 • 1997 • 1998 • 1999 • 2000 • 2001 • 2002 • 2003 • 2004 • **2005**

Le Havre, the city rebuilt by Auguste Perret
France
Criteria – Interchange of values; Significance in human history

The city of Le Havre, on the English Channel in Normandy, was severely bombed during the Second World War. The destroyed area was rebuilt according to the plan of a team headed by Auguste Perret, from 1945 to 1964. The site forms the administrative, commercial and cultural centre of Le Havre. Le Havre is exceptional among many reconstructed cities for its unity and integrity. It combines a reflection of the earlier pattern of the town and its extant historic structures with the new ideas of town planning and construction technology. It is an outstanding post-war example of urban planning and architecture based on the unity of methodology and the use of prefabrication, the systematic utilization of a modular grid, and the innovative exploitation of the potential of concrete.

The rebuilt city is more spacious than the old, with its average density reduced from the pre-war 200,000 to 80,000 inhabitants per square kilometre. The Hôtel de Ville (town hall) is the most monumental structure in the whole scheme and its central part is marked by an eighteen-storey tower 70 m high.

Wadi Al-Hitan (Whale Valley)
Egypt
Criteria – Major stages of Earth's history

Wadi Al-Hitan, Whale Valley, in the Western Desert of Egypt, contains invaluable fossil remains of the earliest, and now extinct, suborder of whales, archaeoceti. These fossils represent one of the major stories of evolution: the emergence of the whale as an ocean-going mammal from a previous life as a land-based animal. This is the most important site in the world for the demonstration of this stage of evolution. It portrays vividly the form and life of these whales during their transition. The number, concentration and quality of such fossils here is unique, as is their accessibility and setting in an attractive and protected landscape. The fossils of Al-Hitan show the youngest archaeocetes, in the last stages of losing their hind limbs. Other fossil material in the site makes it possible to reconstruct the surrounding environmental and ecological conditions of the time.

This site uniquely portrays evolution in action, capturing the metamorphosis of whales from land to sea mammals. The fossils have both the typical streamlined body form of modern whales, and certain primitive aspects of skull and tooth structure.

World Heritage site since

• 1982 • 1983 • 1984 • 1985 • 1986 • 1987 • 1988 • 1989 • 1990 • 1991 • 1992 • 1993 • 1994 • 1995 • 1996 • 1997 • 1998 • 1999 • 2000 • 2001 • 2002 • 2003 • 2004 • **2005**

Biblical Tels – Megiddo, Hazor, Beer Sheba
Israel

Criteria – Interchange of values; Testimony to cultural tradition; Significance in human history; Heritage associated with events of universal significance

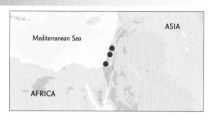

Tels (prehistoric settlement mounds) are characteristic of the flatter lands of the eastern Mediterranean, particularly Lebanon, Syria, Israel and eastern Turkey. Of more than 200 tels in Israel, Megiddo, Hazor and Beer Sheba are representative of those that contain substantial remains of cities with biblical connections. Tel Megiddo was one of the most powerful cities in Canaan and Israel. Its twenty major strata

contain the remains of around thirty different cities. The three tels also preserve the remains of their impressive underground water catchment systems, which reflect sophisticated engineering solutions to water storage. The water at Megiddo came from a spring at the foot of the mound, which was carried by an 80 m long aqueduct beneath the city wall to the bottom of a vertical shaft in the city.

Beer Sheba was a planned city rather than one that evolved gradually. The Iron Age plan shows an oval outline, encircled by a wall and gate to the south. The city was divided into three blocks by peripheral streets and the residential quarters were of uniform size. All streets led to a main city square.

Tel Megiddo.
▼

World Heritage site since

• 1982 • 1983 • 1984 • 1985 • 1986 • 1987 • 1988 • 1989 • 1990 • 1991 • 1992 • 1993 • 1994 • 1995 • 1996 • 1997 • 1998 • 1999 • 2000 • 2001 • 2002 • 2003 • 2004 • **2005**

Incense Route – Desert Cities in the Negev
Israel

Criteria – Testimony to cultural tradition; Traditional human settlement

The four Nabatean towns of Haluza, Mamshit, Avdat and Shivta are spread along routes linking them to the Mediterranean end of the incense and spice routes. Together they reflect the hugely profitable trade in frankincense and myrrh from south Arabia to the Mediterranean, which flourished from the third century BC until the second century AD. The Romans used

frankincense in enormous quantities as incense, medicine and cosmetics. Such was the demand that its price was at times higher than gold. The Nabateans grew rich on the profits of the spice trade, and the remains of their towns, forts, caravanserai and sophisticated agricultural systems demonstrate an outstanding response to a hostile environment.

The transport of goods across the desert to the Mediterranean coast, a distance of some 1,800 km, was made possible by the knowledge of the desert-dwelling Nabateans. They were able to bridge the 'impassable' desert and travel into the southern Arabian Peninsula, a world unknown to the Romans and those living along the coast of the Mediterranean.

Remains of Nekarot Fortress, on the Incense Route. ▼

World Heritage site since

• 1982 • 1983 • 1984 • 1985 • 1986 • 1987 • 1988 • 1989 • 1990 • 1991 • 1992 • 1993 • 1994 • 1995 • 1996 • 1997 • 1998 • 1999 • 2000 • 2001 • 2002 • 2003 • 2004 • **2005**

Dong Phayayen-Khao Yai Forest Complex
Thailand
Criteria – Significant natural habitat for biodiversity

The Dong Phayayen-Khao Yai Forest Complex spans 230 km between Ta Phraya National Park on the Cambodian border in the east, and Khao Yai National Park in the west. The site is home to more than 800 species of fauna, including 112 mammal species, among them 2 species of gibbon, 392 bird species and 200 reptile and amphibian species. It is internationally important for the conservation of globally threatened and endangered mammal, bird and reptile species, among them nineteen that are vulnerable, four that are endangered, and one that is critically endangered. The area contains substantial and important tropical forest ecosystems, which can provide a viable habitat for the long-term survival of these species.

The forest is a rugged mountainous area that is home to globally endangered species including tiger (pictured below), elephant, leopard cat and banteng. It also plays an important role in the conservation of migratory birds, including the spot-billed pelican and greater adjutant.

Osun-Osogbo Sacred Grove
Nigeria
Criteria – Interchange of values; Testimony to cultural tradition; Heritage associated with events of universal significance

The dense forest of the Osun Sacred Grove, on the outskirts of the city of Osogbo, is one of the last remnants of primary high forest in southern Nigeria. Regarded as the abode of the goddess of fertility Osun, one of the pantheon of Yoruba gods, the landscape of the grove and its meandering river is dotted with sanctuaries and shrines, sculptures and art works in honour of Osun and other deities. The sacred grove, which is now seen as a symbol of identity for all Yoruba people, is probably the last in Yoruba culture. It testifies to the once widespread practice of establishing sacred groves outside all settlements.

The grove covers 0.75 km² of ring-fenced forest alongside the Osun River on the outskirts of Osogbo. Ritual paths lead devotees to forty shrines, dedicated to Osun and other Yoruba deities, and to nine specific worship points beside the river.

World Heritage site since

• 1982 • 1983 • 1984 • 1985 • 1986 • 1987 • 1988 • 1989 • 1990 • 1991 • 1992 • 1993 • 1994 • 1995 • 1996 • 1997 • 1998 • 1999 • 2000 • 2001 • 2002 • 2003 • 2004 • **2005**

West Norwegian Fjords – Geirangerfjord and Nærøyfjord
Norway

Criteria – Natural phenomena or beauty;
Major stages of Earth's history

The two fjords, Geirangerfjord and Nærøyfjord, are considered archetypical fjord landscapes and among the most scenically outstanding anywhere in the world. Their exceptional natural beauty is derived from their narrow and steep-sided crystalline rock walls that rise up to 1,400 m from the Norwegian Sea and extend 500 m below sea level. The sheer walls of the fjords have numerous waterfalls, while free-flowing rivers cross their deciduous and coniferous forests from glacial lakes, glaciers and rugged mountains. The landscape features a range of supporting natural phenomena, both terrestrial and marine, such as submarine moraines and marine mammals. Remnants of old and now mostly abandoned transhumant farms add a cultural aspect to the dramatic natural landscape that complements and adds human interest to the area.

Situated in southwestern Norway, 120 km from one another, Geirangerfjord and Nærøyfjord are part of the west Norwegian fjord landscape that stretches from Stavanger in the south to Andalsnes, 500 km to the northeast. The two fjords are among the world's longest and deepest, and are considered distinctive in a country of spectacular fjords. 'Fjord' is a word of Norwegian origin, meaning a glacially over-deepened valley, usually narrow and steep-sided and extending below sea level. Norway's fjords are among the most extensive on Earth and are considered the type locality for study of fjord landscapes.

Both the fjords developed along faults and fracture zones at right angles, giving them a characteristic zigzag form. They are submarine hanging valleys with floors between 300–500 m deep in ice-scoured basins, and between 1 and 2 km wide. They are surrounded by mountains with old transhumance farms in the hanging valleys, and high glacial lakes.

Climate is transitional between oceanic and continental and varies markedly with aspect and altitude. The vegetation is moderately diverse due to the range of gradients from coast to inland, from north to south, from sea level to 1800 m and to the consequent variety of terrain and microclimates.

Wildlife includes four species of deer, arctic fox, otter, and many marine species such as Atlantic salmon, seals, porpoise, dolphins and whales. Over 100 bird species have been recorded.

The two areas that comprise the property complement each other in their characteristics. The more southerly Nærøyfjord is located 100 km inland near the end of Sognefjord. Its surrounding mountains are smooth-topped with high glacial lakes and a plateau glacier. The uplands preserve much of the rounded landforms of the pre-glacial landscape.

Geirangerfjord (pictured on the right) lies to the north, 60 km inland on the upper end of Storfjord. Its mountains are more Alpine in character. Block fields are more prevalent and there is still permafrost and several small glaciers on the highest summits.

World Heritage site since

• 1982 • 1983 • 1984 • 1985 • 1986 • 1987 • 1988 • 1989 • 1990 • 1991 • 1992 • 1993 • 1994 • 1995 • 1996 • 1997 • 1998 • 1999 • 2000 • 2001 • 2002 • 2003 • 2004 • **2005**

Historical Centre of the City of Yaroslavl
Russian Federation
Criteria – Interchange of values; Significance in human history

The historic city of Yaroslavl is renowned for its numerous seventeenth-century churches and is an outstanding example of urban planning reform. Situated at the confluence of the Volga and Kotorosl rivers some 250 km northeast of Moscow, the city developed into a major commercial centre from the eleventh century. It was renovated in the neoclassical style in 1763 when Empress

Catherine the Great ordered town planning reform for the whole of Russia. The resulting blend of retained historic structures and new radial urban plan presents an outstanding example of the interchange of cultural and architectural influences between western Europe and the Russian Empire.

The town has also kept important elements from the sixteenth century in the Spassky Monastery, one of the oldest in the Upper Volga region. This was built on the site of a pagan temple in the late twelfth century but has been reconstructed over time.

Yaroslavl Kremlin Tower.
▼

World Heritage site since

• 1982 • 1983 • 1984 • 1985 • 1986 • 1987 • 1988 • 1989 • 1990 • 1991 • 1992 • 1993 • 1994 • 1995 • 1996 • 1997 • 1998 • 1999 • 2000 • 2001 • 2002 • 2003 • 2004 • **2005**

Coiba National Park and its Special Zone of Marine Protection
Panama

Criteria – Significant ecological and biological processes; Significant natural habitat for biodiversity

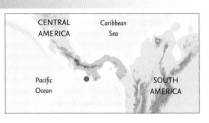

The ecosystems in the marine zone are repositories of great biodiversity, with 760 marine fish species, 33 types of shark and 20 species of cetaceans along with a significant population of Indo-Pacific fish now established in these eastern Pacific waters.

Coiba National Park, off the southwest coast of Panama, protects Coiba Island, thirty-eight smaller islands and the surrounding marine areas within the Gulf of Chiriqui. Protected from the cold winds and effects of El Niño, Coiba's Pacific tropical moist forest maintains exceptionally high levels of endemism of mammals, birds and plants due to the ongoing evolution of new species. It is also the last refuge for a number of threatened species such as the crested eagle. The property is an outstanding natural laboratory for scientific research and provides a key ecological link to the tropical eastern Pacific for the transit and survival of pelagic fish and marine mammals.

Plantin-Moretus House-Workshops-Museum Complex
Belgium

Criteria – Interchange of values; Testimony to cultural tradition; Significance in human history; Heritage associated with events of universal significance

Antwerp's booming prosperity attracted 140 printers, publishers and booksellers to the town by the mid-sixteenth century. It became the centre of the book business for Europe north of the Alps, and one of the three leading cities of early European printing and typography along with Paris and Venice.

The Plantin-Moretus Museum is a printing plant and publishing house dating from the Renaissance and Baroque periods. Situated in Antwerp, it is associated with the history of the invention and spread of typography. Its name refers to the greatest printer-publisher of the second half of the sixteenth century: Christophe Plantin c. 1520–89. The monument is of outstanding architectural value. It contains exhaustive evidence of the life and work of what was the most prolific printing and publishing house in Europe in the late sixteenth century. The company remained in activity until 1867. The building contains a large collection of old printing equipment, including two of the oldest surviving printing presses in the world, an extensive library, invaluable archives and works of art, among them a painting by Rubens.

World Heritage site since

• 1982 • 1983 • 1984 • 1985 • 1986 • 1987 • 1988 • 1989 • 1990 • 1991 • 1992 • 1993 • 1994 • 1995 • 1996 • 1997 • 1998 • 1999 • 2000 • 2001 • 2002 • 2003 • 2004 • **2005**

Soltaniyeh
Islamic Republic of Iran

Criteria – Interchange of values; Testimony to
cultural tradition; Significance in human history

The mausoleum of Oljaytu was constructed
in 1302–12 in the city of Soltaniyeh, the capital
of the Ilkhanid dynasty, which was founded
by the Mongols. Situated in the province of
Zanjān, Soltaniyeh is one of the outstanding
examples of the achievements of Persian
architecture and a key monument in the
development of its Islamic architecture. The
octagonal building is crowned with a 50-m-
tall dome covered in turquoise-blue faïence
and surrounded by eight slender minarets. It
is the earliest existing example of the double-
shelled dome in Iran. The mausoleum's
interior decoration is also outstanding and
scholars such as A.U. Pope have described the
building as 'anticipating the Taj Mahal'.

When Oljaytu came
to power in 1304 he
made the existing
town his capital,
enlarging it and
renaming it
Soltaniyeh (Imperial).
The city was a major
trading centre
between Asia and
Europe but gradually
declined in the
sixteenth–seventeenth
centuries.

◀

Mausoleum of
Oljaytu in Saltaniyeh

Qal'at al-Bahrain – Ancient
Harbour and Capital of
Dilmun
Bahrain

Criteria – Interchange of values; Testimony to
cultural tradition; Significance in human history

Qal'at al-Bahrain is a typical tell – an artificial
mound created by many successive layers
of human occupation. The strata of the
300–600 m tell testify to continuous human
presence from about 2300 BC to the
sixteenth century AD. About 25 per cent of
the site has been excavated, revealing
structures of different types: residential,
public, commercial, religious and military.
They testify to the importance of the site, a
trading port, over the centuries. On the top
of the 12-m mound there is the impressive
Portuguese fort, which gave the whole site
its name, qal'a (fort). The site was the capital
of the Dilmun, one of the most important
ancient civilizations of the region. It
contains the richest remains inventoried
of this civilization, which was hitherto only
known from written Sumerian references.

The once thriving and
important city of
Qal'at al-Bahrain was
finally abandoned
when its access
channel through the
coral reef silted up,
bringing about
the gradual
transformation from
a 4,500-year-old
settlement to an
archaeological site.

World Heritage site since

• 1982 • 1983 • 1984 • 1985 • 1986 • 1987 • 1988 • 1989 • 1990 • 1991 • 1992 • 1993 • 1994 • 1995 • 1996 • 1997 • 1998 • 1999 • 2000 • 2001 • 2002 • 2003 • 2004 • **2005**

Struve Geodetic Arc
Belarus, Estonia, Finland, Latvia, Lithuania, Norway, Moldova, Russian Fed., Sweden and Ukraine

Criteria – Interchange of values; Testimony to cultural tradition; Heritage associated with events of universal significance

The first accurate measuring of a long segment of a meridian, helping to establish the exact size and shape of the world, exhibits an important step in the development of earth sciences. The Struve Arc is a chain of survey triangulations stretching from Hammerfest in Norway to the Black Sea over 2,820 km away. These are points of a survey, carried out between 1816 and 1855 by the astronomer Friedrich Georg Wilhelm Struve, which represented the first accurate measuring of a long segment of a meridian. It is an extraordinary example of scientific collaboration among scientists from different countries, and of collaboration between monarchs for a scientific cause.

Thirty-four of the original station points established by Struve and his colleagues, in ten countries, exist today. These are commemorated by different marks: a drilled hole in rock, an iron cross, cairns, or built obelisks.

Vredefort Dome
South Africa

Criteria – Major stages of Earth's history

The site contains high quality and accessible geological (outcrop) sites that demonstrate a range of geological evidences of a complex meteorite impact structure.

Vredefort Dome, approximately 120 km southwest of Johannesburg, is a representative part of a larger meteorite impact structure, or astrobleme. Dating back 2,023 million years, it is the oldest astrobleme yet found on Earth. With a radius of 190 km, it is also the largest and the most deeply eroded. Vredefort Dome bears witness to the world's greatest known single energy release event, which had devastating global effects including, according to some scientists, major evolutionary changes. It provides critical evidence of the Earth's geological history and is crucial to the understanding of the evolution of the planet. Despite the importance of impact sites to the planet's history, geological activity on the Earth's surface has led to the disappearance of evidence from most of them, and Vredefort is the only example to provide a full geological profile of an astrobleme below the crater floor.

World Heritage site since

• 1982 • 1983 • 1984 • 1985 • 1986 • 1987 • 1988 • 1989 • 1990 • 1991 • 1992 • 1993 • 1994 • 1995 • 1996 • 1997 • 1998 • 1999 • 2000 • 2001 • 2002 • 2003 • 2004 • **2005**

Shiretoko
Japan

Criteria – Significant ecological and biological processes; Significant natural habitat for biodiversity

Shiretoko Peninsula has a central spine of volcanoes that produce geothermal features such as geysers and thermally heated pools. It is one of Japan's most unspoiled areas.

Shiretoko Peninsula is located in the northeast of Hokkaido, the northernmost island of Japan. The site includes the land from the central part of the peninsula to its tip, Shiretoko Cape, and the surrounding marine area. It provides an outstanding example of the interaction of marine and terrestrial ecosystems as well as extraordinary ecosystem productivity, largely influenced by the formation of seasonal sea ice at the lowest latitude in the northern hemisphere. It has particular importance for a number of marine and terrestrial species, some of them endangered and endemic, such as Blackiston's fish owl and the *Viola kitamiana* plant. The site is globally important for threatened seabirds and migratory birds, a number of salmonid species, and for marine mammals including Steller's sea lion and some cetacean species.

Architectural, Residential and Cultural Complex of the Radziwill Family at Nesvizh
Belarus

Criteria – Interchange of values; Significance in human history, Heritage associated with events of universal significance

The ten interconnected buildings of the castle include the palace, the galleries, the residence and the arsenal, all of which are set within the remains of the sixteenth-century fortifications. The castle is connected via a dam to the Church of Corpus Christi.

The Architectural, Residential and Cultural Complex of the Radziwill Family at Nesvizh is located in central Belarus. The Radziwill dynasty, who built and kept the ensemble from the sixteenth century until 1939, gave birth to some of the most important personalities in European history and culture. Due to their efforts, the town of Nesvizh came to exercise great influence in the sciences, arts, crafts and architecture. The complex consists of the residential castle and the mausoleum Church of Corpus Christi with their setting. The castle has ten interconnected buildings, which developed as an architectural whole around a six-sided courtyard. The palaces and church became important prototypes marking the development of architecture throughout central Europe and Russia.

World Heritage site since

• 1982 • 1983 • 1984 • 1985 • 1986 • 1987 • 1988 • 1989 • 1990 • 1991 • 1992 • 1993 • 1994 • 1995 • 1996 • 1997 • 1998 • 1999 • 2000 • 2001 • 2002 • 2003 • 2004 • **2005**

Urban Historic Centre of Cienfuegos
Cuba

Criteria – Interchange of values; Significance in human history

Cienfuegos was founded in 1819 on the Caribbean coast of southern-central Cuba, at the heart of the country's sugar cane, mango, tobacco and coffee production. Trading powered the city's growth, with wax production, as well as timber and sugar, becoming increasingly important in the nineteenth century. This historic town exhibits an important interchange of cultural and social influences based on the Spanish Enlightenment. It is also the first and finest example of an architectural ensemble representing the new ideas of modernity, hygiene and order in urban planning as developed in Latin America from the nineteenth century.

In its two centuries of existence, Cienfuegos has always been a particularly important trading city. Despite its success, the heritage area has retained its historic fabric without the drastic changes common in many other cities.

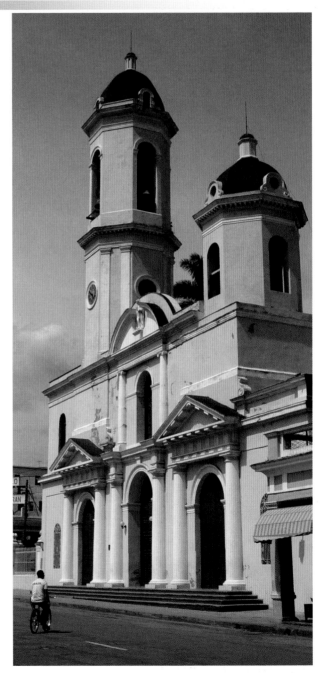

The cathedral of Cienfuegos. ▶

Kunya-Urgench
Turkmenistan
Criteria – Interchange of values; Testimony to
cultural tradition

The monuments of
Kunya-Urgench
testify to outstanding
achievements in
architecture and
craftsmanship. Their
influence reached as
far south and west as
Iran and Afghanistan,
and later extended to
the architecture of the
Mogul Empire of
sixteenth-century
India.

The origins of Kunya-Urgench go back to
the sixth or fifth centuries, the early
Achaemenid period. Situated at the crossing
of trade routes, it was the capital of
Khorezm from the twelfth century and the
second city after Bukhara in central Asia. The
site has three distinct sections: the southern
section contains a series of monuments
dating mainly from the eleventh–sixteenth
centuries, including a mosque, the gates of a
caravanserai, fortresses, mausoleums and a
60-m-high minaret; the northern section
consists of a large Muslim graveyard with a
group of three mausoleums at its centre;
the western section is a small area in the
western part of the old town containing the
monument of Ibn Khajib.

Syracuse and the Rocky
Necropolis of Pantalica
Italy
Criteria – Interchange of values; Testimony to
cultural tradition; Significance in human history;
Heritage associated with events of universal
significance

Situated on the
Mediterranean coast
in southeastern Sicily
and enjoying a
favourable climate,
the sites have been
inhabited since
protohistoric times.
The Syracuse-
Pantalica area is
remarkable for its
cultural diversity.

The site consists of two separate elements,
containing outstanding vestiges dating back
to Greek and Roman times: The Necropolis
of Pantalica contains over 5,000 tombs cut
into the rock near open stone quarries, most
of them dating from the thirteenth to
seventh centuries BC. Vestiges of the
Byzantine era also remain in the area, notably
the foundations of the Anaktoron Prince's
Palace. The other part of the property, Ancient
Syracuse, includes the nucleus of the city's
foundation as Ortygia by Greeks from
Corinth in the eighth century BC. The site of
the city, which Cicero described as 'the
greatest Greek city and the most beautiful of
all', retains vestiges such as the Temple of
Athena, fifth century BC, later transformed to
serve as a cathedral, a Greek theatre, a
Roman amphitheatre, a fort and more. Many
remains bear witness to the troubled history
of Sicily, from the Byzantines to the
Bourbons, interspersed with the Arabo-
Muslims, the Normans, Frederick II of the
Hohenstaufen dynasty 1197–1250, the
Aragons and the Kingdom of the Two Sicilies.
Historic Syracuse offers a unique testimony
to the development of Mediterranean
civilization over three millennia.

World Heritage site since

• 1983 • 1984 • 1985 • 1986 • 1987 • 1988 • 1989 • 1990 • 1991 • 1992 • 1993 • 1994 • 1995 • 1996 • 1997 • 1998 • 1999 • 2000 • 2001 • 2002 • 2003 • 2004 • 2005 • **2006**

Sichuan Giant Panda Sanctuaries - Wolong, Mt Siguniang and Jiajin Mountains
China

Criteria – Significant natural habitat for biodiversity

Sichuan Giant Panda Sanctuaries, home to more than 30 per cent of the world's pandas which are classed as highly endangered, covers 9,245 km² with seven nature reserves and nine scenic parks in the Qionglai and Jiajin Mountains. The sanctuaries constitute the largest remaining contiguous habitat of the giant panda, a relic from the palaeo-tropic forests of the Tertiary Era. It is also the species' most important site for captive breeding. The sanctuaries are home to other globally endangered animals such as the red panda, the snow leopard and clouded leopard. They are among the botanically richest sites of any region in the world outside the tropical rainforests, with between 5,000 and 6,000 species of flora in over 1,000 genera.

The giant panda is recognized as a 'National Treasure' of China and is the flagship for global conservation efforts. In the wild it feeds almost exclusively on bamboo, and its preferred habitat is between altitudes of 2,200 m and 3,200 m. As a unique single species and family, the giant panda is very important for studying mammal classification and evolution.

A young panda cub in the Sichuan Giant Panda Sanctuaries. ▼

World Heritage site since

• 1983 • 1984 • 1985 • 1986 • 1987 • 1988 • 1989 • 1990 • 1991 • 1992 • 1993 • 1994 • 1995 • 1996 • 1997 • 1998 • 1999 • 2000 • 2001 • 2002 • 2003 • 2004 • 2005 • 2006

Centennial Hall in Wroclaw
Poland

Criteria – Human creative genius; Interchange of values; Significance in human history

The Centennial Hall, a landmark in the history of reinforced-concrete architecture, was erected in 1911–3 by the architect Max Berg as a multi-purpose recreational building, situated in the Exhibition Grounds. In form it is a symmetrical quatrefoil with a vast circular central space that can seat some 6,000 persons. The 23-m-high dome is topped with a lantern in steel and glass. The Centennial Hall is a pioneering work of modern engineering and architecture,

which exhibits an important interchange of influences in the early twentieth century, becoming a key reference in the later development of reinforced-concrete structures.

With its diameter of 65 m, the Centennial Hall dome was at the time the largest ever built. Before then, the largest dome was that of the Pantheon in Rome, completed by AD 126. The Centennial Hall dome was twice as big: this stunning achievement was made possible by the new material (ferroconcrete) and Berg's innovative approach to structural design.

Harar Jugol, the Fortified Historic Town
Ethiopia

Criteria – Interchange of values; Testimony to cultural tradition; Significance in human history; Traditional human settlement

The fortified historic town of Harar is located in the eastern part of the Ethiopia on a plateau with deep gorges surrounded by desert and savanna. The walls surrounding this sacred Muslim city were built between the thirteenth and sixteenth centuries. Harar Jugol, said to be the fourth holiest city of Islam, has eighty-two mosques, three of which date from the tenth century, and 102 shrines, but the townhouses with their exceptional interior design constitute the most spectacular part

of Harar's cultural heritage. The impact of African and Islamic traditions on the development of the town's building types and urban layout make for its particular character and uniqueness.

Harar Jugol is the centre of an Islamic region within otherwise Christian Ethiopia. The World Heritage site comprises the entire historic walled city of Jugol, the name 'Jugol' referring to the defensive wall as well as to the fortified town.

◄
One of Harar Jugol's city gates.

World Heritage site since

• 1983 • 1984 • 1985 • 1986 • 1987 • 1988 • 1989 • 1990 • 1991 • 1992 • 1993 • 1994 • 1995 • 1996 • 1997 • 1998 • 1999 • 2000 • 2001 • 2002 • 2003 • 2004 • 2005 • **2006**

Old town of Regensburg with Stadtamhof
Germany

Criteria – Interchange of values; Testimony to cultural tradition; Significance in human history

A feature of Regensburg are the towers built by patrician families, for which there are no other comparable examples north of the Alps. Similar in form to north Italian towers, they were built more for the purpose of display than for protection. The Goldene Turm (twelfth-century) is nearly 50 m high while the seven-storey Baumburgerturm was built in 1270.

Located on the Danube River in Bavaria, this medieval town contains many buildings of exceptional quality that testify to its history as a trading centre and to its influence on the region from the ninth century. A notable number of historic structures span some two millennia and include ancient Roman, Romanesque and Gothic buildings. Regensburg's eleventh- to thirteenth-century architecture – including the market, city hall and cathedral – still defines the character of the town marked by tall buildings, dark and narrow lanes, and strong fortifications. The buildings include medieval patrician houses and towers, a large number of churches and monastic ensembles as well as the twelfth-century Old Bridge. The town is also remarkable for the vestiges testifying to its rich history as one of the centres of the Holy Roman Empire that turned to Protestantism.

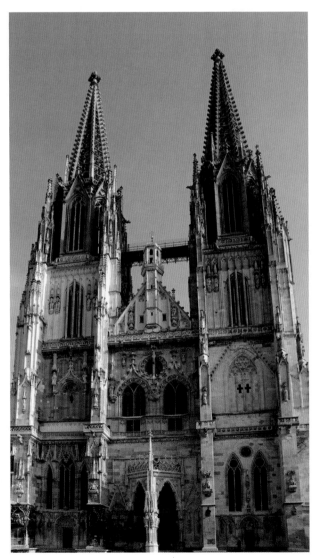

▶
Regensburg Cathedral.

World Heritage site since

• 1983 • 1984 • 1985 • 1986 • 1987 • 1988 • 1989 • 1990 • 1991 • 1992 • 1993 • 1994 • 1995 • 1996 • 1997 • 1998 • 1999 • 2000 • 2001 • 2002 • 2003 • 2004 • 2005 • 2006

Agave Landscape and Ancient Industrial Facilities of Tequila
Mexico

Criteria – Interchange of values; Significance in human history; Traditional human settlement; Heritage associated with events of universal significance

The Tequila area's poor soils and rough terrain are the ideal environment for growing the agave plant, used in numerous manufactures since prehistoric times. Tequila spirit became associated first with the Jalisco region in the eighteenth century and with Mexico as a whole after the revolution of 1910 onwards. Agave culture is now seen as part of Mexican national identity.

Stretching between the Tequila Volcano foothills and the deep Rio Grande valley is a 347-km² landscape of blue agave. Cultivation of the plant, a staple since prehistoric times, has shaped the area, and the agave landscape and local architecture of haciendas, distilleries, factories and tabernas have stimulated Mexican national cultural expressions that have been promoted around the world.

The area encloses a living, working landscape of cultivated fields and the settlements of Tequila, Arenal, and Amatitan together with working distilleries where the agave 'pineapple' is fermented and distilled into tequila.

The site also bears testimony to the Teuchitlan cultures that shaped the Tequila area from AD 200–900. They used agave for the manufacture of basic necessities including fabric, building materials, weapons, sugar, honey, medicines, paper and alcohol. Teuchitlan society grew rich on the monopoly of agave resources.

World Heritage site since

• 1983 • 1984 • 1985 • 1986 • 1987 • 1988 • 1989 • 1990 • 1991 • 1992 • 1993 • 1994 • 1995 • 1996 • 1997 • 1998 • 1999 • 2000 • 2001 • 2002 • 2003 • 2004 • 2005 • 2006

Stone Circles of Senegambia
Gambia and Senegal

Criteria – Human creative genius; Testimony to cultural tradition

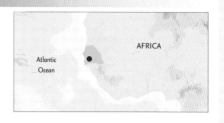

The site consists of four large groups of stone circles that represent an extraordinary concentration of over 1,000 monuments in a band 100 km wide along some 350 km of the river Gambia. The four groups, Sine Ngayène, Wanar, Wassu and Kerbatch, cover ninety-three stone circles and numerous tumuli, (burial mounds), some of which have been excavated to reveal

material that suggest dates between the third century BC and sixteenth century AD.

The stones forming the circles have been quarried with iron tools from nearby laterite quarries and skilfully shaped into almost identical pillars, either cylindrical or polygonal in section, on average around 2 m in height and weighing up to 7 tonnes. Each circle contains between eight and fourteen pillars and has a diameter of 4 to 6 m.

◄
Wassu stone circle.

Kondoa Rock-Art Sites
Tanzania

Criteria – Testimony to cultural tradition; Heritage associated with events of universal significance

On the eastern slopes of the Masai escarpment bordering the Great Rift Valley are natural rock shelters, overhanging slabs of sedimentary rocks fragmented by rift faults, whose vertical planes have been used for rock paintings for at least two millennia. The spectacular collection of images from over 150 shelters over 2,336 km², many with high artistic value, displays sequences that provide a unique testimony to the changing socio-economic base of the area from hunter-gatherer to agro-pastoralist, and the beliefs and ideas associated with the different societies. Some of the shelters are still considered to have ritual associations with

the people who live nearby, reflecting their beliefs, rituals and cosmological traditions.

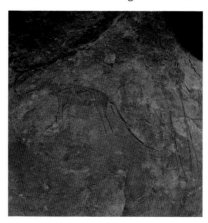

The Kondoa sites are testimony to the lives of hunter-gatherers and agriculturalists who have lived in the area for several millennia. Rock art is still relevant to local communities, who use some sites in rituals for rainmaking, divining and healing.

World Heritage site since

• 1983 • 1984 • 1985 • 1986 • 1987 • 1988 • 1989 • 1990 • 1991 • 1992 • 1993 • 1994 • 1995 • 1996 • 1997 • 1998 • 1999 • 2000 • 2001 • 2002 • 2003 • 2004 • 2005 • **2006**

Chongoni Rock-Art Area
Malawi

Criteria – Testimony to cultural tradition;
Heritage associated with events of universal
significance

Situated within a cluster of forested granite hills and covering an area of 126.4 km², high up the plateau of central Malawi, the 127 sites of this area feature the richest concentration of rock art in central Africa. They reflect the comparatively scarce tradition of farmer rock art, as well as paintings by BaTwa hunter-gatherers who inhabited the area from the late Stone Age. The Chewa agriculturalists, whose ancestors lived there from the late Iron Age, practised rock painting until well into the twentieth century. The symbols in the rock art, which are strongly associated with women, still have cultural relevance amongst the Chewa, and the sites are actively associated with ceremonies and rituals.

The dense and extensive collection of rock-art shelters reflects a remarkable persistence of cultural traditions over many centuries, connected to the role of rock art in women's initiations, in rain making and in funeral rites. These traditions make the Chongoni landscape a powerful force in Chewa society and a significant place for the whole of southern Africa.

Malpelo Fauna and Flora Sanctuary
Colombia

Criteria – Natural phenomena or beauty;
Significant ecological and biological processes

Located some 506 km off the coast of Colombia, the site includes Malpelo Island (3.5 km²) and the surrounding marine environment (8,572 km²). This vast marine park, the largest no-fishing zone in the eastern tropical Pacific, provides a critical habitat for internationally threatened marine species, and is a major source of nutrients resulting in large aggregations of marine biodiversity. It is in particular a 'reservoir' for sharks, giant grouper and billfish. Widely recognized as one of the top diving sites in the world, due to the steep walls and caves of outstanding natural beauty, these deep waters support important populations of large predators and pelagic species in an undisturbed environment where they maintain natural behavioural patterns.

Malpelo Island is thought to be a geological hotspot – a product of the welling up of the Earth's mantle. Its rocky surface supports a sparse vegetation of ferns, lichen, mosses and algae which are sustained by guano.

World Heritage site since

• 1983 • 1984 • 1985 • 1986 • 1987 • 1988 • 1989 • 1990 • 1991 • 1992 • 1993 • 1994 • 1995 • 1996 • 1997 • 1998 • 1999 • 2000 • 2001 • 2002 • 2003 • 2004 • 2005 • **2006**

Cornwall and West Devon Mining Landscape
United Kingdom

Criteria – Interchange of values; Testimony to cultural tradition; Significance in human history

The success of the copper, tin and arsenic mines of Cornwall and West Devon was based on deep-shaft mining made possible by technological innovations; these included the safety fuse for blasting and developments in steam-driven pumping.

The substantial remains of the copper- and tin-mining industries are a testimony to the contribution of Cornwall and West Devon to the Industrial Revolution in Britain and to the area's fundamental influence on the mining world at large. The area was the heartland from which mining technology rapidly spread and its expertise and technology, in the form of engines, engine houses and mining equipment, was exported around the world.

Much of the local landscape was transformed in the eighteenth and early nineteenth centuries as a result of the rapid growth of mining. The deep underground mines, engine houses, foundries, new towns, great houses and estates, smallholdings, ports and harbours, together with ancillary industries such as smelting, canals and railways, reflect the prolific innovation which led to the region producing two-thirds of the world's copper supply in the early nineteenth century.

When mining in the area declined in the 1860s, many miners emigrated, taking Cornish traditions to South Africa, Australia and Central and South America.

Tonwanroath pumping engine house at Wheal Coates mine, St Agnes in Cornwall. ▼

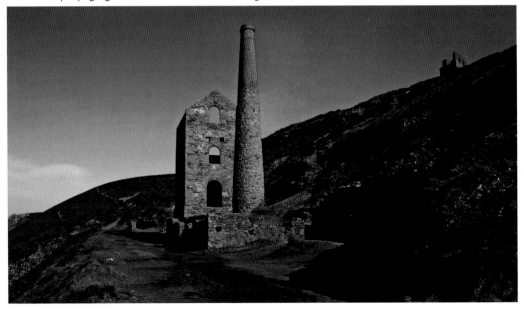

World Heritage site since

• 1983 • 1984 • 1985 • 1986 • 1987 • 1988 • 1989 • 1990 • 1991 • 1992 • 1993 • 1994 • 1995 • 1996 • 1997 • 1998 • 1999 • 2000 • 2001 • 2002 • 2003 • 2004 • 2005 • **2006**

Vizcaya Bridge
Spain

Criteria – Human creative genius; Interchange
of values

EUROPE

Atlantic
Ocean

Mediterranean Sea

AFRICA

Vizcaya Bridge was
designed by the noted
Basque architect
Alberto de Palacio,
a student of Gustave
Eiffel. The bridge
structure is 45 m high
and spans 160 m
across the river.

Vizcaya Bridge (Bizkaiko Zubia in Basque)
which straddles the mouth of the Ibaizabal
estuary in the Basque Country, was the first
bridge in the world of its type, carrying people
and traffic over the river on a suspended
gondola. It is among the outstanding
architectural iron constructions of the
Industrial Revolution.

The bridge represents the solution to the
problem of connecting the towns of
Portugalete and Getxo without disrupting
shipping on the river. Its construction
combined nineteenth-century ironworking
traditions with then-innovative technology
using lightweight twisted steel ropes. Its
success meant that it became a model for
many similar bridges in Europe, Africa and
the Americas, only a few of which still survive.

The bridge suffered bomb damage during
the Spanish Civil War but has otherwise
been in continuous operation since it
opened in 1893.

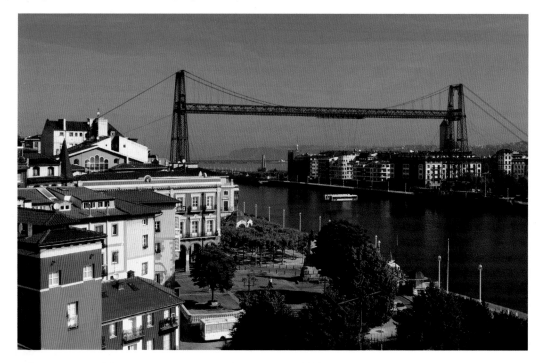

World Heritage site since

• 1983 • 1984 • 1985 • 1986 • 1987 • 1988 • 1989 • 1990 • 1991 • 1992 • 1993 • 1994 • 1995 • 1996 • 1997 • 1998 • 1999 • 2000 • 2001 • 2002 • 2003 • 2004 • 2005 • **2006**

Genoa: Le Strade Nuove and the system of the Palazzi dei Rolli
Italy

Criteria – Interchange of values; Significance in human history

The Strade Nuove and the system of the Palazzi dei Rolli in Genoa's historic centre date from the late sixteenth and early seventeenth centuries when the Republic of Genoa was at the height of its financial and seafaring power. The site represents the first example in Europe of an urban development project parcelled out by a public authority within a unitary framework and associated with a particular system of 'public lodging' in private residences, as decreed by the Senate in 1576. The site includes an ensemble of Renaissance and Baroque palaces along the so-called 'new streets', Strade Nuove. The Palazzi dei Rolli offer an extraordinary variety of different solutions, achieving universal value in adapting to the particular characteristics of the site and to the requirements of a specific social and economic organization. They also offer an original example of a public network of private residences designated to host state visits.

The palaces (palazzi) are generally three- or four-storeys high with spectacular open staircases, courtyards and loggias overlooking gardens, all in a relatively tight space. Their owners' obligation to host state visits led to a widespread knowledge of this architectural model.

Yin Xu
China

Criteria – Interchange of values; Testimony to cultural tradition; Significance in human history; Heritage associated with events of universal significance

The archaeological site of Yin Xu, close to the city of Anyang, some 500 km south of Beijing, is an ancient capital city of the late Shang Dynasty 1300–1046 BC. It testifies to the golden age of early Chinese culture, crafts and sciences, a time of great prosperity of the Chinese Bronze Age.

A number of royal tombs and palaces, prototypes of later Chinese architecture, have been unearthed on the site, including the Palace and Royal Ancestral Shrines Area, with more than eighty house foundations, and the only tomb of a member of the royal family of the Shang Dynasty to have remained intact, the Tomb of Fu Hao. The large number and superb craftsmanship of the burial accessories found there testify to the advanced level of Shang crafts industry. Inscriptions on oracle bones found in Yin Xu bear invaluable testimony to the development of one of the world's oldest writing systems, ancient beliefs and social systems.

The oracle-bone script found at Yin Xu is one of the oldest known writing forms. Oracle bones, or turtle shell, were heated and the resulting cracks were used for divination; the results were then inscribed on the bones.

World Heritage site since

• 1983 • 1984 • 1985 • 1986 • 1987 • 1988 • 1989 • 1990 • 1991 • 1992 • 1993 • 1994 • 1995 • 1996 • 1997 • 1998 • 1999 • 2000 • 2001 • 2002 • 2003 • 2004 • 2005 • 2006

Aflaj Irrigation Systems of Oman
Oman
Criteria – Traditional human settlement

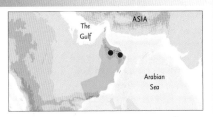

The property includes five *aflaj* irrigation systems and is representative of some 3,000 such systems still in use in Oman. The origins of this system of irrigation may date back to AD 500, but archaeological evidence suggests that irrigation systems existed in this extremely arid area as early as 2500 BC. Using gravity, water is channelled from underground sources or springs to support agriculture and domestic use. The fair and effective management and sharing of water in villages and towns is still underpinned by mutual dependence and communal values and guided by astronomical observations. Numerous watchtowers built to defend the water systems form part of the site, reflecting the historic

dependence of communities on the *aflaj* system. Threatened by the falling level of the underground water table, the *aflaj* represent an exceptionally well-preserved form of land use.

The word 'aflaj' is the plural of 'falaj', which means 'to divide into shares'. Equitable sharing of a scarce resource to ensure sustainability remains the hallmark of this ancient irrigation system.

Aapravasi Ghat
Mauritius
Criteria – Heritage associated with events of universal significance

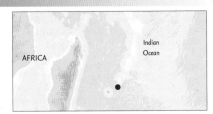

In the district of Port Louis, lies the 1,640 m² site where the modern indentured labour diaspora began. In 1834, the British Government selected the island of Mauritius to be the first site for what it called 'the great experiment' in the use of 'free' labour to replace slaves. Between 1834 and 1920, almost half a million indentured labourers

arrived from India at Aapravasi Ghat to work in the sugar plantations of Mauritius, or to be transferred to Réunion Island, Australia, southern and eastern Africa or the Caribbean. The buildings of Aapravasi Ghat are among the earliest explicit manifestations of what was to become a global economic system and one of the greatest migrations in history.

The immigration depot that received the Indian immigrants is a complex of buildings in Port Louis. Of the original facility founded in the mid-nineteenth century, only around 15 per cent remains today.

World Heritage site since

• 1983 • 1984 • 1985 • 1986 • 1987 • 1988 • 1989 • 1990 • 1991 • 1992 • 1993 • 1994 • 1995 • 1996 • 1997 • 1998 • 1999 • 2000 • 2001 • 2002 • 2003 • 2004 • 2005 • **2006**

Crac des Chevaliers and Qal'at Salah El-Din
Syrian Arab Republic

Criteria – Interchange of values; Significance in human history

Crac des Chevaliers guarded the route from Syria to the Holy Land and was one of a chain of Crusader castles commanding the eastern Mediterranean. British soldier and scholar T.E. Lawrence called it 'perhaps the best preserved and most wholly admirable castle in the world'.

Qal'at Salah El-Din was renamed in 1957 in honour of its conqueror, Muslim leader Saladin.

Crac des Chevaliers and Qal'at Salah El-Din are among the foremost examples of medieval fortified castles in the world. Both were vital Crusader strongholds. The Crac des Chevaliers (Fortress of the Knights) or Qala'at al-Hosn was built on the site of an existing fortification by the Order of St John of Jerusalem, the Knights Hospitaller, who held it from 1142, turning it into the largest Crusader fortress in the Holy Land. It finally fell to a Mameluke siege in 1271. Still towering over the surrounding landscape, between Homs and Tartous, the magnificent Crac is largely restored to its original state.

The Qal'at Salah El-Din (Fortress of Saladin) is partly in ruins but retains features from its tenth-century Byzantine construction, its reinforcement by the Crusaders in the twelfth century, and modifications by the Ayyubids who captured it under Saladin, Sultan of Egypt and Syria, in 1188.

Crac des Chevaliers. ▼

World Heritage site since

• 1983 • 1984 • 1985 • 1986 • 1987 • 1988 • 1989 • 1990 • 1991 • 1992 • 1993 • 1994 • 1995 • 1996 • 1997 • 1998 • 1999 • 2000 • 2001 • 2002 • 2003 • 2004 • 2005 • **2006**

Sewell Mining Town
Chile
Criteria – Interchange of values

Situated at 2,000 m in the Andes, 60 km to the east of Rancagua, in an environment marked by extremes of climate, Sewell Mining Town was built by the Braden Copper company in 1905 to house workers at what was to become the world's largest underground copper mine, El Teniente. It is an outstanding example of the company towns that were born in many remote parts of the world from the fusion of local labour and resources from an industrialized nation, to mine and process high-value natural resources. The town was

built on a terrain too steep for wheeled vehicles around a large central staircase rising from the railway station. Along its route formal squares of irregular shape with ornamental trees and plants constituted the main public spaces or squares of the town. The buildings lining the streets are timber, often painted in vivid green, yellow, red and blue. At its peak Sewell numbered 15,000 inhabitants, but was largely abandoned in the 1970s.

The only transport that served the town, built on a hillside generally too steep for cars, was the railway. There were no roads within the town, paths ran along contours off the central staircase to smaller squares and secondary stairs linking the different levels. It was known as 'the city of stairs.'

Bisotun
Islamic Republic of Iran
Criteria – Interchange of values; Testimony to cultural tradition

Bisotun is located along the ancient trade route linking the Iranian high plateau with Mesopotamia and features remains from prehistoric times to the Median, Achaemenid, Sassanian, and Ilkhanid periods. The principal monument of this archaeological site is the bas-relief and cuneiform inscription ordered by Darius I,

The Great, when he rose to the throne of the Persian Empire in 521 BC. It bears witness to the interchange of influences in the development of monumental art and writing in the region of the Persian Empire.

Roughly 15 m high and 25 m long, the bas-relief on Mount Bisotun depicts Darius triumphant over a rival. Below and around are cuneiform inscriptions, in three languages – Elamite, Babylonian and Old Persian– detailing the king's battles.

World Heritage site since

• 1984 • 1985 • 1986 • 1987 • 1988 • 1989 • 1990 • 1991 • 1992 • 1993 • 1994 • 1995 • 1996 • 1997 • 1998 • 1999 • 2000 • 2001 • 2002 • 2003 • 2004 • 2005 • 2006 • 2007

Sydney Opera House
Australia

Criteria – Human creative genius

The Opera House comprises three groups of interlocking vaulted 'shells' which roof two main performance halls and a restaurant. These shell-structures are set upon a vast platform and are surrounded by terrace areas that function as pedestrian concourses.

Inaugurated in 1973, the Sydney Opera House is a great architectural work of the twentieth century that brings together multiple strands of creativity and innovation in both architectural form and structural design. A great urban sculpture set in a remarkable waterscape, at the tip of a peninsula projecting into Sydney Harbour, the building has had an enduring influence on architecture. In 1957, when the project of the Sydney Opera House was awarded by an international jury to Danish architect Jørn Utzon, it marked a radically new approach to construction. Utzon's original design concept and his unique approach to building gave impetus to a collective creativity of architects, engineers and builders. Ove Arup's engineering achievements helped make Utzon's vision a reality.

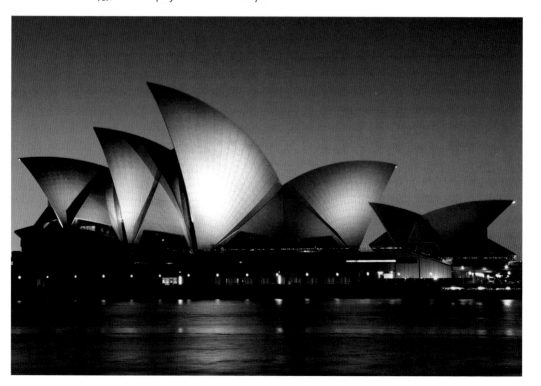

World Heritage site since

• 1984 • 1985 • 1986 • 1987 • 1988 • 1989 • 1990 • 1991 • 1992 • 1993 • 1994 • 1995 • 1996 • 1997 • 1998 • 1999 • 2000 • 2001 • 2002 • 2003 • 2004 • 2005 • 2006 • 2007

Iwami Ginzan Silver Mine and its Cultural Landscape
Japan

Criteria – Interchange of values; Testimony to cultural tradition; Traditional human settlement

The Iwami Ginzan Silver Mine, in the southwest of Honshu Island, is a cluster of mountains, rising to 600 m and interspersed with deep river valleys featuring the archaeological remains of large-scale mines, smelting and refining sites and mining settlements worked between the sixteenth and twentieth centuries. The mines contributed substantially to the overall economic development of Japan and southeast Asia in the sixteenth and

seventeenth centuries, prompting the mass production of silver and gold in Japan. The mining area is now heavily wooded. Included in the site are fortresses, shrines, parts of Kaidô transport routes to the coast, and three port towns, Tomogaura, Okidomari and Yunotsu, from where the ore was shipped to Korea and China.

Japan was a major silver producer. By the first half of the seventeenth century, when production at Iwami Ginzan was at its peak, it is estimated that its output accounted for almost a third of all world silver production.

Richtersveld Cultural and Botanical Landscape
South Africa

Criteria – Significance in human history; Traditional human settlement

The 1,600 km² Richtersveld Cultural and Botanical Landscape of dramatic mountainous desert in northwestern South Africa, constitutes a cultural landscape communally owned and managed. This site sustains the semi-nomadic pastoral livelihood of the Nama people, reflecting seasonal patterns that may have persisted for as much as two millennia in southern Africa. It is the only area where the Nama still construct portable rush-mat houses

(haru om), and includes seasonal migrations and grazing grounds, together with stock posts. The pastoralists collect medicinal and other plants and have a strong oral tradition associated with different places and attributes of the landscape.

The extensive communal grazed lands are a testimony to land management processes that have ensured the protection of the succulent Karoo vegetation. The seasonal pastoral grazing regimes of the Nama, which sustain the extensive biodiversity of the area, were once much more widespread and are now vulnerable.

World Heritage site since

• 1984 • 1985 • 1986 • 1987 • 1988 • 1989 • 1990 • 1991 • 1992 • 1993 • 1994 • 1995 • 1996 • 1997 • 1998 • 1999 • 2000 • 2001 • 2002 • 2003 • 2004 • 2005 • 2006 • **2007**

Red Fort Complex
India

Criteria – Interchange of values; Testimony to cultural tradition; Heritage associated with events of universal significance

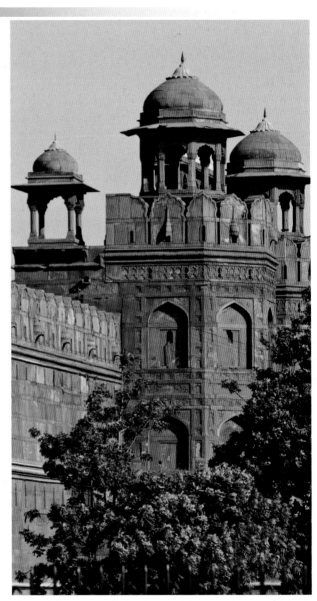

The Red Fort, completed in 1648, represents the zenith of Mughal creativity. The palace plan is based on standard Islamic designs but each pavilion displays architectural elements typical of Mughal building – a fusion of Persian, Timurid, Hindu and Islamic traditions.

Emperor Shah Jahan established his capital at Shahjahanabad and built the Red Fort Complex as his palace fort, enclosing it in ornate red sandstone walls that stretch for 2.5 km. The innovative planning, gardens and architectural style of the fort complex strongly influenced later building and garden design in Rajasthan, Delhi and Agra.

The Red Fort has been a powerful symbol for the Indian nation since its construction. The British Army captured it after the Indian Mutiny of 1857–8 and held it until India gained independence in 1947. It has remained at the centre of national independence celebrations ever since.

The Mughal Empire in India lasted from 1526 until the mid-eighteenth century. It reached the height of its power around 1700, when it encompassed almost the whole subcontinent. The empire's most notable existing legacy is its architecture: Shah Jahan, who built the Red Fort, was also the builder of the Taj Mahal.

World Heritage site since

• 1984 • 1985 • 1986 • 1987 • 1988 • 1989 • 1990 • 1991 • 1992 • 1993 • 1994 • 1995 • 1996 • 1997 • 1998 • 1999 • 2000 • 2001 • 2002 • 2003 • 2004 • 2005 • 2006 • 2007

Teide National Park
Spain

Criteria – Natural phenomena or beauty;
Major stages of Earth's history

Situated on the island of Tenerife, Teide National Park features the Teide-Pico Viejo stratovolcano – at 3,718 m, the highest peak on Spanish soil. Rising 7,500 m above the ocean floor, it is regarded as the world's third-tallest volcanic structure and stands in a spectacular environment. The visual impact of the site is all the greater due to

atmospheric conditions that create constantly changing textures and tones in the landscape and a 'sea of clouds' that forms a visually impressive backdrop to the mountain. Teide is of global importance in providing evidence of the geological processes that underpin the evolution of oceanic islands.

Mount Teide is an exceptional example of a relatively old, slow moving, geologically complex and mature volcanic system. With diverse and accessible features in a relatively limited area, it has long been a major centre for international research with a significant history of influence on the study of geology and geomorphology.

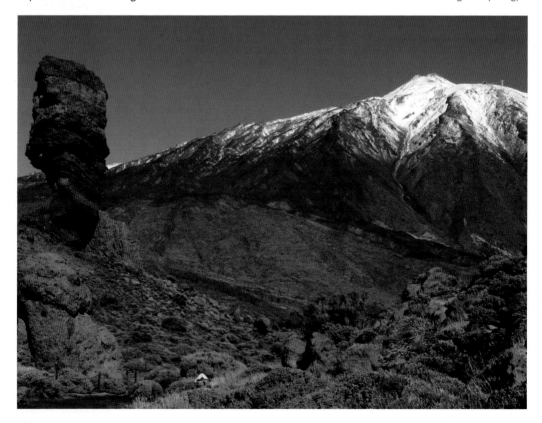

World Heritage site since

• 1984 • 1985 • 1986 • 1987 • 1988 • 1989 • 1990 • 1991 • 1992 • 1993 • 1994 • 1995 • 1996 • 1997 • 1998 • 1999 • 2000 • 2001 • 2002 • 2003 • 2004 • 2005 • 2006 • 2007

Samarra Archaeological City
Iraq

Criteria – Interchange of values; Testimony to cultural tradition; Significance in human history

Samarra Archaeological City is the site of a powerful Islamic capital city that ruled for a century over the provinces of the Abbasid Empire, extending from Tunisia to central Asia. Located on both sides of the river Tigris, 130 km north of Baghdad, the length of the site from north to south is 41.5 km; its width varying from 8 km to 4 km. It testifies to the architectural and artistic innovations that developed there and spread to other regions of the Islamic world and beyond. The ninth-century Great Mosque and its spiral minaret are among the numerous remarkable architectural monuments of the site, 80 per cent of which remain to be excavated.

Samarra contains two of the largest mosques and the largest palaces in the Islamic world. Carved stucco, known as the Samarra style, was developed there and spread to other parts of the region. A new type of ceramic, known as lustre ware, was also developed in Samarra, imitating utensils made of precious metals such as gold and silver.

Gobustan Rock Art Cultural Landscape
Azerbaijan

Criteria – Testimony to cultural tradition

Gobustan Rock Art Cultural Landscape covers three areas of a plateau of rocky boulders rising out of the semi-desert of east-central Azerbaijan, with an outstanding collection of more than 6,000 rock engravings bearing testimony to 40,000 years of rock art. The site also features the remains of inhabited caves, settlements and burials, all reflecting an intensive human use by the inhabitants of the area during the wet period that followed the last Ice Age, from the Upper Paleolithic to the Middle Ages. The site, which covers an area of 5.4 km², is part of the larger Gobustan Reservation.

The rock art at Gobustan is detailed and wide-ranging: it includes plants and animals, and human figures dancing, hunting, fighting and travelling in boats. Nearby are inscriptions left by troops of Alexander the Great and Roman soldiers of the Emperor Trajan.

◄

Animal rock-art engraving, Gobustan.

World Heritage site since

• 1984 • 1985 • 1986 • 1987 • 1988 • 1989 • 1990 • 1991 • 1992 • 1993 • 1994 • 1995 • 1996 • 1997 • 1998 • 1999 • 2000 • 2001 • 2002 • 2003 • 2004 • 2005 • 2006 • 2007

South China Karst
China

Criteria – Natural phenomena or beauty;
Major stages of Earth's history

Shilin stone forest in ▶
Yunnan province.

The South China Karst region extends over a surface of 500,000 km² lying mainly in Yunnan, Guizhou and Guangxi provinces. The region displays a series of karst landforms in a variety of humid, subhumid, tropical and subtropical climate conditions, and geographical settings. It comprises three clusters: Shilin Karst, Libo Karst and Wulong Karst.

Shilin, in Yunnan province, contains classic examples of stone-forest landscapes, noted for high limestone pinnacles and towers decorated with deep, sharp karren (see photo on the right). They formed over some 270 million years during four major geological time periods from the Permian to present, illustrating the episodic nature of the evolution of these karst features. The stone forests of Shilin are considered superlative natural phenomena and a world reference with a wider range of pinnacle shapes than other karst landscapes, and a higher diversity of shapes and changing colours.

Libo contains carbonate outcrops of different ages that erosive processes shaped over millions of years into impressive cone and tower karsts. It contains a combination of numerous tall karst peaks, deep dolines, sinking streams and long river caves. Libo is also noted for its biodiversity, with over 314 vertebrate species and 1,532 plant species, including several endemics and a number of plants and animals that are globally or nationally endangered.

Wulong represents high inland karst plateaus that have experienced considerable uplift, and includes giant collapse depressions and high natural bridges between stretches of deep, unroofed caves. Its giant dolines and bridges are representative of south China's Tiankeng landscapes. Wulong's landscapes contain evidence for the history of one of the world's great river systems, the Yangtze and its tributaries.

Minority peoples live in two of the karst areas and make up most of the population. There is a strong relationship between karst and the cultural identity and traditions of the people. In Shilin, the Yi people have developed a lifestyle adapted to the karst environment and the stone forests are reflected in every aspect of their culture. The Shui people in Libo have managed their lands for at least a thousand years and provide an exemplary example of sustainable forest management.

Four types of karst landscape in the area are considered outstanding. These are: 'fengcong' karst (cone karst), characterised by linked conical hills and depressions, valleys and gorges; 'fenglin' karst (tower karst), comprising isolated cones or towers on broad plains; stone forests, with a wide diversity of closely spaced pinnacles and towers, and 'tiankeng' karst (giant dolines) – massive circular collapse structures often in close proximity to spectacular gorges and decorated caves, where cave or doline collapse can create natural rock bridges.

World Heritage site since

• 1984 • 1985 • 1986 • 1987 • 1988 • 1989 • 1990 • 1991 • 1992 • 1993 • 1994 • 1995 • 1996 • 1997 • 1998 • 1999 • 2000 • 2001 • 2002 • 2003 • 2004 • 2005 • 2006 • 2007

Central University City Campus of the Universidad Nacional Autónoma de México (UNAM)
Mexico

Criteria – Human creative genius; Interchange of values; Significance in human history

The ensemble of buildings, sports facilities and open spaces of the Central University City Campus of the Universidad Nacional Autónoma de México (UNAM), was built from 1949 to 1952 by more than sixty architects, engineers and artists who were involved in the project. As a result, the campus constitutes a unique example of twentieth-century modernism integrating urbanism, architecture, engineering, landscape design and fine arts with references to local traditions, especially to Mexico's pre-Hispanic past. The ensemble embodies social and cultural values of universal significance and is one of the most significant icons of modernity in Latin America.

The Biblioteca Central (Central Library) of UNAM is the university's most famous and iconic building. Tiled murals, the work of Mexican artist Juan O'Gorman, cover the four walls and represent historic and modern Mexico and the university.

Twyfelfontein or /Ui-//aes
Namibia

Criteria – Testimony to cultural tradition; Traditional human settlement

Twyfelfontein or /Ui-//aes has one of the largest concentrations of rock petroglyphs (engravings) in Africa. Most of these well-preserved engravings represent rhinoceros, elephant, ostrich and giraffe, as well as drawings of human and animal footprints. The site also includes six painted rock-shelters with motifs of human figures in red ochre. The objects excavated from two sections, date from the Late Stone Age. The site forms a coherent, extensive and high-quality record of ritual practices relating to hunter-gatherer communities in this part of southern Africa over at least 2,000 years.

Over 2,000 figures have been documented, most of which are recognisable depictions of animals together with engravings of their tracks. It is thought the imagery was linked to the beliefs of hunter-gatherers who dominated this area until around AD 1000.

World Heritage site since

• 1984 • 1985 • 1986 • 1987 • 1988 • 1989 • 1990 • 1991 • 1992 • 1993 • 1994 • 1995 • 1996 • 1997 • 1998 • 1999 • 2000 • 2001 • 2002 • 2003 • 2004 • 2005 • 2006 • 2007

Old Town of Corfu
Greece

Criteria – Significance in human history

The fortifications of Corfu have been actively involved in many conflicts between the west and the east Mediterranean from the fifteenth to the twentieth centuries. During rebuilding they have been altered to allow for developments in weapons of attack and principles of defence, successively by the Venetians and by the British.

The Old Town of Corfu, on the island of Corfu off the western coasts of Albania and Greece, is located in a strategic position at the entrance to the Adriatic Sea, and has its roots in the eighth century BC. The three forts of the town, designed by renowned Venetian engineers, were used for four centuries to defend the maritime trading interests of the Republic of Venice against the Ottoman Empire. In the course of time, the forts were repaired and partly rebuilt several times, more recently under British rule in the nineteenth century. The mainly neoclassical housing stock of the Old Town is partly from the Venetian period, partly of later construction, notably the nineteenth century. As a fortified Mediterranean port, Corfu's urban and port ensemble is notable for its high level of integrity and authenticity.

World Heritage site since

• 1984 • 1985 • 1986 • 1987 • 1988 • 1989 • 1990 • 1991 • 1992 • 1993 • 1994 • 1995 • 1996 • 1997 • 1998 • 1999 • 2000 • 2001 • 2002 • 2003 • 2004 • 2005 • 2006 • **2007**

Primeval Beech Forests of the Carpathians and the Ancient Beech Forests of Germany
Germany, Slovakia and Ukraine

Criteria – Significant ecological and biological processes

The Primeval Beech Forests of the Carpathians are an outstanding example of undisturbed, complex temperate forests and were inscribed onto the list in 2007. In 2011 the site was extended to include five forests in Germany totalling 4,391 hectares. Together they comprise the largest area of virgin forests of European beech (fagus sylvatica) in existence. They represent all stages of beech forest in age and development, and they contain the largest and tallest beech specimens in the world. In all, the forests constitute an invaluable genetic reservoir of beech and many species associated with, and dependent on, these forest habitats.

The areas contain complete naturally functioning ecosystems. Flora and fauna are rich and include rare and unique plants and animals. Some species, such as black stork, are associated with, and depend on, undisturbed forest habitats.

These forests represent examples of on-going post-glacial biological and ecological evolution of terrestrial ecosystems and are indispensable to understanding the spread of the beech in the Northern Hemisphere across a variety of environments.

The Primeval Beech Forests of the Carpathians and the Ancient Beech Forests of Germany represent the largest remaining 'virgin' forests of the European beech (Fagus sylvatica) covering almost 34,000 hectares in this tri-national site. They are also home to the largest and tallest beech specimens in the world.

World Heritage site since

• 1984 • 1985 • 1986 • 1987 • 1988 • 1989 • 1990 • 1991 • 1992 • 1993 • 1994 • 1995 • 1996 • 1997 • 1998 • 1999 • 2000 • 2001 • 2002 • 2003 • 2004 • 2005 • 2006 • 2007

Rideau Canal
Canada

Criteria – Human creative genius; Significance in human history

The Rideau Canal, built by the British to defend Canada against the USA, was one of the first canals designed for steam-powered vessels. It is the only canal from the great North American canal-building era that remains operational along its original line with most of its structures intact. The site also features an ensemble of fortifications in Kingston, a reminder of the period when Britain and the USA vied for control of the region.

The Rideau was one of several canals the British built after the war of 1812, when Britain defended Upper Canada against American invasion. It was intended as an alternative route to the St Lawrence River, which was vulnerable to American blockade. In the event, the canal was never used for military purposes but instead has served important commercial and recreational purposes since its construction.

The Rideau Canal was completed in 1832 and covers 202 km of the Rideau and Cataraqui rivers, from Ottawa south to Kingston on Lake Ontario. It is the best-preserved example of a slack-water canal in North America, demonstrating the use of this European technology on a large scale.

Rideau Canal and The Houses of Parliament, Parliament Hill, Ottawa.
▼

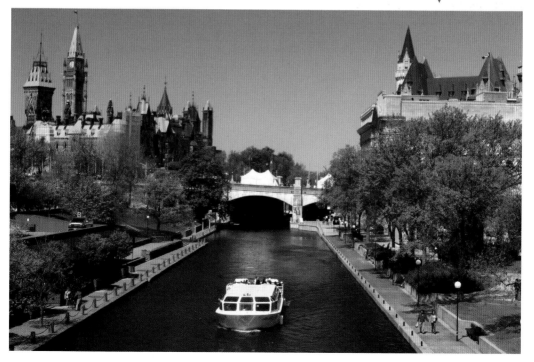

World Heritage site since

• 1984 • 1985 • 1986 • 1987 • 1988 • 1989 • 1990 • 1991 • 1992 • 1993 • 1994 • 1995 • 1996 • 1997 • 1998 • 1999 • 2000 • 2001 • 2002 • 2003 • 2004 • 2005 • 2006 • **2007**

Kaiping Diaolou and Villages
China

Criteria – Interchange of values; Testimony to cultural tradition; Significance in human history

Kaiping Diaolou and Villages feature the diaolou, multi-storeyed defensive village houses in Kaiping, which display a complex and elaborate fusion of Chinese and Western structural and decorative forms. The main towers, with their settings and through their flamboyant display of wealth, are a type of building that reflects the significant role of émigré Kaiping people in the development of several countries in south Asia, Australasia and North America, during the late nineteenth and early twentieth centuries. There are four groups

of diaolou and twenty of the most symbolic ones are inscribed on the World Heritage List. These buildings take three forms: communal towers built by several families and used as temporary refuge, residential towers built by individual rich families and used as fortified residences, and watch towers. They are built of stone, pisé (rammed earth or clay), brick or concrete and retain a harmonious relationship with the surrounding landscape.

The building of defensive towers was a local tradition in the Kaiping area since Ming times. The conspicuous wealth of the returning Chinese émigrés contributed to the spread of banditry in the area and the 'diaolou' were an extreme response to the threat. Those in the site represent the final flourishing of a centuries-old tradition.

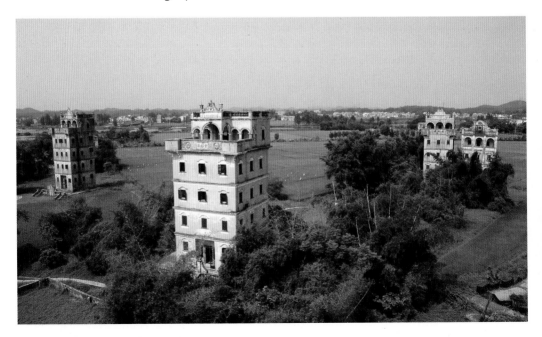

World Heritage site since

• 1984 • 1985 • 1986 • 1987 • 1988 • 1989 • 1990 • 1991 • 1992 • 1993 • 1994 • 1995 • 1996 • 1997 • 1998 • 1999 • 2000 • 2001 • 2002 • 2003 • 2004 • 2005 • 2006 • 2007

Bordeaux, Port of the Moon
France

Criteria – Interchange of values; Significance in human history

The Port of the Moon, port city of Bordeaux in southwest France, is inscribed on the World Heritage List as an inhabited historic city, an outstanding urban and architectural ensemble, created in the age of the Enlightenment, whose values continued up to the first half of the twentieth century, and with more protected buildings than any other French city except Paris. It is also recognized for its historic role as a place of exchange of cultural values over more than 2,000 years, particularly since the twelfth

century, due to commercial links with Britain and the Low Countries. Urban plans and architectural ensembles of the early eighteenth century onwards place the city as an outstanding example of innovative classical and neoclassical trends and give it an exceptional urban and architectural unity and coherence. Its urban form represents the success of philosophers who wanted to make towns into melting pots of humanism, universality and culture.

The age of Enlightenment produced Bordeaux's best known architectural and urban features. Louis-Urbain Aubert, Marquis de Tourny, arrived in Bordeaux in 1743, staying there until 1757. He undertook major projects for the renovation and opening up the medieval city, especially to the façades of buildings on the quays along the river Garonne, the vital commercial artery of the community.

The water mirror and Place de la Bourse. ▼

World Heritage site since

• 1984 • 1985 • 1986 • 1987 • 1988 • 1989 • 1990 • 1991 • 1992 • 1993 • 1994 • 1995 • 1996 • 1997 • 1998 • 1999 • 2000 • 2001 • 2002 • 2003 • 2004 • 2005 • 2006 • **2007**

Gamzigrad-Romuliana, Palace of Galerius
Serbia

Criteria – Testimony to cultural tradition; Significance in human history

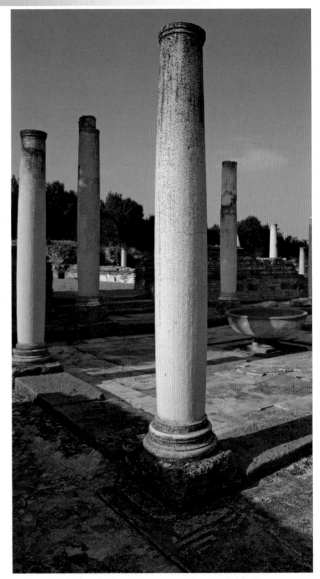

Gamzigrad-Romuliana, the Palace of Galerius in the east of Serbia, is one of the most important Late Roman sites. A fortified palace compound and memorial complex, it was built by the Tetrarch Galerius Maximianus (c. AD 260–311), between the late third and early fourth centuries.

The association of rulers with the divine hierarchy was one of the characteristics of the tetrarchy, and the palace is representative of Late Roman imperial and religious symbolism: the glorification of the emperor as all-powerful ruler and as a god underlies its construction.

The site consists of fortifications, a palace, basilicas, temples, hot baths, a memorial complex and a tetrapylon.

The buildings' intertwining of ceremonial and memorial functions is unique, as are the spatial and visual relationships between the palace and the memorial complex, where the mausoleums of Galerius and his mother Romula are located.

Gamzigrad-Romuliana was built as a place to which Galerius could retire, much like the palace built at Split by his successor, the Emperor Diocletian, who had instituted the tetrarchy in the Roman Empire. The palace was known as Felix Romuliana after the emperor's mother.

Lavaux, Vineyard Terraces
Switzerland

Criteria – Significance in human history

The Lavaux Vineyard Terraces stretch for about 30 km along the south-facing northern shores of Lake Geneva from the Chateau de Chillon to the eastern outskirts of Lausanne in the Vaud region, covering the lower slopes of the mountainside between the villages and the lake. Conditions in the area are ideal for the production of the Chasselas grape.

The Lavaux vineyard terraces are an outstanding example of a centuries-long interaction between people and their environment, developed to optimize local resources and so produce a highly valued wine that has long been important to the economy.

Although there is evidence that vines were grown in the area in Roman times, the present vine terraces can be traced back to the eleventh century when monks from Benedictine and Cistercian monasteries cultivated the area. There are more than 10,000 terraces together with buildings – churches, castles, cellars and houses – that reflect the local history from monastic times to the twentieth century, when the landscape took on its present appearance.

The area is a thriving cultural landscape that demonstrates its millennium-long evolution and development through its well-preserved landscape and buildings, and in the continuation and adaptation of long-standing local cultural traditions.

World Heritage site since

• 1984 • 1985 • 1986 • 1987 • 1988 • 1989 • 1990 • 1991 • 1992 • 1993 • 1994 • 1995 • 1996 • 1997 • 1998 • 1999 • 2000 • 2001 • 2002 • 2003 • 2004 • 2005 • 2006 • **2007**

Parthian Fortresses of Nisa
Turkmenistan

Criteria – Interchange of values; Testimony to cultural tradition

Nisa was the capital of a powerful empire. Old Nisa, the royal citadel, is a 0.14 km² tell, or mound, surrounded by a rampart with towers; while the 0.25 km² tell of the city, known as New Nisa, has walls up to 9 m high.

The Parthian Fortresses of Nisa consist of two tells (prehistoric settlement mounds) of Old and New Nisa, indicating the site of one of the earliest and most important cities of the Parthian Empire, a major power from mid-third century BC to the third century AD. They conserve the unexcavated remains of an ancient civilization which skilfully combined its own traditional cultural elements with those of the Hellenistic and Roman west. Archaeological excavations in two parts of the site have revealed richly decorated architecture, illustrative of domestic, state and religious functions. Situated at the crossroads of important commercial and strategic axes, this powerful empire formed a barrier to Roman expansion while serving as an important communication and trading centre between east and west, north and south.

Rainforests of the Atsinanana
Madagascar

Criteria – Significant ecological and biological processes; Significant natural habitat for biodiversity

Madagascar is one of the foremost countries for megadiversity of flora and fauna. The island has around 12,000 endemic plants and is globally significant for its wildlife, especially primates. The site protects key areas of their habitat in original forests.

The Rainforests of the Atsinanana comprise six national parks distributed along the eastern part of the island. These relict forests are critically important for maintaining ongoing ecological processes necessary for the survival of Madagascar's unique biodiversity, which reflects the island's geological history. Having completed its separation from all other land masses more than sixty million years ago, Madagascar's plant and animal life evolved in isolation. The rainforests are inscribed in the World Heritage List for their importance to both ecological and biological processes as well as their biodiversity and the threatened species they support. Many species are rare and threatened, especially primates and lemurs.

World Heritage site since

• 1984 • 1985 • 1986 • 1987 • 1988 • 1989 • 1990 • 1991 • 1992 • 1993 • 1994 • 1995 • 1996 • 1997 • 1998 • 1999 • 2000 • 2001 • 2002 • 2003 • 2004 • 2005 • 2006 • 2007

Mehmed Paša Sokolović Bridge in Višegrad
Bosnia and Herzegovina
Criteria – Interchange of values; Significance in human history

The Mehmed Paša Sokolović Bridge of Višegrad crosses the Drina River and was built between 1571 and 1577. It is considered to be characteristic of the height of Ottoman monumental architecture and civil engineering, and a representative masterpiece of the renowned Ottoman architect Sinan.

The 179.5-m-long bridge has eleven masonry arches with spans of 10.7 m to 15 m, and an access ramp at right angles with four arches on the left bank of the river. The arches are enhanced by architectural features typical of the classical Ottoman period.

The bridge was important in allowing control of the inner Balkans by the Ottoman Empire in Istanbul. It forms a highlight of the route linking the plains of the Danube to Sarajevo and the Adriatic coast, particularly to the port of Dubrovnik.

The Višegrad bridge was commissioned by the Grand Vizier Mehmed Paša Sokolović (1505–79), the foremost minister or adviser to the sultan, who was a Bosnian. The building of the bridge was primarily a tribute to his native region.
▼

World Heritage site since

• 1984 • 1985 • 1986 • 1987 • 1988 • 1989 • 1990 • 1991 • 1992 • 1993 • 1994 • 1995 • 1996 • 1997 • 1998 • 1999 • 2000 • 2001 • 2002 • 2003 • 2004 • 2005 • 2006 • 2007

Jeju Volcanic Island and Lava Tubes
Korea, Republic of

Criteria – Natural phenomena or beauty;
Major stages of Earth's history

Jeju Volcanic Island and Lava Tubes together
display a range and quality of accessible
volcanic features that offer a distinctive and
important contribution to the
understanding of volcanic activity and lava
cave formation.

The volcanic island of Jeju is an area of
outstanding natural beauty and the site
covers an area of 188 km². It comprises three
locations: Geomunoreum lava-tube system
of caves; Seongsan Ilchulbong tuff cone,
rising out of the ocean; and the shield or
shallow-sided volcano of Mount Hallasan,
at 1,950 m, the highest mountain in the
Republic of Korea. Hallasan, with its
waterfalls, multi-shaped rock formations and
lake-filled crater, is the primary volcano, with
the Hallasan Natural Reserve at its summit.
There are around 360 subsidiary cones
around the island, many of which, on
cooling, formed the lava-tube caves.

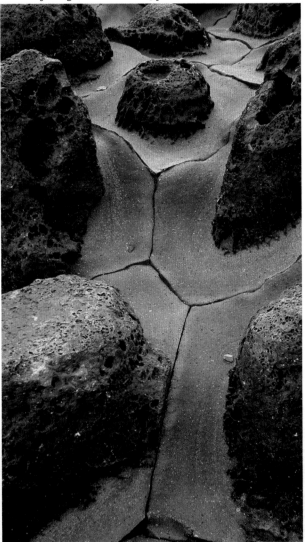

Columnar jointing in the volcanic rock, Jeju. ▼

A lava tube is a conduit that
develops under a lava flow and
through which lava is expelled
during a volcanic eruption. After the
rock cools, the empty, elongated
channel or lava tube remains.

Geomunoreum, with its
multicoloured carbonate roofs
and floors and dark lava walls, is
regarded as the finest lava-tube
system of caves in the world.

World Heritage site since

• 1984 • 1985 • 1986 • 1987 • 1988 • 1989 • 1990 • 1991 • 1992 • 1993 • 1994 • 1995 • 1996 • 1997 • 1998 • 1999 • 2000 • 2001 • 2002 • 2003 • 2004 • 2005 • 2006 • **2007**

Ecosystem and Relict Cultural Landscape of Lopé-Okanda
Gabon

Criteria – Testimony to cultural tradition;
Significance in human history; Significant
ecological and biological processes;
Significant natural habitat for biodiversity

Over 1,550 plant species have been recorded so far in the park and it is anticipated that the final total could reach over 3,000, making Lopé-Okanda one of the most outstanding areas for floral diversity in the Congo rainforest ecoregion.

The Ecosystem and Relict Cultural Landscape of Lopé-Okanda demonstrates an unusual interface between dense and well-conserved tropical rainforest and relict savanna environments with a great diversity of species, including endangered large mammals, and habitats. The site illustrates ecological and biological processes in terms of species and habitat adaptation to post-glacial climatic changes. It contains evidence of the successive passages of different peoples who have left extensive and comparatively well-preserved remains of habitation around hilltops, caves and shelters, evidence of iron-working and a remarkable collection of some 1,800 petroglyphs (rock carvings). The property's collection of Neolithic and Iron Age sites, together with the rock art found there, reflects a major migration route of Bantu and other peoples from west Africa along the river Ogooué valley to the north of the dense evergreen Congo forests and to central, east and southern Africa, that has shaped the development of the whole of sub-Saharan Africa.

World Heritage site since

• 1985 • 1986 • 1987 • 1988 • 1989 • 1990 • 1991 • 1992 • 1993 • 1994 • 1995 • 1996 • 1997 • 1998 • 1999 • 2000 • 2001 • 2002 • 2003 • 2004 • 2005 • 2006 • 2007 • **2008**

Protective town of San Miguel and the Sanctuary of Jesús
Nazareno de Atotonilco
Mexico

Criteria – Interchange of values; Significance
in human history

During its long history the town has also played a part in the struggle for Mexican independence. It was the birthplace of national hero General Ignacio Allende and was renamed San Miguel de Allende in 1926 in his honour.

This fortified town, established in the sixteenth century, reached its apogee in the eighteenth century, when many of its outstanding religious and civic buildings were built in the Mexican Baroque style. It was a melting pot of Spanish, Creole and Amerindian cultures. The Jesuit sanctuary, 14 km away, is one of the finest examples of eighteenth-century Baroque art and architecture in Latin America.

World Heritage site since

• 1985 • 1986 • 1987 • 1988 • 1989 • 1990 • 1991 • 1992 • 1993 • 1994 • 1995 • 1996 • 1997 • 1998 • 1999 • 2000 • 2001 • 2002 • 2003 • 2004 • 2005 • 2006 • 2007 • 2008

San Marino Historic Centre and Mount Titano
San Marino

Criteria – Testimony to cultural tradition

First tower (Guaita) ▶
on Mount Titano.

San Marino is one of the world's oldest republics and the only Italian city-state that survives today. With its unique, uninterrupted continuity as the capital of an independent republic since the thirteenth century, San Marino exemplifies the establishment of a representative democracy based on civic autonomy and self-governance and so represents an important stage in the development of democratic models in Europe and around the world.

The San Marino site covers 0.6 km². The Historic Centre is strategically sited on the top of Mount Titano and its many monuments include fortification towers, walls, gates and bastions; a neoclassical nineteenth-century basilica; fourteenth- and sixteenth-century convents; the nineteenth-century Palazzo Publico; and the Titano Theatre, dating from the eighteenth century.

The state of San Marino is an enclave in the Appenine Mountains and is landlocked and surrounded by Italy. It was the only city-state not to be brought into union with the rest of Italy by Garibaldi during the Risorgimento, the nineteenth-century national unification movement, and maintains its independence today.

Sacred Mijikenda Kaya Forests
Kenya

Criteria – Testimony to cultural tradition; Traditional human settlement; Heritage associated with events of universal significance

Spread out along around 200 km of the Kenyan coast are a number of separate forested sites, mostly on low hills, in which are the remains of fortified villages, kayas, of the Mijikenda people. Tradition tells how kayas were created from the sixteenth century onwards as the Mijikenda migrated south from Somalia. The kayas began to fall out of use in the early twentieth century and are now revered as the repositories of

spiritual beliefs of the Mijikenda people and are seen as the sacred abode of their ancestors. The forests around the kayas have been nurtured by the Mijikenda community to protect the sacred graves and groves and are now almost the only remains of the once extensive coastal lowland forest.

A typical kaya consisted of a circular stockade in a clearing in the forest, approached by well-defined paths. Houses were arranged around the edge of the stockade and within the centre of the village there would be either a grove of trees or a large thatched structure called a moro, places for meetings of the council of elders.

World Heritage site since

• 1985 • 1986 • 1987 • 1988 • 1989 • 1990 • 1991 • 1992 • 1993 • 1994 • 1995 • 1996 • 1997 • 1998 • 1999 • 2000 • 2001 • 2002 • 2003 • 2004 • 2005 • 2006 • 2007 • 2008

Rhaetian Railway in the Albula / Bernina Landscapes
Italy and Switzerland

Criteria – Interchange of values; Significance in human history

The Rhaetian railway brings together two historic mountain railway lines that cross the Swiss Alps through two passes. Opened in 1904, the Albula line is 67 km long. It features an impressive set of structures including forty-two tunnels and covered galleries and 144 viaducts and bridges and reaches a height of 1,819 m. The 61 km Bernina Pass line features thirteen tunnels and galleries and fifty-two viaducts and

bridges and reaches a height of 2,253 m. These railways overcame the isolation of settlements in the central Alps early in the twentieth century, with a major and lasting socio-economic impact on life in the mountains. They display outstanding architectural and civil engineering achievements, built in harmony with the landscapes through which they pass.

The railway crosses the Swiss Alps, to the south of the upper valley of the Rhine, by two passes. It follows the valley and the Albula Pass, and then crosses the upper valley of the Engadin (Saint-Moritz), before crossing the Bernina Pass and descending to the river Adda, in the Italian Veltin.

Berlin Modernism Housing Estates
Germany

Criteria – Interchange of values; Significance in human history

The site consists of six housing estates in Berlin that testify to innovative housing policies from 1910 to 1933, especially during the Weimar Republic, when the city of Berlin was particularly progressive socially, politically and culturally. The estates are an outstanding example of the building reform movement that contributed to improving housing and living conditions for people through novel approaches to town planning, architecture and garden design.

The estates also provide exceptional examples of Modernism, the new architectural style, featuring fresh design solutions, as well as technical and aesthetic innovations. Bruno Taut, Martin Wagner and Walter Gropius were among the leading architects of these projects which exercised considerable influence on the development of housing around the world.

The idea of these Berlin estates was to create housing for all income levels, of equal standard and varying size, with dedicated bathrooms and kitchens and generous loggias and balconies, which faced the sun. The designers not only aimed at creating a new social and spatial order; they also wanted to create beautiful facilities and make the inhabitants happy.

World Heritage site since

• 1985 • 1986 • 1987 • 1988 • 1989 • 1990 • 1991 • 1992 • 1993 • 1994 • 1995 • 1996 • 1997 • 1998 • 1999 • 2000 • 2001 • 2002 • 2003 • 2004 • 2005 • 2006 • 2007 • 2008

Socotra Archipelago
Yemen

Criteria – Significant natural habitat for
biodiversity

Socotra is globally important for biodiversity
conservation because of its exceptionally
rich and distinct flora and fauna; 37 per cent
of its plant species, 90 per cent of its reptile
species and 95 per cent of its land snail
species do not occur anywhere else in the
world. Socotra, one of the most biodiverse
and distinct islands in the world, has been
termed the 'Galápagos of the Indian Ocean'.

▲ Egyptian vulture

The site represents
all the terrestrial and
marine features and
processes essential
for the long-term
conservation of the
archipelago's rich and
distinct biodiversity.
It covers about 75 per
cent of the total land
area, protecting all
the major vegetation
types, areas of high
floral and faunal
values and important
bird areas, and the
most significant areas
of marine biodiversity.

Historic Centre of Camagüey
Cuba

Criteria – Significance in human history;
Traditional human settlement

Camagüey is an exceptional example of a
traditional urban settlement relatively
isolated from main trade routes. It was one
of the first villages founded by the Spaniards
in Cuba and was the centre of a region
dedicated to cattle breeding and the sugar
industry. Settled in its current location in
1528, its irregular urban pattern developed
with large and small squares, winding
streets, alleys and irregular blocks of
buildings, highly unusual for Latin American
colonial towns located on flat land. The

Spanish colonizers followed medieval
European influences in terms of urban
layout and traditional construction
techniques brought to the Americas by their
masons and construction masters. The
centre reflects the influence of numerous
styles including neoclassical, neocolonial,
Art Nouveau and Art Deco.

Religious architecture
reached its peak in the
eighteenth century.
Churches are compact,
usually with
symmetrical façades
with scant decoration.
Some adjoin convents,
hospitals or cemeteries.
As a group, the religious
buildings show extreme
simplicity, but their
historical, artistic and
symbolic value has
contributed to the
naming of Camagüey
as the 'City of
Churches'.

World Heritage site since

• 1985 • 1986 • 1987 • 1988 • 1989 • 1990 • 1991 • 1992 • 1993 • 1994 • 1995 • 1996 • 1997 • 1998 • 1999 • 2000 • 2001 • 2002 • 2003 • 2004 • 2005 • 2006 • 2007 • **2008**

Kuk Early Agricultural Site
Papua New Guinea

Criteria – Testimony to cultural tradition;
Significance in human history

This site consists of 1.2 km² of swamps in the southern highlands of New Guinea, 1,500 m above sea level. Archaeological excavation has established Kuk as the site of the earliest, independent agriculture in Oceania and could indicate that it contributed to the spread of domesticated plants, and of settlement, culture and societies across the region. It contains well-preserved archaeological remains demonstrating the technological leap from plant exploitation to agriculture, initially with taro and yam on wetland margins around 7,000 years ago, and then with organised domestication and cultivation of bananas on drained ground some 4,000 years ago. It is an excellent example of transformation of agricultural practices over time, from cultivation mounds to draining the wetlands through the digging of ditches with wooden tools.

Kuk is one of the few places in the world where archaeological evidence suggests independent agricultural development and changes in agricultural practice over more than 7,000 years. Modern farming activities at Kuk remain relatively low-key and do not intrude upon the archaeological features of the site.

Saryarka – Steppe and Lakes of Northern Kazakhstan
Kazakhstan

Criteria – Significant ecological and biological processes; Significant natural habitat for biodiversity

This site features wetlands of outstanding importance for migratory birds, including the globally threatened Siberian white crane, Dalmatian pelican and Pallas's fish eagle, that travel from Africa, Europe and south Asia to their breeding grounds in western and eastern Siberia. The central Asian steppe provides a valuable refuge for over half the species of the region's steppe flora, a number of threatened bird species and the critically endangered Saiga antelope.

The wetlands of the site are globally important. The Korgalzhyn-Tengiz lakes provide feeding grounds for up to 15–16 million birds, including up to 2.5 million geese. They also support 350,000 nesting waterfowl, while the Naurzum lakes support 500,000 nesting waterfowl.

◄
Dalmatian pelican.

World Heritage site since

• 1985 • 1986 • 1987 • 1988 • 1989 • 1990 • 1991 • 1992 • 1993 • 1994 • 1995 • 1996 • 1997 • 1998 • 1999 • 2000 • 2001 • 2002 • 2003 • 2004 • 2005 • 2006 • 2007 • **2008**

Swiss Tectonic Arena Sardona
Switzerland

Criteria – Major stages of Earth's history

EUROPE

Atlantic
Ocean

Mediterranean
Sea

Adriatic
Sea

The Swiss Tectonic
Arena Sardona lies
in the Alps in
northeastern
Switzerland and
covers a mountainous
area of 329 km²; it
includes seven
peaks that rise above
3,000 m.

The Swiss Tectonic Arena Sardona is an exceptional and dramatic example of the process of mountain building through continental collision. The structures and processes that characterize the phenomenon are displayed in a mountain setting and the area has been a key site for the study of geological sciences since the eighteenth century.

The Glarus Alps are glaciated mountains rising dramatically above narrow river valleys and are the site of the largest post-glacial landslide in the central Alpine region.

The Glarus Overthrust is a key part of the whole site. This is a break in the earth's crust where compression forces the upper side of two tectonic plates further upwards over the lower one. The exposures of the rocks below and above this feature are visible in three dimensions and they have made substantial contributions to the understanding of mountain-building tectonics.

Klöntaler lake and the
Glarus Alps.
▼

World Heritage site since

• 1985 • 1986 • 1987 • 1988 • 1989 • 1990 • 1991 • 1992 • 1993 • 1994 • 1995 • 1996 • 1997 • 1998 • 1999 • 2000 • 2001 • 2002 • 2003 • 2004 • 2005 • 2006 • 2007 • 2008

Fujian Tulou
China

Criteria – Testimony to cultural tradition;
Significance in human history; Traditional human
settlement

Set amongst the rice, tea and tobacco fields
of southwest Fujian Province, this site
contains forty-six extraordinary communal
earthen houses (tulou), built between the
twelfth and the twentieth centuries. They
are up to five storeys high, with an inward-
looking, circular or square floor plan, each
housing a whole clan of up to 800 people.
They were built for defensive purposes
around a central open courtyard with few
windows to the outside and only one
entrance. They feature tall, fortified mud
walls capped by tiled roofs with wide overhanging eaves. The most elaborate
structures date back to the seventeenth and
eighteenth centuries. In contrast with their
plain exterior, the inside of the tulou were
built for comfort and were often highly
decorated.

Tulou functioned as
impregnable village
units and were known
as 'a little kingdom for
the family' or 'a
bustling small city'.
Their lower sections,
reinforced with stone,
were generally
windowless, while the
upper floors were
studded with gun
holes. The main gate
was reinforced, often
with watertanks built
above to extinguish
assault by fire.

Lagoons of New Caledonia: Reef Diversity and Associated Ecosystems
France

Criteria – Natural phenomena or beauty;
Significant ecological and biological processes;
Significant habitat for biodiversity

The tropical lagoons and coral reefs of New
Caledonia are considered to be some of the
most beautiful reef systems in the world,
with a wide variety of shapes and forms
within a comparatively small area. They
feature an exceptional diversity of coral and
fish species and a continuum of habitats
from mangroves to seagrasses. The
excellent ecological condition of the reefs is
remarkable, in particular the number and
diversity of large fish and top predators,
such as sharks and barracuda. The lagoons
provide habitats to a number of threatened
fish, turtles and marine mammals, including
the third largest population of dugongs in
the world. The reefs are of varying age, from
living reefs to ancient fossil reefs, providing
an important source of information on the
natural history of Oceania.

The natural beauty of
the lagoons result
from the combination
of coastal and oceanic
landscapes with a
background of
forested mountains.
This beauty continues
in the clear water
below the surface with
dramatic displays of
coral diversity and
massive coral
structures, together
with arches, caves and
major fissures in the
reefs.

World Heritage site since

• 1985 • 1986 • 1987 • 1988 • 1989 • 1990 • 1991 • 1992 • 1993 • 1994 • 1995 • 1996 • 1997 • 1998 • 1999 • 2000 • 2001 • 2002 • 2003 • 2004 • 2005 • 2006 • 2007 • **2008**

Temple of Preah Vihear
Cambodia
Criteria – Human creative genius

The temple was the scene of battles between the Cambodian army and Khmer Rouge fighters in the 1970s, during Cambodia's civil war. However, despite the country's violent recent history, the temple site remains well preserved.

Preah Vihear, a Hindu temple dedicated to the god Shiva, is an outstanding masterpiece of Khmer architecture in terms of its design, the exceptional quality of its carved stone ornamentation and its relationship to its spectacular setting.

The temple stands in a cliff-top location on the edge of a plateau that dominates the plain of Cambodia. It is a unique complex comprising a series of sanctuaries linked by a system of pavements and staircases that extend over an 800-m-long axis.

The site's origins date from its ninth-century beginnings as a hermitage. In the eleventh and twelfth centuries it was built up as a royal temple under the Khmer kings Suryavarman I and Suryavarman II. The temple was adapted for use by Buddhists after Hinduism declined in the region.

Surtsey
Iceland
Criteria – Significant ecological and biological processes

Geographically isolated, Surtsey has been legally protected since its formation and will continue to provide invaluable data on biological colonisation long into the future. Another part of the evolution of Surtsey is the process of coastal erosion which has already halved the area of the island and is predicted to remove another two-thirds, leaving only the most resistant core.

Surtsey, a volcanic island approximately 32 km from the south coast of Iceland, is a new island formed by volcanic eruptions that took place between 1963 and 1967. Free from human interference, Surtsey has been producing unique long-term information on the colonisation process of new land by plant and animal life. Since 1964, scientists have observed the arrival of seeds carried by ocean currents, the appearance of moulds, bacteria and fungi and, in 1965, the first vascular plant, of which there were ten species by the end of the first decade. By 2004, they numbered sixty, together with seventy-five bryophytes, seventy-one lichens and twenty-four fungi. Eighty-nine species of birds have been recorded on Surtsey, along with 335 species of invertebrates.

World Heritage site since

• 1985 • 1986 • 1987 • 1988 • 1989 • 1990 • 1991 • 1992 • 1993 • 1994 • 1995 • 1996 • 1997 • 1998 • 1999 • 2000 • 2001 • 2002 • 2003 • 2004 • 2005 • 2006 • 2007 • **2008**

Melaka and George Town, Historic Cities of the Straits of Malacca
Malaysia

Criteria – Interchange of values; Testimony to cultural tradition, Significance in human history

Melaka and George Town were forged from the mercantile interaction of Malay, Chinese, and Indian cultures and of three successive European colonial powers over almost 500 years. Each has left its imprint on the local architecture and urban form, technology and monumental art.

The historic cities of Melaka and George Town, on the Straits of Malacca, are remarkable examples of historic colonial towns, demonstrating a succession of cultural influences that derive from their former function as trading ports linking East and West.

The towns complement one another in illustrating different stages of development and successive changes over a period of time. Melaka demonstrates their early history: originating in the fifteenth-century Malay sultanate and the Portuguese and Dutch periods beginning in the early sixteenth century, its notable monuments are its government buildings, churches, squares and fortifications. Residential and commercial buildings feature strongly in George Town, which represents the British era from the end of the eighteenth century until the twentieth century. Together, the two towns constitute a unique architectural and cultural townscape without parallel anywhere in east and southeast Asia.

Stari Grad Plain
Croatia

Criteria – Interchange of values; Testimony to cultural tradition; Traditional human settlement

The agricultural plain of Stari Grad and its environment are an example of very ancient traditional human settlement, which is today under threat from modern economic development, particularly rural depopulation and the abandonment of traditional farming practices.

The fertile plain near the port, now known as Stari Grad, on the Adriatic island of Hvar, was colonized by Ionian Greeks from Paros in the fourth century BC. It quickly became one of the most important Greek colonies of the Adriatic because of its flourishing agriculture. This agricultural activity, based on grapes and olives, has been maintained since Greek times to the present. The site is also a nature reserve. The landscape features ancient stone walls and trims, or small stone shelters, and bears testimony to the regular geometrical system of land division used by the ancient Greeks, the chora, which has remained virtually intact over twenty-four centuries. This system was completed with tanks of varying sizes for the retention of rainwater.

World Heritage site since

• 1985 • 1986 • 1987 • 1988 • 1989 • 1990 • 1991 • 1992 • 1993 • 1994 • 1995 • 1996 • 1997 • 1998 • 1999 • 2000 • 2001 • 2002 • 2003 • 2004 • 2005 • 2006 • 2007 • 2008

Monarch Butterfly Biosphere Reserve
Mexico
Criteria – Natural phenomena or beauty

The millions of monarch butterflies that return to the property every year colour the trees orange, bend branches with their massed weight, fill the sky when they take flight, and sound like light rain with the beating of their wings. To witness this unique phenomenon is an exceptional experience of nature.

The Monarch Butterfly Biosphere Reserve protects key overwintering sites for the monarch butterfly whose concentration in the property is a superlative natural phenomenon.

The 563 km² biosphere lies within rugged forested mountains about 100 km northwest of Mexico City. In a dramatic manifestation of insect migration, up to a billion monarch butterflies return annually from northern breeding areas to land in close-packed clusters within fourteen overwintering colonies in central Mexico's oyamel fir forests. The biosphere reserve protects eight of these colonies and an estimated 70 per cent of the total overwintering population of the monarch butterfly's eastern population.

In the spring the butterflies begin an eight-month round-trip migration that takes them as far as eastern Canada and back, during which four successive generations are born and die.

A monarch butterfly feeding on a flower's nectar.
▼

World Heritage site since

• 1985 • 1986 • 1987 • 1988 • 1989 • 1990 • 1991 • 1992 • 1993 • 1994 • 1995 • 1996 • 1997 • 1998 • 1999 • 2000 • 2001 • 2002 • 2003 • 2004 • 2005 • 2006 • 2007 • 2008

Le Morne Cultural Landscape
Mauritius

Criteria – Testimony to cultural tradition; Heritage associated with events of universal significance

Le Morne, a rugged mountain that juts into the Indian Ocean in the southwest of Mauritius, was used as a shelter by runaway slaves, called 'maroons', through the eighteenth and early years of the nineteenth centuries. Mauritius was a major transhipment place for slaves between Africa, India and the Americas and became known as the 'Maroon republic' because of the comparatively large number of escaped

slaves who were in hiding on Le Morne. Protected by the mountain's isolated, wooded and almost inaccessible cliffs, it offered a retreat against those who hunted them down. Many only survived as free men for a few weeks; others managed to set up small communities on the mountain, around its base, in caves on its sides or on its summit.

Since the abolition of slavery in 1835 the 'maroons' have achieved legendary status as heroic resistance fighters and Le Morne has become the symbol of their suffering, their bid for freedom and their sacrifice. The mountain, together with its surrounding foothills and lagoons, is a place of great scenic beauty.

Armenian Monastic Ensembles of Iran
Islamic Republic of Iran

Criteria – Interchange of values; Testimony to cultural tradition; Heritage associated with events of universal significance

The fortified Armenian monasteries of northwest Iran bear testimony, since the origins of Christianity and certainly since the seventh century, to Armenian culture and its contact with Persian and later Iranian civilizations. The monasteries of St Thaddeus and St Stepanos and the Chapel of Dzordzor are outstanding examples of Armenian architectural and decorative traditions. Situated on the south-eastern fringe of Armenian influence, the

monasteries constituted a major centre for the dissemination of that culture. The monastery of St Thaddeus, the presumed location of the tomb of St Thaddeus, the apostle of Jesus Christ, has always been a place of high spiritual significance for Christians and other inhabitants in the region. It is still a living place of pilgrimage for the Armenian Church.

The monasteries have survived human and natural destruction over the course of 2,000 years and have been rebuilt several times in keeping with Armenian cultural traditions. Today they are the only important vestiges of Armenian culture in this region.

World Heritage site since

• 1985 • 1986 • 1987 • 1988 • 1989 • 1990 • 1991 • 1992 • 1993 • 1994 • 1995 • 1996 • 1997 • 1998 • 1999 • 2000 • 2001 • 2002 • 2003 • 2004 • 2005 • 2006 • 2007 • 2008

Bahá'í Holy Places in Haifa and the Western Galilee
Israel

Criteria – Testimony to cultural tradition; Heritage associated with events of universal significance

The Bahá'í Faith is a monotheistic religion that emphasizes the spiritual unity of all peoples. It was founded by Bahá'u'lláh in Persia in the nineteenth century and it is estimated that there are over five million Bahá'ís around the world.

The Bahá'í Holy Places in Haifa and the Western Galilee are inscribed for their profound spiritual meaning and the testimony they bear to the strong tradition of pilgrimage in the Bahá'í Faith.

The sites include the two most holy places in the Bahá'í religion associated with its founders, the Shrine of Bahá'u'lláh in Acre and the Shrine of the Báb in Haifa, together with their surrounding gardens, associated buildings and monuments. These two shrines are part of a larger complex of buildings, monuments and sites at seven distinct locations in Haifa and the Western Galilee that draw large numbers of pilgrims from around the world.

The two holy Bahá'í shrines are tangible places of great meaning for one of the world's religions.

The Shrine of the Báb and the Bahá'í Gardens, Haifa.
▼

World Heritage site since

• 1985 • 1986 • 1987 • 1988 • 1989 • 1990 • 1991 • 1992 • 1993 • 1994 • 1995 • 1996 • 1997 • 1998 • 1999 • 2000 • 2001 • 2002 • 2003 • 2004 • 2005 • 2006 • 2007 • **2008**

Fortifications of Vauban
France

Criteria – *Human creative genius; Interchange of values; Significance in human history*

The Fortifications of Vauban comprise twelve groups of fortified buildings and sites that together represent the peak of classic bastioned fortification typical of Western military architecture. They are the finest examples of the work of Sébastien Le Prestre de Vauban (1633–1707), the renowned military engineer of King Louis XIV.

The twelve properties in the site form a ring around France's borders. They are at Arras, Besançon, Blaye-Cussac-Fort-Médoc,

Briançon, Camaret-sur-Mer, Longwy, Mont-Dauphin, Mont-Louis, Neuf-Brisach, Saint-Martin-de-Ré, Sant-Vaast-la-Hougue/Tatihou and Villefranche-de-Conflent. The fortifications include towns built from scratch by Vauban, citadels built on plains, urban bastion walls and bastion towers. There are also mountain forts, sea forts, a mountain battery and two mountain communication structures.

Vauban played a major role in the history of fortification. His work crystallized earlier theories of strategy into a rational system of fortifications based on a concrete relationship to the territory to be defended. His theories and models were studied and used across the world and made a major contribution to military architecture.

Fort at Briançon.
▼

World Heritage site since

• 1985 • 1986 • 1987 • 1988 • 1989 • 1990 • 1991 • 1992 • 1993 • 1994 • 1995 • 1996 • 1997 • 1998 • 1999 • 2000 • 2001 • 2002 • 2003 • 2004 • 2005 • 2006 • 2007 • **2008**

Wooden Churches of the Slovak part of the Carpathian Mountain Area
Slovakia

Criteria – Testimony to cultural tradition;
Significance in human history

The wooden churches are an outstanding testimony to the inter-ethnic and inter-cultural character of this small area in the Carpathian Mountains, where Latin and Byzantine cultures met and overlapped, and of tolerance at a time of religious and political upheaval in the Habsburg Empire.

These wooden churches, two Roman Catholic, three Protestant and three Greek Orthodox, were built between the sixteenth and eighteenth centuries, mostly in quite isolated villages, using wood as the main material and traditional construction techniques. They are good examples of a rich local tradition of religious architecture, marked by the meeting of Latin and Byzantine cultures. The buildings exhibit some variations in their floor plans, interior spaces and external appearance due to their respective religious practices. They bear testimony to the development of major architectural and artistic trends during the period of construction, adapted to a specific geographical and cultural context. Interiors are decorated with paintings on the walls and ceilings and other works of art that enrich their cultural significance.

Chief Roi Mata's Domain
Vanuatu

Criteria – Testimony to cultural tradition;
Traditional human settlement; Heritage associated with events of universal significance

The landscape reflects continuing Pacific chiefly systems and respect for this authority through tapu (tabu) prohibitions on the use of Roi Mata's residence and burial that have been observed for over 400 years and that have structured the local landscape and social practices. Roi Mata still lives for many in contemporary Vanuatu as a source of power and inspiration.

The domain comprises three early seventeenth-century sites on the islands of Efate, Lelepa and Artok associated with the life and death of the last paramount chief, or Roi Mata, of what is now central Vanuatu. It includes Roi Mata's residence, the site of his death and Roi Mata's mass burial site. It is closely associated with the oral traditions surrounding the chief and the moral values he espoused.

World Heritage site since

• 1985 • 1986 • 1987 • 1988 • 1989 • 1990 • 1991 • 1992 • 1993 • 1994 • 1995 • 1996 • 1997 • 1998 • 1999 • 2000 • 2001 • 2002 • 2003 • 2004 • 2005 • 2006 • 2007 • **2008**

Joggins Fossil Cliffs
Canada
Criteria – Major stages of Earth's history

The Joggins Fossil Cliffs have been described as the 'coal age Galápagos' due to their wealth of fossils from the Carboniferous (354 to 290 million years ago). These include the remains and tracks of the first known reptiles, and the rainforest in which they lived, left intact and undisturbed. With its 14.7 km of sea cliffs, low bluffs, rock platforms and beaches, the site contains remains of three ecosystems: estuarine bay, floodplain rainforest and fire-prone forested alluvial plain with freshwater pools. Joggins offers the richest assemblage known of the

fossil life in these three ecosystems with 96 genera and 148 species of fossils and 20 footprint groups. It played a vital role in the development of geological and evolutionary principles.

Upright fossil trees are preserved at a series of levels in the cliffs together with animal, plant and trace fossils. These provide environmental context and enable a complete reconstruction to be made of the extensive fossil forests that dominated land at this time, and which are now the source of most of the world's coal deposits.

Mount Sanqingshan National Park
China
Criteria – Natural phenomena or beauty

Mount Sanqingshan National Park contains a unique array of fantastically-shaped granite pillars and peaks, concentrated in a relatively small area. The looming, intricate rock formations intermingled with delicate forest cover and combined with ever-shifting weather patterns create a landscape of arresting beauty. It is located in the west of the Huyaiyu mountain range in the northeast of Jiangxi Province. The area is

subject to a combination of subtropical, monsoonal and maritime influences and forms an island of temperate forest above the surrounding subtropical landscape. It also features numerous waterfalls, some of them 60 m in height, lakes and springs. The access afforded by suspended walking trails in the park permits visitors to appreciate the park's stunning scenery and enjoy its serene atmosphere.

The park is well known for its Taoist cultural relics, stone carvings and temples. Mount Sanqingshan has been a Taoist shrine since a priest, Ge Hong, came to the mountain 400 years ago. The ancient religion of Taoism is based on worship in and of nature, a philosophy much in keeping with conservation ethics now practised here.

World Heritage site since

• 1985 • 1986 • 1987 • 1988 • 1989 • 1990 • 1991 • 1992 • 1993 • 1994 • 1995 • 1996 • 1997 • 1998 • 1999 • 2000 • 2001 • 2002 • 2003 • 2004 • 2005 • 2006 • 2007 • **2008**

Mantua and Sabbioneta
Italy

Criteria – Interchange of values; Testimony to cultural tradition

Mantua and Sabbioneta in the Po valley of northern Italy, are important both for the value of their architecture and also for their prominent role in the dissemination of Renaissance culture. They represent two aspects of Renaissance town planning: Mantua shows the renewal and extension of an already existing city, while 30 km away, sixteenth-century Sabbioneta represents the expression of contemporary theories on the planning of the ideal city.

Typically, Mantua's layout is irregular with regular parts showing different stages of its growth since the Roman period. It includes many medieval buildings, among them an eleventh-century rotunda and a Baroque theatre. Sabbioneta, on the other hand, is a single-period city. Together they offer exceptional testimony to the urban, architectural and artistic realizations of the Renaissance, linked by the vision, planning and work of the local ruling family of Gonzaga.

Mantua was renovated in the fifteenth–sixteenth centuries with hydrological engineering, urban and architectural works. The participation of renowned architects and painters made it a prominent capital of the Renaissance.

Sabbioneta was a new town built according to Renaissance ideals. Its defensive walls, grid-patterned streets, public spaces and monuments make it one of the best examples of European ideal cities.

Mantua from Lago di Mezzo. ▼

World Heritage site since

• 1985 • 1986 • 1987 • 1988 • 1989 • 1990 • 1991 • 1992 • 1993 • 1994 • 1995 • 1996 • 1997 • 1998 • 1999 • 2000 • 2001 • 2002 • 2003 • 2004 • 2005 • 2006 • 2007 • 2008

Al-Hijr Archaeological Site (Madâin Sâlih)
Saudi Arabia

Criteria – Interchange of values; Testimony to cultural tradition

The remarkable archaeological site of Al-Hijr – formerly known as Hegra – is the largest conserved site of the Nabataean civilization south of Petra in modern-day Jordan. It includes a major ensemble of tombs whose architecture and decorations are cut directly into the sandstone of the local landscape.

The site has in total 111 well-preserved monumental tombs, ninety-four of which have decorated façades dating from the first century BC to the first century AD. There are also fifty inscriptions of the pre-Nabataean period and some cave drawings. It is an outstanding illustration of the Nabataeans' specific architectural style and accomplishment.

The site includes a set of wells, most of which were sunk into the rock, demonstrating the Nabataeans' mastery of water techniques for agricultural purposes. Some wells are still in use today.

Al-Hijr is located at a meeting point between various civilizations of late Antiquity, on a trade route between the Arabian Peninsula, the Mediterranean world and Asia. It bears outstanding witness to important cultural exchanges in architecture, decoration, language use and the caravan route. Although abandoned during the pre-Islamic period, the route continued to play its international role for caravans and then for the pilgrimage to Mecca.

World Heritage site since

• 1986 • 1987 • 1988 • 1989 • 1990 • 1991 • 1992 • 1993 • 1994 • 1995 • 1996 • 1997 • 1998 • 1999 • 2000 • 2001 • 2002 • 2003 • 2004 • 2005 • 2006 • 2007• 2008 • **2009**

Cidade Velha, Historic Centre of Ribeira Grande
Cape Verde

Criteria – Interchange of values; Testimony to cultural tradition; Heritage associated with events of universal significance

São Tiago, on which Cidade Velha stands, is part of the Cape Verde archipelago. Portuguese explorers first arrived in 1462 during their explorations of the African coast.

In the fifteenth century, Vasco da Gama and Christopher Columbus stopped off in the port on their voyages to India and the Americas respectively.

The town of Ribeira Grande, renamed Cidade Velha in the late eighteenth century, was the first European colonial town built in the tropics, and it provided an early image of transcontinental geopolitical visions. Its situation, with access to shipping routes between Europe, Africa and the Americas, made it central to further Portuguese colonisation and administration.

It became an important centre in the West African slave trade and the large-scale mixing of European and African cultures and people led to the development in the town of the first Creole culture. The Pillory, for punishing slaves, still stands in the town which is overlooked by the Fortress of São Filipe.

New forms of colonial agriculture, based on its situation between temperate and tropical climate zones, were developed in the Ribeira Grande valley and the town became a platform for the acclimatisation and dissemination of plant species across the world.

Royal Tombs of the Joseon Dynasty
Korea, Republic of

Criteria – Testimony to cultural tradition; Significance in human history; Heritage associated with events of universal significance

The Royal Tombs of the Joseon Dynasty, which ruled in Korea from the fourteenth to the twentieth centuries, were built between 1408 and 1966 to honour the memory of ancestors, show respect for their achievements, assert royal authority, protect ancestral spirits from evil and provide protection from vandalism.

The Royal Tombs of the Korean Joseon Dynasty form a collection of forty tombs scattered over eighteen locations. They are directly associated with a living tradition of ancestral worship through the performance of prescribed rites. The tombs represent an outstanding example of an architectural ensemble and landscape illustrating a significant stage in the development of burial mounds in Korean and East Asian tombs.

Sites of outstanding natural beauty were chosen: typically tombs face south toward water, protected by a hill behind and ideally have mountain ridges in the distance.

Alongside the burial area, each tomb features a ceremonial area, an entrance and associated buildings including a shrine and tomb-keeper's house.

The grounds outside are adorned with stone objects including figures of people and animals.

World Heritage site since

• 1986 • 1987 • 1988 • 1989 • 1990 • 1991 • 1992 • 1993 • 1994 • 1995 • 1996 • 1997 • 1998 • 1999 • 2000 • 2001 • 2002 • 2003 • 2004 • 2005 • 2006 • 2007• 2008 • **2009**

La Chaux-de-Fonds / Le Locle, Watchmaking Town Planning
Switzerland
Criteria – Significance in human history

The small sister cities of La Chaux-de-Fonds and Le Locle in the Jura Mountains are centres of the Swiss watch-making industry and represent outstanding examples of single-industry manufacturing towns which are well preserved and still thriving today.

The local watch-making culture dates to the seventeenth century and the towns were originally planned in the early nineteenth century following extensive damaging fires. The towns' layout, along an open-ended series of parallel strips of intermingled houses and workshops, was designed totally for the single goal of manufacturing.

The planning of both towns has accommodated successfully the transition from the artisanal production of a cottage industry to the more concentrated factory production that replaced it in the late nineteenth and twentieth centuries.

La Chaux-de-Fonds and Le Locle owe their existence solely to the watch-making industry. Their location, 1000 metres up in the Jura Mountains, is a remote and infertile area unsuitable for farming.

In Das Kapital, Karl Marx described La Chaux-de-Fonds as a 'huge factory-town' in his analysis of the division of labour in the watch-making industry of the Jura.

Sacred City of Caral-Supe
Peru
Criteria – Interchange of values; Testimony to cultural tradition; Significance in human history

The Sacred City of Caral-Supe reflects the rise of civilisation in the Americas. As a fully developed state of the third millennium BC, it is remarkable for its social and political complexity and its impact on developing settlements throughout the Supe Valley and beyond.

Exceptionally well preserved, Caral is one of eighteen urban settlements situated in the same area and features complex architectural and spatial elements: in particular, its monumental earthen platform mounds and sunken circular courts are powerful expressions of a consolidated state. These features were to influence and dominate much of the Peruvian coast for centuries.

The city's plan and some of its components, including pyramidal structures and residence of the elite, show clear evidence of ceremonial functions, signifying a powerful religious ideology.

The 5000-year-old, 0.7 km² archaeological site of Caral-Supe stands on a dry desert terrace overlooking the green valley of the Supe River. The city was a centre of the Norte Chico civilisation, a pre-Columbian society claimed to be the oldest known civilisation in the Americas and one of the oldest in the world.

Pontcysyllte Aqueduct and Canal
United Kingdom

Criteria – *Human creative genius; Interchange of values; Significance in human history*

The Pontcysyllte Aqueduct and Canal, completed in the early years of the nineteenth century, is a feat of Industrial Revolution civil engineering. Due to the difficult terrain, the building of the canal required substantial, bold engineering solutions including tunnel construction, especially as it was built without using locks.

The Pontcysyllte Aqueduct is a pioneering masterpiece of engineering and monumental metal architecture, conceived by the noted civil engineers Thomas Telford and William Jessop. The unique production capacities of the British iron industry allowed the use of both cast and wrought iron in the construction of arches that were light and strong, producing an overall effect that is both monumental and elegant.

The site is regarded a masterpiece of creative genius and a synthesis of expertise already acquired in Europe. It is also recognized as an innovative ensemble that inspired many projects all over the world.

The name Pontcysyllte is (approximately) pronounced 'pont-kuh-suh-llt-eh'.

The Pontcysyllte Aqueduct towers at heights of over 37 m above the floor of the steep-sided Dee valley, bearing only a cast-iron, water-filled trough and a towpath with a handrail. Its completion in 1805 came at the end of the canal-building era: the railway age was less than three decades away.

▼

World Heritage site since

• 1986 • 1987 • 1988 • 1989 • 1990 • 1991 • 1992 • 1993 • 1994 • 1995 • 1996 • 1997 • 1998 • 1999 • 2000 • 2001 • 2002 • 2003 • 2004 • 2005 • 2006 • 2007• 2008 • **2009**

Mount Wutai
China

Criteria – Interchange of values; Testimony to cultural tradition; Significance in human history; Heritage associated with events of universal significance

Their mountain landscape is integral to the temples of Mount Wutai. The high peaks, snow-covered for much of the year, thick forests of vertical pines, firs, poplar and willow trees and lush grassland form a landscape of great beauty that has been celebrated by artists since at least the seventh century.

Mount Wutai, with its five flat peaks, is one of four sacred Buddhist mountains in China. Temples were built there from the first century AD to the early twentieth century and many of the country's most important monasteries and temples stand on its slopes. It is the global centre for Buddhist worship of Manjusri, the Bodhisattva of Wisdom.

Mount Wutai received imperial patronage for over 1000 years and the landscape was adorned with buildings, statuary, paintings and stelae (inscribed slabs) in recognition and confirmation of its status as a Buddhist sacred place.

The architecture reflects a fertile exchange of ideas from Nepal and Mongolia and as a whole chronicles over more than a millennium the development of Buddhist architecture in China and its strong influence on both temple- and palace-building.

One of the many temples on Mount Wutai.
▼

World Heritage site since

• 1986 • 1987 • 1988 • 1989 • 1990 • 1991 • 1992 • 1993 • 1994 • 1995 • 1996 • 1997 • 1998 • 1999 • 2000 • 2001 • 2002 • 2003 • 2004 • 2005 • 2006 • 2007• 2008 • 2009

Shushtar Historical Hydraulic System
Iran (Islamic Republic of)

Criteria – Human creative genius; Interchange of values; Traditional human settlement

Shushtar Historical Hydraulic System is a complete and large-scale and therefore unique example of hydraulic techniques developed in ancient times to allow settlement on semi-desert lands. The diversion of a mountain river by means of canals and other civil-engineering structures brought water to a vast territory for urban and domestic supply, agriculture, fish farming, mills, city defence and transport.

In its present form the system dates from the third century AD, probably built on fifth-century BC bases. It synthesises diverse techniques of hydraulic engineering applied over several centuries: from Elamites and Mesopotamians and later, Nabateans skilled in canal irrigation (suggesting Petra's water-management systems may have been influential); and Roman civil engineers contributed to the construction.

In its entirety, the system demonstrates an accomplished and early vision of the possibilities for land development afforded by diversion canals and large weir-dams.

The Kārūn River was diverted around Shushtar to form a moat around which defensive bridges and gates were built. A network of channels or qanāts honeycombs under the city, supplying the river water direct to reservoirs in houses and buildings for domestic use, irrigation, and storage during times of war. Some remnants of these ghanats still exist below older houses.

Sulaiman-Too Sacred Mountain
Kyrgyzstan

Criteria – Testimony to cultural tradition; Heritage associated with events of universal significance

Sulaiman-Too is an exceptional spiritual landscape reflecting both ancient religious and Islamic beliefs and particularly the cult of the horse. Its strong traditions of worship span several millennia and it presents the most complete picture of a sacred mountain in Central Asia.

Its five peaks and slopes contain a large assembly of ancient cult places and caves with petroglyphs, interconnected by a network of ancient paths, together with later mosques.

Sulaiman-Too matches iconic images from Zoroastrian and Vedic tradition: one mountain with a peak dominating four others, in the centre of a river valley and surrounded by other mountains.

With its long tradition of religious worship and rich remains together with its 'ideal' form, Sulaiman-Too has had a profound effect over much of Central Asia.

Sulaiman-Too dominates its landscape of the fertile Fergana Valley and the city of Osh. Medieval Osh stood at an important crossroads on the Central Asian Silk Routes connecting Asia, Africa and the Mediterranean worlds.

World Heritage site since

• 1986 • 1987 • 1988 • 1989 • 1990 • 1991 • 1992 • 1993 • 1994 • 1995 • 1996 • 1997 • 1998 • 1999 • 2000 • 2001 • 2002 • 2003 • 2004 • 2005 • 2006 • 2007• 2008 • **2009**

The Wadden Sea
Germany/Netherlands

Criteria – Major stages of Earth's history;
Significant ecological and biological processes;
Significant natural habitat for biodiversity

North
Sea

EUROPE

Bay of
Biscay

The Wadden Sea is a large temperate coastal-wetland environment and is the world's largest unbroken system of intertidal sand and mudflats.

It encompasses a multitude of transitional zones between the land, sea and freshwater environments with tidal channels, sandy shoals, sea-grass meadows, mussel beds, sandbars, mudflats, salt marshes, estuaries, beaches and dunes.

The availability of food and minimal disturbance makes these coastal wetlands unusually rich in the diversity of their fauna and they are home to numerous plant and animal species, including marine mammals such as the harbour seal, grey seal and harbour porpoise.

They are also a breeding and wintering area for up to 12 millions birds annually and support more than 10 per cent of 29 species. Up to 6.1 million birds can be present at one time.

Biodiversity on a worldwide scale is reliant on the Wadden Sea.

The size and diversity of the Wadden Sea is unique. It is distinctive in being almost entirely a tidal flat and barrier system with only minor river influences. Dynamic natural processes create a constantly changing variety of barrier islands, channels, gullies, saltmarshes and other coastal and sedimentary features. The area provides crucial lessons for wetland and coastal management (important for addressing climate change).
▼

World Heritage site since

• 1986 • 1987 • 1988 • 1989 • 1990 • 1991 • 1992 • 1993 • 1994 • 1995 • 1996 • 1997 • 1998 • 1999 • 2000 • 2001 • 2002 • 2003 • 2004 • 2005 • 2006 • 2007• 2008 • 2009

Stoclet House
Belgium

Criteria – Human creative genius; Interchange of values

The Stoclet House is one of the most complete realisations of the Wiener Werkstätte (Vienna Workshops) community of architects, artists and designers which grew out of the Vienna Secession movement in the early twentieth century. The Brussels house was designed and built by Austrian architect Josef Hoffmann between 1905 and 1911, and is his masterpiece.

From its inception the house was intended as an ideal expression of the arts and the materials used were uniformly of superb quality. A number of artists, including Klimt and Moser, worked under Hoffmann to design and integrate every aspect of the house, fittings, household objects and gardens.

The house has remained influential and inspirational since its completion and was a herald of Art Deco and the Modern Movement.

The Stoclet House is a private dwelling designed and built for banker and art-lover Adolphe Stoclet. His designers and artists enjoyed an unlimited budget and artistic free rein.

The coordinated work of the Wiener Werkstätte architects, artists, designers and craftsmen makes the house a classic and superb example of Gesamtkunstwerk (total artwork), a defining feature of Jugendstil or Art Nouveau.

The Ruins of Loropéni
Burkina Faso

Criteria – Testimony to cultural tradition

The Ruins of Loropéni are the remains of a thousand-year-old fortified stone settlement that played an important role in the trans-Saharan gold trade. Loropéni is the finest remaining example of these West African settlements.

The 11,130 m² property consists of tall, laterite stone perimeter walls, up to 6 m high, surrounding a large settlement.

As the best-preserved of ten similar fortresses in the Lobi area and part of a larger group of around a hundred stone-built enclosures, Loropéni was part of a network of settlements that flourished with the lucrative trans-Saharan gold trade which ran north-south between the seventh and eleventh centuries, linking the gold-hungry Mediterranean economies with sub-Saharan Africa where gold was plentiful.

Loropéni was finally deserted early in the nineteenth century.

Loropéni's size and scope reflect the gold trade's power and influence and its links with the Atlantic coast.

Gold was mined in the area by the Lohron or Koulango peoples who occupied Loropéni and controlled the excavation and refining processes. Production reached its height between the fourteenth and seventeenth centuries.

World Heritage site since

• 1986 • 1987 • 1988 • 1989 • 1990 • 1991 • 1992 • 1993 • 1994 • 1995 • 1996 • 1997 • 1998 • 1999 • 2000 • 2001 • 2002 • 2003 • 2004 • 2005 • 2006 • 2007• 2008 • 2009

Tower of Hercules
Spain

Criteria – Testimony to cultural tradition

The Tower of Hercules is the only fully preserved and functioning Roman lighthouse. It is still used for maritime signalling and is one of the oldest lighthouses in the world. It bears witness to organised and elaborate systems of navigation in ancient times and helps in the understanding of ancient Atlantic sea routes.

The sea area beyond, named Finisterra as the Romans thought it the end of the world, was notorious for dangers to shipping and construction of what was called the Farum Brigantium (Tower of Brigantium) began in the first century AD.

The tower stands on a 57-m-high rock and rises a further 55 m; the Roman core is 34 m high. It is divided into three progressively smaller levels, the first corresponding to the Roman structure.

The tower was restored in neoclassical style in the late eighteenth century.

The Tower of Hercules stands at the entrance of A Coruña (La Coruna) harbour in the Galicia province of Spain. The tower features in several medieval legends of the Roman demigod, Hercules. Within the tower site there is also a sculpture park, Iron Age rock carvings and a Muslim cemetery. ▶

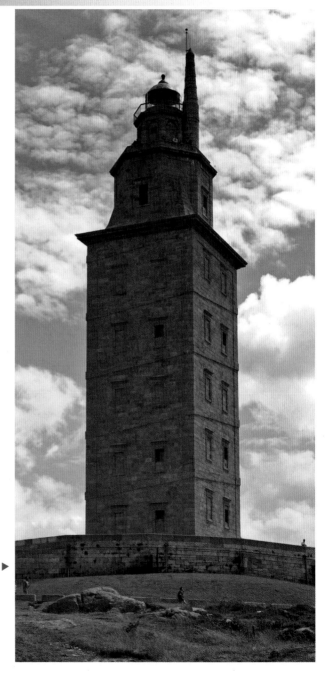

World Heritage site since

• 1986 • 1987 • 1988 • 1989 • 1990 • 1991 • 1992 • 1993 • 1994 • 1995 • 1996 • 1997 • 1998 • 1999 • 2000 • 2001 • 2002 • 2003 • 2004 • 2005 • 2006 • 2007• 2008 • **2009**

The Dolomites
Italy

Criteria – Natural phenomena or beauty; Major stages of Earth's history;

EUROPE

Mediterranean Sea

Ionian Sea

The Dolomites form a limestone mountain range renowned for its natural beauty. They lie over an area of 1400 km² in the northern Italian Alps and include eighteen summits over 3,000 m.

The Dolomites are widely regarded as being among the most distinctive and beautiful mountain landscapes in the world and are of international importance in terms of their geomorphology and geology.

The dramatic pale, vertical peaks of the limestone range are formed in a variety of distinctive sculptural forms that is extraordinary in a global context.

The nine areas within the site present a wide range of landforms fashioned by erosion, tectonism and glaciation.

Spectacular limestone formations are characteristic to the Dolomites and include steeples, pinnacles, long, deep, narrow valleys and some of the highest vertical rock walls in the world. Dynamic processes continue to affect the area with frequent landslides, floods and avalanches.

The site also features excellent examples of the preservation of carbonate platforms, sedimentary systems from the Mesozoic era (up to 251 million years ago), with fossil records.

The mountains rise as peaks with intervening ravines, standing isolated in some places and forming sweeping panoramas in others. Talus (scree) deposits lie below, with forest- and meadow-covered foothills.

▼

World Heritage site since

1987 • 1988 • 1989 • 1990 • 1991 • 1992 • 1993 • 1994 • 1995 • 1996 • 1997 • 1998 • 1999 • 2000 • 2001 • 2002 • 2003 • 2004 • 2005 • 2006 • 2007 • 2008 • 2009 • **2010**

Australian Convict Sites
Australia

Criteria – Significance in human history;
Heritage associated with events of universal
significance

The property includes a selection of eleven
penal sites, among the thousands
established by the British Empire on
Australian soil in the eighteenth and
nineteenth centuries. The sites are spread
across Australia, from Fremantle in Western
Australia to Kingston and Arthur's Vale on
Norfolk Island in the east; and from areas
around Sydney in New South Wales in the
north, to sites located in Tasmania in the
south. Around 166,000 men, women and
children were transported to Australia over

80 years between 1787 and 1868,
condemned by British justice to
transportation to the convict colonies. Each
of the sites had a specific purpose, in terms
both of punitive imprisonment and of
rehabilitation through forced labour to help
build the colony. The property presents the
best surviving examples of large-scale
convict transportation and the colonial
expansion of European powers through the
presence and labour of convicts.

The eleven sites
feature a wide range of
buildings, from the
Parramatta riverside
residence of the first
governors of New
South Wales, with
servants' quarters; to
the barracks, prison,
dockyards and
quarries of the Port
Arthur complex.

The old penal ruins at
Kingston, Norfolk
Island
▼

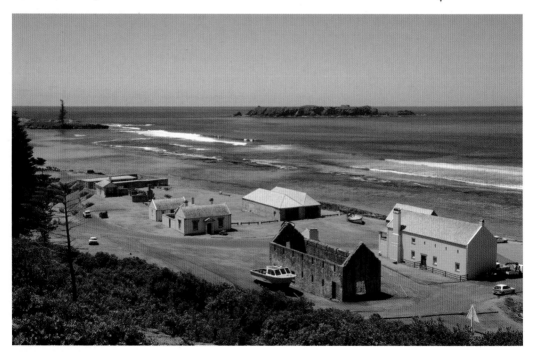

World Heritage site since

1987 • 1988 • 1989 • 1990 • 1991 • 1992 • 1993 • 1994 • 1995 • 1996 • 1997 • 1998 • 1999 • 2000 • 2001 • 2002 • 2003 • 2004 • 2005 • 2006 • 2007 • 2008 • 2009 • **2010**

São Francisco Square in the Town of São Cristóvão
Brazil

Criteria – Interchange of values; Significance in human history

São Cristóvão was founded in its present location in 1607 when Spain and Portugal were united under one crown. The Portuguese designed colonial towns to accommodate local topography, but São Cristóvão is unique in Brazil for its gridded, more formulaic, Spanish-influenced design.

São Francisco Square, in the town of São Cristóvão in northeastern Brazil, is a quadrilateral open space surrounded by substantial early buildings such as São Francisco Church and convent, the Church and Santa Casa da Misericórdia, the Provincial Palace and the associated houses of different historical periods surrounding the Square. This monumental ensemble, together with the surrounding eighteenth- and nineteenth-century houses, creates an urban landscape which reflects the history of the town since its origin. The Franciscan complex is an example of the typical architecture of the religious order developed in this area. The city was the capital of Sergipe del Rey province and attracted the administrative, religious and commercial organisation and architecture attendant on its status.

Bikini Atoll, Nuclear Test Site
Marshall Islands

Criteria – Significance in human history; Heritage associated with events of universal significance

The residual features of the testing include explosion craters, sunken warships and aircraft from simulated battle scenarios, and monitoring bunkers on the islands. Some radioactivity is still present and while much of the ecosystem has regenerated, the human impact on those in and near the blast zones was much more severe. Although deemed safe, Bikini remains uninhabited in 2010.

In the wake of World War II, in what would become the initial stage of the Cold War, the United States of America decided to begin testing nuclear weapons in the Pacific Ocean, on Bikini Atoll in the Marshall Islands. After the displacement of the local inhabitants, sixty-seven nuclear tests were carried out in the Marshall Islands on Bikini and Enewetak Atolls from 1946 to 1958, twenty-three of these on Bikini Atoll. The world's first deliverable hydrogen bomb, the Bravo, was detonated on Bikini Atoll in 1954. Bikini Atoll has conserved direct tangible evidence that is highly significant in conveying the power of the nuclear tests, i.e. the sunken ships sent to the bottom of the lagoon by the tests in 1946, remnants of testing facilities on various islands in the atoll, and the gigantic Bravo crater. The tests had major consequences on the geology and natural environment of Bikini Atoll and on the health of those who were exposed to radiation. Through its history, the atoll symbolises the dawn of the nuclear age, despite its paradoxical image of peace and of earthly paradise. This is the first site from the Marshall Islands to be inscribed on the World Heritage List.

World Heritage site since

1987 • 1988 • 1989 • 1990 • 1991 • 1992 • 1993 • 1994 • 1995 • 1996 • 1997 • 1998 • 1999 • 2000 • 2001 • 2002 • 2003 • 2004 • 2005 • 2006 • 2007 • 2008 • 2009 • **2010**

Historic Monuments of Dengfeng, in the 'Centre of Heaven and Earth'
China

Criteria – Testimony to cultural tradition; Heritage associated with events of universal significance

Mount Songshan is considered to be the central sacred mountain of China. At the foot of this 1500-m-high mountain, close to the city of Dengfeng in Henan province and spread over a 40 km² circle, stand eight clusters of buildings and sites, including three Han Que gates (remains of the oldest religious edifices in China), temples, the Zhougong Sundial Platform and the Dengfeng Observatory. Constructed over

the course of nine dynasties, these buildings are reflections of different ways of perceiving the centre of heaven and earth and the power of the mountain as a centre for religious devotion. The historical monuments of Dengfeng include some of the best examples of ancient Chinese buildings devoted to ritual, science, technology and education.

In Chinese culture, mountains were considered a link between heaven and earth and Mount Songshan was of primary importance, as a centre of mountain worship and the Confucian culture and the birthplace of Chan (Zen) Buddhism.

Sheikh Safi al-Din Khānegāh and Shrine Ensemble in Ardabil
Iran (Islamic Republic of)

Human creative genius; Interchange of values; Significance in human history

Built between the beginning of the sixteenth century and the end of the eighteenth century, this place of spiritual Sufi pilgrimage uses traditional forms of Iranian architecture. Builders knew how to get the most out of a small space in order to provide multiple amenities which include among others, a library, a mosque, a school, a mausoleum, a cistern, a hospital, kitchens, a bakery and some offices.

The site includes a pathway leading to the Sheik's sanctuary laid out over seven floors which reflect the seven stages of Sufi mysticism. These are separated by eight doors which represent the eight attitudes of Sufism. In addition, the site is comprised of richly decorated interiors and façades as well as a remarkable collection of ancient objects. It forms a rare collection of medieval Islamic architecture.

◄

Sheikh Safi Mausoleum, Ardabil

World Heritage site since

1987 • 1988 • 1989 • 1990 • 1991 • 1992 • 1993 • 1994 • 1995 • 1996 • 1997 • 1998 • 1999 • 2000 • 2001 • 2002 • 2003 • 2004 • 2005 • 2006 • 2007 • 2008 • 2009 • **2010**

China Danxia
China

Criteria – Natural phenomena or beauty; Major stages of earth's history

China Danxia is the name given in China to landscapes developed on continental red terrigenous sedimentary beds influenced by constructive forces (including uplift) and destructive forces (including weathering and erosion). The inscribed site comprises six areas found in the subtropical zone of southwest China. They are characterized by spectacular red cliffs and a range of erosional landforms, including dramatic natural pillars, towers, ravines, valleys and waterfalls. These rugged landscapes have helped to conserve subtropical broad-leaved evergreen forests, and host many species of flora and fauna, about 400 of which are considered rare or threatened.

Danxia look at first glance like limestone-based karst landscapes but unlike those are made up of red sandstones. Danxia are unique to southern China and take their name from Mount Danxia, one of the most famous examples of the landform.

Danxia landforms, Yunnan
▼

World Heritage site since

1987 • 1988 • 1989 • 1990 • 1991 • 1992 • 1993 • 1994 • 1995 • 1996 • 1997 • 1998 • 1999 • 2000 • 2001 • 2002 • 2003 • 2004 • 2005 • 2006 • 2007 • 2008 • 2009 • **2010**

Pitons, cirques and remparts of Reunion Island
France

Natural phenomena or beauty; Significant natural habitat for biodiversity

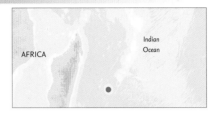

The Pitons, cirques and remparts (ramparts) of Reunion Island site coincides with the core zone of La Réunion National Park. The property covers more than 1000 km² or 40 per cent of La Réunion, an island comprising two adjoining volcanic massifs located in the southwest of the Indian Ocean. Dominated by two towering volcanic peaks, the dormant Piton de Neiges and the highly active Piton de la Fournaise, massive walls and three cliff-rimmed cirques, the property includes a great variety of rugged terrain and impressive escarpments, forested gorges and basins creating a visually striking landscape. It is the natural habitat for a wide diversity of plants, presenting a high level of endemism. There are subtropical rainforests, cloud forests and heaths creating a remarkable and visually appealing mosaic of ecosystems and landscape features.

The variations in topography, climate and altitudes on the island allow the support of a rich and diverse range of plant life, including over 800 indigenous species, many of them not found on the other Mascarene Islands.

Piton de la Fournaise, Réunion
▼

World Heritage site since

1987 • 1988 • 1989 • 1990 • 1991 • 1992 • 1993 • 1994 • 1995 • 1996 • 1997 • 1998 • 1999 • 2000 • 2001 • 2002 • 2003 • 2004 • 2005 • 2006 • 2007 • 2008 • 2009 • **2010**

Episcopal City of Albi
France

Criteria – Significance in human history;
Traditional human settlement

EUROPE

Atlantic
Ocean

On the banks of the Tarn river in southwest France, the old city of Albi reflects the culmination of a medieval architectural and urban ensemble. Today the Old Bridge (Pont-Vieux), the Saint-Salvi quarter and its church are testimony to its initial development (tenth – eleventh centuries). Following the Albigensian Crusade against the Cathar heretics (thirteenth century) it became a powerful episcopal city. Built in a unique southern French Gothic style from local brick in characteristic red and orange colours, the lofty fortified cathedral (late thirteenth century) dominates the city, demonstrating the power regained by the Roman Catholic clergy. Alongside the cathedral is the bishop's vast Palais de la Berbie, overlooking the river and surrounded by residential quarters that date back to the Middle Ages. The Episcopal City of Albi forms a coherent and homogeneous ensemble of monuments and quarters that has remained largely unchanged over the centuries.

The Episcopal City is specifically the part of Albi that grew up around the centrepiece of its austere and magnificent cathedral, Sainte-Cécile d'Albi and associated buildings. Built of red brick in Southern Gothic style between 1282 and 1480, it was intended as a statement of faith and power after the Albigensian Crusade.

Albi Cathedral
▼

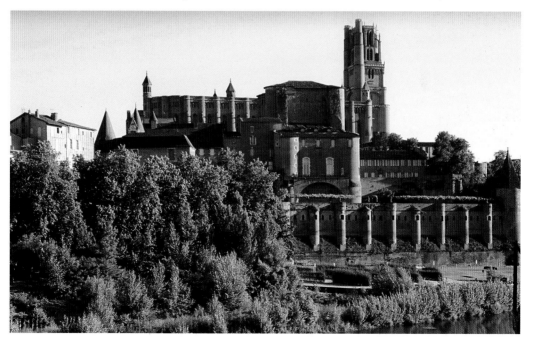

World Heritage site since

1987 • 1988 • 1989 • 1990 • 1991 • 1992 • 1993 • 1994 • 1995 • 1996 • 1997 • 1998 • 1999 • 2000 • 2001 • 2002 • 2003 • 2004 • 2005 • 2006 • 2007 • 2008 • 2009 • **2010**

Jantar Mantar
India

Criteria – Testimony to cultural tradition;
Significance in human history

The Jantar Mantar, in Jaipur, is an astronomical observation site built in the early eighteenth century. It includes a set of some twenty main fixed instruments. They are monumental examples in masonry of known instruments but which in many cases have specific characteristics of their own. Designed for the observation of astronomical positions with the naked eye, they embody several architectural and instrumental innovations. This is the most significant, most comprehensive, and the best preserved of India's historic observatories. It is an expression of the astronomical skills and cosmological concepts of the court of a scholarly prince at the end of the Mughal period.

The Jantar Mantar is said to be the world's largest stone observatory, built between 1727 and 1734 by Maharaja Jai Singh II of Jaipur. Its huge instruments include sundials, instruments to measure time, plot the skies and calculate celestial heights, courses, latitudes and longitudes. They were built according to Ptolemaic cosmology, which placed Earth at the centre of the universe.

◄
Astronomical instruments, Jantar Mantar

Papahānaumokuākea
United States of America

Criteria – Testimony to cultural tradition;
Heritage associated with events of universal significance; Major stages of Earth's history; Significant ecological and biological processes; Significant natural habitat for biodiversity

Papahānaumokuākea is a vast and isolated linear cluster of small, low-lying islands and atolls, with their surrounding ocean, roughly 250 km to the northwest of the main Hawaiian Archipelago and extending over some 1931 km. The area has deep cosmological and traditional significance for living Native Hawaiian culture, as an ancestral environment, as an embodiment

of the Hawaiian concept of kinship between people and the natural world, and as the place where it is believed that life originates and to where the spirits return after death. On two of the islands, Nihoa and Makumanamana, there are archaeological remains relating to pre-European settlement and use.

Much of the monument is made up of pelagic and deepwater habitats, with notable features such as seamounts and submerged banks, extensive coral reefs and lagoons. It is one of the largest marine protected areas in the world.

World Heritage site since

1987 • 1988 • 1989 • 1990 • 1991 • 1992 • 1993 • 1994 • 1995 • 1996 • 1997 • 1998 • 1999 • 2000 • 2001 • 2002 • 2003 • 2004 • 2005 • 2006 • 2007 • 2008 • 2009 • **2010**

Tabriz Historic Bazaar Complex
Iran (Islamic Republic of)

Criteria – Interchange of values; Testimony to
cultural tradition; Significance in human history

Tabriz, in the province of Eastern Azerbaijan,
has been a place of cultural exchange since
antiquity and its historic bazaar complex is
one of the most important commercial
centres on the Silk Road. Tabriz Historic
Bazaar Complex consists of a series of
interconnected, covered, brick structures,
buildings, and enclosed spaces for different
functions. The town and its bazaar were
already prosperous and famous in the
thirteenth century, when the town became
the capital city of the Safavid kingdom. The
city lost its status as capital in the sixteenth
century, but remained important as a
commercial hub until the end of the
eighteenth century, with the expansion of
Ottoman power. It is one of the most
complete examples of the traditional
commercial and cultural system of Iran.
Tabriz Bazaar is among the oldest in the
Middle East and the largest covered bazaar
in the world. Italian traveller Marco Polo
called the city one of the richest trading
centres in the world.

The Bazaar, Tabriz ▶

World Heritage site since

1987 • 1988 • 1989 • 1990 • 1991 • 1992 • 1993 • 1994 • 1995 • 1996 • 1997 • 1998 • 1999 • 2000 • 2001 • 2002 • 2003 • 2004 • 2005 • 2006 • 2007 • 2008 • 2009 • **2010**

Central Sector of the Imperial Citadel of Thang Long – Hanoi
Vietnam

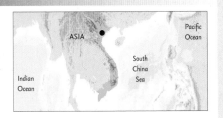

Criteria – Interchange of values; Testimony to cultural tradition; Heritage associated with events of universal significance

The Thang Long Imperial Citadel was built in the eleventh century by the Ly Viet Dynasty, marking the independence of the Dai Viet. It was constructed on the remains of a Chinese fortress dating from the seventh century, on drained land reclaimed from the Red River Delta in Hanoi. It was the centre of regional political power for almost thirteen centuries without interruption. The Imperial Citadel buildings and the remains in the 18 Hoang Dieu Archaeological Site reflect a unique South-East Asian culture specific to the lower Red River valley, at the crossroads between influences coming from China in the north and the ancient Kingdom of Champa in the south.

Most of the buildings in the imperial city of Thang Long, including the royal palaces, were destroyed by the French in the nineteenth century. Their archaeological remains are being excavated today. The parts still extant include Doan Mon gate, the dragon-adorned steps of Kinh Thiên Palace, the Hâu Lâu (Princess Palace) and the Flag Tower.

Camino Real de Tierra Adentro
Mexico

Criteria – Interchange of values; Significance in human history

Camino Real de Tierra Adentro was the Royal Inland Road, also known as the Silver Route. The inscribed property consists of fifty-five sites and five existing World Heritage sites lying along a 1400 km section of this 2600 km route, that extends north from Mexico City to Texas and New Mexico, United States of America. The route was actively used as a trade route for 300 years, from the mid-sixteenth to the nineteenth centuries, mainly for transporting silver extracted from the mines of Zacatecas, Guanajuato and San Luis Potosí, and mercury imported from Europe. Although it is a route that was motivated and consolidated by the mining industry, it also fostered the creation of social, cultural and religious links in particular between Spanish and Amerindian cultures.

The World Heritage site stretches only to the Mexico–US border. The trail encompasses many features, including chapels and haciendas, mountains and bridges, a hospital and cemetery, towns and five cities that are already World Heritage sites in their own right: Guanajuato, Mexico City, Querétaro, San Miguel and Zacatecas.

World Heritage site since

1987 • 1988 • 1989 • 1990 • 1991 • 1992 • 1993 • 1994 • 1995 • 1996 • 1997 • 1998 • 1999 • 2000 • 2001 • 2002 • 2003 • 2004 • 2005 • 2006 • 2007 • 2008 • 2009 • **2010**

Prehistoric Caves of Yagul and Mitla in the Central Valley of Oaxaca
Mexico

Criteria – Testimony to cultural tradition

This property lies on the northern slopes of the Tlacolula valley in subtropical central Oaxaca and consists of two pre-Hispanic archaeological complexes and a series of prehistoric caves and rock shelters. Some of these shelters provide archaeological and rock-art evidence for the progress of nomadic hunter-gatherers to incipient farmers. Ten-thousand-year-old Cucurbitaceae seeds in one cave, Guilá Naquitz, are considered to be the earliest known evidence of domesticated plants in the continent, while corn cob fragments from the same cave are said to be the earliest documented evidence for the domestication of maize. The cultural landscape of the Prehistoric Caves of Yagul and Mitla demonstrates the link between man and nature that gave origin to the domestication of plants in North America, thus allowing the rise of Mesoamerican civilizations.

The site has 147 caves and rock shelters set two or three hundred metres up in the Mixe Mountains. The evidence they contain of plant remains and art is thought to highlight a pivotal point in man's progress to cultivation and settled farming.

In addition to its prehistoric importance, Oaxaca was also home to the pre-Columbian Zapotec civilization from around 500 BC.

Proto-urban Site of Sarazm
Tajikistan

Criteria – Interchange of values; Testimony to cultural tradition

Sarazm, which means 'where the land begins', is an archaeological site bearing testimony to the development of human settlements in Central Asia, from the fourth millennium BC to the end of the third millennium BC. The ruins demonstrate the early development of proto-urbanization in this region. This centre of settlement, one of the oldest in Central Asia, is situated between a mountainous region suitable for cattle rearing by nomadic pastoralists, and a large valley conducive to the development of agriculture and irrigation by the first settled populations in the region. Sarazm also demonstrates the existence of commercial and cultural exchanges and trade relations with peoples over an extensive geographical area, extending from the steppes of Central Asia and Turkmenistan, to the Iranian plateau, the Indus valley and as far as the Indian Ocean.

With a local economy that encompassed agriculture and cattle-rearing, mineral-working and crafts, a prosperous early form of town developed in Sarazm. By the third millennium BC it was Central Asia's most important production centre for metal mining and working, notably copper and tin. Appropriately, the forgotten settlement was only rediscovered in 1976 when a local farmer found a copper dagger at a building site.

World Heritage site since

1987 • 1988 • 1989 • 1990 • 1991 • 1992 • 1993 • 1994 • 1995 • 1996 • 1997 • 1998 • 1999 • 2000 • 2001 • 2002 • 2003 • 2004 • 2005 • 2006 • 2007 • 2008 • 2009 • 2010

Seventeenth-century canal ring area of Amsterdam inside the Singelgracht
Netherlands

North Sea

EUROPE

Criteria – *Human creative genius; Interchange of values; Significance in human history*

The historic urban ensemble of the canal district of Amsterdam was a project for a new 'port city' built at the end of the sixteenth and beginning of the seventeenth centuries. It comprises a network of canals to the west and south of the historic old town and the medieval port that encircled the old town, and was accompanied by the repositioning inland of the city's fortified boundaries, the Singelgracht. This was a long-term programme that involved extending the city by draining the swampland, using a system of canals in concentric arcs and filling in the intermediate spaces. These spaces allowed the development of a homogeneous urban ensemble including gabled houses and numerous monuments. This urban extension was the largest and most homogeneous of its time. It was a model of large-scale town planning, and served as a reference throughout the world until the nineteenth century.

The Dutch Golden Age began in the late sixteenth century. The profits from the worldwide trading networks built by the Dutch East India and West India Companies made Amsterdam not only the leading financial centre but the world's richest city.

Canalside houses, Amsterdam.
▼

World Heritage site since

1987 • 1988 • 1989 • 1990 • 1991 • 1992 • 1993 • 1994 • 1995 • 1996 • 1997 • 1998 • 1999 • 2000 • 2001 • 2002 • 2003 • 2004 • 2005 • 2006 • 2007 • 2008 • 2009 • **2010**

Putorana Plateau
Russian Federation

Criteria – *Natural phenomena or beauty; Significant ecological and biological processes*

ASIA

Pacific Ocean

This site coincides with the area of the Putoransky State Nature Reserve, and is located in the central part of the Putorana Plateau in northern Central Siberia. It is situated about 100 km north of the Arctic Circle. The part of the plateau inscribed on the World Heritage List harbours a complete set of subarctic and arctic ecosystems in an isolated mountain range, including pristine taiga, forest tundra, tundra and arctic desert systems, as well as untouched cold-water lake and river systems. A major reindeer migration route crosses the property, which represents an exceptional, large-scale and increasingly rare natural phenomenon.

The untouched arctic and subarctic ecosystems of the Putorana Plateau are supported by an extraordinary landscape of austere and dramatic beauty. Erosion, sedimentation and tectonic uplift have all played a part in shaping its aspect of basalt, limestone and sandstone stepped massifs intercut by gorges, waterfalls and lakes, often in fjord-type formations.

Waterfall on Dulismar river, Putorana Plateau
▼

World Heritage site since

1987 • 1988 • 1989 • 1990 • 1991 • 1992 • 1993 • 1994 • 1995 • 1996 • 1997 • 1998 • 1999 • 2000 • 2001 • 2002 • 2003 • 2004 • 2005 • 2006 • 2007 • 2008 • 2009 • 2010

At-Turaif District in ad-Dir'iyah
Saudi Arabia

Criteria – Significance in human history; Traditional human settlement; Heritage associated with events of universal significance

This property was the first capital of the Saudi dynasty, in the heart of the Arabian Penisula, northwest of Riyadh. Founded in the fifteenth century, it bears witness to the Najdi architectural style, which is specific to the centre of the Arabian peninsula. From the sixteenth century onwards the area around the ad-Dir'iyah oasis was the Saudi dynasty's powerbase. Ultimately they constructed a complete system of fortifications to defend it, of which at-Turaif, built in the eighteenth century, was the citadel. In the eighteenth and early nineteenth century, its political and religious role increased, and the citadel at at-Turaif became the centre of the temporal power of the House of Saud and the spread of the Wahhabi reform inside the Muslim religion.

The property includes the remains of many palaces and an urban ensemble built on the edge of the ad-Dir'iyah oasis. In 1818 the town fell to the Ottoman Turks who destroyed it when they were forced out by the resurgent Saudis in 1824.

Saad ibn Saud Palace, Diriyah
▼

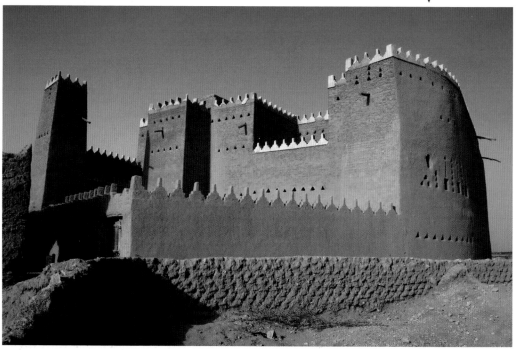

World Heritage site since

1987 • 1988 • 1989 • 1990 • 1991 • 1992 • 1993 • 1994 • 1995 • 1996 • 1997 • 1998 • 1999 • 2000 • 2001 • 2002 • 2003 • 2004 • 2005 • 2006 • 2007 • 2008 • 2009 • 2010

Phoenix Islands Protected Area
Kiribati

Criteria – Natural phenomena or beauty;
Significant ecological and biological processes

Pacific Ocean

OCEANIA

The Phoenix Island Protected Area (PIPA) is a 408,250 km² expanse of marine and terrestrial habitats in the Southern Pacific Ocean. The property encompasses the Phoenix Island Group, one of three island groups in Kiribati, and is the largest designated Marine Protected Area in the world. PIPA conserves one of the world's largest intact oceanic coral archipelago ecosystems, together with fourteen known underwater sea mounts (presumed to be extinct volcanoes) and other deep-sea habitats. The area contains approximately 800 known species of fauna, including about 200 coral species, 500 fish species, 18 marine mammals and 44 bird species. The structure and functioning of PIPA's ecosystems illustrate its pristine nature and importance as a migration route and reservoir.

The Phoenix Island group has been only intermittently populated through its history. Now the islands are virtually uninhabited again, and the almost complete lack of human influence on the marine environment has created an extensive and pristine ocean wilderness.

Coral reef near Enderbury Island, Phoenix Islands Protected Area
▼

Historic Villages of Korea: Hahoe and Yangdong
Korea, Republic of

Criteria – Testimony to cultural tradition; Heritage associated with events of universal significance

Founded between the fourteenth – fifteenth centuries, Hahoe and Yangdong are seen as the two most representative historic clan villages in the Republic of Korea. Their layout and location – sheltered by forested mountains and facing out onto a river and open agricultural fields – reflect the distinctive aristocratic Confucian culture of the early part of the Joseon Dynasty (1392–1910). The villages were located to provide both physical and spiritual nourishment from their surrounding landscapes. They include residences of the

head families, together with substantial timber-framed houses of other clan members, also pavilions, study halls, Confucian academies for learning, and clusters of one-storey mud-walled, thatched-roofed houses, formerly for commoners. The landscapes of mountains, trees and water around the village, framed in views from pavilions and retreats, were celebrated for their beauty by seventeenth- and eighteenth-century poets.

The two villages were designed to reflect Neo-Confucian philosophy in their every aspect. This even related to which group of people lived at a particular altitude or location: the aristocratic classes had tile-roofed houses built on the higher grounds further up the valleys, while the thatched dwellings of lower-class workers were built further down the slopes.

Hahoe village
▼

World Heritage site since

1987 • 1988 • 1989 • 1990 • 1991 • 1992 • 1993 • 1994 • 1995 • 1996 • 1997 • 1998 • 1999 • 2000 • 2001 • 2002 • 2003 • 2004 • 2005 • 2006 • 2007 • 2008 • 2009 • **2010**

Central Highlands of Sri Lanka

Sri Lanka

Criteria – Significant ecological and biological processes; Significant natural habitat for biodiversity

Sri Lanka's highlands are situated in the south-central part of the island. The property comprises the Peak Wilderness Protected Area, the Horton Plains National Park and the Knuckles Conservation Forest. These montane forests, where the land rises to 2,500 m above sea level, are home to an extraordinary range of flora and fauna, including several endangered species such as the western-purple-faced langur, the Horton Plains slender loris and the Sri

Lankan leopard. The richness of the Central Highlands' plant and wildlife derives not just from its ecosystem but from the uplift of the land and the landforms that developed. The region is considered a super biodiversity hotspot.

The rugged and deeply dissected terrain with its isolated valleys allowed species to develop and evolve differently across various locations. Many of these species are endemic and a relatively high proportion globally threatened.

Horton Plains, Sri Lanka
▼

World Heritage site since

1988 • 1989 • 1990 • 1991 • 1992 • 1993 • 1994 • 1995 • 1996 • 1997 • 1998 • 1999 • 2000 • 2001 • 2002 • 2003 • 2004 • 2005 • 2006 • 2007 • 2008 • 2009 • 2010 • **2011**

Longobards in Italy. Places of the power (AD 568-774)
Italy

Criteria – Interchange of values; Testimony to cultural tradition; Significance in human history

The Longobards in Italy, Places of the Power, AD 568–774 comprises seven groups of important buildings (including fortresses, churches, and monasteries) throughout the Italian Peninsula. They testify to the high achievement of the Lombards, who migrated from northern Europe and developed their own specific culture in Italy, where they ruled over vast territories in the 6th to 8th centuries. They gradually converted from nomadism and paganism to settlement and Christianity, which opened up new arenas of artistic expression, such as architecture (especially churches) and its accompanying decorative arts (such as frescoes). The Lombards' synthesis of architectural styles marked the transition from Antiquity to the European Middle Ages, drawing on the heritage of Ancient Rome, Christian spirituality, Byzantine influence and Germanic northern Europe. The serial property testifies to the Lombards' major role in the spiritual and cultural development of Medieval European Christianity, notably by bolstering the monastic movement.

The Longobards were an East Germanic tribe who, in AD 568, left their settlements in the valley of the Danube to invade Byzantine Italy. The 'Lombard Kingdom' they established (later named Kingdom of Italy) lasted until 774, when it was conquered by the Franks. Their influence on Italian political geography lives on in the name of the modern region of Lombardy.

◄

The village Cividale Del Friuli in the province of Udine, north-eastern Italy

World Heritage site since

1988 • 1989 • 1990 • 1991 • 1992 • 1993 • 1994 • 1995 • 1996 • 1997 • 1998 • 1999 • 2000 • 2001 • 2002 • 2003 • 2004 • 2005 • 2006 • 2007 • 2008 • 2009 • 2010 • **2011**

Fagus Factory in Alfeld
Germany

Criteria – Interchange of values; Significance in human history

The Fagus Factory is a ten-building complex that is a landmark in the development of modern architecture and industrial design. Serving all stages of manufacture, storage and dispatch of lasts used by the shoe industry, the complex, which is still operational today, is situated in Alfeld an der Leine in Lower Saxony. The Fagus company was founded in 1910 by Carl Benscheidt and he commissioned the architect Eduard

Werner to build his new factory. He accepted Werner's layout but in 1911 asked Walter Gropius and Adolf Meyer to design the revolutionary façades of the buildings, with their large windows and unsupported corners. The factory was constructed between 1911 and 1913, with some additions and interiors completed by 1925. The complex has been sensitively restored in recent times.

With its ground-breaking use of vast expanses of glass panels and its functionalist aesthetics, the Fagus Factory complex foreshadowed the work of the Bauhaus school (led by Walter Gropius) and is a landmark in the development of architecture in Europe and North America.

The Causses and the Cévennes, Mediterranean agro-pastoral Cultural Landscape
France

Criteria – Testimony to cultural tradition; Traditional human settlement

The 3,023 km² property, in the southern part of central France, is a mountain landscape interspersed by deep valleys that is representative of the relationship between agro-pastoral systems and their biophysical environment, notably through *drailles* (drove roads). Villages and substantial stone farmhouses on deep terraces of the Causses reflect the organization of large abbeys from the eleventh century. Mont Lozère, inside the property, is one of the last places where summer transhumance

is still practised, with farmers moving their livestock from winter pastures in the valleys to high pastures in the hills.

The Cévennes were atmospherically described in the classic travel book, Robert Louis Stevenson's *Travels with a Donkey in the Cévennes*, published in 1879, and the route that he took with his recalcitrant donkey, Modestine, can now be followed as the Stevenson Way.

World Heritage site since

1988 • 1989 • 1990 • 1991 • 1992 • 1993 • 1994 • 1995 • 1996 • 1997 • 1998 • 1999 • 2000 • 2001 • 2002 • 2003 • 2004 • 2005 • 2006 • 2007 • 2008 • 2009 • 2010 • **2011**

Residence of Bukovinian and Dalmatia Metropolitans
Ukraine

Criteria – Interchange of values; Testimony to cultural tradition; Significance in human history

The Residence of Bukovinian and Dalmatian Metropolitans at Chernivtsi represents a masterful synergy of architectural styles built by Czech architect Josef Hlavka from 1864 to 1882. The property, an outstanding example of nineteenth-century historicist architecture, also includes a seminary and monastery, dominated by the domed, cruciform Seminary Church, along with a garden and park. Hlavka created a complex of buildings that draws upon Moorish, Flemish, Byzantine and Romanesque styles and merges these with the local Bukovinian roof style of decorated, glazed tiles. The complex contains three major buildings around an open courtyard, the Metropolitan Palace in the centre, with the Seminary and church on one side and the Presbytery, which included the Guest House, Psalmist School and Icon Painting School, on the other. The interiors of the church and the Metropolitan Palace are elaborately decorated. The buildings now form part of Yuriy Fedkovych Chernivtsi National University, one of Ukraine's oldest universities, founded in 1875.

The Residence of Bukovinian and Dalmatian Metropolitans embodies the powerful presence of the Orthodox Church during the Habsburg rule of this area, reflecting the Austro-Hungarian Empire's policy of religious tolerance. The buildings mirror this in their eclectic mixture of stylistic influences.

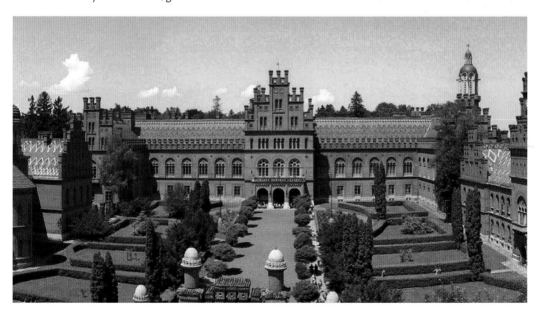

World Heritage site since

1988 • 1989 • 1990 • 1991 • 1992 • 1993 • 1994 • 1995 • 1996 • 1997 • 1998 • 1999 • 2000 • 2001 • 2002 • 2003 • 2004 • 2005 • 2006 • 2007 • 2008 • 2009 • 2010 • **2011**

Selimiye Mosque and its Social Complex
Turkey

Criteria – Human creative genius; Significance in human history

The square Selimiye Mosque, with its single great dome and four slender minarets, dominates the skyline of the former Ottoman capital of Edirne in western Turkey, close to Greece and Bulgaria. The mosque was commissioned by Sultan Selim II and built between 1568 and 1575, although, sadly, Selim died a few months before the mosque was completed. Sinan, the most famous Ottoman architect in the sixteenth century, considered the complex, which includes madrasas (Islamic schools), a covered market, clock house, outer courtyard and library, to be his best work. The interior decoration using Iznik tiles from the peak period of their production testifies to an art form that remains unsurpassed in this material. The complex is considered to be the most harmonious expression ever achieved of the Ottoman külliye, a group of buildings constructed around a mosque and managed as a single institution, and is a high point of Ottoman architecture.

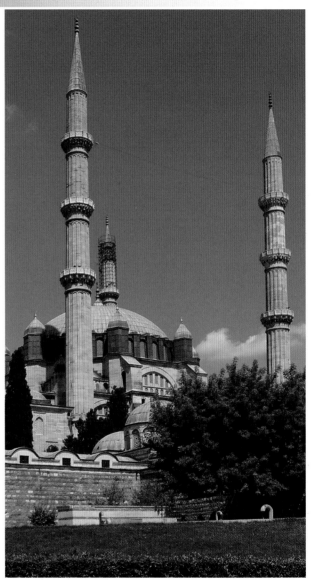

The dome of the Selimiye Mosque spans 31.3 m and is over 43 m high, while the elegant and narrow minarets are 71 m high.

Internally the great dome is supported by eight massive pillars that form an octagon within the square floor plan of the mosque.

World Heritage site since

1988 • 1989 • 1990 • 1991 • 1992 • 1993 • 1994 • 1995 • 1996 • 1997 • 1998 • 1999 • 2000 • 2001 • 2002 • 2003 • 2004 • 2005 • 2006 • 2007 • 2008 • 2009 • 2010 • **2011**

Historic Bridgetown and its Garrison
Barbados

Criteria – Interchange of values; Testimony to cultural tradition; Significance in human history

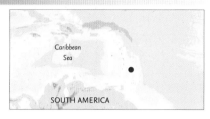

Bridgetown is the capital of Barbados and its historic centre provides an outstanding and well-preserved example of British colonial architecture from the seventeenth–nineteenth centuries, which testifies to the spread of Great Britain's Atlantic colonial empire. The property also includes the nearby military garrison which consists of numerous historic buildings. The garrison was created in the late eighteenth century around Charles Fort, which dates from 1650

and St Ann's Castle (from 1707). Parts of the garrison wall survive as do the Main Guard House, the Drill Hall and the Soldiers' and Officers' Barracks. With its serpentine urban layout, Bridgetown provides a different approach to colonial town-planning compared to the Spanish and Dutch colonial cities of the region, which were built along a grid plan.

The historic core of Bridgetown includes the island's Parliament Building which dates from the 1870s (the Parliament itself was established in 1639), St Michael's Cathedral, which dates from 1629, and the Lord Nelson Statue, in National Heroes Square, which was erected in 1813, one of the first monuments to the great sailor.

León Cathedral
Nicaragua

Criteria – Interchange of values; Significance in human history

Built between 1747 and the early nineteenth century to the design of Guatemalan architect Diego José de Porres Esquivel, León Cathedral expresses the transition from Baroque to Neoclassical architecture. The cathedral is characterized by its restrained Neoclassical interior decoration and the abundance of natural light. The vault of the Sanctuary, however, is richly ornamented. The Cathedral houses important works of art including a wooden Flemish altarpiece, and paintings of the

fourteen stations of the Way of the Cross by Nicaraguan artist Antonio Sarria (late 19th and early 20th centuries).

The strength of the construction of the 18th-century León Cathedral (Basilica de la Asuncion) has ensured that it has survived earthquakes, volcanic eruptions and wars and it remains one of Central America's largest cathedrals.

World Heritage site since

1988 • 1989 • 1990 • 1991 • 1992 • 1993 • 1994 • 1995 • 1996 • 1997 • 1998 • 1999 • 2000 • 2001 • 2002 • 2003 • 2004 • 2005 • 2006 • 2007 • 2008 • 2009 • 2010 • **2011**

Ningaloo Coast
Australia

Criteria – Natural phenomena or beauty;
Significant natural habitat for biodiversity

At 260 km, Ningaloo Reef is one of the world's largest fringing coral reefs. It supports dolphins, dugongs, manta rays, whales, turtles and whale sharks. Adjacent to the reef is an arid landscape with an extensive underground karst system that houses many rare species that contribute to the exceptional diversity of the property.

The 6,045 km² marine and terrestrial property of Ningaloo Coast is on the remote western coast of Australia, approximately 1,200 km north of Perth. It includes one of the longest near-shore reefs in the world and is renowned for the annual gatherings of whale sharks, which come to the reef to feed from March to June. The area supports an abundance of marine life, including 500 species of fish, 300 species of coral and 600 species of mollusc as well as many other marine invertebrates. New species of sponges have also been recently discovered. On land the site features an extensive karst system and a network of underground caves, conduits, and groundwater streams. They support a variety of rare species that contribute to the exceptional biodiversity of the marine and terrestrial site. Many of the 630 plant species are at the end of their geographic range and are considered extremely important from an ecological perspective.

A whale shark on the Ningaloo Reef
▼

World Heritage site since

1988 • 1989 • 1990 • 1991 • 1992 • 1993 • 1994 • 1995 • 1996 • 1997 • 1998 • 1999 • 2000 • 2001 • 2002 • 2003 • 2004 • 2005 • 2006 • 2007 • 2008 • 2009 • 2010 • **2011**

West Lake Cultural Landscape of Hangzhou
China

Criteria – Interchange of values; Testimony to cultural tradition; Significance in human history

Leifeng Pagoda is a five-storey octagonal pagoda built on Sunset Hill on the southern side of the West Lake. Originally built in 975 by Qian Hongchu, King of Wuyue, to celebrate the birth of a son, it was badly damaged by Japanese pirates during the Ming dynasty and finally collapsed in 1924; it has recently been reconstructed.

The West Lake Cultural Landscape of Hangzhou, comprising the West Lake and the hills surrounding it on three sides, has inspired famous poets, scholars and artists since the ninth century. It comprises numerous temples, pagodas, pavilions, gardens and ornamental trees, as well as causeways and artificial islands. These additions have been made to improve the landscape west of the city of Hangzhou to the south of the Yangtze river. The

West Lake has an area of around 6 km^2 – its largest island is called Three Ponds Mirroring the Moon and its oldest is the Mid-Lake Pavilion. The West Lake has influenced garden design in the rest of China as well as Japan and Korea over the centuries and bears an exceptional testimony to the cultural tradition of improving landscapes to create a series of vistas reflecting an idealized fusion between humans and nature.

Sunset at West Lake (Xi Hu), Hangzhou
▼

World Heritage site since

1988 • 1989 • 1990 • 1991 • 1992 • 1993 • 1994 • 1995 • 1996 • 1997 • 1998 • 1999 • 2000 • 2001 • 2002 • 2003 • 2004 • 2005 • 2006 • 2007 • 2008 • 2009 • 2010 • **2011**

Fort Jesus, Mombasa
Kenya

Criteria – Interchange of values; Traditional human settlement

Fort Jesus, built by the Portuguese in 1593–1596 to the designs of Giovanni Battista Cairati to protect the port of Mombasa, is one of the most outstanding and well-preserved examples of sixteenth-century Portuguese military fortification and is a landmark in the history of this type of construction. The fort's layout and form reflected the Renaissance ideal that perfect proportions and geometric harmony are to be found in the human body – and when seen from above it does indeed have a human shape.

Fort Jesus was the first colonial fort in Africa designed to withstand cannon attack. Declared a national monument in 1958, the fort had been used as a prison by the British and as a slave market by the Arab rulers of Mombasa after it fell to the Omanis in 1698.

Saloum Delta
Senegal

Criteria – Testimony to cultural tradition; Significance in human history; Traditional human settlement

The Saloum Delta area of Senegal is on the Atlantic coast over 100 km south of Dakar. Fishing and shellfish gathering have sustained human life in the 5,000 km² property over the centuries. The site comprises brackish channels encompassing over 200 islands and islets, mangrove forest, an Atlantic marine environment, and dry forest. The site is marked by 218 shellfish mounds, some of them several hundred metres long, produced by its human inhabitants over the ages. Burial sites on twenty-eight of the mounds take the form of tumuli where remarkable artefacts have been found. They are important for our understanding of cultures from the various periods of the delta's occupation and testify to the history of human settlement along the coast of West Africa.

The Saloum Delta property includes the Saloum Biosphere Reserve, designated by UNESCO in 1982, which is dominated by mangroves and also contains sand dunes, forests and sand islands. There are active community-based schemes to safeguard the mangroves and to encourage reforestation.

World Heritage site since

1988 • 1989 • 1990 • 1991 • 1992 • 1993 • 1994 • 1995 • 1996 • 1997 • 1998 • 1999 • 2000 • 2001 • 2002 • 2003 • 2004 • 2005 • 2006 • 2007 • 2008 • 2009 • 2010 • **2011**

Konso Cultural Landscape
Ethiopia

Criteria – Testimony to cultural tradition;
Traditional human settlement

Konso Cultural Landscape is a 55 km²
arid property of contoured stone-walled
terraces (kabata), pictured top right, and
fortified settlements in the Konso highlands
of Ethiopia. It constitutes a spectacular
example of a living cultural tradition
stretching back twenty-one generations
(more than 400 years) adapted to its
dry hostile environment. The landscape
demonstrates the shared values, social
cohesion and engineering knowledge of its
communities. The Konso live in dry-stone
walled towns (paletea) located on high hills
selected for their strategic and defensive
advantage and which are remarkable for the
beauty and simplicity of their workmanship,
constructed entirely from local natural
materials. In the centre of communities are
the moras, community meeting places, and
the pafta, where adult males sleep at night,
in case they need to protect their settlement.
The paletea are ringed by dry-stone walls,
at least a metre thick and three metres
high. Stone steles in the towns express a
complex system of marking the passing of
generations of leaders.

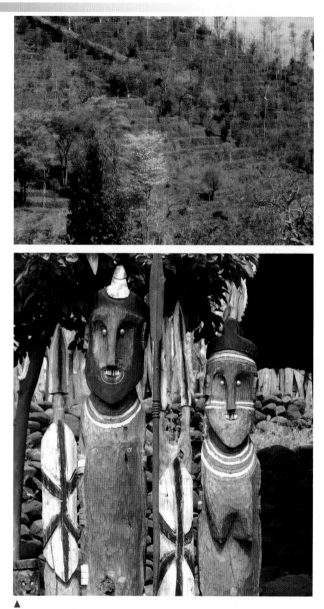

▲
The Konso Cultural Landscape also features anthropomorphic wooden
statues (waka) – grouped to represent respected members of their communities
and particularly heroic events – which are an exceptional living testimony to
funerary traditions that are on the verge of disappearing.

World Heritage site since

1988 • 1989 • 1990 • 1991 • 1992 • 1993 • 1994 • 1995 • 1996 • 1997 • 1998 • 1999 • 2000 • 2001 • 2002 • 2003 • 2004 • 2005 • 2006 • 2007 • 2008 • 2009 • 2010 • **2011**

Wadi Rum Protected Area
Jordan

Criteria – Testimony to cultural tradition;
Traditional human settlement; Natural
phenomena or beauty

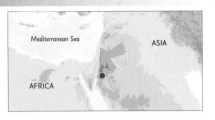

Wadi Rum is the largest wadi, or dry river
valley, in Jordan, covering an area of
740 km². Situated close to the border
with Saudi Arabia, this dramatic desert
wilderness has a wide range of natural and
cultural treasures.

The landscape features sandstone and
granite mountains that rise sharply to
heights of over 1,700 m from wide sandy
valleys. Narrow gorges and fissures have
been carved through the rocks and there

are many natural arches and caves. There
are more than 25,000 rock carvings with
20,000 inscriptions attesting to 12,000
years of human occupation and interaction
with the natural environment. They trace
the evolution of human thought and the
early development of the alphabet. The
site illustrates the evolution of pastoral,
agricultural and urban activity in the region.

T.E. Lawrence helped
secure the support
of the Wadi Rum
Bedouin tribes during
the Arab Revolt in
1917/18, and he made
several references to
Wadi Rum in his book
*The Seven Pillars of
Wisdom*. This book's
title was inspired
by one of Rum's
most spectacular
mountains.

World Heritage site since

1988 • 1989 • 1990 • 1991 • 1992 • 1993 • 1994 • 1995 • 1996 • 1997 • 1998 • 1999 • 2000 • 2001 • 2002 • 2003 • 2004 • 2005 • 2006 • 2007 • 2008 • 2009 • 2010 • **2011**

Cultural Sites of Al Ain (Hafit, Hili, Bidaa Bint Saud and Oases Areas)
United Arab Emirates

Criteria – Testimony to cultural tradition; Significance in human history; Traditional human settlement

The Cultural Sites of Al Ain (Hafit, Hili, Bidaa Bint Saud and Oases Areas) constitute a serial property that testifies to sedentary human occupation of a desert region since the Neolithic period with vestiges of many prehistoric cultures. Remarkable structures in the property include circular stone tombs (ca. 2500 BC), wells and a wide range of adobe constructions: residential buildings, towers, palaces and administrative buildings. Hili moreover features one of the oldest examples of the sophisticated aflaj irrigation system which dates back to the Iron Age. This remarkable engineering feat is not only significant as a method of transporting water, but also for the way in which it allowed settlements to develop. The property provides important testimony to the transition of cultures in the region from hunting and gathering to a sedentary way of life.

Excavations of one of the tombs at Hili discovered pottery with parallels to the Kulli culture of southern Baluchistan and relief carvings of humans and animals. The tomb also features two 5,000-year-old petroglyphs – one of two people and an oryx, another of two cheetahs catching a gazelle.

The Persian Garden
Iran (Islamic Republic of)

Criteria – Human creative genius; Interchange of values; Testimony to cultural tradition; Significance in human history; Heritage associated with events of universal significance

The Persian Garden in the Islamic Republic of Iran is a property that includes nine separate gardens in as many provinces. These exemplify the diversity of Persian garden designs that evolved and adapted to different climate conditions while retaining principles that have their roots in the times of Cyrus the Great, king of Persia from ca. 558–529 BC. Always divided into four sectors, with water playing an important role for both irrigation and ornamentation, the Persian garden was conceived to symbolize Eden and the four Zoroastrian elements of sky, earth, water and plants. These gardens, dating back to different periods since the 6th century BC, also feature buildings, pavilions and walls, as well as sophisticated irrigation systems. The harmony and beauty of the properties have created an international legacy, influencing the art of garden design as far as India and Spain.

The classic Persian garden originated as a place to seek both spiritual peace and to enjoy communal recreation with friends. The simple but formal rules of design intended to maximize all that the garden could offer. The Old East Iranian word for garden or enclosed space is 'pairidaeza' which ultimately gave rise to the English word 'paradise'.

World Heritage site since

1988 • 1989 • 1990 • 1991 • 1992 • 1993 • 1994 • 1995 • 1996 • 1997 • 1998 • 1999 • 2000 • 2001 • 2002 • 2003 • 2004 • 2005 • 2006 • 2007 • 2008 • 2009 • 2010 • **2011**

Archaeological Sites of the Island of Meroe
Sudan

Criteria – Interchange of values; Testimony to cultural tradition; Significance in human history; Traditional human settlement

The Archaeological Sites of the Island of Meroe occupy a semi-desert landscape between the Nile and Atbara rivers. From the 8th century BC to the 4th century AD this was the heartland of the Kingdom of Kush, a major power that controlled a vast empire extending from the Mediterranean to the heart of Africa. The property consists of the royal city of the Kushite kings at Meroe, near the River Nile, and the cemetery, and the religious sites of Naqa and Musawwarat es Sufra. It was the seat of the rulers who occupied Egypt for close to a century and features more than two hundred pyramids in three groups as well as temples, domestic buildings and major installations connected to water management. The property testifies to the exchange between the art, architectures, religions and languages of local and outside cultures.

The development of skill in iron working helped Meroe grow into a wealthy kingdom that traded with societies as far away as India and China. At the empire's peak, the rulers of Meroe controlled more than 1,000 km of the Nile valley.

Pyramids of the Kushite rulers at Meroe
▼

World Heritage site since

1988 • 1989 • 1990 • 1991 • 1992 • 1993 • 1994 • 1995 • 1996 • 1997 • 1998 • 1999 • 2000 • 2001 • 2002 • 2003 • 2004 • 2005 • 2006 • 2007 • 2008 • 2009 • 2010 • **2011**

Citadel of the Ho Dynasty
Vietnam

Criteria – Interchange of values; Significance in
human history

The citadel was an
impressive military
stronghold, with walls
5 m high and 3 m thick
protected by deep
ditches. It was also the
site of the royal palace
and the seat of the Ho
Dynasty government
for ten years.

The late fourteenth century Ho Dynasty
citadel is in Hoa Binh Province,
approximately 150 km west of Hanoi.
The citadel's construction testifies to the
flowering of neo-Confucianism in Vietnam
and its spread to other parts of east Asia.
This followed strict feng shui principles, with
the site lying in a landscape of great scenic
beauty on an axis joining the Tuong Son and
Don Son mountains in a plain between the
Ma and Buoi rivers. The rectangular citadel
measured 870.5 m by 883.5 m in length
and had four massive gates. Uniquely
for a building of that time, it was built
from blocks of green granite. The citadel
buildings represent an outstanding example
of a new style of south-east Asian
imperial city.

Ancient Villages of
Northern Syria
Syrian Arab Republic

Criteria – Testimony to cultural tradition;
Significance in human history; Traditional
human settlement

The Ancient Villages
were close to the
great Christian city
of Antioch (now in
Turkey), trade with
which helped the
area support a large
and prosperous
population. After the
Islamic conquest,
Damascus took over
as the capital. The
region subsequently
went into decline,
leaving the villages as
ghost towns.

Some forty villages grouped in eight parks
situated in northwestern Syria provide
remarkable testimony to rural life in late
Antiquity and during the Byzantine period.
Abandoned in the eighth–tenth centuries,
the villages have remained remarkably well-
preserved over the centuries, and among
the ruins are some of the greatest treasures
of Byzantine architecture to be found in the
ancient world. The architectural remains,
which date from the 1st to 7th centuries,
include dwellings, temples, churches,
cisterns and bathhouses that provide a
unique record of Byzantine countryside
habitation. The relict cultural landscape of
the villages also constitutes an important
illustration of the transition from the ancient
pagan world of the Roman Empire to
Byzantine Christianity. Vestiges illustrating
hydraulic techniques, protective walls and
Roman agricultural plot plans furthermore
offer testimony to the inhabitants' mastery
of agricultural production.

World Heritage site since

1988 • 1989 • 1990 • 1991 • 1992 • 1993 • 1994 • 1995 • 1996 • 1997 • 1998 • 1999 • 2000 • 2001 • 2002 • 2003 • 2004 • 2005 • 2006 • 2007 • 2008 • 2009 • 2010 • **2011**

Kenya Lake System in the Great Rift Valley
Kenya

Criteria – Natural phenomena or beauty;
Significant ecological and biological processes;
Significant natural habitat for biodiversity

The Kenya Lake System in the Great Rift Valley is a natural property of outstanding beauty that is home to some of Earth's highest avian diversity. The site comprises three inter-linked relatively shallow lakes (Lake Bogoria, Lake Nakuru and Lake Elementaita) in basins on the floor of the Rift Valley Province of Kenya and covers a total area of 320 km². It is the single most important foraging site for the lesser flamingo anywhere, and a major nesting and breeding ground for great white pelicans. It offers a sanctuary to thirteen globally threatened bird species. Many of Africa's iconic mammal species, including black rhinos, giraffes, lions, Rothschild's giraffe, greater kudu, wild dogs and cheetahs are also found here in abundance. The variety of wildlife in the Kenya Lake System makes it valuable for the study of ecological processes of major importance.

The three lakes are shallow and are hydro-geologically connected through sub-surface seepage of water. They are also alkaline and support the abundant growth of the green algae (Spirulina platensis). This is the favoured food of the lesser flamingo, which congregates on the lakes in vast numbers.

A great white pelican takes to the air with lesser flamingos in the background, Lake Nakuru.
▼

World Heritage site since

1988 • 1989 • 1990 • 1991 • 1992 • 1993 • 1994 • 1995 • 1996 • 1997 • 1998 • 1999 • 2000 • 2001 • 2002 • 2003 • 2004 • 2005 • 2006 • 2007 • 2008 • 2009 • 2010 • **2011**

Prehistoric Pile Dwellings around the Alps
Austria, France, Germany, Italy, Slovenia, Switzerland

Criteria – Testimony to cultural tradition; Traditional human settlement

This serial property of 111 small individual sites encompasses the remains of prehistoric pile-dwelling (or stilt house) settlements in and around the Alps. The dwellings were built from around 5000 to 500 BC on the edges of lakes, rivers or wetlands and are spread across six countries. Excavations, only conducted in some of the sites, have yielded evidence that provides insight into life in prehistoric times during the Neolithic and Bronze Age

in Alpine Europe and the way communities interacted with their environment. Fifty-six of the sites are located in Switzerland. The settlements are a unique group of exceptionally well-preserved and culturally rich archaeological sites, which constitute one of the most important sources for the study of early agrarian societies in the region.

Although many of the sites are either under water or buried under thick layers of sediments, dendrochronologists have been able to precisely date the wooden remains of architectural elements. This has allowed scientists to track the spatial and social development of the prehistoric villages over time.

Cultural Landscape of the Serra de Tramuntana
Spain

Criteria – Interchange of values; Significance in human history; Traditional human settlement

The Cultural Landscape of the Serra de Tramuntana is located on a sheer-sided mountain range parallel to the north-western coast of the island of Mallorca. Millennia of agriculture in an environment with scarce resources has transformed the terrain, and displays an articulated network of devices for the management of water revolving around farming units of feudal origins. The landscape is marked by agricultural terraces and inter-connected water works – including water mills – as well as dry-stone constructions and farms.

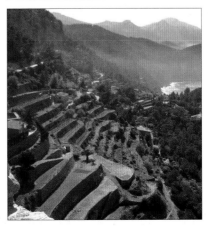

In addition to its cultural heritage, the area is rich in important wildlife, including a wide range of birds of prey such as the osprey and Eleonora's falcon, which visit from Madagascar. The Mallorcan midwife toad was believed extinct until it was rediscovered in 1977 in some of the most remote pools and watercourses of the Serra de Tramuntana.

World Heritage site since

1988 • 1989 • 1990 • 1991 • 1992 • 1993 • 1994 • 1995 • 1996 • 1997 • 1998 • 1999 • 2000 • 2001 • 2002 • 2003 • 2004 • 2005 • 2006 • 2007 • 2008 • 2009 • 2010 • **2011**

Hiraizumi – Temples, Gardens and Archaeological Sites Representing the Buddhist Pure Land

Japan

Criteria – Interchange of values; Heritage associated with events of universal significance

Hiraizumi – Temples, Gardens and Archaeological Sites Representing the Buddhist Pure Land comprises five sites, including the sacred Mount Kinkeisan and the temple complex of Chūson-ji. It features vestiges of government offices dating from the 11th and 12th centuries when Hiraizumi was the administrative centre of the northern realm of Japan and rivalled Kyoto. The realm was based on the cosmology of Pure Land Buddhism, which spread to Japan in the 8th century. It represented the pure land of Buddha that people aspire to after death, as well as peace of mind in this life. In combination with indigenous Japanese nature worship and Shintoism, Pure Land Buddhism developed a concept of planning and garden design that was unique to Japan.

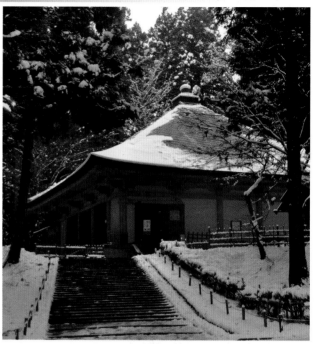

Chūson-ji building containing the Konjikidō (or Golden Hall) ▲

Mōtsū-ji Pure Land garden ▶

World Heritage site since

1988 • 1989 • 1990 • 1991 • 1992 • 1993 • 1994 • 1995 • 1996 • 1997 • 1998 • 1999 • 2000 • 2001 • 2002 • 2003 • 2004 • 2005 • 2006 • 2007 • 2008 • 2009 • 2010 • **2011**

Ogasawara Islands
Japan
Criteria – Significant ecological and biological processes

The Ogasawara Islands form an archipelago some 1,000 km directly south of Tokyo, Japan. The property numbers more than thirty subtropical and tropical islands, clustered in three groups and covers surface area of 74 km². The landscape is dominated by subtropical forest types and sclerophyllous shrublands surrounded by steep cliffs. There are more than 440 species of native vascular plants with exceptionally concentrated rates of endemism as high as 70% in woody plants. The islands are the habitat for more than 100 recorded native land snail species, over 90% of which are endemic to the islands. The Islands serve as an outstanding example of the ongoing evolutionary processes in oceanic island ecosystems.

The Ogasawara Islands form a distinct subtropical moist broadleaf forest ecoregion, with a high degree of biodiversity and endemism. The islands have never been connected with a continent, which has allowed evolution to produce some unique species and ecosystems. The archipelago is sometimes called the 'Galápagos of the Orient'.

Coffee Cultural Landscape of Colombia
Colombia
Criteria – Traditional human settlement; Heritage associated with events of universal significance

This is an exceptional example of a sustainable and productive coffee-growing landscape that was established in the nineteenth century and which is a strong symbol for coffee growing areas worldwide. Within the departments of Antioquia, Caldas, Risaralda, Quindío, and Valle del Cauca it encompasses six farming areas, which include eighteen urban centres on the foothills of the western and central ranges of the Cordillera de los Andes in the west of Colombia. The traditional method of coffee growing is in small plots in the high forest between 1,200 and 1,800 m above sea level and illustrates the way farmers have adapted cultivation to difficult mountain conditions. The urban areas, mainly situated on the relatively flat tops of hills above sloping coffee fields, are characterized by the architecture of the Antioquian colonization with Spanish influence. Building materials were, and remain in some areas, cob and pleated cane for the walls with clay tiles for the roofs.

The majority of Colombia's premium coffee is grown in the Coffee Cultural Landscape. Coffee production is a major component of the Colombian economy and over 80,000 people work in its cultivation.

World Heritage site since

1988 • 1989 • 1990 • 1991 • 1992 • 1993 • 1994 • 1995 • 1996 • 1997 • 1998 • 1999 • 2000 • 2001 • 2002 • 2003 • 2004 • 2005 • 2006 • 2007 • 2008 • 2009 • 2010 • **2011**

Petroglyphic Complexes of the Mongolian Altai
Mongolia

Criteria – Testimony to cultural tradition

The numerous rock carvings and funerary monuments found in these three sites illustrate the development of culture in Mongolia over a period of 12,000 years. The petroglyphs are engraved, scratched, gouged or pecked into the surface of bedrock or boulders. The earliest images reflect a time (11,000–6,000 BC) when the area was partly forested and the valley provided a habitat for hunters of large game. Later images show the transition to herding as the dominant way of life. The most recent images show the transition to a horse-dependent nomadic lifestyle during the early first millennium BC, the Scythian period and the later Turkic period (seventh and eighth centuries AD). The carvings contribute valuably to our understanding of pre-historic communities in northern Asia.

The petroglyphs feature elk, deer, wild goats, horses and hunters, either as single images or compositions of anything up to several hundred motifs. The earliest carvings date from the Late Pleistocene. The property also includes many funerary mounds and groups of standing stones. ▶

Nomads driving cattle in the Mongolian Altai. ▲

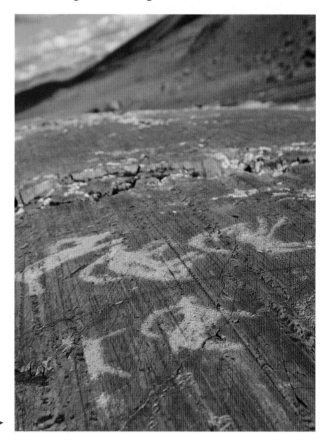

World Heritage site since

1989 • 1990 • 1991 • 1992 • 1993 • 1994 • 1995 • 1996 • 1997 • 1998 • 1999 • 2000 • 2001 • 2002 • 2003 • 2004 • 2005 • 2006 • 2007 • 2008 • 2009 • 2010 • 2011 • **2012**

Lena Pillars Nature Park
Russian Federation
Criteria – Major stages of Earth's history

Lena Pillars Nature Park features spectacular 100-m-high rock columns along the banks of the Lena River in Yakutia. The rock pillars were produced by the region's extreme continental climate, which has an annual temperature range of almost 100 °C (from -60 °C in winter to +40 °C in summer). The pillars form rocky buttresses isolated from each other by deep and steep gullies developed by frost shattering directed along intervening joints. Penetration of water from the surface has facilitated freeze–thaw action, which has widened gullies between pillars leading to their isolation.

Stratigraphic analysis of the area's unique geology has led to the discovery of the earliest currently recorded mass-extinction events in the Earth's history: the Sinsk and Toyonian events, both named after the Lena Pillars' area. The site also contains a wealth of Cambrian fossil remains of numerous species, some of them unique.

Sites of Human Evolution at Mount Carmel: The Nahal Me'arot / Wadi el-Mughara Caves
Israel

Criteria – Testimony to cultural tradition;
Traditional human settlement

Located in the steep-sided Nahal Me'arot/ Wadi el-Mughara valley on the western side of the Mount Carmel range, Tabun, Jamal, el-Wad and Skhul caves contain cultural deposits representing the past half a million years of human evolution. The site is part of one of the best-preserved fossilized reefs of the Mediterranean region and is recognized as providing a definitive chronological framework at a key period of human development. Archaeological evidence covers the appearance of modern humans, deliberate burials, early manifestations of stone architecture and the transition from hunter-gathering to agriculture and animal husbandry. The site demonstrates the unique existence of both Neanderthals and early anatomically modern humans within the same Middle Palaeolithic cultural framework, the Mousterian, and provides an archive of early human life in Southwest Asia.

The archaeological knowledge generated at the Nahal Me'arot/ Wadi el-Mughara site has established the caves and their region as crucial to understanding the biological, behavioural and cultural origins of humans. Research has been ongoing since 1928, and continues to promote multidisciplinary scientific dialogue.

World Heritage site since

1989 • 1990 • 1991 • 1992 • 1993 • 1994 • 1995 • 1996 • 1997 • 1998 • 1999 • 2000 • 2001 • 2002 • 2003 • 2004 • 2005 • 2006 • 2007 • 2008 • 2009 • 2010 • 2011 • **2012**

Rio de Janeiro: Carioca Landscapes between the Mountain and the Sea
Brazil

Criteria – Traditional human settlement; Heritage associated with events of universal significance

Rio is a unique example of a natural landscape that has developed over half a millennium from the interactions brought about by human settlements and the development of the city. The quality of the successive interventions to a site of such great beauty has given rise to an extraordinary set of urban public landscapes, composed of gardens, parks and protected natural landmarks whose natural scientific significance and cultural associations grant them unique value.

The site encompasses the key natural elements that have shaped and inspired the development of the city: from the highest points of the Tijuca National Park's mountains down to the sea. They also include the Botanical Gardens, established in 1808, Corcovado Mountain with its celebrated statue of Christ, and the hills around Guanabara Bay, including the extensive designed landscapes along Copacabana Bay which have contributed to the outdoor living culture of this spectacular city.

Rio de Janeiro is also internationally recognized for the artistic inspiration it has provided to musicians, landscapers and urbanists.

Scientific knowledge of the native plant life, allied to the Romantic ideals prevalent in the second half of the nineteenth century, and increased concerns about environmental preservation led to the reforestation of the Tijuca massif, resulting in an urban forest of unique features. The man-made transformations of the landscape, the mountain and the seafront have made the city a point of reference the world over.

Aerial view of Christ the Redeemer statue on Corcovado Mountain, Rio de Janeiro ▼

Bassari Country: Bassari, Fula and Bedik Cultural Landscapes
Senegal

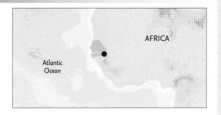

Criteria – Testimony to cultural tradition; Traditional human settlement; Heritage associated with events of universal significance

This site is in the barely accessible northern foothills of the Fouta Djallon Massif in southeastern Senegal, close to the Mali and Guinean borders. The Bassari, Fula and Bedik settled here from the eleventh to the nineteenth centuries. Their agro-pastoral, social, ritual and spiritual practices represent an original response to environmental constraints and human pressures. Terraces and rice paddies interspersed with villages form the Bassari landscape, while villages of dense groups of huts with steeped thatched roofs characterize the Bedik settlements.

Bassari villages were grouped on higher land, so as to control the plains, and consisted of round thatched huts built around a central space. In the middle of the village was a larger hut, called the *ambofor*, where youths – male and female – lived together and where ritual objects were kept.

Chengjiang Fossil Site
China

Criteria – Major stages of Earth's history

The Chengjiang Fossil Site in Yunnan province presents an exceptional record of the rapid diversification of life on Earth 530 million years ago, when almost all of today's major animal groups emerged. It is the most complete record of an early Cambrian marine ecosystem, with food webs capped by sophisticated predators. The quality of the preserved biota is excellent, displaying the anatomy of hard and soft tissues in a very wide variety of organisms, invertebrate and vertebrate. The site documents at least sixteen phyla and a variety of enigmatic groups as well as about 196 species.

Today the area is largely covered with secondary forest and shrubs and there is no industrial activity or permanent human habitation within the site.

The 5 km² property opens a palaeobiological window of great significance to scholarship. The discoveries here range from algae, through sponges and cnidarians to numerous bilaterian phyla, including the earliest known chordates, the phylum to which all vertebrates belong. Almost all of the soft-bodied species discovered at Chengjiang are unknown elsewhere.

World Heritage site since

1989 • 1990 • 1991 • 1992 • 1993 • 1994 • 1995 • 1996 • 1997 • 1998 • 1999 • 2000 • 2001 • 2002 • 2003 • 2004 • 2005 • 2006 • 2007 • 2008 • 2009 • 2010 • 2011 • **2012**

Masjed-e Jāmé of Isfahan
Iran (Islamic Republic of)
Criteria – Interchange of values

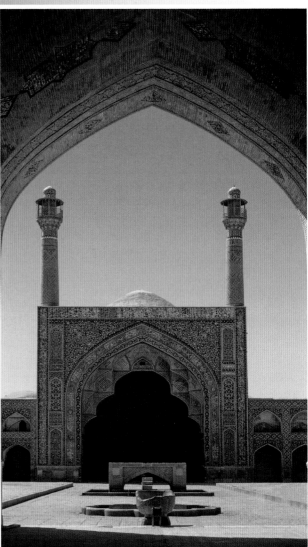

Located in the historic centre of Isfahan, the Masjed-e Jāmé (Friday, or congregational, mosque) is the centrepiece of Islamic religious life in the city. It is the oldest preserved complex of its type in Iran and a prototype for later mosque designs throughout Central Asia. Building started around AD 841 under the Abbasids with the most significant structures dating from the eleventh and twelfth centuries under the Seljuqs. It is a composite of a variety of Iranian Islamic styles of construction and decoration and has even been referred to as a 'museum of mosque architecture'. Upon entering the mosque, the dominant space of the monument is its sahn (courtyard) of 60 m by 70 m, with its four impressive iwans (vaulted halls opening into the courtyard). It was the first Islamic building to adapt this courtyard layout of Sassanid palaces to Islamic religious architecture. The site also features remarkable decorative details representative of stylistic developments over more than a thousand years of Islamic art.

Framed by an entrance arch, the courtyard and minarets of the Friday ▲ mosque in Isfahan, Iran.

The eleventh-century Nezam al-Molk Dome set new engineering standards as the first double-shell ribbed-dome structure in the Islamic world. The smaller but more elaborate Taj al-Molk Dome followed soon after. These domes of the Masjed-e Jāmé influenced domes of later periods and regions of the Islamic world.

World Heritage site since

1989 • 1990 • 1991 • 1992 • 1993 • 1994 • 1995 • 1996 • 1997 • 1998 • 1999 • 2000 • 2001 • 2002 • 2003 • 2004 • 2005 • 2006 • 2007 • 2008 • 2009 • 2010 • 2011 • **2012**

Decorated Farmhouses of Hälsingland
Sweden

Criteria – Traditional human settlement

The farmhouses of Hälsingland combine rich decorative paintings with a highly developed building tradition that reflects the considerable prosperity of the farmers. These decorated farms bear witness to a culture that has disappeared today but has been preserved in an exceptional way. As a group they do not have a parallel.

The seven listed decorative farmhouses of Hälsingland represent the zenith of a regional timber building tradition that dates back to the Middle Ages. They reflect the prosperity of independent farmers who used their wealth in the nineteenth century to build substantial new homes with elaborately decorated ancillary houses or suites of rooms reserved for festivities. The paintings represent a fusion of folk art with the styles favoured by the landed gentry of the time, including the Baroque and Rococo. Decorated by painters, including known and unknown itinerant artists, the properties represent the final flowering of a long cultural tradition.

They are part of an outstanding collection of some 1,000 well-preserved farmhouses with around 400 decorative rooms still in situ. The density of intact and preserved rooms is unparalleled within the entire Northern Taiga.

Western Ghats
India

Criteria – Significant ecological and biological processes; Significant natural habitat for biodiversity

The Western Ghats contains an exceptionally high level of biological diversity and endemism. Of the 650 tree species found in the Western Ghats, 352 are endemic. Animal diversity is also exceptional, and endangered species such as the Lion-tailed macaque, Nilgiri tahr and Nilgiri langur are unique to the area.

Older than the Himalaya mountains, the mountain chain of the Western Ghats represents geomorphic features of immense importance with unique biophysical and ecological processes. The site's high montane forest ecosystems influence the Indian monsoon weather pattern. Moderating the tropical climate of the region, it presents one of the best examples of the monsoon system in the planet. The forests of the site include some of the best representatives of non-equatorial tropical evergreen forests anywhere and are home to at least 325 globally threatened flora, fauna, bird, amphibian, reptile and fish species. It is also recognized as one of the world's eight 'hottest hotspots' of biological diversity.

World Heritage site since

1989 • 1990 • 1991 • 1992 • 1993 • 1994 • 1995 • 1996 • 1997 • 1998 • 1999 • 2000 • 2001 • 2002 • 2003 • 2004 • 2005 • 2006 • 2007 • 2008 • 2009 • 2010 • 2011 • **2012**

Sangha Trinational
Cameroon, Central African
Republic, Congo

Criteria – Significant ecological and biological
processes; Significant natural habitat for
biodiversity

The three contiguous national parks that
form Sangha lie at the nexus of Cameroon,
the Republic of the Congo and the Central
African Republic in the northwestern
Congo Basin. Much of the site is unaffected
by human activity and it features a wide
range of humid tropical forest ecosystems
with rich flora and fauna, including Nile
crocodiles and goliath tigerfish. Forest
clearings support herbaceous species and
Sangha is home to considerable populations
of forest elephants, critically endangered
western lowland gorilla, and endangered
chimpanzee. The site's environment has
preserved the continuation of ecological
and evolutionary processes on a huge scale
and has great biodiversity.

A male western lowland gorilla ▲

Sangha protects a large number
of tree species which are heavily
commercially exploited elsewhere,
such as the critically endangered
Mukulungu. With a total area of
more than 7,500 km², the park is

unlike many other protected areas in
that it is not a remaining fragment
of forest but is part of a much larger
intact and ecologically functional
landscape. This is increasingly rare
and significant in the world today.

World Heritage site since

1989 • 1990 • 1991 • 1992 • 1993 • 1994 • 1995 • 1996 • 1997 • 1998 • 1999 • 2000 • 2001 • 2002 • 2003 • 2004 • 2005 • 2006 • 2007 • 2008 • 2009 • 2010 • 2011 • **2012**

Landscape of Grand Pré
Canada

Criteria – Traditional human settlement; Heritage associated with events of universal significance

In the southern Minas Basin of Nova Scotia, the Grand Pré marshland was developed as agricultural farmland, using dykes and the *aboiteau* wooden sluice system, by French colonists (called Acadians) in the seventeenth century. The cultural landscape contains polder farmland and archaeological elements of the towns of Grand Pré and Hortonville. It is an exceptional example of the adaptation of the first European settlers to the conditions of the North American Atlantic coast.

The site is also a memorial to the Acadian way of life and an iconic place of remembrance of the Acadians' deportation, known as the Grand Dérangement, which commenced in 1755 after the British took control of the French colony of Acadia (which included Nova Scotia).

◄

The Memorial Church of Grand Pré located in the Annapolis Valley of Nova Scotia.

Pearling, Testimony of an Island Economy
Bahrain

Criteria – Testimony to cultural tradition

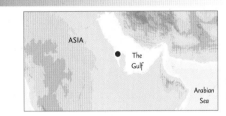

The site is the last remaining complete example of the cultural tradition of pearling and the wealth it generated at a time when the trade dominated the Gulf economy. It consists of seventeen buildings in Muharraq city, three offshore oyster beds, part of the seashore and the Qal'at Bu Mahir fortress on the southern tip of Muharraq Island, from where boats used to set off for the oyster beds. It constitutes an outstanding example of traditional utilization of the sea's resources and human interaction with the environment, which shaped both the economy and cultural identity of the island's society. The buildings listed include residences of wealthy merchants, shops, storehouses and a mosque. They have mostly survived unaltered since the collapse of the pearl industry and now bear witness to the distinctive building traditions that the industry fostered, particularly their high standard of craftsmanship in timber and plaster. In their beautiful, fragile state these buildings evoke memories of that industry and its supporting social and economic structures.

Traditional pearling shaped the single-product economy and cultural identity of Bahrain's island society. The pearl-collecting traditions of Bahrain were amongst the oldest in the world and consistently delivered pearls to the world's market for two millennia, from the second century to the 1930s, when Japan developed cultured pearls and the traditional industry collapsed.

World Heritage site since

1989 • 1990 • 1991 • 1992 • 1993 • 1994 • 1995 • 1996 • 1997 • 1998 • 1999 • 2000 • 2001 • 2002 • 2003 • 2004 • 2005 • 2006 • 2007 • 2008 • 2009 • 2010 • 2011 • **2012**

Nord–Pas de Calais Mining Basin
France

Criteria – Interchange of values; Significance in human history; Heritage associated with events of universal significance

The Nord–Pas de Calais Mining Basin is a well-preserved example of the mining and industrial landscape created by three centuries of coal extraction. It is characterized by its pitheads and their equipment, slag heaps, a dense pattern of mining communities and the urban planning of the mining towns. Significant economic and cultural values are associated with the mines' history in terms of everyday activity, the miners' living conditions, social events and accidents.

Former coal mine at Wallers Arenberg ▲

The Nord–Pas de Calais Mining Basin features collieries (the oldest of which dates from 1850) with pithead lifts, slag heaps (some of which cover 0.9 km² and exceed 140 m in height), coal transport infrastructure, railway stations, owners' and managers' houses, workers' estates and mining villages including schools, religious buildings, health and community facilities.

Gonbad-e Qābus
Iran (Islamic Republic of)

Criteria – Human creative genius; Interchange of values; Testimony to cultural tradition; Significance in human history

Visible from a great distance, this 53-m-high tomb was built in 1006 for the Ziyarid emir Qābus Ibn Voshmgir near the ancient city of Jorjan on the Gorgan River in northeast Iran. It bears testimony to the cultural exchange between Central Asian nomads and the ancient civilization of Iran. The tower is the only remaining evidence of Jorjan, which was destroyed during the Mongols' invasion in the fourteenth and fifteenth centuries.

Designed in accordance with intricate geometric and mathematical principles and constructed of unglazed fired brick, the hollow cylindrical shaft, buttressed by ten triangular flanges, tapers to a conical roof from the 17-m-diameter base. It is an outstanding example of Islamic architecture.

World Heritage site since

1989 • 1990 • 1991 • 1992 • 1993 • 1994 • 1995 • 1996 • 1997 • 1998 • 1999 • 2000 • 2001 • 2002 • 2003 • 2004 • 2005 • 2006 • 2007 • 2008 • 2009 • 2010 • 2011 • **2012**

Garrison Border Town of Elvas and its Fortifications
Portugal

Criteria – Significance in human history

Guarding the key border crossing between Portugal's capital Lisbon and Spain's capital Madrid, in an undulating, riverine landscape, the Garrison Town of Elvas was fortified extensively from the seventeenth to the nineteenth centuries to become the largest bulwarked dry-ditch system in the world. Within its walls, Elvas contains barracks and other military buildings as well as churches and monasteries. The great fortifications began when Portugal regained independence from Spain in 1640. Designed by Dutch Jesuit João Piscásio Cosmander, they are the best surviving example of the Dutch school of fortifications. The Amoreira aqueduct (built 1529–1622) is 7,504 m long and consists largely of arches arranged in up to four tiers, bringing water from the springs to the west of the town to the town fountain (Fonte da Vila) and later to the Fortress Cistern. Outlying forts built on surrounding hills ringed the town to accommodate the changing needs of defensive warfare.

The bulwarked fortifications, designed to protect Elvas against developments in modern artillery, were begun in 1643. They form an unequal polygon of twelve sides with the castle at one corner. The bulwarks are battered, surrounded by a dry ditch and counterscarp and further protected by a number of ravelins.

The Amoreira aqueduct that bought water to Elvas
▼

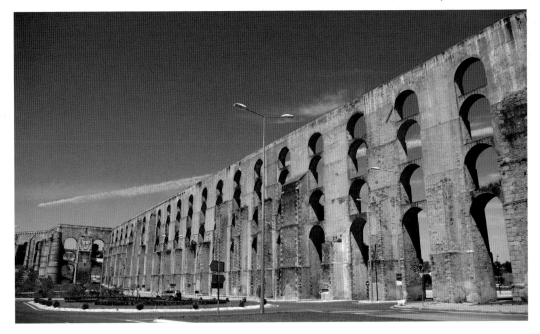

World Heritage site since

1989 • 1990 • 1991 • 1992 • 1993 • 1994 • 1995 • 1996 • 1997 • 1998 • 1999 • 2000 • 2001 • 2002 • 2003 • 2004 • 2005 • 2006 • 2007 • 2008 • 2009 • 2010 • 2011 • **2012**

Site of Xanadu
China

Criteria – Interchange of values; Testimony to cultural tradition; Significance in human history; Heritage associated with events of universal significance

Xanadu, Kublai Khan's fabled capital city in Inner Mongolia, was designed by his Chinese adviser, Liu Bingzhong in 1256, and located in accordance with feng shui principles with hills to the north and a river to the south. It comprises the Palace City, surrounded by the Imperial City laid out along a north–south axis, together with the Outer City to the west and north, the whole a square measuring 2,200 m along each side. From Xanadu, Kublai Khan established

the Yuan Dynasty that ruled China for over a century, and, following a religious debate here in 1258, Tibetan Buddhism spread over northeast Asia. After the overthrow of the Yuan dynasty by the Ming, the city was captured and destroyed in 1368. The surviving remains include fragments of temples, palaces, tombs, city walls and nomadic encampments.

The city became an important stopping place on the Silk Road, receiving many foreign envoys, among them Marco Polo from 1275 to 1292, who recorded his experiences in The Travels of Marco Polo and opened the eyes of the world to China and the marvels of Xanadu.

Archaeological Heritage of the Lenggong Valley
Malaysia

Criteria – Testimony to cultural tradition; Significance in human history

The Perak River flows through Lenggong valley, an essentially agricultural landscape threaded with traditional villages and dotted with limestone massifs. This property includes four archaeological sites in two clusters, which span close to two million years – one of the longest records of early man in a single locality and the oldest outside the African continent. It features open-air and cave sites with Palaeolithic tool workshops providing evidence of early technology. At the Bukit Bunuh site, suevite rocks created by a meteorite impact

1.83 million years ago contain embedded stone handaxes, which are among the oldest so far discovered outside Africa. At Kota Tampan there is an open-air in situ stone tool workshop dated to 70,000 BP, which has become a global reference site for the Palaeolithic in Southeast Asia.

Perak Man, Southeast Asia's oldest most complete human skeleton, radiocarbon dated to 10,120 BP, was found in 1991 in the Gua Gunung Runtuh cave, which was used for habitation and burial purposes from around 13,000 BP until 2,600 BP. Stone tools, animal bones and shells accompanied the skeleton.

World Heritage site since

1989 • 1990 • 1991 • 1992 • 1993 • 1994 • 1995 • 1996 • 1997 • 1998 • 1999 • 2000 • 2001 • 2002 • 2003 • 2004 • 2005 • 2006 • 2007 • 2008 • 2009 • 2010 • 2011 • **2012**

Birthplace of Jesus: Church of the Nativity and the Pilgrimage Route, Bethlehem
Palestine (oPt)*

Criteria – Significance in human history; Heritage associated with events of universal significance

Entrance to the Grotto of the Nativity, Bethlehem ▲

Bethlehem is 10 km south of Jerusalem, and this property is located on the site of a cave identified in Christian tradition since the second century as the birthplace of Jesus. The first church was completed in AD 339. Its octagonal sanctuary allowed worshippers to look down into the cave, and adjoining this was a five-aisled basilica. Its highly elaborate geometric mosaic floors survived a fire in the sixth century which destroyed the rest of the church, and it was then rebuilt by the Emperor Justinian, keeping the form of the nave but incorporating the cave under an apsed chancel. During the Crusader era in the twelfth century, the church was embellished with paintings and mosaics, traces of which survive. The property also includes Greek Orthodox, Franciscan and Armenian convents. Bethlehem and the Church of the Nativity are major pilgrim destinations, and the final part of the traditional route from Jerusalem to the Church is also included in the property.

Two flights of steps lead down from the aisles of the church to the cave of the Nativity. Its marble floor was ornamented in 1717 with a star to mark the birthplace of Jesus. The walls of the cave are partly lined with marble and partly covered with silks and buckram.

World Heritage site since

1989 • 1990 • 1991 • 1992 • 1993 • 1994 • 1995 • 1996 • 1997 • 1998 • 1999 • 2000 • 2001 • 2002 • 2003 • 2004 • 2005 • 2006 • 2007 • 2008 • 2009 • 2010 • 2011 • **2012**

Lakes of Ounianga
Chad

Criteria – Natural phenomena or beauty

AFRICA

Atlantic Ocean

Indian
Ocean

The lakes are fed by fossil groundwater, which compensates for evaporation losses, making the lakes durable features even in the current water-deficit conditions. There are very few permanent lakes of significant size in the Sahara Desert, and the Lakes of Ounianga seem to be unique in their type of fossil groundwater circulation.

The site includes eighteen interconnected lakes in the hyper-arid Ennedi region of the Sahara Desert, part of an exceptional natural landscape of great beauty. Its saline, hyper-saline and freshwater lakes are supplied by groundwater and are found in two groups 40 km apart. Ounianga Kebir comprises four lakes, the largest of which, Yoan, has highly saline waters that only sustain algae and some micro-organisms. The second group, Ounianga Serir, comprises fourteen lakes separated by sand dunes. Floating reeds cover almost half the surface of these lakes, reducing evaporation. With their high quality freshwater, some of these lakes are home to aquatic fauna, particularly fish.

Lake Yoan ▼

World Heritage site since

1989 • 1990 • 1991 • 1992 • 1993 • 1994 • 1995 • 1996 • 1997 • 1998 • 1999 • 2000 • 2001 • 2002 • 2003 • 2004 • 2005 • 2006 • 2007 • 2008 • 2009 • 2010 • 2011 • **2012**

Historic Town of Grand-Bassam
Côte d'Ivoire

Criteria – Testimony to cultural tradition; Significance in human history

The outstanding and well-conserved Historic Town of Grand-Bassam embodies colonial architecture and town planning based on the principles of functionalism and hygiene of the time, adapted to climatic conditions of West Africa. The site also includes a vernacular village that demonstrates the permanency of indigenous cultures.

The first capital of Côte d'Ivoire, the Historic Town of Grand-Bassam is an example of a late nineteenth- and early twentieth-century colonial town planned with quarters specializing in commerce, administration and housing for Europeans and Africans. The site includes the N'zima vernacular fishing village alongside colonial architecture marked by functional houses with galleries, verandas and gardens. It bears witness to the complex social relations between Europeans and Africans, and to the subsequent independence movement. As a vibrant centre of the territory of French trading posts on the Gulf of Guinea, which preceded modern Côte d'Ivoire, it attracted populations from all parts of Africa, Europe and the Mediterranean Levant.

Major Mining Sites of Wallonia
Belgium

Criteria – Interchange of values; Significance in human history

The Walloon mines are one of the oldest and most important places of cultural intermixing through the participation of workers from other regions (Flemish in the nineteenth century), and then through immigration from various European regions in the twentieth century (Italians, Czechs, Hungarians, Poles, Yugoslavs and Russian prisoners).

The four sites of the property form a strip 170 km long by 3–15 km wide, crossing Belgium from east to west, consisting of the best-preserved nineteenth- and twentieth-century coal-mining sites in the country. As a global coal extraction system, the Belgian colliery model was widely disseminated and taught, and the four sites represent the country's best-preserved collieries of this age.

The Grand-Hornu and Bois-du-Luc sites reflect the influence of architectural and urban trends linked to the utopian view of the industrial and workers city that arose in the Age of Enlightenment, notably the Grand-Hornu colliery and workers' city designed by Bruno Renard in the first half of the nineteenth century. Bois-du-Luc includes numerous buildings erected from 1838 to 1909 and is one of Europe's oldest collieries, dating back to the end of the seventeenth century. The last major European mining disaster occurred at the Bois du Cazier colliery in 1956, when 262 miners were killed.

World Heritage site since

1989 • 1990 • 1991 • 1992 • 1993 • 1994 • 1995 • 1996 • 1997 • 1998 • 1999 • 2000 • 2001 • 2002 • 2003 • 2004 • 2005 • 2006 • 2007 • 2008 • 2009 • 2010 • 2011 • **2012**

Margravial Opera House Bayreuth
Germany

Criteria – Human creative genius; Significance in human history

The Margravial Opera House is a masterpiece of Baroque theatre architecture, built between 1745 and 1750. Authentic Baroque court opera culture and acoustics can still be experienced by an audience of 500, as its auditorium retains its original structure of wood and canvas. Commissioned by Margravine Wilhelmine, wife of Frederick, Margrave of Brandenburg–Bayreuth, the interior of the Opera House was designed by the renowned Italian theatre architect Giuseppe

Galli Bibiena. Opening onto a public square, its grand Baroque façade and ceremonial foyer foreshadowed the construction of large public theatres. The highly decorated, bell-shaped auditorium contains tiers of loges (or boxes) whose the rear walls are covered in illusionistic painted canvas reflecting both the traditions of ephemeral ceremonial architecture and the practical requirements of covering cracks in the wood to achieve improved acoustics.

The Opera House's benefactor, Margravine Wilhelmine, was a highly talented composer, artistic director and stage director, performing on her own stage. Hers is a key work in theatre architecture, coming between early Italian theatres that looked to antiquity and large nineteenth-century public opera houses.

Neolithic Site of Çatalhöyük
Turkey

Criteria – Interchange of values; Significance in human history

Çatalhöyük, on the Southern Anatolian Plateau, is a very rare, well-preserved Neolithic settlement comprising two tells. The taller eastern mound (or tell) contains evidence of eighteen levels of Neolithic occupation between 7,400 and 6,200 BC, including wall paintings, reliefs, sculptures and other symbolic and artistic features. The western mound shows the evolution of cultural practices in the Chalcolithic period

from 6,200 to 5,200 BC. The site illustrates the transition from settled villages to urban agglomeration.

Çatalhöyük features a unique street-less settlement of houses clustered back to back, with roof access into the buildings. It is the outstanding settlement type of the Neolithic period and testifies to the evolution of social organization and cultural practices as humans adapted to a sedentary life.

Rabat, Modern Capital and Historic City: a Shared Heritage

Morocco

Criteria – Interchange of values; Significance in human history

Rabat, on the Atlantic coast in northwest Morocco, combines the Ville Nouvelle, built under the French Protectorate from 1912 to the 1930s, with the older parts of the city dating back to the twelfth century. In addition there are archaeological remains in the Chellah district from Mauritanian settlement (seventh–sixth century BC) and from Roman times. The new town, one of the most ambitious urban projects in Africa, was the product of a fertile exchange between the Arabo-Muslim past and Western modernism. It includes royal and administrative areas, residential and commercial developments and the pleasure and botanic gardens, the Jardins d'Essais. A rich repertoire of forms, specific spaces and decorative motifs exists, ranging from the neo-Moorish style to European neoclassicism, and from naturalism to Art Deco and modernism. The synthesis of decorative, architectural and landscape elements, and the interplay between the present and the past, offer a refined urban ensemble of rare quality.

Rabat landmarks include the twelfth-century Almohad ramparts and the Hassan minaret (started in 1184), the only surviving parts of a proposed capital for the Almohad caliphate. The Kasbah and Medina also go back to this period and include buildings from the Moorish, or Andalusian, principality of the seventeenth century.

Bab Oudaïa, the principal gateway into Rabt's Oudaïa Kasbah, was built in the late twelfth century. ▼

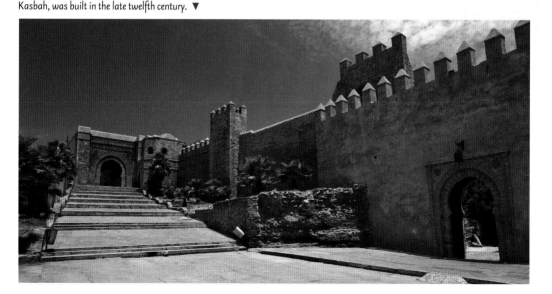

World Heritage site since

1989 • 1990 • 1991 • 1992 • 1993 • 1994 • 1995 • 1996 • 1997 • 1998 • 1999 • 2000 • 2001 • 2002 • 2003 • 2004 • 2005 • 2006 • 2007 • 2008 • 2009 • 2010 • 2011 • **2012**

Heritage of Mercury, Almadén and Idrija
Slovenia, Spain

Criteria – Interchange of values; Significance in human history

The property includes the mining sites of Almadén in Spain, where mercury has been extracted since antiquity, and Idrija in Slovenia, where mercury was first found in AD 1490. The sites represent the two largest mercury mines in the world and were operational until recent times. They bear testimony to the intercontinental trade in mercury between Europe and America.

They also illustrate the social and economic conditions of mercury extraction, and the educational and medical traditions linked to the needs of the mercury mines. The Spanish property includes Retamar Castle, religious buildings and traditional dwellings. The site in Idrija notably features mercury stores and infrastructure, as well as miners' living quarters and a miners' theatre.

Mercury has toxicological properties that make it dangerous to handle, and mean that its residues pollute the environment, which led to the decline in its use at the end of the twentieth century. The great mines of the past, such as Almadén and Idrija, have ceased to function, and have become testimony to a technical and industrial culture that has disappeared.

Rock Islands Southern Lagoon
Palau

Criteria – Testimony to cultural tradition; Traditional human settlement; Natural phenomena or beauty; Significant ecological and biological processes; Significant natural habitat for biodiversity

The Rock Islands Southern Lagoon contains an exceptional variety of habitats within a relatively limited area. The maze of dome-shaped and green Rock Islands, seemingly floating in turquoise lagoons surrounded by coral reefs, is of exceptional aesthetic beauty. There are 445 of these uninhabited limestone islands of volcanic origins. The attractiveness of the site is heightened by a complex reef system featuring over 385 coral species and different types of habitat. They sustain a large diversity of plants, birds and

marine life including dugong and at least thirteen shark species.

The remains of stonework villages, as well as burial sites and rock art, bear testimony to the organization of small island communities over some three millennia. The abandonment of the villages in the seventeenth and eighteenth centuries illustrates the consequences of climate change, population growth and subsistence existence on a society living in a marginal marine environment.

The Rock Islands Southern Lagoon contains the highest concentration of marine lakes anywhere in the world. These are isolated bodies of seawater separated from the ocean by land barriers and are among the islands' most distinctive features. They sustain high endemism of populations which continue to yield new organisms, including five new subspecies of the Mastigias papua jellyfish.

World Heritage site since

1989 • 1990 • 1991 • 1992 • 1993 • 1994 • 1995 • 1996 • 1997 • 1998 • 1999 • 2000 • 2001 • 2002 • 2003 • 2004 • 2005 • 2006 • 2007 • 2008 • 2009 • 2010 • 2011 • **2012**

Cultural Landscape of Bali Province: the Subak System as a Manifestation of the Tri Hita Karana Philosophy
Indonesia

Criteria – Interchange of values; Testimony to cultural tradition; Traditional human settlement; Heritage associated with events of universal significance

This cultural landscape of five rice terraces and their water temples are the focus of a cooperative water management system of canals and weirs, known as *subak*, which dates back to the ninth century. Included in the landscape is the eighteenth-century Royal Temple of Pura Taman Ayun, the largest and most impressive architectural edifice of its type on the island. The water temple networks have managed the ecology of rice terraces at the scale of whole watersheds, and cover 195 km². They provide a unique response to the challenge of supporting a dense population on a rugged volcanic island.

Rice is seen as the gift of god, and the subak system is part of temple culture. Water from springs and canals flows through the temples and out onto the rice paddy fields. The water temples are the focus of a cooperative management of water resource by a group of *subaks*. Today Bali has about 1,200 of these water collectives.

The subak reflects the philosophical concept of Tri Hita Karana, which brings together the realms of the spirit, the human world and nature. This philosophy was born of the cultural exchange between Bali and India over the past 2,000 years and has shaped the landscape of Bali. The subak system has enabled the Balinese to become the most prolific rice growers in the archipelago despite the challenge of supporting a dense population.

Rice terraces of Jatiluwih ▼

World Heritage site since

1990 • 1991 • 1992 • 1993 • 1994 • 1995 • 1996 • 1997 • 1998 • 1999 • 2000 • 2001 • 2002 • 2003 • 2004 • 2005 • 2006 • 2007 • 2008 • 2009 • 2010 • 2011 • 2012 • **2013**

Medici Villas and Gardens in Tuscany
Italy

Criteria – Interchange of values; Significance in human history; Heritage associated with events of universal significance

Twelve villas and two pleasure gardens spread across the Tuscan countryside make up this site which bears testimony to the influence the Medici family exerted over modern European culture through its patronage of the arts. Built between the 15th and 17th centuries, they represent an innovative system of rural construction in harmony with nature and dedicated to leisure, the arts and knowledge. The villas embody an innovative form and function, a new type of princely residence that differed from both the farms owned by rich Florentines of the period and from the military might of baronial castles.

The Medici villas form the first example of the connection between habitat, gardens and the environment, and became an enduring reference for princely residences throughout Italy and Europe. Their gardens and integration into the natural environment helped develop the appreciation of landscape characteristic of Humanism and the Renaissance.

Hill Forts of Rajasthan
India

Criteria – Interchange of values; Testimony to cultural tradition

The serial site, situated in the state of Rajasthan, includes six majestic forts in Chittorgarh, Kumbhalgarh, Sawai Madhopur, Jhalawar, Jaipur and Jaisalmer. The ecclectic architecture of the forts, some up to 20 km in circumference, bears testimony to the power of the Rajput princely states which flourished in the region from the 8th to the 18th centuries. Enclosed within defensive walls are major urban centres, palaces, trading centres and other buildings, including temples that often predate the fortifications, within which an elaborate courtly culture that supported learning, music and the arts developed. Some of the urban centres have survived, as have many of the site's temples and other sacred buildings. The forts use the natural defences offered by the landscape: hills, deserts, rivers and dense forests. They also feature extensive water harvesting structures, largely still in use today.

Chittorgarh Fort is one of the largest forts in India and the grandest in the state of Rajasthan. It is a spacious fort located on an isolated rocky plateau approximately 2 km long and 155 m wide. It is surrounded by a perimeter wall 4.5 km long, beyond which a 45-degree hill slope made it almost inaccessible to enemies.

◄

Chittorgarh Fort is a majestic fort situated on a hilltop near Chittorgarh town in the state of Rajasthan.

World Heritage site since

1990 • 1991 • 1992 • 1993 • 1994 • 1995 • 1996 • 1997 • 1998 • 1999 • 2000 • 2001 • 2002 • 2003 • 2004 • 2005 • 2006 • 2007 • 2008 • 2009 • 2010 • 2011 • 2012 • **2013**

Cultural Landscape of Honghe Hani Rice Terraces
China

Criteria – Testimony to cultural tradition; Traditional human settlement

The Hani people worship the sun, moon, mountains, rivers, forests and other natural phenomena, including fire.

The Cultural Landscape of Honghe Hani Rice Terraces covers 166 km² in southern Yunnan in China. It is marked by spectacular terraces that cascade down the slopes of the towering Ailao Mountains to the banks of the Hong River. Over the past 1,300 years, the Hani people have developed a complex system of channels to bring water from the forested mountain tops to the terraces. They have also created an integrated farming system that involves buffaloes, cattle, ducks, fish and eel, and supports the production of red rice, the area's primary crop. They live in eighty-two villages situated between the mountain-top forests and the terraces. The villages feature traditional thatched 'mushroom' houses. The resilient land management system of the rice terraces demonstrates extraordinary harmony between people and their environment, both visually and ecologically, and is based on exceptional and long-standing social and religious structures.

Tajik National Park (Mountains of the Pamirs)
Tajikistan

Criteria – Natural phenomena or beauty; Major stages of Earth's history

The longest valley glacier outside the Polar region is located among the 1,085 glaciers inventoried in the site, which also numbers 170 rivers and more than 400 lakes.

Tajik National Park covers an area of more than 25,000 km² in the east of Tajikistan, at the centre of the so-called 'Pamir Knot', a meeting point of the highest mountain ranges on the Eurasian continent. It consists of high plateaus in the east and, to the west, rugged peaks, some of which are over 7,000 m high, and features extreme seasonal variations of temperature. A rich variety of flora species of both the southwestern and central Asian floristic regions grow in the Park, which shelters nationally rare and threatened birds and mammals, such as the Marco Polo Argali sheep, Siberian ibex and snow leopard. Subject to frequent strong earthquakes, the Park is sparsely inhabited, and virtually unaffected by agriculture and permanent human settlement. It offers a unique opportunity for the study of plate tectonics and subduction phenomena.

World Heritage site since

1990 • 1991 • 1992 • 1993 • 1994 • 1995 • 1996 • 1997 • 1998 • 1999 • 2000 • 2001 • 2002 • 2003 • 2004 • 2005 • 2006 • 2007 • 2008 • 2009 • 2010 • 2011 • 2012 • **2013**

Historic Centre of Agadez
Niger
Criteria – Interchange of values; Testimony to cultural tradition

The historic centre of Agadez contains numerous earthen dwellings and a well-preserved group of palatial and religious buildings, including a 27-m-high minaret made entirely of mud brick, the highest such structure in the world.

Known as the gateway to the desert, Agadez, on the southern edge of the Sahara desert, developed in the 15th and 16th centuries when the Sultanate of Aïr was established and Tuareg tribes were sedentarized in the city, respecting the boundaries of old encampments, which gave rise to the street pattern still in place today. The historic centre of the city, an important crossroads of the caravan trade, is divided into eleven irregularly-shaped quarters. The site is marked by ancestral cultural, commercial and handicraft traditions still practised today and presents exceptional and sophisticated examples of earthen architecture.

Historic Monuments and Sites in Kaesŏng
Korea, Democratic People's Republic of
Criteria – Interchange of values; Testimony to cultural tradition

The monuments inscribed also include an astronomical and meteorological observatory, two schools (including one dedicated to educating national officials) and commemorative stelae.

Situated in Kaesŏng city, in the south of the country, the site consists of twelve separate components, which together testify to the history and culture of the Koryŏ Dynasty from the 10th to 14th centuries. The geomantic layout of the former capital city of Kaesŏng, its palaces, institutions and tomb complex, defensive walls and gates embody the political, cultural, philosophical and spiritual values of a crucial era in the region's history. The site testifies to the transition from Buddhism to neo-Confucianism in East Asia, and to the assimilation of the cultural, spiritual and political values of the states that existed prior to Korea's unification under the Koryŏ Dynasty. The integration of Buddhist, Confucian, Taoist and geomantic concepts is manifest in the planning of the site and the architecture of its monuments.

◀

Tomb of King Kongmin, a 14th-century mausoleum located in Kaep'ung County, just outside of the city of Kaesŏng.

World Heritage site since

1990 • 1991 • 1992 • 1993 • 1994 • 1995 • 1996 • 1997 • 1998 • 1999 • 2000 • 2001 • 2002 • 2003 • 2004 • 2005 • 2006 • 2007 • 2008 • 2009 • 2010 • 2011 • 2012 • **2013**

University of Coimbra – Alta and Sofia
Portugal

Criteria – Interchange of values; Significance in human history; Heritage associated with events of universal significance

The University of Coimbra offers an outstanding example of an integrated university city with a specific urban typology, as well as its own ceremonial and cultural traditions that have been kept alive through the ages.

Situated on a hill overlooking the city, the University of Coimbra and its colleges grew and evolved over more than seven centuries within the old town. Notable university buildings include the 12th-century Cathedral of Santa Cruz and a number of 16th-century colleges, the Royal Palace of Alcáçova, which has housed the University since 1537, the Joanine Library with its rich baroque decor, the 18th-century Botanical Garden and University Press, as well as the large 'University City' created during the 1940s. The University's edifices became a reference in the development of other institutions of higher education in the Portuguese-speaking world, where the University exerted a major influence on learning and literature.

◄ Paço das Escolas, Coimbra University.

Levuka Historical Port Town
Fiji

Criteria – Interchange of values; Significance in human history

Levuka is an outstanding example of a late 19th-century Pacific port settlement, and reflects the integration of local building traditions by a supreme naval power, leading to the emergence of a unique landscape.

The town and its low line of buildings set among coconut and mango trees along the beach front was the first colonial capital of Fiji, ceded to the British in 1874. It developed from the early 19th century as a centre of commercial activity by Americans and Europeans who built warehouses, stores, port facilities, residences, and religious, educational and social institutions around the villages of the South Pacific island's indigenous population. It is a rare example of a late colonial port town that was influenced in its development by the indigenous community which continued to outnumber the European settlers.

World Heritage site since

1990 • 1991 • 1992 • 1993 • 1994 • 1995 • 1996 • 1997 • 1998 • 1999 • 2000 • 2001 • 2002 • 2003 • 2004 • 2005 • 2006 • 2007 • 2008 • 2009 • 2010 • 2011 • 2012 • 2013

Al Zubarah Archaeological Site
Qatar

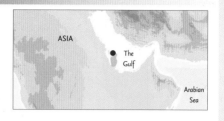

Criteria – Testimony to cultural tradition; Significance in human history; Traditional human settlement

The walled coastal town of Al Zubarah in the Gulf flourished as a pearling and trading centre in the late 18th century and early 19th century, before it was destroyed in 1811 and abandoned in the early 1900s. Founded by merchants from Kuwait, Al Zubarah had trading links across the Indian Ocean, Arabia and western Asia. A layer of sand blown from the desert has protected the remains of the site's palaces, mosques, streets, courtyard houses and fishermen's huts; its harbour and double defensive walls; a canal and cemeteries. Excavation has only taken place over a small part of the site, which offers an outstanding testimony to an urban trading and pearl-diving tradition which sustained the region's major coastal towns, and led to the development of small independent states that flourished outside the control of the Ottoman, European and Persian empires, and eventually led to the emergence of the modern-day Gulf States.

The Zubarah Fort is a historic Qatari military fortress originally built by Sheikh Abdullah bin Jassim Al Thani, an Emir of Qatar, in 1938. It is now a museum displaying diverse exhibits, artworks and archaeological findings.

El Pinacate and Gran Desierto de Altar Biosphere Reserve
Mexico

Criteria – Natural phenomena or beauty; Major stages of Earth's history; Significant natural habitat for biodiversity

The 7,146 km² site comprises two distinct parts: the dormant volcanic Pinacate Shield with black and red lava flows and desert pavements to the east and, in the west, the Gran Altar Desert, with its ever-changing and varied sand dunes that can reach a height of 200 m. The dunes emerge like islands from the sea of sand and harbour distinct and highly diverse plant and wildlife communities, including endemic freshwater fish species and the endemic Sonoran pronghorn, which can only be found in northwestern Sonora and in southwestern Arizona, USA. Ten enormous, deep and almost perfectly circular craters, believed to have been formed by a combination of eruptions and collapses, also contribute to the dramatic beauty of the site whose exceptional combination of features is of great scientific interest. The site is also a UNESCO Biosphere Reserve.

The landscape is one of dramatic contrast and notably features linear, star and dome dunes as well as several arid granite massifs, some as high as 650 m.

World Heritage site since

1990 • 1991 • 1992 • 1993 • 1994 • 1995 • 1996 • 1997 • 1998 • 1999 • 2000 • 2001 • 2002 • 2003 • 2004 • 2005 • 2006 • 2007 • 2008 • 2009 • 2010 • 2011 • 2012 • **2013**

Ancient City of Tauric Chersonese and its Chora
Ukraine

Criteria – Interchange of values;
Traditional human settlement

The site features the remains of a city founded by Dorian Greeks in the 5th century BC on the northern shores of the Black Sea. It encompasses six component sites with urban remains, and agricultural lands divided into several hundreds of *chora*, rectangular plots of equal size. The plots supported vineyards whose product was exported by the city which thrived until the 15th century. The site features several public building complexes and residential neighbourhoods, as well as early Christian monuments alongside remains from Stone and Bronze Age settlements; Roman and medieval tower fortifications and water supply systems; and

exceptionally well-preserved examples of vineyard planting and dividing walls.

In the 3rd century AD, the site was known as the most productive wine centre of the Black Sea region and remained a hub of exchange between the Greek, Roman and Byzantine Empires and populations north of the Black Sea. It is an outstanding example of democratic land organization linked to an ancient polis, reflecting the city's social organization.

◄

The National Preserve of Tauric Chersonese on the shores of the Black Sea.

Red Bay Basque Whaling Station
Canada

Criteria – Testimony to cultural tradition;
Significance in human history

Red Bay, established by Basque mariners in the 16th century at the northeastern tip of Canada on the shore of the Strait of Belle Isle, is an archaeological site that provides the earliest, most complete and best-preserved testimony of the European whaling tradition. Gran Baya, as it was called by those who founded the station

in 1530s, was used as a base for coastal hunting, butchering, rendering of whale fat by heating to produce oil, and storage. The site became a major source of whale oil which was shipped to Europe where it was used for lighting. The station was used for some seventy years, before the local whale population was depleted.

The site, which was used in the summer months, includes remains of rendering ovens, cooperages, wharves, temporary living quarters and a cemetery, together with underwater remains of vessels and whale bone deposits.

World Heritage site since

1990 • 1991 • 1992 • 1993 • 1994 • 1995 • 1996 • 1997 • 1998 • 1999 • 2000 • 2001 • 2002 • 2003 • 2004 • 2005 • 2006 • 2007 • 2008 • 2009 • 2010 • 2011 • 2012 • 2013

Bergpark Wilhelmshöhe
Germany

Criteria – Testimony to cultural tradition;
Significance in human history

Descending a long slope of a hill dominated by a giant statue of Hercules, construction of the monumental water displays of Wilhelmshöhe was started by Landgrave Charles of Hesse-Kassel in 1689 around an east-west axis. The displays were developed further into the 19th century. Reservoirs and channels behind the Hercules monument supply water to a complex system of hydro-pneumatic devices that supply the site's large Baroque water theatre, grotto, fountains and 350-m-long Grand Cascade. Beyond this, channels and waterways wind across the axis, feeding a series of dramatic waterfalls and wild rapids; the geyser-like Grand Fountain which leaps 50 m high; and the lake and secluded ponds that enliven the Romantic garden created in the 18th century by Charles' great-grandson, Elector William I. The great size of the park and its waterworks, along with the towering Hercules statue constitute an expression of the ideals of absolutist monarchy; while the ensemble is a remarkable testimony to the aesthetics of the Baroque and Romantic periods.

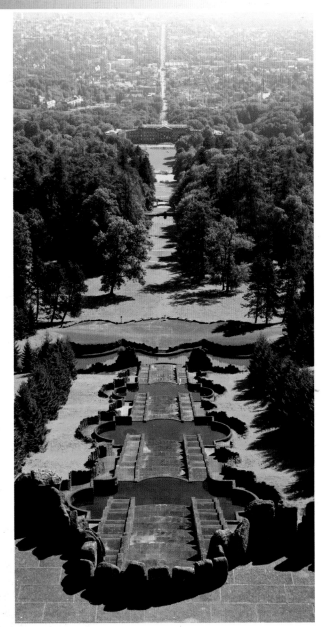

View of the Grand Cascade from the Hercules Statue at the top of ▲ Bergpark Wilhelmshöhe.

World Heritage site since

1990 • 1991 • 1992 • 1993 • 1994 • 1995 • 1996 • 1997 • 1998 • 1999 • 2000 • 2001 • 2002 • 2003 • 2004 • 2005 • 2006 • 2007 • 2008 • 2009 • 2010 • 2011 • 2012 • **2013**

Xinjiang Tianshan
China

Criteria – Natural phenomena or beauty;
Significant ecological and biological processes

Xinjiang Tianshan comprises four components – Tomur, Kalajun-Kuerdening, Bayinbukuke and Bogda – that total an area of 6,068 km². They are part of the Tianshan mountain system of Central Asia, one of the largest mountain ranges in the world. Xinjiang Tianshan presents unique physical geographic features and scenically beautiful areas, including spectacular snow and snowy mountains, glacier-capped peaks, undisturbed forests and meadows, clear rivers and lakes, and red-bed canyons. These landscapes contrast with the vast adjacent desert landscapes, creating a striking visual contrast between hot and cold environments, dry and wet, desolate and luxuriant. The landforms and ecosystems of the site have been preserved since the Pliocene epoch and present an outstanding example of ongoing biological and ecological evolutionary processes.

The site also extends into the Taklimakan Desert, one of the world's largest and highest deserts, known for its large dune formations and great dust storms. Xinjiang Tianshan is moreover an important habitat for endemic and relic flora species, some of which are rare and endangered.

Fujisan, Sacred Place and Source of Artistic Inspiration
Japan

Criteria – Testimony to cultural tradition;
Heritage associated with events of universal significance

The beauty of the solitary and often snow-capped stratovolcano, known around the world as Mount Fuji, rising above villages and tree-fringed sea and lakes, has long inspired artists and poets and been the object of pilgrimages. Its representation in Japanese art goes back to the 11th century, but it is the 19th-century wood block prints that have made Fujisan an internationally recognized icon of Japan and had a deep impact on the development of Western art. The inscribed property consists of twenty-five sites which reflect the essence of Fujisan's sacred landscape. In the 12th century, Fujisan became the centre of training for ascetic Buddhism, which included Shinto elements.

On the upper 1,500-m tier of the 3,776-m-high mountain, pilgrim routes and crater shrines have been inscribed alongside sites around the base of the mountain, including Sengen-jinja shrines, Oshi lodging houses, and natural volcanic features such as lava tree moulds, lakes, springs and waterfalls, which are revered as sacred.

◄

Mount Fuji from Lake Kawaguchi.

World Heritage site since

1990 • 1991 • 1992 • 1993 • 1994 • 1995 • 1996 • 1997 • 1998 • 1999 • 2000 • 2001 • 2002 • 2003 • 2004 • 2005 • 2006 • 2007 • 2008 • 2009 • 2010 • 2011 • 2012 • **2013**

Golestan Palace
Iran (Islamic Republic of)

Criteria – Human creative genius;
Interchange of values; Testimony to cultural
tradition; Significance in human history

The spectacular
throne known as
Takht-e Marmar
(Marble Throne)
consists of sixty-five
marble stone pieces
and is made of the
famous yellow marble
of Yazd province. The
throne's supports are
carved in the shape of
men, women, fairies
and demons.

The lavish Golestan Palace is a masterpiece
of the Qajar era, embodying the successful
integration of earlier Persian crafts and
architecture with Western influences. The
walled Palace, one of the oldest groups of
buildings in Teheran, became the seat of
government of the Qajar family, who came
into power in 1779 and made Teheran the
capital of the country. Built around a garden
featuring pools as well as planted areas, the
Palace's most characteristic features and
rich ornaments date from the 19th century.
It became a centre of Qajari arts and
architecture of which it is an outstanding

example, and has remained a source
of inspiration for Iranian artists and
architects to this day. It represents a new
style incorporating traditional Persian arts
and crafts and elements of 18th-century
architecture and technology.

◄

The Takht-e Marmar
(Marble Throne) was
built in 1806.

Wooden Tserkvas of the Carpathian Region in Poland and Ukraine
Poland, Ukraine

Criteria – Testimony to cultural tradition;
Significance in human history

The tserkvas are
built on a tripartite
plan surmounted by
open quadrilateral or
octagonal domes and
cupolas. They feature
wooden bell towers,
iconostases, and
interior polychrome
decorations, as well
as churchyards,
gatehouses and
graveyards.

Situated on the eastern fringe of eastern
Europe, this transnational property includes
a selection of sixteen tserkvas – churches
built of horizontal wooden logs between
the 16th and 19th centuries by communities
of the Eastern Orthodox and Greek
Catholic faiths. They represent the cultural
expression of four ethnographic groups

and the formal, decorative and technical
characteristics they developed over time.
The tserkvas bear testimony to a distinct
building tradition rooted in Orthodox
ecclesiastic design, interwoven with elements
of local tradition, and symbolic references to
their communities' cosmogony.

World Heritage site since

1990 • 1991 • 1992 • 1993 • 1994 • 1995 • 1996 • 1997 • 1998 • 1999 • 2000 • 2001 • 2002 • 2003 • 2004 • 2005 • 2006 • 2007 • 2008 • 2009 • 2010 • 2011 • 2012 • **2013**

Mount Etna
Italy

Criteria – Major stages of Earth's history

Mount Etna is an iconic site encompassing 192 km² of uninhabited terrain on the highest part of Mount Etna, on the eastern coast of Sicily. Mount Etna is the highest Mediterranean island mountain and the most active stratovolcano in the world. The eruptive history of the volcano can be traced back 500,000 years and at least 2,700 years of this activity has been documented. The almost continuous eruptive activity of Mount Etna continues to influence volcanology, geophysics and other earth science disciplines. The volcano also supports important terrestrial ecosystems including endemic flora and fauna and its

activity makes it a natural laboratory for the study of ecological and biological processes.

The diverse and accessible range of volcanic features such as summit craters, cinder cones, lava flows and the Valle del Bove depression have made the site a prime destination for research and education.

◄

One of the many craters of Mount Etna, Sicily.

Namib Sand Sea
Namibia

Criteria – Natural phenomena or beauty; Major stages of Earth's history; Significant ecological and biological processes; Significant natural habitat for biodiversity

Namib Sand Sea is the only coastal desert in the world that includes extensive dune fields influenced by fog. Covering an area of over three million hectares and a buffer zone of 8,995 km², the site is composed of two dune systems – an ancient semi-consolidated one overlain by a younger active one. The desert dunes are formed by the transportation of

materials carried thousands of kilometres from the hinterland by river, ocean current and wind. The desert features gravel plains, coastal flats, rocky hills, inselbergs within the sand sea, a coastal lagoon and ephemeral rivers, resulting in a landscape of exceptional beauty.

Fog is the primary source of water in the site, accounting for a unique environment in which endemic invertebrates, reptiles and mammals adapt to an ever-changing variety of microhabitats and ecological niches.

World Heritage and UNESCO's World Heritage Mission

Heritage is our legacy from the past, what we live with today, and what we pass on to future generations. Our cultural and natural heritage are both irreplaceable sources of life and inspiration. Places as unique and diverse as the wilds of East Africa's Serengeti, the Pyramids of Egypt, the Great Barrier Reef in Australia and the Baroque cathedrals of Latin America make up our world's heritage.

The United Nations Educational, Scientific and Cultural Organization (UNESCO) seeks to encourage the identification, protection and preservation of cultural and natural heritage around the world considered to be of outstanding universal value to humanity. This is embodied in a unique international treaty, called the Convention Concerning the Protection of the World Cultural and Natural Heritage adopted by UNESCO in 1972 (see http://whc.unesco.org/en/conventiontext).

One of the world's most successful conservation instruments, the World Heritage Convention is exceptional in that it links together in a single document the concepts of nature conservation and the preservation of cultural properties. It is also significant in its universal application – World Heritage sites belong to all the peoples of the world, irrespective of the territory on which they are located. By regarding heritage as both cultural and natural, the Convention recognizes the ways in which people interact with nature, and of the fundamental need to preserve the balance between the two.

UNESCO's World Heritage mission is to:

- encourage countries to sign the World Heritage Convention and to ensure the protection of their natural and cultural heritage;
- encourage States Parties to the Convention to nominate sites within their national territory for inclusion on the World Heritage List;
- encourage States Parties to establish management plans and set up reporting systems on the state of conservation of their World Heritage sites;
- help States Parties safeguard World Heritage properties by providing technical assistance and professional training;
- provide emergency assistance for World Heritage sites in immediate danger;
- support States Parties' public awareness-building activities for World Heritage conservation;
- encourage participation of the local population in the preservation of their cultural and natural heritage;
- encourage international cooperation in the conservation of our world's cultural and natural heritage.

THE CRITERIA FOR SELECTION

The World Heritage Convention stipulates the creation of a World Heritage List. In a detailed process, properties are inscribed by an intergovernmental twenty-one member elected Committee, only after a preselection, nomination, and evaluation process. Two leading international Non-Governmental Organizations, the International Union for the Conservation of Nature (IUCN) and the International Council on Monuments and Sites (ICOMOS), review and advise on the natural and cultural nominations respectively. The International Centre for the Study of the Preservation and Restoration of Cultural Property provides the Committee with expert advice on conservation of cultural sites. To be included, sites must be of outstanding universal value and meet at least one out of ten selection criteria:

Human creative genius

i. to represent a masterpiece of human creative genius;

Interchange of values

ii. to exhibit an important interchange of human values, over a span of time or within a cultural area of the world, on developments in architecture or technology, monumental arts, town-planning or landscape design;

Testimony to cultural tradition

iii. to bear a unique or at least exceptional testimony to a cultural tradition or to a civilization which is living or which has disappeared;

Significance in human history

iv. to be an outstanding example of a type of building, architectural or technological ensemble or landscape which illustrates (a) significant stage(s) in human history;

Traditional human settlement

v. to be an outstanding example of a traditional human settlement, land-use, or sea-use which is representative of a culture (or cultures), or human interaction with the environment especially when it has become vulnerable under the impact of irreversible change;

Heritage associated with events of universal significance

vi. to be directly or tangibly associated with events or living traditions, with ideas, or with beliefs, with artistic and literary works of outstanding universal significance. (The Committee considers that this criterion should preferably be used in conjunction with other criteria);

Natural phenomena or beauty

vii. to contain superlative natural phenomena or areas of exceptional natural beauty and aesthetic importance;

Major stages of Earth's history

viii. to be outstanding examples representing major stages of Earth's history, including the record of life, significant on-going geological processes in the development of landforms, or significant geomorphic or physiographic features;

Significant ecological and biological processes

ix. to be outstanding examples representing significant on-going ecological and biological processes in the evolution and development of terrestrial, fresh water, coastal and marine ecosystems and communities of plants and animals;

Significant natural habitat for biodiversity

x. to contain the most important and significant natural habitats for in-situ conservation of biological diversity, including those containing threatened species of outstanding universal value from the point of view of science or conservation.

The protection, management, authenticity and integrity of properties are also important considerations. The process is further detailed in the Operational Guidelines for the Implementation of the World Heritage Convention which, along with the actual text of the Convention, is the main working tool on World Heritage.

UNESCO **Worldwide**

Africa

Algeria	Libya
Angola	Madagascar
Benin	Malawi
Botswana	Mali
Burkina Faso	Mauritania
Burundi	Mauritius
Cameroon	Morocco
Cape Verde	Mozambique
Central African Republic	Namibia
Chad	Niger
Comoros	Nigeria
Congo	Rwanda
Côte d'Ivoire	Sao Tome and Principe
Democratic Republic of the Congo	Senegal
Djibouti	Seychelles
Egypt	Sierra Leone
Equatorial Guinea	Somalia
Eritrea	South Africa
Ethiopia	South Sudan
Gabon	Sudan
Gambia	Swaziland
Ghana	Togo
Guinea	Tunisia
Guinea-Bissau	Uganda
Kenya	United Republic of Tanzania
Lesotho	Zambia
Liberia	Zimbabwe

Asia and the Pacific

Afghanistan	New Zealand
Australia	Niue
Bangladesh	Pakistan
Bhutan	Palau
Brunei Darussalam	Papua New Guinea
Cambodia	Philippines
China	Republic of Korea
Cook Islands	Russian Federation
Democratic People's Republic of Korea	Samoa
Fiji	Singapore
India	Solomon Islands
Indonesia	Sri Lanka
Iran, Islamic Republic of	Tajikistan
Japan	Thailand
Kazakhstan	Timor-Leste
Kiribati	Tonga
Kyrgyzstan	Turkey
Lao People's Democratic Republic	Turkmenistan
Malaysia	Tuvalu
Maldives	Uzbekistan
Marshall Islands	Vanuatu
Micronesia (Federated States of)	Viet Nam
Mongolia	
Myanmar	
Nauru	
Nepal	

The regions presented here follow specific UNESCO definitions which do not forcibly reflect geography. They refer to the execution of regional activities of the Organization.
http://www.unesco.org/new/en/unesco/worldwide/

Europe and North America

Albania
Andorra
Armenia
Austria
Azerbaijan
Belarus
Belgium
Bosnia and Herzegovina
Bulgaria
Canada
Croatia
Cyprus
Czech Republic
Denmark
Estonia
Finland
France
Georgia
Germany
Greece
Hungary
Iceland
Ireland
Israel
Italy
Kazakhstan
Latvia
Lithuania

Luxembourg
Malta
Monaco
Montenegro
Netherlands
Norway
Poland
Portugal
Republic of Moldova
Romania
Russian Federation
San Marino
Serbia
Slovakia
Slovenia
Spain
Sweden
Switzerland
Tajikistan
The former Yugoslav Republic of
  Macedonia
Turkey
Ukraine
United Kingdom of Great Britain
  and Northern Ireland
United States of America

Arab States

Algeria
Bahrain
Djibouti
Egypt
Iraq
Jordan
Kuwait
Lebanon
Libya
Malta
Mauritania

Morocco
Oman
Palestine (oPt)*
Qatar
Saudi Arabia
Somalia
Sudan
Syrian Arab Republic
Tunisia
United Arab Emirates
Yemen

* member of UNESCO since 23 November 2011

Latin America and the Caribbean

Antigua and Barbuda
Argentina
Bahamas
Barbados
Belize
Bolivia
Bolivarian Republic of Venezuela
Brazil
Chile
Colombia
Costa Rica
Cuba
Dominica
Dominican Republic
Ecuador
El Salvador
Grenada

Guatemala
Guyana
Haiti
Honduras
Jamaica
Mexico
Nicaragua
Panama
Paraguay
Peru
Saint Kitts and Nevis
Saint Lucia
Saint Vincent and the Grenadines
Suriname
Trinidad and Tobago
Uruguay

Country index

Afghanistan
Cultural Landscape and Archaeological Remains of the Bamiyan Valley **703**
Minaret and Archaeological Remains of Jam **683**

Albania
Butrint **389**
Historic Centres of Berat and Gjirokastra **732**

Algeria
Al Qal'a of Beni Hammad **109**
Djémila **148**
Kasbah of Algiers **379**
M'Zab Valley **145**
Tassili n'Ajjer **145**
Timgad **148**
Tipasa **142**

Andorra
Madriu-Perafita-Claror Valley **732**

Argentina
Cueva de las Manos, Río Pinturas **607**
Iguazu National Park **188**
Ischigualasto / Talampaya Natural Parks **628**
Jesuit Block and Estancias of Córdoba **647**
Jesuit Missions of the Guaranis **159**
Parque Nacional Los Glaciares **111**
Península Valdés **590**
Quebrada de Humahuaca **705**

Armenia
Cathedral and Churches of Echmiatsin and the Archaeological Site of Zvartnots **655**
Monasteries of Haghpat and Sanahin **500**
Monastery of Geghard and the Upper Azat Valley **630**

Australia
Australian Convict Sites **808**
Australian Fossil Mammal Sites (Riversleigh / Naracoorte) **429**
Fraser Island **393**
Gondwana Rainforests of Australia **260**
Great Barrier Reef **122**
Greater Blue Mountains Area **609**
Heard and McDonald Islands **522**
Kakadu National Park **127**
Lord Howe Island Group **136**
Macquarie Island **506**
Ningaloo Coast **830**
Purnululu National Park **699**
Royal Exhibition Building and Carlton Gardens **718**
Shark Bay **368**
Sydney Opera House **763**
Tasmanian Wilderness **143**
Uluru-Kata Tjuta National Park **306**
Wet Tropics of Queensland **311**
Willandra Lakes Region **125**

Austria
City of Graz – Historic Centre and Schloss Eggenberg **585**
Fertö / Neusiedlersee Cultural Landscape **664**
Hallstatt-Dachstein / Salzkammergut Cultural Landscape **531**
Historic Centre of the City of Salzburg **498**
Historic Centre of Vienna **678**
Palace and Gardens of Schönbrunn **502**
Prehistoric Pile Dwellings around the Alps **839**
Semmering Railway **551**
Wachau Cultural Landscape **641**

Azerbaijan
Gobustan Rock Art Cultural Landscape **767**
Walled City of Baku with the Shirvanshah's Palace and Maiden Tower **607**

Bahrain
Pearling, Testimony of an Island Economy **849**
Qal'at al-Bahrain – Ancient Harbour and Capital of Dilmun **746**

Bangladesh
Historic Mosque City of Bagerhat **228**
Ruins of the Buddhist Vihara at Paharpur **222**
The Sundarbans **512**

Barbados
Historic Bridgetown and its Garrison **829**

Belarus
Architectural, Residential and Cultural Complex of the Radziwill Family at Nesvizh **748**
Belovezhskaya Pushcha / Białowieża Forest **61**
Mir Castle Complex **635**
Struve Geodetic Arc **747**

Belgium
Belfries of Belgium and France **575**
Flemish Béguinages **562**
Historic Centre of Brugge **650**
La Grand-Place, Brussels **555**
Major Mining Sites of Wallonia **855**
Major Town Houses of the Architect Victor Horta (Brussels) **648**
Neolithic Flint Mines at Spiennes (Mons) **652**
Notre-Dame Cathedral in Tournai **655**
Plantin-Moretus House-Workshops-Museum Complex **745**
Stoclet House **805**
The Four Lifts on the Canal du Centre and their Environs, La Louvière and Le Roeulx (Hainault) **554**

Belize
Belize Barrier Reef Reserve System **483**

Benin
Royal Palaces of Abomey **232**

Bolivia
City of Potosí **289**
Fuerte de Samaipata **556**
Historic City of Sucre **367**
Jesuit Missions of the Chiquitos **348**
Noel Kempff Mercado National Park **636**
Tiwanaku: Spiritual and Political Centre of the Tiwanaku Culture **634**

Bosnia and Herzegovina
Mehmed Paša Sokolović Bridge in Višegrad **779**
Old Bridge Area of the Old City of Mostar **734**

Botswana
Tsodilo **668**

Brazil
Atlantic Forest South-East Reserves **606**
Brasilia **280**
Brazilian Atlantic Islands: Fernando de Noronha and Atol das Rocas Reserves **668**
Central Amazon Conservation Complex **624**
Cerrado Protected Areas: Chapada dos Veadeiros and Emas National Parks **681**
Discovery Coast Atlantic Forest Reserves **579**
Historic Centre of Salvador de Bahia **208**
Historic Centre of São Luís **537**
Historic Centre of the Town of Diamantina **588**
Historic Centre of the Town of Goiás **674**
Historic Centre of the Town of Olinda **150**
Historic Town of Ouro Preto **108**
Iguaçu National Park **235**
Jesuit Missions of the Guaranis **159**
Pantanal Conservation Area **656**
Rio de Janeiro: Carioca Landscapes between the Mountain and the Sea **844**
Sanctuary of Bom Jesus do Congonhas **223**
São Francisco Square in the Town of São Cristóvão **809**
Serra da Capivara National Park **374**

Bulgaria
Ancient City of Nessebar **165**
Boyana Church, Sofia **60**
Madara Rider **69**
Pirin National Park **179**
Rila Monastery **178**
Rock-Hewn Churches of Ivanovo **69**
Srebarna Nature Reserve **168**
Thracian Tomb of Kazanlak **49**
Thracian Tomb of Sveshtari **234**

Burkina Faso
The Ruins of Loropéni **805**

Cambodia
Angkor **390**
Temple of Preah Vihear **789**

Cameroon
Dja Faunal Reserve **308**
Sangha Trinational **848**

Canada
Canadian Rocky Mountain Parks **194**
Dinosaur Provincial Park **48**
Gros Morne National Park **302**
Head-Smashed-In Buffalo Jump **118**
Historic District of Old Québec **206**
Joggins Fossil Cliffs **796**

Kluane / Wrangell-St Elias / Glacier Bay / Tatshenshini-Alsek **52**
Landscape of Grand Pré **849**
L'Anse aux Meadows National Historic Site **37**
Miguasha National Park **599**
Nahanni National Park **38**
Old Town Lunenburg **463**
Red Bay Basque Whaling Station **865**
Rideau Canal **773**
SGang Gwaay **133**
Waterton Glacier International Peace Park **450**
Wood Buffalo National Park **170**

Cape Verde
Cidade Velha, Historic Centre of Ribeira Grande **799**

Central African Republic
Manovo-Gounda St Floris National Park **313**
Sangha Trinational **848**

Chad
Lakes of Ounianga **854**

Chile
Churches of Chiloé **620**
Historic Quarter of the Seaport City of Valparaíso **696**
Humberstone and Santa Laura Saltpeter Works **736**
Rapa Nui National Park **454**
Sewell Mining Town **762**

China
Ancient Building Complex in the Wudang Mountains **429**
Ancient City of Ping Yao **540**
Ancient Villages in Southern Anhui–Xidi and Hongcun **653**
Capital Cities and Tombs of the Ancient Koguryo Kingdom **722**
Chengjiang Fossil Site **845**
China Danxia **811**
Classical Gardens of Suzhou **518**
Cultural Landscape of Honghe Hani Rice Terraces **861**
Dazu Rock Carvings **584**
Fujian Tulou **788**
Historic Centre of Macao **737**
Historic Ensemble of the Potala Palace, Lhasa **425**
Historic Monuments of Dengfeng, in the 'Centre of Heaven and Earth' **810**
Huanglong Scenic and Historic Interest Area **395**
Imperial Palaces of the Ming and Qing Dynasties in Beijing and Shenyang **277**
Imperial Tombs of the Ming and Qing Dynasties **616**
Jiuzhaigou Valley Scenic and Historic Interest Area **380**
Kaiping Diaolou and Villages **774**
Longmen Grottoes **654**
Lushan National Park **484**
Mausoleum of the First Qin Emperor **300**
Mogao Caves **298**

Mount Emei Scenic Area, including Leshan Giant Buddha Scenic Area **481**
Mount Huangshan **357**
Mount Qincheng and the Dujiangyan Irrigation System **648**
Mount Sanqingshan National Park **796**
Mount Taishan **297**
Mount Wutai **802**
Mount Wuyi **598**
Mountain Resort and its Outlying Temples, Chengde **436**
Old Town of Lijiang **510**
Peking Man Site at Zhoukoudian **298**
Sichuan Giant Panda Sanctuaries – Wolong, Mt Siguniang and Jiajin Mountains **751**
Site of Xanadu **852**
South China Karst **768**
Summer Palace and Imperial Garden in Beijing **552**
Temple and Cemetery of Confucius and the Kong Family Mansion in Qufu **433**
Temple of Heaven: an Imperial Sacrificial Altar in Beijing **559**
The Great Wall **294**
Three Parallel Rivers of Yunnan Protected Areas **700**
West Lake Cultural Landscape of Hangzhou **831**
Wulingyuan Scenic and Historic Interest Area **382**
Xinjiang Tianshan **867**
Yin Xu **759**
Yungang Grottoes **672**

Colombia
Coffee Cultural Landscape of Colombia **841**
Historic Centre of Santa Cruz de Mompox **473**
Los Katíos National Park **426**
Malpelo Fauna and Flora Sanctuary **756**
National Archeological Park of Tierradentro **473**
Port, Fortresses and Group of Monuments, Cartagena **184**
San Agustín Archeological Park **458**

Congo
Sangha Trinational **848**

Congo, Democratic Republic of the
Garamba National Park **94**
Kahuzi-Biega National Park **97**
Okapi Wildlife Reserve **478**
Salonga National Park **186**
Virunga National Park **45**

Costa Rica
Area de Conservación Guanacaste **596**
Cocos Island National Park **516**
Talamanca Range-La Amistad Reserves / La Amistad National Park **162**

Côte d'Ivoire
Comoé National Park **153**
Historic Town of Grand-Bassam **855**
Mount Nimba Strict Nature Reserve **126**
Taï National Park **139**

Croatia
Cathedral of St James in Šibenik **627**
Episcopal Complex of the Euphrasian Basilica in the Historic Centre of Poreč **516**
Historic City of Trogir **533**
Historical Complex of Split with the Palace of Diocletian **82**
Old City of Dubrovnik **86**
Plitvice Lakes National Park **57**
Stari Grad Plain **790**

Cuba
Alejandro de Humboldt National Park **672**
Archaeological Landscape of the First Coffee Plantations in the South-East of Cuba **649**
Desembarco del Granma National Park **583**
Historic Centre of Camagüey **785**
Old Havana and its Fortification System **146**
San Pedro de la Roca Castle, Santiago de Cuba **548**
Trinidad and the Valley de los Ingenios **323**
Urban Historic Centre of Cienfuegos **749**
Viñales Valley **593**

Cyprus
Choirokoitia **554**
Painted Churches in the Troodos Region **210**
Paphos **101**

Czech Republic
Gardens and Castle at Kroměříž **565**
Historic Centre of Český Krumlov **386**
Historic Centre of Prague **384**
Historic Centre of Telč **392**
Holašovice Historical Village Reservation **551**
Holy Trinity Column in Olomouc **637**
Jewish Quarter and St Procopius' Basilica in Třebíč **704**
Kutná Hora: Historical Town Centre with the Church of St Barbara and the Cathedral of Our Lady at Sedlec **469**
Lednice-Valtice Cultural Landscape **493**
Litomyšl Castle **588**
Pilgrimage Church of St John of Nepomuk at Zelená Hora **443**
Tugendhat Villa in Brno **681**

Denmark
Ilulissat Icefjord **708**
Jelling Mounds, Runic Stones and Church **426**
Kronborg Castle **608**
Roskilde Cathedral **452**

Dominica
Morne Trois Pitons National Park **515**

Dominican Republic
Colonial City of Santo Domingo **343**

Ecuador
City of Quito **32**
Galápagos Islands **26**
Historic Centre of Santa Ana de los Ríos de Cuenca **576**
Sangay National Park **171**

Egypt
Abu Mena 49
Ancient Thebes with its Necropolis 74
Historic Cairo 78
Memphis and its Necropolis – the Pyramid
   Fields from Giza to Dahshur 70
Nubian Monuments from Abu Simbel to Philae
   56
St Catherine Area 688
Wadi Al-Hitan (Whale Valley) 738

El Salvador
Joya de Cerén Archaeological Site 416

Estonia
Historic Centre (Old Town) of Tallinn 509
Struve Geodetic Arc 747

Ethiopia
Aksum 98
Fasil Ghebbi, Gondar Region 60
Harar Jugol, the Fortified Historic Town 752
Konso Cultural Landscape 833
Lower Valley of the Awash 102
Lower Valley of the Omo 106
Rock-Hewn Churches, Lalibela 32
Simien National Park 37
Tiya 106

Fiji
Levuka Historical Port Town 863

Finland
Bronze Age Burial Site of Sammallahdenmäki
   599
Fortress of Suomenlinna 378
Kvarken Archipelago 630
Old Rauma 368
Petäjävesi Old Church 436
Struve Geodetic Arc 747
Verla Groundwood and Board Mill 486

Former Yugoslav Republic of Macedonia
Natural and Cultural Heritage of the Ohrid
   region 77

France
Abbey Church of Saint-Savin sur Gartempe 168
Amiens Cathedral 117
Arles, Roman and Romanesque Monuments
   131
Belfries of Belgium and France 575
Bordeaux, Port of the Moon 775
Bourges Cathedral 381
Canal du Midi 480
Cathedral of Notre-Dame, Former Abbey of
   Saint-Rémi and Palace of Tau, Reims 372
Chartres Cathedral 65
Cistercian Abbey of Fontenay 121
Episcopal City of Albi 813
Fortifications of Vauban 794
From the Great Saltworks of Salins-les-Bains
   to the Royal Saltworks of Arc-et-Senans, the
   production of open-pan salt 153
Gulf of Porto: Calanche of Piana, Gulf of
   Girolata, Scandola Reserve 174

Historic Centre of Avignon: Papal Palace,
   Episcopal Ensemble and Avignon Bridge 444
Historic Fortified City of Carcassonne 514
Historic Site of Lyons 561
Jurisdiction of Saint-Emilion 600
Lagoons of New Caledonia: Reef Diversity and
   Associated Ecosystems 788
Le Havre, the city rebuilt by Auguste Perret 738
Loire Valley between Sully-sur-Loire and
   Chalonnes 622
Mont-Saint-Michel and its Bay 58
Nord-Pas de Calais Mining Basin 850
Palace and Park of Fontainebleau 113
Palace and Park of Versailles 62
Paris, Banks of the Seine 360
Place Stanislas, Place de la Carrière and Place
   d'Alliance in Nancy 169
Pitons, cirques and remparts of Reunion Island
   812
Pont du Gard (Roman Aqueduct) 229
Prehistoric Pile Dwellings around the Alps 839
Prehistoric Sites and Decorated Caves of the
   Vézère Valley 44
Provins, Town of Medieval Fairs 669
Pyrénées - Mont Perdu 508
Roman Theatre and its Surroundings and the
   'Triumphal Arch' of Orange 120
Routes of Santiago de Compostela in France
   557
Strasbourg – Grande Île 334
The Causses and the Cévennes, Mediterranean
   agro-pastoral Cultural Landscape 826
Vézelay, Church and Hill 66

Gabon
Ecosystem and Relict Cultural Landscape of
   Lopé-Okanda 781

Georgia
Bagrati Cathedral and Gelati Monastery 435
Historical Monuments of Mtskheta 437
Upper Svaneti 481

Germany
Aachen Cathedral 33
Abbey and Altenmünster of Lorsch 379
Bauhaus and its Sites in Weimar and Dessau
   484
Bergpark Wilhelmshöhe 866
Berlin Modernism Housing Estates 784
Castles of Augustusburg and Falkenlust at
   Brühl 193
Classical Weimar 549
Collegiate Church, Castle, and Old Town of
   Quedlinburg 441
Cologne Cathedral 474
Fagus Factory in Alfeld 826
Frontiers of the Roman Empire 273
Garden Kingdom of Dessau-Wörlitz 610
Hanseatic City of Lübeck 281
Historic Centres of Stralsund and Wismar 690
Luther Memorials in Eisleben and Wittenberg
   503
Margravial Opera House, Bayreuth 856
Maulbronn Monastery Complex 407
Messel Pit Fossil Site 456

Mines of Rammelsberg and Historic Town of
   Goslar and Upper Harz Water Management
   System 387
Monastic Island of Reichenau 640
Museumsinsel (Museum Island), Berlin 578
Muskauer Park / Park Muzakowski 719
Old Town of Regensburg with Stadtamhof 753
Palaces and Parks of Potsdam and Berlin 346
Pilgrimage Church of Wies 176
Prehistoric Pile Dwellings around the Alps 839
Primeval Beech Forests of the Carpathians and the
   Ancient Beech Forests of Germany 772
Roman Monuments, Cathedral of St Peter and
   Church of Our Lady in Trier 251
St Mary's Cathedral and St Michael's Church
   at Hildesheim 225
Speyer Cathedral 128
The Wadden Sea 804
Town of Bamberg 406
Town Hall and Roland on the Marketplace of
   Bremen 727
Upper Middle Rhine Valley 684
Völklingen Ironworks 441
Wartburg Castle 589
Würzburg Residence with the Court Gardens
   and Residence Square 132
Zollverein Coal Mine Industrial Complex in
   Essen 667

Ghana
Asante Traditional Buildings 94
Forts and Castles, Volta, Greater Accra, Central
   and Western Regions 44

Greece
Acropolis, Athens 282
Archaeological Site of Aigai (modern name
   Vergina) 504
Archaeological Site of Delphi 262
Archaeological Site of Mystras 341
Archaeological Site of Olympia 336
Archaeological Sites of Mycenae and Tiryns 574
Delos 353
Historic Centre (Chorá) with the Monastery of
   Saint John 'the Theologian' and the Cave of
   the Apocalypse on the Island of Pátmos 603
Medieval City of Rhodes 324
Meteora 332
Monasteries of Daphni, Hosios Loukas and Nea
   Moni of Chios Greece 342
Mount Athos 309
Old Town of Corfu 771
Paleochristian and Byzantine Monuments of
   Thessalonika 313
Pythagoreion and Heraion of Samos 388
Sanctuary of Asklepios at Epidaurus 315
Temple of Apollo Epicurius at Bassae 240

Guatemala
Antigua Guatemala 73
Archaeological Park and Ruins of Quirigua 130
Tikal National Park 88

Guinea
Mount Nimba Strict Nature Reserve 126

Haiti
National History Park – Citadel, Sans Souci, Ramiers 139

Holy See
Historic Centre of Rome, the Properties of the Holy See in that City Enjoying Extraterritorial Rights and San Paolo Fuori le Mura 92
Vatican City 180

Honduras
Maya Site of Copán 90
Río Plátano Biosphere Reserve 142

Hungary
Budapest, including the Banks of the Danube, the Buda Castle Quarter and Andrássy Avenue 274
Caves of Aggtelek Karst and Slovak Karst 456
Early Christian Necropolis of Pécs (Sopianae) 619
Fertő / Neusiedlersee Cultural Landscape 664
Hortobágy National Park - the Puszta 583
Millenary Benedictine Abbey of Pannonhalma and its Natural Environment 479
Old Village of Hollókő and its Surroundings 293
Tokaj Wine Region Historic Cultural Landscape 686

Iceland
Surtsey 789
Þingvellir National Park 709

India
Agra Fort 161
Ajanta Caves 156
Buddhist Monuments at Sanchi 342
Champaner-Pavagadh Archaeological Park 730
Chhatrapati Shivaji Terminus (formerly Victoria Terminus) 723
Churches and Convents of Goa 237
Elephanta Caves 271
Ellora Caves 160
Fatehpur Sikri 247
Great Living Chola Temples 276
Group of Monuments at Hampi 252
Group of Monuments at Mahabalipuram 204
Group of Monuments at Pattadakal 308
Hill Forts of Rajasthan 860
Humayun's Tomb, Delhi 403
Jantar Mantar 814
Kaziranga National Park 224
Keoladeo National Park 216
Khajuraho Group of Monuments 249
Mahabodhi Temple Complex at Bodh Gaya 688
Manas Wildlife Sanctuary 215
Mountain Railways of India 576
Nanda Devi and Valley of Flowers National Parks 333
Qutb Minar and its Monuments, Delhi 413
Red Fort Complex 765
Rock Shelters of Bhimbetka 694
Sun Temple, Konârak 183
Sundarbans National Park 271
Taj Mahal 154
Western Ghats 847

Indonesia
Borobudur Temple Compounds 376
Cultural Landscape of Bali Province: the Subak System as a Manifestation of the Tri Hita Karana Philosophy 859
Komodo National Park 370
Lorentz National Park 604
Prambanan Temple Compounds 373
Sangiran Early Man Site 503
Tropical Rainforest Heritage of Sumatra 712
Ujung Kulon National Park 374

Iran, Islamic Republic of
Armenian Monastic Ensembles of Iran 792
Bam and its Cultural Landscape 710
Bisotun 762
Golestan Palace 868
Gonbad-e Qābus 850
Masjed-e Jāmé of Isfahan 846
Meidan Emam, Esfahan 38
Pasargadae 714
Persepolis 68
Sheikh Safi al-Din Khānegāh and Shrine Ensemble in Ardabil 810
Shushtar Historical Hydraulic System 803
Soltaniyeh 746
Tabriz Historic Bazaar Complex 815
Takht-e Soleyman 691
Tchogha Zanbil 88
The Persian Garden 835

Iraq
Ashur (Qal'at Sherqat) 697
Hatra 215
Samarra Archaeological City 767

Ireland
Brú na Bóinne – Archaeological Ensemble of the Bend of the Boyne 401
Skellig Michael Monastery 492

Israel
Bahá'í Holy Places in Haifa and the Western Galilee 793
Biblical Tels – Megiddo, Hazor, Beer Sheba 739
Incense Route – Desert Cities in the Negev 740
Masada 676
Old City of Acre 680
Sites of Human Evolution at Mount Carmel: The Nahal Me'arot / Wadi el-Mughara Caves 843
White City of Tel-Aviv – The Modern Movement 694

Italy
Archaeological Area of Agrigento 542
Archaeological Area and the Patriarchal Basilica of Aquileia 565
Archaeological Areas of Pompei, Herculaneum and Torre Annunziata 524
Assisi, the Basilica of San Francesco and Other Franciscan Sites 632
Botanical Garden (Orto Botanico), Padua 532
Castel del Monte 506
Cathedral, Torre Civica and Piazza Grande, Modena 520
Church and Dominican Convent of Santa Maria delle Grazie with 'The Last Supper' by Leonardo da Vinci 95
Cilento and Vallo di Diano National Park with the Archeological sites of Paestum and Velia, and the Certosa di Padula 558
City of Verona 618
City of Vicenza and the Palladian Villas of the Veneto 428
Costiera Amalfitana 538
Crespi d'Adda 465
Early Christian Monuments of Ravenna 487
Eighteenth-Century Royal Palace at Caserta with the Park, the Aqueduct of Vanvitelli, and the San Leucio Complex 527
Etruscan Necropolises of Cerveteri and Tarquinia 729
Ferrara, City of the Renaissance, and its Po Delta 453
Genoa: Le Strade Nuove and the system of the Palazzi dei Rolli 759
Historic Centre of the City of Pienza 495
Historic Centre of Florence 134
Historic Centre of Naples 448
Historic Centre of Rome, the Properties of the Holy See in that City Enjoying Extraterritorial Rights and San Paolo Fuori le Mura 92
Historic Centre of San Gimignano 358
Historic Centre of Siena 460
Historic Centre of Urbino 567
Isole Eolie (Aeolian Islands) 625
Late Baroque Towns of the Val di Noto (South-Eastern Sicily) 690
Longobards in Italy. Places of the power (568-774 AD) 824
Mantua and Sabbioneta 797
Medici Villas and Gardens in Tuscany 860
Monte San Giorgio 704
Mount Etna 869
Piazza del Duomo, Pisa 265
Portovenere, Cinque Terre, and the Islands (Palmaria, Tino and Tinetto) 513
Prehistoric Pile Dwellings around the Alps 839
Residences of the Royal House of Savoy 541
Rhaetian Railway in the Albula / Bernina Landscapes 784
Rock Drawings in Valcamonica 76
Sacri Monti of Piedmont and Lombardy 695
Su Nuraxi di Barumini 546
Syracuse and the Rocky Necropolis of Pantalica 750
The Dolomites 807
The Sassi and the Park of the Rupestrian Churches of Matera 399
The Trulli of Alberobello 501
Val d'Orcia 724
Venice and its Lagoon 268
Villa Adriana, Tivoli 595
Villa d'Este, Tivoli 673
Villa Romana del Casale 546

Japan
Buddhist Monuments in the Horyu-ji Area 415
Fujisan, Sacred Place and Source of Artistic Inspiration 867

Gusuku Sites and Related Properties of the
    Kingdom of Ryukyu **643**
Himeji-jo **409**
Hiraizumi – Temples, Gardens and
    Archaeological Sites Representing the
    Buddhist Pure Land **840**
Hiroshima Peace Memorial (Genbaku Dome)
    477
Historic Monuments of Ancient Kyoto (Kyoto,
    Uji and Otsu Cities) **438**
Historic Monuments of Ancient Nara **560**
Historic Villages of Shirakawa-go and
    Gokayama **462**
Itsukushima Shinto Shrine **486**
Iwami Ginzan Silver Mine and its Cultural
    Landscape **764**
Ogasawara Islands **841**
Sacred Sites and Pilgrimage Routes in the Kii
    Mountain Range **726**
Shirakami-Sanchi **415**
Shiretoko **748**
Shrines and Temples of Nikko **604**
Yakushima **400**

Jordan
Petra **212**
Quseir Amra **221**
Um er-Rasas (Kastrom Mefa'a) **713**
Wadi Rum Protected Area **834**

Kazakhstan
Mausoleum of Khoja Ahmed Yasawi **707**
Petroglyphs within the Archaeological Landscape
    of Tamgaly **729**
Saryarka – Steppe and Lakes of Northern
    Kazakhstan **786**

Kenya
Fort Jesus, Mombasa **832**
Kenya Lake System in the Great Rift Valley **838**
Lake Turkana National Parks **517**
Lamu Old Town **682**
Mount Kenya National Park / Natural Forest
    508
Sacred Mijikenda Kaya Forests **782**

Kiribati
Phoenix Islands Protected Area **821**

Korea, Democratic People's Republic of
Complex of Koguryo Tombs **715**
Historic Monuments and Sites in Kaesŏng **862**

Korea, Republic of
Changdeokgung Palace Complex **521**
Gochang, Hwasun and Ganghwa Dolmen
    Sites **626**
Gyeongju Historic Areas **642**
Haeinsa Temple Janggyeong Panjeon, the
    Depositories for the Tripitaka Koreana
    Woodblocks **462**
Historic Villages of Korea: Hahoe and
    Yangdong **822**
Hwaseong Fortress **536**
Jeju Volcanic Island and Lava Tubes **780**
Jongmyo Shrine **468**

Royal Tombs of the Joseon Dynasty **799**
Seokguram Grotto and Bulguksa Temple **457**

Kyrgyzstan
Sulaiman-Too Sacred Mountain **803**

Lao People's Democratic Republic (Laos)
Town of Luang Prabang **464**
Vat Phou and Associated Ancient Settlements
    within the Champasak Cultural Landscape
    679

Latvia
Historic Centre of Riga **544**
Struve Geodetic Arc **747**

Lebanon
Anjar **205**
Baalbek **191**
Byblos **192**
Ouadi Qadisha (the Holy Valley) and the Forest
    of the Cedars of God (Horsh Arz el-Rab) **569**
Tyre **197**

Lesotho
Maloti-Drakensberg Park **611**

Libya
Archaeological Site of Cyrene **136**
Archaeological Site of Leptis Magna **144**
Archaeological Site of Sabratha **149**
Old Town of Ghadamès **261**
Rock-Art Sites of Tadrart Acacus **234**

Lithuania
Curonian Spit **615**
Kernavė Archaeological Site (Cultural Reserve of
    Kernavė) **715**
Struve Geodetic Arc **747**
Vilnius Historic Centre **421**

Luxembourg
City of Luxembourg: its Old Quarters and
    Fortifications **424**

Madagascar
Rainforests of the Atsinanana **778**
Royal Hill of Ambohimanga **663**
Tsingy de Bemaraha Strict Nature Reserve
    352

Malawi
Chongoni Rock-Art Area **756**
Lake Malawi National Park **190**

Malaysia
Archaeological Heritage of the Lenggong Valley
    852
Gunung Mulu National Park **638**
Kinabalu Park **631**
Melaka and George Town, Historic Cities of the
    Straits of Malacca **790**

Mali
Cliff of Bandiagara (Land of the Dogons) **340**
Old Towns of Djenné **310**

Timbuktu **321**
Tomb of Askia **725**

Malta
City of Valletta **93**
Hal Saflieni Hypogeum **98**
Megalithic Temples of Malta **96**

Marshall Islands
Bikini Atoll, Nuclear Test Site **809**

Mauritania
Ancient Ksour of Ouadane, Chinguetti, Tichitt
    and Oualata **478**
Banc d'Arguin National Park **340**

Mauritius
Aapravasi Ghat **760**
Le Morne Cultural Landscape **792**

Mexico
Agave Landscape and Ancient Industrial
    Facilities of Tequila **754**
Ancient Maya City of Calakmul, Campeche **687**
Archaeological Monuments Zone of Xochicalco
    605
Archaeological Zone of Paquimé, Casas
    Grandes **563**
Camino Real de Tierra Adentro **816**
Central University City Campus of the
    Universidad Nacional Autónoma de México
    (UNAM) **770**
Earliest 16th-Century Monasteries on the Slopes
    of Popocatepetl **432**
El Pinacate and Gran Desierto de Altar
    Biosphere Reserve **864**
El Tajin, Pre-Hispanic City **394**
Franciscan Missions in the Sierra Gorda of
    Querétaro **703**
Historic Centre of Mexico City and Xochimilco
    284
Historic Centre of Morelia **369**
Historic Centre of Oaxaca and Archaeological
    Site of Monte Albán **286**
Historic Centre of Puebla **284**
Historic Centre of Zacatecas **419**
Historic Fortified Town of Campeche **577**
Historic Monuments Zone of Querétaro **496**
Historic Monuments Zone of Tlacotalpan **548**
Historic Town of Guanajuato and Adjacent
    Mines **318**
Hospicio Cabañas, Guadalajara **534**
Islands and Protected Areas of the Gulf of
    California **733**
Luis Barragán House and Studio **722**
Monarch Butterfly Biosphere Reserve **791**
Pre-Hispanic City of Chichen-Itza **330**
Pre-Hispanic City and National Park of
    Palenque **299**
Pre-Hispanic City of Teotihuacan **288**
Pre-Hispanic Town of Uxmal **489**
Prehistoric Caves of Yagul and Mitla in the
    Central Valley of Oaxaca **817**
Protective Town of San Miguel and the
    Sanctuary of Jesús Nazareno de Atotonilco
    781

Rock Paintings of the Sierra de San Francisco
419
Sian Ka'an 267
Whale Sanctuary of El Vizcaino 401

Moldova, Republic of
Struve Geodetic Arc 747

Mongolia
Orkhon Valley Cultural Landscape 719
Petrogylphic Complexes of the Mongolian Altai
842
Uvs Nuur Basin 693

Montenegro
Durmitor National Park 107
Natural and Culturo-Historical Region of
Kotor 84

Morocco
Archaeological Site of Volubilis 543
Historic City of Meknes 494
Ksar of Aït-Ben-Haddou 305
Medina of Essaouira (formerly Mogador) 666
Medina of Fez 119
Medina of Marrakesh 218
Medina of Tétouan (formerly known as Titawin)
522
Portuguese City of Mazagan (El Jadida) 717
Rabat, Modern Capital and Historic City:
a Shared Heritage 857

Mozambique
Island of Mozambique 365

Namibia
Namib Sand Sea 869
Twyfelfontein or /Ui-//aes 770

Nepal
Chitwan National Park 196
Kathmandu Valley 50
Lumbini, the Birthplace of the Lord Buddha 512
Sagarmatha National Park 85

Netherlands
Defence Line of Amsterdam 488
Droogmakerij de Beemster (Beemster Polder)
580
Historic Area of Willemstad, Inner City and
Harbour, Curaçao 528
Ir. D.F. Woudagemaal (D.F. Wouda Steam
Pumping Station) 566
Mill Network at Kinderdijk-Elshout 523
Rietveld Schröderhuis (Rietveld Schröder House)
636
Schokland and Surroundings 449
Seventeenth-century canal ring area of
Amsterdam inside the Singelgracht 818
The Wadden Sea 804

New Zealand
New Zealand Sub-Antarctic Islands 556
Te Wahipounamu – South West New Zealand
354
Tongariro National Park 349

Nicaragua
León Cathedral 829
Ruins of León Viejo 619

Niger
Aïr and Ténéré Natural Reserves 367
Historic Centre of Agadez 862
W National Park of Niger 485

Nigeria
Osun-Osogbo Sacred Grove 741
Sukur Cultural Landscape 587

Norway
Bryggen 43
Røros Mining Town and the Circumference
104
Rock Art of Alta 232
Struve Geodetic Arc 747
Urnes Stave Church 81
Vegaøyan – the Vega Archipelago 716
West Norwegian Fjords – Geirangerfjord and
Nærøyfjord 742

Oman
Aflaj Irrigation Systems of Oman 760
Archaeological Sites of Bat, Al-Khutm and
Al-Ayn 322
Bahla Fort 303
Land of Frankincense 614

Pakistan
Archaeological Ruins at Moenjodaro 102
Buddhist Ruins at Takht-i-Bahi and
Neighbouring City Remains at Sahr-i-Bahlol
110
Fort and Shalamar Gardens in Lahore 124
Historical Monuments at Makli, Thatta 118
Rohtas Fort 532
Taxila 109

Palau
Rock Islands Southern Lagoon 858

Palestine (oPt)*
Birthplace of Jesus: Church of the Nativity and
the Pilgrimage Route, Bethlehem 853

Panama
Archaeological Site of Panamá Viejo and
Historic District of Panamá 529
Coiba National Park and its Special Zone of
Marine Protection 745
Darien National Park 130
Fortifications on the Caribbean Side of Panama:
Portobelo-San Lorenzo 99
Talamanca Range-La Amistad Reserves / La
Amistad National Park 162

Papua New Guinea
Kuk Early Agricultural Site 786

Paraguay
Jesuit Missions of La Santísima Trinidad de
Paraná and Jesús de Tavarangue 407

Peru
Chan Chan Archaeological Zone 238
Chavín (Archaeological site) 210
City of Cuzco 158
Historic Centre of Lima 326
Historic Sanctuary of Machu Picchu 172
Historical Centre of the City of Arequipa 617
Huascarán National Park 214
Lines and Geoglyphs of Nasca and Pampas de
Jumana 434
Manú National Park 296
Río Abiseo National Park 356
Sacred City of Caral-Supe 800

Philippines
Baroque Churches of the Philippines 402
Historic Town of Vigan 582
Puerto-Princesa Subterranean River National
Park 601
Rice Terraces of the Philippine Cordilleras 466
Tubbataha Reefs Natural Park 412

Poland
Auschwitz Birkenau, German Nazi
Concentration and Extermination Camp
(1940-1945) 40
Belovezhskaya Pushcha / Białowieża Forest 61
Castle of the Teutonic Order in Malbork 547
Centennial Hall in Wrocław 752
Churches of Peace in Jawor and Swidnica 675
Historic Centre of Kraków 30
Historic Centre of Warsaw 89
Kalwaria Zebrzydowska: the Mannerist
Architectural and Park Landscape Complex
and Pilgrimage Park 594
Medieval Town of Toruń 526
Muskauer Park / Park Muzakowski 719
Old City of Zamość 382
Wieliczka and Bochnia Royal Salt Mines 36
Wooden Churches of Southern Małopolska
702
Wooden Tserkvas of the Carpathian Region in
Poland and Ukraine 868

Portugal
Alto Douro Wine Region 662
Central Zone of the Town of Angra do
Heroismo in the Azores 162
Convent of Christ in Tomar 175
Cultural Landscape of Sintra 447
Garrison Border Town of Elvas and its
Fortifications 851
Historic Centre of Évora 258
Historic Centre of Guimarães 682
Historic Centre of Oporto 482
Landscape of the Pico Island Vineyard Culture
731
Laurisilva of Madeira 602
Monastery of Alcobaça 337
Monastery of Batalha 177
Monastery of the Hieronymites and Tower of
Belém in Lisbon 163
Prehistoric Rock-Art Sites in the Côa Valley and
Siega Verde 563
University of Coimbra – Alta and Sofia 863

Qatar
Al Zubarah Archaeological Site 864

Romania
Churches of Moldavia 412
Dacian Fortresses of the Orastie Mountains 597
Danube Delta 362
Historic Centre of Sighişoara 592
Monastery of Horezu 408
Villages with Fortified Churches in Transylvania 404
Wooden Churches of Maramureş 581

Russian Federation
Architectural Ensemble of the Trinity Sergius Lavra in Sergiev Posad 420
Central Sikhote-Alin 664
Church of the Ascension, Kolomenskoye 427
Citadel, Ancient City and Fortress Buildings of Derbent 698
Cultural and Historic Ensemble of the Solovetsky Islands 392
Curonian Spit 615
Ensemble of the Ferrapontov Monastery 643
Ensemble of the Novodevichy Convent 728
Golden Mountains of Altai 557
Historic and Architectural Complex of the Kazan Kremlin 646
Historic Centre of Saint Petersburg and Related Groups of Monuments 344
Historic Monuments of Novgorod and Surroundings 383
Historical Centre of the City of Yaroslavl 744
Kizhi Pogost 356
Kremlin and Red Square, Moscow 350
Lake Baikal 476
Lena Pillars Nature Park 843
Natural System of Wrangel Island Reserve 716
Putorana Plateau 819
Struve Geodetic Arc 747
Uvs Nuur Basin 693
Virgin Komi Forests 449
Volcanoes of Kamchatka 490
Western Caucasus 601
White Monuments of Vladimir and Suzdal 396

Saint Kitts and Nevis
Brimstone Hill Fortress National Park 596

Saint Lucia
Pitons Management Area 711

San Marino
San Marino Historic Centre and Mount Titano 782

Saudi Arabia
Al-Hijr Archaeological Site (Madâin Sâlih) 798
At-Turaif District in ad-Dir'iyaha 820

Senegal
Bassari Country: Bassari, Fula and Bedik Cultural Landscapes 845
Djoudj National Bird Sanctuary 121
Island of Gorée 29
Island of Saint-Louis 626

Niokolo-Koba National Park 116
Saloum Delta 832
Stone Circles of Senegambia 755

Serbia
Gamzigrad-Romuliana, Palace of Galerius 776
Medieval Monuments in Kosovo 717
Stari Ras and Sopoćani 76
Studenica Monastery 250

Seychelles
Aldabra Atoll 133
Vallée de Mai Nature Reserve 171

Slovakia
Bardejov Town Conservation Reserve 645
Caves of Aggtelek Karst and Slovak Karst 456
Historic Town of Banská Štiavnica and the Technical Monuments in its Vicinity 414
Levoča, Spišský Hrad and the Associated Cultural Monuments 417
Primeval Beech Forests of the Carpathians and the Ancient Beech Forests of Germany 772
Vlkolínec 418
Wooden Churches of the Slovak part of the Carpathian Mountain Area 795

Slovenia
Heritage of Mercury, Almadén and Idrija 858
Prehistoric Pile Dwellings around the Alps 839
Škocjan Caves 261

Solomon Islands
East Rennell 558

South Africa
Cape Floral Region Protected Areas 720
Fossil Hominid Sites of South Africa 593
iSimangaliso Wetland Park 575
Maloti-Drakensberg Park 611
Mapungubwe Cultural Landscape 693
Richtersveld Cultural and Botanical Landscape 764
Robben Island 569
Vredefort Dome 747

Spain
Alhambra, Generalife and Albayzín, Granada 202
Aranjuez Cultural Landscape 658
Archaeological Ensemble of Mérida 410
Archaeological Ensemble of Tárraco 621
Archaeological Site of Atapuerca 647
Burgos Cathedral 200
Catalan Romanesque Churches of the Vall de Boí 644
Cathedral, Alcázar and Archivo de Indias in Seville 266
Cave of Altamira and Paleolithic Cave Art of Northern Spain 220
Cultural Landscape of the Serra de Tramuntana 839
Doñana National Park 430
Garajonay National Park 250
Heritage of Mercury, Almadén and Idrija 858
Historic Centre of Córdoba 198

Historic City of Toledo 242
Historic Walled Town of Cuenca 505
Ibiza Biodiversity and Culture 572
La Lonja de la Seda de Valencia 485
Las Médulas 535
Monastery and Site of the Escurial, Madrid 193
Monuments of Oviedo and the Kingdom of the Asturias 217
Mudéjar Architecture of Aragon 256
Old City of Salamanca 328
Old Town of Ávila with its Extra-Muros Churches 233
Old Town of Cáceres 253
Old Town of Segovia and its Aqueduct 209
Palau de la Música Catalana and Hospital de Sant Pau, Barcelona 528
Palmeral of Elche 639
Poblet Monastery 366
Prehistoric Rock-Art Sites in the Côa Valley and Siega Verde 563
Pyrénées - Mont Perdu 508
Renaissance Monumental Ensembles of Úbeda and Baeza 697
Rock Art of the Mediterranean Basin on the Iberian Peninsula 562
Roman Walls of Lugo 649
Route of Santiago de Compostela 397
Royal Monastery of Santa María de Guadalupe 416
San Cristóbal de La Laguna 587
San Millán Yuso and Suso Monasteries 535
Santiago de Compostela (Old Town) 211
Teide National Park 766
Tower of Hercules 806
University and Historic Precinct of Alcalá de Henares 568
Vizcaya Bridge 758
Works of Antoni Gaudí 182

Sri Lanka
Ancient City of Polonnaruwa 140
Ancient City of Sigiriya 151
Central Highlands of Sri Lanka 823
Golden Temple of Dambulla 363
Old Town of Galle and its Fortifications 320
Sacred City of Anuradhapura 138
Sacred City of Kandy 314
Sinharaja Forest Reserve 316

Sudan
Archaeological Sites of the Island of Meroe 836
Gebel Barkal and the Sites of the Napatan Region 695

Suriname
Central Suriname Nature Reserve 658
Historic Inner City of Paramaribo 687

Sweden
Agricultural Landscape of SouthernÖland 640
Birka and Hovgården 404
Church Village of Gammelstad, Luleå 504
Decorated Farmhouses of Hälsingland 847
Engelsberg Ironworks 408
Hanseatic Town of Visby 459
High Coast 630

Laponian Area **497**
Mining Area of the Great Copper Mountain in
    Falun **667**
Naval Port of Karlskrona **553**
Rock Carvings in Tanum **432**
Royal Domain of Drottningholm **371**
Skogskyrkogården **435**
Struve Geodetic Arc **747**
Varberg Radio Station **725**

Switzerland
Abbey of St Gall **176**
Benedictine Convent of St John at Müstair **159**
La Chaux-de-Fonds / Le Locle, Watchmaking
    Town Planning **800**
Lavaux, Vineyard Terraces **777**
Monte San Giorgio **704**
Old City of Berne **157**
Prehistoric Pile Dwellings around the Alps **839**
Rhaetian Railway in the Albula / Bernina
    Landscapes **784**
Swiss Alps Jungfrau-Aletsch **660**
Swiss Tectonic Arena Sardona **787**
Three Castles, Defensive Wall and Ramparts of
    the Market-Town of Bellinzone **610**

Syrian Arab Republic (Syria)
Ancient City of Aleppo **236**
Ancient City of Bosra **105**
Ancient City of Damascus **39**
Ancient Villages of Northern Syria **837**
Crac des Chevaliers and Qal'at Salah El-Din
    761
Site of Palmyra **100**

Tajikistan
Proto-urban Site of Sarazm **817**
Tajik National Park (Mountains of the Pamirs)
    861

Tanzania
Kilimanjaro National Park **278**
Kondoa Rock-Art Sites **755**
Ngorongoro Conservation Area **42**
Ruins of Kilwa Kisiwani and Ruins of Songo
    Mnara **116**
Selous Game Reserve **137**
Serengeti National Park **112**
Stone Town of Zanzibar **612**

Thailand
Ban Chiang Archaeological Site **388**
Dong Phayayen-Khao Yai Forest Complex **741**
Historic City of Ayutthaya **359**
Historic Town of Sukhothai and Associated
    Historic Towns **375**
Thungyai-Huai Kha Khaeng Wildlife
    Sanctuaries **364**

The Gambia
Kunta Kinteh Island and Related Sites **698**
Stone Circles of Senegambia **755**

Togo
Koutammakou, the Land of the Batammariba
    726

Tunisia
Amphitheatre of El Jem **80**
Dougga / Thugga **530**
Ichkeul National Park **97**
Kairouan **335**
Medina of Sousse **317**
Medina of Tunis **72**
Punic Town of Kerkuane and its Necropolis **220**
Site of Carthage **46**

Turkey
Archaeological Site of Troy **550**
City of Safranbolu **442**
Göreme National Park and the Rock Sites of
    Cappadocia **230**
Great Mosque and Hospital of Divriği **225**
Hattusha: the Hittite Capital **237**
Hierapolis-Pamukkale **329**
Historic Areas of Istanbul **226**
Nemrut Dağ **292**
Neolithic Site of Çatalhöyük **856**
Selimiye Mosque and its Social Complex **828**
Xanthos-Letoon **333**

Turkmenistan
Kunya-Urgench **750**
Parthian Fortresses of Nisa **778**
State Historical and Cultural Park 'Ancient
    Merv' **573**

Uganda
Bwindi Impenetrable National Park **422**
Rwenzori Mountains National Park **430**
Tombs of Buganda Kings at Kasubi **663**

Ukraine
Ancient City of Tauric Chersonese and its Chora
    865
Kiev: Saint-Sophia Cathedral and Related
    Monastic Buildings, Kiev-Pechersk Lavra **347**
L'viv – the Ensemble of the Historic Centre **564**
Primeval Beech Forests of the Carpathians and
    the Ancient Beech Forests of Germany **772**
Residence of Bukovinian and Dalmatia
    Metropolitans **827**
Struve Geodetic Arc **747**
Wooden Tserkvas of the Carpathian Region in
    Poland and Ukraine **868**

United Arab Emirates
Cultural Sites of Al Ain (Hafit, Hili, Bidaa Bint
    Saud and Oases Areas) **835**

United Kingdom
Blaenavon Industrial Landscape **620**
Blenheim Palace **270**
Canterbury Cathedral, St Augustine's Abbey,
    and St Martin's Church **327**
Castles and Town Walls of King Edward in
    Gwynedd **257**
City of Bath **290**
Cornwall and West Devon Mining Landscape
    757
Derwent Valley Mills **675**
Dorset and East Devon Coast **671**
Durham Castle and Cathedral **246**

Frontiers of the Roman Empire **273**
Giant's Causeway and Causeway Coast **244**
Gough and Inaccessible Islands **468**
Heart of Neolithic Orkney **570**
Henderson Island **321**
Historic Town of St George and Related
    Fortifications, Bermuda **621**
Ironbridge Gorge **239**
Liverpool – Maritime Mercantile City **707**
Maritime Greenwich **507**
New Lanark **659**
Old and New Towns of Edinburgh **470**
Palace of Westminster and Westminster Abbey
    including Saint Margaret's Church **272**
Pontcysyllte Aqueduct and Canal **801**
Royal Botanic Gardens, Kew **692**
St Kilda **241**
Saltaire **665**
Stonehenge, Avebury and Associated Sites **254**
Studley Royal Park including the Ruins of
    Fountains Abbey **248**
Tower of London **312**

Uruguay
Historic Quarter of the City of Colonia del
    Sacramento **472**

USA
Cahokia Mounds State Historic Site **151**
Carlsbad Caverns National Park **446**
Chaco Culture **285**
Everglades National Park **53**
Grand Canyon National Park **54**
Great Smoky Mountains National Park **164**
Hawaii Volcanoes National Park **264**
Independence Hall **64**
Kluane / Wrangell-St Elias / Glacier Bay /
    Tatshenshini-Alsek **52**
La Fortaleza and San Juan National Historic
    Site in Puerto Rico **166**
Mammoth Cave National Park **126**
Mesa Verde National Park **28**
Monticello and the University of Virginia in
    Charlottesville **304**
Olympic National Park **128**
Papahānaumokuākea **814**
Redwood National Park **103**
Statue of Liberty **187**
Taos Pueblo **380**
Waterton Glacier International Peace Park **450**
Yellowstone National Park **34**
Yosemite National Park **184**

Uzbekistan
Historic Centre of Bukhara **405**
Historic Centre of Shakhrisyabz **629**
Itchan Kala **348**
Samarkand – Crossroad of Cultures **670**

Vanuatu
Chief Roi Mata's Domain **795**

Venezuela
Canaima National Park **431**
Ciudad Universitaria de Caracas **644**
Coro and its Port **398**

Vietnam
Central Sector of the Imperial Citadel of Thang
Long – Hanoi **816**
Citadel of the Ho Dynasty **837**
Complex of Hué Monuments **411**
Ha Long Bay **440**
Hoi An Ancient Town **586**
My Son Sanctuary **579**
Phong Nha-Ke Bang National Park **706**

Yemen
Historic Town of Zabid **398**
Old City of Sana'a **245**
Old Walled City of Shibam **152**
Socotra Archipelago **785**

Zambia
Mosi-oa-Tunya / Victoria Falls **338**

Zimbabwe
Great Zimbabwe National Monument **240**
Khami Ruins National Monument **257**
Mana Pools National Park, Sapi and Chewore
Safari Areas **186**
Matobo Hills **696**
Mosi-oa-Tunya / Victoria Falls **338**

Index

A
Aachen Cathedral Germany **33**
Aapravasi Ghat Mauritius **760**
Abbey and Altenmünster of Lorsch Germany
379
Abbey Church of Saint-Savin sur Gartempe
France **168**
Abbey of St Gall Switzerland **176**
Abomey, Royal Palaces of Benin **232**
Abu Mena Egypt **49**
Abu Simbel, Nubian Monuments Egypt **56**
Acre, Old City of Israel **680**
Acropolis, Athens Greece **282**
ad-Dir'iyah, At-Turaif District in Saudi Arabia
820
Aeolian Islands Italy **625**
Aflaj Irrigation Systems of Oman Oman **760**
Agave Landscape and Ancient Industrial
Facilities of Tequila Mexico **754**
Aggtelek Karst and Slovak Karst, Caves of
Hungary and Slovakia **456**
Agra Fort India **161**
Agricultural Landscape of Southern Öland
Sweden **640**
Agrigento, Archaeological Area of Italy **542**
Aigai, Archaeological Site of (modern Vergina)
Greece **504**
Aïr and Ténéré Natural Reserves Niger **367**
Ait-Ben-Haddou, Ksar of Morocco **305**
Ajanta Caves India **156**
Aksum Ethiopia **98**
Al Ain (Hafit, Hili, Bidaa Bint Saud and
Oases Areas), Cultural Sites of United Arab
Emirates **835**
Al Qal'a of Beni Hammad Algeria **109**
Al-Ayn Oman **322**
Al-Hijr Archaeological Site (Madâin Sâlih)
Saudi Arabia **798**
Al-Khutm Oman **322**
Al Zubarah Archaeological Site Qatar **864**
Albayzín, Granada Spain **202**
Alberobello, The Trulli of Italy **501**
Albi, Episcopal City of France **813**
Albula / Bernina Landscape, Rhaetian Railway
in the Italy and Switzerland **784**
Alcalá de Henares, University and Historic
Precinct of Spain **568**
Alcázar, Seville Spain **266**
Alcobaça Monastery of Portugal **337**
Aldabra Atoll Seychelles **133**
Alejandro de Humboldt National Park Cuba
672

Aleppo, Ancient City of Syrian Arab Republic
(Syria) **236**
Algiers, Kasbah of Algeria **379**
Alhambra, Generalife and Albayzín, Granada
Spain **202**
Almadén and Idrija, Heritage of Mercury
Slovenia and Spain **858**
Alps, Prehistoric Pile Dwellings around the
Switzerland, Austria, France, Germany, Italy
and Slovenia **839**
Alta, Rock Art of Norway **232**
Altai, Golden Mountains of Russian Federation
557
Altamira, Cave of Spain **220**
Alto Douro Wine Region Portugal **662**
Ambohimanga, Royal Hill of Madagascar **663**
Amiens Cathedral France **117**
Amphitheatre of El Jem Tunisia **80**
Amsterdam, Defence Line of Netherlands **488**
Amsterdam inside the Singelgracht, Seventeenth-
century canal ring area of Netherlands **818**
Ancient Building Complex in the Wudang
Mountains China **429**
Ancient City of Aleppo Syrian Arab Republic
(Syria) **236**
Ancient City of Bosra Syrian Arab Republic
(Syria) **105**
Ancient City of Damascus Syrian Arab Republic
(Syria) **39**
Ancient City of Nessebar Bulgaria **165**
Ancient City of Ping Yao China **540**
Ancient City of Polonnaruwa Sri Lanka **140**
Ancient City of Sigiriya Sri Lanka **151**
Ancient City of Tauric Chersonese and its Chora
Ukraine **865**
Ancient Ksour of Ouadane, Chinguetti, Tichitt
and Oualata Mauritania **478**
Ancient Maya City of Calakmul, Campeche
Mexico **687**
Ancient Merv Turkmenistan **573**
Ancient Thebes with its Necropolis Egypt **74**
Ancient Villages in Southern Anhui–Xidi and
Hongcun China **653**
Ancient Villages of Northern Syria Syrian Arab
Republic (Syria) **837**
Andrássy Avenue, Budapest Hungary **274**
Angkor Cambodia **390**
Angra do Heroismo in the Azores, Central Zone
of the Town of Portugal **162**
Anjar Lebanon **205**
Antigua Guatemala Guatemala **73**
Anuradhapura, Sacred City of Sri Lanka **138**
Apocalypse, Cave of the Greece **603**
Aquileia, Archaeological Area and the
Patriarchal Basilica of Italy **565**

Aragon, Mudéjar Architecture of Spain **256**
Aranjuez Cultural Landscape Spain **658**
Arc-et-Senans, Royal Saltworks of France **153**
Archaeological Area of Agrigento Italy **542**
Archaeological Area and the Patriarchal Basilica
of Aquileia Italy **565**
Archaeological Areas of Pompei, Herculaneum
and Torre Annunziata Italy **524**
Archaeological Ensemble of Mérida Spain **410**
Archaeological Ensemble of Tárraco Spain **621**
Archaeological Heritage of the Lenggong Valley
Malaysia **852**
Archaeological Landscape of the First Coffee
Plantations in the South-East Cuba **649**
Archaeological Monuments Zone of Xochicalco
Mexico **605**
Archaeological Park and Ruins of Quirigua
Guatemala **130**
Archaeological Ruins at Moenjodaro Pakistan
102
Archaeological Site of Aigai (modern name
Vergina) Greece **504**
Archaeological Site of Atapuerca Spain **647**
Archaeological Site of Cyrene Libya **136**
Archaeological Site of Delphi Greece **262**
Archaeological Site of Leptis Magna Libya **144**
Archaeological Site of Mystras Greece **341**
Archaeological Site of Olympia Greece **336**
Archaeological Site of Panamá Viejo and
Historic District of Panamá Panama **529**
Archaeological Site of Sabratha Libya **149**
Archaeological Site of Troy Turkey **550**
Archaeological Site of Volubilis Morocco **543**
Archaeological Sites of Bat, Al-Khutm and Al-
Ayn Oman **322**
Archaeological Sites of Mycenae and Tiryns
Greece **574**
Archaeological Sites of the Island of Meroe
Sudan **836**
Archaeological Zone of Paquimé, Casas
Grandes Mexico **563**
Architectural Ensemble of the Trinity Sergius
Lavra in Sergiev Posad Russian Federation
420
Architectural, Residential and Cultural Complex
of the Radziwill Family at Nesvizh Belarus
748
Archivo de Indias, Seville Spain **266**
Ardabil, Sheikh Safi al-Din Khānegāh and
Shrine Ensemble in Islamic Republic of Iran
810
Area de Conservación Guanacaste Costa Rica
596
Arequipa, Historical Centre of the City of Peru
617

Arles, Roman and Romanesque Monuments France **131**
Armenian Monastic Ensembles of Iran Islamic Republic of Iran **792**
Asante Traditional Buildings Ghana **94**
Ashur (Qal'at Sherqat) Iraq **697**
Askia, Tomb of Mali **725**
Asklepios at Epidaurus, Sanctuary of Greece **315**
Assisi, the Basilica of San Francesco and Other Franciscan Sites Italy **632**
Asturias, Kingdom of the Spain **217**
At-Turaif District in ad-Dir'iyah Saudi Arabia **820**
Atapuerca, Archaeological Site of Spain **647**
Athens, Acropolis Greece **282**
Athos, Mount Greece **309**
Atlantic Forest South-East Reserves Brazil **606**
Atol das Rocas Reserve Brazil **668**
Atsinanana, Rainforests of the Madagascar **778**
Augustusburg and Falkenlust at Brühl, Castles of Germany **193**
Auschwitz Birkenau, German Nazi Concentration and Extermination Camp (1940-1945) Poland **44**
Australian Convict Sites Australia **808**
Australian Fossil Mammal Sites (Riversleigh / Naracoorte) Australia **429**
Avebury United Kingdom **254**
Avignon, Historic Centre of France **444**
Ávila with its Extra-Muros Churches, Old Town of Spain **233**
Awash, Lower Valley of the Ethiopia **102**
Ayutthaya, Historic City of Thailand **359**

B
Baalbek Lebanon **191**
Baeza, Renaissance Monumental Ensembles of Spain **697**
Bagerhat, Historic Mosque City of Bangladesh **228**
Bagrati Cathedral and Gelati Monastery Georgia **435**
Bahá'í Holy Places in Haifa and the Western Galilee Israel **793**
Bahla Fort Oman **303**
Bahrain, Pearling, Testimony of an Island Economy Bahrain **849**
Baikal, Lake Russian Federation **476**
Bali Province: the Subak System as a Manifestation of the Tri Hita Karana Philosophy, Cultural Landscape of Indonesia **859**
Baku, Walled City of Azerbaijan **607**
Bam and its Cultural Landscape Islamic Republic of Iran **710**
Bamberg, Town of Germany **406**
Bamiyan Valley, Cultural Landscape and Archaeological Remains of the Afghanistan **703**
Ban Chiang Archaeological Site Thailand **388**
Banc d'Arguin National Park Mauritania **340**
Banská Štiavnica, Historic Town of Slovakia **414**
Barcelona, Palau de la Música Catalana and Hospital de Sant Pau Spain **528**
Bardejov Town Conservation Reserve Slovakia **645**
Baroque Churches of the Philippines Philippines **402**

Barumini, Su Nuraxi di Italy **546**
Bassae, Temple of Apollo Epicurius at Greece **240**
Bassari Country: Bassari, Fula and Bedik Cultural Landscapes Senegal **845**
Bat Oman **322**
Batalha, Monastery of Portugal **177**
Batammariba, The Land of the Togo **726**
Bath, City of United Kingdom **290**
Bauhaus and its Sites in Weimar and Dessau Germany **484**
Bayreuth, Margravial Opera House Germany **856**
Bedik, Fula and Bassari Cultural Landscapes, Bassari Country: Senegal **845**
Beemster Polder Netherlands **580**
Beer Sheba, Tel Israel **739**
Béguinages, Flemish Belgium **562**
Belfries of Belgium and France Belgium and France **575**
Belize Barrier Reef Reserve System Belize **483**
Bellinzone Switzerland **610**
Belovezhskaya Pushcha / Białowieża Forest Belarus and Poland **61**
Benedictine Convent of St John at Müstair Switzerland **159**
Berat, Historic Centre of Albania **732**
Bergpark Wilhelmshöhe Germany **866**
Berlin Modernism Housing Estates Germany **784**
Berlin, Palaces and Parks of Germany **346**
Bermuda, Historic Town of St George and Related Fortifications United Kingdom **621**
Berne, Old City of Switzerland **157**
Bernina Landscape, Rhaetian Railway in the Italy and Switzerland **784**
Bethlehem, Birthplace of Jesus: Church of the Nativity and the Pilgrimage Route Palestine **853**
Bhimbetka, Rock Shelters of India **694**
Białowieża Forest Belarus and Poland **61**
Biblical Tels – Megiddo, Hazor, Beer Sheba Israel **739**
Bikini Atoll, Nuclear Test Site Marshall Islands **809**
Birka and Hovgården Sweden **404**
Birthplace of Jesus: Church of the Nativity and the Pilgrimage Route, Bethlehem Palestine **853**
Bisotun Islamic Republic of Iran **762**
Blaenavon Industrial Landscape United Kingdom **620**
Blenheim Palace United Kingdom **270**
Bodh Gaya, Mahabodhi Temple Complex at India **688**
Bom Jesus do Congonhas, Sanctuary of Brazil **223**
Bordeaux, Port of the Moon France **775**
Borobudur Temple Compounds Indonesia **376**
Bosra, Ancient City of Syrian Arab Republic (Syria) **105**
Botanical Garden (Orto Botanico), Padua Italy **532**
Bourges Cathedral France **381**
Boyana Church, Sofia Bulgaria **60**
Brasilia Brazil **280**

Brazilian Atlantic Islands: Fernando de Noronha and Atol das Rocas Reserves Brazil **668**
Bremen, Town Hall and Roland on the Marketplace of Germany **727**
Bridgetown and its Garrison, Historic Barbados **829**
Brimstone Hill Fortress National Park Saint Kitts and Nevis **596**
Brno, Tugendhat Villa in Czech Republic **681**
Bronze Age Burial Site of Sammallahdenmäki Finland **599**
Brugge, Historic Centre of Belgium **650**
Brú na Bóinne – Archaeological Ensemble of the Bend of the Boyne Ireland **401**
Bryggen Norway **43**
Buda Castle Quarter, Budapest Hungary **274**
Budapest, including the Banks of the Danube, the Buda Castle Quarter and Andrássy Avenue Hungary **274**
Buddhist Monuments at Sanchi India **342**
Buddhist Monuments in the Horyu-ji Area Japan **415**
Buddhist Ruins at Takht-i-Bahi and Neighbouring City Remains at Sahr-i-Bahlol Pakistan **110**
Buganda Kings, Tombs of Uganda **663**
Bukhara, Historic Centre of Uzbekistan **405**
Bukovinian and Dalmatia Metropolitans, Residence of Ukraine **827**
Bulguksa Temple Republic of Korea **457**
Burgos Cathedral Spain **200**
Butrint Albania **389**
Bwindi Impenetrable National Park Uganda **422**
Byblos Lebanon **192**

C
Cáceres, Old Town of Spain **253**
Cahokia Mounds State Historic Site USA **151**
Cairo, Historic Egypt **78**
Calais Mining Basin, Nord-Pas de France **850**
Calakmul, Ancient Maya City of Mexico **687**
Camagüey, Historic Centre of Cuba **785**
Camino Real de Tierra Mexico **816**
Campeche, Historic Fortified Town of Mexico **577**
Canadian Rocky Mountain Parks Canada **194**
Canaima National Park Venezuela **431**
Canal du Centre, The Four Lifts on the Belgium **554**
Canal du Midi France **480**
Canterbury Cathedral, St Augustine's Abbey, and St Martin's Church United Kingdom **327**
Cape Floral Region Protected Areas South Africa **720**
Capital Cities and Tombs of the Ancient Koguryo Kingdom China **722**
Cappadocia, Rock Sites of Turkey **230**
Caracas, Ciudad Universitaria de Venezuela **644**
Caral-Supe, Sacred City of Peru **800**
Carcassonne, Historic Fortified City of France **514**
Carioca Landscapes between the Mountain and the Sea, Rio de Janeiro: Brazil **844**
Carlsbad Caverns National Park USA **446**
Carlton Gardens, Melbourne Australia **718**

Carpathian Mountain Area, Wooden Churches
of the Slovak part of the Slovakia **795**
Carpathians and Ancient Beech Forests of
Germany, Primeval Beech Forests of the
Germany, Slovakia and Ukraine **772**
Cartagena Colombia **184**
Carthage, Site of Tunisia **46**
Casas Grandes, Archaeological Zone of
Paquimé Mexico **563**
Caserta, Eighteenth-Century Royal Palace at
Italy **527**
Castel del Monte Italy **506**
Castle of the Teutonic Order in Malbork Poland
547
Castles and Town Walls of King Edward in
Gwynedd United Kingdom **257**
Castles of Augustusburg and Falkenlust at Brühl
Germany **193**
Catalan Romanesque Churches of the Vall de
Boí Spain **644**
Çatalhöyük, Neolithic Site of Turkey **856**
Cathedral and Churches of Echmiatsin and the
Archaeological Site of Zvartnots Armenia **655**
Cathedral of Notre-Dame, Former Abbey of
Saint-Rémi and Palace of Tau, Reims France
372
Cathedral of St James in Šibenik Croatia **627**
Cathedral, Alcázar and Archivo de Indias in
Seville Spain **266**
Cathedral, Torre Civica and Piazza Grande,
Modena Italy **520**
Caucasus, Western Russian Federation **601**
Causeway Coast United Kingdom **244**
Causses and the Cévennes, Mediterranean
agro-pastoral Cultural Landscape,The
France **826**
Cave of Altamira and Paleolithic Cave Art of
Northern Spain Spain **220**
Cave of the Apocalypse on the Island of Pátmos,
Historic Centre (Chorá) with the Monastery
of Saint John 'the Theologian' and the Greece
603
Caves of Aggtelek Karst and Slovak Karst
Hungary and Slovakia **456**
Cedars of God, Forest of the Lebanon **569**
Centennial Hall in Wroclaw Poland **752**
Central Amazon Conservation Complex Brazil
624
Central Highlands of Sri Lanka Sri Lanka **823**
Central Sector of the Imperial Citadel of Thang
Long – Hanoi Vietnam **816**
Central Sikhote-Alin Russian Federation **664**
Central Suriname Nature Reserve Suriname **658**
Central University City Campus of the
Universidad Nacional Autónoma de México
(UNAM) Mexico **770**
Central Zone of the Town of Angra do
Heroismo in the Azores Portugal **162**
Cerrado Protected Areas: Chapada dos
Veadeiros and Emas National Parks Brazil
681
Certosa di Padula Italy **558**
Cerveteri and Tarquinia, Etruscan Necropolises
of Italy **729**
Český Krumlov, Historic Centre of Czech
Republic **386**

Chaco Culture USA **285**
Champaner-Pavagadh Archaeological Park
India **730**
Champasak Cultural Landscape Lao People's
Democratic Republic (Laos) **679**
Chan Chan Archaeological Zone Peru **238**
Changdeokgung Palace Complex Republic of
Korea **521**
Chapada dos Veadeiros National Park Brazil
681
Chartres Cathedral France **65**
Chavín (Archaeological site) Peru **210**
Chengde, Mountain Resort and its Outlying
Temples China **436**
Chengjiang Fossil Site China **845**
Chewore Safari Area Zimbabwe **186**
Chhatrapati Shivaji Terminus (formerly Victoria
Terminus), Mumbai India **723**
Chichen-Itza, Pre-Hispanic City of Mexico
330
Chief Roi Mata's Domain Vanuatu **795**
Chiloé, Churches of Chile **620**
China Danxia China **811**
Chinguetti, Ancient Ksour of Mauritania **478**
Chiquitos, Jesuit Missions of the Bolivia **348**
Chitwan National Park Nepal **196**
Choirokoitia Cyprus **554**
Chola Temples, Great Living India **276**
Chongoni Rock-Art Area Malawi **756**
Chorá Greece **603**
Church and Dominican Convent of Santa
Maria delle Grazie with 'The Last Supper' by
Leonardo da Vinci Italy **95**
Church of the Ascension, Kolomenskoye Russian
Federation **427**
Church of the Nativity and the Pilgrimage
Route, Bethlehem, Birthplace of Jesus:
Palestine **853**
Church Village of Gammelstad, Luleå Sweden
504
Churches and Convents of Goa India **237**
Churches of Chiloé Chile **620**
Churches of Moldavia Romania **412**
Churches of Peace in Jawor and Swidnica
Poland **675**
Cidade Velha, Historic Centre of Ribeira Grande
Cape Verde **799**
Cienfuegos, Urban Historic Centre of Cuba **749**
Cilento and Vallo di Diano National Park with
the Archeological sites of Paestum and Velia,
and the Certosa di Padula Italy **558**
Cinque Terre Italy **513**
Cistercian Abbey of Fontenay France **121**
Citadel, Ancient City and Fortress Buildings of
Derbent Russian Federation **698**
Citadel of the Ho Dynasty Vietnam **837**
City of Bath United Kingdom **290**
City of Cuzco Peru **158**
City of Graz – Historic Centre and Schloss
Eggenberg Austria **585**
City of Luxembourg: its Old Quarters and
Fortifications Luxembourg **424**
City of Potosí Bolivia **289**
City of Quito Ecuador **32**
City of Safranbolu Turkey **442**
City of Valletta Malta **93**

City of Verona Italy **618**
City of Vicenza and the Palladian Villas of the
Veneto Italy **428**
Ciudad Universitaria de Caracas Venezuela **644**
Classical Gardens of Suzhou China **518**
Classical Weimar Germany **549**
Cliff of Bandiagara (Land of the Dogons) Mali
340
Côa Valley and Siega Verde, Prehistoric Rock-
Art Sites in the Portugal and Spain **563**
Cocos Island National Park Costa Rica **516**
Coffee Cultural Landscape of Colombia
Colombia **841**
Coffee Plantations in the South-East of Cuba,
Archaeological Landscape of the First Cuba
649
Coiba National Park and its Special Zone of
Marine Protection Panama **745**
Collegiate Church, Castle, and Old Town of
Quedlinburg Germany **441**
Cologne Cathedral Germany **474**
Colonia del Sacramento, Historic Quarter of the
City of Uruguay **472**
Colonial City of Santo Domingo Dominican
Republic **343**
Comoé National Park Côte d'Ivoire **153**
Complex of Hué Monuments Vietnam **411**
Complex of Koguryo Tombs Democratic People's
Republic of Korea **715**
Confucius, Temple and Cemetery of China **433**
Convent of Christ in Tomar Portugal **175**
Copan, Maya Site of Honduras **90**
Córdoba, Historic Centre of Spain **198**
Córdoba, Jesuit Block and Estancias of
Argentina **647**
Corfu, Old Town of Greece **771**
Cornwall and West Devon Mining Landscape
United Kingdom **763**
Coro and its Port Venezuela **398**
Costiera Amalfitana Italy **538**
Crac des Chevaliers and Qal'at Salah El-Din
Syrian Arab Republic (Syria) **761**
Crespi d'Adda Italy **465**
Cuenca, Historic Walled Town of Spain **505**
Cueva de las Manos, Río Pinturas Argentina
607
Cultural Landscape and Archaeological Remains
of the Bamiyan Valley Afghanistan **703**
Cultural and Historic Ensemble of the
Solovetsky Islands Russian Federation **392**
Cultural Landscape of Bali Province: the Subak
System as a Manifestation of the Tri Hita
Karana Philosophy Indonesia **859**
Cultural Landscape of Honghe Hani Rice
Terraces China **861**
Cultural Landscape of Sintra Portugal **447**
Cultural Landscape of the Serra de Tramuntana
Spain **839**
Cultural Sites of Al Ain (Hafit, Hili, Bidaa
Bint Saud and Oases Areas) United Arab
Emirates **835**
Curonian Spit Lithuania and Russian Federation
615
Cuzco, City of Peru **158**
Cyrene, Archaeological Site of Libya **136**

D

Dacian Fortresses of the Orastie Mountains Romania **597**
Dahshur Egypt **70**
Damascus, Ancient City of Syrian Arab Republic (Syria) **39**
Dambulla, Golden Temple of Sri Lanka **363**
Danube, Banks of the, Budapest Hungary **274**
Danube Delta Romania **362**
Daphni, Monastery of Greece **342**
Darien National Park Panama **130**
Dazu Rock Carvings China **584**
Decorated Farmhouses of Hälsingland Sweden **847**
Defence Line of Amsterdam Netherlands **488**
Delos Greece **353**
Delphi, Archaeological Site of Greece **262**
Dengfeng in the 'Centre of Heaven and Earth' Historic Monuments of China **810**
Derbent, Ancient City of Russian Federation **698**
Derwent Valley Mills United Kingdom **675**
Desembarco del Granma National Park Cuba **583**
Dessau, Bauhaus and its Sites in Germany **484**
Dessau-Wörlitz, Garden Kingdom of Germany **610**
Diamantina, Historic Centre of the Town of Brazil **588**
Dilmun, Ancient Harbour and Capital of Bahrain **746**
Dinosaur Provincial Park Canada **48**
Diocletian, Palace of Croatia **82**
Discovery Coast Atlantic Forest Reserves Brazil **579**
Divriği, Great Mosque and Hospital of Turkey **225**
Dja Faunal Reserve Cameroon **308**
Djémila Algeria **148**
Djenné, Old Towns of Mali **310**
Djoudj National Bird Sanctuary Senegal **121**
Dogons, Land of the Mali **340**
Dolomites, The Italy **807**
Doñana National Park Spain **430**
Dong Phayayen-Khao Yai Forest Complex Thailand **741**
Dorset and East Devon Coast United Kingdom **671**
Dougga / Thugga Tunisia **530**
Drakensberg Park South Africa **611**
Droogmakerij de Beemster (Beemster Polder) Netherlands **580**
Drottningholm, Royal Domain of Sweden **371**
Dubrovnik, Old City of Croatia **86**
Dujiangyan Irrigation System China **648**
Durham Castle and Cathedral United Kingdom **246**
Durmitor National Park Montenegro **107**

E

Earliest 16th-Century Monasteries on the Slopes of Popocatepetl Mexico **432**
Early Christian Monuments of Ravenna Italy **487**
Early Christian Necropolis of Pécs (Sopianae) Hungary **619**
East Devon Coast United Kingdom **671**

East Rennell Solomon Islands **558**
Echmiatsin, Cathedral and Churches of Armenia **655**
Ecosystem and Relict Cultural Landscape of Lopé-Okanda Gabon **781**
Edinburgh, Old and New Towns of United Kingdom **470**
Eighteenth-Century Royal Palace at Caserta with the Park, the Aqueduct of Vanvitelli, and the San Leucio Complex Italy **527**
Eisleben and Wittenberg, Luther Memorials in Germany **503**
El Jadida Morocco **717**
El Jem, Amphitheatre of Tunisia **80**
El Pinacate and Gran Desierto de Altar Biosphere Reserve Mexico **864**
El Tajin, Pre-Hispanic City Mexico **394**
El Vizcaino, Whale Sanctuary of Mexico **401**
Elche, Palmeral of Spain **639**
Elephanta Caves India **271**
Ellora Caves India **160**
Elvas and its Fortifications, Garrison Border Town of Portugal **851**
Emas National Park Brazil **681**
Emei, Mount China **481**
Engelsberg Ironworks Sweden **408**
Ensemble of the Ferrapontov Monastery Russian Federation **643**
Ensemble of the Novodevichy Convent Russian Federation **728**
Epidaurus, Sanctuary of Asklepios at Greece **315**
Episcopal City of Albi France **813**
Episcopal Complex of the Euphrasian Basilica in the Historic Centre of Poreč Croatia **516**
Escurial, Monastery and site of the Spain **193**
Essaouira (formerly Mogador), Medina of Morocco **666**
Essen, Zollverein Coal Mine Industrial Complex in Germany **667**
Etruscan Necropolises of Cerveteri and Tarquinia Italy **729**
Euphrasian Basilica, Episcopal Complex of the Croatia **516**
Everest, Mount Nepal **85**
Everglades National Park USA **53**
Évora, Historic Centre of Portugal **258**

F

Fagus Factory in Alfeld Germany **826**
Falkenlust Castle at Brühl Germany **193**
Falun, Mining Area of the Great Copper Mountain in Sweden **667**
Fasil Ghebbi, Gondar Region Ethiopia **60**
Fatehpur Sikri India **247**
Fernando de Noronha and Atol das Rocas Reserves Brazil **668**
Ferrapontov Monastery, Ensemble of the Russian Federation **643**
Ferrara, City of the Renaissance, and its Po Delta Italy **453**
Fertö / Neusiedlersee Cultural Landscape Austria and Hungary **664**
Fez, Medina of Morocco **119**
Flemish Béguinages Belgium **562**
Flint Mines, Neolithic Belgium **652**
Florence, Historic Centre of Italy **134**

Fontainebleau, Palace and Park of France **113**
Fontenay, Cistercian Abbey of France **121**
Fort and Shalamar Gardens in Lahore Pakistan **124**
Forts and Castles, Volta, Greater Accra, Central and Western Regions Ghana **44**
Fortifications of Vauban France **794**
Fortifications on the Caribbean Side of Panama: Portobelo-San Lorenzo Panama **99**
Fort Jesus, Mombasa Kenya **832**
Fortress of Suomenlinna Finland **378**
Fossil Cliffs, Joggins Canada **796**
Fossil Hominid Sites of South Africa South Africa **593**
Fossil Mammal Sites (Riversleigh / Naracoorte) Australia **429**
Fountains Abbey, Ruins of United Kingdom **248**
Four Lifts on the Canal du Centre and their Environs, La Louvière and Le Roeulx (Hainault), The Belgium **554**
Franciscan Missions in the Sierra Gorda of Querétaro Mexico **703**
Frankincense, Land of Oman **614**
Fraser Island Australia **393**
Frontiers of the Roman Empire United Kingdom and Germany **273**
Fuerte de Samaipata Bolivia **556**
Fujian Tulou China **788**
Fujisan, Sacred Place and Source of Artistic Inspiration Japan **867**
Fula, Bassari and Bedik Cultural Landscapes, Bassari Country: Senegal **845**

G

Galápagos Islands Ecuador **26**
Galerius, Palace of Serbia **776**
Galle and its Fortifications, Old Town of Sri Lanka **320**
Gammelstad, Church Village of, Luleå Sweden **504**
Gamzigrad-Romuliana, Palace of Galerius Serbia **776**
Ganghwa Dolmen Republic of Korea **626**
Garajonay National Park Spain **250**
Garamba National Park Dem. Rep. of the Congo **94**
Garden Kingdom of Dessau-Wörlitz Germany **610**
Gardens and Castle at Kroměříž Czech Republic **565**
Garrison Border Town of Elvas and its Fortifications Portugal **851**
Gaudí, Antoni Spain **182**
Gebel Barkal and the Sites of the Napatan Region Sudan **695**
Geghard, Monastery of Armenia **630**
Geirangerfjord Norway **742**
Gelati Monastery Georgia **435**
Genbaku Dome Japan **477**
Generalife, Granada Spain **202**
Genoa: Le Strade Nuove and the system of the Palazzi dei Rolli Italy **759**
Geoglyphs and Lines of Nasca and Pampas de Jumana Peru **434**
George Town, Historic City of the Straits of Malacca Malaysia **790**
Ghadamès, Old Town of Libya **261**

Giant's Causeway and Causeway Coast United Kingdom **244**
Girolata, Gulf of France **174**
Giza Egypt **70**
Gjirokastra, Historic Centre of Albania **732**
Glacier Bay Canada and USA **52**
Goa, Churches and Convents of India **237**
Gobustan Rock Art Cultural Landscape Azerbaijan **767**
Gochang, Hwasun and Ganghwa Dolmen Sites Republic of Korea **626**
Goiás, Historic Centre of the Town of Brazil **674**
Gokayama, Historic Villages of Japan **462**
Golden Mountains of Altai Russian Federation **557**
Golden Temple of Dambulla Sri Lanka **363**
Golestan Palace Islamic Republic of Iran **868**
Gonbad-e Qābus Islamic Republic of Iran **850**
Gondwana Rainforests of Australia Australia **260**
Gorée, Island of Senegal **29**
Göreme National Park and the Rock Sites of Cappadocia Turkey **230**
Goslar, Historic Town of Germany **387**
Gough and Inaccessible Islands United Kingdom **468**
Granada, Spain **202**
Grand-Bassam, Historic Town of Côte d'Ivoire **855**
Grand Canyon National Park USA **54**
Grand Pré, Landscape of Canada **849**
Graz and Schloss Eggenberg, Historic Centre of the City of Austria **585**
Great Barrier Reef Australia **122**
Great Copper Mountain in Falun, Mining Area of the Sweden **667**
Great Living Chola Temples India **276**
Great Mosque and Hospital of Divriği Turkey **225**
Great Rift Valley, Kenya Lake System in the Kenya **838**
Great Saltworks of Salins-le-Bains France **153**
Great Smoky Mountains National Park USA **164**
Great Wall, The China **294**
Great Zimbabwe National Monument Zimbabwe **240**
Greater Blue Mountains Area Australia **609**
Greenwich, Maritime United Kingdom **507**
Grimeton, Varberg Radio Station Sweden **725**
Gros Morne National Park Canada **302**
Group of Monuments at Hampi India **252**
Group of Monuments at Mahabalipuram India **204**
Group of Monuments at Pattadakal India **308**
Guadalajara, Hospicio Cabañas Mexico **534**
Guanacaste, Area de Conservación Costa Rica **596**
Guanajuato, Historic Town of Mexico **318**
Guaranis, Jesuit Missions of the Argentina and Brazil **159**
Guimarães, Historic Centre of Portugal **682**
Gulf of California, Islands and Protected Areas of the Mexico **733**
Gulf of Porto: Calanche of Piana, Gulf of Girolata, Scandola Reserve France **174**
Gunung Mulu National Park Malaysia **638**

Gusuku Sites and Related Properties of the Kingdom of Ryukyu Japan **643**
Gwynedd, Castles and Town Walls of King Edward in United Kingdom **257**
Gyeongju Historic Areas Republic of Korea **642**

H

Ha Long Bay Vietnam **440**
Haeinsa Temple Janggyeong Panjeon, the Depositories for the Tripitaka Koreana Woodblocks Republic of Korea **462**
Haghpat and Sanahin, Monasteries of Armenia **500**
Hahoe and Yangdong, Historic Villages of Korea: Republic of Korea **822**
Haifa, Bahá'í Holy Places in Israel **793**
Hal Saflieni Hypogeum Malta **98**
Hallstatt-Dachstein / Salzkammergut Cultural Landscape Austria **531**
Hälsingland, Decorated Farmhouses of Sweden **847**
Hampi, Group of Monuments at India **252**
Hangzhou, West Lake Cultural Landscape of China **831**
Hanseatic City of Lübeck Germany **281**
Hanseatic Town of Visby Sweden **459**
Harar Jugol, the Fortified Historic Town Ethiopia **752**
Hatra Iraq **215**
Hattusha: the Hittite Capital Turkey **237**
Havana, Old Cuba **146**
Hawaii Volcanoes National Park USA **264**
Hazor, Tel Israel **739**
Head-Smashed-In Buffalo Jump Canada **118**
Heard and McDonald Islands Australia **522**
Heart of Neolithic Orkney United Kingdom **570**
Henderson Island United Kingdom **321**
Heraion of Samos Greece **388**
Herculaneum, Archaeological Area of Italy **524**
Hercules, Tower of Spain **806**
Heritage of Mercury, Almadén and Idrija Slovenia and Spain **858**
Hierapolis-Pamukkale Turkey **329**
Hieronymites, Monastery of the Portugal **163**
High Coast Sweden **630**
Hildesheim, St Mary's Cathedral and St Michael's Church Germany **225**
Hill Forts of Rajasthan India **860**
Himeji-jo Japan **409**
Hiraizumi – Temples, Gardens and Archaeological Sites Representing the Buddhist Pure Land Japan **840**
Hiroshima Peace Memorial (Genbaku Dome) Japan **477**
Historic and Architectural Complex of the Kazan Kremlin Russian Federation **646**
Historic Area of Willemstad, Inner City and Harbour, Curaçao, Netherlands **528**
Historic Areas of Istanbul Turkey **226**
Historic Bridgetown and its Garrison Barbados **829**
Historic Cairo Egypt **78**
Historic Centre (Chóra) with the Monastery of Saint John 'the Theologian' and the Cave of the Apocalypse on the Island of Pátmos Greece **603**

Historic Centre (Old Town) of Tallinn Estonia **509**
Historic Centre of the City of Pienza Italy **495**
Historic Centre of the City of Salzburg Austria **498**
Historic Centre of the Town of Diamantina Brazil **588**
Historic Centre of the Town of Goiás Brazil **674**
Historic Centre of the Town of Olinda Brazil **150**
Historic Centre of Agadez Niger **862**
Historic Centre of Avignon: Papal Palace, Episcopal Ensemble and Avignon Bridge France **444**
Historic Centre of Brugge Belgium **650**
Historic Centre of Bukhara Uzbekistan **405**
Historic Centre of Camagüey Cuba **785**
Historic Centre of Český Krumlov Czech Republic **386**
Historic Centre of Córdoba Spain **198**
Historic Centre of Évora Portugal **258**
Historic Centre of Florence Italy **134**
Historic Centre of Guimarães Portugal **682**
Historic Centre of Kraków Poland **30**
Historic Centre of Lima Peru **326**
Historic Centre of Macao China **737**
Historic Centre of Mexico City and Xochimilco Mexico **284**
Historic Centre of Morelia Mexico **369**
Historic Centre of Naples Italy **448**
Historic Centre of Oaxaca and Archaeological Site of Monte Albán Mexico **286**
Historic Centre of Oporto Portugal **482**
Historic Centre of Prague Czech Republic **384**
Historic Centre of Puebla Mexico **284**
Historic Centre of Riberia Grande Cape Verde **799**
Historic Centre of Riga Latvia **544**
Historic Centre of Rome, the Properties of the Holy See in that City Enjoying Extraterritorial Rights and San Paolo Fuori le Mura Italy **92**
Historic Centre of Saint Petersburg and Related Groups of Monuments Russian Federation **344**
Historic Centre of Salvador de Bahia Brazil **208**
Historic Centre of San Gimignano Italy **358**
Historic Centre of Santa Ana de los Ríos de Cuenca Ecuador **576**
Historic Centre of Santa Cruz de Mompox Colombia **473**
Historic Centre of São Luís Brazil **537**
Historic Centre of Shakhrisyabz Uzbekistan **629**
Historic Centre of Siena Italy **460**
Historic Centre of Sighişoara Romania **592**
Historic Centre of Telč Czech Republic **392**
Historic Centre of Urbino Italy **567**
Historic Centre of Vienna Austria **678**
Historic Centre of Warsaw Poland **89**
Historic Centre of Zacatecas Mexico **419**
Historic Centres of Berat and Gjirokastra Albania **732**
Historic Centres of Stralsund and Wismar Germany **690**
Historic City of Ayutthaya Thailand **359**
Historic City of Meknes Morocco **494**
Historic City of Sucre Bolivia **367**

Historic City of Toledo Spain **242**
Historic City of Trogir Croatia **533**
Historic District of Old Québec Canada **206**
Historic District of Panamá Panamá **529**
Historic Ensemble of the Potala Palace, Lhasa China **425**
Historic Fortified City of Carcassonne France **514**
Historic Fortified Town of Campeche Mexico **577**
Historic Inner City of Paramaribo Suriname **687**
Historical Monuments at Makli, Thatta Pakistan **118**
Historic Monuments and Sites in Kaesŏng Democratic People's Republic of Korea **862**
Historic Monuments of Ancient Kyoto (Kyoto, Uji and Otsu Cities) Japan **438**
Historic Monuments of Ancient Nara Japan **560**
Historic Monuments of Dengfeng in the 'Centre of Heaven and Earth' China **810**
Historic Monuments of Novgorod and Surroundings Russian Federation **383**
Historic Monuments Zone of Querétaro Mexico **496**
Historic Monuments Zone of Tlacotalpan Mexico **548**
Historic Mosque City of Bagerhat Bangladesh **228**
Historic Quarter of the City of Colonia del Sacramento Uruguay **472**
Historic Quarter of the Seaport City of Valparaíso Chile **696**
Historic Sanctuary of Machu Picchu Peru **172**
Historic Site of Lyons France **561**
Historic Town of Banská Štiavnica and the Technical Monuments in its Vicinity Slovakia **414**
Historic Town of Grand-Bassam Côte d'Ivoire **855**
Historic Town of Guanajuato and Adjacent Mines Mexico **318**
Historic Town of Ouro Preto Brazil **108**
Historic Town of St George and Related Fortifications, Bermuda United Kingdom **621**
Historic Town of Sukhothai and Associated Historic Towns Thailand **375**
Historic Town of Vigan Philippines **582**
Historic Town of Zabid Yemen **398**
Historic Villages of Korea: Hahoe and Yangdong Republic of Korea **822**
Historic Villages of Shirakawa-go and Gokayama Japan **462**
Historic Walled Town of Cuenca Spain **505**
Historical Centre of the City of Arequipa Peru **617**
Historical Centre of the City of Yaroslavl Russian Federation **744**
Historical Complex of Split with the Palace of Diocletian Croatia **82**
Historical Monuments of Mtskheta Georgia **437**
Ho Dynasty, Citadel of the Vietnam **837**
Hoi An Ancient Town Vietnam **586**
Holašovice Historical Village Reservation Czech Republic **551**
Hollókő, Old Village of Hungary **293**

Holy Trinity Column in Olomouc Czech Republic **637**
Hongcun, Southern Anhui China **653**
Horezu, Monastery of Romania **408**
Horta, Victor Belgium **648**
Hortobágy National Park - the Puszta Hungary **583**
Horyu-ji Area, Buddhist Monuments in the Japan **415**
Hosios Loukas, Monastery of Greece **342**
Hospicio Cabañas, Guadalajara Mexico **534**
Hospital de Sant Pau, Barcelona Spain **528**
Hovgården Sweden **404**
Huanglong Scenic and Historic Interest Area China **395**
Huangshan, Mount China **357**
Huascarán National Park Peru **214**
Hué Monuments, Complex of Vietnam **411**
Humayun's Tomb, Delhi India **403**
Humberstone and Santa Laura Saltpeter Works Chile **736**
Hwaseong Fortress Republic of Korea **536**
Hwasun Republic of Korea **626**

Iberian Peninsula, Rock Art of the Mediterranean Basin on the Spain **562**
Ibiza, Biodiversity and Culture Spain **572**
Ichkeul National Park Tunisia **97**
Idrija and Almadén, Heritage of Mercury Slovenia and Spain **858**
Iguaçu National Park Brazil **235**
Iguazu National Park Argentina **188**
Ilulissat Icefjord Denmark **708**
Imperial Citadel of Thang Long – Hanoi, Central Sector of the Vietnam **816**
Imperial Garden, Beijing China **552**
Imperial Palaces of the Ming and Qing Dynasties in Beijing and Shenyang China **277**
Imperial Tombs of the Ming and Qing Dynasties China **616**
Incense Route – Desert Cities in the Negev Israel **740**
Independence Hall, Philadelphia USA **64**
Ingenios, Valley de los Cuba **323**
Ir. D.F. Woudagemaal (D.F. Wouda Steam Pumping Station) Netherlands **566**
Ironbridge Gorge United Kingdom **239**
Ironworks, Völklingen Germany **441**
Ischigualasto / Talampaya Natural Parks Argentina **628**
Isfahan, Masjed-e Jāmé of Islamic Republic of Iran **846**
iSimangaliso Wetland Park South Africa **575**
Island of Gorée Senegal **29**
Island of Mozambique Mozambique **365**
Island of Saint-Louis Senegal **626**
Islands and Protected Areas of the Gulf of California Mexico **733**
Isole Eolie (Aeolian Islands) Italy **625**
Istanbul, Historic Areas of Turkey **226**
Itchan Kala Uzbekistan **348**
Itsukushima Shinto Shrine Japan **486**
Ivanovo, Rock-Hewn Churches of Bulgaria **69**
Iwami Ginzan Silver Mine and its Cultural Landscape Japan **764**

J
Jam, Minaret and Archaeological Remains of Afghanistan **683**
Jantar Mantar India **814**
Jawor and Swidnica, Churches of Peace in Poland **675**
Jeju Volcanic Island and Lava Tubes Republic of Korea **780**
Jelling Mounds, Runic Stones and Church Denmark **426**
Jerusalem and its Walls, Old City of **114**
Jesuit Block and Estancias of Córdoba, Argentina **647**
Jesuit Missions of the Chiquitos Bolivia **348**
Jesuit Missions of the Guaranis Argentina and Brazil **159**
Jesuit Missions of La Santísima Trinidad de Paraná and Jesús de Tavarangue Paraguay **407**
Jesús Nazareno de Atotonilco, Sanctuary of Mexico **781**
Jewish Quarter and St Procopius' Basilica in Třebíč Czech Republic **704**
Jiajin Mountains, Giant Panda Sanctuary China **751**
Jiuzhaigou Valley Scenic and Historic Interest Area China **380**
Joggins Fossil Cliffs Canada **796**
Jongmyo Shrine Republic of Korea **468**
Joseon Dynasty, Royal Tombs of the Republic of Korea **799**
Joya de Cerén Archaeological Site El Salvador **416**
Jumana, Pampas de Peru **434**
Jungfrau-Aletsch Switzerland **660**
Jurisdiction of Saint-Emilion France **600**

K
Kahuzi-Biega National Park Dem. Rep. of the Congo **97**
Kaiping Diaolou and Villages China **774**
Kakadu National Park Australia **127**
Kalwaria Zebrzydowska: the Mannerist Architectural and Park Landscape Complex and Pilgrimage Park Poland **594**
Kamchatka, Volcanoes of Russian Federation **490**
Kandy, Sacred City of Sri Lanka **314**
Karlskrona, Naval Port of Sweden **553**
Kasbah of Algiers Algeria **379**
Kastrom Mefa'a (Um er-Rasas) Jordan **713**
Kasubi, Tombs of Buganda Kings at Uganda **663**
Kathmandu Valley Nepal **50**
Kazan Kremlin, Historic and Architectural Complex of the Russian Federation **646**
Kazanlak, Thracian Tomb of Bulgaria **49**
Kaziranga National Park India **224**
Kenya, Mount Kenya **50**
Kenya Lake System in the Great Rift Valley Kenya **838**
Keoladeo National Park India **216**
Kerkuane, Punic Town of Tunisia **220**
Kernavė Archaeological Site (Cultural Reserve of Kernavė) Lithuania **715**

Kew, Royal Botanic Gardens United Kingdom 692

Khajuraho Group of Monuments India 249

Khami Ruins National Monument Zimbabwe 257

Khoja Ahmed Yasawi, Mausoleum of Kazakhstan 707

Kiev: Saint-Sophia Cathedral and Related Monastic Buildings, Kiev-Pechersk Lavra Ukraine 347

Kii Mountain Range, Sacred Sites and Pilgrimage Routes in the Japan 726

Kilimanjaro National Park Tanzania 278

Kilwa Kisiwani, Ruins of Tanzania 116

Kinabalu Park Malaysia 631

Kinderdijk-Elshout Mill Network Netherlands 523

King Edward, Castles and Town Walls of United Kingdom 257

Kizhi Pogost Russian Federation 356

Kluane / Wrangell-St Elias / Glacier Bay / Tatshenshini-Alsek Canada and USA 52

Koguryo Kingdom, Capital Cities and Tombs of the Ancient China 722

Koguryo Tombs, Complex of Democratic People's Republic of Korea 715

Kolomenskoye, Church of the Ascension Russian Federation 427

Komodo National Park Indonesia 370

Konârak, Sun Temple India 183

Kondoa Rock-Art Sites Tanzania 755

Kong Family Mansion in Qufu China 433

Konso Cultural Landscape Ethiopia 833

Kosovo, Medieval Monuments in Serbia 717

Kotor, Natural and Culturo-Historical Region of Montenegro 84

Koutammakou, the Land of the Batammariba Togo 726

Kremlin and Red Square, Moscow Russian Federation 350

Kromdraai, Fossil Hominid Site South Africa 593

Kroměříž, Gardens and Castle at Czech Republic 565

Kronborg Castle Denmark 608

Ksar of Ait-Ben-Haddou Morocco 305

Kuk Early Agricultural Site Papua New Guinea 786

Kunta Kinteh Island and Related Sites The Gambia 698

Kunya-Urgench Turkmenistan 750

Kutná Hora: Historical Town Centre with the Church of St Barbara and the Cathedral of Our Lady at Sedlec Czech Republic 469

Kvarken Archipelago Finland 630

Kyoto (Kyoto, Uji and Otsu Cities), Ancient Historic Monuments of Japan 438

L

La Amistad National Park Costa Rica and Panama 162

La Chaux-de-Fonds, Watchmaking Town Planning Switzerland 800

La Fortaleza and San Juan National Historic Site in Puerto Rico USA 166

La Grand-Place, Brussels Belgium 555

La Lonja de la Seda de Valencia Spain 485

La Louvière Belgium 554

La Santísima Trinidad de Paraná and Jesús de Tavarangue, Jesuit Missions of Paraguay 407

Lagoons of New Caledonia: Reef Diversity and Associated Ecosystems France 788

Lahore, Fort and Shalamar Gardens in Pakistan 124

Lake Baikal Russian Federation 476

Lake Malawi National Park Malawi 190

Lake Turkana National Parks Kenya 517

Lakes of Ounianga Chad 854

Lalibela, Rock-Hewn Churches Ethiopia 32

Lamu Old Town Kenya 682

Land of Frankincense Oman 614

Landscape of Grand Pré Canada 849

Landscape of the Pico Island Vineyard Culture Portugal 731

L'Anse aux Meadows National Historic Site Canada 37

Laponian Area Sweden 497

Las Médulas Spain 535

Late Baroque Towns of the Val di Noto (South-Eastern Sicily) Italy 690

Laurisilva of Madeira Portugal 602

Lavaux, Vineyard Terraces Switzerland 777

Le Havre, the city rebuilt by Auguste Perret France 738

Le Locle, watchmaking town planning Switzerland 800

Le Morne Cultural Landscape Mauritius 792

Le Roeulx (Hainault) Belgium 554

Le Strade Nuove and the system of the Palazzi dei Rolli, Genoa Italy 759

Lednice-Valtice Cultural Landscape Czech Republic 493

Lena Pillars Nature Park Russian Federation 843

Lenggong Valley, Archaeological Heritage of Malaysia 852

León Cathedral Nicaragua 829

León Viejo, Ruins of Nicaragua 619

Leptis Magna, Archaeological Site of Libya 144

Leshan Giant Buddha Scenic Area China 481

Levoča, Spišský Hrad and the Associated Cultural Monuments Slovakia 417

Levuka Historical Port Town Fiji 863

Lhasa, Historic Ensemble of the Potala Palace China 425

Lijiang, Old Town of China 510

Lima, Historic Centre of Peru 326

Lines and Geoglyphs of Nasca and Pampas de Jumana Peru 434

Lisbon, Monastery of the Hieronymites and Tower of Belém in Portugal 163

Litomyšl Castle Czech Republic 588

Liverpool – Maritime Mercantile City United Kingdom 707

Loire Valley between Sully-sur-Loire and Chalonnes, The France 622

Lombardy and Piedmont, Sacri Monti of Italy 695

Longmen Grottoes China 654

Longobards in Italy. Places of the power (568-774 AD) Italy 824

Lopé-Okanda, Ecosystem and Relict Cultural Landscape of Gabon 781

Lord Howe Island Group Australia 136

Lorentz National Park Indonesia 604

Loropéni, The Ruins of Burkina Faso 805

Lorsch, Abbey and Altenmünster of Germany 379

Los Katíos National Park Colombia 426

Lower Valley of the Awash Ethiopia 102

Lower Valley of the Omo Ethiopia 106

Luang Prabang, Town of Lao People's Democratic Republic (Laos) 464

Lübeck, Hanseatic City of Germany 281

Lugo, Roman Walls of Spain 649

Luleå Gammelstad, Church Village of Sweden 504

Luis Barragán House and Studio Mexico 722

Lumbini, the Birthplace of the Lord Buddha Nepal 512

Lunenburg, Old Town Canada 463

Lushan National Park China 484

Luther Memorials in Eisleben and Wittenberg Germany 503

Luxembourg, City of Luxembourg 424

L'viv – the Ensemble of the Historic Centre Ukraine 564

Lyons, Historic Site of France 561

M

Macao, Historic Centre of China 737

Machu Picchu, Historic Sanctuary of Peru 172

Macquarie Island Australia 506

Madâin Sâlih Saudi Arabia 798

Madara Rider Bulgaria 69

Madeira, Laurisilva of Portugal 602

Madrid, Monastery and Site of the Escurial Spain 193

Madriu-Perafita-Claror Valley Andorra 732

Mahabalipuram, Group of Monuments at India 204

Mahabodhi Temple Complex at Bodh Gaya India 688

Maiden Tower, Baku Azerbaijan 607

Major Mining Sites of Wallonia Belgium 855

Major Town Houses of the Architect Victor Horta (Brussels) Belgium 648

Makli, Historical Monuments at Pakistan 118

Malbork, Castle of the Teutonic Order in Poland 547

Maloti-Drakensberg Park Lesotho and South Africa 611

Malpelo Fauna and Flora Sanctuary Colombia 756

Mammoth Cave National Park USA 126

Mana Pools National Park, Sapi and Chewore Safari Areas Zimbabwe 186

Manas Wildlife Sanctuary India 215

Mannerist Architectural and Park Landscape Complex Poland 594

Manovo-Gounda St Floris National Park Central African Republic 313

Mantua and Sabbioneta Italy 797

Manú National Park Peru 296

Mapungubwe Cultural Landscape South Africa 693

Maramureş, Wooden Churches of Romania 581

Margravial Opera House Bayreuth Germany 856

Maritime Greenwich United Kingdom 507

Marrakesh, Medina of Morocco 218

Masada Israel **676**
Masjed-e Jāmé of Isfahan Islamic Republic of Iran **846**
Matera, The Sassi and the park of the Rupestrian Churches of Italy **399**
Matobo Hills Zimbabwe **696**
Maulbronn Monastery Complex Germany **407**
Mausoleum of the First Qin Emperor China **300**
Mausoleum of Khoja Ahmed Yasawi, Turkestan Kazakhstan **707**
Maya Site of Cópan Honduras **90**
Mazagan (El Jadida), Portuguese City of Morocco **717**
McDonald Island Australia **522**
Medici Villas and Gardens in Tuscany Italy **860**
Medieval City of Rhodes Greece **324**
Medieval Monuments in Kosovo Serbia **717**
Medieval Town of Toruń Poland **526**
Medina of Essaouira (formerly Mogador) Morocco **666**
Medina of Fez Morocco **119**
Medina of Marrakesh Morocco **218**
Medina of Sousse Tunisia **317**
Medina of Tétouan (formerly known as Titawin) Morocco **522**
Medina of Tunis Tunisia **72**
Megalithic Temples of Malta Malta **96**
Megiddo, Tel Israel **739**
Mehmed Paša Sokolović Bridge in Višegrad Bosnia and Herzegovina **779**
Meidan Emam, Esfahan Islamic Republic of Iran **38**
Meknes, Historic City of Morocco **494**
Melaka and George Town, Historic Cities of the Straits of Malacca Malaysia **790**
Melbourne, Royal Exhibition Building and Carlton Gardens Australia **718**
Memphis and its Necropolis – the Pyramid Fields from Giza to Dahshur Egypt **70**
Mercury, Heritage of, Almadén and Idrija Slovenia and Spain **858**
Mérida, Archaeological Ensemble of Spain **410**
Meroe, Archaeological Sites of the Island of Sudan **836**
Merv, Ancient Turkmenistan **573**
Mesa Verde National Park USA **28**
Messel Pit Fossil Site Germany **456**
Meteora Greece **332**
Miguasha National Park Canada **599**
Mijikenda Kaya Forests, Sacred Kenya **782**
Mill Network at Kinderdijk-Elshout Netherlands **523**
Millenary Benedictine Abbey of Pannonhalma and its Natural Environment Hungary **479**
Minaret and Archaeological Remains of Jam Afghanistan **683**
Mines of Rammelsberg and Historic Town of Goslar and Upper Harz Water Management System Germany **387**
Ming and Qing Dynasties in Beijing and Shenyang, Imperial Palaces of the China **277**
Ming and Qing Dynasties, Imperial Tombs of the China **616**
Mining Area of the Great Copper Mountain in Falun Sweden **667**
Mir Castle Complex Belarus **635**

Mitla, Prehistoric Caves of Mexico **817**
Modena Italy **520**
Moenjodaro, Archaeological Ruins at Pakistan **102**
Mogador (Medina of Essaouira) Morocco **666**
Mogao Caves China **298**
Moldavia, Churches of Romania **412**
Monarch Butterfly Biosphere Reserve Mexico **791**
Monasteries of Daphni, Hosios Loukas and Nea Moni of Chios Greece **342**
Monasteries of Haghpat and Sanahin Armenia **500**
Monastery and Site of the Escurial, Madrid Spain **193**
Monastery of Alcobaça Portugal **337**
Monastery of Batalha Portugal **177**
Monastery of Geghard and the Upper Azat Valley Armenia **630**
Monastery of Horezu Romania **408**
Monastery of the Hieronymites and Tower of Belém in Lisbon Portugal **163**
Monastic Island of Reichenau Germany **640**
Mongolian Altai, Petroglyphic Complexes of the Mongolia **842**
Mons, Neolithic Flint Mines at Belgium **652**
Mont-Saint-Michel and its Bay France **58**
Monte Albán, Archaeological Site of Mexico **286**
Monte San Giorgio Italy and Switzerland **704**
Monticello and the University of Virginia in Charlottesville USA **304**
Monuments of Oviedo and the Kingdom of the Asturias Spain **217**
Morelia, Historic Centre of Mexico **369**
Morne Trois Pitons National Park Dominica **515**
Mosi-oa-Tunya / Victoria Falls Zambia and Zimbabwe **338**
Mostar, Old Bridge Area of the Old City of Bosnia and Herzegovina **734**
Mount Athos Greece **309**
Mount Carmel: The Nahal Me'arot / Wadi el-Mughara Caves, Sites of Human Evolution at Israel **843**
Mount Emei Scenic Area, including Leshan Giant Buddha Scenic Area China **481**
Mount Etna Italy **869**
Mount Huangshan China **357**
Mount Kenya National Park / Natural Forest Kenya **508**
Mount Nimba Strict Nature Reserve Côte d'Ivoire and Guinea **126**
Mount Qingcheng and the Dujiangyan Irrigation System China **648**
Mount Sanqingshan National Park China **796**
Mount Taishan China **297**
Mount Wutai China **802**
Mount Wuyi China **598**
Mountain Railways of India **576**
Mountain Resort and its Outlying Temples, Chengde China **436**
Mozambique, Island of Mozambique **365**
Mtskheta, Historical Monuments of Georgia **437**
Mudéjar Architecture of Aragon Spain **256**
Mumbai, Chhatrapati Shivaji Terminus (formerly Victoria Terminus) India **723**

Museumsinsel (Museum Island), Berlin Germany **578**
Muskauer Park / Park Muzakowski Germany and Poland **719**
Müstair, Benedictine Convent of St John at Switzerland **159**
My Son Sanctuary Vietnam **579**
Mycenae, Archaeological Site of Greece **574**
Mystras, Archaeological Site of Greece **341**
M'Zab Valley Algeria **145**

N

Nærøyfjord Norway **742**
Nahal Me'arot / Wadi el-Mughara Caves, Sites of Human Evolution at Mount Carmel Israel **843**
Nahanni National Park Canada **38**
Namib Sand Sea Namibia **869**
Nancy, Place Stanislas, Place de la Carrière and Place d'Alliance in France **169**
Nanda Devi and Valley of Flowers National Parks India **333**
Napatan Region, Gebel Barkal and the Sites of the Sudan **695**
Naples, Historic Centre Italy **448**
Nara, Historic Monuments of Ancient Japan **560**
Naracoorte, Fossil Mammal Site Australia **429**
Nasca, Lines and Geoglyphs of Peru **434**
National Archeological Park of Tierradentro Colombia **473**
National History Park – Citadel, Sans Souci, Ramiers Haiti **139**
Natural and Cultural Heritage of the Ohrid region Former Yugoslav Republic of Macedonia **77**
Natural and Culturo-Historical Region of Kotor Montenegro **84**
Natural System of Wrangel Island Reserve Russian Federation **716**
Naval Port of Karlskrona Sweden **553**
Nea Moni of Chios, Monastery of Greece **342**
Negev, Desert Cities in the Israel **740**
Nemrut Dağ Turkey **292**
Neolithic Flint Mines at Spiennes (Mons) Belgium **652**
Neolithic Site of Çatalhöyük Turkey **856**
Nessebar, Ancient City of Bulgaria **165**
Nesvizh, Architectural, Residential and Cultural Complex of the Radziwill Family at Belarus **748**
New Caledonia, Lagoons of France **788**
New Lanark United Kingdom **556**
New Zealand Sub-Antarctic Islands New Zealand **556**
Ngorongoro Conservation Area Tanzania **42**
Niger, W National Park of Niger **485**
Nikko, Shrines and Temples of Japan **604**
Nimba Strict Nature Reserve, Mount Côte d'Ivoire and Guinea **126**
Ningaloo Coast Australia **830**
Niokolo-Koba National Park Senegal **116**
Nisa, Parthian Fortresses of Turkmenistan **778**
Noel Kempff Mercado National Park Bolivia **636**
Nord-Pas de Calais Mining Basin France **850**

Northern Syria, Ancient Villages of Syrian Arab Republic **837**
Notre-Dame, Cathedral of, Reims France **372**
Notre-Dame Cathedral in Tournai Belgium **655**
Novgorod and Surroundings, Historic Monuments of Russian Federation **383**
Novodevichy Convent, Ensemble of the Russian Federation **728**
Nubian Monuments from Abu Simbel to Philae Egypt **56**
Nuclear Test Site, Bikini Atoll Marshall Is **809**

O

Oaxaca, Historic Centre of Mexico **286**
Ogasawara Islands Japan **841**
Ohrid region, Natural and Cultural Heritage of the Former Yugoslav Republic of Macedonia **77**
Okapi Wildlife Reserve Dem. Rep. of the Congo **478**
Öland, Agricultural Landscape of Southern Sweden **640**
Old Bridge Area of the Old City of Mostar Bosnia and Herzegovina **734**
Old and New Towns of Edinburgh United Kingdom **470**
Old City of Acre Israel **680**
Old City of Berne Switzerland **157**
Old City of Dubrovnik Croatia **86**
Old City of Jerusalem and its Walls **114**
Old City of Salamanca Spain **328**
Old City of Sana'a Yemen **245**
Old City of Zamość Poland **382**
Old Havana and its Fortification System Cuba **146**
Old Rauma Finland **368**
Old Town of Ávila with its Extra-Muros Churches Spain **233**
Old Town of Cáceres Spain **253**
Old Town of Corfu Greece **771**
Old Town of Galle and its Fortifications Sri Lanka **320**
Old Town of Ghadamès Libya **261**
Old Town of Lijiang China **510**
Old Town of Regensburg with Stadtamhof Germany **753**
Old Town of Segovia and its Aqueduct Spain **209**
Old Town Lunenburg Canada **463**
Old Towns of Djenné Mali **310**
Old Village of Hollókő and its Surroundings Hungary **293**
Old Walled City of Shibam Yemen **152**
Olinda, Historic Centre of the Town of Brazil **150**
Olomouc, Holy Trinity Column in Czech Republic **637**
Olympia, Archaeological Site of Greece **336**
Olympic National Park USA **128**
Omo, Lower Valley of the Ethiopia **106**
Oporto, Historic Centre of Portugal **482**
Orange, Roman Theatre and its Surroundings and the 'Triumphal Arch' of France **120**
Orastie Mountains, Dacian Fortresses of the Romania **597**
Orkhon Valley Cultural Landscape Mongolia **719**

Orkney, Heart of Neolithic United Kingdom **570**
Osun-Osogbo Sacred Grove Nigeria **741**
Otsu Japan **438**
Ouadane, Ancient Ksour of Mauritania **478**
Ouadi Qadisha (the Holy Valley) and the Forest of the Cedars of God (Horsh Arz el-Rab) Lebanon **569**
Oualata, Ancient Ksour of Mauritania **478**
Ounianga, Lakes of Chad **854**
Our Lady at Sedlec, Cathedral of Czech Republic **469**
Ouro Preto, Historic Town of Brazil **108**
Oviedo and the Kingdom of the Asturias, Monuments of Spain **217**

P

Padua, Botanical Garden (Orto Botanico) Italy **532**
Padula, Certosa di Italy **558**
Paestum Italy **558**
Paharpur, Ruins of the Buddhist Vihara at Bangladesh **222**
Painted Churches in the Troodos Region Cyprus **210**
Palace and Gardens of Schönbrunn Austria **502**
Palace and Park of Fontainebleau France **113**
Palace and Park of Versailles France **62**
Palace of Westminster and Westminster Abbey including Saint Margaret's Church United Kingdom **272**
Palaces and Parks of Potsdam and Berlin Germany **346**
Palau de la Música Catalana and Hospital de Sant Pau, Barcelona Spain **528**
Palazzi dei Rolli, Genoa Italy **759**
Palenque, Pre-Hispanic City and National Park of Mexico **299**
Paleochristian and Byzantine Monuments of Thessalonika Greece **313**
Paleolithic Cave Art of Northern Spain Spain **220**
Palladian Villas of The Veneto Italy **428**
Palmaria Italy **513**
Palmeral of Elche Spain **639**
Palmyra, Site of Syrian Arab Republic (Syria) **100**
Pampas de Jumana Peru **434**
Panamá Viejo, Archaeological Site of Panama **529**
Pannonhalma and its Natural Environment, Millenary Benedictine Abbey of Hungary **479**
Pantalica, Rocky Necropolis of Italy **750**
Pantanal Conservation Area Brazil **656**
Papahānaumokuākea USA **814**
Papal Palace, Avignon France **444**
Paphos Cyprus **101**
Paquimé, Archaeological Zone of Mexico **563**
Paramaribo, Historic Inner City of Suriname **687**
Paris, Banks of the Seine France **360**
Parque Nacional Los Glaciares Argentina **111**
Parthian Fortresses of Nisa Turkmenistan **778**
Pasargadae Islamic Republic of Iran **714**
Pátmos, Island of Greece **603**
Pattadakal, Group of Monuments at India **308**
Pearling, Testimony of an Island Economy Bahrain **849**

Pécs (Sopianae), Early Christian Necropolis of Hungary **619**
Peking Man Site at Zhoukoudian China **298**
Península Valdés Argentina **590**
Perdu, Mont France and Spain **508**
Persepolis Islamic Republic of Iran **68**
Persian Garden, The Islamic Republic of Iran **835**
Petäjävesi Old Church Finland **436**
Petra Jordan **212**
Petrogylphic Complexes of the Mongolian Altai Mongolia **842**
Petroglyphs within the Archaeological Landscape of Tamgaly Kazakhstan **729**
Philae, Nubian Monuments Egypt **56**
Philippine Cordilleras, Rice Terraces of the Philippines **466**
Phoenix Islands Protected Area Kiribati **821**
Phong Nha-Ke Bang National Park Vietnam **706**
Piana, Calanche of France **174**
Piazza del Duomo, Pisa Italy **265**
Piazza Grande, Modena Italy **520**
Pico Island Vineyard Culture, Landscape of the Portugal **731**
Piedmont and Lombardy, Sacri Monti of Italy **695**
Pienza, Historic Centre of the City of Italy **495**
Pilgrimage Church of St John of Nepomuk at Zelená Hora Czech Republic **443**
Pilgrimage Church of Wies Germany **176**
Pilgrimage Park Poland **594**
Pilgrimage Route and the Church of the Nativity, Bethlehem, Birthplace of Jesus Palestine **853**
Ping Yao, Ancient City of China **540**
Pirin National Park Bulgaria **179**
Pisa, Piazza del Duomo Italy **265**
Pitons, cirques and remparts of Reunion Island France **812**
Pitons Management Area Saint Lucia **711**
Place Stanislas, Place de la Carrière and Place d'Alliance in Nancy France **169**
Plantin-Moretus House-Workshops-Museum Complex, Antwerp Belgium **745**
Plitvice Lakes National Park Croatia **57**
Po Delta Italy **453**
Poblet Monastery Spain **366**
Polonnaruwa, Ancient City of Sri Lanka **140**
Pompei, Archaeological Area of Italy **524**
Pont du Gard (Roman Aqueduct) France **229**
Pontcysyllte Aqueduct and Canal United Kingdom **801**
Popocatepetl, Earliest 16th-Century Monasteries on the Slopes of Mexico **432**
Poreč, Episcopal Complex of the Euphrasian Basilica in the Historic Centre of Croatia **516**
Port, Fortresses and Group of Monuments, Cartagena Colombia **184**
Porto, Gulf of: Calanche of Piana, Gulf of Girolata, Scandola Reserve France **174**
Portobelo-San Lorenzo Panama **99**
Portovenere, Cinque Terre, and the Islands (Palmaria, Tino and Tinetto) Italy **513**
Portuguese City of Mazagan (El Jadida) Morocco **717**

Potala Palace, Historic Ensemble of the China 425
Potosí, City of Bolivia 289
Potsdam and Berlin, Palaces and Parks of Germany 346
Prague, Historic Centre of Czech Republic 384
Prambanan Temple Compounds Indonesia 373
Preah Vihear, Temple of Cambodia 789
Pre-Hispanic City of Chichen-Itza Mexico 330
Pre-Hispanic City, El Tajin Mexico 394
Pre-Hispanic City and National Park of Palenque Mexico 299
Pre-Hispanic City of Teotihuacan Mexico 288
Pre-Hispanic Town of Uxmal Mexico 489
Prehistoric Caves of Yagul and Mitla in the Central Valley of Oaxaca Mexico 817
Prehistoric Pile Dwellings around the Alps Switzerland, Austria, France, Germany, Italy and Slovenia 839
Prehistoric Rock-Art Sites in the Côa Valley and Siega Verde Portugal and Spain 563
Prehistoric Sites and Decorated Caves of the Vézère Valley France 44
Primeval Beech Forests of the Carpathians and the Ancient Beech Forests of Germany Germany, Slovakia and Ukraine 772
Protective Town of San Miguel and the Sanctuary of Jesús Nazareno de Atotonilco Mexico 781
Proto-urban Site of Sarazm Tajikistan 817
Provins, Town of Medieval Fairs France 669
Puebla, Historic Centre of Mexico 284
Puerto Rico, La Fortaleza and San Juan National Historic Site in USA 166
Puerto-Princesa Subterranean River National Park Philippines 601
Punic Town of Kerkuane and its Necropolis Tunisia 220
Purnululu National Park Australia 699
Putorana Plateau Russian Federation 819
Pyramid Fields from Giza to Dahshur Egypt 70
Pyrénées - Mont Perdu France and Spain 508
Pythagoreion and Heraion of Samos Greece 388

Q
Qābus, Gonbad-e Islamic Republic of Iran 850
Qal'at al-Bahrain – Ancient Harbour and Capital of Dilmun Bahrain 746
Qal'at Salah El-Din Syrian Arab Republic (Syria) 761
Qal'at Sherqat (Ashur) Iraq 697
Qin Emperor, Mausoleum of the First China 300
Qing Dynasty, Imperial Tombs of the China 616
Qingcheng, Mount, and the Dujiangyan Irrigation System China 648
Québec, Old, Historic District of Canada 206
Quebrada de Humahuaca Argentina 705
Quedlinburg, Old Town of Germany 441
Queensland, Wet Tropics of Australia 311
Querétaro, Franciscan Missions in the Sierra Gorda of Mexico 703
Querétaro, Historic Monuments Zone of Mexico 496
Qufu, Temple and Cemetery of Confucius and the Kong Family Mansion in China 433

Quirigua, Archaeological Park and Ruins of Guatemala 130
Quito, City of Ecuador 32
Quseir Amra Jordan 221
Qutb Minar and its Monuments, Delhi India 413

R
Rabat, Modern Capital and Historic City: a Shared Heritage Morocco 857
Radziwill Family at Nesvizh, Architectural, Residential and Cultural Complex of the Belarus 748
Rainforests of the Atsinanana Madagascar 778
Ramiers Haiti 139
Rammelsberg, Mines of Germany 387
Rapa Nui National Park Chile 454
Ravenna, Early Christian Monuments of Italy 487
Red Bay Basque Whaling Station Canada 865
Red Fort Complex India 765
Red Square, Moscow Russian Federation 350
Redwood National Park USA 103
Regensburg with Stadtamhof, Old Town of Germany 753
Reichenau, Monastic Island of Germany 640
Reims, Cathedral of Notre-Dame France 372
Renaissance Monumental Ensembles of Úbeda and Baeza Spain 697
Residence of Bukovinian and Dalmatia Metropolitans Ukraine 827
Residences of the Royal House of Savoy Italy 541
Reunion Island, Pitons, cirques and remparts of France 812
Rhaetian Railway in the Albula / Bernina Landscapes Italy and Switzerland 784
Rhine Valley, Upper Middle Germany 684
Rhodes, Medieval City of Greece 324
Ribeira Grande, Historic Centre of Cape Verde 799
Rice Terraces of the Philippine Cordilleras Philippines 466
Richtersveld Cultural and Botanical Landscape South Africa 764
Rideau Canal Canada 773
Rietveld Schröderhuis (Rietveld Schröder House), Utrecht Netherlands 636
Riga, Historic Centre of Latvia 544
Rila Monastery Bulgaria 178
Río Abiseo National Park Peru 356
Rio de Janeiro: Carioca Landscapes between the Mountain and the Sea Brazil 844
Río Pinturas, Cueva de las Manos, Argentina 607
Río Plátano Biosphere Reserve Honduras 142
Riversleigh, Fossil Mammal Site Australia 429
Røros Mining Town and the Circumference Norway 104
Robben Island South Africa 569
Rock Art of Alta Norway 232
Rock Art Cultural Landscape, Gobustan Azerbaijan 767
Rock Art of the Mediterranean Basin on the Iberian Peninsula Spain 562

Rock Carvings in Tanum Sweden 432
Rock Drawings in Valcamonica Italy 76
Rock Islands Southern Lagoon Palau 858
Rock Paintings of the Sierra de San Francisco Mexico 419
Rock Shelters of Bhimbetka India 694
Rock-Art Area, Chongoni Malawi 756
Rock-Art Sites, Kondoa Tanzania 755
Rock-Art Sites in the Côa Valley, Prehistoric Portugal 563
Rock-Art Sites of Tadrart Acacus Libya 234
Rock-Hewn Churches, Lalibela Ethiopia 32
Rohtas Fort Pakistan 532
Roman Empire, Frontiers of the United Kingdom and Germany 273
Roman Monuments, Cathedral of St Peter and Church of Our Lady in Trier Germany 251
Roman Theatre and its Surroundings and the 'Triumphal Arch' of Orange France 120
Roman Walls of Lugo Spain 649
Rome, Historic Centre of Italy 92
Roskilde Cathedral Denmark 452
Route of Santiago de Compostela Spain 397
Routes of Santiago de Compostela France 557
Royal Botanic Gardens, Kew United Kingdom 692
Royal Domain of Drottningholm Sweden 371
Royal Exhibition Building and Carlton Gardens, Melbourne Australia 718
Royal Hill of Ambohimanga Madagascar 663
Royal Monastery of Santa María de Guadalupe Spain 416
Royal Palaces of Abomey Benin 232
Royal Saltworks of Arc-et-Senans France 153
Royal Tombs of the Joseon Dynasty Republic of Korea 799
Ruins of the Buddhist Vihara at Paharpur Bangladesh 222
Ruins of Kilwa Kisiwani and Ruins of Songo Mnara Tanzania 116
Ruins of León Viejo Nicaragua 619
Ruins of Loropéni Burkina Faso 805
Rwenzori Mountains National Park Uganda 430
Ryukyu, Gusuku Sites and Related Properties of the Kingdom of Japan 643

S
Sabbioneta Italy 797
Sabratha, Archaeological Site of Libya 149
Sacred City of Anuradhapura Sri Lanka 138
Sacred City of Caral-Supe Peru 800
Sacred City of Kandy Sri Lanka 314
Sacred Mijikenda Kaya Forests Kenya 782
Sacred Sites and Pilgrimage Routes in the Kii Mountain Range Japan 726
Sacri Monti of Piedmont and Lombardy Italy 695
Safranbolu, City of Turkey 442
Sagarmatha National Park Nepal 85
Sahr-i-Bahlol Pakistan 110
St Augustine's Abbey, Canterbury United Kingdom 327
St Barbara, Church of, Kutná Hora Czech Republic 469
St Catherine Area Egypt 688
St Gall, Abbey of Switzerland 176

St George, Historic Town of, Bermuda United Kingdom **621**
St James, Cathedral of, Šibenik Croatia **627**
St John of Nepomuk at Zelená Hora, Pilgrimage Church of Czech Republic **443**
Saint John 'the Theologian', Monastery of, Greece **603**
St Kilda United Kingdom **241**
Saint Margaret's Church, Westminster United Kingdom **272**
St Mary's Cathedral and St Michael's Church at Hildesheim Germany **225**
St Martin's Church, Canterbury United Kingdom **327**
St Peter, Cathedral of, Trier Germany **251**
Saint Petersburg and Related Groups of Monuments,Historic Centre of Russian Federation **344**
St Procopius' Basilica in Třebíč Czech Republic **704**
Saint-Emilion, Jurisdiction of France **600**
Saint-Louis, Island of Senegal **626**
Saint-Rémi, Former Abbey of France **372**
Saint-Savin sur Gartempe, Abbey Church of France **168**
Saint-Sophia Cathedral and Related Monastic Buildings, Kiev-Pechersk Lavra Ukraine **347**
Salamanca, Old City of Spain **328**
Salins-les-Bains, Great Saltworks of France **153**
Salonga National Park Dem. Rep. of the Congo **186**
Saloum Delta Senegal **832**
Saltaire United Kingdom **665**
Salvador de Bahia, Historic Centre of Brazil **208**
Salzburg, Historic Centre of the City of Austria **498**
Salzkammergut Cultural Landscape Austria **531**
Samaipata, Fuerte de Bolivia **556**
Samarkand – Crossroad of Cultures Uzbekistan **670**
Samarra Archaeological City Iraq **767**
Sammallahdenmäki, Bronze Age Burial Site of Finland **599**
Samos, Pythagoreion and Heraion of Greece **388**
San Agustín Archeological Park Colombia **458**
San Cristóbal de La Laguna Spain **587**
San Francesco, Basilica of Italy **632**
San Gimignano, Historic Centre of Italy **358**
San Juan National Historic Site, Puerto Rico USA **166**
San Leucio Complex Italy **527**
San Lorenzo Panama **99**
San Marino Historic Centre and Mount Titano San Marino **782**
San Miguel and the Sanctuary of Jesús Nazareno de Atotonilco, Protective Town of Mexico **781**
San Millán Yuso and Suso Monasteries Spain **535**
San Paolo Fuori le Mura Italy **92**
San Pedro de la Roca Castle, Santiago de Cuba Cuba **548**
Sana'a, Old City of Yemen **245**
Sanahin, Monastery of Armenia **500**
Sanchi, Buddhist Monuments at India **342**
Sanctuary of Asklepios at Epidaurus Greece **315**

Sanctuary of Bom Jesus do Congonhas Brazil **223**
Sangay National Park Ecuador **171**
Sangha Trinational Cameroon, Central African Republic and Congo **848**
Sangiran Early Man Site Indonesia **503**
Sanqingshan, Mount, National Park China **796**
Sans Souci Haiti **139**
Sant Pau, Hospital de, Barcelona Spain **528**
Santa Ana de los Ríos de Cuenca, Historic Centre of Ecuador **576**
Santa Cruz de Mompox, Historic Centre of Colombia **473**
Santa María de Guadalupe, Royal Monastery of Spain **416**
Santa Maria delle Grazie with 'The Last Supper' by Leonardo da Vinci, Church and Dominican Convent of Italy **95**
Santiago de Compostela, Route of Spain **397**
Santiago de Compostela in France, Routes of France **557**
Santiago de Compostela (Old Town) Spain **211**
Santiago de Cuba, San Pedro de la Roca Castle Cuba **548**
São Cristóvão, Saõ Francisco Square in the Town of Brazil **809**
Santo Domingo, Colonial City of Dominican Republic **343**
Saõ Francisco Square in the Town of São Cristóvão Brazil **809**
Saõ Miguel das Missões, Ruins of Brazil **159**
Sapi Safari Area Zimbabwe **186**
São Luís, Historic Centre of Brazil **537**
Sarazm, Proto-urban Site of Tajikistan **817**
Saryarka – Steppe and Lakes of Northern Kazakhstan Kazakhstan **786**
Sassi and the Park of the Rupestrian Churches of Matera, The Italy **399**
Savoy, Residences of the Royal House of Italy **541**
Scandola Reserve France **174**
Schloss Eggenberg, City of Graz – Historic Centre and Austria **585**
Schokland and Surroundings Netherlands **449**
Schönbrunn, Palace and Gardens of Austria **502**
Segovia, Old Town of Spain **209**
Seine, Banks of the France **360**
Selimiye Mosque and its Social Complex Turkey **828**
Selous Game Reserve Tanzania **137**
Semmering Railway Austria **551**
Senegambia, Stone Circles of The Gambia and Senegal **755**
Seokguram Grotto and Bulguksa Temple Republic of Korea **457**
Serengeti National Park Tanzania **112**
Serra da Capivara National Park Brazil **374**
Serra de Tramuntana, Cultural Landscape of the Spain **839**
Seuthopolis, Thracian Tomb of Kazanlak Bulgaria **49**
Seventeenth-century canal ring area of Amsterdam inside the Singelgracht Netherlands **818**
Seville, Cathedral, Alcázar and Archivo de Indias in Spain **266**
Sewell Mining Town Chile **762**

SGang Gwaay Canada **133**
Shakhrisyabz, Historic Centre of Uzbekistan **629**
Shark Bay, Western Australia Australia **368**
Sheikh Safi al-Din Khānegāh and Shrine Ensemble in Ardabil Islamic Republic of Iran **810**
Shenyang, Imperial Palaces of the Ming and Qing Dynasties China **277**
Shibam, Old Walled City of Yemen **152**
Shirakami-Sanchi Japan **415**
Shirakawa-go and Gokayama, Historic Villages of Japan **462**
Shiretoko Japan **748**
Shirvanshah's Palace, Baku Azerbaijan **607**
Shrines and Temples of Nikko Japan **604**
Shushtar Historical Hydraulic System Islamic Republic of Iran **803**
Sian Ka'an Mexico **267**
Šibenik, The Cathedral of St James in Croatia **627**
Sichuan Giant Panda Sanctuaries – Wolong, Mt Siguniang and Jiajin Mountains China **751**
Siega Verde, Prehistoric Rock-Art Sites in the Côa Valley and Portugal and Spain **563**
Siena, Historic Centre of Italy **460**
Sierra de San Francisco, Rock Paintings of the Mexico **419**
Sierra Gorda of Querétaro, Franciscan Missions in the Mexico **703**
Sierra Maestra, Archaeological Landscape of the First Coffee Plantations Cuba **649**
Sighișoara, Historic Centre of Romania **592**
Sigiriya, Ancient City of Sri Lanka **151**
Siguniang, Mt, Giant Panda Sanctuary China **751**
Sikhote-Alin, Central Russian Federation **664**
Simien National Park Ethiopia **37**
Singelgracht, Seventeenth-century canal ring area of Amsterdam inside the Netherlands **818**
Sinharaja Forest Reserve Sri Lanka **316**
Sintra, Cultural Landscape of Portugal **447**
Site of Carthage Tunisia **46**
Site of Palmyra Syrian Arab Republic (Syria) **100**
Site of Xanadu China **852**
Sites of Human Evolution at Mount Carmel: The Nahal Me'arot / Wadi el-Mughara Caves Israel **843**
Skellig Michael Monastery Ireland **492**
Škocjan Caves Slovenia **261**
Skogskyrkogården Sweden **435**
Slovak Karst, Caves of Aggtelek Karst and Hungary and Slovakia **456**
Socotra Archipelago Yemen **785**
Sofia, Boyana Church Bulgaria **60**
Solovetsky Islands, Cultural and Historic Ensemble of the Russian Federation **392**
Soltaniyeh Islamic Republic of Iran **746**
Songo Mnara, Ruins of Tanzania **116**
Sopianae (Pécs), Early Christian Necropolis of Hungary **619**
Sopoćani Serbia **76**
Sousse, Medina of Tunisia **317**
South China Karst China **768**
Southern Little Poland, Wooden Churches of Poland **702**

Speyer Cathedral Germany 128
Spiennes (Mons), Neolithic Flint Mines at Belgium 652
Spišský Hrad and the Associated Cultural Monuments Slovakia 417
Split, Historical Complex of Croatia 82
Srebarna Nature Reserve Bulgaria 168
Sri Lanka, Central Highlands of Sri Lanka 823
Stari Grad Plain Croatia 790
Stari Ras and Sopoćani Serbia 76
State Historical and Cultural Park 'Ancient Merv' Turkmenistan 573
Statue of Liberty USA 187
Sterkfontein, Fossil Hominid Site of South Africa 593
Stoclet House Belgium 805
Stone Circles of Senegambia The Gambia and Senegal 755
Stone Town of Zanzibar Tanzania 612
Stonehenge, Avebury and Associated Sites United Kingdom 254
Stralsund, Historic Centre of Germany 690
Strasbourg – Grande Île France 334
Struve Geodetic Arc Belarus, Estonia, Finland, Latvia, Lithuania, Norway, Republic of Moldova, Russian Federation, Sweden and Ukraine 747
Studenica Monastery Serbia 250
Studley Royal Park including the Ruins of Fountains Abbey United Kingdom 248
Su Nuraxi di Barumini Italy 546
Sucre, Historic City of Bolivia 367
Sukhothai, Historic Town of Thailand 375
Sukur Cultural Landscape Nigeria 587
Sulaiman-Too Sacred Mountain Kyrgyzstan 803
Sumatra, Tropical Rainforest Heritage of Indonesia 712
Summer Palace and Imperial Garden in Beijing China 552
Sun Temple, Konârak India 183
Sundarbans, The Bangladesh 512
Sundarbans National Park India 271
Suomenlinna, Fortress of Finland 378
Surtsey Iceland 789
Suso Monastery Spain 535
Southern Anhui, Ancient Villages in Xidi and Hongcun China 653
Suzdal, White Monuments of Russian Federation 396
Suzhou, Classical Gardens of China 518
Sveshtari, Thracian Tomb of Bulgaria 234
Swartkrans, Fossil Hominid Site South Africa 593
Świdnica, Church of Peace Poland 675
Swiss Alps Jungfrau-Aletsch Switzerland 660
Swiss Tectonic Arena Sardona Switzerland 787
Sydney Opera House Australia 763
Syracuse and the Rocky Necropolis of Pantalica Italy 750

T

Tabriz Historic Bazaar Complex Islamic Republic of Iran 815
Tadrart Acacus, Rock-Art Sites of Libya 234
Taï National Park Côte d'Ivoire 139

Taishan, Mount China 297
Tajik National Park (Mountains of the Pamirs) Tajikistan 861
Taj Mahal India 154
Takht-e Soleyman Islamic Republic of Iran 691
Takht-i-Bahi, Buddhist Ruins at Pakistan 110
Talamanca Range-La Amistad Reserves / La Amistad National Park Costa Rica and Panama 162
Talampaya Natural Park Argentina 628
Tallinn, Historic Centre (Old Town) of Estonia 509
Tamgaly, Petroglyphs within the Archaeological Landscape of Kazakhstan 729
Tanum, Rock Carvings in Sweden 432
Taos Pueblo USA 380
Tarquinia, Etruscan Necropolises of Italy 729
Tárraco, Archaeological Ensemble of Spain 621
Tasmanian Wilderness Australia 143
Tassili n'Ajjer Algeria 145
Tatshenshini-Alsek Canada and USA 52
Tau, Palace of France 372
Taxila Pakistan 109
Tchogha Zanbil Islamic Republic of Iran 88
Te Wahipounamu – South West New Zealand New Zealand 354
Teide National Park Spain 766
Tel-Aviv, White City of – The Modern Movement Israel 694
Telč, Historic Centre of Czech Republic 392
Tels, Bibilical – Megiddo, Hazor, Beer Sheba Israel 739
Temple of Apollo Epicurius at Bassae Greece 240
Temple and Cemetery of Confucius and the Kong Family Mansion in Qufu China 433
Temple of Heaven: an Imperial Sacrificial Altar in Beijing China 559
Temple of Preah Vihear Cambodia 789
Ténéré Natural Reserve Niger 367
Teotihuacan, Pre-Hispanic City of Mexico 288
Tequila, Agave Landscape and Ancient Industrial Facilities of Mexico 754
Tétouan (formerly known as Titawin), Medina of Morocco 522
Thang Long – Hanoi, Central Sector of the Imperial Citadel of Vietnam 816
Thatta Pakistan 118
The Causses and the Cévennes, Mediterranean agro-pastoral Cultural Landscape France 826
The Dolomites Italy 807
The Four Lifts on the Canal du Centre and their Environs, La Louvière and Le Roeulx (Hainault) Belgium 554
The Great Wall China 294
The Persian Garden Islamic Republic of Iran 835
The Sassi and the park of the Rupestrian Churches of Matera Italy 399
The Sundarbans Bangladesh 512
The Trulli of Alberobello Italy 501
The Wadden Sea Germany and Netherlands 804
Thebes, Ancient Egypt 74
Thessalonika, Paleochristian and Byzantine Monuments of Greece 313
Þingvellir National Park Iceland 709
Thracian Tomb of Kazanlak Bulgaria 49

Thracian Tomb of Sveshtari Bulgaria 234
Three Castles, Defensive Wall and Ramparts of the Market-Town of Bellinzone Switzerland 610
Three Parallel Rivers of Yunnan Protected Areas China 700
Thugga Tunisia 530
Thungyai-Huai Kha Khaeng Wildlife Sanctuaries Thailand 364
Tichitt, Ancient Ksour of Mauritania 478
Tierradentro, National Archeological Park of Colombia 473
Tikal National Park Guatemala 88
Timbuktu Mali 321
Timgad Algeria 148
Tinetto Italy 513
Tino Italy 513
Tipasa Algeria 142
Tiryns, Archaeological Site of Greece 574
Titano, Mount San Marino 782
Titawin, Medina of Morocco 522
Tiwanaku: Spiritual and Political Centre of the Tiwanaku Culture Bolivia 634
Tiya Ethiopia 106
Tlacotalpan, Historic Monuments Zone of Mexico 548
Tokaj Wine Region Historic Cultural Landscape Hungary 686
Toledo, Historic City of Spain 242
Tomar, Convent of Christ in Portugal 175
Tomb of Askia Mali 725
Tombs of Buganda Kings at Kasubi Uganda 663
Tongariro National Park New Zealand 349
Torre Annunziata, Archaeological Area of Italy 524
Torre Civica, Modena Italy 520
Toruń, Medieval Town of Poland 526
Tournai, Notre-Dame Cathedral in Belgium 655
Tower of Belém Portugal 163
Tower of Hercules Spain 806
Tower of London United Kingdom 312
Town of Bamberg Germany 406
Town of Luang Prabang Lao People's Democratic Republic (Laos) 464
Town Hall and Roland on the Marketplace of Bremen Germany 727
Transylvania, Villages with Fortified Churches in Romania 404
Trier, Roman Monuments, Cathedral of St Peter and Church of Our Lady in Germany 251
Trinidad and the Valley de los Ingenios Cuba 323
Trinity Sergius Lavra in Sergiev Posad, Architectural Ensemble of the Russian Federation 420
Tripitaka Koreana Woodblocks, The Depositories for Republic of Korea 462
Trogir, Historic City of Croatia 533
Troodos Region, Painted Churches in the Cyprus 464
Tropical Rainforest Heritage of Sumatra Indonesia 712
Troy, Archaeological Site of Turkey 550
Trulli of Alberobello, The Italy 501
Třebíč, Jewish Quarter and St Procopius' Basilica in Czech Republic 704

Tsingy de Bemaraha Strict Nature Reserve Madagascar 352
Tsodilo Botswana 668
Tubbataha Reefs Natural Park Philippines 412
Tugendhat Villa in Brno Czech Republic 681
Tunis, Medina of Tunisia 72
Twyfelfontein or /Ui-//aes Namibia 770
Tyre Lebanon 197

U

Úbeda and Baeza, Renaissance Monumental Ensembles of Spain 697
/Ui-//aes, Twyfelfontein or Namibia 770
Uji Japan 438
Ujung Kulon National Park Indonesia 374
Uluru-Kata Tjuta National Park Australia 306
Um er-Rasas (Kastrom Mefa'a) Jordan 713
Universidad Nacional Autónoma de México (UNAM), Central University City Campus of the Mexico 770
Universitaria de Caracas, Ciudad Venezuela 644
University and Historic Precinct of Alcalá de Henares Spain 568
University of Coimbra – Alta and Sofia Portugal 863
University of Virginia in Charlottesville USA 304
Upper Azat Valley Armenia 630
Upper Harz Water Management System Germany 387
Upper Middle Rhine Valley Germany 684
Upper Svaneti Georgia 481
Urban Historic Centre of Cienfuegos Cuba 749
Urbino, Historic Centre of Italy 567
Urnes Stave Church Norway 81
Uus Nuur Basin Mongolia and Russian Federation 693
Uxmal, Pre-Hispanic Town of Mexico 489

V

Val di Noto (South-Eastern Sicily), Late Baroque Towns of the Italy 690
Val d'Orcia Italy 724
Valcamonica, Rock Drawings in Italy 76
Vall de Boí, Catalan Romanesque Churches of the Spain 644
Vallée de Mai Nature Reserve Seychelles 171
Valletta, City of Malta 93
Valley of Flowers National Parks India 333
Valparaíso, Historic Quarter of the Seaport City of Chile 696
Vanvitelli, Aqueduct of Italy 527
Varberg Radio Station, Grimeton Sweden 725
Vat Phou and Associated Ancient Settlements within the Champasak Cultural Landscape Lao People's Democratic Republic (Laos) 679
Vatican City Holy See 180
Vauban, Fortifications of France 794
Vegaøyan – the Vega Archipelago Norway 716
Velia Italy 558
Veneto, Palladian Villas of the Italy 428
Venice and its Lagoon Italy 268
Vergina, Archaeological Site of Greece 504
Verla Groundwood and Board Mill Finland 486
Verona, City of Italy 618
Versailles, Palace and Park of France 62

Vézelay, Church and Hill France 66
Vézère Valley, Prehistoric Sites and Decorated Caves of the France 44
Vicenza, City of Italy 428
Victoria Falls Zambia and Zimbabwe 338
Victoria Terminus, India 723
Vienna, Historic Centre of Austria 678
Vigan, Historic Town of Philippines 582
Villa Adriana, Tivoli Italy 595
Villa d'Este, Tivoli Italy 673
Villa Romana del Casale, Piazza Armerina Italy 546
Villages with Fortified Churches in Transylvania Romania 404
Vilnius Historic Centre Lithuania 421
Viñales Valley Cuba 593
Virgin Komi Forests Russian Federation 449
Virunga National Park Dem. Rep. of the Congo 45
Visby, Hanseatic Town of Sweden 459
Višegrad, Mehmed Paša Sokolović Bridge in Bosnia and Herzegovina 779
Vizcaya Bridge Spain 758
Vladimir and Suzdal, White Monuments of Russian Federation 396
Vlkolínec Slovakia 418
Volcanoes of Kamchatka Russian Federation 490
Völklingen Ironworks Germany 441
Volubilis, Archaeological Site of Morocco 543
Vredefort Dome South Africa 747

W

W National Park of Niger Niger 485
Wachau Cultural Landscape Austria 641
Wadden Sea, The Germany and Netherlands 804
Wadi Al-Hitan (Whale Valley) Egypt 738
Wadi el-Mughara / The Nahal Me'arot Caves, Sites of Human Evolution at Mount Carmel: Israel 843
Wadi Rum Protected Area Jordan 834
Walled City of Baku with the Shirvanshah's Palace and Maiden Tower Azerbaijan 607
Wallonia, Major Mining Sites of Belgium 855
Warsaw, Historic Centre of Poland 89
Wartburg Castle Germany 589
Waterton Glacier International Peace Park Canada and USA 450
Weimar and Dessau, Bauhaus and its Sites in Germany 484
Western Caucasus Russian Federation 601
Western Galilee, Bahá'í Holy Places in the Israel 793
Western Ghats India 847
West Lake Cultural Landscape of Hangzhou China 831
Wet Tropics of Queensland Australia 311
Whale Sanctuary of El Vizcaino Mexico 401
Whale Valley (Wadi Al-Hitan) Egypt 738
White City of Tel-Aviv – The Modern Movement Israel 694
White Monuments of Vladimir and Suzdal Russian Federation 396
Wieliczka and Bochnia Royal Salt Mines, Poland 36

Wies, Pilgrimage Church of Germany 176
Willandra Lakes Region Australia 125
Willemstad, Inner City and Harbour, Curaçao Historic Area of Netherlands 528
Wismar, Historic Centre of Germany 690
Wittenberg, Luther Memorial in Germany 503
Wolong Giant Panda Sanctuary China 751
Wood Buffalo National Park Canada 170
Wooden Churches of the Slovak part of the Carpathian Mountain Area Slovakia 795
Wooden Churches of Maramureş Romania 581
Wooden Churches of Southern Małopolska Poland 702
Wooden Tserkvas of the Carpathian Region in Poland and Ukraine Poland and Ukraine 868
Works of Antoni Gaudí Spain 182
Wrangel Island Reserve, Natural System of Russian Federation 716
Wrangell-St Elias Canada and USA 52
Wrocław, Centennial Hall in Poland 752
Wudang Mountains, Ancient Building Complex in the China 429
Wulingyuan Scenic and Historic Interest Area China 382
Würzburg Residence with the Court Gardens and Residence Square Germany 132
Wutai, Mount China 802
Wuyi, Mount China 598

X

Xanadu, Site of China 852
Xanthos-Letoon Turkey 333
Xidi, Southern Anhui China 653
Xinjiang Tianshan China 867
Xochicalco, Archaeological Monuments Zone of Mexico 605
Xochimilco Mexico 284

Y

Yagul, Prehistoric Caves of Mexico 817
Yakushima Japan 400
Yangdong, Historic Villages of Korea: Hahoe and Republic of Korea 822
Yaroslavl, Historical Centre of the City of Russian Federation 744
Yellowstone National Park USA 34
Yin Xu China 759
Yosemite National Park USA 184
Yungang Grottoes China 672
Yunnan Protected Areas, Three Parallel Rivers of China 700

Z

Zabid, Historic Town of Yemen 398
Zacatecas, Historic Centre of Mexico 419
Zamość, Old City of Poland 282
Zanzibar, Stone Town of Tanzania 612
Zelená Hora, Pilgrimage Church of St John of Nepomuk at Czech Republic 443
Zhoukoudian, Peking Man Site at China 298
Zollverein Coal Mine Industrial Complex in Essen Germany 667
Zvartnots, Archaeological Site of Armenia 655

Acknowledgements

Concept, design, maps, editorial and project management by the staff at Collins Geo, Glasgow.

Text edited by Collins Geo. Based on official information made available by the United Nations Educational, Scientific and Cultural Organization (UNESCO) and its World Heritage Centre.

With thanks to:
The UNESCO World Heritage Centre and its staff.

The freelance editors, copywriters, cartographers and pre-press individuals and organizations.

Image credits

Images supplied by www.shutterstock.com unless noted with an asterisk. All photographers credited unless unknown.

▲ picture located on the upper half of the page
▼ picture located on the lower half of the page

27▲ ©javarman; 27▼ ©javarman; 28 ©Duncan Gilbert; 29 ©faberfoto; 31 ©Wiktor Bubniak; 32▲*©UNESCO/Jim Williams; 32▼ ©Jennifer Stone; 33▲ ©skyfish; 33▼ ©skyfish; 35 ©Katrina Leigh; 36*©Anna Rosinska-Renaud; 37©Will Davies; 39 ©Olga Kolos; 41 ©Wiktor Bubniak; 42▲ ©Kitch Bain; 42▼ ©Kitch Bain; 43 ©PixAchi; 45*©Africa Conservation Fund/www.gorilla.cd; 47▲ ©WitR; 47▼ ©Danijela Pavlovic Markovic; 48 ©Ryan Morgan; 49*©Tito Dupret; 51 ©Om Prakash Yadav; 52 ©Mariusz S. Jurgielewicz; 53 ©John A. Anderson; 55 ©Anton Foltin; 56▲ ©Mirek Hejnicki; 56▼ ©Vladimir Wrangel; 57 ©Maugli; 59 ©Cristina Ciochina; 60*©Tito Dupret; 61 ©Aleksander Bolbot; 63 ©Marek Slusarczyk; 64 ©Tony Strong; 65 ©Gautier Willaume; 67 ©Sofilou; 68 ©steba; 71 ©Vladamir Wrangel; 72 ©Piotr Sikora; 73 ©Daniel Loncarevic; 75 ©Connors Bros.; 77 ©Ljupco Smokovski; 79 ©W H Chow; 80 ©PavleMarjanovic; 81 ©Andrea Seemann; 83 ©Krkr; 84 ©Svetlana Tikhonova; 85 ©Jason Maehl; 87 ©paradoks_blizanaca; 88*©Tito Dupret; 89 ©Copestello; 90 ©Sam Chadwick; 91 ©Grigory Kubatyan; 92 ©Iexan; 93 ©PixAchi; 94*©Nuria Ortega; 95 ©Belle Momenti Photography; 96 ©William Attard McCarthy; 97*©UNESCO/Marc Patry; 98*©T6 Ecosystem/UNESCO; 99 ©Matt Ragen; 100 ©OPIS; 101 ©Ioannis Ioannou; 102▲*©Tito Dupret; 102▼*©Tito Dupret; 103 ©Andrew Ferguson; 104 ©Inger Anne Hulbækdal; 105 ©OPIS; 106▲*©Tito Dupret; 106▼*©Tito Dupret; 107 ©Milan Ljubisavljevic; 108 ©David Davis; 109▼*©Tito Dupret; 110*©Tito Dupret; 111 ©David Thyberg; 112 ©Stephane Angue; 113 ©Darja Vorontsova; 115▲ ©Bomshtein; 115▼ ©Stavchansky Yakov; 116*©Tito Dupret; 117 ©Claudio Giovanni Colombo; 118*©Waqas Muhammad/Wikipedia; 119 ©Thomas Cristofoletti; 120 ©Philip Lange; 121 ©Norman Bateman; 123▲ ©tororo reaction; 123▼ ©tororo reaction; 124*(CC by sa 2.5) ©Ali Imran; 125 ©Sam DCruz; 126*©Prof. Dr Mark-Oliver Rödel; 127 ©Sam DCruz; 129 ©Natalia Bratslavsky; 131 ©Claudio Giovanni Colombo; 132 ©Khirman Vladimir; 133 ©Holger Ehlers; 135 ©Sailorr; 136*©UNESCO/Giovanni Boccardi; 137 ©faberfoto; 138 ©Mirek Hejnicki; 141 ©Emma Holmwood; 143 ©Ashley Whitworth; 144 ©WitR; 147 ©Leonid Katsyka; 149 ©Clara; 150 ©ostill; 151*©Tito Dupret; 152 ©Vladimir Melnik; 155 ©Luciano Mortula; 156 ©JeremyRichards; 157 ©Marek Slusarczyk; 158 ©Chris Howey; 160 ©JeremyRichards; 161 ©Jarno Gonzalez Zarraonandia; 163 ©Matt Trommer; 164 ©Carolina K. Smith M.D.; 165 ©Andreas Gradin; 167 ©Bryan Busovicki; 169 ©Lazar Mihai-Bogdan; 170*(CC by sa 3.0) ©Alan D. Wilson; 173 ©Jarno Gonzalez Zarraonandia; 174 ©Bensliman; 175 ©Matt Trommer; 177 ©ultimathule; 178 ©sunnyfrog; 179 ©Ljupco Smokovski; 181 ©Slawomir Kruz; 182 ©WH Chow; 183 ©JeremyRichards; 185 ©Susan McKenzie; 187 ©Marcio Jose Bastos Silva; 189 ©urosr; 190 ©Dennis Albert Richardson; 191 ©javarman; 194 ©Palis Michael; 195▲*©Mark Steward; 195▼ ©Nelu Goia; 196 ©Jason Maehl; 197 ©javarman; 199 ©Brandus Dan Lucian; 200 ©Vladimir Korostyshevskiy; 201 ©quantz; 203 ©Rafael Ramirez Lee; 204 ©omkar.a.v; 205 ©Olga Kolos; 207 ©Kenneth V. Pilon; 208 ©Jose Miguel Hernandez Leon; 209 ©Justin Black; 210*©Alonzo Addison; 211 ©Francisco Turnes; 213 ©Joseph Calev; 214 ©Jakub Cejpek; 216 ©Larsek; 217 ©Rafael Angel Garcia Dobarganes; 219 ©Dainis Derics; 221 ©Factoria singular fotografia; 222*©Tito Dupret; 223*(CC by sa 2.0) ©Glauco Umbelino; 224 ©JeremyRichards; 227 ©ImageDesign; 228*©Tito Dupret; 229 ©Elena Elisseeva; 231 ©Jaroslaw Grudzinski; 233 ©Oscar F. Chuyn; 235 ©Jason Maehl; 236 ©Holger Mette; 237*©Tito Dupret; 238 ©Chris Howey; 239 ©Jean Frooms; 241 ©Joe Gough; 242 ©aguilarphoto; 243 ©Fotowan; 244 ©Joe Gough; 245 ©Vladimir Melnik; 246 ©Gail Johnson; 247 ©Nikolay Titov; 248 ©pdtnc; 249 ©Asit Jain; 251 ©Jeremy R. Smith Sr.; 252 ©Mikhail Nekrasov; 253 ©LianeM; 255 ©John Evans; 256 ©Lola; 257 ©Gail Johnson; 259 ©inacio pires; 260 ©Ralph Loesche; 263 ©dr. Le Thanh Hung; 264 ©Bryan Busovicki; 265 ©edobric; 266 ©sokolovsky; 267 ©Joseph Calev; 269▲*©Mark Steward; 269▼*©Mark Steward; 270 ©Rachael Russell; 271▲*©Tito Dupret; 271▼*©Tito Dupret; 272 ©Vinicius Tupinamba; 273 ©SmarterMedium; 275 ©Zsolt Nyulaszi; 276 ©Sankar; 277 ©sunxuejun; 279 ©enote; 280 ©ostill; 281 ©rubiphoto; 282 ©Michael Avory; 285 ©Zack Frank; 287 ©Michael Levy; 287 ©Ian D Walker; 288*©Tito Dupret; 289 ©Chris Howey; 291 ©Tamara Kulikova; 292 ©Nathan Chor; 293 ©Mary Lane; 295 ©russal; 296 ©Joseph Calev; 297 ©emily2k; 298▲*©Tito Dupret; 298▼*©Tito Dupret; 299 ©Ales Liska; 301 ©Jack Cronkhite; 302 ©Duncan de Young; 303 ©Martin Preston; 304 ©PRANAV VORA; 305 ©Bidouze Stéphane; 307 ©pandeqiang; 308*©Tito Dupret; 309 ©Koylias Ioannis; 310 ©Jam.si; 311 ©tororo reaction; 312 ©Mary Lane; 313▲*©UNESCO/APF-José Kalpers - Africa Parks Foundation; 313▼ ©Panos Karapanagiotis; 314 ©Ewen Cameron; 315 ©Ivan Montero Martinez; 316 ©Mithila Somasiri; 317 ©LouLouPhotos; 319 ©Bill Perry; 320 ©Evgeniapp; 322*©Tito Dupret; 323 ©Alexey Goosev; 325 ©Jozsef Szasz-Fabian; 326 ©Thomas Barrat; 327 ©hauhu; 328 ©VanHart; 329 ©Clara; 331 ©Joseph Calev; 332 ©Andrew Buckin; 333 ©Bill McKelvie; 334*©Sjoerd van der Wal; 335 ©Aneta Skoczewska; 336 ©Richard Bowden; 337 ©Pedro Pinto; 339 ©Korobanova; 341 ©Ioannis Nousis; 342*©Tito Dupret; 343 ©rj lerich; 345 ©Fast Snail; 346 ©Dainis Derics; 347 ©Dmytro Korolov; 348*©Tito Dupret; 349 ©Sam DCruz; 351 ©Dimon; 352 ©Tito Dupret; 353 ©POZZO DI BORGO Thomas; 353 ©rj lerich; 355 ©Sander van Sinttruye; 356 ©Artem Samokhvalov; 357 ©Tan Kim Pin; 358 ©MASSIMO MERLINI; 359 ©akva; 361▲ ©CHRISTOPHE ROLLAND; 361▼*©Mark Steward; 362 ©Mircea BEZERGHEANU; 363 ©Magdalena Bujak; 364*©Tito Dupret; 365 ©Grigory Kubatyan; 366 ©Sofilou; 367*©Dieter Biskamp; 368 ©Alexander Studentschnig; 369 ©Bill Perry; 370 ©Specta; 371 ©Mikael Damkier; 372 ©ultimathule; 373 ©Cristina CIOCHINA; 374*©Tito Dupret; 375 ©John Hemmings; 377 ©Elena Pokrovskaya; 378 ©Juha Sompinmäki; 380*©Tito Dupret; 381 ©POZZO DI BORGO Thomas; 382*©Tito Dupret; 383 ©Alexander Maksimov; 385 ©Ferenc Cegledi; 386 ©robert paul van beets; 387 ©Philip Lange; 388*©Tito Dupret; 389 ©Netfalls; 391 ©Luciano Mortula; 392 ©Olga Kolos; 394 ©Holger Mette; 394 ©Grigory Kubatyan; 395*©Tito Dupret; 396 ©Dmitriy Bryndin; 397 ©MCales; 398▲*©Tito Dupret; 398▼*©Carmen Daly Schelbert; 399 ©Olga Zaporozhskaya; 400 ©tororo reaction; 402 ©Alan Kraft; 403 ©paul prescott; 404 ©PixAchi; 405 ©enote; 406 ©Khirman Vladimir; 409 ©Martin Mette; 410 ©Jarno Gonzalez Zarraonandia; 411 ©Valery Shanin; 413 ©JeremyRichards; 414 ©Jozef Sedmak; 415 ©Sam DCruz; 417 ©Wiktor Bubniak; 418 ©jpatava; 420 ©krechet; 421 ©tfrischg9; 423 ©Steffen Foerster Photography; 424 ©Fedor Selivanov; 425 ©Pichugin Dmitry; 427 ©Svetlana Tikhonova; 428 ©Thomas M Perkins; 429*©Tito Dupret; 431 ©rm; 433 ©Bill Perry; 434 ©Jarno Gonzalez Zarraonandia; 436*©Tito Dupret; 437 ©Tomasz Parys; 439 ©Huang Yuetao; 440 ©Kris Vandereycken; 442 ©tolobalaguer; 443 ©vospalej; 445 ©carlos sanchez pereyra; 446 ©Michael J Thompson; 447 ©Ungor; 448 ©Danilo Ascione; 449 ©Motordigitaal;

451 ©2009fotofriends; 452 ©Alan Kraft; 453 ©Gianluca Figliola Fantini; 455 ©Andrzej Gibasiewicz; 456 ©Falk Kienas; 457 ©Keith Brooks; 458 ©Mark Van Overmeire; 459 ©Daniel Gustavsson; 461 ©edobric; 462*©Tito Dupret; 463 ©Helen & Vlad Filatov; 464 ©Willem Tims; 465 ©Claudio Giovanni Colombo; 467 ©Jonald Morales; 468*©Tito Dupret; 469 ©Jiri Krajicek; 471▲ ©godrick; 471▼©Ron Urquhart; 472 ©Joel Blit; 475 ©Peter Zurek; 476 ©Kochergin; 477 ©koi88; 478*©Reto Kuster; 479 ©Mary Lane; 480 ©Xavier MARCHANT; 481*©Tito Dupret; 482 ©Jorge Felix Costa; 483 ©Joe Barbarite; 484*©Tito Dupret; 487 ©Valeria73; 489 ©Alex Garaev; 491 ©Pichugin Dmitry; 492 ©Sean Prior; 493 ©BESTWEB; 494 ©kirych; 495 ©L F File; 496 ©Bryan Busovicki; 497 ©Andreas Gradin; 499▲ ©Tobias Guttmann; 499▼ ©Marek Slusarczyk; 500 ©Zorik Galstyan; 501 ©Valeria73; 502 ©Aron Brand; 503*©Tito Dupret; 505 ©aguilarphoto; 507 ©Benson HE; 509 ©Veronika Trofer; 511 ©szefei; 512▲*©Tito Dupret; 512▼*©Tito Dupret; 513 ©Dan Breckwoldt; 514 ©Lagui; 515 ©Maksym Kalyta; 517*©Tito Dupret; 519 ©Mikhail Nekrasov; 520 ©MASSIMO MERLINI; 521 ©Shapiro Svetlana; 522 ©Angels at Work; 523 ©Floris Slooff; 525 ©Perov Stanislav; 526 ©Tomasz Szymanski; 527 ©Dino; 528 ©Angels at Work; 529 ©rj lerich; 530 ©WitR; 531 ©Razvan Stroie; 532*©Tito Dupret; 533 ©Slawomir Kruz; 534 ©Bill Perry; 536 ©Chris102; 537 ©ostill; 539 ©ollirg; 540*©Tito Dupret; 541 ©Mauro Bighin; 542 ©Tobias Machhaus; 543 ©Dainis Derics; 545 ©Vladimirs Koskins; 547 ©Marcin-linfernum; 549 ©Uwe Bumann; 550 ©MaxFX; 551*©Austrian National Tourist Office/Diejun; 552 ©Buddhadl; 553 ©Joerg Hausmann; 555 ©Ivo Brezina; 557▲ ©Pichugin Dmitry; 557▼ ©MARTAFR; 559 ©sunxuejun; 560 ©Laitr Keiows; 561 ©lexan; 562*©Tito Dupret; 564 ©Andy Z.; 566*©Tito Dupret; 567 ©luri; 568 ©photooiasson; 569▲*©Tito Dupret; 569▼*©Jethro Lennox; 571 ©David Woods; 572 ©Factoria singular fotografia; 573*©Tito Dupret; 574 ©Jan Schuler; 576*©David Barrie/Darjeeling Himalayan Railway Society; 577 ©Alfredo Schaufelberger; 578 ©Philip Lange; 579 ©Le Do; 580*©M. L. Slot-Dekker; 581 ©Tudor Stanica; 582*©Tito Dupret; 584*©Tito Dupret; 585 ©OPIS; 586 ©Guillermo Garcia; 589 ©Joerg Humpe; 591 ©Pablo H Caridad; 592 ©Sorin Popa; 593 ©robert paul van beets; 594 ©Bartlomiej K. Kwieciszewski; 595 ©Valeria73; 597 ©Insuratelu Gabriela Gianina; 598 ©Sam DCruz; 599*©Tito Dupret; 600 ©riekephotos; 601*©Tito Dupret; 602 ©Ales Liska; 603 ©baldovina; 604 ©WH CHOW; 605 ©Tootles; 606 ©kwest; 607 ©Marc C. Johnson; 609*(CC by 2.0) ©sridgway; 610 ©Fedor Selivonov; 611 ©EcoPrint; 613 ©Albo; 614*©Tito Dupret; 615 ©Birute Vijeikiene; 616 ©zhouhui8525; 617 ©Jarno Gonzalez Zarraonandia; 618 ©Vladimir Daragan;

621 ©Ismael Montero Verdu; 623 ©St. Nick; 624 ©Joao Virissimo; 625 ©slava_vn; 626*©Tito Dupret; 627 ©Hano Uzeirbegovic; 628 ©rm; 629*©Tito Dupret; 630 ©Alexey Averiyanov; 631 ©Chong Wei Jin; 633 ©Ivonne Wierink; 634 ©javarman; 635 ©Tim Arbaev; 636*©Tito Dupret; 637 ©Karel Gallas; 638 ©Chow Shue Ma; 639 ©Miguel Angel Pallardo del Rio; 640 ©Vladimir Korostyshevskiy; 641 ©Larky; 642*©Tito Dupret; 645 ©zicci; 646 ©Pavel K; 648*©Tito Dupret; 648*©Tito Dupret; 651©Wojciech Zbieg; 652*©Tito Dupret; 653 ©Craig Hanson; 654 ©Buddhadl; 655 ©Zorik Galstyan; 655*©Tito Dupret; 657 ©ecoventuretravel; 658 ©Eric Gevaert; 659 ©rubiphoto; 661 ©Julia R.; 662 ©Sílvia Antunes; 663*©Tito Dupret; 665 ©Gyrohype; 666 ©Seleznev Oleg; 668*(CC by 2.0) ©Sara & Joachim; 669 ©Graham Bloomfield; 670 ©javarman; 671 ©Daniel Gilbey; 672*©Tito Dupret; 673 ©Joseph Calev; 674 ©Mark Breck; 677*©Israel Ministry of Tourism www.goisrael.com; 678 ©Alexander Cyliax; 679 ©Juha Sompinmäki; 680 ©Rostislav Glinsky; 681 ©Nestor Noci; 682*©Tito Dupret; 683*©UNESCO/Claudio Margottini; 685 ©LianeM; 686 ©Falk Kienas; 689 ©PavleMarjanovic; 690 ©mirabile; 691*©Tito Dupret; 692 ©jeff gynane; 693*©NASA/GSFC/METI/ERSDAC/JAROS and the U.S./Japan ASTER Science Team and Jesse Allen; 694*©Tito Dupret; 697*©UNESCO/Giovanni Boccardi; 699 ©urosr; 701 ©mastiffliu; 702 ©Wiktor Bubniak; 703*©Tito Dupret; 704 ©AND Inc.; 705 ©rm; 706*©Tito Dupret; 707 ©Andrew Barker; 708*©MODIS/NASA; 709 ©Eirikur Kristjansson; 710 ©Igor Alyukov; 711 ©lidian; 712 ©Michael Steden; 713*©Tito Dupret; 714*(CC by sa 2.0) ©Sorosh; 715 ©fotique; 718 ©Joern; 721*©Fleur Gayet; 723 ©Holger Mette; 724 ©Stuart Blyth; 727*(CC by 2.0) ©Crazy Joe Devola; 727 ©Joerg Humpe; 728 ©Eremin Sergey; 730 ©Plotnikoff; 731 ©Horácio José Lopes dos Santos; 733 ©alysta; 736*©UNESCO/Alessandro Balsamo; 737 ©Ng Wei Keong; 739*©Doron Nissim; 740*©Tsvika Tsuk; 741*©beltsazar; 743 ©GagarinART; 744 ©Zimins@NET; 745*©Tito; 746*©Tito Dupret; 749 ©Rafael Martin-Gaitero; 751 ©newphotoservice; 752▲ ©Kate Kotova; 752▼*©Tito Dupret; 753 ©manfredxy; 754 ©Jesus Cervantes; 755▲*(CC by sa 2.0) ©shaunanmullally; 755*©Tito Dupret; 757 ©Richard Griffin; 758 ©Ruta Saulyte-Laurinaviciene; 760*©Tito Dupret; 761 ©Holger Mette; 763 ©Neale Cousland; 765 ©Holger Mette; 766 ©Vlad Zharoff; 767 ©Tonis Valing; 769 ©Andy Lim; 770 ©ECOPRINT; 771 ©Petros Tsonis; 772 ©Brykaylo Yuriy; 773 ©Vlad Ghiea; 774*©Tito Dupret; 775 ©Coquilleau; 776 ©El Choclo; 777 ©lavigne herve; 779 ©PavleMarjanovic; 780 ©Connors Bros.; 783 ©Aleksandrs Jermakovichs; 785 ©Vladimir Melnik; 786 ©Jens Stolt; 787 ©Peter Wey; 791 ©Lori Skelton ; 793 ©Tatiana Belova ;

794 ©Katarzyna Mazurowska; 795*(CC by 2.0) ©PhillipC; 796*©Tito Dupret; 797 ©RookCreations; 798 ©Salem Alforaih; 801*(CC by sa 2.5) ©Adrian Pingstone; 802*(CC by sa 2.0) ©serapio; 804*Satellite image ©Jacques Descloitres, MODIS Rapid Response Team, NASA/GSFC; 804*(CC by sa 2.0) ©Mogens Engelund, Wikipedia; 806 ©rubiphoto; 807 ©Dan Breckwoldt; 808 ©thewhiteview; 810*(CC by sa 2.0) ©Marmoulak; 811 ©zhu difeng; 812*(CC by sa 3.0) ©B.navez; 813 ©ziggysofi; 814 ©Jeremy Richards; 815*(CC by sa 2.0) ©Ensie & Matthias; 818 ©Gregory James Van Raalte; 819 ©Dmitry Zamorin; 820 ©Fedor Selivanov; *821(CC 3.0) ©Dr. Randi Rotjan, New England Aquarium. www.neaq.org; 822 ©Stephan Scherhag; 823 ©Stephan Scherhag; 824 ©Jessmine; 826*(CC by 2.0) ©Chris Scott; 827*(CC by 2.0) ©cherniutsi_112; 828*(CC by 2.0) ©Sholeh; 829 ©rj lerich; 830 ©Fred Kamphues; 831*(CC by 2.0) ©Pedrenet; 832 ©wiw; 833 ©UNESCO; 834 ©Carlos Neto; 836 ©urosr; 838 ©alanf; 839*(CC by 2.0) ©Llonguet; 840▲*(CC by 2.0) ©kanegen; 840▼*(CC by 2.0) ©chaojikazu; 842▲*(CC by 2.0) ©Pichugin Dmitry; 842▼*(CC by 2.0) ©hunta; 844 ©mangostock; 846 ©Dashutter; 847 ©EMJAY SMITH; 848 ©Uryadnikov Sergey; 849 ©V. J. Matthew; 850▲ ©Shifted; 850▼*(CC by sa 2.5); 851 ©inacio pires; 853 ©Zvonimir Atletic; 854*©Sven Oehm (sven.oehm@gmail.com); 856 ©muratart; 857 ©Witr; 859 ©Jason Ho; 860 ©Igor Plotnikov; 862 ©Anton_Ivanov; 863 ©Olga Meffista; 865 ©Mikhail Markovskiy; 866 ©elxeneize; 867 ©Vacclav; 868 ©Aleksandar Todorovic; 869 ©Ivan Smuk

CC by 2.0

CC by sa 2.0

CC by sa 2.5

CC by sa 3.0

Tito Dupret/WHTour.org

(www.worldheritage-tour.org) is a non-profit organization documenting World Heritage sites in panography – 360 degree imaging – thanks to the support of the J. M. Kaplan Fund from New York, USA.